CQ Researcher on
Controversies in Law and Society

CQ Researcher on
Controversies in Law and Society

CQ PRESS

A Division of Congressional Quarterly Inc.
Washington, D.C.

CQ Press
A Division of Congressional Quarterly Inc.
1414 22nd Street, N.W.
Washington, D.C. 20037

(202) 822-1475; (800) 638-1710

www.cqpress.com

Printed and bound in the United States of America

05 04 03 02 01   5 4 3 2 1

∞ The paper used in this publication meets the minimum requirements of the American National Standard for Information Sciences—Permanence of Paper for Printed Library Materials, ANSI Z39.48-1992.

Library of Congress Cataloging-in-Publication Data

CQ researcher on controversies in law and society.
    p. cm.
  Includes bibliographical references and index.
  ISBN 1-56802-672-2 (cloth: alk.paper)
  1. Law—United States. 2. Sociological jurisprudence. I. CQ researcher.

KF379.C7 2001
340'.115—dc21   00-069476

Appendix: The publisher wishes to thank Kathryn L. Schwartz for permission to use *A+ Research and Writing for High School and College Students,* copyright 1997 by Kathryn L. Schwartz. Published by the Internet Public Library: http://www.ipl.org.

Contents

MEDICINE AND THE LAW

THE INTERNET AND THE LAW

Annotated Table of Contents

The 16 *CQ Researcher* articles reprinted in this book have been reproduced essentially as they appeared when first published. In a few cases in which important new developments have occurred since an article came out, these developments are mentioned in the following overviews, which highlight the principal issues that are examined.

CIVIL LIBERTIES

DNA Databases

DNA identification has moved from an experimental technique to an established crime-solving tool for police and prosecutors in the United States, as well as other nations. Now, law enforcement agencies are creating DNA databases of criminal offenders that can be used to link criminals or suspects to unsolved crimes. All 50 states have laws requiring DNA profiling of some offenders, and some law enforcement officials want to compile DNA profiles of arrestees as well. Defense lawyers are also using DNA analysis to challenge old convictions: more than 60 prisoners—some on death row—have been exonerated by DNA testing. But civil liberties and privacy advocates say expanding government DNA databases will lead to misuse of sensitive personal information that can be gleaned from DNA analysis.

Adoption Controversies

Recently, Oregon voters approved a ballot initiative that would allow adopted children to obtain their original birth records when they turn 21, regardless of the wishes of their birth parents. Legal challenges have prevented the Oregon law from taking immediate effect, but adoption rights activists began working to put similar measures before voters in other states. The controversy over open adoption records is one of several highly emotional issues dividing the adoption community. Controversies linger over whether gays and lesbians should be allowed to adopt and whether to allow parents to adopt children of another race.

Gay Rights

Vermont has become the first state to grant marriagelike status to gay and lesbian couples. Elsewhere in the country, however, opposition to same-sex marriage remains strong. Meanwhile, other gay-rights measures are gaining support despite continuing opposition from conservatives. Eleven states and some 124 municipalities have anti-discrimination legislation, and many school districts have allowed high school students to form "gay-straight" alliance clubs. On the military front, the Defense Department is promising a crackdown on anti-gay harassment but defending the "don't ask, don't tell" policy. The issues divided the major presidential candidates: Democrat Al Gore backed gay-rights measures, while Republican George W. Bush was opposed.

CRIMINAL JUSTICE

Prison-Building Boom

The number of Americans behind bars has grown to nearly 2 million, requiring federal and state governments to build an unprecedented number of prisons. Conservatives argue that while regrettable, the prison-building boom has helped to bring down the nation's high crime rate. But liberals and others say the United States is building prison cells when it should be combating crime by spending more money on education and drug treatment. In addition, they argue, other tough-on-crime measures, such as mandatory minimum sentences and truth-in-sentencing laws, are simply keeping minor felons in jail too long, at great expense to the taxpayers. But proponents of tough sentencing laws counter that they are needed as an antidote to lenient judges.

Policing the Police

Police departments around the country have been on the defensive because of accusations of abuse of authority. Los Angeles has been rocked by a corruption scandal involving planted evidence and shooting unarmed suspects. New York City officers have been convicted of torturing a suspect and covering up the crime but acquitted in the shooting death of an unarmed civilian. State and local law enforcement agencies are accused of using "racial profiling" in traffic stops. Critics say stronger controls are needed. Law enforcement groups say most police obey the law and that the abuses are being exaggerated. Meanwhile, the U.S. Supreme Court considered a controversial law aimed at partly overturning the famous *Miranda* decision on police interrogation.

Drug Policy

The federal government spends billions fighting drugs, yet illegal drug use remains high. Critics say the answer to the drug problem is not more law enforcement but policies that focus on reducing the harm that results from both drug use and the efforts to stop it. But drug-policy officials charge that most "harm reduction" proposals are little more than veiled attempts to legalize dangerous substances. They say a better approach is the growing system of drug courts, which require addicted drug offenders to undergo treatment. Meanwhile, states are taking innovative approaches to the drug problem. Voters in several states have approved initiatives allowing the medical use of marijuana, and have considered proposals to divert some drug offenders from prison to treatment programs.

SETTING THE BOUNDARIES OF BUSINESS

Antitrust Policy

For more than a century, federal law has sought to encourage competition by prohibiting monopoly behavior and other anti-competitive business practices. Now District Judge Thomas Penfield Jackson has ordered the breakup of Microsoft Corp., saying that the company did not appear to have accepted his ruling that it had broadly violated antitrust laws. The government had charged, and Jackson agreed, that Microsoft used its monopoly in operating systems to put competitors at a disadvantage and stifle innovation. Microsoft Chairman William H. Gates called the judge's ruling "an unwarranted and unjustified intrusion into the software marketplace, a marketplace that has been the engine of economic growth for America." Microsoft said it would appeal the case to the Court of Appeals, while the government plans to seek an immediate review by the Supreme Court. The high-

stakes court action comes as the Justice Department and the Federal Trade Commission are also more closely scrutinizing corporate mergers that may restrict competition. With a record wave of mergers, some people are cheering on more aggressive policies, and some want the government to do even more, but others say the government should let the marketplace alone.

Utility Deregulation

The $220 billion U.S. electricity market—sometimes dubbed the last great government-sanctioned monopoly—has slowly been opening to competition. Many states have passed deregulation plans that allow residential and commercial consumers to choose their electricity supplier, and at least as many other states have begun studying free-market proposals. Already, several deregulated states have delivered lower electric rates, particularly to large industrial power users, as well as giving consumers the option to support the production of non-polluting "green power." But the federal government hasn't developed an overall strategy for deregulating the nation's retail power market. Serious questions remain about the future of the nation's power grid, the potential for discriminatory pricing and contingencies to avoid regional blackouts.

PUBLIC POLICY IN THE COURTROOM

Closing In on Tobacco

The tobacco industry is facing a new round of legal and regulatory challenges in the protracted war over smoking and health. The Supreme Court ruled that the Food and Drug Administration should not regulate tobacco products, while the Justice Department is suing tobacco companies for the costs of treating smoking-related illnesses under Medicare and other federal health programs. These moves came in the wake of the tobacco industry's agreements to pay state governments $246 billion to settle similar reimbursement suits. For its part, the country's largest tobacco company, Philip Morris, is now acknowledging that smoking causes lung cancer and heart disease. But all the tobacco companies are resisting the latest governmental moves against the industry and defending their right to sell a "legal product" in a "responsible manner."

High-Impact Litigation

The states' successful litigation against the tobacco industry has spawned a new legal offensive—against gun manufacturers. Thirty local governments want to force gunmakers to pay damages for gun-related injuries, change gun design and alter marketing practices. Cities and gun-control advocates say the suits follow established legal principles, but critics say the litigation amounts to extortion and an end-run around the legislative process. Meanwhile, plaintiffs' attorneys are pressing private class-action suits against other businesses, including health maintenance organizations and giant Microsoft Corp. Business interests say the disputes do not belong in the courts, but defenders say litigation often is the only way to hold industry accountable and force decisions on pressing social problems.

MEDICINE AND THE LAW

Patients' Rights

The continuing growth of managed-care health plans is provoking a powerful backlash. Many patients say managed care makes it harder simply to see a doctor, let alone get insurance coverage for needed treatment. Doctors are also chafing under restrictions that limit the way they treat patients. The managed-care industry insists, however, that it is improving the quality of health care and slowing the rise in costs. More than 30 states have passed laws strengthening patients' rights in dealing with insurers. Congress continues to consider imposing new regulations on managed-care companies. Patient and consumer groups are pushing for reforms as part of so-called Patients' Bill of Rights legislation, but insurers' and employers' groups warn that the result may be higher premiums and more uninsured workers.

Embryo Research

The use of embryos and aborted fetuses in scientific research is again under scrutiny, thanks to the landmark isolation of primordial human embryonic stem cells. These "master cells" are capable of evolving into virtually every kind of tissue in the body and could be the key to cures for conditions such as Parkinson's disease and diabetes. They also offer a never-before-seen glimpse into the earliest stages of human development. But anti-abortion groups and other critics contend the privately funded work runs counter to a 1995 congressional ban on embryo research and want to bar taxpayer money from subsidizing the research, regardless of the potential benefits. Congress and the National Institutes of Health are trying to devise new guidelines and sidestep political minefields.

Medical Mistakes

Many more patients are hurt by medical mistakes than hospitals ever acknowledge. In fact, a recent report by the Institute of Medicine confirms what medical experts have long known: medical errors kill more people every year than AIDS, breast cancer or car crashes. The IOM says that encouraging doctors to admit their mistakes could help hospitals prevent future errors. President Clinton has urged the states to require the reporting of medical errors, but medical lobbyists and consumers are at odds over how public the reports should be. Consumer advocates and large employers, including General Motors, say hospitals should be required to report their mistakes publicly. But hospitals and doctors want their identities protected to avoid malpractice suits and to encourage candor.

THE INTERNET AND THE LAW

Internet Privacy

Privacy advocates warn that many Web sites try to collect personal information from on-line users, but few of these sites guarantee how that data will be used. Privacy advocates also say the federal government should establish standards to protect privacy online. But Internet businesses and others contend that they can safeguard users' privacy without resorting to government interference. Law-enforcement agencies, meanwhile, favor government limitations on the use of sophisticated encryption technology, which makes on-line communications secure—even from the police. They fear that strong encryption software will aid criminals in hiding their activities. But privacy advocates argue that encryption technology assures companies and consumers that their online communications are not being tampered with.

Digital Commerce

Once known mainly for chat rooms, e-mail and pornography, the Internet has rapidly transformed into a powerful commercial selling tool. U.S. business transactions on the World Wide Web totaled $43 billion in 1998 and could rise to $1.3 trillion by 2003. Companies increasingly go online to order parts, schedule shipments and obtain business services. Consumers are clicking on Web sites that sell books, recordings and high-tech equipment. But all of the activity is posing difficult questions for regulators, who must set rules for the thriving marketplace. Among the chief issues are taxing sales in cyberspace, defining appropriate commercial speech used on Web sites and applying antitrust laws to an industry often likened to the Wild West.

Copyright and the Internet

Millions of Internet users are downloading the latest CDs onto their personal computers—and the recording industry is up in arms. But the legal battle over Napster is just one of many new copyright disputes spawned by the digital revolution. Movie studios are trying to limit the availability of a software program that allows movie fans to copy encrypted digital videodisks. The film industry is also suing a California company that provides a Web-based video playback service—what the founder calls a "virtual VCR." The recording and movie industries claim that the Internet-based services amount to "piracy." But computer and consumer groups say copyright law needs to adapt to new technologies that make it easier and less expensive to disseminate creative works.

Introduction

A society creates a system of laws to resolve conflict fairly and impartially, to protect the basic rights of its citizens and to reflect its norms and values. Every citizen has a stake in the rigorous application of the law, yet many people disagree about how it should be practiced and adjudicated—from the regulation of commerce, to the fight against crime, to the guarantee of civil rights. At times, there are no obvious winners in legal arguments, and *Controversies in Law and Society* does not take sides or champion a particular perspective. Instead, through balanced accounts, readers can thoroughly and fairly explore opposing sides of today's problems in law and society. This volume is a compilation of 16 recent articles from *The CQ Researcher,* a weekly report that brings into focus the often complicated and controversial issues on the public agenda. *The CQ Researcher* makes complex issues less intimidating. Difficult concepts are not oversimplified but are explained in plain English. Offering in-depth, objective and forward-looking reporting on a specific topic, each selection chronicles and analyzes past legislative and judicial actions as well as current and possible future developments. *Controversies in Law and Society* is designed to encourage discussion, to help readers think critically and actively about these vital issues and to facilitate future research. Adding color and depth, real-world examples give a flavor of the substantive detail in a variety of areas while showing how legal issues at all levels of government—federal, state and local—affect students' lives and futures.

The readings, organized into six subject areas—Civil Liberties, Criminal Justice, Setting the Boundaries of Business, Public Policy in the Courtroom, Medicine and the Law and the Internet and the Law—were chosen to expose students to a wide range of legal issues.

The CQ Researcher

The CQ Researcher, founded in 1923 as *Editorial Research Reports,* was sold primarily to newspapers for research purposes. The magazine was given its current name and a design overhaul in 1991. *The CQ Researcher* is still sold to many newspapers, some of which reprint all or part of each issue. But today, students, not journalists, are the primary audience for *The CQ Researcher.*

Chapter Format

Each issue of the *Researcher,* and therefore each selection in this book, is structured in the same way, beginning with an introductory overview of the topic. This first section briefly touches on the areas that will be explored in greater detail in the rest of the chapter. Following the introduction is a section that explains the important debates in the field. The section is structured around a number of questions known as "Issue Questions," such as "Should the government try to regulate Internet content?" or "Should mandatory-minimum sentences for drug offenses be abolished?" This section is the core of each selection: the questions raised are often highly controversial and usually the object of much argument among those who work and think in the field. Hence, the answers provided by the writer are never conclusive. Instead, each answer details the range of opinion within the field.

Next is the "Background" section, which provides a history of the issue being examined. This look back includes important legislative and executive actions and court decisions from the past. Readers will be able to see how current policy has evolved. An examination of existing policy (under the heading "Current Situation") follows the background section. Each "Current Situation" provides an overview of important developments that were occurring when the article was published. Each selection concludes with an "Outlook" section, which gives a sense of what might happen in the near future.

All selections contain other regular features to augment the main text. Each selection has two or three sidebars that examine issues related to the topic. An "At Issue" page provides opposing answers to a relevant question, from two outside experts. Also included are a chronology that cites important dates and events, and an annotated bibliography that details some of the sources used by the author of each article.

1 DNA Databases

KENNETH JOST

New York City police arrested Isaac Jones in April outside a pawnshop in the Bronx. He was waiting in a car while his girlfriend redeemed a diamond pendant that had been taken from a rape victim. [1]

At first, Jones denied any knowledge of the attack, according to police. When detectives threatened to charge his girlfriend, however, Jones reportedly admitted that he was the man police had been hunting in a string of rapes dating back to 1993.

Jones, who had previous convictions for sodomy and unlawful imprisonment of a woman, could not recall details of the other attacks, police said, so they charged him in only four assaults. But an analysis of the DNA contained in a sample of Jones' blood showed a likely match with DNA samples obtained in many other rapes.* "We have 17 positive hits of DNA evidence leading back to Isaac Jones as the rapist," First Deputy Police Commissioner Patrick Kelleher told reporters.

Acquaintances from Jones' Bronx apartment house and the New York office building where he worked as a floor polisher described Jones as polite and friendly and voiced surprise at his arrest. "The DNA evidence speaks for itself as to what kind of individual he really is," Kelleher responded. "We got a very, very dangerous individual off the streets of New York."

---

* DNA — deoxyribonucleic acid — is the basic genetic substance of all living cells. Embedded in the giant DNA molecules — identical throughout the body — is the hereditary information that determines everything from eye color to predisposition to some diseases. In addition, a DNA molecule contains stretches of chemical building blocks with repetitive patterns that vary from individual to individual.

From *The CQ Researcher,*
May 28, 1999.

Introduced in U.S. and British courtrooms in 1987, DNA profiling, or so-called genetic fingerprinting, has evolved from a controversial forensic novelty to a powerful and widely accepted tool for identification in criminal investigations and prosecutions. [2] DNA identification has also been used in some 60 cases in the United States to exonerate defendants wrongfully convicted years ago — freeing inmates from death rows or long prison sentences. (*See story, p. 5*)

"It's the most significant advancement in investigative tools at least in this century," says Christopher Asplen, a federal prosecutor who is currently serving as executive director of the Justice Department's National Commission on the Future of DNA Evidence. "It's one of the most accurate technologies we have. It has an incredible ability not just to convict the guilty but also to exonerate the innocent."

Walter Rowe, a leading academic forensic scientist, says that DNA typing, in fact, is going beyond the identification technique introduced at the turn of the century: fingerprinting. "Now we're probably more likely to recover usable DNA from a scene than a fingerprint," says Rowe, a professor at George Washington University in Washington, D.C. "We're now starting to do DNA work from animals and plants. It may be the greatest advance in forensic science in history."

Most of the early controversies about the science of DNA identification have faded away. But some civil liberties and privacy advocates are assailing moves by law enforcement agencies to construct a nationwide computer database of DNA profiles of criminal offenders. Law enforcement officials say police and prosecutors can use the databases to link suspects and offenders to crimes that otherwise would either go unsolved or require substantial amounts of time and money to solve.

Critics, however, fear the databases will be abused. "There is a frightening potential for a brave new world where genetic information is routinely collected and its use results in abuse and discrimination," says Barry Steinhardt, associate director of the American Civil Liberties Union (ACLU). Employers and insurers, for example, could uncover a worker's predisposition to disease and use the information to exclude him from employment or insurance coverage.

The same biological sample used for DNA identification "can also be used for a full biological dissection of that person," says geneticist Paul Billings, who edited a collection of critical essays about DNA identification several years ago. [3]

Law enforcement officials note, however, that the DNA used for identification purposes actually does not contain genes and thus provides no genetic information about a person: "junk DNA," they call it. But critics emphasize that law enforcement agencies retain the original samples collected from criminal offenders — usually blood or saliva — making it possible to use the samples for other purposes. "Whoever holds those samples has full access to all the genetic information about that person," Billings says.

Steinhardt also warns against what

DNA Databases 1

he calls the "creeping expansion" of databases. The earliest databases were limited to sex offenders, but over time they have been expanded in some states to include people convicted of other crimes. "We've gone very quickly from data banks for persons convicted of sex offenses to data banks for most felonies to proposals to test all arrestees and even to test all newborns," says Steinhardt (See story, p. 16)

So far, the criticisms of DNA data-banking are having little effect. All 50 states have passed laws providing for DNA databases on convicted sexual offenders. Four of those states collect samples from anyone convicted of a felony (see p. 12).

The FBI, which established its own database in 1990, is now working to create a national database comparable to its national criminal fingerprint file. Twelve states have connected to the FBI's system — known as CODIS for Combined DNA Identification System — since it was officially announced in October; FBI officials hope to have all 50 states connected within a year or so.

But the states face significant funding and logistical problems — including a backlog of nearly a half-million DNA samples that have been collected but not analyzed. And some states have yet to set up their databases — including Louisiana, the only state with a law on the books for collecting DNA samples from people who simply have been arrested for felonies, as well as those who have been convicted.

Despite those difficulties, lawmakers and law enforcement officials in many states are actively debating expansion of DNA databases. New York City Police Commissioner Howard Safir stirred the controversy in December by proposing that DNA samples be collected from all arrestees in the city, saying it would help reduce crime. He coupled the proposal with some safeguards, such as expunging the DNA identification of anyone who was not convicted. Even so, civil liberties advocates fiercely denounced the idea, while even some DNA database advocates said practical considerations weighed against the idea for the time being. (See "At Issue," p. 15)

The issue is one of many questions concerning the use of DNA evidence being considered by the national DNA commission, which is expected to complete its work by August. As the commission, appointed by Attorney General Janet Reno, sifts through a variety of issues, here are some of the major questions being debated:

Should the use of DNA databases be expanded?

Carolyn and Tony Sievers, of Virginia Beach, Va., have no doubts about the value of DNA databases. Virginia's database helped solve the murder of their 22-year-old daughter, Hope Hall, more than two years after she was raped and killed in her suburban Richmond, Va., apartment. Her killer, Shermaine Johnson, was identified after he had begun serving a long prison sentence for rape and abduction in southeastern Virginia. Johnson was identified when the DNA sample he had provided after his conviction — as required under Virginia law — was matched in August 1996 in a computerized "cold hit" to DNA collected at the scene of the 1994 crime. Johnson was convicted in July 1998 of Hall's murder and sentenced to death.

The Sievers have created the "Hope Denise Hall Action Memorial" Web site to advocate more funding for national and international DNA databases to identify and prosecute criminal offenders. "Instead of convicting a criminal of one crime," the Sievers write, "we can identify him for all the crimes he committed, and then he goes to prison for the rest of his life or is properly executed if warranted." [4]

Such cases explain why law enforcement officials view DNA databases as an important tool in fully realizing the benefits of DNA evidence. "It's not just crimes that occur today," says Steve Niezgoda, program manager for the FBI's DNA database. "It's crimes that occurred in the past: women raped five or six years ago."

Niezgoda says there have been more than 600 cold hits through the FBI's DNA database since it was established in 1990. The database also produces benefits that are less susceptible to quantifying, he says. "A database hit saves a lot of police resources," Niezgoda says. "And it might lead to longer sentences, or less cost with the trial, because the evidence is of higher quality."

Critics of DNA databases are hard-pressed to dispute the benefits to law enforcement. "Of course, there would be benefits for the criminal justice system," says Philip Bereano, a professor of technology and public policy at the University of Washington in Seattle. "There would be benefits if we let police knock down doors at random in search of criminal activity. I'm sure they would find some, but the Fourth Amendment wouldn't permit it."

"Law enforcement is always looking for new tools to investigate crime," says the ACLU's Steinhardt. "We still have problems with the notion of mass testing of individuals based not on reasonable cause that they are a suspect in the crime but just on their status" as a convicted offender or arrestee.

So far, however, civil liberties challenges to creating DNA databases of convicted offenders have failed in state and federal courts. Three federal appeals courts have upheld state laws allowing the collection of DNA samples from inmates and parolees, and the only state court ruling to bar the practice — by a lower court judge

DNA Testing Frees Many Convicted Offenders

At least 62 convicted offenders have been freed from prison in the United States after DNA testing of evidence established their innocence or cast sufficient doubt on their guilt to warrant their release. A Justice Department report published in 1996 analyzed the 28 cases known at that time. All but one of the defendants were convicted by juries; the one guilty plea involved a defendant with a mental disability. All of the cases involved some form of sexual assault. The inmates served an average of seven years before their release. Three of the freed inmates had been sentenced to death, and six others received life terms. Here are synopses of those cases:

Case Name/ Location	Primary Charges/ Date of Conviction/ Sentence	Selected Evidence at Trial	Result of DNA Testing; Time Served
Bloodsworth, Kirk Baltimore, Md.	Murder, rape (1985); death, reduced to life	Five witness IDs; self-incriminating statements	Excluded by test of panties; 9 yrs.
Cotton, Ronald Burlington, N.C.	Rape, 2 counts (1985, '87); life + 54 yrs.	Victim ID; similarity of shoes, flashlight	Excluded by test of panties, vaginal swabs; 10-$\frac{1}{2}$ yrs.
Cruz, Rolando Chicago, Ill.	Murder, kidnapping, rape (1985); death	Witness statements; "dream visions" of murder	Excluded by test of semen-stained underwear; 11 yrs.
Daye, Frederick Rene San Diego, Calif.	Rape, 2 counts; kidnapping (1984); life	Victim, witness ID; blood analysis	Excluded by test of semen-stained jeans; 10 yrs.
Hernandez, Alejandro Chicago, Ill.	Murder, kidnapping, rape (1985); death	Witness statements; self-incriminating statements	Excluded by test of semen-stained underwear; 11 yrs.
Honaker, Edward Nelson County, Va.	Rape, sexual assault, sodomy (1985); 3 life terms + 34 yrs.	Victim, witness IDs; hair analysis	Excluded by test of vaginal swab; 10 yrs.
Jones, Joe C. Topeka, Kan.	Rape, kidnapping (1986); life + 10-25 yrs.	Victim, witness IDs; proximity to crime scene	Excluded by test of vaginal swab; 6-$\frac{1}{2}$ yrs.
Nelson, Bruce Allegheny Co., Pa.	Murder, rape (1982); life	Codefendant testimony; inculpatory statements	Excluded by test of crime-scene evidence; 9 yrs.
Woodall, Glen Huntington, W. Va.	Sexual assault, kidnapping (1987); 2 life terms + 203-335 yrs.	Blood, hair analysis; victim ID	Excluded by tests of vaginal swabs, clothing; 4 yrs. + 1yr. electronic confinement

Source: U.S. Department of Justice, Convicted by Juries, Exonerated by Science: Case Studies in the Use of DNA Evidence to Establish Innocence After Trial *(1996).*

in Boston — was overturned by Massachusetts' highest court in April.

The successes in matching convicted offenders to unsolved crimes, combined with the favorable court rulings, lead some DNA advocates to call for expanding the databases. "We need to have the databases as comprehensive as possible to get the maximum benefit," says George Washington's Rowe.

Civil libertarians naturally oppose any further expansion of the databases. But many law enforcement officials and other DNA database advocates also oppose the idea of collecting samples from arrestees — at least for the time being — for pragmatic reasons.

"On the face of it, it sounds good, but it does present some problems," says Rowe. "Right now, you just don't have the capability to do anything with it. And if [a suspect] is acquitted, there's some case law that would say he would have the right to have the sample destroyed and the record expunged."

"If we get to the point where our DNA labs can start turning these [samples] around in a month, and we start collecting all the samples owed and analyzing all the samples from crime scenes, once that happens, come back and talk to us about typing all arrestees," says Barry Scheck, a defense lawyer, member of the national commission and director of the Innocence Project at Yeshiva University's Cardozo Law School in New York. Scheck, who came to national prominence as the DNA evidence expert on the defense team in O.J. Simpson's 1995 murder trial, is a DNA database advocate.

Still, some law enforcement officials who oppose including arrestees for now also say there would be benefits in the future. "If we took samples from suspects at arrest and searched a database of samples from crime scenes, the advantages to public safety are going to be tremendous," says

Paul B. Ferrara, director of Virginia's Forensic Science Division.

Critics, however, say that collecting samples from arrestees is just one more step down a slippery slope that could lead someday to universal genetic registration — a system that they say is fraught with privacy implications.

"This is a technology that powerful groups will want to use eventually to monitor all of us, not just the bad people, but the rest of us," Bereano says. "That's what this technology is about."

Do DNA databases pose a danger for individual rights?

"Danny," a 7-year-old California boy, was diagnosed several years ago with a gene that predisposes him to a heart disorder. The family's doctor prescribed medication to lower the risk of a heart attack. But when Danny's father changed health insurers, the company refused to insure the boy, saying the genetic trait amounted to a "pre-existing condition" that disqualified him from coverage.

The Council for Responsible Genetics, a bioethics advocacy group in Cambridge, Mass., cites Danny's case as one of 200 instances of what it labels genetic discrimination. [5] Critics of DNA databases say the risk of genetic discrimination will necessarily increase with the increasing number of DNA profiles being collected in both private and government computers that can readily be interconnected.

"We have a forensic, data-banking system based in the states, some more developed than others, but completely designed so that they will share information and cross state lines for doing searches of the sort we're talking about," says geneticist Billings, who reported Danny's case and others several years ago. "What's the reason for thinking that you won't be able to cross agencies?"

"The government is increasingly collecting biological samples that

contain DNA, and there are no real controls over how that information can be used and for what purposes," says Steinhardt of the ACLU. "We believe that inexorably databases created for one purpose wind up being used for other purposes."

Advocates of using DNA evidence in court have acknowledged potential risks to privacy since the early days of the technology. "When data banks are established in such a way that state and federal law-enforcement authorities can gain access to DNA profiles, not only of persons convicted of violent crimes but of others as well, there is a serious potential for abuse of confidential information," the National Academy of Sciences concluded in its first report on DNA profiling, in 1992. [6]

Law enforcement officials today, however, insist that the state and FBI DNA databases pose no real risk to privacy rights. They insist that the DNA profiles are strictly safeguarded and, in any event, are nothing more than "junk DNA" that contains no sensitive information about a person's health or background.

"These aren't genes," Ferrara says. "They don't tell us anything about medical conditions."

Steinhardt and other critics acknowledge that the DNA profiles themselves are useful only for identification not for other genetic information. But they note that law enforcement agencies retain the blood samples used to obtain the DNA used in profiling and that those samples could be used — or misused — at a later time to find out more personal information. "If the states and FBI were serious about limiting the use of these samples to law enforcement purposes, they would be destroying these samples rather than retaining them indefinitely," Steinhardt says.

"There are real and valid reasons for keeping those samples," counters the FBI's Niezgoda. First, he notes that

DNA Testing Helps Free Inmates After Years in Prison

DNA profiling was too new to be of use when Ronald Williamson and Dennis Fritz were tried in 1988 for the rape-murder of a waitress in Ada, Okla. Prosecutors did have some scientific evidence, though. An expert from the state's crime laboratory testified that the 17 hairs found on the victim were an exact match to either Fritz or Williamson. In addition, the expert said that semen found on the victim could have come from the two men. [1]

The scientific evidence, combined with testimony from two jailhouse informers and a convicted felon, satisfied the jury of the two defendants' guilt. Williamson, a local sports hero and former professional baseball player, was sentenced to death. Fritz, a junior high school science teacher and coach, received a life prison sentence.

In April, the two men were both freed from prison after DNA tests showed that the semen found on the victim's body could not have come from either Williamson or Fritz. Instead, the tests showed a match with one of the witnesses against the two men: Glen Gore, who was serving three 40-year prison sentences on kidnapping charges at the time of the original trial.

When they walked to freedom after a decade behind bars, Williamson, 46, and Fritz, 49, became the 61st and 62nd inmates known to have been freed from prison in the United States because of post-conviction DNA testing. Defense lawyers say many more inmates could show they were wrongfully convicted if evidence used in their own trials was subjected to DNA analysis.

"We will get thousands of people out," Barry Scheck, a lawyer for Fritz and professor at Yeshiva University's Benjamin Cardozo School of Law in New York, told *The New York Times* after the two men were released. Scheck, the DNA expert on O.J. Simpson's defense team, directs a legal clinic at the law school — known as the Innocence Project — that has used DNA testing to challenge convictions in scores of cases.

Fritz had been asking for DNA testing since as early as 1989, but officials turned him down. The DNA tests that exonerated the two men resulted instead from a federal court's decision in 1995 ordering a new trial for Williamson because of ineffective legal assistance in the 1988 trial. Williamson's new lawyers — Mark Barrett and Sara Bonnell of the Oklahoma Indigent Defense System — requested the DNA test as part of the preparation for the new trial.

Law enforcement officials acknowledge the importance of DNA testing in examining the validity of convictions

Dennis Fritz, left, and Ronald Williamson

AP Photo/J. Pat Carter

obtained before widespread use of the technology. "DNA aids the search for truth by exonerating the innocent," Attorney General Janet Reno wrote three years ago in the introduction to a Justice Department report that examined 28 such cases. [2] The report showed that the 28 inmates — most of them convicted in the mid-to-late 1980s — served a total of 197 years in prison, or an average of seven years each, before being released. Reno cited the report earlier this year as one of the reasons for creating the National Commission on the Future of DNA Evidence.

Now the commission is working on recommendations that would ease the way for post-conviction DNA testing for some defendants. Meeting May 7 and 8 in Santa Fe, N.M., the commission approved a recommendation that prosecutors, defense attorneys and judges should allow DNA testing of evidence in old criminal cases if the results could conclusively establish the defendant's innocence.

"If everyone agrees that an exclusion would, in fact, exclude someone, everyone should agree to do the testing," says Christopher Asplen, the commission's executive director.

The recommendations — due to be prepared in final form within the next two months — also include model state legislation to waive statutory deadlines that might block inmates' requests for DNA tests. Williamson's lawyer, Barrett, calls the recommendations "excellent" but said he would go further. "I think it would be worthwhile to have the DNA evidence automatically considered significant if the prosecution considered it significant when they were getting a conviction," Barrett says.

Scheck, who serves on the DNA commission, says the group's recommendations will help inmates get DNA testing to challenge their convictions. But Asplen, a federal prosecutor, cautions against allowing such testing too freely. "We cannot open cases for victims and prosecutors where it would be frivolous to do so," he says.

In its draft recommendation, the commission concludes, "The need for post-conviction DNA testing will wane over time. Within the decade, DNA testing with highly discriminatory results will be performed in all cases in which biological evidence is relevant, and advanced technologies will become commonplace in all laboratories."

[1] Background from *The New York Times*, April 19, 1999, p. A12.

[2] U.S. Department of Justice, "Convicted by Juries, Exonerated by Science: Case Studies in the Use of DNA Evidence to Establish Innocence After Trial," 1996.

All States Provide for DNA Databases

All the states have passed laws to establish databases containing DNA profiles of convicted offenders. All the laws at least cover sexual offenders. In addition, a majority of the states maintain DNA profiles for offenses against children or murder. Four states — Alabama, New Mexico, Virginia and Wyoming — require DNA profiles of all convicted felons. One state, Louisiana, has a law requiring DNA profiling of arrestees as well as convicted offenders, but the law has not been put into effect.

	Date	Sex Offenses	Murder	Assault	Offenses Against Children	Robbery	Burglary	Kidnapping	Juveniles	Felonies Only	Stalking
Alabama	1994	X	X	X	X	X	X	X		X	X
Alaska	1996	X	X	X	X	X		X	X	X	
Arizona	1989	X			X						
Arkansas	1995	X			X						
California	1989	X	X	X	X				X	X	
Colorado	1988	X			X						
Connecticut	1994	X									
Delaware	1994	X			X						
Florida	1990	X	X								
Georgia	1992	X			X						
Hawaii	1992	X	X		X						
Idaho	1997	X	X	X	X	X		X	X		
Illinois	1990	X			X						
Indiana	1996	X	X	X	X	X	X	X		X	
Iowa	1989	X	X	X			X	X			
Kansas	1991	X	X		X				X		
Kentucky	1992	X								X	
Louisiana	1997	X	X	X	X	X		X		X	
Maine	1995	X	X	X	X	X	X	X	X	X	
Maryland	1994	X			X						
Massachusetts	1997	X	X	X	X	X	X	X			
Michigan	1990	X		X							
Minnesota	1989	X							X		
Mississippi	1995	X									
Missouri	1991	X								X	

the technology used in DNA typing changed in the 1990s, requiring the retesting of old samples. "Without those samples in the freezer," he says, "they'd have to collect [new] samples if the technology changes again."

In addition, Niezgoda says that holding onto the samples would al-

low retesting if a DNA profile were challenged. "No one's made a mistake yet on a hit that I know of," he says. But two states — California and Florida — do reanalyze samples after a match is made, just to double-check.

Ferrara has made similar argu-

ments in the past about keeping samples, but today he is prepared to change his position. "The forensic science community has now settled on a standardized [procedure] in DNA profiling," Ferrara remarked in an interview in his office earlier this month. "If I got rid of the samples,

	Date	Sex Offenses	Murder	Assault	Offenses Against Children	Robbery	Burglary	Kidnapping	Juveniles	Felonies Only	Stalking
Montana	1995	X	X	X	X	X		X	X		
Nebraska	1997	X	X		X			X		X	X
Nevada	1989	X			X						
New Hampshire	1996	X							X	X	
New Jersey	1994	X									
New Mexico	1997	X	X	X	X	X	X	X	X	X	
New York	1994	X	X	X						X	
North Carolina	1993	X	X	X	X	X		X			X
North Dakota	1995	X			X						
Ohio	1995	X	X		X		X	X	X		
Oklahoma	1991	X	X	X	X			X			
Oregon	1991	X	X		X		X		X		
Pennsylvania	1995	X	X		X				X		X
Rhode Island	1998	X	X							X	
South Carolina	1995	X		X					X		
South Dakota	1990	X			X						
Tennessee	1991	X							X		
Texas	1995	X			X		X	X			
Utah	1994	X	X		X		X				
Vermont	1998	X	X	X	X	X	X	X			
Virginia	1990	X	X	X	X	X	X	X		X	X
Washington	1990	X	X	X	X	X		X	X		
West Virginia	1995	X	X	X	X	X		X			X
Wisconsin	1993	X	X	X	X		X	X			
Wyoming	1997	X	X	X	X	X	X	X		X	
TOTALS		50	29	22	36	15	13	20	16	14	6

Note: Congress has not passed a law requiring DNA profiling for federal offenders, including those in the District of Columbia.

Source: FBI Laboratory Division, June 1998

I could live with it today because I know it's all right."

Steinhardt says destruction of samples would allay some of his concerns, but he still worries about the "creeping expansion" of DNA databases. And he predicts that the public's attitude toward DNA databases will change as a result.

"Once you take it outside the criminal context, there will be substantial opposition to government databanking," Steinhardt continues. "Criminals don't have much of a lobby, but

newborns do. Average individuals do."

Law enforcement officials acknowledge the public concerns about privacy issues. "When you say government and computers and DNA, people's hair raises," the FBI's Niezgoda says.

"You've got to decide how much of your personal freedom you're willing to give up in return for security," Niezgoda adds. "I can tell you that from what I hear people are in favor of the data bank, even in favor of testing all arrestees." ∎

BACKGROUND

The Power of DNA

The first use of DNA as a tool for identification came more than a century after the substance was discovered by the German biochemist Friedrich Miescher in 1869 and some three decades after its molecular structure — the famous "double helix" of complementary strands of nucleotides — was accurately described in 1953 by the American biochemist James D. Watson and the British molecular biologist Francis Crick. [7]

The development of DNA typing resulted from genetic research by scientists in the United States and England: Roy White of the Howard Hughes Medical Institute at the University of Utah and a British geneticist, Alec Jeffreys, at the University of Leicester.

White developed a technique in 1980 that "revolutionized modern biology," according to Harlan Levy, a former federal prosecutor who traced the development of DNA identification in his book *And the Blood Cried Out*. [8]

White discovered that when a DNA molecule was cut, certain repetitive patterns could be identified. These strands of DNA had no known purpose, but they could be used to help locate specific genes. As Levy explains, the technique was called restriction fragment length polymorphism (RFLP) because a restrictive enzyme was used to cut DNA into various fragment lengths and the differences, or polymorphisms, were then analyzed.

Four years later, in 1984, Jeffreys discovered that some of those repetitive patterns at particular locations on the DNA "ladder" showed great variability between different people and thus could be used for purposes of identification. He published his findings the next year in the British journal, *Nature*, describing the results as a "genetic fingerprint." He listed several potential medical applications of the technique but also added that it could be useful for paternity or maternity testing and in forensic sciences.

Within three years, the technique in fact did move from the laboratory into

an English courtroom in an episode that DNA advocates like Levy today cite as evidence of the unique power of DNA typing both to convict the guilty and exonerate the innocent. [9]

The small village of Narborough had been shaken by the rape-murders of two teenage girls — in 1983 and 1986. Police identified a teenage suspect in the second killing, who initially confessed, then recanted and then confessed again. The suspect's father recalled later that he had heard of Jeffreys' work and asked his son's lawyer to "look into it." Police claimed they turned to Jeffreys on their own.

In any event, DNA analysis of semen from both crimes showed that the offenses were committed by the same person — but not by the suspect in custody. Police then decided to gather DNA samples — "voluntarily" — from thousands of men in the area: 4,582 in all. None of the samples matched, but one villager reported to police that he had heard a man in a pub saying that he had paid someone else to provide a sample for him.

When police went to question the man, he confessed to both crimes. In Colin Pitchfork's 1987 trial, the judge gave credit to DNA typing for the arrest. "If it wasn't for DNA, you might still be at large today," the judge said. Today, law enforcement experts are also quick to note that the technique cleared someone who was innocent. "The first use was just as important for its exonerative ability as its ability to convict people," says the DNA commission's Asplen.

Civil liberties advocates, on the other hand, see the story as a harbinger of DNA dragnets: mass collection of DNA samples from people without any need for police to show probable cause or even reasonable suspicion on an individual basis. "There are DNA dragnets, they've already occurred and it's only going to increase," says Benjamin Keehn, a Massachusetts public defender. He

notes that police investigating a recent rape at a Massachusetts nursing home asked all male workers at the facility to "cooperate, quote-unquote," and provide a DNA sample.

In the United States, DNA typing made its debut more as courtroom evidence than as an investigative tool, according to Asplen. The first conviction using DNA evidence appears to have come in January 1987, when a Florida teenager was found guilty of sexual battery after prosecutors used DNA analysis of semen taken from a rape victim, along with traditional blood and hair tests, to link him to the crime. [10]

Prosecutors scored at least two other convictions with DNA evidence in 1987, but also failed to win a conviction in an Oklahoma murder case despite a DNA match between blood found in the hose of the defendant's vacuum cleaner and the blood of a presumed murder victim.

By 1989, experts were estimating that DNA evidence had been introduced in at least 80 murder or rape cases in 27 states. Prosecutors were enamored of the technique, judges and juries seemingly impressed. But some doubts were being raised — doubts that would be aired and argued in courtrooms and elsewhere over the next several years.

Fighting for Acceptance

The infatuation with DNA was still fresh in January 1988 when California's attorney general, John Van de Kamp, sounded a cautionary note. "We can botch a golden opportunity by rushing too quickly into court," Van de Kamp said. [11] Over the next few years, police and prosecutors worked to develop expertise in DNA technology, while defense lawyers often tried to discredit DNA

Chronology

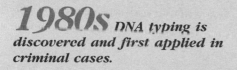

1950s *Molecular structure of DNA — deoxyribonucleic acid, the basic genetic material of all living cells — is discovered.*

1953
J.D. Watson and Francis Crick demonstrate "double helix" structure of DNA. Discovery lays basis for development of modern genetics.

———— • ————

1980s *DNA typing is discovered and first applied in criminal cases.*

1980
U.S. researcher Roy White discovers technique for cutting repetitive patterns of DNA: restriction fragment length polymorphism or RFLP.

1984
British geneticist Alec Jeffreys discovers RFLP technique can be applied for identification purposes; labels the DNA profile "genetic fingerprinting."

1985
U.S. geneticist Kary Mullis and others publish first paper describing "polymerase chain reaction" (PCR) to amplify small quantities of DNA for analysis.

1986-1987
DNA profiling exonerates suspect in rape-murder case in England; police use mass DNA screening of villagers to locate perpetrator.

1987
DNA identification is introduced in criminal cases in the U.S.

1988
Colorado passes law requiring genetic samples from convicted sex offenders before parole.

———— • ————

1990s *All 50 states establish DNA databases for some criminal offenders.*

1990
Twelve states pass legislation requiring DNA samples from some offenders; Virginia is first to require samples from all felons.

1991
Scientists debate whether DNA experts are exaggerating significance of DNA matches within ethnic or racial groups.

1992
National Academy of Sciences' report endorses general reliability of DNA evidence, but calls for higher standards for laboratories and more cautious approach in describing the frequency of occurence of a particular DNA profile in some instances.

1994
DNA Identification Act establishes guidelines for national DNA database, authorizes $25 million over five years in grants to states for setting up databases.

1995
O.J. Simpson is acquitted in sensational murder trial after defense lawyers attack prosecutors' DNA evidence.

1996
National Academy of Sciences' second report says reliability of DNA evidence is "not in doubt"; softens stance on laboratory standards, racial and ethnic identification.

1997
Louisiana passes law requiring DNA testing of arrestees, but implementation is delayed by financial and logistical issues. Attorney General Janet Reno creates national commission to study future of DNA evidence.

April 1998
Trial judge in Boston rules Massachusetts' law requiring DNA sampling of non violent offenders unconstitutional.

December 1998
New York City Police Commissioner Howard Safir calls for taking DNA samples from all arrestees; proposal is criticized by civil liberties advocates.

April 13, 1999
Massachusetts' highest court upholds DNA sampling of all convicted felons, reversing trial court decision that had ruled the practice unconstitutional.

May 8, 1999
National DNA commission endorses recommendations to ease inmates' use of DNA evidence to challenge convictions; panel also decides to oppose DNA profiling of arrestees.

September 1, 1999
Louisiana law requiring DNA samples from all arrestees due to take effect, but likely to be delayed because of funding, technical difficulties.

evidence in court. Some scientific experts supported some of the critiques — in particular, over the issue of the degree of certainty that could be given to a DNA match within a particular racial or ethnic grouping. In the face of some scientific uncertainty, some courts initially were slow to accept the evidence. By the middle of the 1990s, however, the legal doubts were largely suppressed and the admissibility of DNA typing in court firmly established.

The debate over racial and ethnic groupings was densely statistical, but fiercely fought and critical to courtroom use of DNA typing. The issue was publicly aired in the scientific community in a pair of articles in the journal *Science* in December 1991. A prominent Harvard geneticist, Richard Lewontin, and a colleague from Washington University in St. Louis, Daniel Hartl, argued that DNA advocates were ignoring genetic similarities within specific ethnic subgroups and consequently overstating the significance of a DNA match. Without subpopulation studies, they wrote, the high probabilities of identification being testified to in court were "unjustified and generally unreliable."

In an unusual step, the journal published a simultaneous rebuttal by two other geneticists: Ranajit Chakraborty of the University of Texas and Yale's Kenneth Kidd. They insisted that genetic differences were great even within population subgroups and that what they called "conservative" estimates of a match provided "overwhelming evidence that cannot be coincidental." [12]

A National Academy of Sciences committee on DNA technology gave further airing to the issue in April 1992 in a comprehensive report on the use of DNA evidence in court. [13] The report opened by describing DNA typing as a "powerful tool for criminal investigation and justice," but cautioned that the technology was "vul-

nerable to error" and interpretation of results required "an appreciation of the principles of population genetics."

On the racial grouping issue, the report recommended a conservative approach — known as "the ceiling principle" — that limited the statistical significance to be given to a DNA match in comparison to the so-called product rule favored by more enthusiastic DNA advocates. The report noted that varying approaches had produced wild variations in courtroom testimony about the possibility of a coincidental match — ranging from one in 500 to one in 739 billion in one case cited. The more conservative approach, the report concluded, represented "the most prudent course for the future."

The report also recommended a series of safeguards for laboratories performing DNA analyses. The issue reflected a concern about quality assurance at the private laboratories that were the first to offer DNA typing — and that had a financial incentive in promoting use of the technology. The report's recommendations appeared to be so restrictive that *The New York Times* initially described them as amounting to a "moratorium" on DNA evidence. When the report was actually released, the committee's chairman, Victor McKusick of Johns Hopkins University, said the Times report was wrong — and the newspaper ran a corrected story the next day under a headline that admitted the previous story was "in error."

Even with that high-level correction, the report still attracted strong criticism from many scientists and law enforcement advocates of DNA evidence. The result, according to Levy's account, was "an extraordinary victory" for the scientific critics of the report. The academy itself agreed to create a new committee to re-examine the issues of race and ethnicity in DNA identifications, and courts did not require expert witnesses to com-

ply with the committee's methodology in giving their testimony. [14]

Today, the issue has diminished in importance because DNA profiles are based on an examination of a larger number of "loci," or sites, on the DNA molecule: The FBI standard of 13 loci is now in more or less universal use. With each additional site, the likelihood of a coincidental match is diminished and the resulting "identification" can be stated with greater statistical certainty. "The forensic community has more or less all agreed that this is the way we'll calculate these numbers," Ferrara says. "When you have a declared match, for all intents and purposes that's an identification."

Gaining Acceptance

By the middle of the 1990s, DNA evidence was no longer a scientific curiosity but an established forensic technique. Police and prosecutors used it in investigations and criminal trials, while defense lawyers discovered the technology sometimes could produce powerful evidence to exonerate a defendant years after his conviction. Courts accepted the evidence in trials and sometimes even in post-conviction challenges. And the public, too, came to regard DNA evidence as valid and reliable.

Levy cites one especially telling demonstration of the power of DNA evidence: a Baltimore rape case in which the victim identified the wrong person as the perpetrator. [15] The victim in the 1990 assault told police that she had been attacked by her estranged boyfriend. After the boyfriend's arrest, however, a DNA analysis showed that semen recovered from the woman came from somebody else. The stunned prosecutors arranged for the man's release and pressed police to investigate further.

Databases and DNA Dragnets Aid Police in England

England is far ahead of the United States in building a DNA database of criminal offenders and using DNA profiling in criminal investigations. But Americans would rebel at some of the tactics that English police use, according to U.S. law enforcement officials and civil liberties advocates.

The United States is still working to establish a nationwide DNA database, four years after the Forensic Science Service for England and Wales established the world's first such computer linked file of DNA profiles of criminal offenders in 1995. Today, the British database includes profiles of more than 360,000 offenders and about 27,000 crime scene samples. That's much bigger than the FBI's data bank, which currently has about 150,000 offenders and 7,000 crime scene samples despite the United States' greater population and higher crime rate. Only 12 states are hooked up to the FBI's database so far.

Police in England and Wales say the DNA database is a valuable crime-fighting tool on a daily basis. "We've solved a large number of cases that were originally based solely on DNA profiles," says Peter Gammon, president of the Police Superintendents Association. As of last fall, the independent forensic service said the DNA database had matched 28,000 individuals to crime scenes — roughly, an average of 700 a month over the life of the data bank — and made 6,000 links between crime scenes. By comparison, the FBI counted only 182 "offender hits" and 233 crime-scene hits from its DNA database through July 1998.

The starkest contrast between the two countries, though, is the use of mass DNA screening — in effect, DNA dragnets — to investigate crimes in Britain. In several high-profile cases, police in England or Wales have collected DNA samples from hundreds or even thousands of people from the area where the crime occurred in an effort to identify a suspect. Theoretically, cooperation with the investigation is "voluntary," though police sometimes make clear that anyone who refuses to provide a DNA sample may face more intensive investigation as a result.

In fact, the first application of DNA profiling in a criminal case entailed the use of mass DNA screening of more than 4,000 people to try to flush out a suspect in a pair of rape-murders in a small village in the English Midlands in 1986. The apprehension of the suspect and his subsequent conviction were the subject of a best-selling book, *The Blooding*, written by the American crime author, Joseph Wambaugh. More recently, police in South Wales took DNA samples from about 2,000 men in a Cardiff neighborhood in 1995 to solve another rape-murder of a teenage girl. [1] And Gammon recalled that police in Bristol, England, solved a 1997 rape-murder case with mass DNA

screening. In that case, police discovered that a suspect had fled to South Africa without providing a sample, but South African police obtained a DNA sample from the man and sent it back to England for profiling.

Police in the United States have not used such tactics and would not be able to force anyone to provide a DNA sample without a search warrant based on specific information implicating the individual. By contrast, Gammon says Britons appear to have no problem with the technique. "People in this country, thankfully, still are shocked by heinous crimes, and they want to help the police in any way they can," he says.

U.S. law enforcement officials acknowledge that the United States lags behind Britain on working with DNA profiling. "It was really [Britain] that took the lead," says Christopher Asplen, executive director of the Justice Department's National Commission on the Future of DNA Evidence. But Asplen and others also acknowledge that civil liberties and privacy concerns are stronger in the United States than in Britain. "In the United States we have a different perspective on privacy and on the extent to which we would be willing to depend on a database," he says.

Civil liberties advocates say more directly that Britain's experience has little relevance to the United States. "They don't have a Bill of Rights. They have different views of civil liberties than we do," says Barry Steinhardt, associate director of the American Civil Liberties Union. "We fought a revolution against England because of our opposition to the kind of general searches that were conducted by the British colonial powers. That's why we have the Fourth Amendment. It was a direct reaction to standardless searches conducted by the British, and that's what these DNA searches are."

Gammon, however, did draw opposition in England last year when he called for establishing a universal DNA database — with profiles from the entire population. "It would save a lot of time and money," Gammon says. But he acknowledges the plan "has some real ramifications in terms of civil liberties."

The police group shelved the idea after it was criticized both on both privacy grounds and on practical considerations: the cost of establishing the database was put at 20 million pounds (about $32 million). Instead, police are now talking about a voluntary database of DNA profiles. Gammon says the broader database could still help police even if it did not include everyone. "It's an interesting development, and it hasn't been written off," he says.

---

[1] See *The Washington Post*, Feb. 2, 1996, p. A21; April 14, 1995, p. A1.

Finally, police came upon a second man, a friend of the original defendant and a former boyfriend of the victim's roommate. The two men resembled each other enough to explain the misidentification. The victim clung to her original identification, however, even after a DNA analysis showed the semen was the friend's. Prosecutors decided to accept a guilty plea with a 40-year prison sentence. Without the DNA evidence, the prosecutor in the case told Levy, the wrong man "would have been sent to prison."

The use of DNA evidence was also boosted by application of a different technology that made it possible to analyze samples containing minute amounts of blood or semen. The technique — known as polymerase chain reactions or PCR — had been developed in the 1980s by American biochemist Kary Mullis, then working with the Cetus Corp., a California biogenetics firm. [16] Mullis, who was researching the genetics of sickle cell anemia, figured out a way to get around the recurrent problem of having too little DNA to work with. By introducing a DNA sample in a biological substance (known as a polymerase), Mullis produced a chain reaction in which the original DNA was repeatedly replicated. The technique allowed a minute trace of DNA to be "amplified" a millionfold or more.

Mullis was awarded the Nobel Prize in chemistry in 1993 for his discovery. Despite its obvious applications to crime scene investigations, however, the technique did not gain immediate acceptance in police forensics — in part because the FBI was slow in developing guidelines for its use. Gradually, though, the technology became more common and its value recognized. The technique was also refined by the use of additional, easier-to-locate stretches of DNA for analysis — known as "short-tandem repeats" or STRs.

One dramatic application of PCR analyses came in the case of one of the suspects in the Feb. 26, 1993, bombing of the World Trade Center in New York City. Three days after the bombing, *The New York Times* received an anonymous letter claiming responsibility for the blast. Police recovered saliva from the envelope flap and had a PCR analysis performed, which showed a possible match with a suspect, Nidal Ayyad, who had previously been implicated by circumstantial evidence. The DNA "identification" was weak: the possibility of a coincidental match was one in 50. But it combined with the other evidence to satisfy the jury. Ayyad was convicted.

The most visible use of DNA evidence — less auspicious for DNA advocates — came in 1995, with the sensational murder trial of O.J. Simpson, the former football star, for the stabbing deaths of his former wife, Nicole Brown Simpson, and a friend of hers, Ronald Goldman. [17] The prosecutors had DNA evidence to show that blood with DNA matching Simpson's was found at Brown's house and that blood spots in Simpson's car and at Simpson's house contained DNA matching Nicole Simpson's and Goldman's.

Against such seemingly powerful evidence, a defense team led by Scheck mounted a determined attack to show that the DNA evidence was either tainted by laboratory contamination or planted by corrupt police officers. The strategy worked. To the vast surprise of the worldwide audience for the trial, the Los Angeles jury on Oct. 3, 1995, found Simpson not guilty.

DNA advocates worried that the Simpson verdict could be a setback for the technique, but the fears proved to be unfounded. Within a year, the National Research Council decisively reaffirmed the validity of DNA typing and softened some of the recommendations of its first report on the issue

four years earlier. "The admissibility of properly collected and analyzed DNA should not be in doubt," stated the report — which came to be known as NRC II. [18] The report backed away from some of the recommended safeguards in the earlier report and, most significantly, endorsed the less restrictive methodology for characterizing the significance of a DNA match. Levy says the report — without mentioning the Simpson case by name — "seemed to limit some key avenues of attack" that his attorneys had used in the trial. [19]

Creating Databases

The idea of creating DNA databases emerged quickly after the technology was introduced into courtrooms and police laboratories, both in England and in the United States. States began passing laws requiring genetic samples from some convicted offenders as early as 1988. Congress gave its support to the idea in 1994 by authorizing grants to the states and establishing guidelines for a national database. Defense lawyers and civil liberties advocates criticized many of the moves along the way and argued in court against the most expansive database proposals. So far, federal and state courts have uniformly upheld DNA sampling from convicted offenders, but the issue of testing arrestees or others has yet to be squarely joined in court.

FBI officials were predicting as early as 1988 that DNA typing would become as routine as fingerprinting and were talking about the possibility of linking state databases to a national system comparable to the bureau's national fingerprint files. [20] Colorado passed a law in 1988 requiring genetic sampling of convicted sex offenders before they could be paroled. California began considering the creation of a statewide database the next year. Virginia became the first state to require DNA samples from all convicted felons in 1990 — one of 12 states to pass some form of DNA sampling legislation that year. By 1994, 29 states had passed such laws; by 1998, all had done so. [21]

Congress threw its support behind the creation of DNA databases in 1994. The DNA Identification Act, part of the omnibus Violent Crime Control and Law Enforcement Act, specifically authorized the FBI to establish a national index of DNA identification records of "persons convicted of crimes" and analyses of DNA samples recovered from crime scenes and samples recovered from "unidentified human remains." Disclosure of the information was permitted only to criminal-justice agencies "for law enforcement purposes," in judicial proceedings, and for limited research or quality-control purposes after removal of personally identifiable genetic information. The act also authorized $25 million over a five-year period in grants to the states to help set up similar databases; states seeking grants had to abide by the same safeguards on disclosure.

Court cases challenging the DNA databases began soon after their creation. The federal appeals court in Richmond, Va., ruling in 1992 in a suit brought by six Virginia inmates, upheld the state's law enacted two years earlier requiring DNA sampling of all convicted felons. The majority opinion called DNA testing "a dramatic new tool for the law enforcement effort to match suspects and criminal conduct" and called the collection of samples a "minimal" intrusion comparable to fingerprinting all arrestees at the time of booking.

But in a dissenting opinion, Judge Francis Murnaghan discounted the usefulness of taking DNA samples from non-violent offenders and

warned that Virginia was "taking significant strides toward the establishment of a future police state." Three years later, a federal appeals court upheld, in another split opinion, a narrower Oregon law requiring DNA sampling only of violent and sexual offenders. Inmates in each case asked the U.S. Supreme Court to review the decisions, but the justices declined to take up the issue. [22]

State court cases challenging DNA databases were similarly unsuccessful, allowing the expansion of the databases to proceed without legal obstacles. Even as some states were beginning to set up DNA databases, other states that initially collected samples only from certain groups of criminals — most commonly, sex offenders — were changing their laws to take samples from all felons. But states did face practical constraints in expanding the databases: money, time and expertise. Hundreds of thousands of DNA samples were collected but went unanalyzed. Today, the backlog is estimated at 480,000 and is continuing to grow. In addition, states have failed to collect samples from tens of thousands of offenders who are required by law to provide them. "There are a tremendous number of people who should be in the system but aren't in the system," Asplen says.

After an uninterrupted string of courtroom victories, advocates of DNA databases suffered their first legal defeat last August when a lower court judge in Boston invalidated the Massachusetts law requiring sampling from violent and sexual offenders. The judge agreed with the inmates' claim that the 1997 law — not yet put into effect at the time — amounted to an unreasonable search under both the federal and state constitutions. In April, however, the state's highest court reversed the decision in a unanimous opinion. "The state has an established and indisputable interest in

preserving a permanent record of convicted persons for resolving past and future crimes," the court declared, "and now will use DNA identification for these purposes." [23] ∎

CURRENT SITUATION

Expanding Databases

Gov. George E. Pataki, R-N.Y., was flanked by police, prosecutors and his own criminal justice chief when he unveiled details last month of a legislative proposal to dramatically enlarge the state's DNA data bank. Pataki's plan, announced at a news conference on April 13, calls for expanding the database to include anyone convicted in the state of a felony or attempted felony. In addition, Pataki also wants the director of his criminal justice service to study the possibility of including arrestees in the data bank. [24]

The proposal — if enacted and fully implemented — would take samples from about 50,000 offenders a year and would expand the database more than tenfold. It currently includes samples from about 6,000 people convicted since 1994 of any of 21 crimes, including sex offenses, homicide or felony assault. "The untapped potential for advancing public safety is enormous," Pataki told reporters.

The governor failed to acknowledge, however, that even the present value of the state's existing database is itself untapped. When Pataki first called for expanding the database in his annual state of the state speech in January, the newspaper *Newsday* reported that only 1,500 of the 6,000 samples had actually been analyzed. In addition, the library of profiles was not being used because guidelines had yet to be drawn up for its operation — nearly five years after enactment of the law creating the database and three years after the first samples were drawn. Officials were hoping to complete the guidelines by the end of the year, the newspaper reported. [25]

New York's example is typical. All 50 states have DNA database laws, but many of the databases are on paper rather than on-line. The FBI's national database was announced with fanfare in October, but only 12 states have hooked up so far, according to Niezgoda. The database includes about 150,000 offenders — a tiny fraction of the 33 million individuals in the FBI's criminal fingerprint files — and about 7,000 DNA profiles from crime-scene evidence.

Louisiana, the only state with a law on the books to collect DNA samples from arrestees, has no statewide database yet — two years after the law was passed. The law is theoretically due to take effect on Sept. 1, but Louisiana officials say funding and implementation problems will likely result in another delay. "We would like to see it get through," says Pat Wojtkiewicz, who runs a regional forensic science laboratory in Shreveport that serves northern Louisiana. "We think we could solve a lot of cases that way."

Nationwide, a daunting backlog of DNA samples has been collected but not analyzed. Virginia, which has been taking DNA samples from all felons since 1990, has the biggest individual backlog: about 180,000 samples collected but awaiting analysis. To try to whittle that number down, Ferrara has contracted with a private laboratory in Northern Virginia, Bode Technology, which is processing some 2,000 samples a week.

If no new samples were added, it would still take two years to eliminate the backlog.

Ferrara also joined with other members of the DNA commission in calling for federal funds to help states do the work. "This would be the one area where it would be useful to throw money at the problem and see some results," Ferrara explains. The commission asked for $22.5 million in the coming fiscal year; the Clinton administration included $15 million in its proposed budget.

Even more worrisome, Niezgoda says, is the backlog of unanalyzed crime-scene evidence. "We've got thousands of rape kits that are just sitting in lockers," Niezgoda says. "It's like having a database of fingerprint cards but never dusting for fingerprints."

"It's more than just money," Niezgoda adds. "The crime-scene side needs people and needs training, both in the forensic science and in the courtroom."

Despite the implementation problems, lawmakers in many states are taking up proposals this legislative season to expand the coverage of their state database laws. There is also a bill pending in Congress to require DNA sampling of federal offenders, including offenders in the District of Columbia. The bill, introduced by Sens. Mike DeWine, R-Ohio, and Herb Kohl, D-Wis., would fill a seemingly inadvertent gap; it would require sampling of offenders convicted of murder, armed robbery and burglary, among other crimes. [26]

Civil liberties advocates concede that expansion of DNA databases to cover more convicted offenders is difficult, if not impossible, to stop. Steinhardt concedes the federal bill is likely to be passed if it gets to the floor, and observers in New York predict the legislature will approve some expansion of the state's database. But financial and logistical

considerations may weigh against covering all convicted felons.

Working the Cases

When sheriff's deputies in Maricopa County, Ariz., found Denise Johnson's body in a remote location outside Phoenix several years ago, one of the clues at the scene was a scar on a nearby tree that looked as though it might have resulted from a collision with a pickup truck. By a fortunate coincidence, the tree was an unusual type that grows wild and was susceptible to DNA identification. When deputies later arrested Mark Bogan for the killing, they found seedpods in the bed of his pickup truck — seedpods that a DNA analysis showed were a likely match for seedpods from the tree at the murder scene. The evidence convinced a jury that Bogan was lying when he denied being at the murder scene; he was convicted of first-degree murder and sentenced to life imprisonment.

Bogan's 1993 murder conviction — believed to be the first case in the United States based on plant DNA identification — gives one more indication of the variety of uses of DNA technology in the courtroom. "There is nothing comparable to that in the fingerprint area," says George Washington's Rowe. "We have this extremely powerful tool. We just don't know how far we'll be able to run with it. It's just a question of how imaginative we can be with the use of DNA."

Police and prosecutors are already using their imagination to use DNA technology in investigating and prosecuting more cases. When DNA typing was first developed, advocates cautioned that it would be useful only in a relatively few cases — mostly rapes and homicides — where the perpetrator's blood or semen could

At Issue:

Should DNA samples be collected from arrestees and included in law enforcement databases?

HOWARD SAFIR
New York City Police Commissioner

WRITTEN FOR *THE CQ RESEARCHER*, MAY 1999.

*e*xpanding the use of DNA data-banking will greatly assist law enforcement in its crime-fighting efforts. The sooner in the process that this reliable and powerful technology is employed, the greater the benefits. That is why I am calling for the taking of DNA samples from all those arrested for a fingerprintable offense. By excluding suspects early in the process, valuable time and resources will be saved.

In addition to identifying the guilty, it will also quickly exonerate the innocent. Sixty people have been exonerated through post-conviction DNA analysis. Unfortunately, there may be others who have been wrongly convicted of crimes. Taking DNA samples from all arrestees will prevent such unfortunate mistakes from happening.

Data-banking arrestee profiles will also enhance our ability to solve crimes. We simply need to look at England's experience with DNA data-banking. There, DNA samples are taken from anyone arrested for a misdemeanor or felony. Since 1995, they have linked 36,000 suspects to crime scenes and 6,700 crime scenes to other scenes.

While the existing convicted-offender data banks are a good start, they do not go far enough. Only the FBI and 12 states participate in the national convicted-offender data-bank system, to date, only 450 matches have been made. England has at least that many hits in a week. Additionally, my staff reviewed 100 forcible sexual assault cases; only 18 offenders had previous convictions that would have included them in this state's data bank. Under the law I propose, 75 would have been included.

Using this technology, however, carries an obligation to protect individual rights and privacies. Safeguards should be put in place to control the operation of the data bank. If a person is acquitted or not prosecuted, their profile would be expunged from the data bank and the sample destroyed. The information contained in the data bank would be used for law enforcement identification purposes only. It would not be used for medical research or insurance purposes, and it would be a crime to misuse the information.

We need to responsibly use the technology available to solve crimes and prevent others from being victimized. My proposal to take DNA samples from arrestees offers the right balance between a person's privacy rights and the right of all citizens to live in a crime-free society. It will act as both a sword and a shield, identifying the guilty and exonerating the innocent.

BARRY STEINHARDT
Associate Director, American Civil Liberties Union

WRITTEN FOR *THE CQ RESEARCHER*, MAY 1999.

*t*he proposed creation of wholesale DNA data banks of anyone who is arrested for any reason presents a frightening potential for a "brave new world" in which genetic information is routinely collected and used in ways that will result in abuse and discrimination.

Let's start with what should be the obvious. Arrest does not equal guilt and no one should suffer the consequences of guilt until after they have been convicted. Forcing arrestees to provide blood samples does not serve any legitimate security concern when there are ample other means of confirming identity. The only possible justification is investigatory, and if law enforcement has reason to suspect an individual then it can and should seek a warrant.

It also should be obvious that DNA is not analogous to a fingerprint. DNA samples can provide insights into the most intimate workings of the human body, including the likelihood of the occurrence of over 4,000 types of genetic conditions and diseases. Given the scope of information how can anyone justify forced testing of a person arrested for jaywalking or taking part in a political demonstration?

Our country has a long history of creating databases for one purpose that later assume additional functions. For example, census records created for general statistical purposes were used during World War II to round up innocent Japanese-Americans and to place them in internment camps.

Notwithstanding the constitutional impediments, the single greatest obstacle to the DNA database proposal now is the existing backlog of 450,000 unprocessed samples. With an estimated 15 million arrests last year, it makes no sense for law enforcement even to consider putting its dollars into collecting and processing samples from people who have never been convicted of a crime. Wouldn't it make more sense to put scarce resources into processing the overwhelming backlog of samples, not to mention those that will continue to be generated under the existing program?

For those who think otherwise, prepare for this modification of the Miranda warning: "You are under arrest. Anything in your DNA can and will be held against you and your family in a court of law . . . and by insurance companies, medical researchers and hackers who break into the system." By the time you call your lawyer, it may be too late.

DNA Testing of Newborns Stirs Privacy Debate

I magine your worst nightmare as a parent: Your child is missing — perhaps abducted, maybe feared lost in a plane crash or some natural disaster. A body is recovered. It may be your child, but the normal forensic techniques cannot make a positive identification. What to do?

One answer being pushed by some law enforcement officials and missing-child advocacy groups is DNA profiling of children at birth. But some civil liberties advocates fear that an idea now being discussed as a voluntary option for parents could be expanded in the future to become mandatory registration of DNA identifications for everyone from birth.

In Florida, some 34 hospitals are participating in a program organized by the Florida Department of Law Enforcement to give parents the chance to have their newborns' DNA tested at birth. Parents take the DNA sample home with them on a specially treated card that can be stored for life. Officials stress that the program is voluntary and that neither the hospital nor the state agency keeps a sample.

"Well over 95 percent of the parents who we offered this agreed to have the DNA sample taken," says Warren Jones, vice president for public relations at Tallahassee Memorial Hospital. "Many parents seemed to take some comfort in knowing that that sample would be available if needed."

"We're very proud of it," says Jennifer McCord, spokesperson for the state agency. The program began as a pilot project with Tallahassee Memorial last year and grew quickly to the 34 hospitals participating today.

McCord says the department views the program as a success even though so far none of the DNA samples taken has been put to use in identifying a youngster. But Larry Spalding, legislative counsel for the Florida chapter of the American Civil Liberties Union (ACLU), says he is "nervous" about the idea. "I understand that that would give parents some closure and peace of mind," Spalding says. "But I can also foresee that [in the future] we could have a situation where we had a child who didn't have this identification and we come back and say had this been mandatory, we could have resolved this issue. And

then we're off on a path that we're concerned about."

The Florida House of Representatives passed a bill in March to require hospitals to offer DNA sampling for newborns, but the measure stalled in the state Senate after drawing opposition from the Florida Hospital Association. "We are very supportive of the concept of hospitals' voluntarily offering this," says Bill Bell, the association's lobbyist in Tallahassee. "The problem with this particular piece of legislation is that it mandated that hospitals offer this."

Issues surrounding DNA testing of newborns have flared elsewhere around the country. New York City Mayor Rudolph Giuliani drew sharp criticism in December when he said, in response to a reporter's question, that he would have "no problem" with DNA testing or fingerprinting of all children at birth. "There is absolutely no reason why people should be afraid of being identified," Giuliani said. [1]

"This really does evoke the specter of *Brave New World*," responded Norman Siegel, executive director of the New York Civil Liberties Union. Giuliani's police commissioner, Howard Safir, who advocates expanding DNA testing of criminal offenders to include arrestees, quickly stepped in to stress that he had made no proposal for testing newborns as suggested by the reporter's question.

Meanwhile, more Florida hospitals are expected to join those that are already offering parents the option of DNA sampling for newborns. The cost is relatively nominal — about $1.40, according to Jones.

Rep. Bob Starks, a six-term Republican lawmaker who sponsored the House bill, insists that privacy advocates have no cause for concern. "We have all the safeguards to make sure privacy is protected," he says.

But Spalding disagrees. "We're slowly eroding privacy as technology advances," he says. "The bad part about it is that when you voluntarily give up a right, it's much easier to expand it and say, 'We haven't had any problems so far, so why don't we go further?' "

---

[1] Quoted in *The New York Times*, Dec. 17, 1998, p. B4.

---

be obtained. Today, however, DNA typing can be performed on trace amounts of blood, sweat or saliva that a perpetrator might leave on a murder weapon or an object at a crime scene. Prosecutors in Orange County, Calif., for example, have won murder convictions in three cases where DNA samples were obtained from a base-

ball bat, a hammer and a rope.

In New York City, detectives recently obtained a DNA sample from a murder suspect less directly — from the saliva he left behind on a coffee cup that he had been drinking from while under interrogation. [27] The suspect, Ahron Kee, who had been arrested on a petty theft charge, was

being questioned in connection with a June 1998 slaying. A DNA analysis on Kee's saliva linked him not only to the killing but also to two other homicides and two rapes of teenage girls.

Such deceptive practices concern some civil liberties advocates. "This is a form of search that should be done only after the police have obtained a warrant," says the ACLU's Steinhardt. "It shows how arbitrarily police officers can act and why they should not be given the power to decide who will be DNA tested based on an arrest."

But Safir calls the police tactic "perfectly legal and certainly proper." "If a suspect leaves a coffee cup behind, it's abandoned property," Safir says. "We have every right to use that for investigative purposes."

Police and prosecutors in some places, such as Orange County, are also using DNA databases not only to link suspects to specific crimes but also to try to link crimes with common features. "If we had a crime with a rope that happened in a park, we would put park and rope in there and all the crimes that had a similar situation would automatically come on the screen," explains Tori Richards, a spokeswoman for the Orange County district attorney's office. "If we had somebody who was arrested for that, we could run that person's DNA through the system and link that person with these other offenses."

Meanwhile, a San Diego-based company is working to develop a device to allow police to perform DNA analyses right at a crime scene. [28] The device, about the size of a 3 x 5 index card, is equipped with a microchip in the center that can be connected to a portable computer. A DNA sample can be placed in the device, analyzed on the spot and computer-checked against profiles in a remote database. Officials of Nanogen, the company working on the device under contract with the National Institute of Justice, the research arm of the Justice Department, say the device could be in police cars within two years. Bode Technology Group will be testing prototypes this summer. "The current processes are very, very labor-intensive," says Thomas Bode, president of the Virginia company. "This will

cut down on that labor intensity to a significant degree." The device would also cut the cost of DNA profiles perhaps to as low as $10-$20, less than half of the current cost.

Civil liberties advocates say they have no problems with the technology, but still worry about its application. "The underlying problem is not the technology," says Steinhardt. "It is the existence of large databases and collections of DNA that have great potential for misuse." ∎

OUTLOOK

New Applications

Today, nearly five decades after Watson and Crick discovered the secrets of DNA, the study of genetics enables scientists and doctors to diagnose and treat diseases, develop new plants and vegetables and even to produce clones of adult sheep.

The applications of DNA technology in forensic science are at least as startling and, for many people, as wondrous. But DNA technology does not eliminate the need for old-fashioned police work. DNA evidence is not available in all criminal cases and in many cases is not determinative — for example, in a rape case where the defense is consent.

Beyond the criminal justice system, DNA identification has a host of other applications. It is now often being used in paternity disputes — providing results far more reliable than previous techniques, such as blood typing. Military officials turned to DNA analyses recently to identify a Vietnam-era soldier buried in the Tomb of the Unknowns. Historians used DNA typing to try to determine whether Thomas Jefferson fathered a

child by his African-American slave, Sally Hemmings. Human rights activists applied DNA technology to establish the identity of a young girl whose parents were killed by the Argentine military when she was an infant.

For many people, however, the creation of DNA databases raises concerns that the technology has a dark side, that it will be used to unlock personal genetic secrets. "It's a cost to some people, it's not a cost to others," says Asplen of the Justice Department's DNA evidence commission.

Some advocates of law-enforcement DNA databases acknowledge some dangers for privacy rights in the use of genetic information outside the criminal justice system. "If I have my child tested, who else is going to have access to that information?" Virginia's Ferrara asks. "We're going to have difficult questions to face about who has that information and who has access to that information."

But Ferrara and other law enforcement officials minimize the dangers from DNA databases on criminals. "It's hard for me to look at the convicted-offender databases and think that they're going to abuse those samples," Ferrara says.

Civil liberties advocates are less sanguine. "We are seeing an ever-widening circle of DNA surveillance," says the ACLU's Steinhardt. "Every expansion of data banks and every new use of those data banks increases the risk of abuse and discrimination," Steinhardt says.

Steinhardt says some concerns about criminal-offender databases could be eased if the DNA samples were destroyed after identification information was entered. For any databases that include arrestees, Steinhardt says, profiles should be expunged if no conviction is obtained. New York police Commissioner Safir agrees on the need to expunge DNA profiles in dismissed cases, but sees no special concern in taking DNA samples as part of the normal police booking process. "We take fingerprints at the time of arrest," Safir says, "and there is no reason that we should not pass legislation to take DNA samples."

For its part, the Justice Department commission has now decided to oppose DNA testing of arrestees, at least for the time being, but primarily because of the urgency of dealing with the backlog of already-collected DNA samples awaiting analysis rather than because of civil liberties concerns. "Absent very substantial financial support, taking DNA from arrestees would do more harm than good," Asplen says. The commission will be advising Attorney General Reno of its position in a letter within the next two months.

Whatever law enforcement agencies do, however, one critic warns that the biological samples routinely collected in hospitals and university medical centers could pose an even greater danger to individual privacy.

"If they get analyzed and stored in ways that can be interchanged, then you have an enormously powerful system," Billings says. The result, he says, could be "a potential enhancement for government surveillance that is disproportionate to government control."

Despite those concerns, some public health experts and organizations are today advocating DNA testing of all newborns — a step they say can help in early diagnosis and treatment of genetic diseases. Meanwhile, the government of Iceland has approved a plan to compile a database of genetic, medical and genealogical information about the country's entire population of 270,000. The plan envisions selling the information to biotechnology companies that can use it to find new clues about the nature of disease. Most Icelanders appear to favor the plan despite opposition from some privacy-minded critics. [29]

Billings criticizes the idea, but credits Icelanders with giving the proposal more serious consideration than data-banking has received so far in the United States. "They had a very broad debate about the problem," Billings says. "Such a standard has not been met in the United States."

"The big issue is the balance on privacy," the FBI's Niezgoda acknowledges. "As the technology gets cheaper, and the privacy issues become less theoretical, then as a nation we have decisions to make." ∎

Notes

[1] Background on the Jones case drawn from the *Daily News* (New York), April 8, 1999; April 9, 1999; The Associated Press, April 9, 1999.

[2] For background, see Robert K. Landers, "Solving Crimes With Genetic Fingerprinting," *Editorial Research Reports*, June 30, 1989, pp. 353-364.

[3] See Paul R. Billings (ed.), *DNA on Trial: Genetic Identification and Criminal Justice* (1992). Billings is now the administrator for three veterans hospitals in Texas.

[4] The Web site address is http://www.hope-dna.com.

[5] Council for Responsible Genetics, "Position Paper on Genetic Discrimination," updated Aug. 18, 1997, www.genewatch.org/gendisc.html.

[6] National Research Council, *DNA Technology in Forensic Science*, (1992).

[7] For the early history of human genetics, see Robert Shapiro, *The Human Blueprint: The Race to Unlock the Secrets of Our Genetic Script* (1991).

[8] Harlan Levy, *And the Blood Cried Out: A Prosecutor's Spellbinding Account of the Power of DNA* (1996). Much of the historical material is drawn from Levy's account.

[9] The Narborough murders are recounted in Joseph Wambaugh, *The Blooding: The True Story of the Narborough Village Murders* (1989). Summaries are drawn from Levy, *op. cit.*, pp. 26-31, and Shapiro, *op. cit.*, pp. 302-303.

[10] See Debra Cassens Moss, "DNA — The New Fingerprints," *ABA Journal*, May 1, 1988, pp. 66-70.

[11] Quoted in Moss, *ibid.*, p. 68.

[12] See R.C. Lewontin and Daniel J. Hartl, "Population Genetics in Forensic DNA Typing," *Science*, Dec. 20, 1991, pp. 1745-1750; Ranajit Chakraborty and Kenneth K. Kidd, "The Utility of DNA Typing in Forensic Work," *ibid.*, pp. 1739-1745. For a summary of the debate, see Levy, *op. cit.*, pp. 111-116.

[13] National Research Council, *op. cit.*, See Levy, *op. cit.*, pp. 117-120.

[14] *Ibid.*, p. 121.

[15] Levy, *ibid.*, pp. 87-103.

[16] *Ibid.*, pp. 138-141. See also Paul Rabinow, *Making PCR: A Story of Biotechnology* (1996).

[17] See Levy, *op. cit.*, pp. 159-188.

[18] National Research Council, *The Evaluation of Forensic DNA Evidence* (1996), p. 2.

[19] Levy, *op. cit.*, p. 193.

[20] See Jean L. Marx, "DNA Fingerprinting Takes the Witness Stand," *Science*, June 17, 1988, pp. 1616-1618.

[21] "1998 CODIS DNA Laboratory Survey," FBI Laboratory Forensic Science Systems Unit, January 1999, p. 10.

[22] The cases are *Jones v. Murray*, 4th U.S. Circuit Court of Appeals, April 7, 1992; *Rise v. Oregon*, 9th U.S. Circuit Court of Appeals, July 18, 1995.

[23] The case is *Landry v. Attorney General*, April 12, 1999.

[24] Quotes and background drawn from *New York Law Journal*, April 14, 1999, p. 1.

[25] Matthew Cox, "As Debate Rages, DNA Unused: Guidelines Needed for Database on Criminals," *Newsday*, Jan. 18, 1999, p. A8.

[26] See *Legal Times*, May 10, 1999, p. 1.

[27] See *The New York Times*, March 9, 1999, p. B1.

[28] See *USA Today*, May 4, 1999, p. 4A.

[29] See *The Washington Post*, Jan. 12, 1999, p. A1.

Bibliography

Selected Sources Used

Books

Billings, Paul R. (ed.), *DNA on Trial: Genetic Identification and Criminal Justice,* **Cold Spring Harbor Laboratory Press, 1992.**

The book includes eight essays on a variety of scientific and legal issues, including DNA data-banking, mostly from a critical perspective. Each essay includes reference notes. Billings, a geneticist, is now chief medical officer for a system of three veterans hospitals in Texas.

Levy, Harlan, *And the Blood Cried Out: A Prosecutor's Spellbinding Account of the Power of DNA,* **Basic Books, 1996.**

Levy, now a criminal defense attorney in New York, wrote this account of the use of DNA evidence in criminal investigations and prosecutions based on nine years as a prosecutor in the Manhattan district attorney's office. The book traces the history of DNA sampling, its first application to criminal cases in the 1980s through the controversies over the practice in the United States and what he depicts as its nearly universal acceptance today. The book includes 12 pages of source notes.

Shapiro, Robert, *The Human Blueprint: The Race to Unlock the Secrets of Our Genetic Script,* **St. Martin's Press, 1991.**

Shapiro, a professor of chemistry at New York University, provides an accessible account of the scientific developments in human genetics, including a chapter on DNA identification. The book includes 24 pages of source notes and a three-page bibliography.

Wambaugh, Joseph, *The Blooding: The True Story of the Narborough Village Murders,* **William Morrow, 1989.**

Wambaugh, a former police detective turned author, gives a popular recounting of the use of DNA typing to solve the Narborough murders in England in the early 1980s — exonerating a suspect who had falsely confessed to the rape-murder of one young girl and then, after mass DNA sampling in the village, correctly identifying the man who committed that crime and another similar killing.

Articles

Landers, Robert K., "Solving Crimes With Genetic Fingerprinting," *Editorial Research Reports,* **June 30, 1989, pp. 353-364.**

The article gives a good overview of the development of DNA typing and its early use by police and prosecutors in the United States.

Reports and Studies

National Research Council, *DNA Technology and Forensic Science,* **National Academy Press, 1992.**

This first report by the National Research Council endorsed the use of DNA typing as courtroom evidence but called for careful case-by-case evaluation and safeguards so strict that some experts initially viewed it — mistakenly — as urging a moratorium on its use. The report includes chapter notes and a six-page glossary.

National Research Council, *The Evaluation of Forensic DNA Evidence,* **National Academy Press, 1996.**

This report — sometimes called NRC II — endorsed a less restrictive statistical methodology for evaluating DNA evidence than that recommended by the previous National Academy of Sciences committee. The report includes a 14-page list of references, a five-page glossary and a listing of state court cases on the admissibility of DNA evidence.

U.S. Department of Justice, *Convicted by Juries, Exonerated by Science: Case Studies in the Use of DNA Evidence to Establish Innocence After Trial,* **1996.**

The report summarizes 28 cases in which DNA evidence was used to exonerate defendants who had previously been convicted of crimes — rape or sexual assault and sometimes other offenses. It also includes a discussion of the policy implications of the case studies, commentaries by experts representing a range of views and a two-page glossary.

FOR MORE INFORMATION

American Academy of Forensic Sciences, 410 N. 21st St., Suite 203, Colorado Springs, Colo. 80904-2798; (719) 636-1100; http://www.aafs.org.

American Civil Liberties Union, 125 Broad St., New York, N.Y. 10004-2400; (212) 549-2500; www.aclu.org.

Council for Responsible Genetics, 5 Upland Road, Suite 3, Cambridge, Mass. 02140; (617) 868-0870; www.gene-watch.org.

National Commission on the Future of DNA Evidence, 810 7th St., N.W., Washington, D.C. 20531; (202) 307-5847; www.ojp.usdoj.gov/nij/dna.

2 Adoption Controversies

CHRISTINA L. LYONS

I t was the 1960s, and the woman identified in court documents as Jane Doe No. 7 was 19 and pregnant.

"My story isn't unique," she recalled. "There were thousands of us then as there are now — engaging in sexual activities and making serious mistakes — either by being sexually active in the first place or by not using contraception." [1]

Unwilling to marry the father, have an abortion or raise a child she could not afford, the young woman put her baby up for adoption. "It wasn't an easy choice," Jane continued. "It's hard to carry a child for nine months, give birth, hear the first few cries, then silence as the child is whisked off to the arms of the waiting adoptive parents."

Jane was assured that under state law the original birth certificate and adoption records would remain sealed and that her child would never be able to locate her. After Jane married, she told her husband about her secret but no one else — not her parents, her siblings or her friends.

Then, on Nov. 3, 1998, Jane's secret was threatened. Oregon voters approved a ballot initiative that would allow adopted children to see their birth certificates at age 21, regardless of the natural parents' objections. That would enable adoptees to track down their birth parents more easily.

Terrified at the prospect of her past arriving on her doorstep uninvited, Jane went to court to overturn the initiative, known as Measure 58. Among other things, she and other birth mothers contended that it invaded their constitutional right to privacy. But in July 1999, U.S. Circuit Judge Paul J. Lipscomb ruled against the birth mothers, who are appealing

the verdict. Meanwhile, the law is on hold.

The lawsuit outraged adoptees like Nehalem, Ore., artist Helen Hill, a co-author of Measure 58. Hill, 44, calls the suit "a violation of our civil rights" and argues that the 14th Amendment protects the privileges of all citizens from being abridged.

Moreover, says Shea Grimm, 33, a founder of the Internet-based adoptees'-rights group Bastard Nation, Measure 58 is not just about helping adoptees contact their birth mothers. "Many of us have already done that" despite closed records, says Grimm, a Measure 58 co-author. Rather, she says, the battle for open records is for adoptees' "dignity," for the right to the same piece of paper — a birth certificate — that everyone else has a right to see.

The National Council for Adoption (NCFA), which represents more than 100 private adoption agencies, has led the opposition to open adoption records. "We think the answer is clear and unambiguous," says NCFA President Bill Pierce. Birth parents "were promised confidentiality, and opening records would not only be inconvenient for them but [devastating]."

A similar battle over birth records is playing out in Tennessee, where a 1996 law that permits adult adoptees and close relatives immediate access to sealed birth records has been challenged. The law permits the birth

parent or adoptee to register a "contact veto" if they do not want to be contacted.

Charles Raymond Lokey is one of many adoptees in Tennessee who filed for access to his birth records under the new law, but he has been unable to see them because the law was put on hold.* Lokey contends that the uncertain legal status of the law may have contributed to his brother's death in 1997. [2]

Both Lokey and his brother John were adopted in 1956. In 1997, about a year after Charles applied for access to his adoption records, his brother began having pains in his abdomen. When he belatedly decided to seek treatment, it was too late. He collapsed on the hospital steps and died in the emergency room.

Doctors said John died of a massive heart attack and had suffered from coronary disease — usually a genetic condition. "Had my brother and I had access to our adoption records and an opportunity to contact our birth parents and learn our family medical histories, my brother might have been less likely to disregard his pains, and he might be alive today," Charles asserted. [3]

In all the states except Kansas and Alaska, birth records of adoptees are sealed to provide privacy for the birth mother as well as the adoptive families, who often fear birth parents might later want their children back. Kansas and Alaska give adoptees age 18 and over unconditional access to their birth records. Nineteen other states allow limited access.

Birth mothers who want to remain anonymous say the children they gave up for adoption years ago have no right to barge into their lives unannounced and without permission. "Forcing a reunion is tantamount

---

* The law was only in effect for 18 days before it was challenged and put on hold; it does not apply in cases of rape or incest.

21 States Give Adoptees Access to Birth Records

Only two states, Alaska and Kansas, permit adoptees age 18 and over to have unconditional access to their birth records. Nineteen other states allow access under certain conditions.

State	Conditions for Access
Alaska	Age 18.
Colorado	Age 18 for adoptions after June 9, 1999, unless birth parent objects.
Delaware	Age 21, unless birth parent objects.
Hawaii	Age 18 for adoptions after Jan. 1, 1991, unless birth parent objects.
Indiana	Pre-1940 records open.
Iowa	Pre-1941 records open.
Kansas	Age 18.
Kentucky	Age 21, with birth parent's consent.
Maryland	Pre-1947 records open.
Minnesota	Age 19 for adoptions after 1982, unless birth parent objects.
Montana	Records before July 1, 1967, open; court orders needed for records from July 1, 1967, to Sept. 30, 1997; records open at age 18 from Oct. 1, 1997 to present, unless birth parent objects.
Nebraska	Age 25, with birth parent's consent, but adoptive parent can veto.
Ohio	Pre-1964 records open.
Oklahoma	Post-1991 records open at age 18, unless birth parent vetoes.
Oregon	Age 21; law is on hold because of a challenge.
Pennsylvania	Age 18, if birth parent files waiver giving consent.
Tennessee	Age 21, unless the adoptee is a product of rape or incest; birth parent can veto any contact with adoptee; law is under challenge.
Vermont	Pre-1986 records open at age 18 with birth parent's consent; on later adoptions, birth parent can veto.
Virginia	Records for adoptions on or after July 1, 1994, are open to adoptees at 18 and adoptive and birth parents.
Washington	Post-Oct. 1, 1993, records open unless birth parent vetoes.
Wisconsin	Age 18, with birth parent's consent.

Sources: Bastard Nation, The Evan B. Donaldson Adoption Institute

to an emotional rape," says "Cindy," who gave up her daughter for adoption after being raped.

But adoptees cite a variety of reasons for seeking access to their records. Some want medical and genealogical information. Others are curious about their parents' religion and country of origin. Still others just want to meet their parents, the people who gave them life. A wide range of organizations representing adoption agencies, birth parents and adoptive families also support opening birth records.

Some adoptive parents want to help their children find their birth parents when the children reach an appropriate age. Some even welcome birth parents into their family. Others, however, are terrified that access to birth records will enable birth parents to arrive on the scene and steal the affections of the child.

As an alternative to open access, some organizations support the creation of a national adoption registry that would allow adoptees and birth parents to obtain information about each other if both agree.

Two other adoption issues also continue to generate heated debate: adoptions by gays and lesbians and adoptions of children of another race. Those who support such adoptions point to the high number of foster children waiting to be adopted and a 1996 federal law intended to speed up the movement of children out of the foster-care system. As of January 1999, 520,000 children were in the system, and 110,000 were eligible for adoption. About 36,000 foster children were adopted in 1998. [4]

Recent estimates show the number of adoptions from foster care is increasing, to a large extent because of innovative adoption programs being implemented in the states, particularly New York and Illinois. (*See story, p. 27.*) With adoptions on the increase, however, concerns are being raised about the use of the

Internet to promote adoptions, the need for stricter regulations on international adoptions and increasing allegations of so-called wrongful adoption.

As courts, officials and parents and adoptees grapple with these issues, here are some of the key questions being asked:

Should adoption records be opened?

Movies and TV shows, not to mention the news media, often find high drama in the reunions of birth mothers and adoptees. In reality, however, adoptees' original birth records in many states can be opened only through a court order.

Most states give adoptees a birth certificate with the names of their adoptive parents but not the original certificate showing their biological parents. To locate their birth mothers (or vice versa), they must turn to search handbooks in public libraries, adoption registries, private investigators or the Internet. (*See story, p. 32.*)

Advocates of open access argue that society's views on adoption have changed radically since the mid-20th century, when original birth records of adoptees were first sealed. Even the Child Welfare League of America (CWLA), which was once opposed to opening records, now favors state laws that would allow adult adoptees to obtain information about their birth parents, provided the birth parents consent to the disclosure.

Wanting information about one's biological parents is perfectly normal, according to adoption researchers. In a 1996 survey, they found that 72 percent of adopted adolescents wanted to know why they were adopted, 65 percent wanted to meet

their birth parents and 94 percent wanted to know which birth parent they resembled. [5]

Moreover, research also suggests that keeping birth parents and adoptees separated can cause psychological and emotional problems for all parties involved — adoptive parents as well as adoptees. [6]

Research also strongly indicates that birth mothers want to reconnect with their children. According to a 1989 survey in Maine, every birth parent contacted — 130 in all —

Gay adoptive parents Jon Holden, left, and Michael Galluccio legally adopted their son Adam after New Jersey courts cleared the way for gay and lesbian couples to adopt children jointly.

AP Photo/Mike Derer

wanted to be found by the child they had placed, and 95 percent of the adoptees surveyed wanted to be found by their birth parents. Other studies report similar findings. [7]

"Birth mothers really validate the findings," says Madelyn Freundlich, executive director of the Evan B. Donaldson Adoption Institute in New York City. "So many of these women say it was always their hope that their children would" locate and contact

them, she says.

Frank Hunsaker, a lawyer who represents the birth mothers challenging Measure 58 in Oregon, takes a different view. "What about the few who don't want to be contacted?" he asks. He concedes that some birth mothers who oppose the measure may even want to be contacted, but "this statute takes it out of their control completely. Reunions can be forced on someone without their control."

The NCFA's Pierce opposes open records because, he says, "In any society, laws should be designed to protect the rights of the minority." Pierce and other opponents of open records also dispute the research on methodological grounds. They argue that the samples often are self-selected rather than random and that birth mothers who are trying to maintain their privacy would not participate in such surveys. (*See "At Issue," p. 35.*)

Many birth mothers expected "that their identity would be protected and honored by all parties associated with the adoption for their entire lives," Josette P. Marquess, a Florida adoption official, told a House subcommittee in 1998. "I can tell you from my professional experience that not all adoption reunions are happy, wanted or in the best interest of all who are reunited." [8]

Cindy, the birth mother who was raped, says the maternity facility where she placed her baby for adoption said her identity would be revealed only if she signed up at a mutual-consent registry when the child was 18. "There were laws promising me confidentiality," she insists.

Lauren Greenbaum, lead adoption counsel for the Boys and Girls Aid

Society, a private, child-welfare organization in Oregon, says it supports Measure 58 in principle but opposes changing the rules retroactively. In the 1950s and '60s, she says, there was shame around being an unwed mother, and "people chose adoption with the idea they did not have to give their identity. If you're going to change the rules, you need to give these people a chance to say 'no.' Measure 58 doesn't do that."

But New York attorney Fred Greenman, who is involved in defending the open-records laws in both Tennessee and Oregon, insists no written promises of confidentiality or privacy were ever made. And Judge Lipscomb ruled in Oregon that the "plaintiffs have failed to demonstrate either any contractual right to absolute privacy and confidentiality, or any impermissible impairment of such rights."

Measure 58 co-author Hill contends that a child's birth records don't belong to the birth parents. Therefore, she says, "They can't own a right to privacy with someone else's document." Further, she points out, if a mother doesn't want to meet her child, she can always say "no" if she gets a phone call.

A common reason cited among adoptees for wanting contact with birth parents is to obtain medical information. Most states require birth parents to provide adoptees with a family medical history. But the records in adoption files are often inadequate, Greenman says. "They reflect what a scared 18-year-old remembered of her family medical history 20 or 30 years ago," he says.

Some have suggested that the way to resolve the birth records debate is with a "mutual consent" registry simi-lar to the one proposed by Sen. Carl Levin, D-Mich. The American Adoption Congress, the CWLA and other organizations support Levin's proposal, which would allow adoptees and birth parents who want to be contacted by each other to signal their interest in sharing information by signing a registry.

Supporters of open records say a registry would be inadequate. "You still don't get a birth certificate," Hill

Longtime foster parents Steven Lofton and Roger Croteau cannot adopt 8-year-old Bert (front) because of a Florida statute barring adoption by a homosexual. In May, the American Civil Liberties Union challenged the law on behalf of Lofton and other Florida gays and lesbians. The family now lives in Oregon.

Courtesy of Steven Lofton

says. "It remains sealed." The birth certificate also could provide clues to an adoptee's social history, Hill argues. There are many cases in which adoptees have discovered, for example, that they were raised in a religion different from their birth parents' religion.

Hill also points out that registries are ineffective because some birth parents have died, particularly those of older adoptees, eliminating the possibility of obtaining consent.

Some adoptive parents think registries are much safer than opening birth records. The "Baby Jessica" case is often cited by adoptive parents who fear open records. The case drew worldwide attention when the courts in Detroit, Mich., forced foster parents who had cared for the child for more than two years to return the toddler to her birth parents after they changed their minds. [9] The fear that biological parents will reappear to reclaim their children prompts many people to adopt children from overseas, according to a recent NCFA survey.

But Joe Kroll, executive director of the North American Council on Adoptable Children (NACAC), says that "99 percent of the adoption community has really changed its thinking on records." He says adoptees and often their adoptive families want a variety of information, such as medical histories, which often can be obtained only by contacting the birth parents.

Jane Nast, an adoptive parent in Morristown, N.J., knows the fear that comes with being contacted by a birth parent. Nast says that when her adopted son's birth parents asked to meet him she was scared. But she eventually agreed to the reunion and now believes it was good for everyone.

In fact, Nast and her husband later helped their adopted daughter meet with her birth mother. The reunions "brought us closer to our kids," says Nast, president of the American Adoption Congress, a volunteer organization dedicated to opening birth records.

Should gays and lesbians be allowed to adopt?

Steven Lofton, 41, and Roger Croteau, 43, are the only parents 8-

year-old Bert and his two siblings have ever really known. Steve is the at-home dad, getting the children ready for school and taking them to swimming lessons and other activities. Roger, a nurse, supports the family. Both are active in the PTA, and both are called "Dad" by the children. "We do all the things that other families do," Lofton says. "We eat dinner together every night. We go on family outings."

Lofton also keeps busy administering medication. All of the children they have taken into their home as foster children, five in all, were HIV-positive at birth, including two who later died of AIDS.

When Bert became eligible for adoption, Lofton filled out the adoption forms but left one question blank: "Are you gay or bisexual?" He was told he would not be able to adopt unless he answered the question. "I felt it was an invasion of my personal privacy," he says. "It's discriminatory — if I answer truthfully, I'm disqualified; if I lie I'm in trouble."

Nevertheless, Bert has remained with Lofton and Croteau, even when the family moved to Oregon to be closer to relatives. "If Florida would give up its jurisdiction over Bert, I could adopt him legally in Oregon," Lofton says. But Florida won't budge. According to a Florida statute, "No person . . . may adopt if that person is a homosexual." Florida is the only state that expressly bars homosexuals from adopting.

In May, the American Civil Liberties Union (ACLU) filed a class-action lawsuit challenging the statute on behalf of Lofton and other gays and lesbians in Florida. The case is being closely watched for its potential landmark implications. [10]

The actual number of children living with gay or lesbian parents is unknown, particularly since many states do not require single parents who adopt to reveal their sexual preference. None-

theless, according to the ACLU, researchers estimate that 6-14 million children live with at least one gay parent. [11] Gays and lesbians form their families through a variety of methods, including adoption; the availability of donor banks and surrogate mothers; and artificial insemination.

New Jersey in 1997 became the first state to permit adoptions by homosexuals and unmarried couples under state law. The state agreed to change its policy to settle a lawsuit filed by more than 200 gay couples who charged that New Jersey's rule barring adoptions by gay couples violated both state law and their right to equal protection. Previously, gays in New Jersey only could adopt as individuals, forcing couples to undergo a lengthy and expensive adoption process twice.

The majority of organizations representing adoption agencies or adoptive families support adoptions by homosexuals. [12] Judges increasingly have given custody and visitation rights to homosexual parents. According to the ACLU, 22 states have allowed lesbians and gays to adopt through state-run or private adoption agencies.

But a few states still consider a parent's sexual orientation in adoption decisions. Those that oppose placements with homosexuals often express concern that the children will become gay or be pressured to become gay, that they will be living in an "immoral environment," that they may be molested by the homosexual adoptive parents or that they may be exposed to AIDS. [13]

The ACLU's complaint in the Florida case alleges the law ignores the best interests of children by precluding an entire class of qualified adults from adopting. It claims the state adoption policy violates the children's and adults' constitutional rights to equal protection, privacy, intimate association and family integrity.

Deb Harder, former program ser-

vices manager for Adoptive Families of America, says she has seen many children benefit from placement with a homosexual couple, particularly foster children from abused or neglected backgrounds and children of different races and ethnicities. "People of different sexual orientation are so familiar with bias they make very good parents for children who are different or victimized by bias and prejudice," she says.

"We have seen enough adoption success stories to say this is a different family configuration," Harder adds, "but it doesn't devalue from the health and well-being of the child."

Ann Sullivan, director of adoption services at the CWLA, says that children have a fundamental need for a family and that an atypical family arrangement shouldn't automatically be ruled out based on just one criterion.

"I'm seeing a tendency to oppose all single parents because of a fear of gay and lesbian parents," Sullivan says. "And a lot of good parents could be denied an opportunity to adopt."

Several studies have indicated that children raised by homosexuals do not suffer psychologically or physically, and that the parenting instincts and skills of gays and lesbians do not differ from those of heterosexuals. [14]

According to Charlotte Patterson, a professor of psychology at the University of Virginia, the sexual orientation of the parent is not a predictor of how well children adjust. "The quality of parenting a child receives is more important than a biological connection or the gender of a parent," Patterson testified in a 1996 Hawaii case regarding same-sex marriage. [15]

Many conservative groups still argue that placing children with homosexuals is morally and ethically wrong, and that the studies of homosexual parenting are seriously flawed.

When newborn twins from Texas were adopted in January by two high-profile Washingtonians, Elizabeth

Birch, executive director of the AIDS group Human Rights Campaign, and her partner, record-industry lobbyist Hilary Rosen, the conservative Family Research Council (FRC) denounced the adoption.

"A mountain of social science, the world's major religions, common sense and observation tell us that children have the best chance to thrive in married, mother-and-father-based families," Robert H. Knight, the group's director of cultural studies, said. "Placing babies in a lesbian household deliberately deprives these children of a father's love."

Conservative groups like the FRC also are concerned that children with homosexual parents will have a tendency to experiment in "homosexual behavior" or become gay themselves. Lynn Wardle, a law professor at Brigham Young University, contends that the studies indicating no damaging psychological or emotional effects on children of homosexual parents are "ludicrous. They don't come close to meeting the standards" of adequate research, he says, noting that many studies use samples that are too small or flawed technically.

"Most of the studies of homosexual parenting are based on very unreliable quantitative research, flawed methodologically and analytically ... and provide a very tenuous empirical basis for setting public policy," Wardle wrote. [16]

Wardle also argues against homosexual adoptive parents because homosexual relationships have a "tremendous" breakup rate, as well as AIDS and other health problems associated with a homosexual lifestyle. Children in foster care have experienced possibly years of abuse or neglect, he says, and "you want to provide the best chance you can for

those children because they already have been through the mill."

As for newborn children, both Wardle and the FRC argue that all infants available for adoption can be placed in homes with a mother and a father because of the greater demand for infants.

Earlier this year an Oklahoma legislator failed to get passage of a bill that would have barred joint adoption by any couple — heterosexual or homosexual — living together in any manner "not solemnized as marriage" by state law. Homosexual marriage is banned by Oklahoma law.

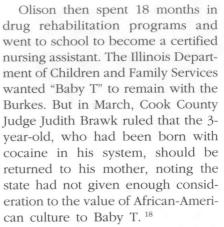

Eric Goldscheider and his wife Debbi Friedlander of Amherst, Mass., adopted Rebecca Maisha (left) from Kenya and Joshua from Jamaica.

"Homosexual people are unstable in their lifestyle — period," said the bill's sponsor, Republican Rep. Tim Pope. "They say you can't legislate morality. Why not? We legislate morality every day of the week." [17]

Should children be adopted outside their race?

In February 1996, a powerful Chicago alderman, Edward M. Burke, and his wife Anne, a state appellate judge — both white — became foster parents for a black child whose mother, Tina Olison, was a drug abuser.

Olison then spent 18 months in drug rehabilitation programs and went to school to become a certified nursing assistant. The Illinois Department of Children and Family Services wanted "Baby T" to remain with the Burkes. But in March, Cook County Judge Judith Brawk ruled that the 3-year-old, who had been born with cocaine in his system, should be returned to his mother, noting the state had not given enough consideration to the value of African-American culture to Baby T. [18]

The National Association of Black Social Workers (NABSW) ignited the fight over transracial adoptions in the early 1970s, when it vehemently opposed placing black children in white homes "for any reason." [19] The group's stand prompted many adoption agencies to encourage same-race adoptions — which in turn ignited many court battles.

Many adoption experts thought the debate over transracial adoption would end with the 1994 Multi-Ethnic Placement Act (MEPA), which prohibited an agency that receives federal funds from denying the placement of a child on the basis of race or national origin.

But the debate continued, largely because many social workers found the law unclear on a key point: Could race be considered a factor at all? So in 1996 Congress amended MEPA with the Interethnic Adoption Provisions, which prohibits an agency from denying placement of a child for adoption solely on the basis of race.

Supporters say the law addresses the problem of too many minority children languishing in foster care. But critics say that placing a child with a family of different race or ethnicity can be threatening to the

Cutting Red Tape in Illinois

Judy and Gary Berman of Buffalo Grove, Ill., agonized for six years while they awaited various court rulings and state agency decisions that finally allowed them to adopt their first foster child, a boy they had cared for since he was 10 months old.

But that was years before the Illinois Department of Child and Family Services and the local court system overhauled their procedures. By the time they adopted their fifth child, in 1998, their wait had been cut down to a little more than 18 months.

Judy says the waiting was difficult for her and her husband, as well as the children. "When you take a child as a foster child, you take them as somebody else's children," she says. "You fall in love with them, but still feel they're someone else's child. I think the children feel the same thing. Once you adopt them, and they know they're your children, it's a different feeling."

Many states like Illinois have overhauled their programs and moved a record number of children into permanent homes. In fiscal 1998, 36,000 foster children were adopted in 42 states, up more than 20 percent over the average number of adoptions from the previous three years, according to the North American Council on Adoptable Children. The increases are attributed to recent changes in public opinion, political support and laws that have shortened foster-care stays and designated new resources to support adoptions.

Illinois reported one of the most dramatic increases. In fiscal 1991, adoptions numbered about 708. By fiscal 1998, the number reached a record 4,293. And for fiscal 1999, which ended June 30, preliminary estimates indicate that more than 7,000 adoptions from foster care took place, according to Jess McDonald, director of the Illinois Department of Children and Family Services.

McDonald says most of the increase has taken place in the Chicago area alone, where about 5,500 adoptions have occurred in the past fiscal year — up 70 percent from the previous year.

In 1997 the Illinois General Assembly passed legislation that requires the courts and the state to move children to permanent homes more quickly. The legislation requires judges to hold a hearing within 12 months to decide on a permanency goal for the child and to review it six months later. Shortly thereafter, Congress passed the Adoption and Safe Families Act of 1997, which called on states to move children more quickly into permanent homes

and provided additional adoption assistance for families.

McDonald attributes much of the success in Illinois to his partnership with Judge Nancy Salyers, who meets with representatives of the courts, the state attorney's office, public defenders and adoption-services providers. McDonald and Salyers have been closely involved in the development of legislation, particularly the so-called permanency legislation, which has helped families like the Bermans.

McDonald's agency also slashed the number of children each caseworker was assigned — from 75 children to 25 children per worker. And in some cases, it was just a matter of requiring workers to show up and do their job, McDonald says.

The state also introduced performance contracting, indicating to public and private agencies what the expectations were for getting kids adopted or reunified with their families. Other changes have included an expansion of the state's adoption information center, which lists every child that is available for adoption, launching a new Web site and a partnership with the Freddie Mac Foundation, which has donated $960,00 to finance "Wednesday's Child," a weekly NBC television program that promotes adoption.

But McDonald says the improvements have also come from the "subtle things — just picking up the phone and saying, 'We have a problem judge, let's solve it.' "

Meanwhile, the system also has seen a 150 percent increase in cases in which children are reunified with their natural parents, partly due to changes in the child-protection system that enable the state to assure the safety of the child.

There also has been an increase in the number of subsidized guardianships, usually by a relative who does not want to formally adopt. In fiscal 1998, subsidized guardianships reached 1,129. In 1999 the number is expected to reach 2,250 — including up to 1,800 children in Cook County alone.

Judy Berman applauds the changes that have helped her and her husband adopt six foster children, and they hope the state will allow them to adopt two more. She says it would make it easier still if the courts could work faster.

And, she adds, Illinois needs to stick to the 12-to-18-month time frame to place the children in permanent homes. "That's all these kids should have to wait to know that this is forever."

child's racial identity. Moreover, they say white parents cannot properly prepare a minority child for the racism of the real world, and that the law should do more to recruit adop-tive parents of color.

But waiting for a family of color is dangerous to the child, says Gloria Hochman, communications director of the National Adoption Center. "The longer children remain without a permanent family," she says, "the more damaging it is to their identity, self-esteem and chances for growing into healthy adulthood."

Former Sen. Howard Metzenbaum, D-Ohio, author of MEPA, says opposing transracial adoption is counterproductive. "Black social workers are so determined that white families not adopt black children that they're willing to keep them in foster homes . . . rather than [help] white families adopt the children," he said. [20]

Historian Elizabeth Bartholet says there just aren't enough black families for all the black children waiting for homes and that the search for scarce, same-race families keeps black children in foster care longer than white children. And the longer they are in foster care, she says, the lower their chances of getting adopted because most adoptive parents want young children.

According to the U.S. Department of Health and Human Services (HHS), about 60 percent of the children in foster care in the United States are African-American and other minorities, and 35 percent are white. [21]

The NABSW counters that adoption agencies simply are not working hard enough to recruit black families. It points to special programs designed to recruit black families as evidence that such recruitment can work. The program One Church, One Child, for example, has been recruiting families from the African-American Chicago community since 1980, when it was started by Father George Clements, then pastor of Holy Angels Roman Catholic Church.

Others, like the NACAC's Kroll, say large numbers of qualified blacks are available to adopt black infants and foster children but are excluded from consideration or don't try.

Olison feels racism is the problem in Illinois. She and six other parents filed a federal lawsuit in July claiming that Illinois' welfare system discriminates against African-American parents and their children. The suit claims that although African-American children comprised 19 percent of the child population in Illinois, they constituted 78 percent of the children in state custody in 1997. The suit also contends that the family-reunification rate for white children in state custody is almost double the rate for African-Americans.

Rita Simon, a professor in the

Unsealed birth records in Florida enabled Michael Chalek of Boca Raton to learn he had been sold as a baby by his young, unwed mother. He is seeking a new birth certificate naming his actual parents.

AP Photo/Gary I. Rothstein

School of Public Affairs at American University, says the 1994 law apparently has had little effect on the number of transracial adoptions.

According to the HHS, of the 31,000 children adopted from the public welfare system in fiscal 1997, fewer than 10,000 were adopted transracially or transculturally.

"It's a very emotional issue," says Hochman of the National Adoption Center. "There are workers at agencies who still believe that same-race placements are the best for a child. At the same time, I think there are many agencies that are trying to comply with the law. But you still can't wipe out years of attitude with legislation."

But many opponents of transracial adoptions say they are simply looking out for the children. Kroll says he and his wife were very naive when they adopted a Korean infant, who is now 23. While he doesn't regret adopting his daughter, he says he has learned that race plays a critical role in the development of children and that, despite all their efforts, he and his wife were unable to prepare their daughter for the real world, where racism exists.

Now Kroll helps other families cope with transracial adoptions, even though he still thinks children are better with families of the same race.

The Child Welfare League also opposed the MEPA. The league's Sullivan thinks there's been an overly strict interpretation of the law. "We still do think culture is important to children," she says, "and there is a tendency to minimize this importance when it comes to African-American children."

Almost a dozen studies indicate that about 75 percent of transracially adopted preadolescent and younger children adjust well in their adoptive homes. [22]

Critics of transracial adoption have argued that black children may do fine in white families through the elementary years but will become increasingly uncomfortable with their racial identity as they encounter prejudice at dating age and adulthood. However, a 20-year study of 200 white parents and their predominantly black adopted children reached a different conclusion. Researchers who contacted the children

Jesse Helms Zeroes in on Adoption

Thousands of foreign infants and children are adopted by Americans every year. But Sen. Jesse Helms, R-N.C., is concerned about American children being adopted by foreign families. More specifically, he wants to prevent it.

Helms, chairman of the Senate Foreign Relations Committee, and Sen. Mary L. Landrieu, D-La., are pushing legislation that would implement the Hague Convention on Protection of Children and Cooperation in Respect of Intercountry Adoption, which seeks to unify worldwide standards on adoption. The United States signed the treaty in 1994, but the Senate has not ratified it. So far 30 countries have signed it, and 16 have implemented it.

While the legislation primarily focuses on standards to protect parents adopting children from overseas, it also seeks to provide some standards on the adoption of U.S. children by foreign parents.

There are no firm statistics on how many U.S. children are adopted by foreign families because there are no regulations on such adoptions, according to Maurine Evans, executive director of the Joint Council on International Children Services. Canada and Western Europe are believed to be the main countries receiving the estimated 300 children a year, she says. Under the Helms-Landrieu legislation, the number would be closely tracked.

Adoption organizations are not concerned about the tracking, but they have raised a loud cry about two other provisions in the legislation, one stipulating that the children must not go to single-parent families. Many adoption organizations believe the provision aims to prevent children from being adopted by homosexuals.

An aide to Helms denies that the provision targets homosexuals. Rather, she says, it's about "trying to bring some stability" into the children's lives. And "when you're sending a child out of our borders, you are losing total control."

Other countries have implemented such provisions, according to Evans. South Korea, for example, only places children with married couples. Many countries will allow placement of children with single women but not with single men. China doesn't place children with homosexual men or women, she says. Still other countries "look at it on a case-by-case basis."

Another provision of the legislation would require a 12-month waiting period before a child can be placed with a family outside the United States.

"A prohibition against adopting for 12 months will delay placement into permanent families," Evans says. "It creates a delay that is inevitably detrimental to the child. Another concern is that other countries will reciprocate and impose a delay."

Helms' aide says the provision is intended to allow parents in the United States an opportunity to adopt all the available American children. She says that with so many would-be parents on waiting lists to adopt infants, agencies should be able to find suitable homes domestically for their children.

The aide said the senators are trying to negotiate with members of the adoption community on these provisions. One consideration is to give babies available for adoption a higher priority than older children waiting in foster care. She said the senators would not want to unnecessarily continue to delay a foster child's wait for a permanent family, but that they would like to see the available infant babies go to the many parents who are on waiting lists.

The focus of the Helms-Landrieu legislation is foreign children adopted by U.S. parents. In fiscal 1989, the State Department reported that 8,102 overseas children were adopted by U.S parents, including 3,544 from Korea. In fiscal 1998, 15,774 children were adopted from foreign countries, with the majority this time (4,491 children) coming from Russia.

Under the Helms-Landrieu legislation, agencies would have to be accredited to provide intercountry adoption. The State Department would be the central authority in charge of monitoring agencies, which would have to provide medical reports in English, six weeks of preadoption counseling, liability insurance and permit examination of their practices and records.

Evans says the Hague Convention should give adoptive parents peace of mind knowing that any agency they use is accredited. The convention also should allay birth parents' and adoptees' fears regarding how the children are treated by adoptive or birth families in other countries, she says.

Immigrant Visas Issued to Orphans Coming to the U.S., 1998

Russia	4,491
China	4,206
South Korea	1,829
Guatemala	911
Vietnam	603
Other	3,734
Total	15,774

Source: National Health Adoption Information Clearinghouse, March 9, 1999

when they were in their 20s found they were comfortable with their racial identity and did not have any trauma during dating and adolescence. Other studies have indicated similar findings. [23] ■

BACKGROUND

Focus of Concern Shifts

Adoptions were not regulated by statute in the United States until 1851, when Massachusetts became the first state to pass an adoption law. It required the written consent of the birth parents, a joint petition by both adoptive parents, an adoption decree by a judge and legal separation between the child and the birth parents. [24]

After World War I, the large number of orphaned and illegitimate children increased the appeal of adoption. The rising influence of psychiatry also reinforced the public's acceptance of adoption as a way to re-create a nurturing parent-child relationship.

Despite the growing concern about protecting the welfare of children, courts generally supported the efforts of biological parents to prevent their children from being taken away. The U.S. Supreme Court's landmark 1923 ruling in *Meyer v. Nebraska* held that the 14th Amendment protects an individual's right to raise his children. Thereafter, court decisions consistently upheld natural parenthood as a constitutionally protected right.

Nevertheless, social workers and psychologists continued to debate whether the parents' or the child's interest should be considered first. In the meantime, many children languished in

foster care, and the burdens on the states' welfare systems grew.

In 1980, Congress passed the Adoption Assistance and Child Welfare Act, aimed at getting children out of foster homes and returned to their biological families. The law also provided financial subsidies to couples, including those on welfare, as an inducement to adopt children who were unlikely to be adopted otherwise.

In the next decade, however, the focus of concern in the adoption community gradually shifted to giving more attention to the child's welfare. President Clinton has called for improved efforts to increase adoptions out of foster care. On Dec. 14, 1996, he issued an executive memorandum urging adoption officials to move children more quickly into permanent homes.

In 1997, Congress reflected the changing attitudes about adoption by passing the Adoption and Safe Families Act (ASFA). It encouraged courts and social workers to put more emphasis on children's safety rather than returning them to dangerous family situations. The legislation also gave financial incentives to states to find adoptive parents. It authorized $20 million per year per state from fiscal 1999-2003 to all states that exceeded the average number of adoptions they had completed during fiscal 1995-1997.

Sealed Records

The court records of adoption proceedings traditionally have been kept confidential to protect the privacy of those involved. In the early 20th century, courts began to seal the records and birth certificates, initially only denying natural parents access to the information, and later adult adoptees. [25]

In 1925, the New York Court of Appeals set a legal precedent supporting sealed records when it refused a mother's plea that the Spence Alumnae Society, an adoption agency, turn over the name and address of the couple who had adopted her son. "[S]ecrecy is the foundation underlying all adoption, and if this secrecy is not to continue this great work must suffer," the court said. [26] By the early 1950s, almost every state had statutes sealing adoption records.

After World War II, a growing number of middle-class, single mothers relinquished their children born out of wedlock and demanded secrecy. Later, however, adult adoptees and natural parents launched an "Adoption Rights Movement," pleading for information to conduct searches for one another, according to historian Wayne Carp.

In 1978, the publication of *Adoption Triangle* influenced the debate over sealed vs. open records. Written by three researchers, the book advocated changing laws to allow adult adoptees access to original birth records. [27]

In 1979, the Adoptees' Liberty Movement Association filed a class-action federal lawsuit seeking to open New York's sealed adoption records law. It argued that adoptees had a constitutional right — under the First, 13th and 14th amendments — to the information contained in the adoption records. But the courts, including the 2nd U.S. Circuit Court of Appeals, ruled the adoptees did not have a "fundamental" right to learn the identities of their birth parents. [28]

Unable to get help from the courts in the search process, adoptees and birth parents turned to mutual-consent registries, which allowed parties to an adoption to register if they wanted to find one another. Once a match was made, the two sides would be notified and sometimes provided counseling. In 1979 Maine and Nevada became the first two states to

Chronology

1800s *View of adoption as a means for adults to gain heirs or servants gives way to treatment of adoptees as biological offspring.*

1851
First U.S. adoption statute is passed in Massachusetts.

1881
Michigan requires judges to investigate adopting families before issuing adoption decrees.

— • —

1900-1950s
Thousands of children are left homeless after the world wars. The Supreme Court gives primacy to the rights of natural parents.

1923
In *Meyer v. Nebraska*, the Supreme Court rules that the 14th Amendment protects the birth parents' right to bring up their children.

1925
In *Henderson v. Spence Alumnae Society*, the New York Court of Appeals calls secrecy "the foundation underlying all adoption."

— • —

1960s-1970s
Legalization of abortion and increased acceptance of unwed motherhood reduce the number of healthy, white infants available for adoption. Stigma of adoption also begins to lift and adoptees want records opened.

1978
National Association of Black Social Workers says transracial adoptions deprive black children of their cultural heritage.

1979
In *ALMA v. New York*, U.S. Court of Appeals rules adoptees do not have a "fundamental" right to learn the identities of their birth parents. Maine and Nevada implement mutual-consent adoption registries.

1980
Congress passes the Adoption Assistance and Child Welfare Act, aimed at finding permanent homes for hard-to-place children.

1982
Minnesota reforms its sealed records law, stating that biological parents must file an affidavit asserting their privacy rights and expressly denying consent to release of any information.

1987
New Hampshire makes it illegal for homosexuals to adopt.

— • —

1990s
Criticism grows that adoption laws do not adequately address the best interests of children. State policies discouraging interracial adoption come under fire.

1994
Congress passes the Multi-Ethnic Placement Act (MEPA).

1996
Congress passes amendments to 1994 law to make it clear that race or national origin could not be the sole reason for rejecting a child's placement with an adoptive family. Tennessee passes law permitting all adult adoptees and certain close relatives immediate access to the formerly sealed birth records, except in cases of rape or incest.

1997
The Adoption and Safe Families Act makes the health and safety of children the primary consideration in placement decisions. New Jersey becomes the first state to permit adoptions by homosexuals and unmarried couples.

1998
Oregon voters approve Measure 58, a ballot initiative allowing adoptees to see their original birth certificate when they turn 21, regardless of the wishes of the natural parents. Group of birth mothers immediately files lawsuit to overturn it.

1999
New Hampshire legislature reverses law prohibiting gays and lesbians from adopting. ACLU files suit to overturn Florida ban on adoptions by gays and lesbians. Illinois judge awards black mother with history of crack addiction custody of her own 3-year-old child rather than white foster parents. Judge says state's recommendation that child remain with foster parents did not give enough weight to the value of African-American culture.

Click If You Want to Adopt Darlene

Darlene, age 5, is a "bright, friendly and happy girl who likes to dance and play outdoors. . . . Darlene is working on social interaction with other children and how to avoid being aggressive with them."

Termain is an "adorable little boy who loves to watch Barney and TV ads. . . . You must be able to manage Termain's ongoing medical needs, daily medication and therapy visits. He is susceptible to infection and should not be exposed to a large number of people."

Darlene and Termain are among the hundreds of foster children whose stories, pictures and sometimes even voices can be found on the Internet. The World Wide Web has become an increasingly popular way for state agencies to advertise the children who need a permanent home, many of them with special needs.

"The Internet seems to be a very effective way" to find homes, says Marianne Clarke, deputy executive director of the National Adoption Center (NAC). In 1995, aided by a $150,000 annual federal grant, the NAC worked with a similar agency, Child Awaiting Parents, to create the first Web site showing children awaiting permanent homes. The center's Faces of Adoption site now features more than 1,800 children, and the number continues to grow in the wake of a 1997 law that called on states to move more rapidly to find permanent homes for the thousands of children waiting in foster care.

The Edmonds family of Anchorage, Alaska, adopted Steven (back row, left) after seeing him on Faces of Adoption. *Steven, 19, was the first child to be placed by the Web site.*

Last month, 20 children were adopted as a direct result of being advertised on the site, and to date 108 children have found homes through the project.

The NAC has helped some 40 states and the District of Columbia to post pictures of their foster children. The center also works with several states to help them create their own Web sites. Now at least 31 states have created Web sites, according to the Evan B. Donaldson Adoption Institute in New York City.

Many of the children have special needs, such as being born with crack cocaine in their system, fetal alcohol syndrome and emotional scars from physical or sexual abuse. Some Web sites provide descriptions of mental retardation, sickle-cell anemia or other problems that the children may have and how families can cope with such problems.

Some critics fear, however, that the Web could dangerously expose the children to molesters and pedophiles. Larry Sinnett, program administrator in Denver's Department of Human Services' Family and Children's Division, encountered such fears when he first proposed advertising foster children available for adoption on-line.

"My first reaction is, 'Why?" said Denver City Council member Ramona Martinez when she first heard the idea. "It sounds pretty insensitive to me." [1]

Council member Ed Thomas, a former Denver police

create registries. By 1985, 16 states had enacted legislation calling for the creation of registries.

In 1994, the Chicago-based National Conference of Commissioners on Uniform State Laws proposed a model state adoption code. The aim was to prevent the kinds of struggles that often ended up in court by setting clear deadlines and definitions of all parties' rights. The most controversial provision, calling for the sealing of adoption records for 99

years, has not been adopted by any state, according to Freundlich of the Donaldson Adoption Institute.

Racial Policies

Traditionally, children being put up for adoption were matched with their adoptive families by ethnicity, race and religion. But with

the advent of the civil rights movement in the 1960s, a growing number of white couples expressed interest in interracial adoption, prompting some adoption agencies to loosen their policies.

In 1978, however, the National Association of Black Social Workers took a strong stand against transracial adoptions, saying they deprived black children of their cultural heritage. In response, many state and private adoption agencies discouraged such

officer, agreed. "One of the most accommodating vehicles for pedophilia is the Internet, and the Denver Department of Social Services is giving pedophiles the key." [2]

Bill Pierce, executive director of the National Council for Adoption, raises similar concerns about the use of the Internet. "What is on the Internet is there forever." He said the Web is a "happy hunting ground" for pedophiles, and that it also could invade the privacy of parents who are seeking children by ex-posing them to fraud.

But Sinnett says such fears are "based on ignorance, not on under-standing." He says his site, which will feature video and audio of the children, will not release anything confidential. Only first names will be listed, as on other sites.

Clarke says she has heard fears similar to those voiced by the Denver City Council members, but "not the reality." She says on the Faces of Adoption site, no confidential information about the children is released, "so it's no different from placing a child in the newspaper or television."

"No research I know of indicates child molesters and perpetrators go to the extreme of adopting in order to access children," Clarke adds.

Last year, President Clinton announced plans to create by 2001 a Web site listing all U.S. foster children awaiting homes. The proposal was part of his initiative to double the number of foster children placed in permanent homes by 2002.

"We can use the Internet to promote adoptions while protecting the confidentiality of children and families," Clinton said. "Technology has given us an important tool, and we should use it."

But selecting a child from a Web site doesn't mean instant placement. An agency must complete a home study to ensure the would-be parent can provide a safe and healthy environment, and visits with the child must take place Then a social worker decides whether the family would meet the child's needs.

Some also say the Web doesn't provide an easy solution to boosting the number of adoptions. Jess McDonald, director of the Illinois Department of Children and Family Services, said his Web site so far accounts for very few of their placements. "We rely on other avenues," he says.

But Sinnett insists that the tools of the Internet, particularly audio and video, will continue to grab the hearts of more parents. He said when he played back some audio he was preparing of foster children reciting their ABCs, co-workers all around him were talking about adopting a child.

"That's why I'm so excited about it," he says.

The National Adoption Center's "Faces of Adoption" Web site features 1,800 children awaiting adoption.

[1] Susan Greene, "Online Adoption Ads Spark Debate," *The Denver Post*, April 13, 1999.

[2] *Ibid.*

adoptions. The number of transracial adoptions dropped dramatically, but a subsequent rise in the number of children in foster care began to worry social workers.

Native American leaders in the 1970s also began to agitate against adoptions outside the Indian community. They charged that state agencies were taking children from poor, un-educated Indians who did not know their rights, alleging that they were unfit and placing the children in non-

Indian homes. In response, Congress in 1978 passed the Indian Child Welfare Act, which gives priority in adoption first to the child's extended family, second to members of the tribe and third to non-tribe members.

In 1994, then-Sen. Metzenbaum sought to end the courtroom battles over interracial adoptions. While he supported the principle of keeping children with families of the same race, he argued that same-race placement was not an option for an "over-

whelming majority of children in foster care homes." [29]

Metzenbaum's Multi-Ethnic Placement Act (MEPA) bars any child-welfare agency that receives federal funds from considering race, color or national origin as the only factor when making foster care or adoptive placements. Adoption cases continue to end up in court despite the act, however, and in some cases agencies themselves are coming under scrutiny. The HHS Office of Civil Rights is investigating adoption placements in Hamilton County, Ohio, because of a lawsuit that accuses the county of illegally delaying or denying adoptions for racial reasons. ■

CURRENT SITUATION

Open-Access Initiatives

Only two states — Kansas and Alaska — permit all adult adoptees to obtain a copy of their original birth certificate. Two other states, Montana and Ohio, allow more limited access.

In at least 20 states, agencies have tried to help by setting up voluntary adoption registries, which allow a birth parent and an adoptee to register, thus indicating that they want to exchange information.

Some state registries maintain lists of relatives of deceased adult adoptees and biological parents who had consented earlier to information being released about them. In some states, a biological father's access to the registry depends on whether he has admitted to being the father of the child. In many cases, his participation is not required for a match to occur between the adoptee and the birth mother.

More than 25 states, even some with registries, have "search and consent" statutes that authorize a public or private agency, or designated individual, to act as intermediary between adoptees and their birth parents. Usually the process requires a

court to authorize disclosure once both parties consent to meet.

Supporters of mutual-consent registries often complain that they are only able to aid those who were adopted in the states where the registries are established, and that some adoptees don't know where they were adopted. Sen. Levin has tried for several years to gain support for a national registry.

Meanwhile, legislation similar to that being challenged in Oregon and Tennessee has come under consideration in several states. A New Jersey bill that would have granted access to birth records was withdrawn before full debate this year due to fears

President Clinton holds LaTasha Washington at a White House celebration of National Adoption month on Nov. 24, 1998. The 3-year-old was legally adopted at the event along with 29 other children.

it would not pass. In Texas, a measure to allow adoptees access to original birth certificates was defeated. In Delaware, a new law went into effect in January allowing adult adoptees to apply for their original birth certificate. The law also allows birth mothers to request that the files stay sealed.

Bastard Nation has failed for two years to pass an open-records bill in Washington state but plans to renew its efforts next year. The group also hopes to put forward a similar mea-

sure in California. It also is busy battling laws — like those in Delaware — that allow birth parents to say they do not want to be contacted, as well as legislation in several states that would only create an adoption registry but not allow open records

And if the law stands in Tennessee, Bastard Nation vows to oppose it. Grimm says the group did not support the Tennessee legislation because it would block adoptees who were conceived during a rape or incest from accessing their birth records, and because it includes a "contact veto" provision.

The search for birth records is also of growing concern to adoptees from foreign countries. For example, Korean adoptees, many adopted in the late 1950s, are now going back to Korea to look at their records, according to Maurine Evans, executive director of the Maryland-based Joint Council on International Children Services, representing nonprofit, international adoption agencies and parent advocacy groups.

For foreign-born adoptees, "it's hit or miss," Evans says. "Sometimes there is information, sometimes not. Different countries have different rules." Some countries won't give adoptees anything, others will hand over everything in their files. In Russia, adoptees likely will have a hard time because records are not always kept or complete.

Meanwhile, many states are still trying to interpret and implement ASFA. Numerous state agencies have reported large increases in adoptions as a result of policies that encourage foster children to be placed in a permanent home rather then forced to wait in foster care in hope that someday they can be reunited with their biological families.

At Issue:

Should birth records of adopted children be unsealed?

JANE C. NAST
President, American Adoption Congress

WRITTEN FOR *THE CQ RESEARCHER*, AUGUST 1999.

*a*s an adoptive parent, I have spent two decades working with and for those whose lives have been impacted by closed adoption laws, and learned that secrecy, sealed records and the failure to recognize loss issues are the major flaws of the current system.

Who loses? Adopted persons and their adoptive families, who are denied medical and social history — sometimes with life-threatening results that reverberate through future generations. Birth families, who lose the right to ever know the fate of the child they relinquished for adoption.

Who benefits? An industry lobbying for government regulations that deny adopted persons access to information that belongs to them.

Lawmakers closed adoption records because they were convinced by the social work community that records must be hidden from the "prying eyes of the public" to "protect" adoptive parents from birth families and spare adopted children the "stigma of illegitimacy." It was also believed environment superseded heredity. In my opinion, it was a social experiment based on the mores and limited scientific knowledge of those times. In today's society, the system of sealed records and secrecy is archaic.

Currently, opponents of honesty and openness in adoption claim that "confidentiality was promised to birth parents"; that birth mothers "would abort" if they believed their unborn children might one day learn their names; and that state mutual-consent registries work. These allegations are undocumented and anecdotal. None have ever been confirmed by a single shred of evidence.

Oregon's Measure 58, a referendum passed in November 1998, allows adoptees access to their original birth certificates. In July 1999, Oregon Circuit Judge Paul Lipscomb ruled: "Although some, and perhaps many may now quarrel with where that [balance between right of privacy and right to know] has been struck, this court may not set aside Measure 58 unless it runs afoul of the Oregon or United States Constitutions. It is my conclusion that it does not."

In this country, the non-adopted have free access to their birth information. To deprive adult adoptees of the right to know the basic facts of their birth, social and genetic history in the name of "birth parent confidentiality" or adoptive parent "concerns" is morally wrong, and the American Adoption Congress is working for adoption reform nationwide to right that wrong.

WILLIAM L. PIERCE
President, National Council on Adoption

WRITTEN FOR *THE CQ RESEARCHER*, AUGUST 1999.

*p*rivacy should be protected for past adoptions because contractual agreements were made between parents and the agencies or others who served as society's agents. Women were assured: "If you continue this pregnancy and plan adoption, we promise you privacy."

Secondly, retroactively opening birth records is not sufficiently important to change public policy. There are alternative ways for persons who have life-threatening conditions to receive medical and genetic information. And in every jurisdiction but one, there's a legal way for persons to seek a birth mother (or, conversely, an adopted adult), often through a registry. In other states, that procedure is a system where the court or law allows a neutral party to contact the person being sought.

Retroactively opening records substantially impairs the obligation of adoption contracts entered into by people, usually unmarried women, and serves no important public or societal goal. Opening records retroactively violates the Contract Clause of the United States Constitution.

Opening records is also unconstitutional because it harms many women and would allow privacy only for one class of citizens, women who manage pregnancies by obtaining abortions, while denying the same privilege to another class of citizens, women who manage their pregnancies by planning adoption. The Due Process Clause of the Constitution would be violated by retroactive opening of records, because the competing interests of those who seek to open records and those who desire to maintain their privacy would not be balanced. Court decisions clearly emphasize that the balance favors the privacy and contract rights of the birth parents.

Opening records infringes on the right to religious liberty under the Free Exercise Clause of the First Amendment. Pregnant women refusing to abort because of religious beliefs may choose adoption, only to be faced with irreparable psychological injury from loss of privacy. No relationship is closer than between a mother and child. No decision is more personal than how to handle a pregnancy, especially in the cases of rape or incest. For a mother to face the loss of confidentiality and anonymity when she exercises her religious belief not to abort clearly interferes with the mother's right to freely exercise her religion. No loss of religious freedom and privacy is visited upon a biological mother as a result of a decision to abort.

These are a few among many reasons why opening records is wrong. Protecting privacy is essential in a civilized society.

But with the increase in adoptions, states have found that the federal funds that ASFA provided as an incentive are not enough to deal with post-adoption counseling and other services. "We'll see a system unable to develop programs that offer support to families" unless more money is provided, says Harder.

The CWLA and other organizations have been pushing congressional leaders for additional funding. The House in June passed a proposal, as an amendment to an unrelated foster care bill, that would authorize $43 million for post-adoption services for fiscal 2000, and lobbyists hope the Senate will pass a similar provision.

To help families that are trying to adopt children, House Commerce Committee Chairman Thomas J. Bliley Jr., R-Va., and Sen. Larry E. Craig, R-Idaho, have been seeking support for a bill that would increase the adoption tax credit and make it permanent. Current law provides $5,000 tax credits for adoptions of normal children and $6,000 for children with special needs; the credits end on Dec. 31, 2001. The proposed measure would increase both credits to $10,000 and apply to both domestic and foreign adoptions. ■

OUTLOOK

"Wrongful Adoption"

Although there is widespread support for the heightened federal and state efforts to find adoptive parents for foster children, there are concerns about the consequences of the pressure to find homes quickly. Some experts fear that agencies under time constraints won't be able to uncover and disclose all the details of a child's past and make sure parents understand the difficulties they may face with a child from a neglected or abused background.

Even before Congress passed the ASFA in 1997, the number of "wrongful adoption" lawsuits being filed by adoptive families had been increasing. They claimed that adoption agencies had withheld critical information about the youngsters being adopted, leaving them unprepared for later problems and facing huge bills for medical and psychological treatment.

What is considered the country's first wrongful adoption case, *Burr v. Board of County Commissioners*, was decided in Ohio in 1986 in favor of the adoptive parents. The court ruled against the agency being sued, holding that it did not reveal full medical and family history of the adopted child. Since the *Burr* decision, courts in several states have heard wrongful-adoption actions, and at least half the states have passed laws requiring agencies to release complete information.

"All the information should be available to the adoptive family," says Harder, "including whether the parent was a drug abuser, the quality of prenatal care, whether any physical or sexual abuse occurred. But if you're dealing with a birth mother whose child is being taken away, she's not going to be real forthcoming with information."

Judith Ashton, executive director of the New York State Citizens' Coalition for Children, which advocates more disclosure by adoption agencies, said ASFA incentive payments to states for each child who is adopted create a "kind of a time bomb." She said the incentives may lead to the recruitment of a growing number of adoptive families that aren't given all the information, training and support they need to raise their new children. [30]

Harder says that even when all the information is presented to families, much post-adoption counseling is needed. But she and others say more money is needed, and that ASFA does not provide enough.

Freundlich of the Donaldson Adoption Institute doubts that the 1997 law will increase the states' caseloads of wrongful-adoption cases. She says the cases now surfacing grew out of agency practices from the 1960s and '70s, when there was a clear desire not to disclose too much and cause undue anxiety for the adoptive parents. The rulings in these cases have encouraged states and agencies to change their policies, she says.

"The cases have been clear," she says. "Social workers have a responsibility to share what information they have. I want to think agencies will continue to do that." ■

Notes

[1] From "Plaintiff's Exhibit" in *Doe v. Oregon*.

[2] See "Affidavit" in *Doe v. Sundquist*.

[3] Quoted from *Ibid*.

[4] U.S. Department of Health and Human Services, "The AFCARS Report," January 1999.

[5] L.A. Babb, "Statistics on U.S. Adoption," *The Decree*, 1996.

[6] Annette Baran and Reuben Pannor, "An Open Adoption Policy is Best," in David Bender and Bruno Leone, eds., *Adoption: Opposing Viewpoints* (1995), pp. 229-237.

[7] Maine Department of Human Resources, Task Force on Adoption, "Adoption: A Lifelong Process" (1989). See also P. Sachdev, "Achieving Openness in Adoption: Some Critical Issues in Policy Formation," *American Journal of Orthopsychiatry*, Vol. 61, No. 2 (1991), pp. 241-249.

[8] Testimony before Ways and Means Subcommittee on Human Resources, June 11, 1998.

[9] For background, see Sarah Glazer, "Adoption," *The CQ Researcher*, Nov. 26, 1993, pp. 1033-1056.

[10] The ACLU is joined in the lawsuit (*Lofton v. Butterworth*) by the Children First Project, a Broward County, Fla., children's advocacy group that represents the two foster

children in the lawsuit, one of whom is Bert.

[11] American Civil Liberties Union, "ACLU Fact Sheet: Overview of Lesbian and Gay Parenting, Adoption and Foster Care," April 6, 1999.

[12] See Caryle Murphy, "Gay Parents Find More Acceptance," *The Washington Post,* June 14, 1999, p. A1.

[13] Ann Sullivan, "Policy Issues," in *Issues in Gay and Lesbian Parenting: Proceedings of the Fourth Annual Peirce-Warwick Adoption Symposium,* Child Welfare League of America (1995), p. 3.

[14] See David K. Flaks, "Research Issues," in *Ibid.,* pp. 21-38, and Charlotte J. Patterson, "Lesbian Mothers, Gay Fathers, and Their Children," in *Lesbian, Gay, and Bisexual Identities Over the Lifespan* (1995).

[15] The case was *Baehr v. Miike,* Sept. 10, 1996.

[16] Lynn D. Wardle, "The Potential Impact of Homosexual Parenting on Children," *University of Illinois Law Review,* No. 3 (1997), p. 844.

[17] Quoted in Sean Scully, "States Target Adoptions by Gays; Oklahoman Seeks to 'Legislate Morality,'" *The Washington Times,* April 12, 1999, p. A1. The House passed the bill 97-2, but it died in the Senate.

[18] Mike Robinson, "Ex-addict Mother Gets Custody of Son," *USA Today,* March 9, 1999.

[19] "NABSW Opposes Trans-Racial Adoption," National Association of Black Social Workers, *Workers News,* 1972.

[20] Quoted in Stacy A. Teicher, "Fight Over Mixed-Race Adoptions," *The Christian Science Monitor,* April 14, 1999.

[21] U.S. Department of Health and Human Services, *op. cit.*

[22] See A.R. Silverman, "Outcomes of Transracial Adoption," *Future of Children,* Vol. 3, No. 1, (1993), pp. 104-118.

[23] Rita Simon, "Transracial Adoption: High-lights of a Twenty-year Study," *Reconstruction,* Vol. 2, No. 2 (1993), pp. 130-131. See also Rita Simon, Howard Alstein and Marygold S. Melli, "Transracial Adoptions Should Be Encouraged," in *Adoption: Opposing Viewpoints* (1995), pp. 197-213.

[24] Elizabeth Bartholet, *Family Bonds: Adoption and the Politics of Parenting* (1993).

[25] Wayne Carp, *Family Matters: Secrecy and Disclosure in the History of Adoption* (1998), p. 11.

[26] *Ibid.,* pp. 101-105.

[27] Arthur D. Sorosky, Annette Baran and Reuben Pannor, *Adoption Triangle* (1978).

[28] Carp, *op. cit.,* pp. 178-180.

[29] Howard M. Metzenbaum, "Commentary: In Support of Multiethnic Placement Act," *Duke Journal of Gender Law & Policy,* Vol. 2, No. 165 (1995), pp. 165-166).

[30] Quoted in Barbara Vobejda, "Billy's Story: Adopting a Child and His Demons," *The Washington Post,* Nov. 28, 1998, p. A1.

Bibliography
Selected Sources Used

Books

Bartholet, Elizabeth, *Family Bonds: Adoption and the Politics of Parenting,* **Houghton Mifflin, 1993.**
Harvard University law Professor Bartholet questions the stigmas and barriers attached to adoption from the vantage point of her personal effort to adopt two South American children.

Bender, David, and Brune Leone, eds., *Adoption: Opposing Viewpoints,* **Greenhaven Press, 1995.**
This collection of articles summarizes opposing viewpoints about a variety of contentious issues being debated, such as the rights of birth parents vs. those of adoptive parents, transracial adoption, sealed adoption records and foreign adoptions.

Carp, Wayne E., *Family Matters: Secrecy and Disclosure in the History of Adoption,* **Harvard University Press, 1998.**
Historian Carp reviews the rise of adoption and the origins of sealed adoption records and follows the emergence of the Adoption Rights Movement that battled to open birth records of adoptees.

Freundlich, Madelyn, and Lisa Peterson, *Wrongful Adoption: Law, Policy and Practice,* **CWLA Press, 1998.**
This book from the Child Welfare League of America examines the historical and social context of adoption practice in relation to disclosure of background information and provides recommendations to improve agencies' practices and eliminate "wrongful adoptions."

Articles

Freundlich, Madelyn, "Access to Identifying Information: What the Research Tells Us," *CWLAdoption News,* **summer 1998, p. 4-5.**
Research primarily indicates that adoptees want to be located by their birth mothers.

Kopels, Sandra, "Wrongful Adoption Litigation and Liability," *The Journal of Contemporary Human Services,* **January 1995, pp. 20-28.**
The author examines the potential impact of agencies not disclosing health and background information about children and the legal theories on which wrongful-adoption cases are based.

Teicher, Stacy A, "Fight Over Mixed-Race Adoptions," *The Christian Science Monitor,* **April 14, 1999.**
A Rhode Island case shows how changes in federal law have not resulted in changes in attitude about transracial adoptions.

Wardle, Lynn D., "The Potential Impact of Homosexual Parenting on Children," *University of Illinois Law Review,* **1997, No. 3.**
Professor Wardle argues that the legal, academic and social-science communities have come to the defense of gay parenting too hastily, without considering the effects on children. Other researchers, he says, have relied on studies that are flawed methodologically.

Reports and Studies

"Issues in Gay and Lesbian Adoption: Proceedings of the Fourth Annual Peirce-Warwick Adoption Symposium," Child Welfare League of America, 1995.
The papers in this compilation grew out of presentations made at a 1994 symposium focused on issues in gays and lesbian adoption. Authors cover the policy and legal issues involved in adoptions by homosexuals and review the research that has been done concerning children adopted by gays or lesbians.

U.S. Department of Health and Human Services, *The AFCARS Report,* **January 1999.**
This semi-annual report provides demographic data from the states on children in foster care, such as their race, age and length of time in foster care.

National Adoption Information Clearinghouse, *Adoption: Numbers and Trends,* **undated.**
Provides the latest studies on adoptions, such as the number of placements from foster care and the percentage of transracial adoptions.

National Adoption Information Clearinghouse, *A Quick Guide to Adoption Law,* **undated.**
Provides a wide range of information on adoption, such as who can be adopted, who can place a child for adoption, how the court process works and the rights of unwed fathers.

Smith, Debra G., *Adoption: Where Do I Start?,* **National Adoption Information Clearinghouse, undated.**
This primer on adoption lays out basic adoption laws and explains who can adopt a child, and how to go about it.

3 Gay Rights

Holly Puterbaugh and Lois Farnham have lived a quiet, loving life together for 28 years. But up until last July a cloud of uncertainty hung over them because their relationship was unrecognized in law.

"If we were in a car accident on the way home," Puterbaugh explained, "there's no guarantee that I'd be able to go see her, to sit with her, because I'm not 'family.' "

For the past three years, the two Vermont women have fought a legal battle to change that. They joined two other same-sex couples in an historic lawsuit that forced the state legislature to pass a law recognizing "civil unions" with essentially the same rights as heterosexual marriage — including property rights, insurance coverage, and child custody.

Puterbaugh, who teaches mathematics at the University of Vermont, and Farnham, a school nurse supervisor, were among many Vermonters who took advantage of the new law on the day it went into effect: July 1.

"I think it's about time, after 27½ years," Farnham told reporters outside the South Burlington town clerk's office. "It's nice after all this time to call Holly my spouse."[1]

Gay rights advocates hailed the Vermont law. The measure "represents a sea change in the entire framework in which gay and lesbian rights are fought," says Beatrice Dohrn, legal director of the New York-based Lambda Legal Defense and Education Fund.

Anti-gay rights groups opposed the law, but agreed that it had broader implications than giving legal rights to same-sex couples. "This isn't just

Originally published April 14, 2000.
Updated by Kenneth Jost,
December 8, 2000.

The three couples who sought the right to same-sex marriage in Vermont are Holly Puterbaugh and Lois Farnham, front, and rear, from left, Stacy Jolles and Nina Beck and Stan Baker and Peter Harrigan.

about them wanting their rights," said John Paulk, who handles homosexuality issues for Focus on the Family, a Colorado-based Christian organization. "What they want is societal approval and sanction of homosexuality."

Same-sex marriage is one of several gay rights issues that have risen to the top of the national agenda over the past year. Gay rights advocates have been pressing their efforts to modify or repeal the military's "don't ask, don't tell" policy on homosexuality ever since the murder of a young soldier believed to be gay at an Army base in Kentucky in July 1999. They renewed their arguments in March with the release of a Defense Department report that found evidence of widespread harassment of gay and lesbian servicemembers *(see p. 50)*.

Vice President Al Gore, campaigning as the Democratic presidential nominee, vowed to repeal the policy, if elected. Texas Gov. George W. Bush, the Republican nominee, said he favored the existing policy.

Gore also called for passage of federal legislation to prohibit job discrimination due to sexual orientation. Gay rights groups have won

passage of anti-discrimination legislation in 11 states and some 165 municipalities, but have failed to get a federal bill through either the House or the Senate. Bush opposed such legislation *(see p. 51)*.

Meanwhile, the U.S. Supreme Court acted on a closely watched New Jersey case testing whether the Boy Scouts of America can enforce a policy of barring open homosexuals as leaders. The New Jersey Supreme Court ruled that the policy violated the state's anti-discrimination law. But the high court sided with the Boy Scouts in July, holding that the New Jersey ruling infringed on their First Amendment rights *(see p. 49)*.

In addition, some school districts are contending with the issue whether to allow high school students to form so-called "gay-straight alliance" clubs. Proponents say the clubs help promote tolerance and combat harassment of gay and lesbian students. Critics say they promote homosexuality. *(See story, p. 54; "At Issue," p. 53.)*

In Vermont, the state Supreme Court forced the legislature's hand by ruling that lawmakers had to allow same-sex couples either to marry or to form a "domestic partnership" or some alternative relationship.[2] The decision in *Baker v. State* was based on a provision in the Vermont constitution and therefore could not be appealed to the U.S. Supreme Court, which cannot override a state court's interpretation of state law.[3]

The legislature quickly turned to the issue in January, the month after the state high court's ruling. Most lawmakers rejected marriage for same-sex couples and turned instead to a bill allowing homosexuals to form a "civil union" with essentially all the legal rights of marriage. The

Laws Prohibiting Discrimination

Legislation prohibiting discrimination in private employment based on sexual orientation is in force in 11 states, the District of Columbia and some 124 municipalities and counties. Similar federal legislation has failed in the House and Senate.

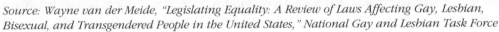

Source: Wayne van der Meide, "Legislating Equality: A Review of Laws Affecting Gay, Lesbian, Bisexual, and Transgendered People in the United States," National Gay and Lesbian Task Force

Vermont House of Representatives narrowly approved the bill in March; the more liberal state Senate followed suit in April; and the state's Democratic governor, Howard Dean, signed it into law on April 26.

Opponents had mounted a strong lobbying campaign against legal recognition for homosexual couples. "I disagree with the concept that they're entitled to the same things that heterosexual couples are entitled to," said Michele Cummings, president of the ad hoc lobbying group Take It to the People. "We do not believe that benefits should be awarded on the basis of sexual activity."

Nationally, social conservative advocacy groups make similar arguments. "If you say two men constitute a marriage, you are creating a counterfeit," says Robert Knight, di-

rector of cultural studies for the Family Research Council. "Homosexual relationships are not a facsimile of marriage. They are entirely different."

Gay rights advocates, however, contend that the reasons for refusing to recognize same-sex relationships are outdated. "Our social context of marriage has changed so much," says Paula Ettelbrick, director of the family law project of the National Gay and Lesbian Task Force (NGLTF). "It's really about economic benefits and the support systems that government provides to family. It's much less about being a proper procreative form or having a male head of household."

The opposing advocacy groups also clashed on the role of the courts in dealing with the issue. "We feel that it needed to be taken to the

people, that five judges shouldn't make that decision for all of us," Cummings said.

"The very reason for being of the judicial branch of government is to protect the rights of the minority against the majority," countered Susan Murray, a Burlington lawyer and one of the attorneys for the three same-sex couples in the Vermont case. "If we waited for the majority to grant rights that they're not interested in thinking about granting, it would take a heck of a longer time."

The Vermont measure represents a major victory — both substantively and symbolically — for the gay rights movement. But one leading gay rights advocate says the new civil unions recognized under the law can also be viewed as a "second best" status. "The glass is still at least half-empty," says William Rubenstein, a law professor at UCLA. "No same-sex couple can be married anywhere in the United States."

Rubenstein, formerly director of the American Civil Liberties Union's national lesbian and gay rights project, says gay rights advocates have comparable records in other areas. "There has been enormous progress in the last 30 years, but alongside that is there still an enormous amount of work to go," he says. Only a minority of states have enacted anti-discrimination laws, he notes, while some 19 states have refused to repeal anti-sodomy laws once widely used to prosecute homosexuals for consensual sexual behavior (see map, p. 44).

Nonetheless, a *Newsweek* poll last spring showed that Americans are becoming more comfortable with homosexuality. In 1998, 54 percent said homosexuality was a sin compared with 46 percent today.

Critics and opponents, however, accuse the gay rights movement of fostering legal and social changes that they say are undermining traditional morality.

"When you have corporations promoting open homosexuality, when you have ordinances on the books of many cities adding sexual orientation to civil rights laws, you are well on the way to suppressing dissent on the issue," Knight says. "But like any good activist, they say they are never satisfied. Just a few years ago they were demanding tolerance. Now they're demanding gay marriages and homosexual curriculums in the schools. That's quite an advance, particularly for such a tiny segment of the population."

The debate — part political, part legal, part cultural — continued as gay rights groups held a major march in Washington in April to highlight their agenda (see p. 52). Here are some of the issues they and their opponents are debating:

Should same-sex relationships be legally recognized?

Over the past five years, attorneys Murray and Beth Robinson talked to dozens of church and civic groups in Vermont as they made the case for legal recognition of same-sex relationships. Audiences were skeptical initially, Murray recalls, but most meetings ended with greater sympathy for their position.

"If we can talk to Vermonters about the tangible benefits that married couples obtain simply by obtaining a marriage certificate, fair-minded Vermonters sit back and say, 'Wow, I've never thought of it that way; of course, gay couples deserve that,' " she says.

By the time Vermont lawmakers took up the issue in March, a poll — commissioned by the Vermont Freedom to Marry Task Force — found that most people supported allowing homosexual partners either to marry (30 percent) or to form "civil unions" (25 percent). Only 40 percent opposed either legal recognition for same-sex couples.

Across the nation, however, same-sex marriage still draws fire. National polls consistently show solid majorities opposed to homosexual marriages. [4] And Congress and some 30 states have passed laws to block recognition of same-sex marriages.

Gay-rights advocates view the government's refusal to recognize same-sex relationships as outright discrimination. "The issue is not so much marriage, it's a denial of equal benefits," Ettelbrick says. "That's the constitutional problem. That's where the state most fundamentally treats same-sex partners differently."

Opponents, however, insist that recognizing same-sex relationships would lead to myriad practical problems. "Marriage is about more than the two individuals involved," the Family Research Council's Knight says. "It's how kinship develops and family names are passed down and the generations are linked and property is distributed and where new life is created."

Advocates of same-sex marriage say legal recognition would benefit homosexuals as well as society at large. "Same-sex marriage is good for gay people and good for America," writes Yale Law School Professor William Eskridge Jr., "and for the same reason: It civilizes gays, and it civilizes America." [5]

Eskridge argues that recognizing same-sex marriage would encourage the broad social trend toward tolerance for homosexuality while reducing promiscuity among homosexuals, especially gay men. Other gay-rights advocates, however, back away from any such claim.

"I see the issues as different," UCLA's Rubenstein says. "There's the question of legal recognition, and there's the question of sexual practices."

Indeed, some gay-rights advocates are less than enthusiastic about marriage for homosexual couples. Ettelbrick, for example, has previously denounced marriage as a "patriarchal" institution. "I don't think marriage should be the only way that we describe or support families," she says. "Good public policy will accept and provide economic support for people who are caring for each other whether they're married or not." [6]

In any event, opponents are unconvinced that recognizing same-sex marriage would reduce the incidence of multiple sexual partners among homosexuals. "That is a disingenuous argument," says Lynn Wardell, a law professor at Brigham Young University in Provo, Utah. "I'm waiting to see the evidence."

Given the strong opposition to same-sex marriage, gay-rights organizations began working in the 1980s for a less ambitious goal: winning workplace benefits such as health insurance for same-sex couples. On that front, there has been what Ettelbrick calls "tremendous success." Thousands of employers, including many of the country's biggest businesses, today allow unmarried employees — homosexuals as well as heterosexuals — to designate their partners for health insurance coverage.

Anti-gay-rights groups, however, also object to domestic partnerships — though perhaps not as fiercely. "If you want the benefits of marriage, you have to meet the qualifications," Knight says, "the first of which is that

Military Discharges for Homosexual Conduct

President Clinton was forced to back away from a post-election promise to lift the strict Pentagon ban on homosexuals and in 1993 fashioned a compromise known as "don't ask, don't tell." Despite the seeming liberalization of the policy, the number of servicemembers discharged for homosexuality has increased since 1993 along with the reported incidence of anti-gay harassment.

Total discharged

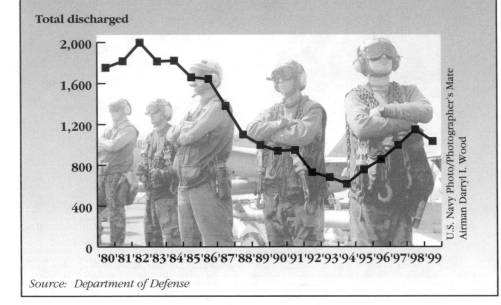

U.S. Navy Photo/Photographer's Mate
Airman Darryl I. Wood

'80'81'82'83'84'85'86'87'88'89'90'91'92'93'94'95'96'97'98'99

Source: Department of Defense

you have to open your life to a person of the opposite sex and make a life-long commitment."

Wardell agrees, though he says he would allow some recognition for same-sex couples — for example, in hospital visitation. "Hospital visitation ought not depend on a marital relationship," he says.

Vermont's civil union law goes further than any previous law or employer policy in providing same-sex couples the rights enjoyed by heterosexuals. The Family Research Council called the measure "nothing short of an endorsement of 'same-sex marriage.' "

For her part, though, attorney Murray said the law does not go far enough. "Marriage, of course, is the only thing that gives gay and lesbian couples true equality," she says. "This is a very good bill, but it is a first step, not the end of the road."

Should the military's "don't ask, don't tell" policy be changed?

Pfc. Barry Winchell suffered through four months of taunting, harassment and anti-gay epithets from fellow soldiers at Fort Campbell in Kentucky before his murder on July 5, 1999. Two soldiers have been convicted in the killing: Pvt. Calvin Glover, who shattered Winchell's skull with a baseball bat, and Spec. Justin Fisher, who gave Glover the bat.

Gay-rights groups, however, believe the real culprit in the Winchell case is the Army itself — for tolerating anti-gay harassment — as well as the military's "don't ask, don't tell" policy — for forcing homosexual servicemembers to conceal their identities in order to serve their country.

"There is no safe haven for military members to turn to if they are harassed or threatened," says Michelle Benecke,

co-director of the Service-members Legal Defense Network (SLDN). "How many people have to be harassed or murdered before people take this problem seriously?"

SLDN says that despite the seeming liberalization of "don't ask, don't tell," the number of servicemembers discharged for homosexuality has increased since 1993 along with the incidence of anti-gay harassment. (*See graph.*) Winchell's murder did prompt the Defense Department to adopt more explicit anti-gay-harassment policies. But the "don't ask, don't tell" policy remains in effect, seven years after its adoption as a compromise of sorts following President Clinton's failure to win support for lifting the ban on homosexuals in the military altogether.

The Winchell episode did renew debate in Washington and across the country over the military's policy. But some opponents of homosexuals in the military say that the harassment issue has been exaggerated, and they remain convinced that homosexuality is "incompatible" with military service — just as Congress declared in 1993 in a Defense Department authorization bill that Clinton signed into law.

"There are no doubt incidents in which drill sergeants and platoon leaders have used derogatory language, and they're wrong," says Robert Maginnis, a retired Army lieutenant colonel and now director of national security and foreign affairs at the Family Research Council. "But I don't think that it's part of the dominant culture."

Maginnis calls Winchell's killing "a terrible situation." But he discounts SLDN's statistics on anti-gay harassment and considers the new anti-harassment policy an overreaction.

"Why are we getting so bent out of shape about a group of people that we've decided ought to be excluded?" he asks.

Gay-rights advocates continue to regard "don't ask, don't tell" as unfair to gay and lesbian servicemembers. The policy "discriminates against lesbian, gay and bisexual servicemembers," Benecke says. "Gay people are kicked out for saying and doing the same thing straight people do every day."

In addition, Benecke and other critics say the policy is bad for the military at a time when the services are having difficulty recruiting and retaining personnel. "This law is forcing commanders to kick good people out of the military," she says.

Supporters of the policy continue to defend the restrictions on open expressions of homosexuality as necessary to protect the rights of straight servicemembers forced to live with fellow soldiers and sailors in close quarters.

"You're talking about the privacy rights of straights as well as gays," says Charles Moskos, a professor of sociology at Northwestern University in Evanston, Ill., and an adviser to the administration at the time of the policy's adoption. "It might be that in the future people won't mind," he says, "but that's not the era we live in right now."

Maginnis cites other reasons for opposing homosexuals in the military, including the risk of sexually transmitted diseases and what he says is an adverse effect on the morale of individual units. "When we throw the ingredient of sex in, whether it's heterosexual or same-sex attraction, it undermines the confidence and trust we must have in these teams," he says.

Gay-rights advocates say they want the military to honor the "don't ask, don't tell" policy by ensuring that commanders do not investigate servicemembers suspected of being homosexual and that they crack down

on anti-gay harassment. In the long term, though, they believe the policy should be replaced by one that permits homosexuals to serve openly.

"Ultimately, this law should be replaced with a principle of non-discrimination where everyone is evaluated according to their merit rather than a characteristic that has nothing to do with their performance," Benecke says.

Maginnis, on the other hand, wants to reinstitute an outright ban on service by homosexuals — the policy that he says is prescribed by law but circumvented by the Clinton administration's regulations. "The law is very clear: it's an exclusion policy," Maginnis says. The administration, he says, "has forced something on the military that is not in the best interest of the service."

Moskos, however, sees no better alternative than the current policy. "It's much like what Winston Churchill said about democracy," Moskos says. "It's the worst system possible, except for any other."

Are additional laws needed to prohibit discrimination on the basis of sexual orientation?

Dwayne Simonton claimed in a federal civil rights suit that his co-workers at the Farmingdale, N.Y., post office mercilessly ridiculed him because of his homosexuality. A federal judge in June 1999 found their conduct "offensive" but dismissed Simonton's sexual-harassment lawsuit. The reason: The federal Civil Rights Act does not prohibit discrimination on the basis of sexual orientation. [7]

Gay-rights advocates have been pushing for two decades for passage of laws to prohibit discrimination against homosexuals in the workplace, in housing and in public accommodations. "There's a tremendous amount of individual bias against gay people," says Beatrice Dohrn, legal director for the Lambda

Legal Defense and Education Fund. "Some people want us to continue having second-class status."

Polls show that a substantial majority of Americans — more than 80 percent — believe that homosexuals should not be discriminated against in the workplace. (See poll, p. 48.) But efforts to enact anti-gay-discrimination laws have fallen short in Washington and in most state capitals in the face of a swirl of arguments raised by conservative advocacy groups.

They warn of a parade of horribles that would result, in particular, from a proposed federal law, the Employment Non-Discrimination Act (ENDA): job quotas, heavy-handed federal enforcement, invasive questioning about employees' sexual orientation and intrusions on the religious liberties of faith-based employers. Most broadly, opponents say the law would undermine traditional morality and give "special rights" to a group that neither needs nor deserves special legal protections.

ENDA "requires the federal government to abandon its commitments to the traditions of marriage and family and to declare that all sexual preferences are equally valid," says a Family Research Council position paper. The bill "affords special protection to a group that is not disadvantaged," the paper continues. "Homosexuals, as a group, outpace most other Americans economically and educationally, and no one can dispute their political power and savvy."

Lobbyists insist the opponents are exaggerating or misstating the provisions of the federal bill. "This is a very modest piece of legislation," says Winnie Stachelberg, political director of Human Rights Campaign (HRC), a gay-rights organization. "All it would say is you can't be fired from your job for sexual orientation — because of a factor that has nothing to do with your job performance."

Sixteen States Still Have Anti-Sodomy Laws

Anti-sodomy laws historically have been used to prosecute homosexuals for oral and anal sex, although they also typically apply to heterosexuals. The laws are rarely enforced today but are still used, according to gay-rights advocates, to deny employment and child custody and visitation rights to gays. Supporters say that even if the laws are rarely enforced, they help to safeguard the legal and moral status of the family and to contain sexual conduct that is a factor in sexually transmitted diseases.

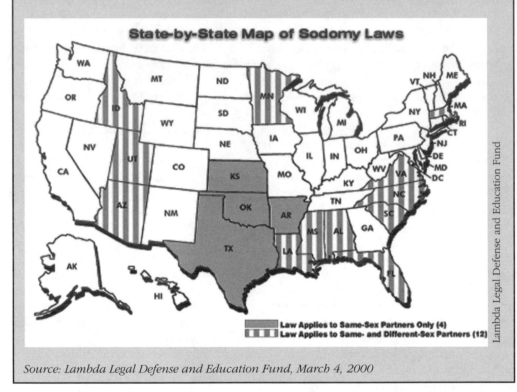

State-by-State Map of Sodomy Laws

Law Applies to Same-Sex Partners Only (4)
Law Applies to Same- and Different-Sex Partners (12)

Lambda Legal Defense and Education Fund

Source: Lambda Legal Defense and Education Fund, March 4, 2000

religious exemption so big you could push the National Cathedral through it," Dohrn says.

Despite the failure of the federal bill, some 11 states, the District of Columbia and 124 municipalities and counties have passed gay-rights measures — almost all of them with employment-discrimination provisions. Gay-rights advocates say, somewhat regretfully, that the laws have not generated the kind of rush of litigation that opponents have warned about.

"The laws are underused, and that's because using them is an expensive, uphill battle," Dohrn says. "Coming out is still a dangerous proposition in many parts of the country, and litigating against your employer is always a risky proposition."

Congress has had only one recorded vote on the federal bill: in the Senate in September 1996. The measure failed 49-50, with one senator absent. The vote was largely symbolic since the House would have had no time to act on the measure late in the session. Since that time, Stachelberg says, the Republican leadership in the House and the Senate has kept the bill "bottled up."

The Family Research Council's Knight acknowledges that more states and municipalities are likely to pass such laws, though he doubts Congress will. But he also sees a likely backlash. "You're going to see more of these laws challenged," he says. "People will say you shouldn't create a sweeping new category" for civil rights laws.

But Dohrn thinks the movement

Opponents acknowledge that the bill bars the use of quotas or preferences for homosexuals. But they contend that administrative enforcement and litigation will pressure employers into adopting such schemes anyway. "Employers will be forced to learn more about their employees' sex lives," the Family Research Council warns, "in order to defend themselves against possible lawsuits."

Supporters of the bill dismiss such fears as groundless. "I don't think there's any reason to believe that having laws [in some states] has injected all sorts of sexual-orientation questions into the workplace," Dohrn says. "The laws provide an incentive for employers to leave the subject out." In any event, the notion of quotas is "kind of ridiculous," she says. "There is no way in the world to count how many people are gay."

Opponents also warn that the bill could force religious organizations to hire homosexuals despite religious convictions against homosexuality. They acknowledge the bill includes an exemption for religious organizations but say it does not extend to individuals and might not apply to some church-sponsored social services. Supporters again say the warnings are off base. The bill "has a

to enact such laws will continue. "It's remarkable how many people think that discrimination on the basis of sexual orientation is already illegal," she says. "Eventually, the law will conform to people's expectations about the law." ∎

BACKGROUND

Birth of a Movement

H omosexuals were largely invisible, politically unorganized and legally vulnerable from the founding of the United States until the early 20th century. When homosexual subcultures started becoming more visible, the social pressures against homosexuality turned into legal strictures with expansively written "crime-against-nature" laws.

The legal crackdown on homosexuals increased from the 1920s through the decades after World War II. Ironically, the crackdown spawned the gay-rights movement, as homosexuals organized first to protect themselves from prosecution and then to demand legal recognition and equal rights. [8]

The legal crackdown on homosexuality was multifaceted. Under the 1917 Immigration Act, the government barred "sexual perverts" from entering the country, much as a 1921 Army regulation permitted exclusion for "sexual perversion." Homosexual organizations were shut down through the use of disorderly-conduct laws. Gay bars found their licenses suspended or revoked. Most dramatically, homosexuals were subject to criminal prosecution for sodomy, lewd conduct or other offenses. On the eve of World War II, Yale's Eskridge writes, "a homosexual with

an active social life had a good chance of spending time in jail." [9]

The pursuit of homosexuals intensified after World War II, when Eskridge estimates that as many as 100,000 gays per year, mostly men, were arrested for consensual sexual behavior. Some states moved to bar homosexuals as teachers or as lawyers. Thousands of soldiers and sailors were discharged on grounds of homosexuality, proven or suspected.

The crackdown finally engendered resistance — and the first stirrings of the gay-rights movement. The leading resistance group was the Mattachine Society, formed in Los Angeles in 1951. Taking its name from a medieval Italian court jester who expressed unpopular truths from behind a mask, the group vowed to unify homosexuals and to assist "our people who are victimized daily as a result of our oppression." [10]

The Mattachine Society and the Daughters of Bilitis — the first lesbian organization, founded in San Francisco in 1955 — both adopted assimilationist strategies. Mattachine wanted to educate homosexuals and heterosexuals alike to an "ethical homosexual culture," while the Daughters advocated "a mode of behavior and dress acceptable to society."

The non-confrontational approach combined with liberalizing trends in politics, law and society to produce some tangible gains. Illinois became the first state to decriminalize sodomy in 1961. The California Supreme Court acted to protect gay bars from arbitrary closures, and the U.S. Supreme Court limited the Post Office's power to censor male physique magazines.

The number of gay organizations increased in the 1960s — from 15 in 1966 to nearly 50 three years later — and the groups became both more visible and more aggressive. [11] Then in 1969, two days of disturbances touched off by a police raid at a

dilapidated — and unlicensed — gay dance bar in New York City gave new impetus and militancy to the gay-rights movement. [12] Plainclothes officers ordered patrons out of Greenwich Village's Stonewall Inn on June 28 and loaded three men dressed as women into paddywagons. When the crowd threw cans and bottles, the police retreated and reinforcements arrived to clear the streets.

The next night, as hundreds of protesters gathered, the mood was camp rather than revolution. But a milestone had been reached. Gay people, author Eric Marcus writes, "were finally pushed to the point where they'd had enough, and they fought back." A month later, activists in Greenwich Village organized what they called the city's "first gay-power vigil.

"Do you think homosexuals are revolting?" a leaflet asked, capturing the movement's new sense of pride and militancy. "You bet your sweet ass we are," it answered in capital letters. [13]

Successes and Setbacks

T he gay-rights movement made fitful advances over the next two decades. Anti-sodomy statutes were repealed or invalidated in many states, while a few states and many municipalities prohibited discrimination against homosexuals. But social conservatives — the so-called New Right — responded with lobbying and citizen initiatives to block gay-rights measures or in a few cities to repeal ordinances already enacted.

The Supreme Court also dealt the movement a setback, upholding state anti-sodomy statutes. Meanwhile, same-sex marriage made no headway in the courts, although some cities enacted domestic partnership laws. And the Pentagon actually toughened its policy on homosexuality, explicitly excluding homosexuals from the military. [14]

The movement's broadest success came in eradicating sodomy laws. Connecticut followed Illinois' lead in repealing its anti-sodomy statute in 1971. By 1992, similar laws had been repealed in some 19 other state legislatures and nullified by court rulings in four others.

Nonetheless, the U.S. Supreme Court in 1986 voted 5-4 to uphold the constitutionality of enforcing sodomy statutes against private, consensual homosexual conduct. Writing for the majority in *Bowers v. Hardwick*, Justice Byron White said Georgia's law could be justified on the basis of "the presumed belief of a majority of the electorate in Georgia that homosexual conduct is immoral and unacceptable."

Gay-rights advocates began winning enactment of anti-discrimination laws at the local level in the 1970s and then in a handful of states in the '80s. Generally, the laws prohibited discrimination in government or private employment on the basis of sexual orientation; some also barred discrimination in housing or public accommodations.

Opponents succeeded in several cities in overturning ordinances through the referendum process — notably in Miami-Dade County, Fla., in a 1977 campaign led by pop singer Anita Bryant and fueled by conservative religious groups. At the state level, opponents succeeded in stalling bills or — for example, in California in 1985 — in persuading the governor to veto a measure approved by lawmakers. Despite the difficulties, by 1992 gay-rights laws were on the books in seven states and some 90 municipalities — mostly large cities or university towns.

Advocates of same-sex marriage made no headway before the 1990s. A few couples brought suits, but courts rejected their constitutional claims almost out of hand. None of the major gay and lesbian organizations supported their efforts. The community was, in fact, divided on the issue, with many gay and lesbian activists viewing marriage as the kind of hierarchical institution that the movement should seek to displace.

In the 1980s, gay-rights groups did support the emerging effort to win workplace equality through recognition of domestic partnerships. The San Francisco Board of Supervisors passed a domestic partnership bill in 1981, but it was vetoed by then-Mayor Dianne Feinstein. A year later, Berkeley, Calif., became the first city to enact such an ordinance. By 1991, another two dozen cities had followed suit — including San Francisco.

Gay-rights advocates suffered one clear setback — in the military. Regulations dating back to World War II had prohibited service by homosexuals, but they were often ignored. Pentagon officials began rewriting the regulations in the late 1970s, under President Jimmy Carter; the revamping was completed in the first year of President Ronald Reagan's administration in 1981.

The new regulations reiterated the description of homosexuality as "incompatible with military service" but expanded the definition to include anyone who "engages in, desires to engage in or intends to engage in homosexual acts."

As author Randy Shilts put it, "The military had, in effect, banned homosexual thoughts." [15] The new regulations were more rigorously enforced: nearly 17,000 servicemembers were discharged for homosexual conduct during the 12 years of Reagan's and George Bush's presidencies.

"A Seat at the Table"

Despite continuing resistance, the movement made remarkable strides in the 1990s, legally and politically. Gay rights became a focus of national debate for the first time during the 1992 presidential election. The Clinton administration and the Democratic Party aligned themselves for the rest of the decade with many of the issues on the gay-rights agenda.

Still, there were setbacks: the "don't ask, don't tell" policy; Congress' failure to pass a gay civil-rights law; and the adoption of defense of marriage laws by Congress and a majority of states.

Clinton signaled his support for the cause by appearing at a 1992 Los Angeles fund-raiser organized by gay activists. [16] The Clinton campaign netted $100,000 — and the gay community showed it could flex its considerable financial muscle to further its aims. For his part, Clinton said gay Americans represented "a community of our nation's gifted people that we have been willing to squander." He pledged to undo the Pentagon's policy, crack down on anti-gay hate crimes and include an HIV-positive speaker at the Democratic National Convention.

In office, Clinton proved unable to deliver on his promises. Most dramatically, his effort to open military service to homosexuals fell short in the face of a strong backlash from military leaders, members of Congress from both parties and the public. [17]

Clinton was forced to back away from a post-election promise to lift the ban on homosexuals by executive order and then fashioned a short-term compromise — soon known as "don't ask, don't tell." Gay servicemembers derisively termed it "don't tell, don't touch."

Congress kept at the issue, however, and eventually approved a provision in the Defense Department authorization that codified the ban on homosexuals

Chronology

Before 1945
Homosexuals are politically unorganized, legally vulnerable.

— • —

1945-1970 *Initial stirrings of gay-rights movement.*

1951
Mattachine Society is founded in Los Angeles to provide support for male homosexuals. Four years later, Daughters of Bilitis is founded in San Francisco as first U.S. lesbian organization.

1961
Illinois becomes first state to remove penalty for consensual homosexual relations between adults.

June 1969
Police raid on the Stonewall Inn, a popular gay bar in New York City, becomes defining moment for modern gay-rights movement.

— • —

1970s *Gay rights becomes national issue, but gains are limited.*

1977
Miami-Dade County, Fla., adopts ordinance prohibiting discrimination against gay men and lesbians; ordinance overturned by referendum six months later.

1979
First national gay-rights march held in Washington.

1980s *Gay rights advances, but social conservatives stiffen opposition; AIDS becomes an epidemic.*

1981
Wisconsin becomes first state to bar discrimination against homosexuals in employment, housing and public accommodations.

1984
Berkeley, Calif., becomes first city to provide domestic-partner benefits for gays and lesbians.

1986
U.S. Supreme Court upholds state laws against consensual homosexual sodomy.

— • —

1990s *Gay-rights movement combines political clout and legal initiatives to make significant gains against continuing resistance.*

1992
Democratic presidential candidate Bill Clinton promises support for several gay-rights proposals; after his election, Clinton repeats vow to end military policy excluding gays.

1993
Congress forces Clinton to accept "don't ask, don't tell" policy on gays in military; Hawaii Supreme Court says state must justify law prohibiting same-sex marriages; third gay-rights march on Washington.

1994
Massachusetts becomes first state to outlaw discrimination against gays in public schools.

1996
Colorado initiative prohibiting legal protections for homosexuals nullified by Supreme Court.

July 5, 1999
Pfc. Barry Winchell is beaten to death by a fellow soldier after being taunted for being gay; Defense Secretary William Cohen announces policy against harassment of gays a month later.

Aug. 4, 1999
New Jersey Supreme Court says Boy Scouts' exclusion of gays violates state civil rights law.

Dec. 20, 1999
Vermont Supreme Court says state must allow same sex couples to enjoy legal benefits accorded to heterosexuals.

— • —

2000s *New decade opens with gay-rights issues high on political, legal agendas.*

Apr. 25, 2000
Vermont legislature gives final approval to law permitting "civil unions" for same-sex couples; law takes effect July 1.

Apr. 30, 2000
Hundreds of thousands join Millennium March on Washington for gay rights.

June 28, 2000
U.S. Supreme Court upholds Boy Scouts' policy of excluding gays.

Fall 2000
Democrat Al Gore and Republican George W. Bush differ on gay rights issues in presidential campaign.

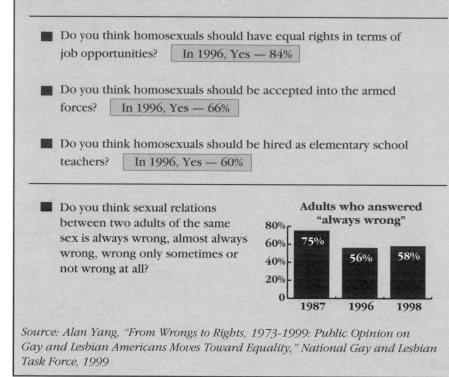

How Americans Feel About Gay Rights

Public opinion polls indicate solid majority support for giving homosexuals "equal rights in terms of job opportunities." Most Americans, however, believe that sexual relations between two adults of the same sex are "always wrong," though the disapproval rate has fallen significantly in the last decade.

■ Do you think homosexuals should have equal rights in terms of job opportunities?   In 1996, Yes — 84%

■ Do you think homosexuals should be accepted into the armed forces?   In 1996, Yes — 66%

■ Do you think homosexuals should be hired as elementary school teachers?   In 1996, Yes — 60%

■ Do you think sexual relations between two adults of the same sex is always wrong, almost always wrong, wrong only sometimes or not wrong at all?

Adults who answered "always wrong"

75%	56%	58%
1987	1996	1998

Source: Alan Yang, "From Wrongs to Rights, 1973-1999: Public Opinion on Gay and Lesbian Americans Moves Toward Equality," National Gay and Lesbian Task Force, 1999

while leaving intact the administration's decision not to ask recruits about their sexual orientation and not to initiate investigations except after receiving "credible information" of homosexual conduct. Clinton signed the bill.

The administration was also unable to win support for a gay civil rights bill or special federal penalties for anti-gay hate crimes. The 1990 Hate Crime Statistics Act, signed by President George Bush, does include anti-gay offenses as one category in an annual data compilation by the Justice Department. [18]

Gay-rights advocates continued to press their efforts both in Washington and before state and local legis-lative bodies. By the end of the decade, the number of gays was still increasing, two states had domestic-partnership schemes and the number of states with anti-sodomy statutes had dwindled to 19. [19]

Opponents tried to thwart gay-rights advocates with initiatives in several states aimed at blocking state or local governments from enacting laws to prohibit discrimination on the basis of sexual orientation. Colorado voters approved such a measure in 1992, but voters in three other states rejected similar initiatives: Idaho and Oregon in 1994 and Maine in 1995.

Then in 1996, the U.S. Supreme Court appeared to bar the tactic by ruling that the Colorado initiative violated the U.S. Constitution's Equal Protection Clause. The law had no rational basis, Justice Anthony Kennedy wrote in *Romer v. Evans*. It was, instead, a "status-based enactment" born out of "animosity toward homosexuals." [20]

The Hawaii Supreme Court's ruling on same-sex marriages in 1993 provoked a similar but stronger backlash. Opponents lobbied Congress and state legislatures to pass laws aimed at barring recognition of same-sex marriages. Congress cleared the federal Defense of Marriage Act on Sept. 10, 1996, just two months before the presidential election. [21]

The measure — which Clinton signed almost surreptitiously at 12:50 a.m. on Sept. 21 — said that states were not obligated to recognize same-sex marriages from other states and defined marriage for purposes of federal law as a union between people of opposite sexes. By decade's end, 30 states had similar laws — including Alaska and Hawaii itself, where voters approved constitutional amendments to ward off recognition of homosexual marriages. ■

CURRENT SITUATION

Debating "Civil Unions"

T he Vermont Supreme Court's ruling in the same-sex marriage case touched off a wide-ranging debate from one end of the state to another. Most Vermonters — lawmakers and citizens alike — appeared to oppose marriage for homosexual couples. But with little maneuvering room

Court Upholds Boy Scouts' Rights to Exclude Gays

James Dale became a Cub Scout at age 6 and graduated to Boy Scouts 4 years later. He went on to earn 30 merit badges and achieve scouting's highest honors: Eagle Scout and the Order of the Arrow.

As a young man, Dale wanted to continue as a Scout leader, to give something back to an organization he believed in. But Dale's local Boy Scouts council in Monmouth, N.J., summarily expelled him in 1990 after it learned from a newspaper story that Dale is gay.

Dale challenged the expulsion in a high-profile legal dispute with the Boy Scouts of America (BSA) that pitted anti-discrimination principles against freedom of speech and association. He won a ruling from New Jersey courts that the action violated the state's law against discrimination on the basis of sexual orientation in "public accommodations." But the U.S. Supreme Court overruled that decision, holding that the Boy Scouts had a First Amendment right to enforce their policy of excluding homosexuals.

Dale's attorneys said the case, *Boy Scouts of America v. Dale,* was important not only for Dale but also for gay youths generally. "Gay youths need the same opportunity for socialization and fun and community service as their non-gay brothers and sisters do," said Evan Wolfson, senior attorney with the Lambda Legal Defense and Education Fund.

But BSA national spokesman Greg Shields said homosexuality is inconsistent with Scouting. "The Boy Scouts of America have long taught traditional family values based on the Scout oath and law," Shields says. "The Boy Scouts of America believe that an acknowledged homosexual would not be a role model for those values."

Dale came out as a homosexual while attending Rutgers University in Newark, N.J. While co-president of the gay and lesbian student organization, he attended a seminar in July 1990 on psychological and health needs of homosexual teenagers. The local newspaper ran a story on the seminar along with Dale's picture and a caption identifying his role in the gay organization.

Days later, the Monmouth Boy Scouts council sent Dale a letter that revoked his membership. When Dale asked for a reason, BSA officials responded by saying the organization "specifically forbids membership to homosexuals." Two years later, Dale sued the Scouts under New Jersey's "Law Against Discrimination."

The Boy Scouts had won five similar cases after courts decided that states' civil rights laws did not apply to private membership organizations. A lower court in New Jersey reached the same conclusion in Dale's case. But in August 1999 the New Jersey Supreme Court unanimously ruled that the BSA is a "public accommodation" for purposes of the state's civil rights law and that forcing the organization to accept homosexuals as leaders would not violate its First Amendment freedom of speech or association.

In two rulings in the 1980s, the U.S. Supreme Court did uphold the enforcement of state civil rights laws to require private organizations — the Jaycees and the Rotary Club — to admit women.[1] In a concurring opinion in the Jaycees case, however, Justice Sandra Day O'Connor mentioned the Boy Scouts as an example of an organization that might have a First Amendment right to select its members without running afoul of anti-discrimination laws.

In arguments before the high court, the Scouts' lawyer, George Davidson, defended the policy. "This case is about the freedom of a voluntary association to choose its own leaders," Davidson said. Wolfson countered that the Scouts were asking the court to "specially excuse" it from New Jersey's civil rights laws.

Wolfson insisted that the Scout oath and law — requiring scouts to be "morally straight" and "clean" — had "literally nothing" to do with homosexuality. But Justice Anthony M. Kennedy appeared skeptical. "Who is better qualified to determine the expressive purpose of the Boy Scouts: the Boy Scouts or the New Jersey courts?" he asked.

The court divided along conservative-liberal lines in its 5-4 ruling backing the Scouts on June 28, the final day of the 1999-2000 term. Writing for the conservative majority, Chief Justice William H. Rehnquist said application of the New Jersey law would burden the Scouts' "freedom of expressive association."

"The forced inclusion of an unwanted person in a group infringes the group's freedom of expressive association," Rehnquist wrote, "if the presence of that person affects in a significant way the group's ability to advocate public or private viewpoints."

Writing for the four liberal dissenters, Justice John Paul Stevens disagreed that admitting Dale would burden the Scouts' message. "It is plain as the light of day that neither one of these principles, 'morally straight' and 'clean,' says the slightest thing about homosexuality."

Ruth Harlow, deputy legal director of the Lambda Legal Defense Fund, called the ruling a "hollow, Pyrrhic" victory for the Scouts. "The Boy Scouts have fought long and hard for something that has marginalized the institution," Harlow said.

Dale himself, who had moved to New York and was working as an advertising director for a magazine for people who are HIV-positive, was disappointed both with the ruling and with his beloved Scouts. "The Boy Scouts are making themselves extinct," Dale told reporters, "and it's a very sad thing."

---

[1] The cases are *Board of Directors of Rotary International v. Rotary Club of Duarte* (1987) and *Roberts v. United States Jaycees* (1984). O'Connor's concurring opinion came in the Jaycees case.

under the high court's ruling, the legislature inexorably moved toward approving a "civil union" bill giving gay and lesbian couples rights broader than homosexuals can enjoy in any other state.

The plaintiffs' lawyers — Robinson, Murray and Mary Bonauto of Boston-based Gay and Lesbian Advocates and Defenders (GLAD) — based their case on a provision of the Vermont Constitution known as the common-benefits clause. It provides that government is "instituted for the common benefit, protection and security of the people . . . and not for the particular emolument or advantage of any single person, family or set of persons."

They argued that a law allowing only heterosexual couples to enjoy all the legal benefits of marriage violated that provision. The state's lawyers offered one principal rationale for limiting marriage to heterosexuals: the government's interest in promoting the link between procreation and child-rearing.

In his 45-page opinion for the court, Chief Justice Jeffrey Amestoy pointed out that many heterosexual couples marry "for reasons unrelated to procreation." In addition, he noted that "a significant number of children" are now being raised by same-sex couples and that the state legislature had actually removed legal barriers for same-sex couples to adopt and raise children.

With the state's main argument rejected, Amestoy concluded: "We hold that the State is constitutionally required to extend to same-sex couples the common benefits and protections that flow from marriage under Vermont law."

Nationally, gay-rights advocates were enthused about the ruling. "This decision marks the start of a tremendous sea change that will surely improve life for lesbian and gay families," Lambda's Dohrn declared. On the opposite side, the Family Research Council called the decision "dangerously wrong" because it would "force the people of Vermont to support what is essentially a sin registry."

Opinion was similarly divided in Vermont. [22] A statewide poll conducted a month after the court's ruling found 38 percent in favor of the decision and 52 percent opposed. A near majority — 49 percent — favored a constitutional amendment to overturn the decision, with 44 percent opposed.

In the legislature, the House took first crack at the issue. The Judiciary Committee sent to the House floor a detailed bill establishing "civil union" status for homosexual couples with virtually all the benefits and responsibilities of marriage. The bill declared the state's "strong interest in promoting stable and lasting families, including families based upon a same-sex couple." After lengthy debate, the House passed the measure on March 16 by a narrow margin: 76-69.

The Senate passed a comparable bill, 19-11, on April 19 on a mostly party line vote, with Democrats in favor and all but two Republicans opposed. That bill went back to the House, which gave final legislative approval to the measure on April 25. Gov. Howard Dean, a Democrat, signed the bill the next day with no public ceremony, unusual for a major piece of legislation. "The healing process now begins," he told reporters later.

The state drew national attention when town clerks began issuing civil union licenses on July 1 — some to Vermont couples and others to couples from out of state. The issue continued to divide Vermonters through the fall. Opponents of the legislation mounted a "Take Back Vermont" campaign aimed at defeating Dean and electing Republicans to the legislature. Dean won re-election — gaining a 50 percent majority in a three-way race — but Republicans captured control of the House. An exit poll by Voter News Service found that 49 percent of voters were enthusiastic or supportive of the legislation, while 48 percent were either opposed or angry.

"Disturbing" Harassment

Anti-gay harassment is pervasive and widely tolerated in the U.S. military. That is the conclusion not only from gay-rights groups but also from the Pentagon itself.

A survey of some 71,500 servicemembers conducted by the Defense Department's Office of Inspector General and released on March 24 found that 37 percent had witnessed or experienced serious forms of anti-gay harassment, and 80 percent had heard offensive speech or jokes or derogatory names or remarks about homosexuals during the past year. Most of the harassment was not reported up the chain of command, the survey found, and no action was taken in three-fourths of those cases where senior officers were informed. [23]

"The report shows that military leaders must do more to make it clear that harassment based on sexual orientation violates military values," Defense Secretary William Cohen said.

Gay-rights groups took satisfaction from the report. "This is the first time that the Pentagon has realized that it has a serious problem on its hands," said C. Dixon Osborne, co-director of the Servicemembers Legal Defense Network. But they also called for stronger action.

"Nothing is going to change until the uniformed military leadership, from the Joint Chiefs of Staff on down, send clear and unambiguous signals that this type of harassment will not be tolerated," said HRC Communications Director David Smith.

Opponents of military service by homosexuals questioned the survey's findings, noting that the report itself acknowledged that individual respondents were not randomly selected. "You can't paint the entire military with these results," the Family Research Council's Maginnis says. "That's political spin."

The survey's results suggested the limitations of the military's efforts to date to translate the "don't ask, don't tell" policy into actual practice. Most of the servicemembers surveyed — 57 percent — said they had received no training on the policy. About half — 54 percent — said they understood the policy, but only one-fourth of those correctly answered three questions designed to test their knowledge.

The military had already moved to make training in the policy universal. The Pentagon announced on Feb. 1 that every member of the armed forces would undergo training by the end of the year to prevent anti-gay harassment. [24] The hourlong training session is to include a slide presentation along with role-playing exercises and pamphlets. One of the slides reads, "Zero Tolerance for Harassment."

Reporters who watched some of the early training sessions observed instances of puzzlement among servicemembers taking part. At Fort Campbell — where Winchell was killed — an officer asked whether a gay soldier should be reported for asking another soldier on a date. "No, it's just associational behavior," the training officer, Maj. James Garrett, answered. [25]

At Fort Meade, Md., outside Washington, one of the soldiers attending a training session also worried about harassment of straight servicemembers, according to *The Washington Post*. "If I'm in the shower, and somebody comes up and starts groping me," the Post quoted the soldier as saying, "my first instinct is not to go to the commander. My first instinct is, 'You better get off of me.'" [26]

Cohen responded to the report by creating a high-level working group to draft an "action plan" to address anti-gay harassment. The group's report, issued on July 21, detailed 13 steps aimed at reducing harassment of gay servicemembers. The recommendations were mostly reiterations of existing policy, including providing universal training and holding commanders responsible for policy infractions. "Today's recommendations, if implemented, would be a very good start," Servicemembers Legal Defense Network co-director Benecke said afterward.

The Defense Department on the same day, however, announced that it had cleared Fort Campbell commanders of creating the climate that led to Winchell's murder in 1999. The report found that the general command climate was "favorable." The post's former commander, Maj. Gen. Robert Clark, moved to a Pentagon job in June.

Playing Politics

A week after Al Gore narrowly beat Bill Bradley in New Hampshire's Democratic presidential primary, the HRC Board of Directors met to consider making an endorsement in the race. Since both candidates had staked out pro-gay-rights positions, there was an argument to stay neutral. Nonetheless, with crucial primaries coming up in states with sizable gay voting blocs — California and New York — the board decided on Feb. 9 to back Gore.

"The vice president has toiled at our side over the last seven years," said President Elizabeth Birch. "We thought we better make a decision while it is valuable and relevant." [27]

The competition between Gore and Bradley for gay votes and the HRC's explicitly political calculation in supporting Gore indicated both the changing political climate on gay-rights issues and the gay and lesbian community's increasing political sophistication.

"This is a community to be dealt with, and it can't be taken for granted," says Human Rights Campaign's Stachelberg.

The climate is different in the Republican Party. Gov. Bush snubbed the gay Log Cabin Republicans by refusing to meet with its leaders, though he later met with a selected handful of gay GOP officeholders.

During the primaries, Bush backed the "don't ask, don't tell" policy on gays in the military and opposed civil rights legislation. And during the crucial South Carolina primary he appeared to back away from previous statements that he would have no problem with appointing homosexuals to administration positions. "An openly known homosexual is somebody who probably wouldn't share my philosophy," Bush said. [28]

The Republicans' control of Congress has helped bottle up gay-rights legislation in Congress. "It is terribly disappointing that we still can't get a hate-crimes bill that includes sexual orientation, and we can't get the Employment Non-Discrimination Act passed," Stachelberg says. "Those two bills remain blocked by the leadership in Congress." At the same time, lawmakers in both parties rushed to approve the Defense of Marriage Act in 1996 to try to ward off what they saw as the threat of same-sex marriage.

Gay-rights groups see the climate as more favorable at the state and local level. In an end-of-year review in December 1999, the NGLTF said pro-gay-rights bills outnumbered "unfavorable" bills during the 1999 state legislative season, and "favorable" bills progressed in several states farther than in the past, even if they were not enacted.

Still, the review pointed to only a handful of gay-rights measures actually enacted into law. The biggest victories came in California, where a new Democratic governor, Gray Davis, signed measures establishing domestic-partnership benefits for same-sex couples, prohibiting employment and housing discrimination on the basis of sexual orientation and protecting gay and lesbian students against discrimination. [29]

Vermont's civil union bill topped the gay-rights movement's accomplishments in 2000. In an offsetting defeat, however, Mississippi banned gay and lesbian adoptions, joining Florida as the only other state with a statutory ban.

Gore and Bush continued to diverge on some gay rights issues after winning their parties' nominations in the summer. Gore actively courted the gay vote and continued to tout his support for allowing gay servicemembers to serve openly and for passing the federal Employment Nondiscrimination Act. For his part, Bush generally avoided dealing specifically with gay rights issues. "Governor Bush believes in treating all individuals with dignity and respect," campaign spokesman Scott McClellan told *The Advocate*, a gay magazine. "He does not tolerate discrimination in any fashion." [30]

The parties' platforms directly clashed on the same-sex marriage issue. The GOP platform "supports the traditional definition of 'marriage' as the legal union of one man and one woman." The Democratic platform endorsed "the full inclusion of gay and lesbian families in the life of the nation," including "an equitable alignment of benefits." But Gore hedged on the issue. "I'm in favor of legal protections for domestic partnership, but I'm not in favor of changing the institution of marriage as it is presently understood — between a man and a woman," he told *The Advocate*. [31]

On election night, exit polls by Voter News Service indicated that 70 percent of self-identified gay and lesbian voters cast ballots for Gore, 23 percent for Bush, and 4 percent for Green Party candidate Ralph Nader. Using those figures, the *Washington Blade,* a gay newspaper, calculated that gay and lesbian voters provided Gore a margin of victory in at least four states — Iowa, Minnesota, New Mexico, and Wisconsin — and gave Bush his winning margin in one: New Hampshire. [32] ■

OUTLOOK

Marching in Washington

National gay rights advocates spent the early spring preparing for what they hoped would be a massive gathering of gay, lesbian, bisexual and transgendered people in Washington over the April 29-30 weekend.

Organizers said the "Millennium March on Washington" — the fourth national event of its kind and the first since 1993 — was aimed in part at showcasing the gay community's growing political clout. "We have to show to the world how many people we are, what our voting bloc is and what we bring to the table," explained Dianne Hardy-Garcia, executive director of the march.

The march was marred, however, by organizational missteps and disagreements within the gay community over political priorities. Many gay activists complained that the time and money being spent on the march — the event was expected to cost about $1.73 million and take in about $1.95 million — would have been better used at the state and local level. "Our folks need to be at home doing serious political work, not having a tchotchke sale on the mall," Rick Garcia, of Equality Illinois, told *The Washington Post*.

Hardy-Garcia, who is also executive director of the Lesbian and Gay Rights Lobby of Texas, dismissed the criticism. "There's nothing like coming to your national capital and realizing you're part of a larger movement," she said.

Some gay scholars as well as gay rights opponents predicted that the march would not surpass the numbers of the 1993 event, which drew an estimated 300,000 people. "There is no widely perceived need for a march on Washington right now," said John D'Emilio, a professor at the University of Illinois in Chicago and author of a history of the early gay rights movement. "Most of the areas of advocacy that have a prospect of success and most of the advocacy energy have been focused on state and local issues, not on Washington."

In the end, law enforcement officials estimated that the march — held on the National Mall on April 30 following a previous day of festivals and concerts — at about 200,000. President Clinton addressed the crowd by videotape. He urged the crowd to lobby Congress to pass the Hate Crime Prevention Act, which would impose extra penalties for violent crimes motivated by animosity based on sexual orientation among other categories.

The march appeared to have no immediate political impact, however.

At Issue:

Should high schools permit "gay-straight alliance" clubs?

JIM ANDERSON

Communications director, Gay, Lesbian and Straight Education Network

WRITTEN FOR *THE CQ RESEARCHER*

Considerable media attention has been paid over the past few months, to gay-straight alliance (GSA) controversies in Utah, Louisiana and Orange County, Calif. In each instance, school boards either considered or took action to prevent students from exercising their federally protected right under the Equal Access Act.

While these battles and controversies have been intriguing, it is, perhaps, more interesting to consider the stories that have not made the news.

Little attention has been paid to the approximately 700 gay-straight alliances that are currently meeting in high schools from coast-to-coast. These school communities accepted or embraced the students and their efforts, and not as a result of judicial mandate. Instead, they recognized their professional, if not moral, responsibility to do so.

Should other high schools permit the creation of gay-straight alliances? To answer the question, we need to define gay-straight alliances and to discuss why students are forming them in such numbers. A gay-straight alliance is formed by lesbian, gay, bisexual and transgender (LGBT) students and their straight classmates. These students join together to support one another and to address concerns about the misinformation and ignorance that too often result in anti-gay harassment or violence at school.

Their concerns are well-founded. Studies by the federal Centers for Disease Control and Prevention (CDC) show that lesbian, gay and bisexual students are more than four times as likely as their heterosexual classmates to be threatened with or injured by a weapon while at school.

The Gay, Lesbian and Straight Education Network found similarly disturbing trends. In a recent national survey, we found that 61 percent of LGBT students experience verbal harassment, 27 percent physical harassment and 14 percent outright physical assault while at school.

This harassment and isolation may negatively affect students' self-esteem and school performance. Such experiences may explain why national mainstream organizations such as the American Counseling Association and the National Association of Social Workers have recently endorsed gay-straight alliances.

Every student is entitled to a supportive, safe and affirming learning environment. With this goal in mind, we urge schools not only to permit gay-straight alliances but also to encourage and foster their existence.

PETER LaBARBERA

Senior analyst, Family Research Council

WRITTEN FOR *THE CQ RESEARCHER*

School districts should not allow the formation of gay-straight alliances on their campuses. These groups, where they already exist, have become de facto homosexuality booster clubs — causing unnecessary divisions and distractions and subjecting the entire student body to one-sided propaganda. Moreover, they are part of a movement that promotes radical identities and dangerous sexual practices to vulnerable, confused teens.

The gay-straight alliances are part of an ingenious strategy by pro-homosexuality and transsexuality groups like the Gay, Lesbian and Straight Education Network (GLSEN) to inject their unhealthy sexual and gender ideologies into the classroom. Students rally around the "rights" of gay, bi or even trans (transgender) classmates who, it is true, are ostracized and sometimes mistreated by their peers.

But while GLSEN and other groups have artfully "spun" the issue of youth homosexuality into one of "discrimination," it is really about behavior and parents' rights to guide their children's moral decisions.

In Massachusetts, taxpayers subsidize the formation of gay-straight alliances — there are now 185 — through state grants for GSA projects.

Across the country, educators are wasting valuable school time by allowing GSAs to promote extreme notions to the entire student body. Students rarely get to hear the other side of the debate, and they fear expressing their opposition to homosexuality because of the schools' politically correct embrace of homosexuality.

The National Education Association, the American Civil Liberties Union, GLSEN and their allies promote GSAs in the name of school "safety." But schools shouldn't promote homosexual identities to troubled kids when studies show that homosexual males have drastically shorter life spans. This is due to the risky sexual behavior that flourishes in the promiscuous "gay" world. At a March conference sponsored by GLSEN's Boston affiliate, speakers from the state's Education Department approvingly discussed "queer sex" acts to an audience made up mostly of students ages 14-21.

Parents must resist an agenda that uses schools' authority to confirm impressionable youth in harmful lifestyles. As one former homosexual has noted, "From every medical and health aspect — up to and including the probability of becoming infected with AIDS — it is tragic, even criminal, to lead a child into homosexuality because he or she showed some degree of confusion in adolescence."

Gay-Straight Club Divides California Community

Anthony Colin wanted to make his school in Orange, Calif., a better place for homosexual teenagers like himself. His efforts in founding a so-called gay-straight alliance club at El Modena High School have brought him national publicity and a local human rights award, as well as daily name-calling in school and a draining federal court battle with the local school board.

"I knew I was going to be facing a lot of opposition, but I didn't know just how far it would go," said Anthony, a 16-year-old sophomore.[1]

The controversy over the club — one of some 700 gay-straight alliances at high schools around the country — has divided the 2,000-student school and the community. Students opposed to the club appeared at an early school board meeting carrying signs that read, "Grades, Not AIDS."

Nationally, gay-rights groups and social conservatives sharply disagree over such clubs. Supporters say they are needed to give homosexual high school students a safe place to talk about issues affecting their lives and to promote tolerance among gay and straight students alike.

"Gay-straight alliances help one of most vulnerable populations feel a little safer, a little more accepted," says Kevin Jennings, executive director of the New York-based Gay, Lesbian and Straight Education Network (GLSEN).

"Gay youth are typically very unsupported in schools, unsupported in other aspects of their life, too," says Barbara Rienzo, a professor of health sciences at the University of Florida in Gainesville and co-author of a book on local gay-rights disputes. "Schools are one of the places where we could do a lot of things to intervene and help make schools a safe and healthy place for all youth."

But Robert Knight, director of cultural studies for the conservative Family Research Council, says the clubs promote homosexuality.

"Gay-straight school clubs are a method by which homosexuality is introduced into schools," Knight says. "This is dangerous because some kids are undoubtedly sexually confused and have intense feelings toward same-sex classmates, which is normal. They can be seriously damaged by taking their healthy emotional drives and detouring into homosexuality because they're told it's cool and that they have no alternative."

Anthony was moved to start the club by the killing of Matthew Shepard, the gay University of Wyoming student who was beaten, tied to a fence and left to die in October 1998. Anthony and high school senior Shannon MacMillan applied for recognition of the club to the school's principal, Nancy Murray, saying its mission was "to raise public awareness and promote tolerance by providing a safe

And a new controversy erupted in early May when the organizers of the march disclosed that they had not received about $750,000 due from the company that produced the festival. The FBI was called in to investigate.

As gay rights organizations prepared for the fall elections, Hardy-Garcia insisted that the movement was becoming a factor in political campaigns. "We're 5 percent of the vote, on par with the Jewish and Latino vote," she said. "We've seen politicians respond to that."

Still, the movement had no assurance of tangible progress even if the gay vote helped elect supportive candidates. Clinton received strong support from gay political groups, but was unable to get Congress to approve lifting the ban on gays in the military, barring discrimination against gays, or passing the gay hate crimes measure.

The November elections kept Republicans in control of Congress. And, as the presidential contest remained undecided, the race seemed certain to end with a backward step for gay rights advocates no matter who emerged as the winner. Bush had opposed most of the gay rights legislative proposals, while Gore seemed unlikely to have much political capital to push their agenda on Capitol Hill.

In state and local races, gay rights groups did claim victories for an increasing number of gay and lesbian candidates, including the first openly gay state legislators in Georgia and Michigan. But Maine voters rejected an initiative to prohibit job discrimination against homosexuals. And two more states — Nebraska and Nevada

— adopted constitutional amendments aimed at prohibiting same-sex marriage.

Still, supporters and opponents acknowledge the gay rights movement's growing strength. "The gay rights movement has never been stronger, more influential, more diverse, more organized, or better prepared for anything than it is today," says Eric Marcus, a New York writer and author of a history of the gay rights movement.

From an opposing viewpoint, Knight, of the Family Research Council, credits the gay rights movement with "taking over" mainstream media and other organizations. "They have been successful at using what most Americans regarded as mainstream organizations to push a radical agenda," Knight says.

From its start, however, gay rights

forum for discussion of issues related to sexual orientation and homophobia."

Contrary to normal policy, however, school administrators had instructed principals in 1998 to forward applications for gay-student clubs to the school board for decision. The seven-member Orange Unified School District school board held an open forum on the issue in November 1999 and then voted unanimously to deny the application.

Board member Kathy Ward, author of the resolution to reject the application, said the club's mission intruded on the school's sex-education curriculum. "Sex-based discussions have no place in a school club," Ward said. Other board members were harsher. The application, William Lewis said, "asks us to legitimize sin."

Colin and club co-president Heather Zetin responded by suing the School Board under the Equal Access Act. The 1984 federal law requires schools to be evenhanded in allowing use of school facilities by student groups.

"When a school allows one non-curricular club to meet at school during non-instructional times, they have to allow all groups that want to meet," says Myron Dean Quon, a lawyer with Lambda Legal Defense and Education Fund in Los Angeles, who is representing the club.

In February 2000, U.S. District Judge David Carter agreed that the school board's action probably violated the law and issued a preliminary injunction allowing the club to organize and meet in school.

"Defendants cannot censor the students' speech to avoid discussions on campus that cause them discomfort or represent an unpopular viewpoint," Carter wrote in his 23-page ruling.

The club met several times in the remaining months of the school year, with as many as 50-60 members, according to Quon. But opposition from parents and school board members persisted. "Parents say that there are things they don't want their children exposed to in high school," board member Terri Sargeant said.[2]

In September, the school board agreed to settle the suit by reversing its decision to ban the club. As part of the settlement, the board adopted rules prohibiting student clubs from discussing sexual activity and creating a system to allow parents to object to a child's participation in any school group.

Quon said students were happy with the outcome. "We're happy the kids can go back to being regular school kids and not under such great public scrutiny," he said.

[1] Quoted in *The Orange County Register*, March 26, 2000, p. B1. For background, see *The New York Times*, Feb. 10, 2000, p. A20; *Time*, Feb. 21, 2000, p. 52.
[2] Quoted in *The Orange County Register*, Feb. 11, 2000, p. A19.

has been both a personal and a political struggle — a process of individual self-acceptance as well as collective mobilization. The gay community's growing visibility makes that process less difficult than in previous generations, but the process is no less important. "These marches are like rites of passage," Hardy-Garcia says. "There's nothing like being somebody from Lubbock, Texas, and being on the mall with hundreds of thousands of people and realizing you're not alone."

"The direction has been positive for a long time," Marcus says. "And there's no reason at this time to believe that we won't continue to make progress as long as gay and lesbian people come out and as long as those who love us support us in ever greater numbers." ■

Notes

[1] Background and quotes drawn from *The Boston Globe*, Dec. 21, 1999, p. A28; *USA Today*, June 28, 2000, p. 1A; *The Washington Post*, July 2, 2000, p. A3.
[2] For background, see Richard L. Worsnop, "Gay Rights," *The CQ Researcher*, March 5, 1993, pp. 193-216; and Richard L. Worsnop, "Domestic Partners," *The CQ Researcher*, Sept. 4, 1992, pp. 761-784.
[3] The text of the decision can be found on the Web site of the National Gay and Lesbian Task Force: www.ngltf.org.
[4] See Alan Yang, "From Wrongs to Rights: Public Opinion on Gay and Lesbian Americans Moves Toward Equality," National Gay and Lesbian Task Force, 1999, p. 14. In the most recent poll cited, 29 percent of those surveyed in 1998 said marriages between homosexuals should be "recognized as legal by the law."
[5] William N. Eskridge Jr., *Gaylaw: Challenging the Apartheid of the Closet* (1999).

[6] For opposing views, see Thomas B. Stoddard, "Why Gay People Should Seek the Right to Marry," OUT/LOOK, *National Gay and Lesbian Quarterly*, No. 6 (fall 1989), and Paula L. Ettelbrick, "Since When Is Marriage a Path to Liberation?", *ibid.*, reprinted in Suzanne Sherman (ed.), *Lesbian and Gay Marriage: Private Commitments, Public Ceremonies* (1992), pp. 13-26.
[7] For background, see Sarah Glazer, "Crackdown on Sexual Harassment," *The CQ Researcher*, July 19, 1996, pp. 625-648.
[8] Background drawn from Eskridge, *op. cit.*
[9] *Ibid.*, p. 43.
[10] See Barry D. Adam, *The Rise of a Gay and Lesbian Movement* (rev. ed.) (1995), pp. 67-68. For background on the post-World War II decades, see John D'Emilio, *Sexual Politics, Sexual Communities: The Making of a Homosexual Minority in the United States, 1940-1970* (1983) and Dudley Clendinen and Adam Nagourney, *Out for Good: The Struggle to Build a Gay-Rights Movement in America* (1999).

[11] See Paul Varnell, "Stonewall: Get a Grip," *The Windy City Times*, June 10, 1999. The article appears on the Independent Gay Forum's Web site: www. indegayforum.org.

[12] Account drawn from Eric Marcus, "Stonewall Revisited" (www.indegayforum.org). The article was written for the defunct gay magazine *Ten Percent* to mark the 25th anniversary of Stonewall in 1994.

[13] Cited in Clendinen and Nagourney, *op. cit.*, p. 30.

[14] Background and data drawn from William B. Rubenstein, Lesbians, *Gay Men and the Law* (1st ed.) (1993).

[15] Randy Shilts, *Conduct Unbecoming: Gays and Lesbians in the U.S. Military* (1993), p. 380.

[16] Account drawn from Clendinen and Nagourney, *op. cit.*, pp. 566-573. The authors note that Clinton's appearance was covered the next day in both *The New York Times* and, on the front page, in *The Washington Post*.

[17] For background, see Kenneth Jost, "Hate Crimes," *The CQ Researcher*, Jan. 8, 1993, pp. 1-24.

[18] See *1993 Congressional Quarterly Almanac*, pp. 454-462.

[19] See Wayne van der Meide, *Legislating Equality: A Review of Laws Affecting Gay, Lesbian, Bisexual, and Transgendered People in the United States*, Policy Institute of the National Gay and Lesbian Task Force (1999) (www.ngltf.org).

[20] See Kenneth Jost, *The Supreme Court Yearbook, 1995-1996* (1996), pp. 34-38.

[21] See *1996 Congressional Quarterly Almanac*, pp. 526-529.

[22] Some background drawn from *The New York Times*, Feb. 3, 2000, p. A1. The two major opposing advocacy groups in Vermont have Web sites: www.vtfreetomarry.org; www.takeittothepeople.org.

[23] See Office of the Inspector General, Department of Defense, "Military Environment with Respect to the Homosexual Conduct Policy," Report No. D-2000-101, March 16, 2000 (www.dodig.osd.mil). Reaction drawn from *The New York Times*, March 25, 2000, p. A1; *The Washington Post*, March 25, 2000, p. A1.

[24] See *The New York Times*, Feb. 2, 2000, p. A15.

[25] Reported in *The New York Times*, Feb. 14,

FOR MORE INFORMATION

American Family Association, P.O. Box 2440, Tupelo, Miss. 38803; (662) 844-7370; www.afa.net. Founded by the Rev. Donald Wildmon in 1977, it opposes same-sex marriage and "the movement to normalize homosexual behavior."

Family Research Council, 801 G St., N.W., Washington, D.C. 20001; (202) 393-2100; www.frc.org. The council opposes legal recognition of same-sex relationships, legislation to prohibit discrimination on the basis of sexual orientation and military service by homosexuals.

Gay, Lesbian and Straight Education Network, 121 W. 27th St., Suite 804, New York, N.Y. 10001; (212) 727-0135; www.glsen.org. The organization promotes non-discrimination policies and helps support high school-based "gay-straight alliance" clubs.

Human Rights Campaign, 919 18th St., N.W., Suite 800, Washington, D.C. 20006; (202) 628-4160; www.hrc.org. The organization is a political campaign and lobbying organization working for lesbian and gay equal rights.

Independent Gay Forum, www.indegayforum.org. The forum comprises a group of generally conservative-leaning gay writers, academics, attorneys and activists described as in favor of equality for homosexuals but "dissatisfied" with the current discussion of gay-related issues.

Lambda Legal Defense and Education Fund, Inc., 120 Wall St., Suite 1500, New York, NY 10005-3904; (212) 809-8585; www.lambdalegal.org. The legal center handles a wide array of gay-rights litigation, including employment discrimination, parenting issues, HIV- and AIDS-related discrimination, military and immigration.

National Center for Lesbian Rights, 870 Market St., Suite 570, San Francisco, Calif. 94102; (415) 392-6257; www.nclrights.org. The legal center handles various lesbian-rights issues, with special emphasis on child custody and same-sex adoption issues.

National Gay and Lesbian Task Force, 1700 Kalorama Rd., N.W., Washington, D.C. 20009; (202) 332-6483; www.ngltf.org. The task force, founded in 1973, works for civil rights for gay, lesbian, bisexual and transgendered people.

Servicemembers Legal Defense Network, P.O. Box 65301, Washington, D.C. 20035-5301; (202) 328-3244; www.sldn.org. The organization assists U.S. servicemembers affected by the military's policies on homosexuality.

2000, p. A1.

[26] *The Washington Post*, March 26, 2000, p. C3.

[27] The Associated Press, Feb. 10, 2000.

[28] Quoted in *The New York Times*, March 19, 2000, p. A24.

[29] Christina L. Lyons, "Adoption Controver-sies," *The CQ Researcher*, Sept. 10, 1999, p. 782.

[30] *The Advocate*, July 4, 2000.

[31] The full interview was published on *The Advocate's* Web site: www.advocate.com.

[32] *The Washington Blade*, Nov. 10, 2000, p. 24.

Bibliography

Selected Sources Used

Books

Adam, Barry D., *The Rise of a Gay and Lesbian Movement* (rev. ed.), Twayne Publishers, 1995.

Adam, a professor of sociology at the University of Windsor, Ontario, relates the rise of gay and lesbian movements in the United States and around the world. The book includes chapter notes, a list of works cited and a three-page bibliography.

Button, James W., Barbara A. Rienzo and Kenneth D. Wald, *Private Lives, Public Conflicts: Battles over Gay Rights in American Communities*, CQ Press, 1997.

Three University of Florida professors examine local conflicts over gay-rights laws and the impact of those struggles on local schools.

Clendinen, Dudley, and Adam Nagourney, *Out for Good: The Struggle to Build a Gay Rights Movement in America*, Simon & Schuster, 1999.

The authors sympathetically trace the rise of the gay-rights movement from the Stonewall Inn riots in 1969 through the late 1980s. The book includes a three-page bibliography. Clendinen is an editorial writer and Nagourney a political reporter for *The New York Times*.

D'Emilio, John, *Sexual Politics, Sexual Communities: The Making of a Homosexual Minority in the United States, 1940-1970* (2d ed.), University of Chicago Press, 1998.

D'Emilio, a professor of gender and women's studies at the University of Illinois in Chicago, traces the early history of the gay-rights movement from the 1940s to the formation and increasing assertiveness of gay-rights groups in the 1950s and '60s. The book was originally published in 1983; the 1998 edition includes a new preface and afterword.

Eskridge, William N. Jr., *Gaylaw: Challenging the Apartheid of the Closet*, Harvard University Press, 1999.

Eskridge, a law professor at Yale, traces the history of anti-gay legislation and enforcement in the United States and examines the advance of gay rights along with the continuation of anti-gay inequities in the law. The book includes several appendices and detailed notes.

—, *The Case for Same-Sex Marriage: From Sexual Liberty to Civilized Commitment*, Free Press, 1996.

Eskridge expanded his unsuccessful representation of a Washington, D.C., gay couple's effort to legally marry into a comprehensive argument for permitting same-sex marriage based on history, law and morality. The book includes detailed source notes, an appendix of court cases, and a 19-page bibliography.

Magnuson, *Are Gay Rights Right?: Making Sense of the Controversy*, Multnomah Press, 1990.

The Minneapolis trial lawyer mounts a sharp attack on what he calls the homosexual-rights movement on grounds of religion, morality, law, and public health.

Marcus, Eric, *Making History: The Struggle for Gay and Lesbian Equal Rights, 1945-1990, An Oral History*, HarperCollins, 1992.

Author Marcus presents first-person accounts by some 50 people who figured in the history of the gay-rights movement since World War II.

Rubenstein, William B., *Cases and Materials on Sexual Orientation and the Law* (2d ed.), West Publishing, 1997.

This law school casebook includes court decisions, statutory provisions and other materials on the full range of gay-rights issues. Rubenstein is an acting professor at UCLA School of Law. The first edition of the casebook was published as *Lesbians, Gay Men and the Law*.

Shilts, Randy, *Conduct Unbecoming: Gays and Lesbians in the U.S. Military*, St. Martin's Press, 1993.

Shilts, a *San Francisco Chronicle* reporter until his death from AIDS in 1994, recounts the largely unacknowledged history of homosexuals in the U.S. military in order to mount a strongly argued attack on the then-existing ban on gay or lesbian servicemembers. The current "don't ask, don't tell" policy is not covered. The book includes detailed source notes and a four-page bibliography.

Articles

Leland, John, "Shades of Gay," *Newsweek*, March 20, 2000.

The cover story in this package of articles on gay-related issues depicts increased tolerance for homosexuals in schools, churches, offices, family life, and politics and government. The story notes a new Newsweek poll that for the first time found that less than a majority of those surveyed — 46 percent — believe homosexuality is a sin.

Reports and Studies

Yang, Alan, "From Wrongs to Rights, 1973-1999: Public Opinion on Gay and Lesbian Americans Moves Toward Equality," National Gay and Lesbian Task Force, 1999.

The report, based on opinion polls over the past decade or longer, finds increasing support for gay rights on a range of issues although most Americans continue to oppose same-sex marriage and believe homosexual relations wrong. Yang is a Columbia University researcher.

4 Prison-Building Boom

DAVID MASCI

T he inmates quietly file into the room and begin emptying their pockets — cigarettes, lighters, pens — onto a big table. As a guard reads out their names, they step through a metal detector, then pick up their possessions and go into an adjacent room to wait.

"Twenty-eight!" the guard in the next room calls out, confirming the count after the last man has been checked in. Then an automatic iron door between the rooms clangs shut, and a new group of inmates enters.

It's lunchtime at the Maryland Correctional Institution in Hagerstown, Md., and inmates returning from their jobs in the prison's factories are hungry. But the check-in process can't be rushed. After passing through the metal detector, they will be searched and counted again. Then they must wait in another locked room until they are finally allowed into the cafeteria.

"This is a totally controlled environment," says Lloyd "Pete" Waters, warden of the medium-security institution. "We tell them where to sleep, what to eat and when to work. Everything."

The entire 2,000-inmate facility is designed to give Waters and his staff of 660 complete control at every moment. No prisoner can travel more than a few hundred feet down any hallway without running into a gate or guard. "We need to know where these people are at all times," Waters says, "or we would lose control."

Though he runs the prison with tough and determined efficiency, Waters is not considered a harsh taskmaster. As he walks among the men, many greet him with a "Good morning, sir" or a "How's it going, warden?"

Waters proudly points out that he has reduced the level of tension and

From *The CQ Researcher,*
September 17, 1999.

AP Photo/Damian Dovarganes

violence at the facility during his eight years there, in part by greatly increasing the number of activities and opportunities available to prisoners.

"I don't give up on any of these men," he says. "I try to make a difference with each of them."

Making a difference isn't always easy, he admits. For one thing, Waters says, the offenders who come to Hagerstown are often "broken men." Many were drug abusers, and some are unable to read. A large percentage had long juvenile records.

Indeed, Waters says, more needs to be done to ensure that there are fewer broken men in the future. "Prevention is always better than reaction," he says, "and I don't think we do enough of that. Every time I hear that states like California or Florida spend more on prisons than on education, it makes me cringe."

The warden's views are widely shared by liberal criminal justice experts and others, who say the United States has gone on a prison-building binge at the expense of education, drug treatment and other programs that might help prevent

crimes. They say that over the last 25 years the states and the federal government have spent billions of scarce tax dollars to build hundreds of new correctional facilities. As a result, the United States now has four times as many people behind bars as it did in 1975 and has the world's second-highest incarceration rate.

Opponents of increased prison building argue that while locking up violent criminals makes society safer, the current policy is akin to drift-net fishing: Also scooped up with the truly bad actors are many less dangerous felons, who could be more inexpensively and effectively punished without resorting to incarceration.

"We have 1.8 million people in prisons today, and I think we reached a point a while ago where there is nothing but diminishing returns for continuing this policy," says Marc Mauer, assistant director of The Sentencing Project, a criminal justice think tank.

Mauer and others contend that community-based solutions like parole and probation are being underutilized in favor of the so called get-tough approach. As a result, many men who have committed lesser, non-violent offenses are being removed from their neighborhoods, unable to work and support their families. "People in these communities are often already struggling," he says, "and this just makes it worse."

In addition, critics like Mauer argue that at least some of the billions directed toward prison building each year should be reallocated to programs proven to prevent crime, like after-school and drug-treatment programs.

"The bottom line is we need more social workers and fewer policemen on the street," says Jamie Fellner, associate counsel at Human Rights Watch in New York.

But while Waters would like to see more money directed at preven-

U.S. Criminal Justice Census at a Glance

Nearly 6 million Americans were in jail or prison, or on probation or parole in 1998 — 2.8 percent of all U.S. adults. The number of inmates in state and federal prisons increased more than fivefold from 1970 to 1998.

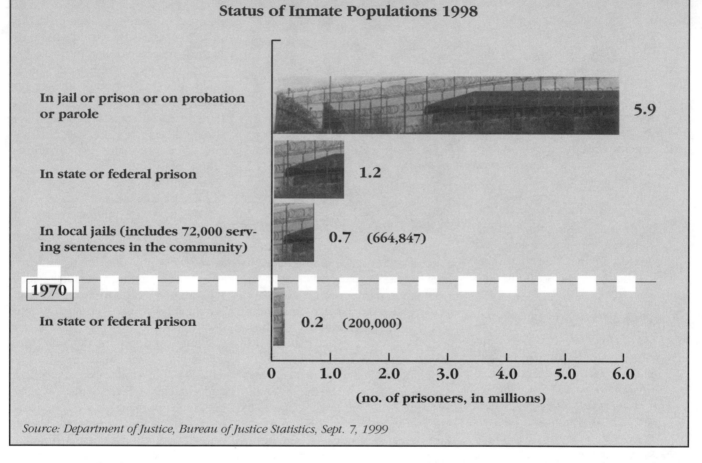

Status of Inmate Populations 1998

In jail or prison or on probation or parole — 5.9

In state or federal prison — 1.2

In local jails (includes 72,000 serving sentences in the community) — 0.7 (664,847)

1970

In state or federal prison — 0.2 (200,000)

0   1.0   2.0   3.0   4.0   5.0   6.0

(no. of prisoners, in millions)

Source: Department of Justice, Bureau of Justice Statistics, Sept. 7, 1999

tion programs, he doesn't necessarily believe, as do many on the left, that society has become too punitive or overly reliant on prisons. "Prison does prevent crime," he says. "It's common sense: If you lock up the bad guys, crime will go down."

Waters' view of prison as a crime deterrent coincides with the views of many conservatives, who argue that the most effective way to fight crime is to put a substantial portion of the criminal element behind bars.

"Prisons work to prevent crime by simply isolating criminals from the rest of society," says Morgan Reynolds, director of the Criminal

Justice Center at the nonprofit National Center for Policy Analysis in Dallas. "Prison, while unpleasant and expensive, is effective."

In addition, Reynolds and others say, increased incarceration sends a message to criminals that the system is capable of meting out adequate punishment when the law is broken. Indeed, they say, during the 1960s and '70s, the crime rate increased, in part because lenient judges and overcrowded jails often meant less or even no prison time for those who had committed serious offenses. "The system lost its credibility," Reynolds says, "and things got much worse."

But building additional prisons does more than just give the system the wherewithal to protect the public. It also improves community life by reducing the power of the criminal element in a given area. This, conservatives argue, can be more effective in preventing future crime than new spending on social programs because it takes offenders out of the vicinity of children and other law-abiding citizens.

At the same time that the number of prisons has been growing, there has been a parallel increase in the amount of time inmates serve. Many states accomplished this through mandatory minimum sentences for certain crimes and so-called truth-in-sentencing laws, which require an inmate to serve out most of his sentence before being released. Half the states have enacted "three-strikes" laws, which usually require a judge to sentence a defendant to life in prison after a third felony, generally for violent offenses.

Here too, conservatives say, the trends have largely been positive. They argue that tough sentencing laws assure the public that criminals will serve "real time for real crimes." "Sure there are exceptions, but most of these people are dangerous criminals who need to be put away for a long time," says Washington lawyer Richard Willard, a former assistant U.S. attorney general.

Willard and others also see tough sentencing laws as an antidote to the trend toward small sentences for big crimes, which began in the 1960s.

"It used to be if you got lucky and drew the right judge, you could get a low sentence, which basically meant getting away with it," says Kurt Scheidegger, legal director of the Criminal Justice Legal Foundation, a conservative think tank in Sacramento, Calif.

But liberals and others say that mandatory minimums and similar laws are a simpleminded and brutish weapon in the war against crime. The biggest problem, they say, is that tens of thousands of mostly young, black men are going to prison for a long time for what are, in many cases, minor drug crimes. "I don't think people realize how many tragic stories there are because of these laws," says Julie Stewart, president of Fami-

lies Against Mandatory Minimums.

Stewart and others contend that taking sentencing discretion away from judges and imposing a one-size-fits-all solution to the problem has created a system that is both unfair and ineffective. In addition to imposing Draconian sentences on minor criminals — and taking up space needed to hold more serious offenders — the new laws have clogged the nation's jails and prisons with inmates who could probably be better dealt with through supervised release and access to drug treatment.

"We've chosen an expensive way to deal with these kids," Stewart says.

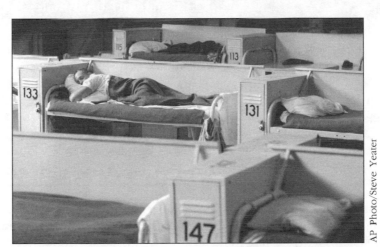

Due to overcrowding, a converted gymnasium is used to house California prisoners at the Deuel Vocational Institute in Tracy.

Right now, it's an expense most people seem willing to bear. But polls show that while most Americans have little sympathy for adult criminals, they don't give much thought to the penal system and how many lives it touches. According to the most recent figures released by the Justice Department's Bureau of Justice Statistics (BJS), 5.9 million persons, or almost 3 percent of the nation's adult population, are in prison or jail or on probation or parole. Almost all of these people, it's safe to assume, have family members and friends who must also cope with their incarceration.

As experts and others ponder these and other statistics, here are some of the questions they are asking:

Should some of the resources being devoted to building prisons be redirected to educational and other social spending?

In 1983, federal District Judge William Wayne Justice assumed direct control of the state prison system in Texas. Overcrowding had caused such bad conditions, Justice said, that prisoners' constitutional rights were being violated — specifically the Eighth Amendment prohibition on cruel and unusual punishment. [1]

Texas responded to the ruling with a massive prison-building campaign. In the last two decades, the state penal system has grown nearly tenfold — from about 15 prisons housing 18,000 inmates to 110 facilities incarcerating 150,000 inmates. [2]

Many other states also went on prison-building sprees in recent years, though none grew as fast as Texas. From 1990 to 1995 alone, Texas and the other states spent almost $15 billion on prison construction, adding almost 400,000 new beds. The federal government also was busy, building 45 new prisons during the same period. [3]

As in Texas, prison construction around the nation was the result of overcrowding caused by increased crime and harsher sentencing laws enacted since the 1980s.

"We've built more prisons because we've needed to take more criminals off the streets," says Todd Gaziano, a senior fellow in legal studies at the Heritage Foundation, a conservative think tank. "It's as simple as that."

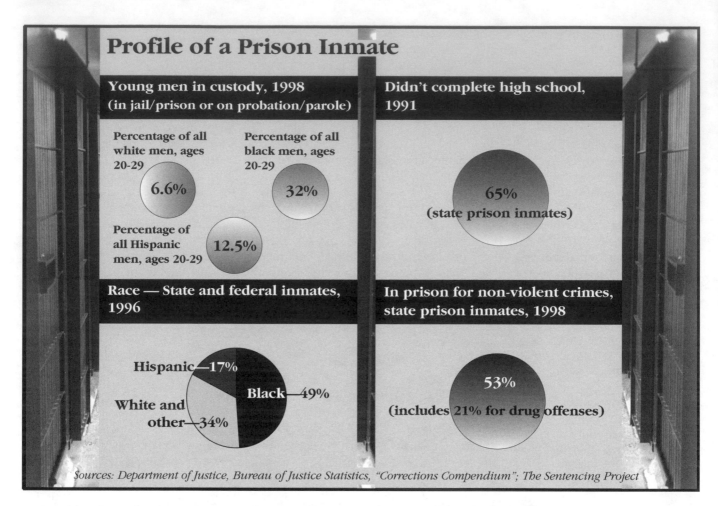

Profile of a Prison Inmate

Young men in custody, 1998
(in jail/prison or on probation/parole)

Percentage of all white men, ages 20-29 — **6.6%**

Percentage of all black men, ages 20-29 — **32%**

Percentage of all Hispanic men, ages 20-29 — **12.5%**

Didn't complete high school, 1991

65%
(state prison inmates)

Race — State and federal inmates, 1996

Hispanic—17%

White and other—34%

Black—49%

In prison for non-violent crimes, state prison inmates, 1998

53%
(includes 21% for drug offenses)

Sources: Department of Justice, Bureau of Justice Statistics, "Corrections Compendium"; The Sentencing Project

But liberals and others contend that it is actually not so simple. They say the prison-building boom itself has been an overly simplistic way of dealing with the complex societal problems that are associated with crime. "We've taken the easy and expedient way out by saying that we'll deal with these problems by locking people up," says Jenni Gainsborough, communications director for the Campaign for an Effective Crime Policy.

The Sentencing Project's Mauer agrees, pointing out that the current wave of prison construction will inevitably lead to more and more prisoners, regardless of whether the crime rate rises or falls. "We've made a serious commitment to long-term imprisonment," he says. "And that means that as we build more and

more prisons the number of prisoners inevitably increases, because the prison population always expands to fill the extra space."

Moreover, Mauer and others argue, policies that rely on incarceration are having a devastating effect on many communities around the country, particularly inner-city neighborhoods. "In some places, kids see more people go to prison than they do leave for work every morning," Mauer says. "What kind of message is that sending?"

In addition, critics say, creating more convicts will likely lead to a larger criminal class. "Going to prison makes getting a job much harder when you get out," says Human Rights Watch's Fellner. "So you have these people, many of whom are already on the edge, returning to society with

the odds even further against them." And that makes them more likely to return to crime, she adds.

Finally, critics of the construction boom say, all the money being spent on prisons is diverting scarce resources from programs that focus on preventing crime without putting people behind bars. "What's really tragic about this whole thing is that it has sucked so much money away from important things that could really make a difference," Gainsborough says.

Tonya McClary, research director for the Criminal Justice Project at the NAACP Legal Defense Fund, agrees. "We've become a throwaway society, throwing people away in prison as an alternative to trying to genuinely help them and their communities."

For instance, McClary and others

argue, society would be better served by funding more drug treatment programs, both in prisons and in neighborhoods. "Every study we have has shown that dollar for dollar drug treatment is more effective [at deterring crime] than prison," Mauer says.

In addition, critics say, more funding should be directed to community-based sanctions like parole and probation, which could be both more effective and infinitely cheaper than incarceration. "Right now, these programs are so underfunded that they are thought of as a joke," Gainsborough says.

Gainsborough and others also argue that money needs to be put into programs that strengthen the family and community. "There's so much we can do, like after-school programs to keep kids busy and off the street," she says. "Studies show that most juvenile crime occurs between the time children leave school and when mom and dad come home."

But many conservatives say that while some programs aimed at preventing crime might help a little, prison will remain a key component of society's crime-fighting strategy as long as felons walk the streets. "No matter what they might say, we haven't discovered a magic bullet, be it drug treatment or something else, to solve the crime problem," Willard says.

And, Willard and others argue, society is unlikely to find a "magic bullet" any time soon, no matter how much money is spent on drug treatment and after-school programs.

"The whole idea that a lot more social spending can reduce the crime rate is a Great Society pipe dream," says the Criminal Justice Legal Foundation's Scheidegger, referring to the programs championed by President Lyndon B. Johnson.

Scheidegger points out that earlier in the century, when poverty and racism were much more prevalent, the incidence of criminal behavior was actually much lower. "The problem [today] is a general cultural rot, a decline in attitudes, that has led people to feel alienated from society and justified in breaking its rules," he says.

Putting more criminals in prison counters this trend, according to Scheidegger and others, by making would-be criminals think twice about breaking the law. "The criminal element on the outside needs to fear and respect the [criminal justice] system or it's meaningless," says Reynolds of the National Center for Policy Analysis.

In addition, many conservatives say, taking criminals off the street improves communities in general and the prospects for children in particular. "Crime begets more crime," Willard says. "One reason young people in some areas commit crimes is that they are surrounded by criminals."

Finally, supporters of prison building say, incarcerating more criminals is simply the most effective means of fighting crime. "It's pretty obvious that the best way to deal with crime is to lock up the criminals," Willard says. "Prisons are the best form of prevention we have."

Not surprisingly, proponents of prison building credit the recent construction boom for at least part of the drop in violent and other types of crime over the last seven years. "There's no question that it's played a significant part in reducing crime in America," Gaziano says.

Gaziano and others argue that the crime rate rose in the 1960s, '70s and '80s in part because the penal system was not big enough to incarcerate the number of criminals being processed through the courts. "It's helpful to go back 10 or 15 years and find out what prompted this movement to build prisons," he says. "Things had gotten so bad, prisons so over-crowded, that some states were letting people convicted of serious crimes go free after only serving a tenth of their sentences."

Reynolds agrees. "Many on the left believed and still do that punishment was outmoded and ineffective," he says. "But the bottom line is, it works, and you can see that in the statistics."

Today, Gaziano and others say, most states have the facilities to keep the worst offenders off the streets for significant periods of time. In addition, they say, criminals know that they're unlikely to be released after serving only a small fraction of their sentence. "Criminals today know that they're going to get hammered pretty badly if they get caught," Reynolds says. "Don't think that doesn't make a difference."

But liberals and others question the correlation between prison building and falling crime rates. "This is a pick-your-statistics game," Gainsborough says, noting, for example, that while violent crime has declined, drug use is up, in spite of the fact that drug arrests have skyrocketed.

According to Fellner, the real impetus behind prison building has more to do with attitudes than statistics. "They've transformed mean-spiritedness into public policy under the guise of cracking down on crime," she says.

But conservatives counter that building more prisons is nothing more or less than a necessary evil. "When liberals talk about the rising numbers" of prisoners, Scheidegger says, "they never mention that we're incarcerating more people because the crime rate has risen so dramatically in the last 30 years."

Conservatives think that liberals should shift some of their concern away from those in prison and toward law-abiding citizens. "We need to care more about innocent victims of crime than we do about convicted criminals," Gaziano says. "So if we're

U.S. Has Second-Highest Incarceration Rate

The United States has the second-highest incarceration rate (after Russia) among 59 other nations in Asia, Europe and North America. The U.S. rate is generally six to 10 times the rate for most nations in Western Europe.*

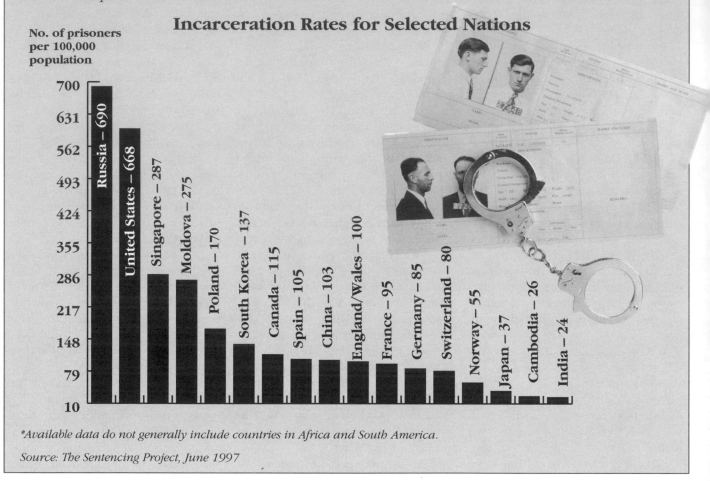

Incarceration Rates for Selected Nations

No. of prisoners per 100,000 population

Values: Russia – 690, United States – 668, Singapore – 287, Moldova – 275, Poland – 170, South Korea – 137, Canada – 115, Spain – 105, China – 103, England/Wales – 100, France – 95, Germany – 85, Switzerland – 80, Norway – 55, Japan – 37, Cambodia – 26, India – 24

Y-axis: 700, 631, 562, 493, 424, 355, 286, 217, 148, 79, 10

*Available data do not generally include countries in Africa and South America.

Source: The Sentencing Project, June 1997

faced with a difficult policy question, we need to err on the side of public safety."

Should mandatory sentencing, three-strikes statutes and similar laws be repealed or scaled back?

On March 11, 42-year-old Odalis Harris was sentenced to life in prison for robbing a shoestore in Roanoke, Va. Harris, who had served time twice before for robbery, was sentenced under the state's "three-strikes" law. The 1994 statute requires juries to sentence convicted felons to life if they had two prior felony convictions, at least one involving violence. [4]

To opponents of three-strikes laws, mandatory minimum sentences and truth-in-sentencing acts, Harris' case is just one of the many miscarriages of justice that have occurred since legislatures began passing such statutes in the 1970s and '80s.

"It's really amazing how many of these horror stories there are," says Stewart of Families Against Mandatory Minimums. "These cases are not the exception, but the rule." Critics like Stewart say that life terms and other long sentences should be re-

served only for the most serious offenders.

Supporters of mandatory minimums challenge Stewart's contention that "horror stories" are common. But all sides agree that mandatory minimums and similar laws have become widely used during the last 25 years. In fact, a majority of states as well as the federal government impose mandatory minimums for crimes ranging from drug offenses to weapons violations.

Also increasingly popular in recent years are truth-in-sentencing laws, which require persons convicted of certain crimes to serve out a large portion of their sentence in prison. Less common are "three-strikes" laws, such as the one used in the Harris case. In addition to Virginia, only a few states have such laws, most notably California.

As many opponents see it, the problem with such laws is that they try to impose a one-size-fits-all solution to individual cases that are all very different. The result, they say, is a system that regularly sentences relatively minor felons to unnecessarily long and cruel jail terms.

"We have tens of thousands of people in prison serving unjust sentences," says Eric Sterling, who helped write federal mandatory minimum laws while working as a counsel for the House Judiciary Committee during the 1980s. Now president of the Criminal Justice Policy Foundation, he is vehemently opposed to the laws he helped draft.

Calling his work on the issue "the greatest tragedy of my professional life," Sterling says that mandatory minimums destroy the entire concept of what is a just sentence. Human Rights Watch's Fellner agrees, "There are a whole host of factors that go into deciding a sentence," he says, "but this boils it down to one or two."

"When it comes to sentencing, you have to look at each individual to determine what the best sanction is," Gainsborough says. "The problem with mandatory minimums is that judges can't do that."

Many judges, in fact, are among the most vehement critics of mandatory minimums, arguing that it takes away their ability to find a punishment to fits the crime. "Judges hate them because they don't allow them

to do what they were appointed to do," Stewart says.

Opponents contend that the new laws have, in essence, given the prosecutor primary authority for imposing sentence. "Because your sentence often depends on what you're convicted of, the real decision-maker in this process becomes the prosecutor," Fellner says, "because he or she

---

Critics of mandatory minimum sentences say they clog the prison system with low-level drug offenders. Supporters say that most offenders convicted under tough sentencing laws are hardened criminals with long records who need to be taken off the street.

---

decides what you'll be charged with."

The power wielded by prosecutors is particularly troublesome, Fellner says, because prosecutors make their charging decisions behind closed doors, without any real information about the defendant's background. "They're not like judges, who have the defendant's whole record, their life history, in front of

them," she says. "And a judge's decisions can be reviewed and reversed by higher courts."

In addition, critics of mandatory minimum laws argue that they end up clogging the prison system with low-level drug offenders and other non-violent criminals who could be dealt with in less expensive and more effective ways.

"We've decided that it's better to warehouse these people rather than try other things like drug treatment and community-based sanctions like parole or probation," Fellner says. "I mean, they say these laws are meant to put drug kingpins away, but most of the time its low-level kids, usually poor, usually minority, that end up serving these sentences."

As evidence, Fellner and others point to a recent study by the Justice Policy Institute, which shows that the new, tough sentencing laws have increased the number of inmates convicted of non-violent offenses in the nation's prisons and jails to more than 1 million, or more than half of all people behind bars. [5]

And in New York state, which has some of the toughest mandatory minimum sentencing laws in the nation, a March 1999 report from Human Rights Watch said that one in four felons recently sent to a state prison had been convicted of a low-level, non-violent drug offense. [6] Opponents of mandatory minimums often point to the five-year prison sentence that must be imposed on anyone convicted in federal court of selling five or more grams of crack cocaine.

But conservatives argue that mandatory minimums and similar laws are an effective way of fighting crime. "Most of the people who are sentenced under these laws are hardened criminals with long criminal records who need to be taken off the street for a long period of time," says former Assistant U.S. Attorney General Willard.

Take drug dealers, for instance, says Gaziano. "Liberals always talk about 'low-level drug dealers,' but what does that mean? What's a low-level drug dealer? What if it's someone who provides drugs to little kids? They may not be a so-called kingpin, but these are bad people we're talking about."

Moreover, conservatives say, the new, tough sentencing laws are largely fair and are not putting away good kids who have made one small mistake. "Most of the people in prison today are hardened criminals, with long histories of criminal activity, not some kid caught with a small amount of drugs," Willard says.

Reynolds agrees, arguing that liberals have found the occasional example where the sentence might not have fit the crime in order to give the impression that these laws are too Draconian. "You can find horror stories if you look for them, but this isn't some sort of problem that's run amok," he says.

Indeed, he and others say, it was horror stories of another kind that led to the enactment of mandatory minimums, truth-in-sentencing and three-strikes laws. According to conservatives, many judges in the 1960s and '70s were meting out laughably light sentences for very serious crimes.

"There's no question that some judges were not handing down stiff enough sentences," Scheidegger says. "A lot of them didn't take some crimes, especially drug crimes, seriously enough."

Another problem, they say, was that many inmates who had been given appropriate sentences were being released after serving only a

small portion of their time. "You had people serving a tenth of their sentences, and for serious crimes," Gaziano says. "In Texas, for instance, you had rapists doing a year or two."

But liberals argue that while a few judges might have been too lenient, the vast majority were handing down appropriate sentences. "It's a myth that people were getting short sentences for rape and murder," Gainsborough says. "What do they think, that judges don't care about public safety? That's ridiculous."

In addition, many liberals say, politicians have fostered the misperception that judges are lenient and out of touch in order to score easy political points with voters. "The 'tough on crime' stand is a winner for [politicians] because unlike almost every other issue, such as the environment, there's no powerful interest on the other side," Sterling says.

But conservatives dispute the notion that support for these tough sentences was whipped up by politicians looking for easy campaign issues. "I don't think politicians created this opinion," says John Lott Jr., a professor of law at the University of Chicago. "They followed the voters, and the voters innately realize that deterrence works." ∎

BACKGROUND

A Rising Population

T he United States incarcerates more people than any other country in the world. Even China, with more than four times America's population, has fewer total inmates.[7] And, of those countries that report the size of their inmate populations, only Russia has a greater percentage of its citizenry in

prison. (*See graph, p. 64.*)

According to the Bureau of Justice Statistics, the United States currently incarcerates 1.8 million of its citizens and residents. The majority of these inmates, about 1.1 million people, are held in state prisons. Another 100,000 reside in federal facilities. The remaining 650,000 are held in local jails, which are used to incarcerate those awaiting trial or convicts serving short sentences. (*See graph, p. 60.*)

To put these numbers in a different perspective, Eric Schlosser writes in *The Atlantic*, "imagine the combined populations of Atlanta, St. Louis, Pittsburgh, Des Moines and Miami behind bars."[8]

The high U.S. rate of incarceration is a relatively recent phenomenon. Until the early 1970s, the incarceration rate was only about 110 inmates per 100,000 people in the United States. But beginning in the mid-to-late '70s, the numbers began to increase, doubling in the '80s and again in the '90s. Today, there are approximately 668 inmates for every 100,000 persons in the United States.[9]

But in the last few years the rise in the incarceration rate has slowed down a bit. In 1998, the total number of inmates increased by 59,900, or 4.8 percent, below the 6.7 percent average growth rate since 1990.[10]

The makeup of the nation's prison population bears little resemblance to the country's overall demographics. The vast majority of people currently in prison and jail tend to come from low-income households and often have a history of substance-abuse problems. In addition, prisoners tend to be poorly educated — only a third are able to read and write when they arrive.[11]

The overwhelming majority of inmates are men, though the country itself is roughly divided in half by gender. Only 78,000 persons, or 6

Chronology

1970s Rising crime rates set off a debate about the best way to protect society.

1971
Gov. Nelson A. Rockefeller, R-N.Y., proposes the toughest anti-drug laws in the nation.

1972
There are 330,000 local, state and federal prisoners in the U.S.

1976
After serving time in connection with the Watergate burglary, Charles Colson founds the Prison Fellowship Ministry.

1979
Texas Judge Wayne Justice takes control of the state's prisons after declaring that the over-crowded system was violating prisoners' constitutional right to protection from cruel and un-usual punishment.

——— • ———

1980s Increasing drug use and other crimes prompt many states to pass tougher sentencing laws. The inmate population begins to climb dramatically.

1980
There are nearly 500,000 people incarcerated in the United States.

1984
The Corrections Corporation of America opens the nation's first privately run prison in Texas.

1985
There are 750,000 people incarcerated in the United States.

1986
Congress passes the Anti-Drug Abuse Act, which includes 28 new mandatory minimum sentences for drug-related crimes.

1987
Parole is abolished in the federal system.

1988
The infamous Willie Horton advertisement used by George Bush during his race for the presidency helps to make crime a top campaign issue. Horton, a convicted murderer, raped a Maryland woman while on furlough from a Massachusetts prison.

1989
Sixty-seven new prisons are built by the states and federal government, adding 31,642 new beds.

——— • ———

1990s Incarceration rates reach record levels as the crime rate's rise begins to slow down.

1991
The U.S. Supreme Court upholds a Michigan law imposing a mandatory life sentence without the possibility of parole to anyone convicted of possessing more than 650 grams of cocaine.

1992
The Bush administration releases a report entitled "The Case for More Incarceration," arguing that longer prison terms will lower the crime rate.

April 1993
Riot in the Lucasville, Ohio,

prison kills nine inmates and a corrections officer.

November 1993
Washington state voters approve the first so-called "three-strikes" law, mandating life without parole for third-time serious offenders.

March 1994
California enacts a tough three-strikes law.

August 1994
The Omnibus Crime Bill authorizes almost $8 billion in prison-building grants to the states. The legislation also includes tough federal sentencing laws.

September 1994
Virginia passes a truth-in-sentencing law that requires convicted felons to serve 85 percent of their sentences.

1995
One of every three black men in the United States between the ages of 20 and 29 is either in prison, jail, on parole or probation at any given moment.

1997
Riots at the newly opened Northeast Ohio Correctional Facility in Youngstown spark a debate on the merits of private prisons. Twenty-five new state prisons (including six in North Carolina alone) and six federal facilities are built, adding 25,248 new beds.

1999
There are 1.8 million Americans behind bars.

Losing the Vote

Ten states disenfranchise felony ex-offenders for life.* Only four states allow offenders in prison to vote. Forty-six states and the District of Columbia do not allow convicted felons in prison to vote.

Allow convicted felons in prison to vote

Maine
Massachusetts
New Hampshire
Vermont

Disenfranchise ex-felons

Alabama	*Mississippi*
Delaware	*Nevada*
Florida	*New Mexico*
Iowa	*Virginia*
Kentucky	*Wyoming*
Maryland	

* *Arizona and Maryland disenfranchise offenders for life after a second felony conviction; Tennessee and Washington deny the vote to those convicted before 1986 and 1984, respectively.*

Sources: The Sentencing Project, Human Rights Watch, October 1998

percent of all jail and prison inmates, are female. Still, the number of women in prison has tripled since 1980. Many have been sentenced under the tougher state drug laws.[12] Most, about 75 percent, also leave children behind when they enter prison.

There is an equally big disparity between the nation's racial makeup and its prisons. Although African-Americans make up 12 percent of the general population, they comprise 49 percent of the nation's jail and prison inmates. By contrast, whites and Hispanics make up 33 percent and 17 percent of the inmate population, respectively.[13]

As things stand, one in three black men ages 20-29 has some contact with the criminal justice system on any given day. To many, this statistic shows a terrible bias in the way justice is administered in the United States. "If you're black and poor, your chances of running afoul of the police are good, regardless of what you do," the NAACP's McClary says. "It's simply a question of skin color."

According to McClary, the incarceration of so many African-American men is having a tragic ripple effect throughout black America. In addition to the obvious problems that come with imprisonment — like broken families — there is a set of less visible concerns associated with the fact that so many young, black men are currently in jail. "A lot of these young people won't have children because they'll

spend much or all of their young-adult years in prison," she says. "It's almost genocidal."

McClary also laments the fact that many states now prohibit convicted felons from voting. "These rules disenfranchise a whole generation," she says. "There are now many people who will never be able to participate in our political process, and that's not right." (*See "At Issue," p. 73.*)

But others argue that, as tragic as the racial disparity in incarceration is, it is not based on some overarching bias on the part of the criminal justice system. Instead, they say, young, black men in inner-city areas are simply much more likely to be committing the kinds of drug-related offenses that put people in jail today.

"If you want to question the incarceration of blacks, you need to question the whole notion of locking people up for drug offenses, because that's what's causing this" says the University of Chicago's Lott.

Lott also points out that just as a substantial number of inmates are black, so are many victims of crime, whether they are harmed by violence or drugs. "You can't separate this fact out from the rest of the debate," he adds.

Rehabilitation

Four inmates stand on the stage of the prison auditorium in Hagerstown, harmonizing their way through

Despite Low Pay, Inmates Covet Prison Jobs

The scene could be a furniture factory anywhere in the country. Some men are welding unfinished filing cabinets; others work on pressing machines, turning sheets of metal into tubular legs and other components.

But this isn't anywhere: It's the medium-security Maryland Correctional Institute (MCI) in Hagerstown. The factory, one of three at the prison, makes metal furniture for various state institutions.

"We're currently working on an order for 4,500 beds for the University of Maryland," says Warden Lloyd "Pete" Waters, pointing to a string of unfinished bed frames hanging from a long cable.

Waters is among many prison officials who view prison jobs as one of the best reha-bilitation tools they have.

"This teaches them respon-sibility and to behave properly," Waters says, pointing out that inmates can lose their coveted — if low-paying — jobs if they're not good workers or if they get into trouble. "And besides, it gives them a trade that they can use after they're released."

"I think it has tremendous rehabilitative value," says Kent Scheidegger, legal director of the Criminal Justice Legal Found-ation, a conservative think tank in Sacramento, Calif. "People have to learn to obey the rules and finish the job."

Timothy Brown, an inmate at MCI who operates a pressing machine, says that the program is helping him to turn his life around. "This has taught me to be a responsible person, to work hard and show up on time." It also gives Brown, who has served 10 years of a 35-year sentence for second-degree murder, an opportunity to help his family. "I'm able to send money home to my mother and to my kids, and that's wonderful."

MCI's three factories — there is also a meat-processing plant and another furniture operation — are among 30 factories operated in 26 Maryland prisons by State Use Industries (SUI). The state-run manufacturing operation employs 1,300 inmates, bringing in more than $30 million in revenue each year by supplying the state with office furniture, food products and, of course, license plates. [1]

But SUI only employs 5.7 percent of the states 22,500 inmates. [2] "There's quite a waiting list of people wanting to get in here," Waters says. "We wish we could do more."

To a large extent, Maryland and other states that manufacture products used by state institutions deliberately limit the number of inmates they put to work, and hence limit their output. That's because the use of prison labor draws opposition from both unions and businesses, who complain that the very low wages typically paid to inmates makes profit-making firms unable to compete with prison products. At MCI for instance, inmates usually earn up to $2.50 a day, working from 7:30 a.m. to 3:30 p.m.

"This is a problem, especially for [organized] labor, since inmates make a small fraction of what workers outside do," says Marc Mauer, assistant director of the Washington-based Sentencing Project, which promotes sentencing reform. "I think everyone would feel better about this if prisoners were paid close to the prevailing wage."

Similar concerns attach to proposals for using prison labor in the private sector. Existing federal law bans the interstate sale of products produced by prisoners for private industry. As a result, only about 2,000 prisoners nationwide work for private businesses. [3]

But others say that using more prisoners in the private sector will not negatively impact the economy. "We have a labor shortage in this country right now," says Morgan Reynolds, director of the Criminal Justice Center at the National Center for Policy Analysis in Dallas. "At the same time, we have more than a million able-bodied men who are literally doing nothing and would benefit tremendously from a steady job. It's a no-brainer."

Warden Lloyd "Pete" Waters views prison jobs as an effective rehabilitation tool.

David Masci

[1] Paul Valentine, "Productive Program in Md. Prisons; State Says Giving Jobs to Inmates Pays Off," *The Washington Post*, March 22, 1999.

[2] *Ibid.*

[3] The National Center for Policy Analysis, "Factories Behind Bars," October, 1996.

"The Road Is Long." When they finish, to enthusiastic applause, Brad Keller, the prison's education director, addresses the audience of about 100 prisoners and two-dozen family members and other visitors. "I want to extend my congratulations to everyone here," he says. "A lot of hard work went into making this day happen."

It's graduation day at the institution, and the men in attendance have either earned their high school equivalency diplomas (GED) or a vocational certificate for proficiency in a trade.

The graduation ceremony has many of the usual trappings, including a commencement speaker. On this day, it's Robert Harleston, a retired Army general who currently chairs the Criminal Justice Department at the University of Maryland's Eastern Shore campus. "Studies have shown that success in such programs is consistent with good feelings about oneself and success in further endeavors once you leave this place," he tells the inmates.

Harleston is among many in the criminal justice community who say that educational and similar programs can give at least some inmates a better chance at becoming law-abiding and productive citizens once they are released.

For much of the 20th century, penologists and others have focused on how best to rehabilitate inmates. Only in the 1970s did the pendulum swing more toward using punitive measures as a way to fight crime. During the last few decades, many programs aimed at improving or rehabilitating inmates have been eliminated or scaled back. In one well-publicized example, in 1994, Congress eliminated Pell grant eligibility for those incarcerated.[14] The cash stipends had allowed some inmates to earn university degrees without ever leaving prison.

"We've abandoned the notion of rehabilitation in prison, cutting back on counseling, drug treatment and education programs," says the NAACP Legal Defense Fund's McClary. "And that's a shame because I believe that a lot of these [inmates] could be turned around because we know what works."

What "works," according to Stephen J. Steurer, executive director of the Correctional Education Association, is a combination of programs both in and out of prison. "There are three linchpins in this equation: education, drug programs and help finding a job and other support after they're released," he says. "If we did these three things, we could drop the recidivism rate like a stone."

Still, while efforts at rehabilitation might have slackened in some prison systems, they have not ended. At Hagerstown, for instance, prisoners can take reading and math classes, participate in psychological and substance-abuse counseling, receive vocational training and even work and earn money. There is also a transition program to help ex-inmates find work and readjust to their new lives.

"Most prisoners are going to be released at some time," Warden Waters says, "so anything that will give them a better chance of meeting their responsibilities in the community is worth trying." In addition, he says, these activities are important because keeping the inmates busy makes things easier on themselves and on the staff charged with watching them.

Still, Waters says, some inmates, for one reason or another, can't change for the better. "You've got guys who just won't move forward, no matter what we do," he says. "For some inmates the only form of rehabilitation that works is age," he says, referring to the fact that older inmates are much less likely to commit

a crime after release than a younger prisoner.

Others go much further, arguing that rehabilitation is oversold as a solution. "We really don't know how to rehabilitate people, so I'm very skeptical about a lot of these ideas," Scheidegger says. "Take counseling. I really don't think it does any good."

Lott agrees. "A lot of these guys are gaming the system," he argues. "If you tell someone that you'll reduce their sentence if they get their GED, then you may be giving them an incentive, but what good is it doing?"

He also disputes the studies showing that certain rehabilitative efforts reduce rates of recidivism, arguing that many of the inmates who try out these programs are already determined to go straight. "My concern is that these studies don't take into account the [self-selection] that occurs in prison." ■

CURRENT SITUATION

Prisons for Profit

The fledgling Northeast Ohio Correctional Center in Youngstown has had a rocky startup. In the first 10 months after it opened in 1997, 20 inmates were stabbed, two fatally. Soon afterward, six inmates, including four murderers, escaped. (All were caught.)[15]

While it is not the first prison to have violence and security problems, Youngstown garnered more than its share of headlines because it is part of a small but growing national ex-

Saving Souls in a Texas Prison

A unique experiment in rehabilitation is being tried at Jester II, a minimum-security prison in Sugarland, Texas. The hope is that an intensive program of Bible study and other religious activity can turn offenders away from crime.

"We believe that only through the grace of our Lord Jesus Christ can [prisoners] transform their lives and truly turn themselves around," says Pat Nolan, president of Justice Fellowship, the public policy arm of Prison Fellowship Ministries, which developed the InnerChange Freedom Initiative program at Jester.

The 100 inmates who have enrolled in the 18-month program divide their time between Bible study, prayer and worship and more traditional rehabilitative activities such as counseling, educational classes and job training. Television-watching and other recreational activities are kept to a minimum.

The hope, according to Nolan and others, is to get lawbreakers to acknowledge that they are sinners, repent for what they've done and commit to a life based on Judeo-Christian values and teachings. "We believe that crime isn't a legal problem, but a moral one," says Nolan, an ex-offender. "Until they understand that there are moral laws set down by God that we are all bound to obey, they won't change."

Charles Colson, who served time in prison for the Watergate burglary, founded Prison Fellowship Ministries in 1976. "There has to be something in people that makes them want to do the right thing," he said. "That's what Christian conversion does that nothing else does." [1]

Of course, using religion to rehabilitate criminals is not a new idea. The word penitentiary is derived from penitent, which has obvious religious overtones. In addition, the first major penal reforms in the United States were initiated by Quakers in Pennsylvania. The so-called Philadelphia system kept inmates in solitary confinement to allow them to think about what they had done and repent. [2]

Faith-based programs are already being offered in almost every prison in America, but they are not as comprehensive as InnerChange. They do, however, touch the lives of hundreds of thousands of prisoners, with prayer, counseling, Bible study and other religious activities. Prison Fellowship Ministries alone has 50,000 volunteers and a paid staff of 300.

Although a few Jester II inmates who enrolled in InnerChange have dropped out, most who begin the 18-month program finish. One participant, James Peterson, even successfully petitioned the Texas Department of Criminal Justice to delay his scheduled release so that he could complete InnerChange. [3]

After a year in the program inside the prison, inmates who participate take part in a six-month post-release program that matches them with a church and a mentor and helps them find a job. "This is vitally important," Nolan said, "because most prisoners who leave don't have help making the transition to life on the outside."

The jury is out as to the program's effectiveness. It's only been in operation since April 1997, and a Princeton University study gauging its effectiveness is not yet complete.

Meanwhile, Prison Fellowship Ministries is currently setting up two new programs at prisons in Iowa and Kansas. In addition, 25 other states have expressed interest in establishing similar programs, the group says.

Growing interest in InnerChange has led its supporters to predict that intensely focused, faith-based programs will become the rule rather than the exception in prisons in the future.

"It's like welfare reform — it will begin in a few states and then spread to the rest of the nation once it's shown to work," says Joe Loconte, a fellow at the Heritage Foundation.

"The fact that Texas, with its 'lock 'em up and throw away the key' attitude, is willing to embrace [InnerChange], shows a growing openness among those in law enforcement to something like this," he says. "It may take a generation for this to go mainstream, but it will happen."

Prison Fellowship Ministries founder Charles Colson

Prison Fellowship Ministries

---

[1] Quoted in Joe Loconte, "Jailhouse Rock of Ages," *Policy Review*, July 1997.

[2] Peter N. Carroll and David W. Noble, *The Restless Centuries: A History of the American People* (1979), p. 224.

[3] William R., Mattox Jr., "Prison Program Uses Faith to Transform Lives," *USA Today*, March 15, 1999.

periment in the use of privately owned and operated correctional facilities.

Some saw the trouble in Ohio as an inevitable result of government abrogating its responsibility to incarcerate criminals. Others, who see the growth of private prisons as a positive trend, viewed the Youngstown incidents as regrettable, but not unusual.

Until recently, incarceration was entirely the provenance of the government. But the explosion in the nation's inmate population during the 1980s forced some states to seek alternatives. As a result, the number of private prisons has skyrocketed in recent years, rising from just a few in the mid-1980s to more than 168 in early 1999.

Almost half of the nation's privately run facilities, including the prison in Youngstown, are operated by the Corrections Corporation of America (CCA). With 74 prisons in 26 states and Puerto Rico, Nashville-based CCA is the nation's fourth-largest corrections system, public or private.

As Schlosser points out, private prisons operate much like motels. They often take in inmates from other states, which usually pay between $25-$60 per inmate per day. [16]

Twenty-seven states currently have arrangements for inmate incarceration with for-profit prison companies. About 90,000 inmates, or 6 percent of the national total, are currently held in private facilities. But experts expect the number of private correctional facilities to continue to rise in the coming years, noting that dozens of new, private prisons are currently being constructed or being planned. "It's already a big business," Mauer says.

Critics of the private prison trend, liberals and conservatives alike, argue that the rush to privatize correctional services should at least be slowed and possibly stopped. For one thing, they

say, none of the facilities are adequately supervised by governmental authorities. Nor are they always required to meet minimum standards before receiving inmates.

"What is different and unfortunate about private correctional facilities is their lack of accountability," writes Nancy Mahon, director of the Center on Crime, Communities and Culture at the Open Society Institute in New York. [17] Mahon and other critics also point to a slew of incidents, ranging from severe prisoners beatings to escapes to misuse of inmate labor.

Others worry that for-profit prisons will try to keep inmates incarcerated longer than necessary in order to keep their facilities full and boost earnings. "I could see a situation where fewer people might be paroled due to the profit motive," Mauer says.

Still others argue that the private sector isn't suited to carry out some crucial government functions, like public safety, under any circumstances. "I generally support the free market," says Scheidegger, "but prisons are like the military and police in that they should always be under the control of the state."

But supporters of privatizing correctional services counter that for-profit prisons are generally cheaper and at least as effective as their public counterparts. "The rate of violence, escapes and similar incidents is no higher in private prisons than in the public system," says Pat Cannan, a spokesman for Florida-based Wackenhut Corrections Corp., the second-largest operator of private prisons in the nation with 45 facilities.

He also counters the charge that the profit motive will prompt private prisons to keep inmates longer than is necessary. "The ultimate decision as to who goes and who stays rests with the state, not us."

Cannan admits that some states have not adequately regulated private prisons. "Private corrections is a new phenomenon and some states just haven't caught up with it yet," he says. But "as the industry continues to grow, so will [government] oversight and regulation."

Parole Under Fire

Many more people processed through the criminal justice system walk the streets than are in prison. At the end of 1998, 3.8 million Americans convicted of a crime were either on parole or probation, more than twice the number of people incarcerated.

The idea behind parole is simple: If a convicted offender, after a certain amount of time in prison, no longer seems to be a threat to society, the criminal justice system should at least consider a supervised release. Prisoners are usually eligible for parole after serving a certain portion of their sentence. Likewise, probation, usually given in lieu of a prison sentence, is often intended for first offenders and others deemed less likely to repeat their crimes or threaten people or property.

But particularly since the 1970s, the concept of supervised release has come in for much criticism. Critics contend that allowing early release from prison for good conduct does little or no good. "There's no evidence to suggest that sorting through prisoners and trying to choose the ones who won't commit crimes works," says the University of Chicago's Lott.

In fact, Lott and others say that parole might lead to an increase in the crime rate since it allows many hardened criminals out of prison early. "Most inmates know how to play the

At Issue:

Should convicted felons be allowed to vote after they leave prison?

JAMIE FELLNER AND MARC MAUER
Fellner is associate counsel, Human Rights Watch; Mauer is assistant director, The Sentencing Project

WRITTEN FOR *THE CQ RESEARCHER*, APRIL 1999.

*m*illions of Americans went to the polls last November, but Lawrence Tyrone Hill was not one of them. A computer programmer in New Mexico, Hill spent a few years in prison in the 1980s. Since his release in 1986, he has worked, paid taxes and led an unblemished life. He has the right to acquire property, travel, get married, sign contracts, surf the Web, buy beer, run up his credit card — everything any other adult can do with one remarkable exception. He can't vote. Hill is one of more than 1.4 million Americans who is barred from the ballot box for life because he was once convicted of a crime.

In *Losing the Vote*, a report issued last November, Human Rights Watch and The Sentencing Project documented the impact of disenfranchisement laws in the United States. Few Americans were shocked upon learning that 46 states deny prisoners the vote and 32 deny the vote to felons on probation or parole. But even the most ardent "tough-on-crime" advocates were stunned to death to learn that 14 states deny the vote to former lawbreakers even after they have been released from the criminal justice system.

In these states, the right to vote can be permanently lost upon conviction of even relatively minor crimes, such as passing a bad check or selling marijuana. In most cases, the only way to get the vote back is through gubernatorial action.

Disenfranchisement laws have dramatically curtailed the black vote in several states. Nationwide, disenfranchisement because of felony convictions bars an estimated 13 percent of all black men from voting. In eight states, one in five black men is permanently denied the right to vote because of a felony conviction. At current rates, 30 to 40 percent of the next generation of black men in these states will be disenfranchised as adults. With the exception of certain Southern states, disenfranchisement laws were enacted without any express racist intent. Whatever the intent, however, the current impact clearly disproportionately affects African-Americans.

Denying ex-offenders the vote does not fight crime or have any practical deterrent effect. Some have argued that ex-offenders should be denied suffrage because they lack the judgment needed to vote responsibly. But in a democracy the vote is not reserved for the virtuous or wise.

At the edge of the millennium, it's time to remove disenfranchisement laws and get on with the tough business of deepening democracy by encouraging those who have the right to vote to do so.

JOHN R. LOTT JR.
John M. Olin law and economics fellow, University of Chicago School of Law, and author of **More Guns, Less Crime: Understanding Crime and Gun Control Laws.**

WRITTEN FOR *THE CQ RESEARCHER*, APRIL 1999.

*s*ociety imposes many penalties on convicted criminals after they leave prison. They face difficulties in joining unions, securing public employment, obtaining business licenses and obtaining the licenses necessary to practice occupations regulated by the government. Ex-convicts face many other forms of penalties, such as being prevented from inheriting property, suffering partial or complete divestment of assets, losing life and automobile insurance and losing pension funds (even if they are already retired). Depending upon the state one lives in, conviction affects parental rights, divorce, the ability to hold public office, ownership of firearms and the ability to serve as a juror. In addition, ex-convicts can lose the right to vote.

It is not obvious why only losing the right to vote is generating serious objections. The loss of many other rights, such as parental rights or the right to own a firearm for self defense, may well impose a much greater penalty on the ex-convict. Surely many of these collateral penalties impose a much greater financial hardship on the ex-convict. Yet, just as ex-convicts are deemed unqualified to be a parent or untrustworthy to have a firearm, it is surely just as reasonable that we might consider an ex-convict to lack the proper social concerns when exercising the decision to vote.

For society to function well, there are benefits to having voters who care about the well-being of others. Those who have committed violent crimes have provided information on how little they value other people. States have also claimed that important information about a person's character is obtained from other types of drug or property crimes. A criminal may have served his debt to society by serving out his prison term, but that does not imply that society must accept that prison has corrected his judgment or his values.

Because certain groups of citizens are incarcerated at higher rates than others, many are concerned about the discriminatory impact of denying ex-convicts the right to vote. Even if conscious discrimination were involved and even if different groups of the population were not committing crimes at relatively high rates, it is still not obvious why voting rights are somehow distinct from other lost rights. The most direct approach to solving such problems would seem to be eliminating the discrimination taking place at conviction and sentencing.

game and use the system to their advantage. So a lot of bad people get out early."

Such concerns have prompted 15 states, including California, Illinois, Arizona, Ohio and Mississippi, to abolish their parole boards, which review inmates' records and decide whether early releases are warranted. The federal government has also done away with parole. [18]

Other states are considering eliminating parole. On Jan. 6, Gov. George E. Pataki, R-N.Y., announced that he would push to end his state's use of parole entirely. Instead, Pataki said, prisoners would not only serve out their full sentences but also be required to have their DNA on file in order to make it easier to link them to future crimes and, hopefully, deter criminal activity.

Even in states that retain parole, its use has dropped significantly due in part to the passage of mandatory minimum and truth-in-sentencing laws. In Texas, for instance, the number of inmates eligible for parole fell from 57 percent in 1988 to 20 percent last year. [19] And according to a recent report by the Bureau of Justice Statistics, the average time served by inmates in states that still have parole boards has increased from 23 months in 1990 to 25 months in 1996. [20]

Supporters of parole bemoan the trend away from supervised release, arguing that it hurts public safety as well as inmates. For one thing, they say, parole boards have the authority not to release dangerous convicts on parole but to hold them to the full maximum of their sentences. So, eliminating these boards reduces a state's "ability to keep very dangerous offenders in prison," said Joan Petersilia, a professor of criminology at the University of California at Davis. [21]

Supporters of parole argue that it allows prisons to discharge those

inmates who are clearly not a threat to society and whose cells could be filled by more dangerous felons. "It's so stupid because prison is extremely expensive, and so we're paying all this money to keep these less dangerous people off the streets," says the Sentencing Project's Mauer.

In addition, Mauer argues, parole or probation after prison can help transition an inmate back into society. "Research shows that if you guide and supervise an inmate, get him some counseling, help him get a job, he'll be less likely to commit another crime," Mauer says. "I mean, it's better than letting him serve his entire sentence, giving him a bus ticket home and forgetting about him."

Mauer and others would like to see more money put into making parole work. "The caseloads of parole officers are almost always too large," Sterling says. "So supervision instead of prison is never really given a chance to work." ■

OUTLOOK

Shift in Priorities?

Conservatives and liberals may disagree over how increased incarceration affects the nation's crime rate. But most agree that the growth in prison building and in the prison population is likely to slow or even stop in the near future.

For many conservatives, the prison-building boom of the last two decades was necessary to correct the imbalances brought about by the mistaken, liberal judicial policies of the 1960s and '70s. In other words, they say, now that a more appropriate balance between punishment and crime has been restored, there will

be less need to continue incarcerating more and more people.

"We lost control back then, and the crime rate grew and was able to overwhelm the system," says Morgan of the National Center for Policy Analysis. "Now the system is overwhelming crime."

Scheidegger agrees. "As the crime rate comes down, I think we'll realize that we have it right and won't continue to increase or decrease sentences."

Other conservatives go a step further, predicting that if the crime rate continues to fall, so will spending on prisons. "If things continue going the way they are, we'll start to see a drop in the number of prisoners," says Chicago's Lott. "Soon, the amount of resources people will be willing to spend on [imprisonment] will begin to fall, and it's not clear that that will be wrong."

Liberals generally embrace the shifting of resources away from imprisonment. And many are confident that national policy will begin to turn away from what they see as the overly punitive measures enacted over the last two and a half decades, including mandatory sentences.

"I'm optimistic because some people who were tough-on-crime types are reconsidering their positions," Mauer says. "There's a growing consensus among police and others in the criminal justice community that things are out of balance here and need to be re-examined."

Others agree, but cite different reasons. "I think they'll reconsider this incarceration boom because financial pressure will force them to," says Sterling, the former House Judiciary Committee staffer. "The cost of keeping so many people behind bars will eventually counterweigh the political pressure to put and keep people away."

In addition, Sterling argues, as prison touches more and more people, either directly or indirectly, the sentiment against widescale incarceration will increase. "As more people are related to or know someone in jail, they may become more sensitive to the absurdity of what we've been doing."

But other liberal thinkers, while cautiously optimistic that incarceration rates will begin falling in sync with the crime rate, warn that the national mood is very fickle when it comes to crime.

"People think we're more unsafe than we actually are, and so it's easy to exaggerate the dangers out there," says Gainsborough of the Campaign for an Effective Crime Policy. "All it takes is one well-publicized and heinous crime, and things can shift and we could very quickly undo a lot of progress." ∎

Notes

[1] Rick Lyman, "Judge Rules That Despite Improvements, Prisons in Texas Still Need Federal Oversight," *The New York Times*, March 2, 1999.
[2] Figures cited in Christy Hoppe, "Judge Keeps Supervision of Prisons," *The Dallas Morning News*, March 2, 1999.
[3] Figures cited in Carl M. Cannon, "America: All Locked Up," *The National Journal*, Aug. 15. 1998.
[4] Laurence Hammack, "Third Strike Gets Robber Life in Prison," *The Roanoke Times*, March 12, 1999.

[5] "America's One Million Non-violent Prisoners," Justice Policy Institute, March 1999.
[6] Cited in "Who Goes to Prison for Drug Offenses," *Human Rights Watch*, March 18, 1999.
[7] Marc Mauer, "Americans Behind Bars: U.S. and International Use of Incarceration, 1995," The Sentencing Project, June 1997.
[8] Eric Schlosser, "The Prison-Industrial Complex," *The Atlantic*, December, 1998.
[9] *Ibid.*
[10] Figures cited in "More Than Any Other Democracy," *The Economist*, March 20, 1999.
[11] Data provided by The Sentencing Project.
[12] Ron Stodghill II, "Unequal Justice: Why Women Fare Worse," *Time*, Feb. 1, 1999.
[13] Figures provided by the Bureau of Justice Statistics.

[14] Jan Austin (ed.), *Congressional Quarterly Almanac* (1994), p. 288.
[15] Pam Belluck, "As More Prisons Go Private, States Seek Tighter Controls," *The New York Times*, April 15, 1999.
[16] Schlosser, *op. cit.*
[17] Nancy Mahon, "The Problem with Private Prisons," *The Washington Post*, Nov. 1, 1998.
[18] Fox Butterfield, "Eliminating Parole Boards Isn't a Cure-All, Experts Say," *The New York Times*, Jan. 11, 1999.
[19] Cited in Fox Butterfield, "Inmates Serving More Time," *The New York Times*, Jan. 11, 1999.
[20] *Ibid.*
[21] Quoted in Butterfield, *op. cit.*, "Eliminating Parole Boards Isn't a Cure-All, Experts Say."

Bibliography

Selected Sources Used

Books

Christianson, Scott, *With Liberty For Some: 500 Years of Imprisonment in America*, Northeastern University (1999).
Christianson details the history of penal life in America, from its role as a dumping ground for British criminals during the Colonial period to the recent prison building boom of the 1980s and '90s. He argues that the high rate of incarceration in the United States today is not just the result of the rising rate of crime but also reflects the mean-spirited side of the American character.

Articles

Belluck, Pam, "As More Prisons Go Private, States Seek Tighter Controls," *The New York Times*, April 15, 1999.
Belluck details the debate currently raging over the utility of privately run prisons, focusing on well-publicized problems with certain private facilities.

Butterfield, Fox, "Eliminating Parole Boards Isn't a Cure-All, Experts Say," *The New York Times*, Jan. 10, 1999.
The article examines efforts around the country to abolish parole boards and severely limit supervised release. Butterfield quotes some experts who say the parole system is in such disarray that abolishing parole won't have a significant positive or negative impact on crime.

Clark, Charles S., "Prison Overcrowding," *The CQ Researcher*, Feb. 4, 1994.
This dated but thoroughly researched piece details the debate over whether building more prisons in the future will reduce crime.

Cloud, John, "A Get-Tough Policy That's Failed," *Time*, Feb. 1, 1999.
Cloud argues that mandatory minimum sentences for non-violent offenders are overly harsh and ineffective. The good news, according to Cloud, is that the law enforcement community is slowly coming to believe "that mandatory minimums are foolish."

Loconte, Joe, "The Remarkable Second Career of Chuck Colson," *The Weekly Standard*, June 28, 1999.
Loconte, a fellow at the Heritage Foundation, chronicle's Colson's journey from Watergate felon to the leader of Prison Fellowship Ministries, which aims to rehabilitate inmates through Christian conversion.

Miller, Lisa, "Inside the Competitive New World of Prison Ministries," *The Wall Street Journal*, Sept. 6, 1999.
Miller examines the growing faith-based movement in corrections, detailing the competition that often ensues between Muslim and Christian groups operating inside prisons.

Schlosser, Eric, "The Prison Industrial Complex," *The Atlantic*, December, 1998.
Schlosser takes an in-depth look at the economic pressures that drive prison construction. He concludes that the interest groups and businesses that build and run the nation's prisons — and by definition define many of our criminal-justice policies — are driven by self-interest, not public service.

Swope, Christopher, "Truth and Consequences," *Governing*, April, 1999.
Swope surveys the impact of truth-in-sentencing laws around the nation. While some states have seen their prison population boom as a result of these laws, others have been more cautious in locking up inmates for a long time.

Valentine, Paul W., "Productive Program in Md. Prisons; State Says Giving Jobs to Inmates Pays Off," *The Washington Post*, March 22, 1999.
The article detail's Maryland's efforts to put inmates to work in fields ranging from food processing to furniture making.

Will, George F., "A Jail Break for Geriatrics," *Newsweek*, July 20, 1998.
The conservative columnist decries tough laws that are keeping older prisoners behind bars. He argues that studies showing low rates of recidivism for older inmates make it a waste of their time and taxpayer money to keep many of them in prison.

Reports

***Losing the Vote: The Impact of Felony Disenfranchisement Laws in the United States*, Human Rights Watch and The Sentencing Project, October, 1998.**
A 50-state survey of felony disenfranchisement laws concludes that they are "unreasonable" as well as "racially discriminatory."

5 Policing the Police

KENNETH JOST

Rafael Perez had wanted to be a policeman since childhood After four years in the Marines, he joined the Los Angeles Police Department in 1989. He did well and was assigned to a special anti-gang squad in the Rampart Division, just west of downtown.

The densely populated Rampart area is home to many Asian and Hispanic immigrants and to some of the city's most feared street gangs. When Perez started in the elite squad, Rampart had one of the highest murder rates among the city's 18 police divisions. Today, violent crime has declined there — perhaps a credit to the LAPD's aggressive anti-gang and anti-drug efforts.

The Rampart Division, however, is taking no bows for its work these days. Instead, Rampart has become the name of a stunning scandal of police misconduct ranging from manufacturing evidence and committing perjury to stealing drugs and shooting unarmed suspects. The spreading scandal threatens hundreds, perhaps thousands, of criminal convictions and deals a body blow to the LAPD's efforts to regain public confidence after a troubled decade marked by the Rodney King beating and the O. J. Simpson murder trial. (*See story, p. 80.*)

Perez was once in the middle of the corruption but is now the source of the scandal's most damning disclosures. Facing trial in September on charges of stealing 6 pounds of cocaine from a police evidence room, Perez negotiated a plea bargain by promising to tell all he knew about misconduct in the Rampart Division.

"There's a lot of crooked stuff going on in the LAPD," Perez told authorities, according to transcripts

From *The CQ Researcher,* March 17, 2000.

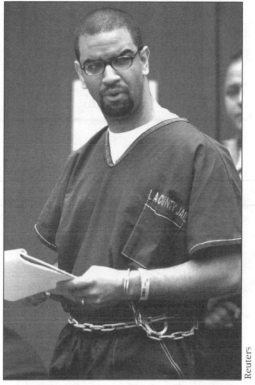

Former LAPD officer Rafael Perez revealed corruption in the Rampart Division as part of a plea bargain on cocaine charges. He was sentenced to five years in prison.

of the interviews obtained by the *Los Angeles Times.* [1]

The Rampart scandal emerged as law enforcement agencies around the country were coming under renewed scrutiny on a variety of issues. The New York City Police Department was still reeling from the brutal sodomizing of a Haitian immigrant in 1997 when four white officers last year shot and killed an unarmed West African immigrant, Amadou Diallo, in the vestibule of his Bronx apartment building. Their trial, moved to Albany because of massive local publicity about the case, ended last month with the officers' acquittal on all counts — a verdict that served only to renew the debate over police tactics and racial attitudes (*see p. 97*).

Meanwhile, civil-rights and civil-liberties organizations were mount-

ing attacks on "racial profiling," the practice of making traffic or other investigative stops on the basis of an individual's race or ethnicity. Two states, Maryland and New Jersey, have signed federal court consent decrees agreeing to end the practice after lawyers from the American Civil Liberties Union (ACLU) gathered evidence showing racial patterns in highway stops by state police. Other suits are pending. Critics also want to require police to collect racial data on traffic stops in other states to determine the extent of the practice — which law enforcement officials insist is not widespread (*see p. 93*).

The public focus on police practices comes at a time of declining crime rates and generally increasing police professionalism. A recent survey of both rank-and-file police personnel and officers suggests that the vast majority of police recognize legal constraints on their conduct, try to stay within the law and disapprove of colleagues who do not. (*See poll, p. 90.*)

Still, policing the police — either through internal management or external review — remains a difficult job. "Cops and teachers exercise the most unsupervised discretion of any government employees in living up to the public trust or not," says Edwin Delattre, dean of Boston University's School of Education and author of a book on police ethics. "If you look at a cop on the street, there's nobody immediately looking over the cop's shoulder."

"The gap between the best and worst police departments is bigger than ever," says Samuel Walker, a professor of criminal justice at the University of Nebraska in Omaha and author of a history of U.S. law enforcement. "In places like San Diego

Black Motorists on I-95 Still Targeted

The state of Maryland settled a racial-profiling suit in January 1995 by agreeing to halt the practice and to furnish racial data on traffic stops to the American Civil Liberties Union of Maryland to monitor the agreement. Despite the settlement, the data showed that a disproportionate number of motorists stopped since then along the I-95 corridor in Maryland — more than two-thirds — were people of color.

Detentions and Searches
January 1995 – June 1999

	Number of Stops	Percent
African-Americans	1,205	60.7%
Hispanics	117	5.9
Whites	641	32.3
Other	23	1.2
Total non-white	1,322	67.8
Total searches	**1,986**	

Note: Total does not add to 100 percent due to rounding.

Source: American Civil Liberties Union of Maryland

and Charlotte, there is good discipline. They care about their citizens. That's simply not true in New York and Los Angeles."

Police officials tend to simultaneously minimize the extent of abusive practices while insisting they are taking steps to prevent them. Abuse-of-force cases are "insignificant arithmetically," says James Powers, chief of the Fredericksburg, Va., police department and an adviser to an International Association of Chiefs of Police (IACP) study on the use of force. "But perception-wise, it's very significant. One misuse of force to us is catastrophic. And for a long, long time, we've been taking every step we know to restrict or prohibit the improper use of force."

"There is no excuse for stopping someone because they're black or Hispanic or because they're a black person in a white neighborhood," says Earl Sweeney, director of the New Hampshire Police Standards and Training Council and chair of the IACP's highway safety committee. But Sweeney says racial-profiling abuses "have been perpetrated by a minority of individuals, in some cases well-motivated but poorly trained. We really think the answer is in policy, training and supervision."

Many of the most volatile police controversies — such as the two recent New York City cases — are racially charged. Public mistrust of police remains high in many minority communities.

"Given the large numbers of African-Americans today in prison or under the jurisdiction of the criminal justice system, there are questions in the black community whether this has resulted from discriminatory practices on the part of the police," says Hubert Williams, president of the Police Foundation, a Washington-based research organization.

In Los Angeles, however, many of the officers implicated so far, including Perez, are Hispanics who were targeting Hispanic offenders and suspects.

"This is not a black-white or white-brown incident," says Elizabeth Schroeder, associate director of the ACLU of Southern California. "You've got minority cops who are beating up minorities."

The efforts to control police conduct from the outside began in earnest in the 1960s, when the U.S. Supreme Court, under Chief Justice Earl Warren, handed down a series of decisions aimed at protecting the rights of suspects and criminal defendants. The best known of those rulings — the so-called *Miranda* decision in 1966 — required police to advise suspects after their arrest of their right to remain silent and to have a lawyer present during any questioning.

At around the same time, efforts were being made to increase the number of minority officers on urban police forces. In addition, police critics sought to establish civilian review boards to receive and in some cases adjudicate complaints regarding police conduct.

Today, those changes are widely, but not universally, accepted. In particular, the *Miranda* rule has become an ingrained police practice — and universally known through three decades of police stories on television and film. But law enforcement groups are lining up behind an effort to relax the *Miranda* decision by breathing life into a 1968 law that sought to partly lift its enforcement in federal courts.

The Justice Department has generally refused to invoke the law — known as Section 3501 — because of doubts about its constitutionality. But the Supreme Court will consider a case next month in which a federal appeals court invoked the law to turn back a defendant's challenge to a confession that he claimed police obtained before giving him his *Miranda* warnings.

"We do not want to be in a situation where officers know that they can torture a suspect to get a confession" says Gene Voegtlin, legislative counsel for the IACP, which filed a brief urging the court to uphold Section 3501. "But we believe you need to have some flexibility so that society is not punished for small oversights by having confessions thrown out and convictions lost."

But Williams says there is no need to relax or overturn *Miranda*. "Why would we — at a time when the crime rate is spiraling down, when we're trying to focus on community policing — why open up the door for inappropriate practices by some officers that in the past have vastly colored the reputation of the whole force?" Williams asks.

As the justices prepare to hear the *Miranda* case, here are some of the questions being debated by police and their critics:

Should the Miranda rule regarding police interrogation be relaxed?

Charles Dickerson was not physically mishandled or psychologically coerced when an FBI agent and an Alexandria, Va., police detective questioned him about a 1997 bank robbery. But a federal judge found that Dickerson — contrary to the FBI agent's testimony — had not been "Mirandized" before he gave a statement linking himself to the getaway vehicle used in the holdup. On that basis, the judge blocked the government from using Dickerson's statement in his scheduled trial.

Three years later, Dickerson has yet to be tried. Instead, his case goes

Demonstrators on Fifth Avenue in New York City protest the Feb. 25 acquittal of four NYPD officers in the shooting death of Amadou Diallo, an unarmed street vendor from West Africa. He was shot in the vestibule of his apartment building while reaching for his wallet.

before the U.S. Supreme Court next month in a crucial test of the federal law aimed at partially overturning *Miranda* — Section 3501. Critics of *Miranda* hope the court will use the case to relax the application of a decision that they say has hurt law enforcement by making confessions harder to get and allowing some defendants to avoid conviction because of technical mistakes unrelated to any improper conduct by police.

"When you have technical errors or inadvertent oversights — good-faith mistakes — you end up punishing society by excluding evidence that could be used to keep dangerous people off the streets," says Voegtlin of the police chiefs' association.

Supporters of the *Miranda* decision deny that the ruling has greatly hampered law enforcement, but also insist that the mandatory warnings are essential to protect suspects' rights in police interrogation.

"It's ridiculous to think that a lay person understands their rights under the Fifth Amendment," says Lisa Kemler, co author of a brief in the case on behalf of the National Association of Criminal Defense Lawyers. "The police setting is inherently coercive. All of the things that the [Supreme Court] talked about in the *Miranda* decision are still true today."

The effects of the *Miranda* decision have been debated ever since the Supreme Court handed down its decision on June 13, 1966. In recent years, an academic critic of the decision, University of Utah law Professor Paul G. Cassell, has sought to prove the ruling's adverse effects on law enforcement in voluminous scholarly articles as well as in court briefs (*see p. 96*).

The Supreme Court case, however, does not directly concern the pros and cons of the *Miranda* ruling. Instead, the case tests Congress' power to pass a law to change a decision that the Supreme Court itself indicated might be subject to legislative revision.

Despite LAPD's Investigation of Rogue Unit . . .

Six months after the Rampart Division scandal broke in Los Angeles, Police Chief Bernard Parks laid out the department's explanation of how a supposedly elite anti-gang unit had turned into a rogue outfit. In a damning 362-page report, investigators blamed the department itself for tolerating sloppy recruiting, inadequate discipline, lax supervision and a general culture of mediocrity.

"We as an organization provided the opportunity," Parks wrote in a preface to the report, which was released on March 1. [1]

Parks, a career cop in his third year as chief of the nation's second-largest police department, hoped the report would convince a skeptical press and public that the department could be trusted to investigate the scandal and institute reforms. But the report did little to quiet criticism of the department or to derail calls for an independent investigation.

"The city and its police department need an independent commission, and we need it now," said Ramona Ripston, executive director of the American Civil Liberties Union (ACLU) of Southern California. "Relying on the police department to ferret out all of the underlying problems is like having a cancer patient operate on himself."

Police experts outside Los Angeles also voiced skepticism and distrust. "The LAPD is incapable of ensuring accountability of itself," Samuel Walker, a professor of criminal justice at the University of Nebraska at Omaha and an expert on police reform, told *The New York Times*.

"Unlike every other major city police department in the country, the Los Angeles Police Department has been able to resist self-scrutiny and reform," says Joseph McNamara, a former Kansas City and San Jose police chief and now a scholar at the Hoover Institution at Stanford University. "The Watts riot in 1965 showed clearly that the department

was insensitive and not geared to providing the kind of service that minority communities needed. They've had one bad case after another, but they continued to embrace a very confrontational style of policing."

The scandal does not lack for other investigations. The Los Angeles District Attorney's office has been reviewing police misconduct in individual cases since the scandal broke. Already, about 40 convictions have been overturned as a result. District Attorney Gil Garcetti said in December that as many as 3,000 cases will have to be reviewed because of the scandal.

In addition, two federal law enforcement agencies recently announced plans to look into the scandal. U.S. Attorney Alejandro Mayorkas said on Feb. 23 that federal prosecutors and at least a dozen FBI agents would begin investigating alleged civil rights abuses by LAPD officers. The next day, the Immigration and Naturalization Service (INS) said it would look into accusations that INS agents helped Rampart Division officers arrange for the deportation of at least 160 Latino immigrants and the prosecution of 40 others for illegal re-entry into the United States.

Prospects for a specially created commission to investigate the scandal, however, are uncertain. Mayor Richard Riordan had high praise for the department's internal report — while acknowledging that he had not read all of it. "I have never been so proud of the Police Department," Riordan told a radio interviewer the day the report was released. Parks himself answered brusquely when a reporter at the news conference asked whether an independent commission was needed. "No," Parks said. "Next question."

Following the beating of black motorist Rodney King by four white police officers a decade ago, an independent commission was created to improve police accountability

Section 3501 of the federal Criminal Code provides that any "voluntary" confession can be introduced in federal courts. The law lists the giving of warnings as two out of five factors for a court to consider in determining whether a statement was voluntary. (*See box, p. 89.*)

The defenders of Section 3501 note that the court itself said that the procedures laid out in the *Miranda* decision might not be the only way to protect suspects' rights.

"*Miranda* itself is not a constitutional

mandate," says Kent Scheidegger, legal director of the California-based Criminal Justice Legal Foundation. "The court created some rules for the implementation of constitutional rights that are not themselves constitutionally required, and those rules are subject to revision by Congress."

Critics of the law, however, insist that Congress had no power to overturn a decision defining constitutional rights. "If Congress can overrule *Miranda* by legislation, then it can overrule anything," says Yale

Kamisar, a University of Michigan law professor and longtime defender of the ruling.

"The *Miranda* opinion says that these warnings aren't the only solution as long as you come up with an alternative that is equally effective," Kamisar adds. "The proponents of the statute never mention the [court's] statement that you'd have to come up with an alternative that is equally effective."

Cassell, who will present the arguments in defense of the law before

... Critics Call for Outside Probe

and oversight. Headed by former Secretary of State Warren Christopher, it called for the establishment of an inspector general's office and the creation of a tracking system for problem officers. Both recommendations were put into effect, but only after several years' delay.

In August 1998, Parks told the Los Angeles Police Commission — the five-member civilian board that exercises nominal authority over the department — that virtually all of the Christopher Commission's recommendations had been implemented. But the new report acknowledges that the computerized system for tracking complaints against officers has fallen short of expectations in part because some personnel investigations never got into the system.

ACLU officials say the problems with implementing the Christopher Commission recommendations demonstrate the need for an independent commission this time, too. "We want to make sure that there is a procedure in place that will do periodic reports on where we stand with regard to the recommendations, so that the public doesn't forget and public officials don't forget that these things are outstanding," says Elizabeth Schroeder, ACLU associate director in Southern California.

So far, 20 Rampart Division police officers have been either fired or suspended or have resigned. The report attributed wrongdoing to "a few individuals" whose behavior "had a contagion effect" on others around them. Schroeder said she was worried that the department had not looked at "the larger problems in the department, other areas outside Rampart."

The report makes 108 recommendations for consideration by the Police Commission, mostly aimed at strengthening management and oversight within the department. (*See box, p. 217.*) The commission itself is apparently divided over how to proceed. Two members — including Chairman Gerald Chaleff, a noted criminal defense attorney — are said to want the commission itself to institute a broad inquiry, while the others are thought either to favor a more limited review or are uncertain.

Meanwhile, Rafael Perez, the officer who blew the whistle on the Rampart scandal, was sentenced last month to five years in prison as part of a plea bargain to charges of stealing 6 pounds of cocaine from the police department's evidence room. Appearing in court in a jail-issued orange jump suit, Perez tearfully apologized for what he called his "atrocities."

The ex-Marine has implicated himself and others in covering up at least three potentially unjustified police shootings, including one fatal incident. In one of the cases, Perez said he and a partner shot an unarmed gang member, Javier Francisco Ovando, and then planted a gun on him to try to justify the shooting. Ovando, whose injuries left him in a wheelchair, was convicted of assault on an officer and given a 23-year prison sentence; he was freed from prison in September.

In court, Perez said that he had allowed himself to be consumed by "the us-against-them ethos of the overzealous cop" while working with the anti-gang unit — which was known by the acronym CRASH (Community Resources Against Street Hoodlums). "We vaguely sensed that we were doing wrong things for the right reasons," Perez said. He concluded, "Whoever chases monsters should see to it that in the process he does not become a monster himself."

---

[1] Coverage drawn from *Los Angeles Times*, March 1, 2000, p. A1; March 2, 2000, p. A1, *The New York Times*, March 2, 2000, *The Washington Post*, March 2, 2000, p. A3. For extensive previous coverage, see the *Los Angeles Times*' Web site: www.latimes.com/rampart. The police department report can be found at www.lapdonline.com.

---

the Supreme Court next month, says that police will "absolutely" continue to give the warnings even if the statute is upheld. "The warnings aren't the problems," Cassell says. "The problems are the vast procedural apparatus that's been erected around the warnings."

In fact, some pro-law enforcement observers say *Miranda* has actually benefited police. "*Miranda* is probably the best thing that's ever happened to police, even though they may not know it," says Craig Bradley, a law professor at Indiana University in Bloomington and former federal prosecutor and Justice Department official.

The ruling "gives police something very easy to comply with," Bradley continues. And compliance with the warnings typically limits further inquiry into police conduct.

"In *Miranda*, the court condemned a number of techniques" such as psychological pressure and deceptive tactics, Bradley says. "After *Miranda*, no one looks into that any more. There's very little examination of police tactics short of outright brutality."

Voegtlin agrees on some of the benefits of the ruling. "The *Miranda* decision gave law enforcement some valuable guidelines," he says. "It put policies and procedures into place to protect officers as well as suspects. Once it was certified that the warnings were given, there wasn't a question of the voluntariness of the confession."

Still, the police chiefs' group is joining other law enforcement organizations in urging the court to uphold the law limiting *Miranda*'s impact. "For someone to go free because of a technical oversight is wrong," Voegtlin says, "and that's what we're trying to remedy."

Are stronger measures needed to prevent use of excessive force by police officers?

Public confidence in New York City's finest was still recovering from the brutal sodomizing of Haitian immigrant Abner Louima in 1997 when it was shaken again a year ago by the Amadou Diallo shooting. But NYPD officials say that the controversy over Diallo's death and the prosecution of four white police officers for the shooting obscures an encouraging trend: a decline in police shootings and civilians killed or wounded by police fire.

In all, New York City police shot and killed 11 civilians in 1999. That figure is sharply down from the previous year's total of 19. Moreover, the number has been declining steadily since 1990, when 41 civilians were killed. The number of wounded also fell to 31 last year from 43 in 1998, and the number of incidents dropped to 155 from 249 in the same period.

"Generally, when it comes to the use of firearms, we are the most restrained large city police department in the United States," New York City Police Commissioner Howard Safir told a *New York Times* columnist last month. [2]

Police organizations nationwide are also trying to reassure the public about improper use of force by offic-ers. A study released by the IACP in January showed that police used force fewer than 3.5 times per 10,000 calls for service, and suspects were injured in fewer than 3 percent of the instances when force was used.

"The incidence of use of force is minuscule compared to the number of citizen contacts, and the incidence of use of improper force is also minuscule in relation to that number," Fredericksburg Police Chief Powers said. [3]

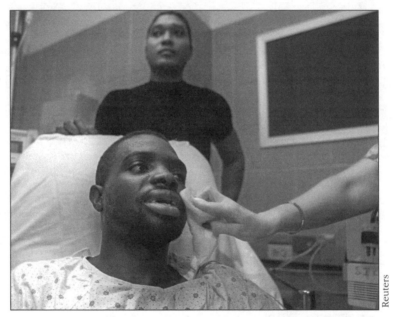

Abner Louima, a Haitian immigrant, was beaten and sodomized with a broken broomstick handle by New York City police officers after a nightclub altercation in 1997.

Outside critics and observers, however, see no cause for complacency. "Excessive force has long been and continues to be a serious problem with enormous racial overtones in New York City," says Norman Siegel, executive director of the New York Civil Liberties Union. "And it will probably continue as long as mayors and police commissioners continue to deny the painful problem of police brutality, until civilian review boards become more effective, until police departments such as New York City's become more racially representative of the people they police and until they get better training."

"Whenever police abuse their authority, it's a social problem that needs to be controlled," says Geoffrey Alpert, a professor at the University of South Carolina's College of Criminal Justice in Columbia and an adviser to police departments on use of force. "It's a very powerful tool that they're given, and to abuse it flies in the face of why we give it to them."

Civil-rights and civil-liberties organizations often emphasize external mechanisms to try to control use of excessive force by police, such as civilian review boards, civil damage suits and criminal prosecutions. The effectiveness of civilian-review mechanisms is a subject of sharp dispute between civil-rights advocates and police unions and public officials in many cities. In New York, for example, Mayor Rudolph Giuliani is strongly opposed to the city's civilian review board, although the City Council voted overwhelmingly several years ago to keep it in existence.

"A number of them are very successful and have documented records of achievements," says the University of Nebraska's Walker, author of a forthcoming book on police accountability. "A number of them are abject failures. It's a question of determining which ones work, and why."

"Civilian review can be useful if it's a cooperative venture that doesn't just have to do with problems," Delattre says. "If the only time they're engaged is over some type of crisis,

The "Rampart Corruption Incident"

The Los Angeles Police Department's Board of Inquiry Report into the "Rampart Corruption Incident" detailed 108 recommendations for improvements in the department. The complete report, with an executive summary tracing the history of the scandals, can be found on the LAPD's Web site: www.lapdonline.com.

Here are some of the board's major recommendations:

■ **Testing and screening of police officer candidates** — Obtain all publicly available information, including criminal records, on candidates; give polygraph examinations to all candidates prior to background investigations.

■ **Personnel practices** — Improve tracking of personnel investigations; "restore integrity" to evaluation system; standardize selection for specialized units; limit tour of duty in specialized units.

■ **Personnel investigations and management of risk** — Expand internal-affairs investigations to cover all but most minor complaints; expand sting operations and checks of officers' financial records; eliminate city charter provisions setting time limits for administrative investigations.

■ **Corruption investigations** — Expand anti-corruption unit within Internal Affairs section; improve consultation with city attorney and district attorney; allow anti-corruption investigations to be conducted from non-city facilities to ensure confidentiality.

■ **Operational controls** — Increase number of field sergeants to improve supervision; improve oversight of specialized units; establish uniform rules on use of informants; strengthen security of Property Division and disposition of evidence; improve review of use of force to detect patterns involving individual officers.

■ **Anti-corruption inspections and audits** — Improve audits of investigations.

■ **Ethics and integrity training** — "Greatly increase" ethics and integrity training for all employees.

■ **Job-specific training** — Improve training in particular for supervisors and watch commanders; develop comprehensive training on cultivating and managing informants.

---

or if it has inordinate power, you're not going to have anything except a higher wall of resistance and silence [from police]."

Legal actions also have mixed results on officer conduct, experts say. Alpert says civil damage suits don't radically affect police behavior. "A lot of that information stays in the legal offices and never filters back to the police department," he says.

As for criminal prosecutions of questionable police behavior — which are relatively few in number in any event — Alpert says officers on patrol often respond by becoming more reluctant to initiate investigations of suspicious circumstances.

"For a lot of these shootings that are relatively close calls, they're likely to say 'the system is just punishing us for doing our jobs' and become more careful in not going out on a limb," he says.

Police officials are more likely to emphasize improved recruitment and training as ways to prevent excessive use of force. "We now give psychological tests and do extensive interviews before hiring," says Fredericksburg Police Chief Powers. "We take every step we can to make sure that officers are not predisposed to that. And we do extensive training and talk about what is the proper use of force."

Categorical rules on use of force also may reduce civilian injuries, according to Carl Klockars, a professor of criminal justice at the University of Delaware in Newark. Departments that specifically prohibit high-speed chases or the use of warning shots, for example, appear to have few civilians killed or injured by police conduct, Klockars says.

"Excessive force has been with us forever, and it's still with us," says the Police Foundation's Williams. "It has not abated significantly at all. But you've got to understand the environment police are working in. It's a very tough job, and in many instances they're just trying to do the best they can do."

Critic Says *Miranda* Hurt Law Enforcement . . .

When he dissented from the Supreme Court's *Miranda* decision in 1966, Justice Byron White bitterly warned that the new rules on police interrogation would result "in some unknown number of cases" in which "a killer, a rapist, or other criminal" was returned to the streets to commit more crimes. After a period of initial opposition, however, police adapted to the new rules, and concern about its impact abated.

Three decades later, *Miranda* is second nature to virtually all police officers and is widely regarded — by police, prosecutors, and criminal-justice experts — as having had little, if any, adverse impact on law enforcement.

For the past five years, however, Paul G. Cassell, a law professor at the University of Utah and former federal prosecutor and Justice Department official, has waged a relentless campaign to reverse the conventional wisdom about the effects of the *Miranda* decision. In a series of eight strongly argued, densely statistical law-review articles, Cassell contends that *Miranda* has resulted in thousands of "lost confessions" over the years and caused a lasting drop in the percentage of crimes "cleared" by police.

"My statistics suggest that *Miranda* is the most devastating blow inflicted on law enforcement in the last half-century," Cassell says.

Other scholars sharply disagree. In one detailed critique, University of Chicago law Professor Stephen J. Schulhofer says *Miranda* has produced "substantial benefits" and "vanishingly small social costs." Another critic, Richard A. Leo, a criminologist at the University of California at Irvine, says *Miranda* "has not had any dramatic rate on how successfully police interrogate and obtain confessions." Cassell "is a one-man panic," Leo says. "He is a brilliant ideologue and an extraordinarily skillful legal advocate. He also manipulates and sometimes misrepresents the data."

Cassell, a former law clerk to Chief Justice Warren E. Burger and to Justice Antonin Scalia when he was on the federal appeals court in Washington, will take his thesis to the Supreme Court itself in a pivotal case involving the *Miranda* ruling next month. He will be asking the high court to uphold a 1968 law — so-called Section 3501 of the federal Criminal Code — that purported to override the use of *Miranda* in federal courts. The high court appointed Cassell to argue the case after the Justice Department decided not to defend the constitutionality of the law.

As one of his major points, Cassell will argue that the court has to defer to Congress' judgment at that time about the effects of the *Miranda* ruling. "Congress' judgment was that *Miranda* did indeed have a harmful effect on law enforcement," Cassell says. "That's the posture that this case will go before the court in, and the court is in no position to second-guess that judgment."

Cassell came to the *Miranda* issue while serving as an associate deputy attorney general in the Justice Department in the late 1980s. One of his assignments was to look for test cases to use Section 3501. After three years as a federal prosecutor in Alexandria, Va., outside Washington, he joined the Utah law faculty and threw himself into a variety of pro-law enforcement issues, including a proposed constitutional amendment on victims' rights.

In his first article on the effects of *Miranda*, Cassell acknowledged that court decisions suppressing confessions or overturning convictions because of *Miranda* violations are "quite rare." But he contended that the true measure of *Miranda*'s effects was the number of confessions "lost" to police because suspects invoked their right to remain silent. Reanalyzing data from a dozen studies done shortly after *Miranda*, Cassell estimated that confessions were

Should the use of "racial profiling" be prohibited?

Christopher Darden and Johnnie Cochran squared off against each other in a Los Angeles courtroom as prosecutor and defense lawyer in the O. J. Simpson murder case. But the two African-American attorneys had something in common before the trial. Both had been victims of what they regarded as racially motivated traffic stops by police while working for the Los Angeles district attorney's office. [4]

Darden and Cochran are just two of the many African-Americans from all walks of life who have stepped forward during recent years to complain about being stopped for the not-so-fictitious offense of DWB — "driving while black." Minority groups representing blacks as well as Hispanics complain that police use racial or ethnic stereotypes in traffic enforcement or other investigative stops.

"This is not a new thing, by any means," says David Harris, a law professor at the University of Toledo who has studied the issue for the ACLU. "What is new is that we have begun over the last few years to see the collection of some of the data to substantiate what blacks and other minorities have been saying for a long time."

Some police officials acknowledge the practice while also expressing strong disapproval. "Whether racial profiling is existent in the United States — I'm sure that it probably is," says Jack Grant, manager of the Division of State and Provincial Police at the police chiefs' association. "We discourage it. Responsible police administrators do everything they

... But Most Experts Disagree, Support Ruling

lost in 16 percent of criminal cases.

Cassell further calculated that confessions were "necessary" to obtain a conviction in 24 percent of criminal cases. On that basis, he calculated that *Miranda* costs law enforcement convictions in about 3.8 percent of cases. Using 1993 figures, Cassell concluded that 28,000 arrests for violent crimes and 79,000 arrests for property offenses that year "slipped through the criminal-justice system due to *Miranda*."[1]

In a response published in the same issue, Schulhofer described Cassell's conclusions as far short of the catastrophic effect that *Miranda*'s critics had predicted. But he proceeded to challenge Cassell's reading of the previous studies and a number of the assumptions he used in making his calculations. On that basis, Schulhofer estimated that *Miranda* caused at most a 4 percent decline in the confession rate and lost convictions in fewer than 1 percent of all arrests.[2]

In a subsequent article, Cassell also blamed *Miranda* for a drop in the crime-clearance rate from about 60 percent before the ruling to about 45 percent after — a level that continues today. Schulhofer responded by contending that the apparent drop was more likely due to the overall increase in crime and the overtaxing of police resources.[3] Others, including Professor Yale Kamisar of the University of Michigan Law School, also have contended that pre-*Miranda* clearance rates were probably inflated and that current figures represent a more accurate picture of police success in identifying and arresting suspects.

Leo weighed in on the academic debate by conducting firsthand observation of more than 180 police interrogations in three unidentified cities.[4] He concluded that police had avoided any dramatic impact from *Miranda* by adapting to the ruling — though sometimes with strategies that "straddle the ambiguous margins of legality." At the same time, Leo credits *Miranda* with improving police professionalism and civility. "Most police like *Miranda*," Leo says. "They've embraced it as a symbol of professionalism."

For his part, Cassell expects most law enforcement officers will continue to give *Miranda* warnings even if the federal statute easing the requirement is upheld. As for the academic debate, "I'm the first to concede that there's conflicting evidence," he says. But he insists that he has punctured a myth that the ruling has had no impact and that law enforcement groups all support the ruling.

"All the leading law enforcement organizations in the country are filing [briefs] in support of [Section 3501]," Cassell says. "All of those groups are coming in and explaining that they're concerned about the harmful effects of *Miranda*."

---

[1] Paul G. Cassell, "Miranda's Social Costs: An Empirical Reassessment," *Northwestern University Law Review*, Vol. 90, No. 2 (winter 1996), pp. 387-499. Cassell has posted his law review articles on a Web site: www.law.utah.c/faculty/bios/cassell.

[2] Stephen J. Schulhofer, "Miranda's Practical Effect: Substantial Benefits and Vanishingly Small Social Costs," *ibid.*, pp. 500-563. Some of Schulhofer's points can be found in the American Civil Liberties Union's brief in the *Dickerson* case: www.aclu.org.

[3] Paul G. Cassell, "All Benefits, No Costs: The Grand Illusion of Miranda's Defenders," *Northwestern University Law Review*, Vol. 90, No. 3 (spring 1996), pp. 1084-1124; Stephen J. Schulhofer, "Miranda and Clearance Rates," *Northwestern University Law Review*, Vol. 91, No. 1 (fall 1996), pp. 278-294. For a rebuttal, see Paul G. Cassell and Richard Fowles, "Handcuffing the Cops? A Thirty-Year Perspective on Miranda's Harmful Effects on Law Enforcement," *Stanford Law Review*, Vol. 50, No. 4 (April 1998), pp. 1055-1145.

[4] Richard A. Leo, "The Impact of Miranda Revisited," *Journal of Criminal Law and Criminology*, Vol. 86, No. 3 (Spring 1996), pp. 621-692.

---

can to prevent it. It cannot be tolerated as a practice in police work."

Many police officials and law enforcement supporters, however, also insist that race can sometimes be a legitimate factor for officers to consider in police investigations. "Racial profiling is wrong," says Cornelius Behan, retired police chief in Baltimore County, Md., "but it gets confused with sensible police procedures. It's wise to try to develop a profile of who the offenders are, and sometimes a legitimate profile would have race in it."

"The distinction is between profiling and discriminatory profiling," Delattre says. "Anybody who says you can enforce the law and protect public safety without profiling is trying to sell you a pipe dream. What you need are clear statements of policy about how to justify responsible profiling from profiling that's based on bigotry and that has the effect that bigotry has."

Racial and ethnic minorities have long been accustomed to being regarded with suspicion when they frequent "white" neighborhoods, whether on foot or in vehicles. The "driving while black" issue has become more visible in recent years because of stepped-up traffic enforcement aimed in large part at detecting drug offenses. "These pretext stops are about drugs," Harris says. "That's what the federal government has trained local law enforcement to use them for."

Harris and other critics of racial profiling say police who target blacks or other minorities in drug-interdiction efforts are operating on a false assumption that use of drugs is highest among African-Americans. "Police are focused on the drug market in the inner city, and that's in African-American communities and other minority communities," the Police Foundation's Williams explains. "They look at the people they're arresting, and that's where they get their profile. So it always winds up with a heavy representation of African-Americans and Hispanics."

Critics also question the value of using traffic stops for drug enforcement, noting that the vast majority of people stopped in drug-related patrolling end up not being charged with any drug offenses. John Crew, director of the ACLU of Northern California's Police Practices Project, says data gathered for a class-action suit against the California Highway Patrol indicate that the CHP stopped about 33,000 motorists in 1997 in drug-related investigations but had a "hit rate" of less than 2 percent. "If you use a tactic that fails 98 percent of the time," Crew says, "normally that's not something that you would view as successful."

But Sweeney, who oversees training for all of New Hampshire's state and local police, defends the use of traffic enforcement for other anticrime purposes. "Aggressive enforcement of the traffic laws keeps crime down," Sweeney says. "You have a tendency to detect people who are violating the laws."

"People who have been arrested tell you that they stay away from communities and areas where there is intensive enforcement of traffic laws," Sweeney continues. "If they're carrying drugs, carrying burglary tools, they're likely to be stopped while driving along that stretch of the highway."

While condemning racial profiling, police officials generally contend the problem is relatively isolated. Critics insist the practice is more widespread. To try to substantiate

their beliefs, the ACLU and other critics favor legislation — passed in two states and pending in Congress and at least 18 other states — to require state and local law enforcement agencies to gather data on the race of persons stopped for traffic violations. Police groups generally oppose such proposals as unnecessary and expensive.

But Crew also notes that many police leaders have become more attuned to the problem, in part because of the effect that the perception of racial profiling has on public confidence in law enforcement.

"It's interesting to hear law enforcement groups talk about this not just as a civil-rights issue, not just a justice issue, but as an effective-policing issue," Crew says. "If they're going to be effective, they can't afford to have a large segment of the American population, people of color, disaffected from police." ■

BACKGROUND

A Checkered Past

T he creation of the first full-time police departments in the United States in Philadelphia and Boston in the 1830s came not long after Sir Robert Peel established what is regarded as the first modern force, the London Metropolitan Police, in 1829. The London police quickly gained a reputation for professionalism, but urban police departments in the United States were beset by continuing scandals through the 19th century. Police departments were guilty of "pervasive brutality and corruption," according to historian Walker, and "did little to prevent crime or provide public services." [5]

A police-reform movement developed in the early 20th century. The reformers sought to rid police departments of political influence and cronyism and turn them into efficient, nonpartisan agencies committed to public service. They wanted police departments to be run by trained experts with job tenure to insulate them from political interference. They also wanted to improve the recruitment and training of officers and to centralize a command structure for better accountability. Some progress was made on all of those goals. Still, a federal crime commission — the famous Wickersham Commission — reported in 1931 that physical brutality was "extensively practiced" by police departments around the country. [6]

The Supreme Court first stepped in to police the interrogation process in 1936 in a flagrant case in which three black tenant farmers "confessed" to the murder of a white farmer after being brutally tortured by local sheriff's deputies in Mississippi. An involuntary confession was unreliable, the court reasoned, and its use in court would violate the 14th Amendment's prohibition against depriving anyone of life or liberty without due process of law. In a second confession case six years later, the court shifted its focus by declaring that the Due Process Clause prohibited the use of any evidence — whether true or false — that police obtained through techniques that "shocked the conscience" of the community or violated fundamental standards of fairness. [7]

The high court ruled on more than 30 confession cases between 1936 and 1964, deciding whether a confession was voluntary by looking at the totality of the circumstances in each case. [8] In some cases, the court established that certain interrogation methods — including physical force, threats of harm or punishment, lengthy or incommunicado question-

Chronology

Before 1900
Corruption and brutality are pervasive in U.S. police forces.

——— • ———

1900-1960 *Police reform movements advance; Supreme Court begins to review confession cases.*

1936
First Supreme Court decision to bar confession as involuntary.

——— • ———

1960s *Warren Court seeks to control police conduct.*

1961
Supreme Court rules illegally seized evidence cannot be used in state court trials.

1966
Supreme Court in *Miranda v. Arizona* requires police to advise suspects of rights.

1968
Kerner Commission warns of deep mistrust of police by African-Americans; Congress passes law aimed at overturning *Miranda* in federal courts.

1970s *Burger Court restricts Miranda, but does not overturn it.*

1971
Confession obtained in violation of *Miranda* can be used to impeach defendant's testimony at trial, Supreme Court rules.

1980s *Conservative era in law enforcement.*

1986
Justice Department unit proposes effort to overturn *Miranda*, but plan is not pursued.

——— • ———

1990s *Police brutality and racial profiling emerge as major issues.*

1991
Black motorist Rodney King is kicked and beaten by white Los Angeles police officers; they are acquitted in state trial in 1992, but two are convicted a year later of civil-rights violations.

1993
Black lawyer Robert Wilkins files anti-racial profiling suit after being stopped by Maryland state troopers; state settles suit in 1995 by agreeing to end racial profiling and provide racial data on traffic stops to ACLU.

1996
Supreme Court upholds pretextual traffic stops for drug enforcement.

1997
Black immigrant Abner Louima is sodomized by white New York police officers; Justin Volpe pleads guilty in 1999 and draws 30-year prison term.

February 1999
Black immigrant Amadou Diallo is fatally shot by four white NYPD officers; murder trial moved to Albany because of publicity in New York City.

April 1999
New Jersey attorney general issues report acknowledging racial profiling by state police; state settles Justice Department suit in December by agreeing to end practice.

September 1999
Rafael Perez implicates himself and other LAPD anti-gang officers in city's Rampart Division in widespread abuse, including planting evidence and shooting suspects.

December 1999
Supreme Court agrees to review appeals court ruling upholding 1968 law aimed at overturning *Miranda* in federal courts.

——— • ———

2000s *Racial profiling, police brutality continue as high-profile issues.*

January 2000
Democratic presidential candidates Al Gore and Bill Bradley oppose racial profiling; GOP front-runner George W. Bush is ambiguous.

Feb. 25, 2000
NYPD officers are acquitted in Diallo shooting; former LAPD officer Perez gets five years in prison for stealing cocaine from police evidence room.

March 1, 2000
LAPD report blames Rampart scandal on lax supervision and "culture of mediocrity."

April 19, 2000
Supreme Court set to hear arguments on anti-*Miranda* law.

Controversial *Miranda* Ruling Still Stands

The U.S. Supreme Court's 1966 *Miranda* decision requiring police to advise suspects of their constitutional rights against self-incrimination before interrogation has been narrowed over the years by subsequent high court decisions, but not overturned.

CASE	VOTE	RULING
Miranda v. Arizona (1966)	5-4	Police must advise suspect before interrogation of right to remain silent, right to a lawyer, right to have lawyer appointed, and give warning that any statement can be used against him; police cannot use any statement obtained without such warnings.
Orozco v. Texas (1969)	6-2	Police must give *Miranda* warnings whenever a suspect is effectively in custody — in this case, in his home.
Harris v. New York (1971)	6-3	Statement obtained in violation of *Miranda* can be used to cross-examine defendant or impeach testimony at trial.
Michigan v. Tucker (1974)	8-1	Police can use statement in violation of *Miranda* as a lead for obtaining other evidence; Rehnquist opinion emphasizes *Miranda* not constitutionally required.
Michigan v. Mosley (1975)	7-2	Police did not violate *Miranda* by questioning suspect who invoked his right to silence about a second offense after they gave a second warning.
United States v. Mandujano (1976)	8-0	No *Miranda* warning needed for grand jury witness.
Brewer v. Williams (1977)	5-4	Police officer's speech pleading for "Christian burial" of child murder victim was "tantamount to interrogation" and violated suspect's *Miranda* rights.
Fare v. Michael C. (1979)	5-4	Probation officer need not give *Miranda* warnings before questioning juvenile suspect.
Rhode Island v. Innis (1980)	6-3	Police appeal to suspect's conscience did not amount to interrogation in violation of *Miranda*.
Edwards v. Arizona (1981)	9-0	Police must stop interrogation after suspect asks for lawyer.
Minnesota v. Murphy (1984)	5-4	No *Miranda* warning needed before interview with probation officer.
New York v. Quarles (1984)	5-4	Police did not violate *Miranda* by asking suspect, "Where's the gun?" before giving warnings; suspect's answer could be used as evidence at trial ("public safety exception").
Withrow v. Williams (1993)	5-4	*Miranda* violation can be basis for challenging state court conviction in federal habeas corpus proceeding.

ing, solitary confinement, denial of food or sleep and promises of leniency — were presumptively coercive and therefore constitutionally impermissible. But the court did not attempt to set out a specific checklist of procedures for police to assure that a suspect's statement would be deemed voluntary and therefore admissible in court.

Police professionalism "continued to make steady advances" during this period, according to historian Walker.[9] A "new generation" of police chiefs provided better leadership, while officers became more productive because of technological advances, such as patrol cars with sophisticated communications systems.

At the same time, racial flareups foreshadowed the crisis in police-community relations that fully developed in the 1960s. Racial disturbances in Detroit and New York City's Harlem in 1943 produced accusations of discriminatory enforcement against the cities' African-American populations, while the "Zoot Suit" riots in Los Angeles exposed tensions between blacks, Hispanics and the city's overwhelmingly white police force.

Some police chiefs and national organizations responded with programs to improve race relations. But, as Walker notes, recruitment of black police officers lagged, and the "pioneering efforts" in improving police-community relations did not keep pace with the rapidly changing context of race relations in the decades after World War II.

By the mid-1960s, the Supreme Court had a liberal majority that was determined to continue the civil-rights revolution it had launched with the landmark school-desegregation rulings of the 1950s. The court also was determined to bring about a due-process revolution in the administration of criminal justice across the country. In 1961 the court ruled that illegally obtained evidence could not be used in state trials; two years later it ruled that the states had to provide lawyers for indigent criminal defendants in felony trials if they could not afford to pay for one themselves.[10]

Then in 1964 the court held in *Escobedo v. Illinois* that a suspect has a right under the Sixth Amendment to consult with his lawyer during police interrogation once an investigation had moved from a general inquiry to focus specifically on him. The implications of the decision were unclear; one reading suggested that it applied only to suspects like Escobedo who already had an attorney.

But two years later the court made clear it had a broader interest in police interrogations by scheduling arguments in four consolidated cases in which defendants challenged their convictions by claiming that police had obtained confessions from them in violation of their constitutional rights.

Miranda's Rights

E rnest Miranda confessed to the kidnap-rape of a Phoenix, Ariz., teenager in 1963 after an interrogation session with no overt indications of coercion. Police found Miranda, a 23-year-old laborer, after tracking the license plate of a truck driven by the

What Cops Say About Police Abuse

Most police officers recognize legal constraints on police and say they reject the so-called code of silence on abuses by colleagues, according to a federally financed survey. The survey found, however, that many officers disagree with strict limits on police behavior. Nearly one-fourth, for example, said it was sometimes justifiable to use more force than legally permitted. "Most officers have the kind of values about police abuse that we want, but there's still a substantial group out there that's saying things that are disturbing," says study director David Weisburd, director of the Institute of Criminology at the Hebrew University Law School in Jerusalem.

Some questions and answers from the survey

- It is sometimes acceptable to use more force than is legally allowable to control someone who physically assaults an officer.

     24.5% agree   75.5% disagree

- Do you think ethics in law enforcement training is effective in preventing abuse of authority?

     82.2% yes   17.8% no

- Do you think human-diversity or cultural-awareness training is effective in preventing abuse of authority?

     74.9% yes   25.1% no

- The code of silence is an essential part of the mutual trust necessary to good policing.

     16.9% agree   83.1% disagree

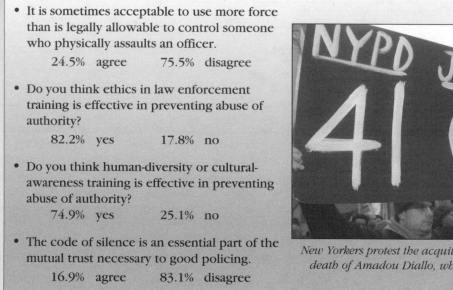

New Yorkers protest the acquittal of four NYPD officers in the death of Amadou Diallo, who died in a hail of 41 bullets.

AP Photo/Tina Fineberg

Source: Police Foundation. The survey consisted of anonymous telephone interviews with 925 officers and rank-and-file street cops conducted in late 1997 and early 1998. The Justice Department's Office of Community Policing Services financed the survey.

assailant. Detectives went to his home, asked him to accompany them to the police station and there began questioning him about the crime. A line-up was inconclusive, but police told Miranda he had been identified. At that point, he admitted that he had raped the girl. [11]

The Supreme Court heard arguments in Miranda's effort to reverse his state court conviction and in three other confession cases on March 2 and 3, 1966. When he announced the decision in the cases on June 13, Chief Justice Warren acknowledged that Miranda's statement might not be deemed involuntary "in traditional terms." But Warren, a former district attorney in California, said that "incommunicado interrogation" and such recognized police techniques of undermining a suspect's will through flattery, isolation or trickery were inherently compulsive and violated the Fifth Amendment's "cherished" principle against self-incrimination.

To protect that right, Warren continued, police must advise a suspect of the right to remain silent, the right to an attorney and the right to have an attorney appointed if he cannot afford one, and must warn that any statement given after waiving those rights could be used in court against him. Warren acknowledged that the Constitution might not require this particular set of safeguards. But unless equally effective safeguards were established, police had to give those warnings for a suspect's statement to be admissible later in court.

The 5-4 decision stopped short of the most restrictive position urged in arguments: an absolute requirement to have an attorney present during any police interrogation. The dissenting justices nonetheless forcefully criticized the ruling. They argued for retaining what Justice Byron White called the "more pliable" method of testing confessions on the totality of the circumstances. And each of the four dissenters warned of a likely adverse effect on law enforcement. "We do know that some crimes cannot be solved without confessions," Justice John Marshall Harlan wrote, "and that the Court is taking a real risk with society's welfare in imposing its new regime on the country."

Those warnings were quickly picked up and amplified by police, prosecutors and politicians. The court, critics said, had "handcuffed" the police. Congress responded in 1968 with a provision in the Omnibus Crime Control and Safe Streets Act seeking to overturn *Miranda* in federal courts and return to a voluntariness test. The main sponsor, Sen. John McClellan, D-Ark., had proposed a constitutional amendment shortly after the decision was announced, but turned to the easier legislative route instead.

Also in 1968, Republican presidential nominee Richard M. Nixon made the Supreme Court's criminal-procedure decisions a major focus of his

campaign and promised to appoint law-and-order justices to the court if elected. The next year, as president, Nixon chose Warren E. Burger, a conservative judge from the federal appeals court in Washington, D.C., to succeed Warren as chief justice.

During Burger's 17 years as chief justice, both supporters and critics of *Miranda* found cause for disappointment. Initially, the court somewhat expanded the ruling — for example, to cover custodial interrogation outside a police station. In 1971, however, Burger and the four *Miranda* dissenters joined in a 6-3 decision carving out a major exception that allowed prosecutors to use a statement obtained in violation of the decision to cross-examine a defendant at trial. Other exceptions and restrictions followed.

Still, the Burger Court stopped short of overturning *Miranda*. And police attitudes toward *Miranda* changed from hostility to acceptance. By the late 1980s, an American Bar Association survey found that "a very strong major-

Looting suspects are arrested during the riots in Los Angeles in May 1992 following the acquittal of four LAPD officers in the videotaped beating of motorist Rodney King.

ity" of police, prosecutors and judges believed *Miranda* "does not present serious problems for law enforcement." [12]

Critics of the Warren Court's criminal-procedure rulings saw a better chance for undoing some of the decisions after President Ronald Reagan chose William H. Rehnquist to succeed Burger as chief justice in 1986. Within the Justice Department, the Office of Legal Policy proposed a direct challenge to *Miranda*, but Solicitor General Charles Fried largely rebuffed the idea.

"Most experienced federal prosecutors in and out of my office were opposed to the project, as was I," Fried wrote in his memoir. [13] Cassell points to cases in which federal prosecutors did try to use Section 3501, and their efforts were supported by the department on appeal.

Still, Justice Antonin Scalia, writing in a 1994 case, complained about the government's "repeated refusal" to invoke the provision in confession cases. [14] And a year earlier, the Rehnquist Court signaled a sort of acceptance of by reaffirming — on a 5-4 vote with Rehnquist in dissent — that federal courts can set aside state court convictions if police violated a suspect's *Miranda* rights during questioning. [15]

Use of Force

Police came under intense, renewed criticism in the 1990s despite the easing of the controversy

Race Colors Attitudes About Police Conduct

Most Americans — including a majority of blacks and a substantial majority of whites — have a favorable opinion of their local police. Aftican-Americans are nearly four times as likely as whites to feel they are treated unfairly by local police, according to a recent Gallup Poll. Among blacks, younger men were nearly twice as likely as younger women to feel unfairly treated. Here are some questi ons from the poll:

1. Do you have a favorable or unfavorable opinion of your local police?

	Favorable	Unfavorable	Don't know
Blacks	58%	36%	6%
Whites	85%	13%	2%

2. Do you feel you're treated fairly by the local police in your area?

	Fairly	Not Fairly	Not Applicable/ Did not answer
Blacks	66%	27%	7%
Whites	91%	7%	2%

3. Do you feel you're treated fairly by the local police in your area?

Black men Ages:	Treated Fairly	Not Treated Fairly
18-34	43%	53%
35-49	71%	23%
50+	68%	22%

Black women Ages:	Treated Fairly	Not Treated Fairly
18-34	67%	26%
35-49	75%	19%
50+	71%	18%

Source: The Gallup Organization. The survey is based on 2,006 phone interviews with a random sample of adults in the continental U.S. from Sept. 24, 1999, to Nov. 16, 1999.

over interrogation practices. The issue was police use of force — a problem that flared up most dramatically in the beating of black motorist King in Los Angeles in 1991 and the sodomizng of Haitian immigrant Louima in New York City in 1997. [16] The incidents provoked new accusations of racism against both police departments from minority and civil rights groups and new concerns among police executives and governments officials about how to con-

trol use of excessive force by police.

Police shootings of black civilians had touched off several of the racial disturbances that had erupted in the nation's big cities three decades earlier. The 1968 report by a presidential panel appointed to study the cause of the riots — the so-called Kerner Commission — found "deep hostility between police and ghetto communities" to have been a "primary cause" of the disorders.

Historian Walker also blames the

lack of controls on the use of force by police. "Even the best departments had no meaningful rules on deadly force," Walker writes, "offering their officers many hours of training on how to shoot but not on when to use their weapons." [17]

Much progress was made over the next 25 years, according to Walker. Civilian review boards — favored by groups seeking to hold police accountable — gradually achieved a measure of acceptance after having been stoutly resisted by police unions, local politicians and some segments of the public. By the 1990s, Walker reports, more than three-fourths of the police departments in the nation's biggest cities had some form of external or civilian review of complaints.

In addition, local police departments began adopting rules to guide officers in the use of force. The rules appeared to bring results. New York City Police Commissioner Patrick Murphy instituted a rule in 1972 allowing officers to shoot only in "the defense of life" and requiring reports and reviews of any weapons discharge. Officer-involved shootings declined 30 percent over the next three years, according to research by James Fyfe, a professor of criminal justice at Temple University in Philadelphia and an expert on use-of-force issues. [18]

The beating of King by four white Los Angeles police officers after a high-speed car chase on March 3, 1991, put the issue of police brutality back on the national agenda. An 81-second videotape shot by a resident of a nearby apartment — broadcast countless times around the world over the next two years — showed the officers repeatedly kicking King and hitting him 56 times with their batons as he lay on the ground.

The episode produced a national outcry, but criminal prosecutions of the officers ended with mixed results. A predominantly white jury in a neighboring county acquitted the officers of state charges in April 1992; two officers were convicted of violating King's civil rights in a federal court trial in April 1993, but they were given relatively light sentences of 30 months each.

Meanwhile, though, a special commission appointed by Los Angeles Mayor Tom Bradley concluded that the incident was merely one example of what it described as "a tolerance within the LAPD of attitudes condoning violence against the public." [19]

Six years after the King beating, police brutality again became a national issue with an episode in New York that had none of the ambiguity or arguable justifications of the Los Angeles incident. New York police officers arrested Louima on Aug. 9, 1997, following an altercation outside a Brooklyn nightclub. Officer Justin Volpe later acknowledged that he struck Louima while taking him to the patrol car. Once at the station house, Volpe took Louima into a restroom and plunged a broken broomstick handle into the Haitian's rectum. Volpe pleaded guilty to six federal charges in May 1999 and was

later sentenced to 30 years in prison; a second officer, Charles Schwarz, was convicted of beating Louima and holding him down during the sodomizing.*

The incident produced universal revulsion, even among sympathetic police observers. "This was clearly a case of sadism and racism," says Boston University's Delattre. Nonetheless, New York Mayor Giuliani, a strong

Los Angeles motorist Rodney King was severely beaten by LAPD officers in 1991 after a high-speed chase. The shocking incident was captured on videotape and shown around the world.

Reuters/Lee Celano

police supporter, saw a positive sign in the willingness of Volpe's fellow

---

* Schwarz was fired from the force; he and two other current officers — Thomas Bruder and Thomas Wiese — were convicted in federal court in Brooklyn on March 6, 2000, of conspiracy to obstruct justice for attempting to cover up the incident; attorneys for the three defendants said they would appeal. Schwarz faces up to a life sentence in the first case; the three face up to five years in the second case.

officers to aid investigators in uncovering the incident and to testify against him. The trial, Giuliani said, "destroys the myth of the blue wall of silence" among police officers.

For his part, though, Walker says the King and Louima cases represented a setback for public perceptions of police accountability.

"All of the positive developments have been obscured by these horrific examples in New York and Los Angeles, which make it appear to the average citizen that nothing has changed, and maybe things have gotten worse," Walker says.

"Driving While Black"

Racial profiling became the new flashpoint of police-community relations during the 1990s. African-Americans from many walks of life testified to their experiences of having been stopped and questioned by police seemingly for no reason other than their race.

By the end of the decade, the leading law enforcement groups were joining civil-rights and civil-liberties groups in saying that race alone should never be the basis for a traffic stop or other police investigation. But police were also continuing to defend the use of race as one factor in criminal profiling, particularly in anti-drug enforcement.

Police explained their use of race in deciding what drivers or pedestrians to stop for investigation by pointing to the statistics showing that African-Americans are more likely than whites to be arrested or convicted of many of the most common crimes, especially drug offenses and so-called street crimes. Courts up to and including the U.S. Supreme Court sanctioned the practice.

In one representative case, the Ari-

Community Policing Widely Accepted . . .

In Boston, police enlisted the help of black ministers to warn drug dealers and young gang members that they risked tough federal prosecutions unless gun violence was curbed.

In San Diego, police gave 1,200 citizen volunteers training and police-like uniforms as part of a neighborhood-based crime-prevention effort.

In Chicago, police work with social-service agencies and organizations to try to improve community life and reduce crime.

The crime-fighting strategies adopted by the three cities reflect different aspects of "community policing," an approach that has advanced over the past decade from experimental innovation to nearly universal acceptance. The philosophy calls for tying police work more closely to citizen concerns, decentralizing police decision-making, and adopting a proactive approach to crime prevention in place of a reactive approach tied to solving crimes after they have occurred. [1]

Proponents say the no-longer-new approach has improved police-community relations and contributed to reducing crimes in cities from coast to coast. "Community policing is what most people would argue is playing a big role in the reductions of crime," says Hubert Williams, a former Newark, N.J., police chief and now president of the Police Foundation. "Large numbers of police officers working in concert with the

public can make a difference."

Critics and skeptics, however, say the results are either disappointing or unproven. "Many people in the field say that it has not really taken root," says Samuel Walker, a professor of criminal justice at the University of Nebraska in Omaha. "It's not clear that this has really changed the fundamental ways that police departments operate."

Some traditionalists also view community policing as soft on serious crime. Some go so far as to dismiss it as more like social work than policing. Proponents scoff at the criticism." It's not soft on crime," says Williams. "It's the key thing to crime control."

"The police are small in numbers, and they cover large areas," Williams continues. "Usually when a crime is occurring, they are not there. It's the public that sees it. They have the information. And that information base is absolutely vital to police solving crimes."

Community policing stems in part from a reaction against an overly technological approach to policing almost universally adopted in the last half-century. "We kind of enclosed ourselves in these metal vehicles and separated ourselves through technology and other means from the people we were serving," Williams says.

Williams, an African-American, says the philosophy also reflects the need for police to gain the confidence of racial and ethnic minority groups. "The problem we have

In Washington, D.C., community policing includes a visit to Young's Supermarket.

CQ Photo/R. Michael Jenkins

zona Supreme Court in 1975 upheld a police officer's decision to question a Mexican male because he was sitting in a parked car in a predominantly white neighborhood. The use of race, the court said, was "a practical aspect of good law enforcement." [20]

Two decades later, the Supreme Court in 1996 gave police a blank check to use traffic violations as a pretext for stopping motorists for suspected drug violations. The ruling in *Whren v. United States* turned aside the plea by two black defendants

that they had been stopped because of their race.

By the 1990s, though, racial profiling was being challenged not only by convicted defendants but also by the innocent victims of the practice — people who were stopped, questioned, perhaps searched and then allowed to go on their way when police found no evidence of crime. The first major victory for critics of the practice came in a case brought by Robert Wilkins, a public defender in Washington, D.C., who was

stopped by Maryland state police in May 1992 while driving with his family back to Washington. When Wilkins refused to consent to a search of his car, troopers called for a trained narcotics dog to try to detect drugs, but no drugs were found.

Wilkins, represented by the ACLU of Maryland and two private Washington lawyers, filed a federal civil rights damage suit in May 1993 contending that the use of a racial profile violated his constitutional rights. The state agreed to settle the suit in Janu-

... But Critics Question the Benefits

is that we are not fully prepared to engage these multicultural communities," he says. "We don't know how to overcome the racial and cultural barriers that exist there."

Walker says the philosophy is akin to an approach called "team policing" that gained popularity in the 1970s but then disappeared in the more conservative '80s. By the early '90s, however, community policing was being widely discussed in law enforcement circles and drawing support from academic circles.

In 1992, Democratic presidential candidate Bill Clinton endorsed the idea. Once in office, his administration has supported community policing with money and other institutional support.

Community policing got another boost — but with a different emphasis — from two conservative-leaning researchers who called for police to give greater emphasis to seemingly minor crimes such as vandalism or public urination and less attention to so-called "index" crimes such as robbery, burglary and the like. In their book *Fixing Broken Windows*, George Kelling and Catherine Coles argued that police could simultaneously improve community life and reduce crime by focusing on these "public order" offenses.

"Crime is prevented by order maintenance," says Kelling, now a professor at Rutgers University's School of Criminal Justice in Newark. [2]

New York City Mayor Rudolph Giuliani and two of his police commissioners — William Bratton and the current commissioner, Howard Safir — put Kelling's philosophy into practice by, for example, cleaning up graffiti in the city's subways. Giuliani and police officials attribute the city's sharp reduction in crime in part to the public-order maintenance approach.

Critics, however, say New York's predominantly white police force has also been guilty of overly aggressive enforcement, especially in minority neighborhoods. They also say that the declining crime rate in the city mirrors trends nationwide that may be due in large part to economic factors, such as the decline in unemployment.

Kelling acknowledges the criticism of New York police in the torture of Haitian immigrant Abner Louima in 1997 and the killing of West African immigrant Amadou Diallo last year. But he calls the Louima case an isolated incident and the Diallo killing a "terrible tragedy" that reflected the risks of police enforcement in high-crime neighborhoods. "The rap that the police of New York City are out there ravaging the African-American community is just a sound bite," Kelling says.

The criticism of New York police, Kelling says, reflects a politicization that obscures a broad consensus in favor of making police departments more accountable on a neighborhood level. "The middle left and the middle right should be rejoicing together," he says.

For his part, Williams says that police themselves have come to view community policing more favorably.

"When I became a police officer 30 years ago, the police didn't want community involvement," Williams says. "We saw that as interference. Now we see the community as a valuable partner in crime control. One of the big changes is this idea that working with the community is positive."

[1] For background, see Richard L. Worsnop, "Community Policing," *The CQ Researcher*, Feb. 5, 1993, pp. 97-120; Samuel Walker, *Popular Justice: A History of American Criminal Justice* (2d ed., 1998), pp. 238-239.

[2] George L. Kelling and Catherine M. Coles, *Fixing Broken Windows: Restoring Order and Reducing Crime in Our Communities* (1996). Coles is a research associate at the Rutgers University School of Criminal Justice, and is Kelling's wife.

---

ary 1995. The state said it would adopt an official policy prohibiting racial profiling and, significantly, maintain detailed records of motorist stops to be provided to the ACLU to monitor any patterns of discrimination. Wilkins and his family were also awarded $50,000 plus attorney fees.

Critics of racial profiling won another settlement late last year after New Jersey officials acknowledged that some state troopers had singled out black and Hispanic motorists for anti-drug enforcement. The long-sim-

mering issue recently erupted in the state when the head of the state police, Carl Williams, was quoted as saying it was "most likely a minority group" that was involved with marijuana or cocaine. The state's Republican governor, Christine Todd Whitman, fired Williams on Feb. 28.

Less than two months later, Whitman appeared with the state's attorney general at a news conference on April 20 to release a two-month study that confirmed a stark racial pattern in traffic stops by troopers at

some stations. At year's end, the state signed an agreement with the U.S. Justice Department mandating an overhaul of the state police to end racial profiling and agreeing to the appointment of a federal monitor to oversee implementation of the accord.

The shift of opinion on the issue could be seen in comments by candidates in the 2000 presidential campaign. The two leading Democrats — Vice President Al Gore and former New Jersey Sen. Bill Bradley — both spoke out against racial profiling in a Jan. 17 debate in Iowa. Bradley drew blood on the issue by challenging Gore to "walk down that hallway" in the White House and get President Clinton to sign an executive order barring racial profiling by federal law enforcement agents. Gore aides later noted that Clinton has ordered federal agencies to collect data on the practice.

For his part, the Republican front-runner, Texas Gov. George W. Bush, also criticized racial profiling in a Jan. 10 campaign debate in Michigan. "No one wants racial profiling to take place in any state," Bush said. But Bush also said, "It's not the federal government's role to run state police departments." The ACLU criticized what it called Bush's "vague" statements and challenged him to issue an executive order in Texas barring the practice. ■

CURRENT SITUATION

Debating *Miranda*

The University of Utah's Cassell began his efforts to undercut the Supreme Court's *Miranda* decision when he worked for the Justice Department in the 1980s. Next month, he finds himself in the unusual position of arguing against an accused bank robber, Charles Dickerson, and the government itself in urging the high court to uphold a statute Congress passed to try to partly overturn *Miranda*.

Cassell has worked with the conservative Washington Legal Foundation (WLF) in several cases in an attempt to validate the law, Section

3501 of the federal Criminal Code, which seeks to replace the *Miranda* rule with a provision allowing the use of any "voluntary" confession. WLF intervened in Dickerson's case as the federal appeals court in Richmond, Va., took up the government's appeal of a trial judge's decision to bar his statements to police on grounds of a *Miranda* violation.

In its appeal, the government ig-

The four LAPD officers accused in the beating of Rodney King in March 1991 were, clockwise from top left, Laurence Powell, Stacey Koon, Theodore Briseno, and Timothy Wind. The four were acquitted in state court, but Koon and Powell were convicted in federal court of violating King's civil rights.

Reuters/Sam Mircovich

nored Section 3501 and instead challenged the judge's finding that Dickerson had not been Mirandized before making a crucial admission that he had driven the pickup truck used by the suspect accused of actually carrying out the robberies. But Cassell argued that the trial judge had been wrong to disregard Section 3501

in determining whether the government could introduce Dickerson's statements as evidence at trial.

The appeals court panel agreed and went on to declare that Congress had acted within its power in passing the law. "Congress has the power to overrule judicially created rules of evidence and procedure that are not required by the Constitution," Judge Michael Williams wrote in the 2-1 decision. "As a consequence, we hold that the admissibility of confessions in federal court is governed by Section 3501, rather than the judicially created rule of *Miranda*." [21]

In urging the Supreme Court to overturn the ruling, Dickerson's attorney, James W. Hundley, argued that the law was unconstitutional. "Only the Supreme Court may alter *Miranda*'s requirements," the Fairfax, Va., lawyer wrote. Hundley acknowledged that the *Miranda* court suggested that Congress and state legislatures might craft their own procedural protections for police interrogation. But Section 3501, he said, "makes no provision whatsoever for procedures at least as effective in apprising individuals of their right to remain silent and assuring that exercise of that right will be honored."

The Justice Department joined Dickerson in urging the high court to invalidate the law. *Miranda* and subsequent cases refining the decision "represent an exercise of this Court's authority to implement and effectuate constitutional rights, and, accordingly, those decisions are binding on Congress," the government lawyers argued. Nor is there any reason to overrule *Miranda*, the government said. The ruling has proved to be easy for both police and courts to administer, the government lawyers argued, and overruling the decision would weaken public confidence in the criminal-justice system as well as in the Supreme Court itself.

With both of the parties urging reversal of the appeals court opinion, the high court appointed Cassell as a "friend of the court" to urge an affirmance. In his brief — filed on March 9 — he insisted that Congress had the power to "modify" what he called *Miranda*'s "overprotective and extraconstitutional features." He also contended that the list of factors cited in the law for evaluating the voluntariness of a confession — including the giving of *Miranda*-type warnings — "amply provides" needed protections for criminal suspects. In fact, Cassell said, police would probably continue to give *Miranda* warnings if the law was upheld. "The statute, as well as numerous other legal rules, makes it very much in every officer's interest to continue to give them," he said.

Civil-liberties groups and law enforcement organizations weighed in with friend-of-the-court briefs on both sides of the case. The ACLU maintained that even with *Miranda*, police go to "sometimes illegal lengths" to get a confession from a suspect. Those incidents, the ACLU warned, "provide a disturbing glimpse of what police practices could become in a world without *Miranda* — where police need not tell citizens of their right to remain silent, and need not respect that right once invoked."

In an opposing brief, however, lawyers representing the IACP, the National Sheriffs Association and Americans for Effective Law Enforcement echoed Cassell's prediction that police would continue to warn suspects of their rights even if the law was upheld. A court ruling upholding

the law, the law enforcement brief concluded, would "take *Miranda*'s salutary purpose of ensuring voluntary confessions to a higher level of refinement and development."

Cassell says he is "optimistic that I'm going to prevail." But Scheidegger of the Criminal Justice Legal Foundation concedes that upholding the law is "an uphill battle. It requires the court to embrace the idea that it imposed rules on the states that aren't required by the Constitution."

On the opposite side, defenders of *Miranda* also expect a close fight, though they expect the court to nullify the law. "It's going to be a really close decision, 5-4, upholding *Miranda*," defense lawyer Kemler predicts.

For his part, though, Indiana law Professor Bradley feels certain that the court will not uphold the law. "There's no reason to think that the Supreme Court's going to do it," Bradley says. "If *Miranda* were gone, the whole voluntariness can of worms would be reopened in every confession. You'd see courts climbing into the whole interrogation thing again."

Judging Police

Four New York City police officers, in plainclothes and an unmarked car, are patrolling a high-crime neighborhood around midnight in the Bronx. They spot a figure that appears to be lurking at the entrance to an apartment building. Their suspicions aroused, they stop, get out of the car, and call out, "Sir, please. New York police. We need a word with you."

The man turns and goes into the vestibule of the building. He does not respond to the officers' request to show his hands. Instead, he reaches in his pocket and pulls out

a black object. "Gun! He's got a gun!" Officer Sean Carroll yells. Carroll and Edward McMellon begin firing. By the end of the incident, they have emptied their pistols — 16 rounds each; officers Kenneth Boss and Richard Murphy fire five and four rounds, respectively.

That is how the four white officers say Amadou Diallo, a 22-year-old immigrant from Guinea, died on the night of Feb. 4, 1999. Only as the West African street vendor lay dying — inside the building where he lived — did the officers realize that the black object in his hand was a wallet, not a gun.

In emotional testimony to a biracial jury in Albany, N.Y., last month, the officers described the incident as a tragic mistake. [22] The jurors — including four black women — apparently agreed. After deliberating for 21 hours over 2½ days, the state court jury on Feb. 25 acquitted the officers of all charges — including murder, manslaughter and reckless homicide.

New Yorkers — politicians and public alike — were divided in their reactions to the verdict. [23] "I think this jury reaffirms our belief in the American system of justice," Giuliani declared. But former Mayor David Dinkins, who is black, was outraged by the verdict. "This will send the wrong message to those members of the Street Crime Unit who walk around saying, 'We own the night,' " Dinkins said.

Lawyers in the case aired similarly divergent views. Defense attorney Stephen Worth, who represented McMellon, said the verdict showed the jurors understood the difficulties faced by police. "The point is the police officers have to be able to do their job and do it the right way." But Bronx District Attorney Robert Johnson said, "This case raises a lot of issues about police tactics."

The acquittals did not end the legal proceedings stemming from the shooting. U.S. Attorney Mary Jo White said her office and the Justice Department's Civil Rights Division will review the case to determine whether any federal civil rights laws were violated. Diallo's parents plan to file a civil lawsuit against the city. And the officers could still face administrative charges within the department.

One expert said the case illustrates the risks of New York's aggressive "zero-tolerance" enforcement — a policing strategy that its supporters say has helped bring down the city's crime rate.

"The strategy is difficult to manage in a way that achieves the crime-control benefits that it is intended to achieve and at the same time respects civil liberties and also doesn't generate ill will in the community," says Robert Worden, a professor of criminal justice and public policy at the State University of New York in Albany.

"It's possible, in principle, to do that, but it's difficult in practice," Worden says. "It's difficult to retain a commitment to that kind of proactive policing while ensuring that the officers do so with respect for the individuals."

Watching for Profiling

Alberto Lovato, a professional musician and preschool teacher, was stopped by Los Angeles police officers last year, ordered out of his truck at gunpoint, forced to lie face down on the ground, handcuffed and accused of being a gang member — all before the officers looked at his driver's license or registration. "I was afraid for my life," Lovato recalled last month at a news conference an-

nouncing a federal civil rights suit brought by three African-Americans and Lovato and a second Latino seeking to block the Los Angeles Police Department from using race as a factor in investigative stops.

All five of the plaintiffs committed no offense other than "driving while black or brown," Ramona Ripston, executive director of the ACLU of

---

"There was a grossly disproportionate number of minority motorists who were being stopped and searched on I-95."

— Deborah Jeon, attorney, ACLU of Maryland

Southern California, remarked at the Feb. 10 news conference. "There is no way in the world what happened to them would have occurred if they were white."

The suit asks for a court order barring racial profiling and requiring the police department to collect and maintain racial data on traffic stops. ACLU officials noted that 70 municipalities in California have already agreed to gather such information on a voluntary basis. LAPD officials declined to comment on the suit or on the general issue of profiling. In the past, however, Chief Bernard Parks, who is black, has said that race can be used "in conjunction with other cir-

cumstances" to justify a detention. [24]

The Los Angeles suit now joins with other ACLU legal attacks on racial profiling on both coasts. The ACLU of Northern California filed suit against the California Highway Patrol and the state's Bureau of Narcotics Enforcement (BNE) last June on behalf of a Latino attorney, Curtis Rodriguez. Rodriguez became suspicious while he was driving on a state highway in June 1998 after he observed five Latino drivers stopped by CHP or BNE officers within a 10-mile stretch. Rodriguez himself was stopped a while later and his car searched without his permission. The officer let him go after 20 minutes without issuing a ticket.

The ACLU's suits in Maryland and New Jersey are both continuing despite agreements by both states to end racial profiling. In Maryland, ACLU lawyers went back into court in late 1996 claiming that the state was not complying with the January 1995 settlement. As evidence, the lawyers cited racial data that the state had agreed to collect and turn over to the ACLU to check implementation of the agreement.

"The numbers began to come in and immediately it jumped out at you that when you looked at the Interstate-95 corridor, there was a grossly disproportionate number of minority motorists who were being stopped and searched," says Deborah Jeon, a managing attorney with the ACLU of Maryland. Jeon says initially about 85 percent of motorists stopped were minorities; the number fell to 70 percent but has remained near that level since.

In New Jersey, the ACLU is proceeding with its class-action suit filed in state court in New Brunswick even though the Justice Department nego-

At Issue:

Is the federal law limiting enforcement of the Miranda *decision* constitutional?

PAUL G. CASSELL
Professor, University of Utah College of Law

BRIEF OF COURT-APPOINTED AMICUS CURIAE, *CHARLES THOMAS DICKERSON v. UNITED STATES,* MARCH 9, 2000

*t*he ultimate question in this case is whether the federal criminal-justice system must exclude from evidence a criminal suspect's voluntary statement, despite an Act of Congress to the contrary. *Miranda v. Arizona* automatically excludes such a statement if it was given in response to custodial questioning without the required warnings. It enforces that exclusion on the basis of an irrebuttable presumption that such questioning by police must in every case have coerced the confession. . . . Nothing in the Constitution requires this uncompromising rule or strips the elected branches of their authority to modify it.

Congress' decision to enact Section 3501 was consistent with the Constitution. *Miranda* did not, and of course could not, simply redraft the Fifth Amendment to include a new constitutional right . . . Later pronouncements by the Court have confirmed that *Miranda*'s exclusionary rule was instead a preventive measure. . . . Because *Miranda*'s exclusionary rule was in this sense judicially improvised, rather than constitutionally required, *Miranda* necessarily accommodates legislative modification. Accordingly, there is neither need nor reason to overrule *Miranda* in order to uphold Section 3501.

The benefits of *Miranda* are preserved virtually intact by Section 3501. There is ample reason to believe that *Miranda* warnings will remain a standard [police] practice, because the statute, as well as numerous other legal rules, makes it very much in every officer's interest to continue to give them.

What Section 3501 changes is not so much the officer's incentive to give warnings but rather *Miranda*'s draconian remedy for any defect in giving them . . . As Congress understood, the automatic character of *Miranda*'s exclusionary rule is excessive because, heedless of the costs, it excludes confessions that manifestly were not produced by the police coercion that was *Miranda*'s principal target.

So long as involuntary confessions remain banned, as they are under Section 3501, and so long as trial courts are empowered [to] thwart any police behavior that produces involuntary confessions — again as they are under the statute — *Miranda*'s automatic exclusionary rule is unnecessary to preserve the full breadth of a suspect's Fifth Amendment right. . . . Because *Miranda*'s automatic rule excluding unwarned statements extends beyond the Fifth Amendment's bar on actually compelled statements, Congress was free to balance for itself the costs and benefits of that automatic rule and to supersede it with a rule more in keeping with the facts of each case and more faithful to the . . . Fifth Amendment.

SETH P. WAXMAN
Solicitor general of the United States

BRIEF FOR THE UNITED STATES, *CHARLES THOMAS DICKERSON v. UNITED STATES,* JAN. 28, 2000

*b*ecause the *Miranda* decision is of constitutional dimension, Congress may not legislate a contrary rule unless this Court were to overrule *Miranda*. We submit that principles of stare decisis do not favor the overruling of *Miranda* . . . In the 34 years since that decision was handed down, it has become embedded in the law. . . . If *Miranda* were to be overruled, this Court would have to disavow a long line of its cases that have interpreted *Miranda*, and it would have to overrule directly at least 11 cases that have reaffirmed that a confession obtained in violation of *Miranda* must be suppressed in the government's [main case]. At this date, there is no sufficient justification to overrule the balance struck in *Miranda* between the need for police questioning and the privilege against compelled self-incrimination, and there are substantial benefits to retaining that balance.

We acknowledge that there is a profound cost to the truth-finding function of a criminal trial when probative evidence is suppressed. . . . In many respects, however, *Miranda* is beneficial to law enforcement. Its core procedures provide clear guidance to law enforcement officers, and thus are not difficult to administer. If those procedures are followed, a defendant will frequently forgo any challenge to the voluntariness of an ensuing confession. . . . By contrast, the totality-of-the-circumstances test that was the sole measure of a confession's admissibility before *Miranda*, and that would govern in its absence, would be much more difficult for the police and the courts to apply and much more uncertain in application.

There is no sufficient change in the factual premises on which this Court based its decision in *Miranda* that would justify revisiting its holding. Although technological changes such as the availability of videotaping — might be of relevance as a part of a package of safeguards intended to provide alternative protection for the Fifth Amendment privilege, Section 3501 does not adopt those safeguards or any others to ensure that a suspect is aware of his rights and has an opportunity to exercise them.

Finally, both the confidence of the public in the fairness of the criminal-justice system and the stability of this Court's constitutional jurisprudence . . . may be expected to suffer if *Miranda* were overruled. Those values weigh heavily against discarding the essence of the balance that the Court struck in *Miranda*. Accordingly, *Miranda* should not be overruled. . . .

tiated an agreement with the state to end racial profiling in December.

"What's in the consent decree hasn't happened yet," says Lenore Lapidus, legal director of the ACLU of New Jersey. "Until we see what changes are actually made, we're not willing to forgo our claims." The ACLU's suit, filed under the state's anti-discrimination law, seeks damages as well as court-ordered changes to bar profiling.

Meanwhile, two states — Connecticut and North Carolina — have begun collecting racial data on traffic stops under laws that went into effect at the start of the year. In California, however, the state's Democratic governor, Gray Davis, vetoed a bill in September that would have required state and local law enforcement agencies to gather such information. ■

OUTLOOK

The Public's Trust

In its report on corruption in the Rampart Division, the LAPD Board of Inquiry acknowledged that the scandal had "devastated our relationship with the public we serve." In New York City, there was also evidence that the Louima and Diallo cases had weakened public confidence in the police.

Some New York prosecutors reported that grand jurors are more skeptical of police officers' testimony than in the past. And a *New York Times* survey of about 100 city residents after the acquittal in the Diallo shooting found that many people believe police show too little respect for citizens — although many also recognized the difficulties police face in doing their jobs. [25]

FOR MORE INFORMATION

American Civil Liberties Union, 125 Broad St., New York, N.Y. 10004; (212) 549-2500; www.aclu.org. The ACLU has been active on racial profiling, use of force and other police practices issues.

Community Policing Consortium, 1726 M St. N.W., Suite 801, Washington, D.C. 20036; (800) 833-3085; www.communitypolicing.org. The federally funded project is a consortium of five law enforcement groups aimed at promoting community-policing projects throughout the country.

Fraternal Order of Police, Grand Lodge, 1410 Donelson Pike, A-17, Nashville, Tenn. 37217; (615) 399-0900; www.grandlodgefop.org. The FOP is the largest membership organization representing rank-and-file law enforcement officers.

International Association of Chiefs of Police, 515 N. Washington St., Alexandria, Va. 22314-2357; (703) 836-6767; www.theiacp.org. The IACP is the world's largest organization of police executives.

National Association of Criminal Defense Lawyers, 1025 Connecticut Ave. N.W., Suite 901, Washington, D.C. 20036; (202) 872-8600; www.criminaljustice.org. NACDL is the largest organization exclusively representing criminal defense lawyers.

Police Foundation, 1201 Connecticut Ave. N.W., Suite 200; Washington, D.C. 20036; (202) 833-1460; www.policefoundation.org. The foundation sponsors research evaluating and promoting innovation in policing.

Americans also have become concerned about police conduct on the issue of racial profiling. A Gallup Poll conducted last fall found that 59 percent of those surveyed believed that racial profiling is "widespread" — including 56 percent of whites and 77 percent of blacks. And 81 percent of respondents said they disapprove of the practice.

Still, the Gallup Poll found that most Americans — including a majority of blacks and a substantial majority of whites — have a favorable opinion of their local and their state police. (*See box, p. 92.*) Some local police departments have their own evidence of public confidence. San Diego's police department — often cited as a model of "community policing" — said that a recent survey by an outside consultant found that 89 percent of those surveyed expressed approval of the police. [26]

Public confidence in police will continue to be tested as the current controversies are played out. In Los Angeles, the police department is continuing with disciplinary investigations against officers implicated in the Rampart scandal. Criminal investigations by the district attorney's office are proceeding slowly, and probes by federal agencies are only now getting under way. The city is also bracing for a flurry of civil lawsuits: The City Council has been told that the city's liability in wrongful-injury and imprisonment cases could reach $120 million.

In New York, meanwhile, the four officers acquitted of criminal charges in the Diallo shooting still face administrative proceedings that could result in anything from a reprimand to dismissal. The Justice Department is promising to complete its review of the incident within a few weeks.

A federal civil-rights prosecution appears unlikely, however, given the lack of evidence of any intent by the officers to violate Diallo's rights.

The Supreme Court's airing of the *Miranda* case next month also will revive public interest in the question of police interrogation and use of confessions. Most legal experts expect the court to reaffirm *Miranda* and strike down the federal law (Section 3501) aimed at limiting the ruling. And some police executives say that a decision to relax *Miranda* would actually unsettle public confidence in police.

"Once you say that a confession is valid without informing people of their rights, you've got problems," says the Police Foundation's Williams.

Police work has clearly changed dramatically in the three decades since the *Miranda* ruling. Today, police chiefs and officers appear to be more careful about staying within legal limits and more willing to discipline individual officers who step over the line. "I've never met a chief who didn't want to prosecute someone" who was found to have used improper force, says Fredericksburg Police Chief Powers.

"It's now more true than it was in the past that officers will report misconduct by other officers," Walker says. "In some of the better departments, they've taken some important steps toward self-policing."

For his part, Boston University's Delattre says the news media's focus on misconduct cases may give the public a misleading image of police.

"I've met a fair number of people who don't belong in policing, who should have been weeded out, and I've met many, many more cops who are basically decent people," Delattre says. "There are a lot of police who belong there, and they don't get much acknowledgment." ■

Notes

[1] Scott Glover and Matt Lait, "L.A. Police Group Often Broke Law, Transcripts Say," *Los Angeles Times*, Feb. 10, 2000, p. A1. For other articles, see the *Times*' Web site: www.latimes.com/rampart.

[2] Clyde Haberman, "Despite Diallo, Data Show Gun Restraint," *The New York Times*, Feb. 4, 2000, p. B1.

[3] International Association of Chiefs of Police, "Police Use of Force in America," October 1999.

[4] See Christopher A. Darden, *In Contempt* (1996), p. 110; "Cochran & Grace," "Johnnie Cochran: Driving While Black," Court TV, March 23, 1997, cited in David A. Harris, "The Stories, the Statistics, and the Law: Why 'Driving While Black' Matters," *Minnesota Law Review*, Vol. 84 (1999), pp. 265-266.

[5] Samuel Walker, *Popular Justice: A History of American Criminal Justice* (1980), p. 61. Other historical background is also drawn from this first edition and from a revised and updated edition published in 1998.

[6] National Commission on Law Observance and Enforcement, *Lawless in Law Enforcement* (1931), p. 103, cited in Walker, *op. cit.*, p. 174.

[7] The cases are *Brown v. Mississippi* (1936) and *Lisenba v. California* (1941).

[8] Background drawn from Yale Kamisar et al., *Modern Criminal Procedure: Cases, Comments, and Questions* (8th ed. 1994), as summarized in Richard A. Leo, "The Impact of Miranda Revisited," *Journal of Criminal Law and Criminology*, Vol. 86, No. 3 (1996), pp. 624-625.

[9] Walker, *op. cit.*, pp. 194-199.

[10] The cases are *Mapp v. Ohio* (1961) and *Gideon v. Wainwright* (1963).

[11] Account of interrogation taken from Paul G. Cassell, "The Statute That Time Forgot: 18 U.S.C. Section 3501 and the Overhauling of Miranda," *Iowa Law Review*, Vol. 85 (1999), pp. 183-191. The teenaged victim said she thought Miranda could be the assailant, but could not be positive. After the line-up, Miranda asked if the teenager and a second assault victim had identified him. "Yes, Ernie, they did," a detective replied.

[12] ABA Special Commission on Criminal Justice in a Free Society, Criminal Justice in Crisis (1988), p. 28.

[13] Charles Fried, *Order and Law* (1990), p. 46.

[14] The case is *Davis v. United States* (1994).

[15] The case is *Withrow v. Williams* (1993).

[16] For background, see Richard L. Worsnop, "Police Brutality," *The CQ Researcher*, Sept. 6, 1991, pp. 633-656.

[17] Walker, *op. cit.* (2d ed.), p. 197.

[18] See *Ibid.*, pp. 232-234.

[19] Cited in Worsnop, *op. cit.*, p. 644.

[20] Cases cited in Randall Kennedy, *Race, Crime, and the Law* (1997), p. 152.

[21] The appeals court ruling in *Dickerson v. United States* can be found on the Web site www.findlaw.com; the decision is also posted on Professor Cassell's Web site: www.law.utah.edu/faculty/bios/cassell, along with many other materials relating to the case.

[22] See *The New York Times*, Feb. 15, 2000, p. A1; Feb. 16, 2000, p. A25.

[23] Reaction drawn from *The New York Times*, Feb. 26, 2000, p. A1; *The Washington Post*, Feb. 26, 2000, p. A1.

[24] See *Los Angeles Times*, Feb. 11, 2000, p. B8.

[25] See *The New York Times*, March 9, 2000 (prosecutors' comments), p. A27; March 5, 2000, p. A1 (public attitudes).

[26] Cited in *The New York Times*, March 4, 2000, p. A1.

Bibliography

Selected Sources Used

Books

Baker, Liva, *Miranda: Crime, Law and Politics*, Atheneum, 1983.

Baker, author of several books on legal topics, traces the history of the *Miranda* case from his initial arrest through the Supreme Court's decision and its political and legal impact over the next decade and a half. The book includes a 15-page bibliography and source notes.

Delattre, Edwin J., *Character and Cops: Ethics in Policing (3d ed.)*, AEI Press, 1996.

Delattre, a philosopher and dean of Boston University's School of Education, examines questions of ethics relating to a variety of police issues, including corruption, discretion, management, recruitment and training.

Fogelson, Robert M., *Big-City Police*, Harvard University Press, 1977.

The book provides a survey history of police in major U.S. cities from the machine-politics days of the late 19th century through the reform efforts of the 20th century, which Fogelson says had stalled as he was writing the book in the mid-1970s. The book includes detailed notes.

Geller, William A., and Hans Toch (eds.), *Police Violence: Understanding and Controlling Police Abuse of Force*, Yale University Press, 1996.

The book includes essays by 20 contributors on issues relating to use of force, including the role of officer selection and training and the role of administrative or outside review. Geller is a former associate director of the Police Executive Research Forum; Toch is a professor at the School of Criminal Justice, State University of New York at Albany. Each chapter has detailed notes; the book also has a 40-page bibliography

Kelling, George F., and Catherine M. Coles, *Fixing Broken Windows: Restoring Order and Reducing Crime in Our Communities*, Free Press, 1996.

This influential book outlines a crime-control strategy for big cities based on maintaining order and devoting attention to disorderly behavior — so-called quality-of-life crimes. Kelling is a professor at Rutgers University's School of Criminal Justice; Coles, his wife, is a research associate at the school.

Kennedy, Randall, Race, *Crime, and the Law*, Pantheon, 1997.

Kennedy, a professor at Harvard Law School, includes a chapter on racial profiling in this strongly argued critique of racial disparities in the criminal-justice system. The book includes detailed notes and a 49-page bibliography.

Rosenbaum, Dennis P. (ed.), *The Challenge of Community Policing: Testing the Promises*, Sage Publications, 1994.

The book includes 19 essays evaluating the impact of community policing within police departments and on communities. Rosenbaum is a professor of criminal justice at the State University of New York in Albany.

Walker, Samuel, *Popular Justice: A History of American Criminal Justice*, Oxford University Press, 1980.

Walker, a professor of criminal justice at the University of Nebraska at Omaha, traces the history of policing in the United States from Colonial times and the creation of the first urban police forces in the 1830s through the professionalization of the police in the 20th century and the changes in policing during the due-process revolution of the 1960s. In a second edition, published in 1998, Walker carries the history through the more conservative law-and-order era of the 1980s and '90s. Walker is also author of the forthcoming *Police Accountability: The Role of Citizen Oversight* (Wadsworth, 2000).

Articles

Harris, David A., "The Stories, the Statistics, and the Law: Why 'Driving While Black' Matters," *Minnesota Law Review*, Vol. 84 (1999), pp. 265-326.

Harris, a law professor at the University of Toledo, provides background about and a strongly argued critique of racial profiling. Harris also authored an earlier report on the issue for the American Civil Liberties Union, "Driving While Black: Racial Profiling on Our Nation's Highways" (June 1999). The report can be found on the ACLU's Web site: www.aclu.org/profiling/report.

Reports and Studies

International Association of Chiefs of Police, "Police Use of Force in America," October 1999.

The 47-page report found that police use force infrequently — about 3.5 times per 10,000 calls for service in 1999 — and that excessive force was used in fewer than one-half of 1 percent of those instances. The report is based on data voluntarily submitted by police forces around the country to a federally funded database.

National Institute of Justice, "Use of Force by Police: Overview of National and Local Data," October 1999.

The 76-page report consists of six chapters written by academic experts on the use of force by police. The report's major conclusion is that the incidence of wrongful use of force by police is "unknown."

6 Drug Policy

Ronald G. is every parent's nightmare. Shortly after he began snorting heroin nine years ago, the 51-year-old Maryland man started selling the drug to feed his own gnawing habit. He pushed heroin for three and a half years in the nearby drug markets of Washington, D.C., contributing to the surging heroin use among the capital's teenagers and young adults.

After undercover police infiltrated Ronald's narcotics ring, he was convicted of conspiracy to distribute heroin and sentenced to 84 months in prison.

Yet to some observers, Ronald is as much a victim of failed social policies as a villain who peddles drugs to kids. When Ronald was 12, his alcoholic father took a fatal spill down a flight of stairs. Ronald started drinking in his late teens but remained steadily employed for three decades, got married and had three children.

After losing his job as a Red Cross bloodmobile driver, Ronald, then 42, became depressed over his inability to find another job and succumbed to a friend's invitation to snort his first line of heroin. It was the beginning of a journey through hell that he is still trying to end.

"When I lost the job, heroin became my buddy," Ronald recalls. "It told me not to worry, that it was just a job. It starts out that way, but after a while it becomes your personality. Soon my job became selling drugs, and heroin was the boss."

The drug's hold over Ronald continued in prison, where narcotics were readily available. Finally, lured by the

From *The CQ Researcher*,
July 28, 2000.

U.S. "drug czar" Barry R. McCaffrey visits Colombia to promote the administration's $1.3 billion anti-narcotics aid package. President Clinton signed the measure into law on July 13, although critics warned that U.S. forces would be sucked into Colombia's civil war without seriously curtailing its drug industry.

promise of early release, he successfully completed a drug-treatment program and was released after serving 42 months of his sentence. As a condition of parole, he enrolled in an outpatient drug-treatment program.

But he returned to heroin, entered another outpatient program and then relapsed again. This time, he enrolled in a six-month residential program run by Second Genesis, a drug and alcohol rehabilitation program in the Washington, D.C., area, where he is today.

"Here, I've gotten the information about myself that I needed to put my life back on track and realize how I've made a mess of my life, as well as my family's and a few friends', too," he says. "At my age, I should be thinking about retirement, but by doing drugs I've delayed my future."

The "war on drugs," the federal government's 30-year-old effort to curb the use of marijuana, heroin, cocaine and other banned substances, was launched to go after men like Ronald.[1] The campaign has consumed billions of dollars in an array

of efforts to eradicate drugs at their source at home and abroad; stop their importation at the border; disrupt street markets; discourage their use through prevention and education programs; and help drug abusers overcome their addictions. Virtually every major federal agency is involved.

Despite these efforts, drug use remains widespread. Ronald is one of more than 13 million Americans who regularly used illicit drugs in 1998, the latest year for which data are available.[2] He's also one of more than 975,000 Americans who used heroin at least once in 1998 — double the number of users in 1993. Similarly, marijuana and cocaine use by teenagers roughly doubled during the 1990s. Although there was a slight decline in teenage drug use from 1997 to 1998, almost 10 percent of youths ages 12 to 17 reported using illicit drugs in 1998.[3]

Such statistics lead critics of U.S. drug policy to conclude that the Clinton administration's anti-crime efforts, including stiffer sentences for drug offenders, have been a dismal failure. Indeed, while the nation's jails and prisons are overflowing with drug offenders, the street prices of some of the most harmful illegal substances have fallen, even as drug purity levels have increased.

"Prohibition didn't work for alcohol in the 1920s, and it's never going to work for drugs," says Kevin B. Zeese, president of Common Sense for Drug Policy, based in Washington, D.C. "When something doesn't work, you have two choices: Face up to the fact and change course, or refuse to admit you're failing and escalate. And that's what's been hap-

Americans Spent $63 Billion on Illegal Drugs

Americans' overall spending on illegal drugs was an estimated $63.2 billion in 1999, a decline of $5.2 billion, or 7.6 percent, since 1997. Spending on cocaine dropped the most — by nearly $5 billion.

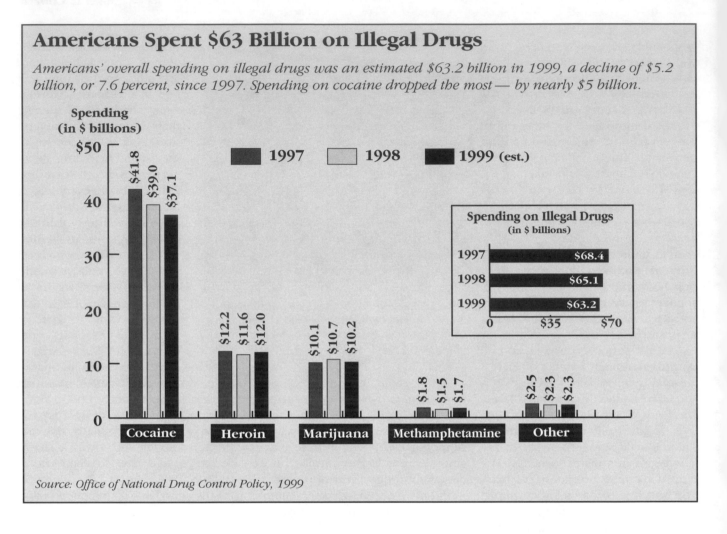

Source: Office of National Drug Control Policy, 1999

pening over the past 20 years."

To the retired Army general leading the war on drugs, however, naysayers like Zeese fail to recognize important gains of current drug policies. "Drug use in America is down dramatically," says Barry R. McCaffrey, director of the Office of National Drug Control Policy — the nation's so-called drug czar. "In the last year the percentage of young people ages 12 to 17 using drugs declined by 13 percent, the average age of first-time use went up and the overall use of pot and other drugs leveled off."

The real measure of the drug policy's effectiveness, McCaffrey says, is clear when viewed over the long term. "The highest rate of drug use in modern history was in 1979, when

14.1 percent of Americans used illegal substances," he says. "Today it's down to 6 percent."

McCaffrey is the first military professional to oversee federal drug policy and its $17.8 billion budget. Despite his background, he describes himself as a reluctant drug czar and even rejects the military terms used to describe his mandate. "The metaphor of a 'war on drugs' is inappropriate," he says. "Drug abuse is more like a cancer affecting American communities."

Indeed, McCaffrey says his experience in the military taught him that treatment is more effective than law enforcement in combating drug abuse. "As many as a third of the people in uniform were using drugs

in the 1970s, and it absolutely wrecked our professional competence," he says. "We worked our way out of it, and we did so not by arresting people, but by running one of the largest drug-treatment programs the world had ever seen. It took us a decade. This is the mindset I brought into this issue."

McCaffrey argues that many critics, in their zeal to denounce the drug policy's failures, overlook the Clinton administration's support of drug prevention and treatment. "We can argue about courses of action, but not about facts, and the facts are that the treatment budget is now over $3.5 billion a year," he says. "The federal drug-prevention budget [from] 1996 to 2000 is up 52 percent, the treatment budget is up 34 percent and the research budget is up 35 percent."

But critics insist that treatment and prevention continue to take a back seat to eradication, interdiction and domestic law-enforcement efforts to reduce the supplies reaching American streets. For evidence, they point to last month's congressional approval of a $1.3 billion aid package to help Colombia eradicate its illegal coca and opium crops, the source of most of the cocaine and heroin in the United States. Clinton signed the measure into law on July 14, after a lengthy debate in Congress in which critics warned that U.S. forces would be sucked into Colombia's civil war without seriously curtailing the country's drug industry. (*See "At Issue," p. 123.*)

Some critics of current drug policy say the place to look for innovative approaches to the drug problem is not in Washington, D.C., but in the states. In recent years, voters in seven states and the District of Columbia have legalized the use of marijuana as a pain reliever for patients with cancer and other diseases. Many advocates of drug-policy reform point to California, where voters this fall will decide on a ballot initiative requiring non-violent drug offenders to get treatment rather than prison the first two times they are arrested.

These and other initiatives fall within a category of policy alternatives that many advocates call "harm reduction."

"This is an approach that acknowl-

edges that both drug use and drug prohibition are going to persist for the foreseeable future and that we need to focus on reducing the harms associated with both of them," says Ethan A. Nadelmann, director of the Lindesmith Center, a drug policy institute in New York City, and a leading advocate of drug-policy reform.

Not all critics of current policy agree with Nadelmann's assessment. "I deeply regret what's going on, because the alternatives that are being

Prisoners line up with their bedding at the Broward County Jail in Fort Lauderdale, Fla., which runs a military-style boot camp for juvenile offenders. Critics say drug-sentencing policies fill prisons with drug users without solving the drug problem.

proposed, including the California initiative, are all hot air," says Mark Kleiman, a professor of policy studies at the University of California, Los Angeles, who was a Justice Department drug official during the Reagan administration. "The California initiative would require offenders to go to treatment, which most of them don't need and which for many of them won't work. But it never allows you to find out whether or not they're complying with a perfectly simple

instruction, which is, 'Don't use.' "

A better way to reduce the harm caused by drug use and drug policies, Kleiman says, would be to focus on "the side effects of drug trafficking — violence, corruption, neighborhood disorder and the use of kids as dealers."

With this approach, often referred to as "coerced abstinence," all drug offenders on parole and probation would be subjected to periodic urine testing. [4] Those who test positive for drug use would be punished with mild sanctions, such as a few days' incarceration. "Instead of sending people to prison, we'd put them on the street in a condition of restricted liberty," he says.

Although several congressional hearings have focused on the war on drugs in recent months, there are few indications of change in federal policy during this election year. Voters in a number of states, however, will be able to choose drug-policy alternatives this fall.

As voters consider current efforts to curb drug abuse, these are some of the issues they will consider:

Should drug prohibition be relaxed?

For years, some critics of drug policy have advocated overturning the entire system of drug prohibition. Just as Prohibition in the 1920s led to a vast black market in alcohol and widespread violence as gangsters fought to control the lucrative trade in bootleg liquor, advocates of drug legalization say current drug laws have only increased crime and suffering.

"Legalization means we educate, regulate, tax and control the estimated $400-billion-a-year drug industry," wrote Gov. Gary E. Johnson, R-N.M., a leading supporter of legalization. "We need to make drugs a controlled substance just like alcohol." [5]

But while legalization would certainly result in reduced drug-related criminal activity, most experts say it would almost certainly lead to increased drug use. "Under a legal regime, the consumption of low-priced, low-risk drugs would increase dramatically," writes drug reform advocate James Q. Wilson, a professor of public policy at Pepperdine University in Malibu, Calif. "We do not know by how much, but the little evidence we have suggests a sharp rise." [6]

Concern about rising drug use prompts many critics of current policies to take a more measured view of drug-law reform, or what Wilson calls a "third way" between the war on drugs and outright legalization. Some, notably billionaire financier George Soros, call for decriminalization of less-dangerous substances, such as marijuana, while retaining bars on access to heroin, cocaine and other addictive drugs. [7]

"We should be aiming for some measure of legally regulating marijuana and then aiming for harm-reduction approaches with respect to the other drugs," says Nadelmann of the Soros-backed Lindesmith Center. "Let's stop pretending that we can be a drug-free society and acknowledge that drugs are here to stay. The challenge is not to get rid of drugs, but to have them

cause the least possible harm."

An immediate goal of the harm reductionists, as Nadelmann and like-minded reformers are often called, is to decriminalize the use of marijuana by people suffering from certain diseases, such as glaucoma and cancer. [8] Medical-marijuana initiatives have been approved in seven states — California, Alaska, Washington, Oregon, Maine, Nevada and Colo-

The Office of National Drug Control Policy uses posters and other advertisements with anti-drug themes to help persuade American youth to reject drugs, alcohol and tobacco.

rado — and the District of Columbia. In June, Hawaii became the first state to legalize medical marijuana through the legislative process.

Skeptics say the ballot initiatives defy federal law and undercut the authority of the medical establishment. "The medicinal use of marijuana is a medical issue that needs to

be answered first and foremost by the medical community," says Steve Dnistrian, executive vice president of the Partnership for a Drug-Free America, a coalition of communications-industry representatives which works to reduce demand for illicit drugs. "We've got to work on a new way to get THC, marijuana's active ingredient, into the bloodstream because smoking it is not the best way."

At least one drug company is working on a form of medicinal marijuana that is not smoked. [9] But like many critics of harm-reduction initiatives, Dnistrian suspects that medical-marijuana initiatives are just a cover for broader legalization efforts.

"This is a well-choreographed and well-financed plan by the same people who have been leading the charge for drug legalization and decriminalization for the past 25 to 30 years," he says, "so naturally we are a little bit suspicious of their true motives."

Needle-exchange programs are another key priority for harm-reduction advocates. Needle sharing by injection drug users is a leading cause of the spread of HIV/AIDS, accounting for some 200,000 current cases. [10] In April 1998, Health and Human Services Secretary Donna Shalala announced, "a meticulous, scientific review has now proven that needle-exchange programs can reduce the transmission of HIV and save lives without losing ground in the battle against illegal drugs." [11]

To the dismay of reformers, however, President Clinton decided not to approve federal AIDS funding for needle exchanges under pressure from critics who said such programs would send the wrong signal on drug

Combating Alcohol and Tobacco Addiction

For all the concern about illegal drug abuse, the two most commonly used mind-altering substances — alcohol and tobacco — take a far greater toll on the health and welfare of Americans. Both substances can be as addictive as many banned drugs, and their consumption poses grave threats to users and non-users alike.

Smoking has long been known to cause cancers of the lung, esophagus and mouth, as well as emphysema, bronchitis and heart disease. More than 430,000 Americans die each year of smoking-related diseases. More recent research has shown that non-smokers exposed to second-hand tobacco smoke are at a higher risk of contracting these diseases than those who live in a smoke-free environment.

Regulation of tobacco sales has tightened as a result of recent court verdicts forcing tobacco manufacturers to pay damages to victims of smoking-related diseases and reimburse states for the costs of treating them. The most recent judgment came on July 14, when a Florida jury awarded $145 billion to sick Florida smokers.

The court verdicts, combined with a 40-year-old public-health campaign warning smokers of the health risks associated with smoking, have reduced tobacco consumption from a peak of 43 percent of the adult population in 1966 to about 25 percent today. [1]

Excessive alcohol consumption also is associated with health risks, especially liver disease. But because of its intoxicating effects, alcoholics aren't the only ones at risk from alcohol abuse. Led by drunken-driving traffic accidents, alcohol-related deaths outnumber deaths related to illicit drugs by four to one. [2]

"Alcohol is a mildly addictive drug that most of us don't have problems with, but since it's widely available, cheap and socially approved, it is without question the single biggest drug-abuse problem in the country," says U.S. "drug czar" Barry R. McCaffrey, director of the Office of National Drug Control Policy. "Around 6 percent of the population, or about 14 million people, have used [illegal] drugs in the past month, and around 5 million of those are chronic addicts. Illegal drugs probably kill around 52,000

people a year and cost us $110 billion in damages. But there are as many as 16 million Americans who are chronically abusing alcohol, and alcohol abuse probably kills 100,000 people a year and costs $150 billion in damages."

Congress included alcohol among the list of banned drugs in 1919 when it passed the 18th Amendment prohibiting the production, sale and consumption of alcohol. But because of alcohol's widespread use, the experiment failed, and lawmakers overturned Prohibition in 1933.

Although anyone 21 or older can easily buy alcohol, and tobacco is available to anyone 18 or older, McCaffrey says both substances are the focus of his education campaign to discourage drug use among young people. "Goal No. 1 of our drug-control strategy is to motivate America's youngsters to reject the use of illegal drugs as well as alcohol and tobacco products," he says.

The drug czar is barred from using appropriated funds to target legal substances, but he does use matching funds to pay for public-service announcements warning young people about the dangers of alcohol abuse. "In my judgment, alcohol abuse probably ought to be added to the National Drug Control Policy director's portfolio," McCaffrey says. Meanwhile, he adds, "We've got the biggest youth anti-alcohol campaign in history going on using matching funds."

McCaffrey is hopeful that alcohol and tobacco use will fall as a result of the war on illegal drugs. "If you solve the drug problem, you'll also reduce adolescent crime, adolescent pregnancy and adolescent alcohol abuse," he says. "They're all wrapped up in the same attitudinal shifts."

Smoking-related illnesses kill more than 430,000 Americans each year, and recent research has shown that non-smokers exposed to secondhand tobacco smoke are also at risk.

AP Photo/The Daily Ledger, Heather Dryer

---

[1] See Judy Packer-Tursman, "Treatment of Choice; Any Time's a Good Time to Quit Smoking," *The Washington Post*, July 11, 2000.

[2] *Millennium Hangover: Keeping Score on Alcohol*, 1999, published by Drug Strategies, a nonprofit research organization that studies drug-policy alternatives.

use. "The federal government has been totally irresponsible in the way [it] handles AIDS prevention and drugs," says Zeese of Common Sense for Drug Policy. "Half the new AIDS cases come from intravenous drug use, and we could cut that rate in half and even reduce drug abuse if we had needle exchange funded fully as part of an AIDS-prevention program."

Supporters of current drug policy say some of the harm-reduction proposals already have been incorporated into the federal drug strategy. "If you're chronically addicted, our strategy says we're trying to organize effective drug treatment to help you break the cycle," McCaffrey says. "The term 'harm reduction' has to some extent been hijacked by some in America who are actually calling for the normalization of drug abuse. So I rarely use the term, but there's no question that much of what we're doing is precisely that."

To some critics, the most damaging effect of the harm-reduction argument is that it distracts attention from drug abuse itself. "This campaign is being fueled by the millions and millions of dollars that George Soros and others have committed to this effort," says Mitchell S. Rosenthal, president and founder of Phoenix House, a nonprofit organization in New York City that runs a nationwide network of drug-treatment programs. "I think it's unfortunate in two ways. First, it takes the focus away from what public policy ought to be about — the drugs — and makes the issue one of legaliza-

tion, or veiled attempts at legalization, which to some extent is what the whole harm-reduction movement is about. Secondly, it is not helping more people access the treatment they need."

Nadelmann rejects the criticism. "Most people in the drug-policy reform movement do not support over-the-counter sales of heroin and cocaine and treating these drugs the way we do alcohol and cigarettes," he says. "The drug czar, the Partnership [for a Drug-Free America] and much of Congress tend to conflate all of our efforts

Gov. Gary E. Johnson, R-N.M., explains his support for drug legalization during a radio call-in show in Albuquerque on Oct. 15, 1999.

as being all about legalization in sheep's clothing. Neither George Soros nor I are out-and-out legalizers. The general public has a hard time understanding the gray areas in all this. As a rhetorical matter, if someone says 'legalize,' it's instantly a headline, but the term 'harm reduction' just isn't going to make the cover of *Time* magazine."

Should mandatory-minimum sentences for drug offenses be abolished?

In the late 1960s and early '70s, as

heroin use rose, Congress and a number of states passed mandatory-minimum sentencing laws, which forced judges to hand out fixed sentences, without parole, as a way to discourage drug use. [12] The most stringent mandatory-sentencing laws were signed in 1973 by Gov. Nelson Rockefeller, R-N.Y., in response to the burgeoning heroin trade in Manhattan. Under the Rockefeller laws, as they are still known, selling small amounts of heroin or cocaine is a Class B felony, comparable in seriousness to armed robbery, first-degree rape and first-degree manslaughter, and brings 15 years to life with no possibility of parole. [13]

More stringent sentencing laws were introduced in the 1980s, including the federal Omnibus Anti-Drug Abuse Act of 1988, which added a mandatory-minimum sentence for possession of crack cocaine.

"When crack hit the newspapers in 1986 and began transforming the inner city and the drug trade, there was a sense of desperation, and a whole lot of new laws were written," says Peter Kerr, a spokesman for Phoenix House. "The drug laws of the 1970s and '80s are now reaping a toll. We've never had this many people in prison, and there are very few countries with as many as we have."

Today about 2 million men and women are being held in state and federal prisons. [14] In fact, the United States has the largest prison population in the world, and is second only to Russia in the proportion of its population behind bars — almost seven inmates for every 1,000 people. [15] Critics say the high incarceration rate has had no visible impact on drug use.

"The main effect of imprisoning drug sellers, we believe, is merely to open the market for another seller," write public-policy experts Anne Morrison Piehl, Bert Useem and John J. DiIulio Jr. For evidence that incarceration has failed to disrupt the market for illegal drugs, they note that the street price of cocaine and other drugs has actually fallen since 1980, at the same time that incarceration rates have increased.

"In sum, it seems to us that the imprisonment of large numbers of drug offenders is not a cost-effective use of public resources," they wrote. [16]

Worse, Kerr says, mandatory-minimum laws deprive judges of their discretionary power to fit the sentence to the gravity of the crime. "The Rockefeller laws that don't allow discretion to judges don't make sense," he says. "A judge has to see whether this is a criminal who's made a fortune out of dealing drugs or a young person who's gotten snared into an addiction and could use treatment."

The plight of non-violent, first-time drug offenders sentenced to years in prison for simple possession has prompted relatives and other critics to organize. In 1991, after her brother received a five-year sentence in federal prison for possession of 36 marijuana plants, Julie Stewart founded Families Against Mandatory Minimums (FAMM), which today has branches in 21 states.

FAMM says the case of 36-year-old Jan Warren illustrates the unfairness of drug-sentencing laws. Warren, who was pregnant and had a teenage daughter, was sentenced in 1987 to 15 years to life for selling 7.83 ounces of cocaine, though she had no prior convictions. At the time of her arrest, an accomplice plea-bargained and

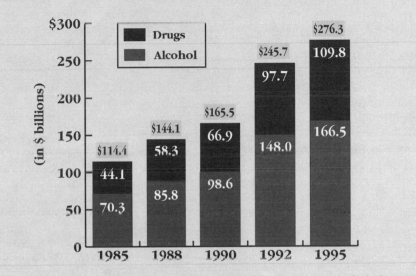

Cost of Substance Abuse Rose

The cost to American society attributed to drug and alcohol abuse from extra health care, lost wages, increased law enforcement and more drug treatment more than doubled from 1985 to 1995. Alcohol abuse was 44 percent more costly than drug abuse in 1995.

Cost of Substance Abuse in U.S., 1985-1995

(in $ billions)

Year	Alcohol	Drugs	Total
1985	70.3	44.1	$114.4
1988	85.8	58.3	$144.1
1990	98.6	66.9	$165.5
1992	148.0	97.7	$245.7
1995	166.5	109.8	$276.3

Sources: National Institute on Drug Abuse, National Institute on Alcohol Abuse and Alcoholism, 1998

received a lighter sentence.

The judge, who said at Warren's sentencing that he "didn't want to do this," later called her sentence a "travesty." [17]

The supporters of current policy tend to dismiss such claims of innocence. "There's a myth about mandatory minimums that a first-time offender who's busted with a dime bag of marijuana goes to jail for 10 years," Dnistrian says. "By and large, that never happens. You have to have a criminal record from here to Chicago."

McCaffrey agrees. "People are not arrested and prosecuted and jailed for first-time possession of a controlled drug for personal addiction," he says. "That almost doesn't happen. People end up behind bars because they break into your house or your car, they steal money from

your business or they're addicted themselves and they're selling drugs to other people to pay for their drug habit. That's why they get arrested and prosecuted."

But some of the strongest criticism of mandatory minimums comes from the law-enforcement community itself. "I believe that mandatory-sentencing laws for drug offenses are in some cases ridiculous," says Dennis Ray Martin, president of the American Police Hall of Fame and a spokesman for the National Association of Chiefs of Police in Saginaw, Mich. "We are filling our jails up, and it's come to the point where one of the top industries in the nation today is building prisons." [18]

Martin, a former police chief of Maple Grove, Mich., says the most serious shortcomings of mandatory

Helping Addicts Get Sober

Getting sober isn't easy. That's why motivational slogans are posted around the Second Genesis drug-treatment facility in Bethesda, Md. They remind residents of the lessons they've learned in therapy.

"Any man can stand up to his opponent; give me the man who can stand up to his friends," reads a sign posted at the door to the dining room. The lesson, a resident explains, is that an important aspect of treatment involves pointing out negative attitudes and behavior to one another.

Founded in 1969, Second Genesis is one of hundreds of local organizations around the country that try to help drug users get off drugs, including alcohol. Once residents complete their stay, generally four months, they move into an adjoining "sober" house for a two-month transition period leading to "graduation." During this phase of treatment, residents work outside the facility.

Statistics show that most drug users took up the habit in their teens or early 20s, so prevention efforts usually are targeted at this age group. Second Genesis recently launched after-school education programs to discourage drug use among middle and high school students. Attendance is voluntary, but students in some schools also can get academic credit for attending the six-week course.

"The prevention program helps kids anticipate their concerns about scary behavior, about things their friends, or even they themselves, may be doing," says Gale Saler, deputy executive director of Second Genesis. "We also provide staff training to help teachers and other school staff deal with the drug problem better. Those who complete this training are extremely good at getting kids to tell them things they never thought they'd tell an adult."

Although Congress has increased funding for drug-abuse prevention programs from $1.4 billion to $2.1 billion since 1996, Saler says she has had to turn to the local community for financial support of the after-school classes. "Prevention programs cost $2,500 a year per high school, and about half that amount for middle schools, where the programs are not conducted at the same intensity," she says.

Most of Second Genesis' efforts are directed toward drug addiction. The organization has both residential and outpatient treatment centers in Washington, D.C., and the surrounding Virginia and Maryland suburbs. Adults in residential programs receive individual and group therapy as well as vocational training and help in developing the social skills needed to prevent relapse. As they progress through the treatment phases, they earn privileges and take on additional responsibilities. To graduate, clients must also obtain full-time employment.

"These people's lives have gotten out of control," Saler explains. "We create an environment to help them get their lives together."

Many residents drop out of Second Genesis before completing the program. In fact, the entrance is locked only from the outside. "You have the option to do treatment or walk out the door," Saler says. "It takes a lot to commit yourself to treatment, and we feel that to make the right choice you have to have the ability to make the wrong choice."

Second Genesis says that 79 percent of the men and women — including pregnant women and women with children — who complete the full program remain free of drugs or alcohol. And fewer than 10 percent were later arrested.

Like many other professionals involved in drug treatment, Saler laments the lack of public support for the services Second Genesis provides. Many residents are former prison inmates, a population that enjoys little public sympathy.

"There's such a stigma attached to drug treatment that it's very, very hard to get people to move past that," she says. "We get so tired of hearing that these are bad people. Compared to mental-health patients, who are supported by a phenomenal mental-health lobby, people in drug treatment have little political voice."

That has a negative impact on the amount of support the treatment community receives from Congress. "It's hard to prove that prevention works," Saler says. "You can't prove a negative. But there is a huge body of studies showing that treatment works. If federal policy were consistent with the research, that would be a really good start."

A staff teacher at Second Genesis, a residential drug-treatment facility in Washington, D.C., assists a client who plans to study for his general-equivalency diploma. Adult education is an integral part of the program's treatment regimen.

Second Genesis

minimums are their ineffectiveness and unintended consequences. "Is the problem actually being addressed?" he asks. "We feel it is not. Personally, I would say the reality is that many of these people, once they are released, have not been positively affected by their incarceration. Many of them have families who have been left destitute, which has really created more problems for society than I think were anticipated."

Still other critics dismiss the controversy over mandatory minimums as a mere distraction from more serious flaws in drug-law enforcement. "Most of the people who go to prison on drug charges aren't the victims of mandatories," Kleiman says. "So if we abolished mandatories tomorrow, nothing important would improve. The question is not whether we have mandatories or not, but what the basis of drug sentencing should be. Right now, it's drugs and quantity, but we need fewer, shorter sentences and sentences more focused on conduct rather than on quantity."

Should parolees be required to abstain from drug use as a condition of their release?

Mandatory-minimum sentences for drug offenses have helped boost the prison population in the United States to about 2 million inmates. Of these, as many as three-quarters tested positive for drug use at the time of arrest. The main defect in current drug policies, law-enforcement officials say, is that drug addicts, once released, tend to return to their neighborhoods and the conditions that prompted them to take drugs in the first place and commit crimes.

"In order to purchase many of these illegal drugs, they have to do illegal acts," Martin says. "A lot of these people can't even hold a job, so they have to generate money in other ways, and that's usually by illegal breaking and entering. They'll steal a $300 television set, which may only bring $25 on the street. So they have to steal larger quantities of mer-

The percentage of youth ages 12 to 17 using drugs fell 13 percent last year and the average age of first-time narcotics users rose. Federal officials say such statistics indicate that their anti-drug strategy is having an affect.

chandise to generate the kind of money they need."

Many experts agree that treatment is the key to stopping the revolving door of incarceration, release and re-arrest. [19] The Clinton administration's main effort to break that cycle is the drug court. Introduced in the late 1980s at the state and local level, drug courts require drug-involved of-

fenders to undergo treatment as part of their sentences. Thanks in part to federal funding, there are more than 600 drug courts around the country.

"If you are arrested at 2 in the morning and you're dazed, drunk or drugged, you're a male street prostitute or you're breaking into a car when arrested, we would like to get you into the drug-court system at the front end," says McCaffrey, the administration's chief booster of drug courts. "If you go into treatment and get a job, we'll arrange the social services and medical care you need, we'll try and keep you out of prison and, indeed, try and not put a formal conviction on your record."

An essential element of the drug-court system, McCaffrey says, is its coercive nature. "It doesn't work without the coercive threat of the drug court," he says. "Say you flunk your drug test because you have a chronically relapsing disorder. You're in misery, you're desperate and you've got this compulsion because you've neurologically modified your brain. When you flunk your drug test, we'll lock you up for a three-day weekend — no boyfriend, no TV — and then release you back into community life."

Some drug-treatment professionals say this approach isn't enough to break the cycle of drug abuse. "We still have in New York and some other states mandatory minimums, where people who are convicted of possession or sale of certain amounts of drugs will have to do long, heavy sentences," says Rosenthal of Phoenix House. "That frequently puts people in jail for what are ludicrously long sentences, when in fact very often these addicted sellers would do much better sentenced in effect to two years of treatment or some lesser prison term with a treatment component in prison. That would be a very significant addition to public policy."

In Rosenthal's experience, the longer drug addicts are in treatment, the more likely they are to overcome their addiction. "We know from the research data that if you keep people in treatment for 12 to 18 months, both in and out of prison, and there's real continuity in treatment, you're going to see positive results over time," he says.

Other critics say the rationale behind both the drug-court system and long-term treatment — that drug abuse is largely a medical condition — is false.

"Most people who use illicit drugs aren't sick, so what are we treating them for?" Kleiman asks. "This policy assumes that if somebody does have a substance-abuse disorder, that somehow there's a treatment process they can go through and then they're cured. Come on. Some people get better, but some people don't. Drug abuse isn't like gonorrhea, where you can just give someone some penicillin to make them well."

A better alternative, in Kleiman's view, would require all people on parole or probation to undergo drug testing as a condition of release. Known as "coerced abstinence," this approach embraces drug testing and immediate, mild sanctions for drug use, generally only a few days in jail. [20]

"The current system puts a lot of people in prison," he says. "If you're on parole and you test dirty, you're

likely to spend 90 days in prison. I want to have a very predictable, mild sanction, which I think will involve less punishment and less drug use in the aggregate than the current system. If harm reduction had its ordinary language meaning, this would be a harm-reduction approach."

But advocates of harm reduction

"Most people who use illicit drugs aren't sick, so what are we treating them for? Drug abuse isn't like gonorrhea, where you can just give someone some penicillin to make them well."

— *Mark Kleiman,*
Professor of Policy Studies,
University of California,
Los Angeles

---

reject coerced abstinence on ideological grounds. "We believe that people should not be punished for what they put in their bodies," Nadelmann says. "People should be held responsible for their actions, whether they're under the influence or not. Therefore, anything that relies on urine testing in a punitive way by definition cannot be harm reduction."

Nadelmann also is skeptical of in-prison treatment programs, saying

they fail to address the underlying problems that lead to drug abuse. "There are a lot of things wrong with coerced drug treatment," he says. "The best place to provide treatment, generally speaking, is outside the criminal-justice system, in the community, where people can get it before they get in trouble. We're hearing more and more stories of people getting arrested just so they can get access to treatment, which is almost ludicrous."

The obvious answer to that problem, Nadelmann says, "Everyone is talking about huge amounts of money flowing into things like coerced drug treatment and drug courts," he says. "At the same time, the money in the community for drug treatment — whether it's methadone maintenance [for heroin addicts] or programs for women who are pregnant and using drugs — all of that is drying up.

"I look at the whole push for more drug courts and coerced drug treatment as a mixed blessing. While I think it's doing some good in moving things somewhat in the right direction, I also think it's hugely corrupting of the long-term picture of what drug treatment should be about." ∎

BACKGROUND

Early Drug Laws

Narcotics use took root in the United States in the late 19th century. Many Civil War veterans who had been treated with morphine for their inju-

Chronology

1900s-1910s
Early drug policy focuses on opium and other opiates.

1906
Pure Food and Drug Act requires manufacturers to list ingredients on product labels.

1912
United States joins the 1912 Hague Opium Convention, the first international agreement to regulate the production and distribution of opium.

1914
Congress passes the nation's first drug law, the Harrison Narcotic Act, which regulates the production and sale of opium and cocaine and is later amended to ban heroin.

1919
Eighteenth Amendment bars the production, sale and consumption of alcohol.

1920s-1930s
Alcohol Prohibition fails and is dropped.

1933
Congress abandons Prohibition by passing the 22nd Amendment, which repeals the 18th Amendment and leaves alcohol regulation to the states.

1937
Marijuana Tax Act extends the drug ban to include marijuana.

1960s-1970s
Growing drug use sparks intensified federal law-enforcement efforts.

1971
President Richard M. Nixon creates the Special Action Office of Drug Abuse Prevention to coordinate drug policy, including prevention efforts, treatment and rehabilitation of drug abusers and research into addiction.

1973
National Institute of Drug Abuse (NIDA) is set up in 1973 to oversee federal prevention and treatment programs.

1973
Gov. Nelson A. Rockefeller, R-N.Y., signs the country's most stringent mandatory-sentencing laws for drug offenses.

1979
Illegal drug use in the United States peaks at 14.1 percent of the population.

1980s *President Ronald Reagan declares a "war on drugs" and oversees dramatic increases in funding for anti-drug policies.*

1986
Anti-Drug Abuse Act provides more than $1.7 billion in new funds, bringing the anti-drug budget to $3.9 billion.

1988
Omnibus Anti-Drug Abuse Act calls for mandatory-minimum sentences for possession of crack cocaine as part of effort to strengthen drug-sentencing laws. The new law also creates the Office of National Drug Policy Control, headed by a Cabinet-level official dubbed the nation's "drug czar."

1990s-2000s
Drug use levels off amid growing criticism of federal policies.

1991
Relatives of incarcerated drug offenders found Families Against Mandatory Minimums with the goal of repealing the Rockefeller laws and similar measures.

1996
California voters approve Proposition 215, legalizing the use of marijuana for medical purposes. Voters in Alaska, Arizona, Maine, Nevada, Oregon, Washington and the District of Columbia later approve similar initiatives, along with lawmakers in Hawaii.

April 1998
Health and Human Services Secretary Donna E. Shalala presents evidence that needle-exchange programs can reduce the spread of AIDS without increasing illegal drug use, but President Clinton later decides not to approve federal funding for such programs.

July 14, 2000
President Clinton signs a controversial $1.3 billion aid package to equip and train Colombian armed forces to combat cocaine and heroin production.

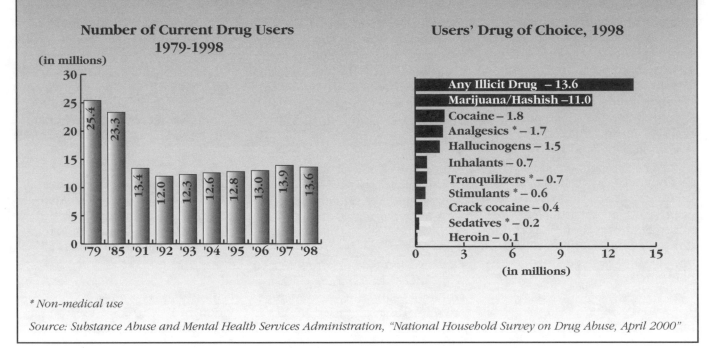

Americans' Illegal Drug Use Has Fallen

More than 13.6 million people, or 6.2 percent of the U.S. population over age 12, used illegal drugs regularly in 1998 (graph at left). Drug use peaked at 25.4 million Americans in 1979 but has remained steady since 1996. The drug of choice for most Americans is marijuana (graph at right).

Number of Current Drug Users 1979-1998
(in millions)

'79	25.4
'85	23.3
'91	13.4
'92	12.0
'93	12.3
'94	12.6
'95	12.8
'96	13.0
'97	13.9
'98	13.6

Users' Drug of Choice, 1998 (in millions)

Any Illicit Drug	13.6
Marijuana/Hashish	11.0
Cocaine	1.8
Analgesics *	1.7
Hallucinogens	1.5
Inhalants	0.7
Tranquilizers *	0.7
Stimulants *	0.6
Crack cocaine	0.4
Sedatives *	0.2
Heroin	0.1

* Non-medical use

Source: Substance Abuse and Mental Health Services Administration, "National Household Survey on Drug Abuse, April 2000"

ries became addicted to opiates. Addiction spread beyond the military with the sale of cough medicines, tonics and other remedies containing opium or cocaine — initially a key ingredient of Coca-Cola. Among the addicted population were middle-class women who self-medicated with narcotics-laced patent medicines. By 1900, there were some 250,000 opiate addicts in the United States. [21]

Reports of adverse reactions to patent medicines fueled public pressure for regulation. Congress responded in 1906 with the Pure Food and Drug Act, which required manufacturers to list ingredients on product labels. Fears about narcotics use, compounded by racial bias, grew with the rapid influx of opium-smoking Chinese railroad laborers in California. Anti-opiate sentiment prompted the United States to help draft and join the 1912 Hague Opium Convention, the first international agreement to regulate the production and distribution of opium.

In 1914, Congress complied with the convention by passing the Harrison Narcotic Act, which regulated the production and sale of opium as well as cocaine. Later amendments to the nation's first drug law prohibited the production and importation of heroin.

The 1937 Marijuana Tax Act extended the drug ban to include marijuana, whose use among Mexican immigrants in the Southwest had sparked the same kind of racially motivated concern about narcotics use earlier targeted at Chinese immigrants and at African-Americans, who were said to commit crimes while high on cocaine.

Another focus of regulation was alcohol, far more commonly consumed than any other mind-altering substance. In 1919, Congress adopted the 18th Amendment barring the production, sale and consumption of alcohol. But prohibiting such a popular substance proved futile. Bootleg alcohol production was widespread, and although alcohol consumption fell, the decline was accompanied by the rapid rise in crime associated with the struggle over control of alcohol distribution. Congress finally repealed the 18th Amendment in 1933, leaving it to the states to regulate alcohol as they saw fit.

The bans on opiates, cocaine and marijuana of the early 1900s formed the foundation of U.S. drug policy. By treating use of these drugs as a criminal offense rather than a public health problem, these early laws also established the emphasis on law enforcement rather than treatment that persists today.

Nixon's Shift

In the 1960s, drug-use patterns changed dramatically. Pot-smoking students and other protesters against U.S. involvement in Vietnam popularized the consumption of marijuana. At the same time, thousands of Vietnam War veterans, introduced during the conflict to heroin produced in the Golden Triangle — Burma, Laos and Thailand — returned addicted, further raising demand for banned substances.

Upon taking office in 1969, President Richard M. Nixon shifted the focus of drug policy from law enforcement to demand reduction. In 1971, he created the Special Action Office of Drug Abuse Prevention to coordinate all aspects of his drug program, including prevention efforts, treatment and rehabilitation of drug abusers and research into addiction.

Another agency, the National Institute of Drug Abuse (NIDA), was set up in 1973 to oversee federal prevention and treatment programs. During the 1970s, federal spending on drug programs expanded from $3 billion from

1970-75 to $5.2 billion from 1976-81. During the first half of the decade, two-thirds of the drug budget went to demand-reduction efforts.

For the rest of the 1970s, Nixon's successors — Presidents Gerald R. Ford (1974-77) and Jimmy Carter (1977-81) — dedicated nearly half

South America supplies most of the cocaine and heroin entering the United States. A farmer in Colombia (top) spreads a load of partially processed cocaine base to dry in the sun. Bolivian authorities burn 20 tons of illegal coca leafs confiscated from growers (bottom).

the budget to prevention and treatment. Efforts to disrupt the supply of drugs focused on arresting traffick-

ers, not users, who were encouraged to seek treatment. To reinforce efforts to reduce demand at home, programs to disrupt the importation of marijuana and heroin, the most commonly used drugs at the time, were carried out in cooperation with source-country governments, especially Mexico and Turkey. [22]

The demand-based drug policy that prevailed for most of the 1970s came at a time of relative tolerance of drug use. The drug culture of the period was so pervasive that six states — Oregon, Alaska, California, Colorado, Maine and Ohio — decriminalized marijuana. Even Robert Dupont, the top drug official during the Nixon and Ford administrations, declared his support for decriminalization.

Reagan's War

America's flirtation with decriminalization soon came to an abrupt halt. Parent groups began calling for government help in curbing pot smoking among teenagers, and state decriminalization laws were quickly overturned. Fulfilling his anti-crime campaign promises, President Ronald Reagan (1981-89) declared an all-out "war on drugs" soon after taking office. He overturned the demand-based focus of drug strategy that had prevailed in the 1970s and reverted to the earlier emphasis on

Spending Focuses on Law Enforcement

Nearly half of the $18.5 billion the federal government will spend this year on the drug war will support domestic law-enforcement efforts. Treatment and prevention programs will receive $6 billion, or 33 percent.

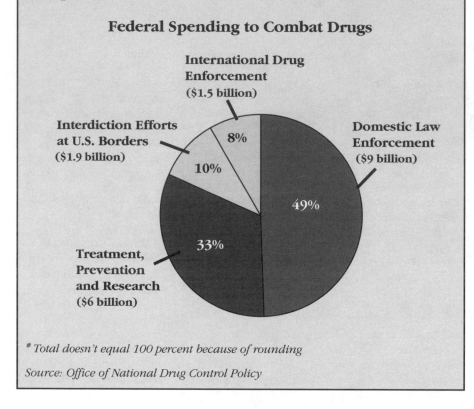

Federal Spending to Combat Drugs

International Drug Enforcement ($1.5 billion) — 8%

Interdiction Efforts at U.S. Borders ($1.9 billion) — 10%

Domestic Law Enforcement ($9 billion) — 49%

Treatment, Prevention and Research ($6 billion) — 33%

* *Total doesn't equal 100 percent because of rounding*

Source: Office of National Drug Control Policy

law enforcement.

Fully 80 percent of the $1.3 billion 1982 drug budget was earmarked for programs intended to reduce the supply of banned substances, largely through interdiction at U.S. borders. Reagan's drug policy downplayed earlier efforts to curtail drug production overseas as well as reduce demand for drugs through treatment.

By 1987, the Reagan administration had more than doubled federal spending for drug control, from $800 million in 1981 to $1.9 billion. About 90 percent of that increase went to law enforcement. Over the same period, funding for drug prevention, education and treatment was slightly reduced, from $404 million to $338

million. The Reagan administration further weakened federal leadership in drug prevention and treatment by shifting funding for these efforts to the states through block grants, which gave the states discretion in apportioning the funds to mental-health services as well as alcohol- and drug-abuse programs. NIDA's role was limited mainly to research.

As a result of these changes, treatment was often inaccessible to addicts who could not afford private care. By 1987, publicly funded treatment was available for less than 4 percent of the estimated 6.5 million drug users in need of help. Despite the Reagan administration's vocal support for prevention and educa-

tion, exemplified by first lady Nancy Reagan's highly visible "Just Say No" campaign, only about 1 percent of federal funding for drug programs went to such efforts.

Cocaine Interdiction

The early 1980s saw a significant rise in the use of cocaine, most of which came from the Andean countries of Bolivia, Peru and Colombia and was smuggled into southern Florida aboard small planes and boats. Then-Vice President George Bush chaired the South Florida Task Force of the National Narcotic Border Interdiction System, an interagency group that included officials from the U.S. Customs Service, the Coast Guard, the Drug Enforcement Administration (DEA) and the Justice and Treasury departments.

But interdiction failed to accomplish its goal; throughout the 1980s, supplies of cocaine were so plentiful that the wholesale price of a kilogram sold in Miami plummeted from $60,000 to less than $10,000. Cocaine's appeal stemmed in part from the Reagan administration's emphasis on interdiction, which had made it harder for traffickers to smuggle marijuana across borders. Increasingly, they turned to cocaine, which in its powder form was far more potent and less bulky than marijuana. As cocaine prices fell, use of the drug rose, especially after the introduction of crack, the cheap, smokable form of the drug. Crack's hold on minority neighborhoods across the country resulted in an explosion of violence as dealers fought over the lucrative crack market.

Mounting evidence that the focus on interdiction was failing to curtail drug use prompted Congress to strengthen U.S. drug policy. The

1986 Anti-Drug Abuse Act provided more than $1.7 billion in new funds, bringing the total anti-drug budget to $3.9 billion. Even though drug supply programs continued to receive three-quarters of the funds, the law more than doubled funding for demand reduction, including a tenfold increase for prevention and education efforts. Reagan publicly welcomed the funding increase, calling for a "national crusade" against drugs, but he subsequently tried to reduce most of the prevention and education funds and all the funding increase for treatment.

Although Congress restored most of the funds targeted for cuts by the Reagan administration, public criticism of drug policy led Congress to pass another Anti Drug Abuse Act in 1988. The new law increased funding for demand reduction and created the Office of National Drug Policy Control, headed by a Cabinet-level official.

President George Bush tapped William Bennett, an outspoken conservative who had served as Education secretary, as the new office's first director, or so-called drug czar. The new law also established harsher penalties for traffickers, including the death penalty for anyone convicted of murder while dealing in drugs. The law called for penalties of up to $10,000 for possession of small amounts of banned substances and authorized courts to deny school loans and other federal benefits to users and dealers alike.

Clinton's Policy

B ill Clinton gave hope to critics of the war on drugs who supported a new strategy based on prevention and greater access to treatment for addicts. [23] Not only was he the first Democrat to occupy the White House in 12 years, but he also had campaigned on a promise to offer addicts treatment on demand. His first drug czar, former New York Police Commissioner Lee Brown, disdained

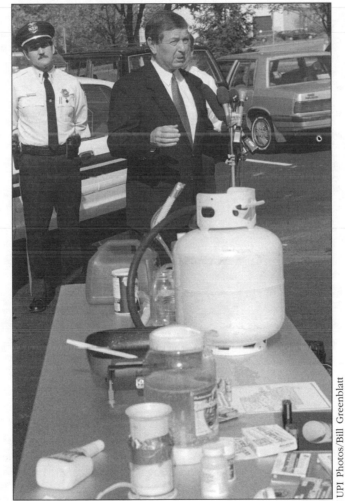

U.S. Sen. John Ashcroft, R-Mo., examines seized equipment used to manufacture methamphetamines. He recently proposed $500,000 in federal funds to root out clandestine meth labs in Missouri's Mark Twain National Forest.

his very title and pledged to reduce the number of people on treatment-center waiting lists across the country — some 200,000 addicts — at the beginning of his term in 1993.

Clinton initially proposed a 9 percent increase in federal drug spending, to $13.2 billion, including an increase for treatment and a cut in interdiction. But new statistics showing the first rise in marijuana use in 14 years, coupled with public support of stricter anti-crime measures, prompted him to emphasize law enforcement. In his 1994 State of the Union address, Clinton reiterated a campaign pledge to put 100,000 new police officers on the streets and called for a new "three-strikes-and-you're-out" law requiring incarceration of three-time felons.

With little support from the White House or Congress for his treatment-based drug strategy, Brown resigned in December 1995. By then, only a third of the drug budget was going to treatment and prevention, the same proportion as in the Bush administration.

To replace Brown, Clinton picked McCaffrey, a four-star general who had distinguished himself in Vietnam and the Persian Gulf War and later commanded U.S. forces in Latin America, including the Pentagon's drug-eradication efforts in Bolivia and Peru. Like his predecessor, McCaffrey has rejected the military connotations of the war on drugs and speaks of the drug problem as a "cancer" requiring greater efforts to reduce demand for drugs at home. But he also

Teens Using More Ecstasy, Cocaine and Heroin

Recent surveys of drug use in the United States send an ambiguous message about the drug war's impact. "Our drug-control strategy is working," says White House "drug czar" Barry R. McCaffrey, director of the Office of National Drug Control Policy. "Drug use in America actually is going down."

But while overall consumption of illicit drugs has leveled off in the last few years after rising in the early 1990s, cocaine and marijuana use by high school students is rising. The Centers for Disease Control and Prevention (CDC) in Atlanta reported that 27 percent of high school students were current users of marijuana in 1999, nearly double the percentage (15 percent) reported in 1991. Cocaine use rose at a similar rate. Four percent of students reported current cocaine use, up from 1.7 percent in 1991, while nearly 10 percent said they had used cocaine at some point in their lives, up from 6 percent in 1991. [1]

Policy-makers are particularly alarmed by a recent increase in teenagers' consumption of heroin. Once largely limited to hard-core junkies in major cities, heroin today is showing up in middle-class suburbs. Since Colombian drug lords began cultivating opium poppies and producing heroin on a massive scale in the early 1990s, larger amounts of the highly addictive drug have entered the United States.

Purity levels of heroin also have increased, enabling users to get high just by sniffing small amounts of the drug, rather than injecting it. Despite the high purity, the average street price for heroin has plummeted, from $3.90 per milligram in 1980 to 80 cents in 1999. [2]

According to McCaffrey's office, the number of heroin addicts also has doubled since 1992. [3] At the same time, the average age of first-time heroin use is falling — from 26 in 1991 to 17 in 1997.

"These stories are becoming all too familiar across America," said Sen. Charles E. Grassley, R-Iowa. "They shatter the stereotype that heroin is just an inner-city drug. These are white-collar professionals and kids who think they are safe by snorting or smoking heroin instead of injecting it. That assumption is dead wrong. Treatment professionals say there is a growing number of kids showing up at suburban treatment centers addicted, or dead in suburban hospitals from overdoses." [4]

Another drug that is enjoying a rise in popularity is Ecstasy, or MDMA (3,4 methylenedioxy methamphetamine), a synthetic chemical that produces a high without the hangover and physical craving that accompany the use of many other drugs. Popular among teenagers and young adults at all-night "rave" parties, Ecstasy goes for about $15 to $25 per pill, and a single pill can sustain a high for hours. By the time they graduate from high school, one teenager in 15 will have used Ecstasy, up from one in 25 just two years ago. [5]

Alarmed by the rise in Ecstasy use, Grassley and Sen. Bob Graham, D-Fla., introduced in May the Ecstasy Anti-Proliferation Act, which would stiffen the federal sentencing guidelines for possession or trafficking in the drug.

The lawmakers' concerns about recent drug trends do not appear to be shared by the general public, however. Sixty percent of respondents to a September 1999 Gallup Poll called drug abuse a "serious problem," down from 63 percent four years earlier. Only 30 percent called it a "crisis," down marginally from 31 percent in 1995. Thirty-eight percent said it was a serious problem in their neighborhoods and schools, down from 44 percent. Eighty-three percent said drugs had not been a cause of trouble in their families, down slightly from 81 percent in 1995. [6]

White House drug policy Director Barry McCaffrey calls Spider-Man an ally in the war against drugs. Marvel comics last year unveiled a series of comics that saturated young readers with anti-drug themes.

AFP Photo/Joyce Naltchayan

---

[1] Centers for Disease Control and Prevention, "Youth Risk Behavior Surveillance — United States, 1999," *Morbidity and Mortality Weekly Report*, June 9, 2000.

[2] U.S. Department of Justice, Drug Enforcement Administration, www.usdoj.gov/dea.

[3] See Annie Gowen, "Heroin Takes Deadly Hold in Md. County," *The Washington Post*, June 18, 2000.

[4] Press release, May 9, 2000.

[5] University of Michigan, Institute for Social Research, "Monitoring the Future," Dec. 17, 1999.

[6] Data posted by the Gallup Organization at www.gallup.com.

has overseen a renewed emphasis on interdiction, especially along the U.S.-Mexican border, the entry point for much of the heroin and cocaine consumed in the United States. ∎

Aid for Colombia

The Clinton administration's most recent drug strategy, released in April, lays out a series of policy goals that appear to be evenly spread between law enforcement and treatment. The first three goals are the prevention of drug use among young people, increasing drug-treatment programs in prison and making treatment available to all who need it. Only the last two goals concern law enforcement and interdiction — stopping the flow of drugs into the United States and helping other countries fight criminal drug organizations. [24]

Interdiction has been in the spotlight in recent months as Congress debated Clinton's "Plan Colombia," a controversial, $1.3 billion aid package that would be used to equip and train Colombian armed forces to combat cocaine and heroin production. Clinton signed the measure, included in an $11.2 billion emergency-spending bill, on July 14.

Critics say that sending aid to Colombia is a futile gesture. "It's just amazing that we're sending military resources into this four-decade-old civil war, where all three sides — the government, the right wing and the left wing — are involved in drug

dealing," says Zeese of Common Sense for Drug Policy. "We're just picking one side. We don't know what we're getting into, what the goal is or how to get out, which are key goals in any military operation. We're just going in because it's the drug war, and it's a big mistake."

Moreover, critics doubt that the Colombia aid package will have the

> "Our purpose is not to take sides in a civil war, but to stand behind the only elected democratic government of Colombia and get a reduction in the explosive rate of growth of cocaine and heroin production in Colombia."
>
> — *Barry R. McCaffrey, Director, Office of National Drug Control Policy*

desired impact on drug use in the United States. "If we're sending money to Colombia, it had better be for Colombia because it's not going to do anything for us," Kleiman says. "In fact, nothing we do in Colombia will change the number of cocaine addicts in the United States by even 1 percent."

Conversely, Kleiman says that subjecting parolees to drug tests would help both countries fight drug abuse. "If we introduced coerced abstinence and shrank the cocaine market by 40 percent, that would be a big help to Colombia," he says "and $1.3 billion a year is about a third of

what we would need to do it."

McCaffrey stands firmly behind the aid package. "Colombia is in trouble," he says. "Our purpose is not to take sides in a civil war, but to stand behind the only elected democratic government of Colombia and get a reduction in the explosive rate of growth of cocaine and heroin production in Colombia."

He points to the alarming rise in heroin production in Colombia at the same time that it continues to be the leading source of cocaine sold in the United States. "Ten years ago, Colombian heroin production was literally at zero, and today probably more than 6 metric tons of heroin come from there each year," he says. "They're in the midst of a gigantic, violent, internal struggle fueled by heroin and cocaine production."

McCaffrey's Approach

The other main criticism of current policy is that federal support of drug-prevention and treatment programs is out of balance. "Obviously, we need law enforcement because a lot of drug users are in the criminal-justice system," says Gale Saler, deputy executive director of Second Genesis. "But the amounts we're spending on drug efforts seem way out of kilter when you consider the effectiveness of programs where most of the money is spent. It we could snap our fingers and all of a sudden

Critics Say the War on Drugs . . .

Critics of the war on drugs complain that many drug policies unfairly target certain groups of people. The most commonly cited example is mandatory-minimum sentences for drug offenders, which critics contend violate African-Americans' civil rights.

A recent report by Human Rights Watch, a New York-based watchdog group, found that 482 of every 100,000 black Americans are in prison for a drug crime, compared with just 36 of every 100,000 white men.[1] But blacks make up only 13 percent of the U.S. population.

"We have an incredibly racist sentencing policy," says Kevin B. Zeese, president of Common Sense for Drug Policy, an advocacy group in Washington, D.C. "If you look at the incarceration of drug offenders through a racial prism, you'll see that the Ku Klux Klan couldn't come up with a policy more damaging to the black community than the drug war."

For instance, one out of every two young African-American males in Washington, D.C., is either in jail or on probation, Zeese says. "How do you expect families, economies or careers to develop in this kind of environment?" he asks.

One reason for the racial disparity in drug sentencing is that the criminal-justice system has meted out longer sentences to those found guilty of trafficking in crack cocaine, the smokable form of the drug whose use is largely restricted to African-Americans. Penalties handed down for powder cocaine, which is associated primarily with middle-class white users, generally have been lighter.

"I have had to look the parents of these young men in the eyes and explain to them that 50 grams of crack translates into a mandatory-minimum sentence of 10 years for their child, and that as little as 5 grams of crack translates into a mandatory minimum of five years," said William B. Moffitt, a criminal lawyer who often represents young, black drug offenders. "I have also looked into the eyes of those parents when I explained to them that this rich, mostly white society has decided that with respect to rich, white people's powdered cocaine, one would have to be involved with 100 times those amounts to get [equivalent] sentences."[2]

Drug-testing practices also have raised questions about civil liberties. During the 1980s, a number of governmental jurisdictions and private employers tried to crack down on drug use by subjecting people with no history of drug offenses to mandatory, random drug testing. After finding that drug testing did little to improve productivity, however, many businesses later dropped their

New York state levies mandatory sentences of 15 years to life for selling small amounts of cocaine (above) and heroin. Critics say the federal Omnibus Anti-Drug Abuse Act of 1988, which sets mandatory minimums for possession of crack cocaine, discriminates against African-Americans, the main users of crack.

Corbis Images

---

stop all drugs at the border, we'd still have a drug problem in this country. We grow our own marijuana, and we produce methamphetamine and pharmaceutical drugs. People with this disease are going to use something until they get high. We need to focus on addiction."

McCaffrey defends the administration's budget priorities. "Drug-treatment dollars have gone up by 34 percent over five budget years," he says. "That's unarguable."

In addition, McCaffrey says the administration has helped make drug treatment available by providing substance-abuse and mental-health coverage to federal workers, to take effect in October. "If you're an oncology patient and have an associated nutrition problem, the hospital will treat you as a holistic challenge," he says. "We want the same thing for drug addiction and mental health. By the way, we'll save a lot of money if we do that. If we treat your sub-stance-abuse problem, we won't then subsequently have to treat you for a quarter-of-a-million-dollar problem because you're HIV-infected or treat you as a traffic-accident victim."

Rosenthal of Phoenix House calls McCaffrey "a really first-rate professional" who has "made real progress," but he says the drug czar cannot ensure broader access to treatment without stronger support by the president. "A Cabinet officer cannot outrun his president," he says. "The public does not

. . . Takes a Toll on Civil Rights

programs. By 1990, almost half the companies with fewer than 50 employees that had introduced drug testing in the '80s had abandoned the practice. [3]

More recently, drug testing has come under judicial review. The Supreme Court upheld federal drug-testing programs in a pair of decisions in 1989 — one involving testing of railway workers after accidents, the other involving mandatory testing of customs officials involved in drug interdiction. Six years later, the court also upheld a local Oregon school board's policy of random drug testing of high school athletes. But in 1997, the court ruled in a Georgia case that states could not force political candidates to be tested for drugs. On June 30, the court overturned a Louisiana law requiring its elected officials to undergo such tests. The law had been challenged as a violation of the Fourth Amendment protection against illegal search and seizure.

The court has three drug-related cases scheduled for argument and decision in its coming term, which opens on the first Monday in October. In one case, the city of Indianapolis is seeking to reinstate a practice — barred by a federal appeals court — of using drug-sniffing dogs at roadblocks set up to catch drunken drivers. In a second case, the court will decide whether a public hospital in Charleston, S.C., conducted unconstitutional searches by testing pregnant women's urine for drugs to report illegal drug use to police. And in the third case, a coal company in Charleston, W.Va., is challenging an arbitrator's decision to reinstate a truck driver who was fired after twice testing positive for marijuana.

Some recent drug-policy proposals also have come under attack. One is a bill introduced by Sen. Bob Graham, D Fla., to combat the sale and use of Ecstasy (MDMA) that would make it a felony to disseminate information about the production of any illegal drug. "This bill is a clear infringement of the First Amendment," said Keith Stroup,

executive director of NORML, a Washington group that supports the decriminalization of marijuana. "It would make it a 10-year felony for someone to help a seriously ill patient cultivate marijuana for medicine, even in those states in which medical marijuana is legal under state law. This is just the latest example of the excesses of the war on drugs." [4]

An innovative drug-policy proposal that has come under scrutiny for potential violations of basic rights would require prisoners to undergo drug testing as a condition for release on parole. Known as "coerced abstinence," the measure recently won the endorsement of Vice President Al Gore, the Democratic candidate in this fall's presidential election. Some critics charge that coerced abstinence would violate parolees' constitutional rights. But supporters defend the idea as a way to reduce prison overcrowding while requiring drug offenders to stay clean.

"If you think that everybody has a constitutional right to use cocaine, then this is a problem," says Mark Kleiman, a professor of policy studies at the University of California, Los Angeles, who strongly endorses coerced abstinence. "I strongly object to workplace and school drug testing, especially on Fourth Amendment grounds. But here we're talking about people on probation and parole. They don't have any constitutional right not to be searched to see whether they're complying with their probation and parole conditions."

---

[1] Human Rights Watch, "Punishment and Prejudice: Racial Disparities in the War on Drugs," May 2000.

[2] Moffitt testified May 10, 2000, before the House Government Reform Subcommittee on Criminal Justice, Drug Policy and Human Resources.

[3] Bureau of Labor Statistics, "Anti-Drug Programs in the Workplace: Are They Here to Stay?" *Monthly Labor Review*, April 1991.

[4] From a statement dated June 8, 2000.

---

really support drug-abuse treatment. In an issue that is basically unpopular politically such as this, interest has to be driven from the top down, and that has not been done sufficiently."

State Initiatives

M ost recent innovations in drug policy have taken place at the

state level. "The last place to look for change is Washington, D.C.," says Nadelmann of the Lindesmith Center, which has helped to organize drug-policy reform ballot initiatives around the country.

"Congress has had so little going on of any serious interest in recent years that it's mostly become a place to read tea leaves and open up some debates," Nadelmann says. "A lot more interesting things are happening in the state legislatures."

The use of voter initiatives as a vehicle for drug-policy reform took off in 1996, when California voters approved Proposition 215 legalizing the use of marijuana for medical purposes. The same year, Arizona voters approved a similar initiative, whose final implementation will be put to a vote this fall.

In 1998, Alaska, Oregon, Washington, Colorado, Nevada and the District of Columbia followed suit. Initiatives took immediate effect in the first

At Issue:

Are mandatory-minimum sentences for drug crimes fair?

GEORGE ALLEN
Former Republican governor of Virginia

FROM TESTIMONY BEFORE THE HOUSE GOVERNMENT REFORM SUBCOMMITTEE ON CRIMINAL JUSTICE, DRUG POLICY AND HUMAN RESOURCES, MAY 11, 2000

*m*andatory-minimum sentences reflect Americans' sense of outrage for certain crimes. . . . And drugs breed so much crime. . . .

One of government's most fundamental responsibilities is to protect the safety of law-abiding citizens. Our nation's crime and drug problems warrant an all-out effort on the federal, state and local level to prevent the devastating effects drugs have on our children and on our society. . . Congress should take the lead. . . .

When I left the House of Representatives in 1993, violent crime was on the rise in Virginia . . . So we took action. We stopped listening to the criminal apologists, and we abolished the lenient, dishonest parole system and established truth in sentencing. We reformed the blissful juvenile-justice system. We took those violent criminals who were selling drugs and using guns to commit crimes, and we sent them a clear message: In Virginia, if you commit the crime, you will do the time — a lot of time.

There was nothing complicated about our approach, just good, old common sense. If the violent criminals are locked up . . . they can't come back into our neighborhoods to prey on new victims. And common sense works. Overall crime is down 24 percent, and violent crime is down 17 percent — the lowest in a decade.

One of the chief causes of violent crime is the scourge of illegal drugs. Drugs destroy young lives, breed crime and tear families apart. We need to make sure we send a message loud and clear to those who would dare to bring drugs into our schools or sell drugs to our children: We are serious about keeping you and the poison you peddle out of our neighborhoods and away from our children. . . .

A recent Office for Civil Rights report . . . cited disparities in federal sentencing guidelines for powder and crack cocaine as discriminating against minorities. I would encourage Congress to fix this — not by making it easier for the crack dealers, but by adopting tougher penalties for powder cocaine, Ecstasy and methamphetamines.

I hold no sympathy and no compassion for those parasites who risk the lives of our children. We should punish these pushers as severely as we would if they forced our children to eat rat poison, because the results can easily be the same.

WADE HENDERSON
Executive director, Leadership Conference on Civil Rights

FROM TESTIMONY BEFORE THE HOUSE GOVERNMENT REFORM SUBCOMMITTEE ON CRIMINAL JUSTICE, DRUG POLICY AND HUMAN RESOURCES, MAY 11, 2000

*t*he mandatory-sentencing laws enacted by Congress and many state legislatures in the mid-1980s have led to racial injustice. These laws establish a minimum penalty that the judge must impose if the defendant is convicted of particular provisions of the criminal code and deprive judges of their traditional discretion to tailor a sentence based on the culpability of the defendant and the seriousness of the crime.

Mandatory-minimum sentencing laws are not truly mandatory because they provide opportunities for prosecutors to grant exceptions. . . . Prosecutors can choose to charge particular defendants with offenses that do not carry mandatory penalties, or they can agree to a plea agreement in which the charges carrying mandatory penalties will be dismissed. And under federal law, only the prosecutor may grant a departure from mandatory penalties by certifying that the defendant has provided "substantial assistance" to law enforcement.

Mandatory minimums, therefore, embody a dangerous combination. They provide the government with unreviewable discretion to target particular defendants or classes of defendants for harsh punishment. But they provide no opportunity for judges to exercise discretion on behalf of defendants in order to check prosecutorial discretion. . . .

[S]ome civil rights supporters originally supported mandatory sentencing as an antidote to racial disparities in sentencing. But the evidence is clear that minorities fare worse under mandatory-sentencing laws than they did under a system of judicial discretion. By depriving judges of the ultimate authority to impose fair sentences, mandatory-sentencing laws put sentencing on autopilot. . . .

The crack/powder [cocaine] sentencing disparity, combined with the almost-exclusive federal targeting of blacks and Hispanics for crack-related crimes, means that minorities in general serve longer sentences for similar drug crimes than do whites. . . .

Although sometimes conceived as a means to combat unwarranted racial disparity in sentencing, mandatory-minimum sentencing laws are, in fact, engines of racial injustice. They have filled America's prisons to the rafters with thousands of nonviolent minority offenders. The repeal of these laws would be a significant step toward restoring balance and fairness to a criminal-justice system that has increasingly come to view incarceration as an end in itself.

At Issue:

Are efforts to curtail drug production abroad worth the investment?

PRESIDENT BILL CLINTON

FROM REMARKS TO THE COUNCIL OF THE AMERICAS, 30th WASHINGTON CONFERENCE, MAY 2, 2000

*t*oday we are called upon to stand for democracy under attack in Colombia. Drug trafficking, civil conflict, economic stagnation [have] combined . . . explosively in Colombia to feed violence, undercut honest enterprise in favor of corruption and undermine public confidence in democracy. Colombia's drug traffickers directly threaten America's security. But first, they threaten Colombia's future.

In the United States, 90 percent of the cocaine and two-thirds of the heroin seized on our streets comes from or through Colombia. Fifty-two thousand Americans die every year from drugs, about as many as died in the wars in Vietnam and Korea. It costs us more than $110 billion a year in crime, accidents, property damage and lost productivity. . . .

President [Andres] Pastrana came to office with a record of risking his own life to take on drug traffic. . . . Once in office, he worked with experts in Colombia and elsewhere to put together Plan Colombia. It's a comprehensive plan to seek peace, fight drugs, build the economy and deepen democracy. The plan costs about $7.5 billion. It includes contributions from . . . Colombia, international financial institutions and other donors.

. . . I've asked our Congress to give it $1.6 billion over two years. That will be a tenfold increase in our U.S. assistance to promote good government, judicial reform, human-rights protection and economic development. It will also enable Colombia's counter-drug program to inflict serious damage on the rapidly expanding drug production activity in areas now dominated by guerrillas or paramilitary groups.

We know this approach can succeed. Over the last five years working with the governments of Peru and Bolivia, we have reduced coca cultivation by more than 50 percent in those countries [and] reduced overall cocaine production in the region by 18 percent. Drug traffickers . . . unfortunately now are consolidating operations in Colombia. But we have an historic opportunity and an historic responsibility to do serious and lasting damage to the international drug trade. . . .

We need to help train and equip Colombia's counter-drug battalion, enhance its interdiction efforts, provide intelligence and logistic supports to the counter-drug mission, including force protection. They need this support. We can provide it, and we ought to provide it. We must not stand by and allow a democracy . . . [to] be undermined and overwhelmed by those who literally are willing to tear the country apart for their own agenda. And make no mistake about it; if the oldest democracy in South America can be torn down, so can others.

SEN. SLADE GORTON, R-WASH.

FROM A SENATE FLOOR DEBATE ABOUT ANTI-DRUG AID FOR COLOMBIA, JUNE 21, 2000

i grant you there is a limitation of no more than 250 American military personnel to accompany the equipment we will be sending to Colombia under the provisions of this bill. But isn't that . . . the way we begin an adventure of this nature, with pious declarations that our participation is limited [that] we are just helping some other country solve its own problems and challenges in some military fashion?

. . . This is a shift from supporting a police force in a friendly country to supporting an army engaged in a civil war, a civil war that it has not been winning, a civil war in which the other side is very well financed — indirectly, at least, in large part by Americans who purchase cocaine — but without the slightest real control over the use of the equipment that the Colombian army will be receiving pursuant to this bill.

How long will it be until we read . . . about some of this equipment showing up in the hands of the rebels? . . . That is what has constantly happened in the past in almost each of the other adventures of this nature in which the United States has found itself.

But my fundamental point . . . is that we are voting money first and asking for the justification later. We should get the justification first and make the determination as to whether to spend this . . . money or how much we ought to spend after we know exactly what the plan is and how the plan promises to lead to any kind of successful conclusion. . . .

Is this the single best way in which to spend the almost three-quarters of a billion dollars that is the subject of this amendment, even on drug interdiction, much less on any other potential program in the United States? Will it help Colombia? Does it really address drug problems in the United States? Is there an exit strategy?

We know there was not any in Bosnia. We know there is not any in Kosovo. And we sure are not told what it is here. . . .

We are asked to engage in another civil war . . . with a major commitment to equipment and training for the Colombian army. Very rarely does this kind of commitment get made without escalating into something more, in money or in personnel or the like. Very rarely are insurgencies such as the one in Colombia successfully met when those insurgencies have as large a source of monetary support as this one seems to have.

three states; the Colorado vote was later nullified following allegations that insufficient signatures had been collected to allow the issue to go on the ballot, while Nevada's Constitution requires a second vote for an initiative to take effect. Medical marijuana will be on ballots again this fall in Colorado and Nevada.

In Washington, Congress forbade District election officials to even tally the medical marijuana vote, citing language in the D.C. appropriations bill barring the use of federal funds to conduct any ballot initiative. After a federal judge overturned the vote-count ban in September, it was found that 69 percent of the electorate had approved the initiative. Last fall, voters in Maine also approved a medical marijuana initiative.

Another initiative, which will be on ballots in Massachusetts, Utah and Oregon, would make it harder for police and prosecutors to seize the property of drug offenders, much as the Civil Asset Forfeiture Reform Act, enacted in April, does at the federal level.

"If police or prosecutors are going to seize people's property, they need to meet a higher burden of proof than they have so far," says Nadelmann, who supports the initiatives. "All around the country, you hear horror stories of people who are totally innocent losing their property and not having the resources to get it back." The state initiatives go beyond the federal model, however, by also requiring that proceeds from the sale of seized property not stay in the hands of law-enforcement

agencies, but be transferred to drug-treatment programs.

Many experts are anticipating the results of a new initiative that will appear on the ballot in California this fall that could have a significant influence on drug policy. The Substance Abuse and Crime Prevention Act would require that anyone who is arrested for simple possession of an illegal substance and who has no record of criminal violence be sent to treatment instead of prison.

A state trooper mows down a marijuana patch in northwestern Missouri. The plant grows wild in many Midwestern states, a holdover from turn-of-the-century days when farmers legally grew hemp as a cash crop.

"The key is that you cannot send these people to jail," Nadelmann says. "The whole idea is that drugs should be treated more as a medical or a public health problem rather than a criminal-justice one." He cites estimates that the initiative would result in as many as 25,000 fewer people being incarcerated on drug-possession charges in the first year and a savings of $12.5 billion over the next five years in prison-building and other costs.

McCaffrey opposes this type of reform because, he says, it would undermine the drug-court system the Clinton administration has carefully fostered. "With this initiative, a drug abuser can basically say, 'Hey, you've got to catch me three times with personal possession of drugs,'" McCaffrey says. "The drug-court system will be completely knocked off its pins by this."

McCaffrey says it costs between $2,000 and $8,000 to prosecute and sentence an offender in drug courts, compared with $26,000 in the traditional criminal-justice system. "But the biggest damages that you, the chronic addict, are going to cause us is if we leave you alone," he says. "If you're a compulsive heroin addict, you're committing as many as 300 felonies a year, you're stealing upwards of $65,000 a year to support your habit. So we feel that a lot of these initiatives that look so appealing on the face of it are very threatening to sensible drug policy." ∎

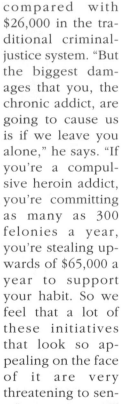

Newsmakers/Timothy Jones

OUTLOOK

Low Campaign Priority?

D rug-policy proposals are not high on the list of campaign promises being made by congressional candidates or the major candidates for the presidency. Only the Libertarian Party's Harry Browne has dealt forcefully with the issue. He has denounced the drug war and promised, if elected, to pardon everyone who is serving prison sentences for nonviolent federal drug offenses.

"The two major candidates aren't dealing with this issue at all," says Zeese of Common Sense for Drug Policy, who sees little to gain for either Vice President Al Gore or Gov. George W. Bush, R-Texas, to take on such a controversial subject. "Bush's base supports the right-wing, law-enforcement approach to drug policy. So where are the progressives going to go but to Gore? For that reason, Gore doesn't gain anything by taking this issue on, and Democrats are always afraid of being looked at as soft on crime."

Given this political calculus, Gore recently surprised some observers when he endorsed mandatory drug testing of all prisoners and parolees. "When inmates have easy access to drugs in prison, but no access to drug treatment and no serious program of drug testing; when inmates are sent back onto the streets unrehabilitated, unrepentant and unskilled — then they're just going to commit more crime and go right back to prison," he said in a May 2 address in Atlanta. "We have to stop that revolving door, once and for all. . . . I believe we

should make prisoners a simple deal: Before you get out of jail, you have to get clean. And if you want to stay out, then you'd better stay clean."

The University of California's Kleiman welcomes Gore's endorsement of his proposal for coerced abstinence. "Necessarily, in a campaign context, he made it sound like an idiotic, tough-guy proposal, but mostly he got it right," Kleiman says. "What's fundamentally new today is that if you take our current policy —

New Jersey state troopers load bales of cocaine and marijuana — street value more than $100 million — seized at a warehouse in Fairview, N.J., on Feb. 5.

which is really building more prisons to put more drug dealers in — nobody respectable is for that any more because it's so radically clear that we can put as many cocaine dealers in prison as we like and not change anything. I've got to regard the fact that coerced abstinence is getting talked about as a good thing."

Some drug-reform advocates are ambivalent about Gore's proposal. "Offering people real treatment can

make a real difference, and in that sense it's right," Nadelmann says. "I think Gore is looking for the politically safe language to advocate the diversion of drug offenders into treatment. But it's not the best solution.

"We know that coercion can work for some people, but we also know that no amount of coercion or incentive will work for others. We should be helping people find ways to reduce their drug use and get their lives together, even if they're not abstinent. Instead, we've set up a system where judges are increasingly empowered to apply neat, little sanctions like throwing someone in jail for two or three days, never mind the impact on their families or their employment." ■

Notes

[1] For background, see Mary H. Cooper, "War on Drugs," *The CQ Researcher*, March 19, 1993, pp. 241-264.

[2] Department of Health and Human Services, "National Household Survey on Drug Abuse: Main Findings 1998," April 2000.

[3] For background, see Sarah Glazer, "Preventing Teen Drug Use," *The CQ Researcher*, July 28, 1995, pp. 674-697.

[4] For background, see Kathy Koch, "Drug Testing," *The CQ Researcher*, Nov. 20, 1998, pp. 1001-1024.

[5] Gary E. Johnson, "Stop Arresting People for Bad Choices," *Cato Policy Report*, November/December 1999.

[6] James Q. Wilson, "A New Strategy for the War on Drugs," *The Wall Street Journal*, April 13, 2000. Wilson is a professor of public policy at Pepperdine University.

[7] See Russ Baker, "George Soros' Long

Strange Trip: A Philanthropist Defies Drug War Orthodoxy," *The Nation*, Sept. 20, 1999, pp. 32-42.

[8] For background, see Kathy Koch, "Medical Marijuana," *The CQ Researcher*, Aug. 20, 1999, pp. 705-728.

[9] See Lawrence K. Altman, "Company Developing Marijuana for Medical Uses," *The New York Times*, April 10, 2000.

[10] Department of Health and Human Services, Public Health Service, Centers for Disease Control and Prevention, "HIV/AIDS Surveillance Report," June 1999. For background, see Adriel Bettelheim, "AIDS Update," *The CQ Researcher*, Dec. 4, 1998, pp. 1049-1072.

[11] See David Murray, "Clean Needles May Be Bad Medicine," *The Wall Street Journal*, April 22, 1998.

[12] For background, see Margaret Edwards, "Mandatory Sentencing," *The CQ Researcher*, May 26, 1995, pp. 465-488.

[13] See Michael Massing, *The Fix* (1998), p. 43.

[14] For background, see David Masci, "Prison-Building Boom," *The CQ Researcher*, Sept. 17, 1999, pp. 801-824.

[15] Dita Smith, "Behind Bars," *The Washington Post*, June 3, 2000.

[16] Anne Morrison Piehl, Bert Useem and John J. DiIulio Jr., "Right-Sizing Justice: A Cost-Benefit Analysis of Imprisonment in Three States," Center for Civic Innovation, Manhattan Institute, September 1999, p. 13.

[17] The case was cited by Families Against Mandatory Minimums at www.famm.org.

[18] Masci, *op. cit.*

[19] For background, see Sarah Glazer, "Treating Addiction," *The CQ Researcher*, Jan. 6, 1995, pp. 1-24.

[20] For more information on coerced abstinence, see John Kaplan, *The Hardest Drug: Heroin and Public Policy* (1983).

[21] Unless otherwise indicated, information in this section is based on Mathea Falco, *Winning the Drug War* (1989), pp. 19-39.

[22] For background, see David Masci, "Mexico's Future," *The CQ Researcher*, Sept. 19, 1997, pp. 817-840.

[23] Information in this section is based on Massing, *op. cit.*, pp. 208-226.

[24] Office of National Drug Control Policy, "National Drug Control Strategy: 2000 Annual Report," April 4, 2000, p. iii.

FOR MORE INFORMATION

Common Sense for Drug Policy, 3220 N St., N.W., Suite 141, Washington, D.C. 20007; (703) 354-5694; www.csdp.org. This nonprofit organization encourages debate about existing drug policy and advocates alternatives such as decriminalizing marijuana.

Families Against Mandatory Minimums (FAMM), 1612 K St., N.W., Suite 1400, Washington, D.C. 20006; (202) 822-6700; www.famm.org. This national organization works to ensure equity and fairness by reforming federal and state mandatory-sentencing laws that remove judicial discretion from the sentencing process.

Lindesmith Center — Drug Policy Foundation, 925 9th Ave., New York, N.Y. 10019; (212) 548-0695; www.lindesmith.org. Founded in 1994 by financier George Soros, the newly merged organizations try to broaden and better inform the public debate on drug policy and related issues. The guiding principle of the center is harm reduction, an alternative approach to drug policy and treatment that focuses on minimizing the adverse effects of both drug use and drug prohibition.

NORML, 1001 Connecticut Ave., N.W., Suite 710, Washington, D.C. 20036; (202) 483-5500; www.norml.org. Founded in 1970, NORML is the principal national advocate for legalizing marijuana. It provides information, advocates for lower penalties for marijuana-related offenses and lobbies state and federal legislators for decriminalization.

National Institute on Drug Abuse (NIDA), 6001 Executive Blvd., Bethesda, Md. 20892-9561; (301) 443-1124; www.nida.nih.gov/NIDAHome1.html. Established in 1974 and part of the National Institutes of Health, NIDA supports more than 85 percent of the world's research on the health aspects of drug abuse and addiction.

Office of National Drug Control Policy, Old Executive Office Building, Washington, D.C. 20503; (202) 395-6700; www.whitehousedrugpolicy.gov. Headed by retired Gen. Barry R. McCaffrey, the White House drug policy office coordinates federal efforts to combat illegal drug use.

Partnership for a Drug-Free America, 405 Lexington Ave., 16th Floor, New York, N.Y. 10174; (212) 922-1560; www.drugfreeamerica.org. This nonprofit coalition of communications industry professionals provides targeted television and print media advertising to discourage drug use among teenagers and young adults.

Phoenix House Foundation, 164 W. 74th St., New York, N.Y. 10023; (212) 595-5810; www.phoenixhouse.org. Phoenix House is the nation's leading nonprofit substance-abuse service organization, providing treatment for more than 5,000 adults and adolescents.

Bibliography

Selected Sources Used

Books

Gray, Michael, *Drug Crazy: How We Got into This Mess and How We Can Get Out*, Random House, 1998.

The author examines past drug policies and concludes that the war on drugs has been a dismal failure. A tightly controlled legal drug market, he writes, would end illicit drug trafficking and the suffering that accompanies it.

Massing, Michael, *The Fix*, University of California Press, 2000.

This well-received review of U.S. drug policy by the winner of a MacArthur Fellowship concludes that the key to success in diminishing drug use depends on a greater emphasis on treatment rather than law enforcement.

Articles

Baker, Russ, "George Soros's Long Strange Trip," *The Nation*, Sept. 20, 1999, pp. 32-42.

Soros, a financier and philanthropist, supports a number of controversial causes, including reform of drug laws. His Lindesmith Center, based in New York City, helps organize voter initiatives around the country to legalize medicinal use of marijuana and adopt other drug reforms.

Collins, Larry, "Holland's Half-Baked Drug Experiment," *Foreign Affairs*, May/June 1999, pp. 82-98.

According to this account, since the Netherlands legalized marijuana in 1976, allowing pot sales in special coffee shops, the country has become "the drug capital of Europe," the center of a thriving market for illegal, synthetic drugs such as Ecstasy and amphetamines.

DiIulio, John J. Jr., "Against Mandatory Minimums," *National Review*, May 17, 1999, pp. 46-51.

A well-known conservative academic explains why he has reversed course on mandatory sentences for drug offenders. Rather than incarcerating non-violent drug users, he writes, law enforcement should target violent criminals involved in the drug trade.

Guillermoprieto, Alma, "Colombia: Violence Without End?" *The New York Review of Books*, April 27, 2000, pp. 31-39.

The $1.3 billion aid package recently signed into law by President Clinton to help Colombia combat drug production may backfire if the Colombian military fails to use the U.S. equipment to defeat the narco-guerrillas, as intended, but joins the lucrative drug trade instead.

Nadelmann, Ethan, "Addicted to Failure," *The Guardian* (London), March 29, 2000.

The author, director of the Lindesmith Center, a drug-reform advocacy group based in New York City, writes that the emphasis on law enforcement that has dominated U.S. drug policy is now coming into question as record incarceration rates have failed to disrupt the market for illegal drugs.

Reports and Studies

Biden, Sen. Joseph R. Jr., "Heroin: Increased Use, Deadly Consequences," Nov. 15, 1999.

Sen. Biden, D-Del., describes the recent rise in heroin use, especially among teens and young adults, and calls for more funding to increase the availability of anti-addiction medications and broader use of drug courts to help addicts get treatment.

Caulkins, Jonathan P., C. Peter Rydell, William L. Schwabe and James Chiesa, "Mandatory Minimum Drug Sentences: Throwing Away the Key or the Taxpayers' Money?" Rand, 1997.

This analysis of the impact of mandatory minimums on cocaine consumption concludes that they are not cost-effective in reducing cocaine use or associated criminal activities.

Human Rights Watch, "Punishment and Prejudice: Racial Disparities in the War on Drugs," May 2000.

Drug-sentencing laws unfairly target African-Americans, who comprise 62 percent of drug offenders in state prisons.

Maginnis, Robert L., "Injecting Drug Use: A 2000 Overview," Family Research Council, May 8, 2000.

A director of this conservative think tank reviews the history of needle-exchange programs and concludes that they do not merit federal support because they encourage drug use and may not slow the spread of AIDS.

Office of National Drug Control Policy, "National Drug Control Strategy: 2000 Annual Report," April 4, 2000.

Director Barry R. McCaffrey outlines his agency's goals, including prevention, treatment, interdiction and eradication programs.

7 Antitrust Policy

KENNETH JOST

It has been called the most valuable square foot of real estate in the world, and it's at the center of a bitter fight between the world's richest man and most powerful nation.

The fight heated up last month when the U.S. government and 20 states launched antitrust suits against Bill Gates' giant Microsoft Corp. At issue is control of that little piece of "real estate" — the first screen that personal computer users see when they boot up machines powered by Microsoft's ubiquitous Windows operating system.

Microsoft chairman and co-founder Gates says the icon-filled screen opens the door for computer users to vast storehouses of information and countless opportunities for enhanced productivity. But Microsoft, he says, should hold the key to that door: His company designed it, sells it and can best be relied on to continue improving it.

Government lawyers say that Windows — used in 90 percent of the world's personal computers — is essentially "the on-ramp to the information superhighway," and no single company should control it. Moreover, they say, Microsoft has abused its power through a host of allegedly anti-competitive practices to boost its business at the expense of rival firms.

The Justice Department's lawsuit, Assistant U.S. Attorney General Joel I. Klein declared on May 18, "seeks to put an end to Microsoft's unlawful campaign to eliminate competition, deter innovation and restrict consumer choice."

Two hours later, an amiable but unyielding Gates answered the charges in a news conference at the company's Redmond, Wash., headquarters. "Federal and state regulators have taken the unprecedented step of trying to intervene in America's most successful and

From *The CQ Researcher,*
June 12, 1998.

growing industry," Gates said. "This is a step backwards for America, for consumers and for the personal computer industry that is leading our nation's economy into the 21st century." [1]

The lawsuits came in the week that Microsoft was scheduled to ship the latest upgrade of its PC operating system, Windows 98, to computer manufacturers in advance of a scheduled release to customers this month.

The suits stop short of seeking to block the release of Windows 98. But they ask a federal judge in Washington, D.C., to order a major change in Microsoft's operating system. The Justice Department and the states are seeking a preliminary injunction to require all future versions of Windows that include Microsoft's Internet Explorer software for browsing the Internet also to include a competing software developed by a rival firm, the Netscape Navigator. [2]

Allowing Microsoft to "bundle" its browser with its monopoly operating system without including Netscape's, Klein told reporters, "could well cause irreversible harm to competition by letting Microsoft unlawfully achieve a second monopoly, this time in Internet browsers."

To back up its charges, the Justice Department included in its 53-page complaint seemingly damaging quotes from internal Microsoft messages and documents suggesting a conscious plan to use

its Windows monopoly to "leverage" its new browser and displace Netscape's earlier — and market-leading — product.

"Pitting browser against browser is hard since Netscape has 80 percent market share, and we have [less than] 20 percent," Microsoft Senior Vice President James Allchin was quoted as telling a colleague in January 1997. "I am convinced we have to use Windows — this is the one thing they don't have."

But Gates and other Microsoft executives depicted the proposed remedy as a punishment for the company's success and a disservice to customers. "Forcing Microsoft to include Netscape's competing software in our operating system is like requiring Coca-Cola to include three cans of Pepsi in every six-pack it sells," Gates said.

As for the internal communications quoted in the Justice Department complaints, Gates and others insisted they were taken out of context. Gates also branded as "absolutely false" the most damning allegation — that he had personally met with Netscape executives in May 1995 to divide up the market, offering to keep Microsoft out of the browser market if Netscape promised not to try to produce a rival operating system. [3]

The lawsuit immediately conjured up images of some of the country's most historic antitrust actions — from the early 20th-century suit that broke up John D. Rockefeller's Standard Oil trust to the more recent litigation that split up AT&T in the 1980s. Microsoft executives offered a less flattering comparison. They likened the suit to the Justice Department's failed antitrust suit against IBM, which lasted for 13 years before the government dropped the case in 1982 for lack of evidence.

The suit against Microsoft comes at a time of increased antitrust activity both at the Justice Department and the Federal Trade Commission (FTC).

Antitrust Activity Has Increased

In the past 10 years, the number of planned corporate mergers rose 35 percent while antitrust investigations quadrupled and cases filed more than doubled.

Premerger Notifications

	1988	1997
Received	*2,747*	*3,702*
Investigations initiated	*56*	*220*
Cases filed	*6*	*14*

Source: Justice Department, Antitrust Division

Antitrust enforcement peaked in the 1960s and early '70s, when many policy-makers viewed corporate size as an inherent economic and political problem. But antitrust laws went out of favor in Washington under President Ronald Reagan, who filled key antitrust posts with avowed advocates of big business and determined skeptics of antitrust laws except in limited circumstances.

President Clinton has not been especially vocal on antitrust issues, but his appointees — Klein and his predecessor at the Justice Department, Anne Bingaman, and Robert Pitofsky as FTC chairman — view antitrust enforcement more positively than their counterparts from the Reagan-Bush era. "It seems to be far more robust than what we had seen earlier," says E. Thomas Sullivan, dean of the University of Minnesota Law School.

"There's a revived interest," says Irwin Stelzer, director of regulatory policy studies at the American Enterprise Institute in Washington. "You've got two good people — Klein and Pitofsky — and they're doing a very good job. They're not crazy like some of the old 'big is bad' people."

The increased interest in antitrust action stems in part from a wave of corporate mergers in the United States and around the world over the past few years. The consolidations — last year's were valued at more than $1 trillion in assets — affect everything from banking and telecommunications to pharmaceuticals and office supplies. [4] *(See chart, p. 144.)*

The Justice Department and FTC have approved some of the mergers while blocking others. "It's hard to accuse the Clinton administration of being either a pushover for transactions or relentlessly hostile," says William E. Kovacic, who teaches antitrust law at George Mason University School of Law in Fairfax, Va.

Some of the biggest deals are still awaiting review, in some cases by other independent agencies. The proposed merger of Citicorp and Travelers is being reviewed by the Federal Reserve Board, while the Federal Communications Commission will study the planned acquisition of MCI Communications by British-based WorldCom Inc. Meanwhile, the Justice Department already had one major antitrust case in court before the Microsoft suit: an effort to block the merger of two giant defense contractors, Lockheed Martin and Northrup Grumman *(see p. 142).*

As Microsoft's Sept. 18 trial date approaches, here are some of the major issues being debated:

Have antitrust laws been good or bad for the economy overall?

The Supreme Court once called the nation's first antitrust law, the 1890 Sherman Act, the "Magna Carta of the free enterprise system" — in effect, a fundamental guarantee for the right of all businesses to fair competition in the marketplace. [5] In the 108 years since then, Congress has periodically reaffirmed that commitment by expanding antitrust laws to cover other business practices besides classic monopolies and cartels *(See chart, p. 132).* And the federal government has repeatedly invoked those laws to break up or control business monopolies — generally to public approval.

Some experts and advocates say the laws have served the country well by promoting and preserving competition. Others maintain that antitrust laws and antitrust enforcers have proved to be too weak to prevent anti-competitive abuses and the growth of giant corporations that wield undue economic power. But still others say that the antitrust laws have been bad for the U.S. economy, even bad for competition — punishing successful companies, protecting inefficient ones and in the end hurting rather than helping consumers.

"It's been an uneven 100 years," says Rudolph Peritz, a professor at New York Law School and author of a recent history of antitrust policy. "Antitrust enforcers and policy-makers have done better at some times and worse at others."

Peritz says the early focus of antitrust laws in breaking up monopolies like the Standard Oil and tobacco trusts established a pattern of generally preventing the creation of single-company industries. But he says the laws have been less effective in dealing with "oligopolies" — industries in which a small number of producers control the market and, according to antitrust advocates, provide less than complete competition.

The more centrist Kovacic says antitrust laws have served an important purpose by committing the federal government to free markets rather than central planning as a central economic principle. "The [Justice Department] antitrust divisions have historically been a voice for promoting private enterprise and rivalry," he says.

More concretely, Kovacic says the laws have discouraged the formation of "producer cartels" — agreements between rival firms to set prices or divide the market. But he notes that price-fixing agreements persist — citing, for example, the recent prosecution of Archer Daniels Midland Inc. that last fall cost the agriprocessing firm a then record $100 million fine for fixing prices on two products. (A price-fixing case against Ucar International, the nation's leading manufacturer of graphite electrodes, a key component in electric arc furnaces, produced a new record fine of $110 million in April.) [6]

Some conservative and libertarian antitrust experts, however, see little but negative effects from the government's use of antitrust laws. In his influential book, *The Antitrust Paradox*, published in 1978, Robert Bork complained that the antitrust laws had evolved into "rules that significantly impair both competition and the ability of the economy to produce goods and services efficiently." [7] Bork, a Yale law professor at the time and later a federal judge and unsuccessful Supreme Court nominee, was one of the leading members of the so-called "Chicago school" that advocated a more strictly economic approach to antitrust issues (*see p. 139*).

Robert Levy, a senior fellow in constitutional studies at the libertarian Cato Institute, says the overall effect of the antitrust laws has been "deleterious."

"I don't think that antitrust laws ever had any legitimate functions," Levy says, "and I don't think they have any legitimate function now given the dynamism of today's markets."

Unlike Levy, most conservatives accept the idea that antitrust laws should prohibit what one of Bork's disciples — federal Judge Frank Easterbrook Jr.— once labeled "plain-vanilla cartels and mergers to monopoly." [8] But they criticize the expansion of antitrust to two other business practices.

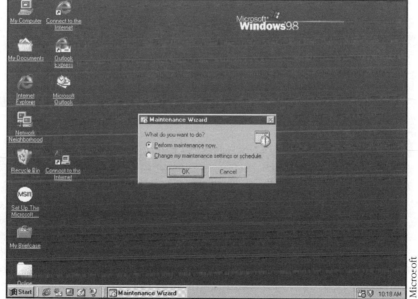

Antitrust suits against Microsoft Corp. contend that it should not require computer makers to include Internet Explorer, Microsoft's browser software, as a condition of using its Windows 98 operating system. Microsoft says Explorer is an integrated feature of Windows that can't be lopped off.

First, they say that antitrust laws should generally not apply to so-called vertical mergers between, for instance, a manufacturer and a retailer, or to vertical "restraints" — such as a restriction by a manufacturer on a dealer's ability to set prices or expand outside a specified territory. Second, they generally defend the legality of so-called "tying" arrangements that condition the sale of one product on the buyer's agreement to purchase a second product. And they believe that the antitrust laws were of-

ten enforced too rigorously, particularly in the 1950s and '60s, against so-called horizontal mergers — combinations between firms producing the same product or service. Conservatives viewed many of these mergers as likely to produce greater efficiencies without adverse effects on competition.

Some more liberal-leaning experts today agree that the Supreme Court under Chief Justice Earl Warren was too strict in disallowing any mergers that would result in increased concentration in the industry. "In retrospect, the antitrust policies of the Earl Warren era were excessive in the way they defined markets," Sullivan says.

For their part, conservatives say that the Supreme Court and lower federal courts have become more sophisticated in handling antitrust issues because of the growing influence of the Chicago school since the late 1970s.

"If the federal government wants to challenge a merger, it has to define a relevant market and then show how the concentration in that market rises to a troublesome level and show why there are barriers to entry," says John Lopatka, a professor at the University of South Carolina Law School. "And if the defendants raise the issue, the government is going to have to explain that the mergers do not generate efficiencies — that is, cost savings — all of which is a proper analysis."

But the emphasis on so-called microeconomics — the study of firm behavior — discomforts liberal antitrust experts. "Microeconomics is a

ANTITRUST POLICY

Major Federal Antitrust Laws

Sherman Act (1890) — *Prohibits any "contract, combination or conspiracy . . . in restraint of trade" (section 1) or monopolizing or attempting to monopolize interstate or foreign trade or commerce (section 2); Justice Department authorized to bring criminal cases or civil suits; criminal violations punishable by up to a year in prison and $5,000 fine; individuals may bring civil suits, with triple damages allowed.*

Clayton Antitrust Act (1914) — *Prohibits price discrimination (section 2), exclusive dealing and "tying" contracts (section 3), and stock acquisitions of other companies (section 7) where effect "may be to substantially lessen competition or tend to create a monopoly in any line of commerce."*

Federal Trade Commission Act (1914) — *Prohibits "unfair methods of competition" and "unfair or deceptive acts or practices" (section 5); creates FTC as independent agency with authority to issue cease-and-desist orders to enforce law.*

Robinson-Patman Act (1936) — *Outlaws "unjustified" price discounts that result in injury to competition (section 2(a)); buyers seeking unjustified price discounts also subject to liability (section 2(f)).*

Celler-Kefauver Act (1950) — *Strengthens Clayton Act's provision against anti-competitive mergers to cover acquisition of assets as well as stock of another company and to cover merger with firms in different line of commerce.*

Antitrust Procedures and Penalties Act (1974) — *Changes price-fixing and other violations from misdemeanors to felonies; raises maximum fines to $1 million for companies and $500,000 for individuals; increases maximum prison sentence to three years. Also requires public disclosure and judicial review of case settlements negotiated by Justice Department.*

Hart-Scott-Rodino Antitrust Improvements Act (1976) — *Requires merging companies above specified size to notify Justice Dept. and FTC before completing transaction; establishes mandatory waiting period for completing transaction or beginning joint operations.*

Source: Ernest Gellhorn and William E. Kovacic, Antitrust Law and Economics in a Nutshell *(1994).*

narrow lens that can tell us at best about one particular kind of economic power: market power," Peritz says. "But firm size reflects another kind of economic power. You can have a merger between two multibillion-dollar companies, like Nynex and Bell Atlantic, that will fly through antitrust scrutiny because they are in different 'markets,' but we all know from our experience that there [was] an increase in economic power of all sorts when those two companies merged."

Is the current wave of mergers good or bad for consumers?

When the government divided AT&T into seven regional telephone companies and a separate long-distance carrier, it hoped to be ushering in an era of wide-open competition that would improve service and lower rates. Long-distance service has become a heartily competitive market, but local telephone service remains a monopoly. Now, some of the so-called Baby Bells are getting back together and promising —

in the face of consumer-group skepticism — that the mergers will enhance competition and bring customers better service and lower prices.

The developments in the telephone industry encapsulate a debate that has raged since the beginning of U.S. antitrust policy: whether corporate mergers help consumers by lowering costs and thereby prices or hurt consumers by reducing competition and thereby the incentives to keep prices low. Despite 100 years of argument and reams of academic research, the issue continues to sharply divide policy-makers, interest groups and experts.

Chicago school experts stoutly insist that most mergers do benefit the economy. "The presumption is that the merger is going to be beneficial," Lopatka says. "If one wants to interfere with the market, one has to prove that interference with the market is going to produce greater benefits than allowing the market to work."

"You can't stop every merger, and it would be bad if you did," says Stelzer, a conservative who does not count himself in the Chicago school.

But Peritz maintains that the view that large firms will be more efficient is overstated. "Efficiency and large size do not correlate so simply," Peritz says. "Large firms are much, much bigger than they need to be to take advantage of economies of scale in production."

The Clinton administration's record on mergers draws mixed reviews. Critics on the right say the administration has been too aggressive. "There's a long list of anti-merger activity," says the Cato Institute's Levy. As one example, he describes the opposition to the planned merger between the two giant office-supply chains, Staples and Office Depot, as "plain silliness."

"There was no evidence at all that there was any monopoly power being exercised by those two companies," Levy says. "There were plenty of competitors in the office-supply market."

Critics on the left, however, say the administration has been too timid in challenging corporate combinations. "The antitrust officials have not been as aggressive in challenging transactions until it gets to an extreme level of concentration," says Gene Kimmelman, co-director of the Washington office of Consumers Union. "I would not call that aggressive enforcement."

A number of experts, however, including several self-described conservatives, give the administration generally good marks in merger cases.

"My impression is that they're applying the law pretty consistently," says Thomas Kauper, a professor at the University of Michigan Law School.

Stelzer agrees. "I think they've got it about right," he says. But Stelzer does fault Klein for not opposing the merger last year of two Baby Bells serving the Eastern and Mid-Atlantic states: Bell Atlantic Corp. and Nynex Corp.

Lopatka also declines to criticize the administration's stance on mergers. He specifically notes that he came to agree with the FTC's opposition to the Staples-Office Depot merger despite his initial skepticism. "They had pretty strong empirical evidence that when the two firms were not competing with each other, the price went up," Lopatka says.

For his part, though, Peritz regrets the reduced concern about corporate growth that dates from the Reagan-Bush presidencies and continues today. One reason for the changed attitude, he says, is that policy-makers have come to focus more on increasing shareholder value than on protecting consumers.

"What's not happening is a sufficient concern for what's happening to consumers, suppliers, and others who deal with these now even more enormous firms," Peritz says.

Should the federal government and the states have filed antitrust suits against Microsoft?

From the moment the suits were filed — indeed, in the several weeks leading up to the filing — the antitrust case against Microsoft was being played out in the political and public relations arenas as much as in court. Members of Congress and newspaper editorials weighed in on opposite sides of the dispute. So did other computer executives.

The suit also drew sharply divided reactions among antitrust experts. Supporters of the suits maintain that they are well-grounded in established antitrust doctrines and that the requested remedies were both appropriate and modest. Critics see the allegations against Microsoft as weak, both factually and legally, and predict either a defeat for the government or at most a fairly weak settlement.

"It was important that the suit was filed," Peritz says. "The remedies that the Justice Department and the state attorneys general are asking for are reasonable, and consistent with the kind of anti-competitive behavior they're claiming Microsoft is engaged in."

"This is an old-time antitrust case in which Bill Gates is trying to establish that high-tech industries are so different from the rest of the world that antitrust laws shouldn't apply," Stelzer says in agreement. "It's a pretty straightforward tying case, a straightforward abuse of monopoly-position case."

But in Lopatka's view, "It's not a very strong complaint, not a very strong theory." Each of the government's theories, he says, presents difficult problems of proof under existing antitrust precedents. "I think the government is going to lose," he concludes.

The Justice Department has already battled Microsoft in court twice, with limited results. It ended its first investigation in July 1994, when Microsoft agreed to a consent decree requiring it to change some of the restrictions in its contracts with PC manufacturers and other software makers. Today, the decree — formally issued in August 1995 after one judge balked at approving it — is widely regarded as weak. "They proposed solutions that became obsolete in a hurry," George Mason's Kovacic says.

Then, last October, the Justice Department returned to court, claiming that Microsoft was violating the 1995 decree by forcing computer makers to include its Internet Explorer browser as a condition of selling Windows 95. U.S. District Judge Thomas Penfield Jackson granted an injunction in December requiring Microsoft to allow computer makers to unbundle the browser. But

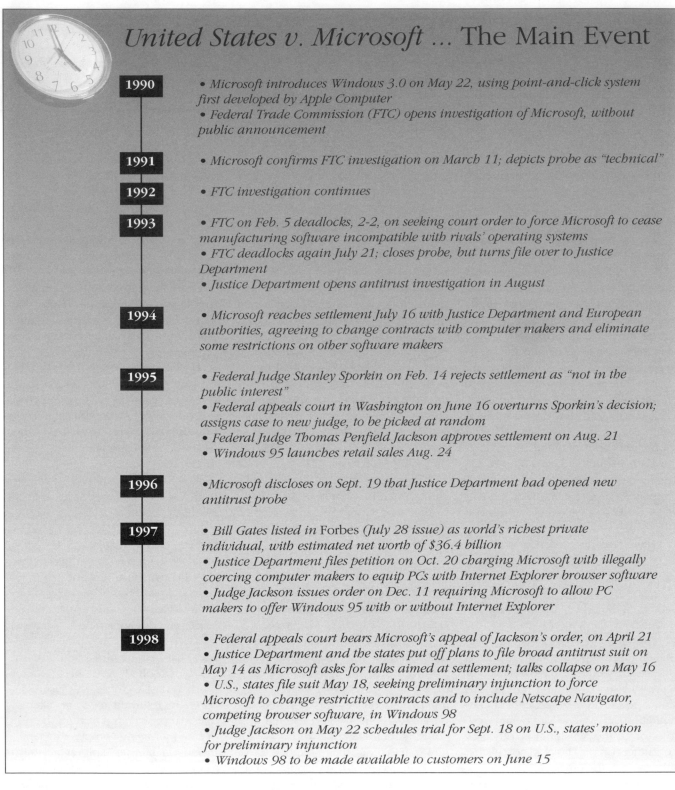

United States v. Microsoft ... The Main Event

1990
- *Microsoft introduces Windows 3.0 on May 22, using point-and-click system first developed by Apple Computer*
- *Federal Trade Commission (FTC) opens investigation of Microsoft, without public announcement*

1991
- *Microsoft confirms FTC investigation on March 11; depicts probe as "technical"*

1992
- *FTC investigation continues*

1993
- *FTC on Feb. 5 deadlocks, 2-2, on seeking court order to force Microsoft to cease manufacturing software incompatible with rivals' operating systems*
- *FTC deadlocks again July 21; closes probe, but turns file over to Justice Department*
- *Justice Department opens antitrust investigation in August*

1994
- *Microsoft reaches settlement July 16 with Justice Department and European authorities, agreeing to change contracts with computer makers and eliminate some restrictions on other software makers*

1995
- *Federal Judge Stanley Sporkin on Feb. 14 rejects settlement as "not in the public interest"*
- *Federal appeals court in Washington on June 16 overturns Sporkin's decision; assigns case to new judge, to be picked at random*
- *Federal Judge Thomas Penfield Jackson approves settlement on Aug. 21*
- *Windows 95 launches retail sales Aug. 24*

1996
- *Microsoft discloses on Sept. 19 that Justice Department had opened new antitrust probe*

1997
- *Bill Gates listed in Forbes (July 28 issue) as world's richest private individual, with estimated net worth of $36.4 billion*
- *Justice Department files petition on Oct. 20 charging Microsoft with illegally coercing computer makers to equip PCs with Internet Explorer browser software*
- *Judge Jackson issues order on Dec. 11 requiring Microsoft to allow PC makers to offer Windows 95 with or without Internet Explorer*

1998
- *Federal appeals court hears Microsoft's appeal of Jackson's order, on April 21*
- *Justice Department and the states put off plans to file broad antitrust suit on May 14 as Microsoft asks for talks aimed at settlement; talks collapse on May 16*
- *U.S., states file suit May 18, seeking preliminary injunction to force Microsoft to change restrictive contracts and to include Netscape Navigator, competing browser software, in Windows 98*
- *Judge Jackson on May 22 schedules trial for Sept. 18 on U.S., states' motion for preliminary injunction*
- *Windows 98 to be made available to customers on June 15*

when the federal appeals court in Washington heard Microsoft's appeal of the injunction in April, the government conceded that no computer maker had exercised that option up to then. [9]

The appellate judges appeared skeptical of the government's case in the April 24 arguments. In any event, the case concerned only Windows 95

U.S. v. Microsoft: The Lines Are Drawn

U.S. Assistant Attorney General Joel I. Klein
Comments accompanying filing of antitrust suit against Microsoft by the Justice Department, May 18, 1998

In essence, what Microsoft has been doing, through a wide variety of illegal business practices, is leveraging its Windows operating system monopoly to force its other software products on consumers. This is like having someone with a monopoly in CD players forcing consumers to take its CDs in order to get the machine. We believe most Americans would prefer to choose their own CDs and, for their matter, their own software products as well. . . .

Microsoft is unwilling to compete fairly and on the merits; rather, it prefers to leverage its Windows monopoly 'to make people use' its browser. The antitrust laws take a very different view of the way the marketplace should work: those laws are premised on the belief that . . . people should be able to choose for themselves what products they use.

. . . [N]othing we are doing here will or should prevent Microsoft from innovating or competing on the merits. What cannot be tolerated — and what the antitrust laws forbid — is the barrage of illegal, anti-competitive practices that Microsoft uses to destroy its rivals and to avoid competition on the merits. That, and that alone, is what this lawsuit is all about.

Bill Gates
Chairman, Microsoft
Comments following filing of federal antitrust suit, May 18, 1998

Forcing Microsoft to include Netscape's competing software in our operating system is like requiring Coca-Cola to include three cans of Pepsi in every six-pack it sells. The changes the government is demanding on the boot-up screen is like telling Coca-Cola that it must remove its name from every can of soda. And saying that we must remove Internet technology from Windows is like telling Coca-Cola that it must take something out of its formula. . . .

Computer users today have more choices than ever before. PC users can already choose between Microsoft's Internet Explorer and any other Web browser, and computer manufacturers are free to install Netscape browsers on any computers they sell. . . . Computer manufacturers choose to configure the first screen differently. They choose to add any browsers. They choose to market whatever productivity software they want . . .

We believe an antitrust lawsuit is counterproductive, costly to the taxpayers, and ultimately will be unsuccessful in the courts. . . . I am confident that in the end, America's judicial system will uphold our right to innovate on behalf of consumers. I look forward to presenting our case in court and continuing to create great software for our consumers.

---

and was already being overshadowed by the broadening investigations of Microsoft.

The government's lawsuit includes four allegations that also appear in the states' complaint. The first charges that Gates and other Microsoft executives unsuccessfully tried to persuade Netscape to divide up the browser and operating-system markets. The government quotes Netscape Executive Vice President Marc Andreesen as describing the no-compete proposal in a meeting between executives of the two companies in June 1995. Gates has vehemently denied the allegation.

The three other claims involve ongoing Microsoft activities: the bundling of Internet Explorer with Windows; restrictions on computer manufacturers' discretion to alter the initial Windows boot-up screen; and Microsoft's agreements with Internet service and content providers that the government says are aimed at promoting Microsoft services and excluding those of competing firms. The states add one other claim in their lawsuit: a contention that Microsoft is also trying to monopolize the market for office-services software through similar tying arrangements and exclusionary contracts.

Peritz says the evidence of antitrust violations is strong. "Microsoft has tried to achieve a monopoly in applications," Peritz says. "They've done that by taking applications and integrating them into the operating system." As for the remedy, he agrees with the government's effort to force Microsoft to include the Netscape browser in its Windows programs — but prefers the states' request that a third browser be included as well. "Just as we don't want Microsoft to dominate that field," he says, "we don't want Microsoft and Netscape to dominate it either."

Lopatka, however, doubts the government's evidence is strong enough to prevail in court. And, if so, he believes the suits are a mistake.

"We have a market that's certainly functioning well, in terms of generating lots of benefits for consumers," The University of South Carolina's Lopatka says. "I don't think you want to interfere with the market on a hunch." ∎

BACKGROUND

Trust Busting

Congress passed the first of the federal antitrust laws in 1890 with bipartisan support at a time of rapid industrial consolidation and rapacious business practices. Four times since then — in 1914, 1950, 1974 and 1976 — Congress approved major revisions of the law aimed at tightening the prohibitions against monopoly power and adding new curbs on unfair business practices. But the executive branch and the federal courts have followed an uneven course in enforcing and interpreting the laws, alternating between periods of somewhat stricter and laxer antitrust enforcement. [10]

The Sherman Act bears the name of Sen. John Sherman, a Republican from Ohio — home of the biggest industrial trust of the late 19th century, John D. Rockefeller's Standard Oil of Ohio. Actually, though, Sherman's original proposal to ban any practices that restrained "full and fair competition" was amended in favor of narrower language prohibiting any contracts or combinations "in restraint of trade." The amended bill passed Congress overwhelmingly in July 1890 and was signed into law by a Republican president, Benjamin Harrison.

Today, Congress' intent in passing the law is one of the major points of disagreement. Bork and others in the so-called Chicago school argue that Sherman himself and Congress as a whole had one goal in mind: "consumer welfare," by which they mean lower prices. "The touchstone of illegality is raising prices to consumers," Bork wrote in an influential law review article in 1966. [11]

Most experts, however, say Bork's thesis ignores the substantial evidence that Congress also wanted to preserve and promote smaller businesses for social and political as well as economic purposes. "His view is far too narrow," says Thomas Sullivan. [12]

Supreme Court Rulings

Whatever Congress' intent, the Sherman Act had a mixed initial reception in the courts. The Supreme Court took a literalist approach in some of its earliest cases — for example, breaking up a rate-fixing agreement in 1897 among 18 freight railroads that lower courts had ruled legal. This literalist approach also led the court to cite antitrust law in curbing the powers of labor unions — an interpretation that Congress eventually put to rest by declaring that labor was not a "commodity" for purposes of antitrust law. At the same time, though, the high court narrowed the scope of the law by ruling in the 1895 "sugar trust" case that the act applied only to "commerce" and not to manufacturing — a doctrine that the court itself repudiated in the late 1930s.

The court created a more durable limitation on the law in 1911 in two decisions that nonetheless broke up Rockefeller's Standard Oil trust and James Duke's American Tobacco trust. Viewing the law as a limitation on constitutionally protected freedom of contract, the court's conservative majority declared that those trusts were illegal only because they were created through "unnatural and wrongful" acts. [13] This so-called Rule of Reason approach to the law prevailed for the next two decades. It then yielded to a more literal "per se" interpretation of the law, but reemerged in the mid-1970s to become

what is now the accepted method for applying the law.

Congress responded to the decisions three years later with a new law expressly aimed at reversing what one senator called the court's "deadly blow to trust litigation." [14] The Clayton Antitrust Act added a laundry list of specifically prohibited business practices, including price discrimination, tying agreements and stock acquisitions, where the effect might be "to substantially lessen competition or tend to create a monopoly." A separate law created a new regulatory agency, the Federal Trade Commission (FTC), with broad power to identify and enjoin unfair commercial conduct.

Despite the Clayton Act's broad language, the Supreme Court again weakened the law through judicial interpretation. By 1950, antitrust-minded lawmakers determined the law needed revision if it was to prevent anti-competitive mergers. The Celler-Kefauver Act strengthened the law in two ways: first, by extending the act's prohibition against mergers achieved through stock acquisitions to the purchase of a competitor's assets as well; and second, by extending the law not only to mergers between competitors but to all corporate mergers with anti-competitive effects.

The law has blocked relatively few of these so-called conglomerate mergers. But the provision is nonetheless very controversial between liberals, who applaud Congress' effort to restrict corporate growth, and conservatives, who see no benefit in restraining mergers between non-competing companies.

A quarter-century later, Congress acted again to stiffen antitrust laws. In 1974, it substantially raised penalties for antitrust violations. Then in 1976 it passed a law, the Hart-Scott-Rodino Antitrust Improvements Act, requiring any company with more than $100 million in assets or sales to give the Justice

Chronology

1890-1950
Congress passes antitrust laws aimed at preventing anti-competitive business practices.

1890
Sherman Act prohibits any "contract, combination or conspiracy . . . in restraint of trade" or monopolizing or attempting to monopolize interstate or foreign trade or commerce.

1911
Supreme Court upholds government's effort to break up Standard Oil trust, but ruling softens Sherman Act by allowing "reasonable" restraints of trade.

1914
Clayton Antitrust Act prohibits a number of anti-competitive practices, including exclusive dealing and "tying" contracts. In the same year, Congress creates Federal Trade Commission (FTC) with power to bar "unfair" competition.

1936
Robinson-Patman Act outlaws "unjustified" price discounts that result in injury to competition.

1941
Report by Temporary National Economic Committee questions economic benefits of mergers.

1945
Appeals court upholds government's antitrust suit against Aluminum Co. of America (ALCOA).

1950
Celler-Kefauver Act strengthens Clayton Act's provision against anti-competitive mergers.

1950s-1960s
Supreme Court adopts strict stance against mergers.

1962
Supreme Court, in *Brown Shoe Co.*, bars manufacturer from acquiring Kinney Shoe Co.; acquisition would have given firm 5 percent of retail market.

1968
Justice Department guidelines call for challenging mergers if four firms would have more than 75 percent of market.

———— • ————

1970s
Antitrust laws are strengthened by Congress but sharply challenged by members of "Chicago school."

1974
Antitrust Procedures and Penalties Act raises penalties for price-fixing and other violations.

1976
Hart-Scott-Rodino Act requires large companies to report planned mergers.

1978
Robert Bork's *The Antitrust Paradox* sharply criticizes antitrust laws.

———— • ————

1980s
Reagan administration severely restricts antitrust enforcement.

1982
Assistant Attorney General William Baxter announces settlement of seven-year-old antitrust suit against AT&T, with agreement for divestiture of local telephone companies; divestiture is completed in 1984. On same day, Baxter announces government is dropping 13-year-old suit against IBM; action is "without merit," Baxter says. Later in year, Justice Department adopts new merger guidelines, raising standard for challenging corporate combinations.

———— • ————

1990s
The Clinton administration adopts stricter antitrust policies; wave of domestic and global mergers begins in mid-decade.

1993
Anne Bingaman appointed assistant attorney general for antitrust; doubles number of mergers challenged by division in two years in office.

1995
Robert Pitofsky appointed FTC chairman; leads commission in challenging mergers or forcing concessions before mergers are approved.

1997
Joel I. Klein named to head Justice Department Antitrust Division; wins Senate confirmation despite criticism for approving Bell Atlantic-Nynex merger.

1998
Justice Department and 20 states file antitrust suits against Microsoft Corp.; FTC launches major antitrust action against Intel Corp. on June 8; both agencies have other major antitrust cases ready for trial.

Private Antitrust Suits Allow Big Awards

Pepsi vs. Coke may sound like a consumer taste test, but it's actually a court case: a high-stakes effort by second-ranked Pepsi Cola to use federal antitrust laws to gain on the long-time industry leader, Coca-Cola Co.

Pepsico Inc. filed suit in federal court in New York last month claiming that Coke was illegally monopolizing the soft-drink market in violation of the Sherman Antitrust Act. The 16-page suit claimed that Coke improperly bars food-service distributors — the companies that supply products for restaurants, theater chains, stadiums and the like — from providing Pepsi products to their customers if they already handle Coke.

A Coca-Cola spokeswoman immediately branded the May 7 suit as "totally without merit." But in a motion to dismiss the complaint, filed on May 28, Coca-Cola acknowledged the heart of the complaint while maintaining that it was perfectly legal to insist that distributors handle only Coke products. Pepsi, the motion said, was "seeking to force Coca-Cola to allow its distributors also to carry the brands of its main competitor."

The court fight between the two soft-drink giants rests on Congress' decision in passing the 1890 Sherman Act to provide for enforcement of the law both by the government and by private individuals and companies. In the century since then, private antitrust suits have allowed consumers and companies injured by anti-competitive conduct to recover big damage awards: Successful plaintiffs can collect three times the amount they lost because of the antitrust violations plus punitive damages and attorney's fees.

In addition, private suits have sometimes pushed the government into taking action on its own. Most notably perhaps, an antitrust suit filed in March 1974 by an upstart long-distance carrier, MCI, against AT&T helped pave the way for the government suit eight months later that eventually forced the breakup of the telephone monopoly.

More recently, competitors of Microsoft Corp. were first to bring unfair competition claims against the computer giant while the Justice Department was still investigating. And the Federal Trade Commission's June 8 complaint against Intel Corp. stems in part from an antitrust claim against the microprocessor manufacturer by a manufacturer of computer work stations.

Private antitrust suits "have had a big impact," says William E. Kovacic, a professor at George Mason University Law School in Fairfax, Va. But he notes that since the mid-1970s the Supreme Court has issued a number of rulings creating substantive or procedural obstacles for antitrust plaintiffs. The trend continues. In October the high court issued a unanimous ruling making it harder for a dealer to challenge a maximum-price requirement imposed by a manufacturer or supplier.

Thomas Kauper, a professor at the University of Michigan Law School, agrees that Supreme Court rulings helped curb private antitrust suits after the boom period of the 1960s and early '70s. But he thinks litigation is now picking up. "My impression is that over the last seven or eight years, we're seeing a good deal more private litigation," Kauper says.

Joe Sims, a private antitrust lawyer in Washington, D.C., agrees, but he also sees a change in the kinds of suits being filed. In the past, Sims says, the most common kinds of suits were class actions brought on behalf of consumers injured by price-fixing or other anti-competitive conduct, or suits by dealers challenging restrictions imposed by manufacturers or suppliers. But Supreme Court rulings have made distribution suits more difficult, Sims says, while class actions have become too expensive to justify the risk.

Instead, Sims says there is an increase in what he calls "strategic litigation" — like the Pepsi-Coke suit. "It's big company vs. big company," Sims explains. "One big company is trying to deal with a business problem by invoking the antitrust laws. That's becoming reasonably common."

Whether brought by the government or by a private company or individual, antitrust litigation is expensive, time-consuming and dicey. But the payoff can be well worth the expense — as MCI's success in the telecommunications industry since 1974 shows. As for Pepsi, Sims says the cost of its antitrust suit is "not very relevant."

"Say it costs you $2-$3 million in legal fees to generate one of these cases," Sims says. "Two or three million dollars in the context of an important business issue is peanuts. If the result of what they do is they gain one or two or three market-share points, that completely overwhelms that expense."

Department and FTC advance notice of any merger valued at more than $15 million. The law also gives state attorneys general power to file civil antitrust suits on behalf of consumers — the provision being used in the states' antitrust suit against Microsoft. [15]

The Politics of Antitrust

The first great "trust-busting" president was a Republican: Theodore Roosevelt, who led the fight to break up Frank Harriman's Northern Pacific trust in 1904 and later bolted from the GOP because of what he saw as weakness on the issue on the part of his successor, William Howard Taft. Since then, support for antitrust enforcement has tended to be stronger in Democratic than in Republican administrations. That partisan split deepened with the conservative shift on antitrust issues during the Reagan and Bush administrations.

The Supreme Court continued to slow antitrust enforcement for a quarter-century after its Standard Oil decision. In 1918 and 1920, for example, the court rejected efforts to break up two giant companies, United Shoe Corp. and U.S. Steel Corp., despite evidence that each controlled more than 80 percent of its industry and had been guilty of questionable business practices. In the 1920s, the court also gave its blessing to the creation of industry trade associations despite concerns among some antitrust advocates that the groups could facilitate price-setting and market divisions among competitors.

President Franklin D. Roosevelt reinvigorated antitrust policy after a failed effort in his first term to link government, business and labor in the National Recovery Administration as a means of lifting the country out of the Great Depression. In his second term, he appointed Yale law Professor Thurman Arnold to head the Justice Department's antitrust division. Arnold viewed antitrust as a tool to eliminate "bottlenecks" that prevented full competition and increased prices to consumers.

His pragmatic approach disappointed some business critics, but it bore fruit in a number of consent decrees reshaping industry practices and some significant court victories after his departure from government — such as a celebrated 1945 decision curbing the Alcoa Co.'s monopoly power in unprocessed aluminum.

Roosevelt also had a lasting impact on antitrust policy through his appointment of liberal justices to the Supreme Court, two of whom — William O. Douglas and Hugo L. Black — each served for more than 30 years. The court's more favorable attitude toward government regulation did not produce an immediate change in antitrust doctrine. In 1947, for example, it issued an important decision rejecting

the government's effort to prove a conspiracy to monopolize because of parallel-pricing policies followed by major film studios vis-a-vis independent theater owners. And in 1956 it rejected an effort to break the duPont chemical company's monopoly on cellophane, reasoning that other wrapping materials competed with duPont's product.

By the 1960s, however, Black and Douglas, along with Chief Justice Earl Warren and others, provided a somewhat reliable liberal majority that produced some of the court's furthest extensions of antitrust law. In the most controversial ruling, the court in 1962 upheld the government's effort to block the merger of Brown Shoe Co., the country's largest shoe manufacturer and third-largest retailer, with another major retailer, Kinney Shoe Co. Together, the two companies would have controlled only 5 percent of the retail market, but the court agreed with the government that the merger would violate the Celler-Kefauver Act by hastening concentration. Most controversially, Warren's opinion declared that the law called for the protection of small businesses even if it meant higher prices for consumers. [16]

The pro-small-business philosophy — derided by critics as "big is bad" — was seen in other court rulings in the decade that broke up mergers in industries that by today's standards would not have been viewed as concentrated. For its part, the Justice Department in 1968 adopted somewhat more lenient merger guidelines that nonetheless promised to oppose combinations even of relatively small firms in industries that were already "highly concentrated" — defined as four or more firms controlling 75 percent of market share.

Outside Washington, however, antitrust doctrine was shifting out from under the government's control. A band of scholars at the University of Chicago

was shaping a new view of antitrust law that would displace the Jeffersonian rhetoric of protecting small businesses with a single-minded focus on economics and a predisposition to permit all but the most evidently anti-competitive mergers and business practices. By the 1980s, this so-called "New Learning" would come to dominate not only academic debate about antitrust issues but also policy decisions by the government and in the courts.

The Chicago School

The so-called Chicago school of antitrust traces its origins to works in the 1950s and '60s by University of Chicago law Professor Aaron Director and economists George Stigler and Ronald Coase. But the two Chicago scholars best known for propagating its tenets are Bork and Richard Posner. [17]

Posner, now a federal appeals court judge, set out what he regarded as a "scientific" theory of economic efficiency — one based on empirical study, not ideology — in two books: *Economic Analysis of Law* (1973) and *Antitrust Law: An Economic Perspective* (1976). [18] In Posner's view, competition was a means to an end — efficiency — rather than an end in itself. On that basis, he argued that "whenever monopoly would increase efficiency, it should be tolerated, indeed encouraged." In addition, as Peritz points out in his critical analysis, Posner focuses solely on maximizing production — "productive efficiency" — and dismisses any concerns about distribution of wealth as "political" or "social" rather than economic.

Bork's *The Antitrust Paradox* followed in 1978 with an even stronger denunciation of antitrust laws and the Supreme Court's decisions interpreting the laws. Antitrust law, he declared, was a "policy at war with itself" because of "mutually incompatible goals." Instead of focusing on the "only legitimate goal . . . the maximization of consumer welfare," antitrust law, he said, was primarily used to protect "the survival or comfort of small business." [19]

With surprising speed, the Chicago school displaced the previously dominant Harvard school of antitrust analysis, which had viewed the growth of large industrial organizations as a problem rather than a natural or even salutary feature of the economy. [20] Bork's book is acknowledged today even by its many critics as perhaps the most influential work on antitrust ever. Chicago school adherents take credit for ushering in an antitrust "revolution" with their emphasis on free-market economics. And, in fact, the Harvard school has all but disappeared, at least in name: The competing intellectual camp today is called the "post-Chicago school."

The Chicago school's anti-regulatory views matched the philosophy that Ronald Reagan brought to the White House after his election as president in 1980. Reagan appointed Chicago school disciples to key policy-making posts: William Baxter to head the antitrust division, James Miller to chair the FTC. Baxter took office saying that he would not consider "industry concentration" as a factor in decision-making. The Justice Department issued new merger guidelines in 1982, significantly relaxing the test for objecting to a combination; through the 1980s, the department challenged only 28 out of the 10,000 merger notifications filed. [21] Reagan also named Bork, Posner and many other Chicago school disciples to the federal bench, where they helped reorient the courts' interpretation of antitrust statutes. [22]

New Court Philosophy

For its part, the Supreme Court had already begun to take a more re-laxed stance on antitrust issues by the mid-1970s. In one important decision, the court in 1974 approved a merger of two coal producers that resulted in a company with 50 percent market share; the opinion was written by Justice Potter Stewart, a dissenter from the court's stricter merger rulings in the 1960s. Three years later, the court in 1977 gave manufacturers leeway to impose restrictions on dealers, such as territorial franchises, even if the result was reduced competition among retailers. In the same year, the court made it somewhat harder for private companies to prove injury in antitrust suits. [23] The high court's conservative trend continued through the 1980s, especially after the Reagan-appointed justices forged a somewhat solid conservative majority under Chief Justice William H. Rehnquist.

The conservative trend did not completely supplant stricter antitrust views. Despite his general orientation, for example, Baxter presided over the completion of the breakup of AT&T in 1984 — and proudly took credit for his role. [24] The Supreme Court in 1985 issued a ruling, little noticed outside the antitrust bar, adopting the view that firms with monopoly power may violate antitrust law by refusing to let competitors use "essential facilities" — a doctrine with potential application to the Microsoft case. [25] Still, by decade's end, conservative antitrust perspectives had clearly come to dominate both the executive branch and, perhaps more significantly, the federal judiciary as well.

Antitrust Revival?

President Clinton gave encouraging signals to antitrust advocates by picking liberals for the government's two top antitrust posts at the FTC and Justice Department. But as a self-styled New Democrat, Clinton was also interested in reassuring both Wall Street and Main Street that the administration was not reflexively pro-regulation or anti-business. In addition, the administration inherited the Reaganized federal judiciary, skeptical of expansive antitrust enforcement, as well as an increasingly globalized economy in which antitrust barriers were widely viewed as anachronistic and counterproductive.

To head the Justice Department's antitrust division, Clinton in 1993 appointed Bingaman, a former law professor and antitrust litigator with a Washington law firm. In her first two years in the antitrust post, Bingaman, the wife of New Mexico's Democratic senator, doubled the number of division cases challenging, restructuring or blocking proposed mergers. [26] But she also presided over one of the division's most embarrassing courtroom defeats when a federal judge in fall 1994 threw out a high-profile criminal price-fixing case against General Electric Co. on grounds the evidence was too weak.

When the term of holdover FTC Chair Janet Steiger expired in 1995, Clinton nominated Robert Pitofsky, a staunch liberal who had served two tours of duty at the agency and gone on to be a professor and dean of Georgetown University Law Center in Washington. Like Bingaman, Pitofsky brought to his post a more skeptical attitude toward mergers that helped thwart a number of proposed combinations submitted to the agency for review in his first year — for example, a $1.8 billion merger between two big drugstore chains, Rite Aid Corp. and Revco D.S. Inc. [27] But some mergers went through even after a hard look from the agency, most notably the 1996 telecommunications marriage of Time Warner Inc. and Turner Broadcasting System Inc. [28]

Klein won Senate confirmation to the Justice Department post last summer, but only after weathering some congressional criticism for approving the Bell Atlantic-Nynex merger while holding the position in an acting capacity. [29] While he continues to say he has no ideological predisposition against mergers, his more activist stand in recent cases has won over some skeptics. "Klein is underrated," Peritz says. "I certainly underrated him until recently." Sen. Ernest F. Hollings, a South Carolina Democrat who criticized Klein over the Bell Atlantic merger, said he "has done a fine job" so far. [30]

The antitrust division's statistics reflect an increase both in corporate marriages and in the Justice Department's scrutiny of the deals. In 1997 the division received 3,702 pre-merger notifications — more than double the number in the early years of the decade and one-third more than in 1988, the last full year of Reagan's presidency. The department initiated investigations in 220 of the cases in 1997 — nearly four times the 56 investigations begun in 1988. *(See box, p. 130.)*

So far this year, the Justice Department has moved in court against two big deals: the Lockheed-Northrup Grumman merger and the plan by a satellite TV company jointly owned by MCI and Rupert Murdoch's News Corp. to merge with one owned by major cable TV companies. In announcing the satellite TV suit on May 12, Klein said, "unless this acquisition is blocked, consumers will be denied the benefits of competition — lower prices, more innovation and better services and quality."

In the same week, Justice Department attorneys and state attorneys general were putting the final touches on their lawsuits against Microsoft. Plans were set for a news conference to announce the suit on Thursday, May 14. But Gates, who had met with Klein privately the week before, made an eleventh-hour bid to try to settle the case without litigation. The suits were put on hold while lawyers on both sides met on Friday and Saturday. But the sessions ended with nothing but recriminations.

Software executives testify during a March 3, 1998 Senate Judiciary Committee hearing on competition and antitrust issues; from left: Bill Gates, Microsoft; Scott McNealy, Sun Microsystems; and Jim Barksdale, Netscape Communications.

After the suit was filed, Gates said he had tried to settle the case, but the government had presented Microsoft with "non-negotiable demands" that were designed to benefit its competitor, Netscape, at consumers' expense. For his part, Klein told reporters that Microsoft had not gone far enough to respond to the antitrust issues in the case. "What they put on the table would not by any means have benefited consumers or eliminated the anti-competitive practices that are alleged in the complaint," Klein said. ∎

CURRENT SITUATION

"Aggressive Competitor"

Until recently, Microsoft has enjoyed the kind of reputation that cannot be bought. In much of the public's mind, the company went from start-up to multibillion-dollar giant in less than two decades on the basis of nothing more than American-style work, smarts and entrepreneurship. "Microsoft should be celebrated as a hero," says James K. Glassman, a senior fellow at the American Enterprise Institute and columnist for *The Washington Post*.

Within the computer industry, however, another image of Microsoft formed in the past few years: that of a greedy monopolist that grew by imitating innovations by other companies and maintained its dominance through hardball negotiations with its partners and ruthless business practices toward its rivals.

"Microsoft is a very aggressive competitor," says James Love, director of the Consumer Project on Technology at the Center for the Study of Responsive Law, founded by Ralph Nader. "They use every conceivable weapon at their disposal to destroy their competitors."

The federal and state suits filed May 18 will give the government and Microsoft an opportunity to air those opposing views of the company in a federal court this fall. Microsoft asked for a seven-month delay before a hearing on the motions for a preliminary injunction, saying it needed time to study the allegations in the suits and the evidence already gathered by the Justice Department and the states. But federal Judge Thomas Penfield Jackson gave Microsoft a first-round defeat by cutting the requested delay nearly in half.

Jackson said he was concerned that a longer delay would allow Microsoft too much time to market Windows 98 without a ruling on the government's effort to force inclusion of Netscape's competing browser software. "By the time you propose to be ready," Jackson said at a May 22 hearing, "16-18 million horses will already be out of the barn, and that's too late."

Heading the Justice Department's team of lawyers at the hearing was David Boies, until recently a star litigator on Wall Street who years earlier led IBM's successful defense of the government's antitrust suit. [31] "This will be resolved very expeditiously," Boies said outside the courtroom.

For his part, Microsoft lead attorney William Neukom told reporters, "We will use the time the court has provided to . . . present a very powerful case."

The dueling press conferences on the day of the suits' filing, along with the complaints themselves and the Justice Department's accompanying 71-page legal memorandum, hint at the arguments both sides will make in the fall.

The most damning accusation — that Gates offered to divide the operating-system and applications markets with Netscape executives in 1995 — was backed up by depositions from Netscape officials. But Gates called the allegation "absolutely false." And Lopatka at the University of South Carolina says that even if the accusation is proved, the government may be entitled to nothing more than an injunction against any collusion in the future. "That

doesn't amount to much," he says.

Lopatka says Microsoft will be able to convince the judge that Microsoft's bundling of the browser software, limits on changing the Windows boot-up screen and restrictive agreements with Internet service and content providers all have sufficient business reasons or consumer benefits to offset any adverse effects on competition.

Other experts view the government's chances more positively, but still hedge their bets. "This is a pretty powerful complaint as complaints go," says AEI's Stelzer. "It's got a lot of good documentary evidence, but you can't say who's going to win."

Meanwhile, the FTC is preparing its own antitrust action against another computer industry giant: Intel Corp., which manufactures the Pentium microprocessing chip used in an estimated 80 percent of PCs. In a complaint filed with an FTC administrative law judge on June 8, the commission charged Intel with abusing its monopoly power by refusing to share technical information with three other computer companies that were both customers and potential competitors: Compaq Computer Corp., Digital Equipment Corp. and Intergraph Corp. The complaint charged that Intel was retaliating against the three companies for their actions in connection with patent-related disputes with Intel. In a statement, Intel denied that it had violated any laws, but executives reportedly acknowledged in interviews many of the facts alleged in the FTC complaint. [32]

The Urge to Merge

Supporters and critics of big business have sharply divergent views of the reasons for the current wave of corporate mergers and their likely effects. Supporters say the combinations stem from a desire to increase efficien-

cies in production and enhance opportunities, all to the ultimate benefit of consumers. Critics, however, say the mergers typically stem from an effort to reduce competition or take advantage of undervalued stock, benefiting corporate managers and shareholders but rarely producing the claimed benefits for consumers.

Many disinterested observers doubt the claims for consumer benefits. "There is scant hard evidence that mergers, hostile or friendly, have in fact generated the promised efficiencies," writes Peter Passell, an economics columnist for The New York Times generally sympathetic to business. [33]

Nonetheless, supporters of mergers appear to be dominating the current debate over the issue both in Washington and among the public at large. When Chrysler Corp. and the German automaker Daimler-Benz AG made the stunning announcement of their planned merger on May 6, hardly anyone was heard raising concerns about the effects on competition or consumers. The Wall Street Journal, the first newspaper to disclose the planned merger, reported after the announcement that antitrust lawyers in Europe and the United States — not specifically identified — expect the deal to be approved "because it wouldn't create a dominant player in the industry." [34]

Critics and observers did raise some concerns a month earlier when two giants in the financial-services industry, Citicorp and Travelers Group Inc., announced their planned merger on April 6. Still, most observers expect the deal to be approved. And the House of Representatives narrowly voted a few weeks later, on May 13, to repeal the federal Glass-Stegall Act, which limits the ability of banks to merge with securities firms. [35]

There is some evidence, however, of an increased willingness in Washington to question or challenge some mergers. The Justice Department's lawsuit filed March 23 to block the Lockheed Martin-Northrup Grumman merger surprised many observers be-

At Issue:

Are antitrust enforcers right to be going after Microsoft?

THE NEW YORK TIMES

FROM AN EDITORIAL, MAY 19, 1998.

*i*n their sweeping antitrust suit against Microsoft, the Justice Department and 20 state attorneys general have made reasonable demands to preserve competition in the world of computers and the Internet. Bill Gates needs to respond with something better than disingenuous countercharges that his company is being punished for its success. Instead of forcing a protracted court battle over remedies, Microsoft should work with federal and state lawyers to reshape the marketplace to help consumers obtain the products they may want. . . .

Much will now depend on whether the Justice Department and attorneys general can prove their charges of illegal anticompetitive conduct. One of the most explosive charges disclosed yesterday was that Microsoft first tried to cut a deal with Netscape, makers of the main rival to its Web browser, to carve up the browser market. Only when that approach failed, said the department, did Microsoft shift tactics and try to muscle Netscape out of the market, fearing that its success on the Internet would supplant Microsoft's dominance in the operating system business. In response, Microsoft says that its conversations with Netscape were innocent and that every one of its decisions was a legal effort to serve its customers.

For all its heated language, the Justice Department stepped back from trying to block the shipment of Microsoft's Windows 98 operating system. . . . Instead, the government wants Microsoft to unbundle its own browser, Internet Explorer, from Windows 98 or to include the rival Netscape browser along with it. The government also wants Microsoft to stop giving preference to its own software products on the screen that first comes up when customers turn on their computers.

Microsoft maintains that everything it is being asked to do is impractical. That is for the courts to decide. But Mr. Gates must know better than to assert that the government's demands are the equivalent of asking Coca Cola to include cans of Pepsi in all its six-packs. Coca Cola is not a monopoly, but Microsoft's operating system is. It would be better if Mr. Gates recognized that reality and stopped behaving as if his company were still a struggling upstart. As he said yesterday, the world awaits an era of accelerating change in computers, with undreamed-of products in voice recognition, artificial intelligence and Internet commerce. The Justice Department and the attorneys general are right that the inventors of products in these areas must be allowed to market them to consumers free of a stranglehold by Microsoft.

THE ROCKY MOUNTAIN NEWS

FROM AN EDITORIAL, MAY 20, 1998.

*i*f the Justice Department's antitrust action against Microsoft is justified — and we emphasis if — it is because the law, as interpreted by the U.S. Supreme Court, prohibits a dominant company in any industry from engaging in ruthless restraint of trade and anti-competitive acts. And while it has yet to be ruled on in court, Microsoft at least appears to have taken occasional unfair advantage of the fact that it's the producer of 90 percent of all computer operating systems in place in this country. . . .

The difficulty for anyone inclined to support the government's lawsuit on those limited grounds is that the Justice Department has much broader and more dubious motives for its lawsuit. While government lawyers apparently don't envision breaking Microsoft up, in the manner of Standard Oil and AT&T, they are intent on regulating the content of Microsoft's products. This is bad business, bad economics and utterly perverse public policy. Federal and state prosecutors must recognize that Microsoft became as dominant as it is through business savvy and ingenuity and because consumers want its products. It is nothing short of alarming that prosecutors should insist that Microsoft either exclude its own browser from its new Windows 98 software or include Netscape's. . . .

The government has no business prescribing what such a product might be like, and becomes something as bad as anti-competitive when it does. It becomes anti-innovative. There are many other extraordinary software features that could soon be coming around the bend, and Microsoft technicians should have an incentive to develop them and stick them in Windows. In what other instance has a firm been told it must diminish what it sells or promote and sell a competitive product? An equally disturbing aspect of the government's case is its focus: the most dynamic sector of the U.S. economy. After all, it is hard to identify the victims of Microsoft's alleged predatory activities. Netscape? Perhaps, although it retains a healthy share of the browser market. Consumers? Hardly. The price of software and other computer products has continued their 20-year plunge. If Microsoft were exploiting consumers and stifling innovation — the classic profile of a monopolist — then a government lawsuit might be more understandable. Instead, Microsoft leads a sector of the economy that is the envy of the world. The truth is that Microsoft represents just a small fraction of all software business and is far from immune to a competitor who has better ideas.

U.S. Mergers Add Up to $Billions

Here are some of the major corporate mergers proposed recently involving U.S. firms:

Companies	Date Proposed	Value	Status
American Home Products Corp., Monsanto Co.	June 1, 1998	$35 billion	Likely to be reviewed by the Federal Trade Commission(FTC)
Citicorp, Travelers Group Inc.	April 6, 1998	$70 billion	Pending review by Federal Reserve Board, Comptroller of the Currency
Daimler-Benz AG, Chrysler Corp.	May 7, 1998	$38 billion	Being reviewed by U.S., European authorities
Lockheed Martin Corp. Northrup Grumman Corp.	July 3, 1997	$2.9 billion	Justice Dept. opposing merger in court
McKesson Corp., AmeriSource Health Corp.	Sept. 23, 1997	$1.7 billion	FTC opposing merger in court, as well as merger of two other wholesalers: Cardinal Health, Inc., and Bergen Brunswig Corp.
NationsBank Corp. BankAmerica Corp.	April 13, 1998	$30 billion	Pending review by banking regulators
SBC Communications Inc., Ameritech Corp.	May 11, 1998	$56.2 billion	Pending review by Federal Communications Commission (FCC), Justice Dept., state regulators
WorldCom Inc., MCI Communications Corp.	Nov. 10, 1997	$37 billion	Pending review by Justice Dept., European Union (EU) Commission
Bell Atlantic Corp., Nynex Corp.	April 21, 1996	$23 billion	Approved by FCC in August 1997, with some pro-competitive conditions; Justice Dept. decided in April 1997 not to oppose deal
Bertlesmann AG, Random House Inc.	March 23, 1998	$1.5 billion	Approved by FTC May 29; FTC initiated "second request" review
Boeing Co., McDonnell Douglas Corp.	Dec. 15, 1996	$13 billion	Completed July 1997 after FTC decision not to oppose deal; some concessions to win approval of European Union
Thomson Corp., West Publishing Co.	Feb. 26, 1996	$3.4 billion	Justice Dept. approved merger, June 1996, after firms agreed to license products, sell some publications
SBC Communications Inc., AT&T Corp.	May 1997 (talks disclosed)	$50 billion	Merger talks called off June 27 because of business disagreements, likely opposition from FCC
SmithKline Beecham PLC, American Home Products Corp.	Jan. 20, 1998 (talks disclosed)	$60 billion (estimate)	British firm called off talks to pursue merger with Glaxo Wellcome PLC; those talks also failed
Staples Inc., Office Depot Inc.	Sept. 4, 1995	$3.4 billion	Merger blocked after federal judge upheld FTC bid to enjoin deal, June 30, 1997

(Left margin labels: PENDING, APPROVED, FAILED)

Source: Facts on File

cause it had failed to move against previous mergers among defense contractors in the past several years, including the $13.4 billion merger between Boeing and McDonnell Douglas last August. [36]

FCC Chairman William Kennard similarly took a tougher line than the agency's previous stance on mergers when SBC and Ameritech announced their planned merger on May 11. The two companies will have "a high burden" to prove that the merger is in consumers' best interest, Kennard told the *Chicago Tribune* the day after the announcement. He said that in approving the Bell Atlantic-Nynex merger and SBC's earlier acquisition of Pacific Telesis, the commission "didn't contemplate further mergers" between the so-called Baby Bells. [37]

Some lawmakers also were raising questions about reduced competition in other industries. The day after American Airlines and US Airways announced plans for a so-called marketing alliance on April 23, Senate Commerce Committee Chairman John McCain, an Arizona Republican, criticized the move and called for legislation to remove what he called "institutional impediments to competition" in the airline industry.

Still, most industry observers appear to expect most of the proposed mergers to win approval either in whole or in part. One recent trend has been for companies to announce merger plans and then gain regulatory approval by making concessions — for example, selling off some parts of one or the other company or agreeing to certain conditions aimed at promoting competition. [38] MCI Communications was following that strategy when it announced plans on May 28 to sell off its Internet facilities in order to win approval from European regulators of its merger with the British-based telecommunications giant, WorldCom. ∎

OUTLOOK

"Hundred Years' War"

When it recently surveyed the history of the U.S. market system in the 20th century, *The Wall Street Journal* prepared a chart with major events characterized either as "promoting" or "restricting" markets. Most of the economic regulatory statutes on the list — like the Food and Drug Act of 1907 or the National Labor Relations Act of 1937 — were shown as restricting markets. But as the century's first important event promoting markets, the newspaper listed, "[Theodore] Roosevelt begins 'trust-busting' campaign." [39]

The view of antitrust laws as an important, even essential, element of a free-market system has lasted for more than a century and still has a powerful hold on the views of policymakers and the public at large. "In the long run, the enormous productivity and wealth of the American economy depends on keeping competitive forces powerful," says the AEI's Stelzer.

But that favorable assessment of antitrust policy has never gone unchallenged. Today, the criticism of antitrust enforcement is gaining strength in some quarters even as the federal government shows greater interest in flexing its muscles to promote competition in the marketplace. "Given innovation, technology and dynamic markets, it's hard to imagine that there is such a thing as a sustainable monopoly absent governmental barriers" to competition, says Levy at the Cato Institute.

The spurt of antitrust enforcement by the Justice Department and the FTC over the past year has been depicted — sometimes positively, sometimes not — as an antitrust "revival." "The temperature is rising," Stelzer says.

But some consumer advocates say that even with the increased activity and interest, both the administration and Congress are too weak in promoting and protecting competition. "This administration has been in the last few years extremely modest and timid to the point of endangering the emergence of competition in key industries," says Kimmelman of Consumers Union. "And Congress and state and federal regulators have eliminated a lot of ownership restrictions and permitted a lot of consolidations to take place."

Federal courts are also less receptive toward antitrust cases than they had been in the past, chiefly from the late 1930s through the mid-'70s. "In the modern era, when the government has been forced to litigate, their track record has not been particularly good," George Mason's Kovacic says.

The likely outcome of the administration's current major antitrust cases is very much uncertain. The Supreme Court precedents on illegal tying arrangements that the administration cites in its suit against Microsoft are viewed by some legal observers as inconclusive. As for the mergers, the high court has not issued a ruling in the area for 25 years. And Kovacic believes one reason for the gap is that the Justice Department has been loath to appeal merger cases to the court for fear of getting a ruling that would raise the standard for blocking corporate combinations.

In his history of "competition policy," Peritz characterizes the period since passage of the Sherman Act as a "hundred years' war" between two competing visions of freedom: freedom from private economic power or freedom from government power. "Because we dread domination — both political and economic — we have called for policy that limits both kinds of power, policy that satisfies commitments to both individual liberty and rough equality," he writes. [40]

"Antitrust policy has been almost a Rorschach test" for social and political values, Peritz adds today. "Has it been successful in serving the dominant interests at the time? Yes. Has there been historical consistency? No, but I don't know that historical consistency is something that we should demand." ∎

Notes

[1] The cases filed in U.S. District Court in Washington, D.C., are *U.S. v. Microsoft Corp.*, 98-1232, and *New York v. Microsoft Corp.*, 98-1233.

[2] The states filing suit were California, Connecticut, Florida, Illinois, Iowa, Kansas, Kentucky, Louisiana, Maryland, Massachusetts, Michigan, Minnesota, New Mexico, New York, North Carolina Ohio, South Carolina, Utah, West Virginia, and Wisconsin. The District of Columbia also joined the suit. See *The Wall Street Journal*, May 28, 1998, p. A24. For background on the Internet, see "Regulating the Internet," *The CQ Researcher*, June 30, 1995, pp. 561-584.

[3] For background on Microsoft and Gates, see Stephen Manes and Paul Andrews, *Gates: How Microsoft's Mogul Reinvented an Industry — And Made Himself the Richest Man in America* (1993), James Wallace and Jim Erickson, *Hard Drive: Bill Gates and the Making of the Microsoft Empire* (1992), and, for a sharply critical account, Jennifer Edstrom and Marlin Eller, *Barbarians Led by Bill Gates: Microsoft from the Inside* (1998).

[4] For background on antitrust policy and professional sports, see "The Business of Sports," *The CQ Researcher*, Feb. 10, 1995, pp. 121-144.

[5] The quote comes from the decision in *United States v. Topco Associates Inc.* (1973).

[6] For background on Archer Daniels Midland, see *The Wall Street Journal*, Oct. 16, 1996, p. A4. The Decatur, Ill.- based company pleaded guilty to two criminal counts for fixing prices with foreign producers of lysine, a livestock-feed additive, and citric acid, an ingredient in numerous foods and beverages. For background on Ucar International, see *The Washington Post*, April 8, 1998, p. C13. Ucar allegedly conspired with unnamed co-conspirators to set prices and production levels in the world market.

[7] Robert H. Bork, *The Antitrust Paradox: A Policy at War With Itself* (1978), p. 4.

[8] Frank H. Easterbrook, "Workable Antitrust Policy," *Michigan Law Review*, Vol. 84, p. 1701 (1986).

[9] Packard Bell NEC Inc. became the first PC maker to take advantage of the option when it announced on May 29 that it would block access to Microsoft's browser in a new line of notebook computers about to be unveiled.

[10] Much of the background is drawn from Rudolph J.R. Peritz, *Competition Policy in America, 1888-1992: History, Rhetoric, Law* (1994).

[11] Robert H. Bork, "Legislative Intent and the Policy of the Sherman Act," *Journal of Law and Economics*, Vol. 9, pp. 7-48 (1966). See also Bork, *The Antitrust Paradox*, op. cit., pp. 50-71. Bork, now a fellow at the American Enterprise Institute, emerged in spring 1998 as a supporter of the government's antitrust actions against Microsoft. Bork said his stance was consistent with his previous views but also acknowledged that he was working as a paid consultant to Microsoft's rival, Netscape. See Robert H. Bork, "What Antitrust Is All About," *The New York Times*, May 4, 1998, p. A19.

[12] For differing interpretations of Congress' intent in passing the Sherman Act, see Robert H. Lande, "Wealth Transfers as the Original and Primary Concern of Antitrust: The Efficiency Interpretation Challenged," *Hastings Law Journal*, Vol. 34 pp. 68-151 (1982), excerpted in Sullivan, op. cit., pp. 71-84; and David Million, "The Sherman Act and the Balance of Power," *Southern California Law Review*, Vol. 61, pp. 1219-92 (1988), excerpted in Sullivan, op. cit., pp. 85-115.

[13] The decisions are *Standard Oil v. United States* and *United States v. American Tobacco Co.* See Peritz, op. cit., pp. 50-52.

[14] The speaker was Sen. James Reed, a Missouri Democrat; quoted in ibid., p. 65.

[15] See *1976 Congressional Quarterly Almanac*, p. 431-438, and *1974 Congressional Quarterly Almanac*, pp. 291-292. For assessments of the impact of the premerger notification rule and other provisions of the law, see "Symposium: Twenty Years of Hart-Scott-Rodino Merger Enforcement," *Antitrust Law Journal*, Vol. 65, spring 1997, pp. 813-927.

[16] The decision is *Brown Shoe Co. v. United States*.

[17] For background, and a critical interpretation, see Peritz, op. cit., pp. 236-245. Peritz cites as a seminal article Ronald Coase, "The Theory of Social Cost," *Journal of Law & Economics*, Vol. 3, 1960, pp. 1-44.

[18] For a summary of Posner's views, contrasted with those of the "Harvard school," see Richard A. Posner, "The Chicago School of Antitrust Analysis," *University of Pennsylvania Law Review*, Vol. 127, pp. 925-948 (1979), excerpted in Sullivan, op. cit., pp. 193-209.

[19] Bork, op. cit., pp. 3-11.

[20] The classic Harvard school text is Carl Kaysen and Donald Turner, *Antitrust Policy: An Economic and Legal Analysis* (1959). For an excerpt, see Sullivan, op. cit., pp. 181-192.

[21] See Peritz, op. cit., p. 278.

[22] See William E. Kovacic, "Reagan's Judicial Appointees and Antitrust in the 1990s," *Fordham Law Review*, Vol. 60, 1991, pp. 49-124.

[23] The cases, in order, are *United States v. General Dynamics* (1974); *Continental T.V., Inc. v. GTE Sylvania, Inc.* (1977); and *Brunswick Corp. v. Pueblo Bowl-O-Mat, Inc.* (1977). See ibid., pp. 97-98.

[24] For an account of the AT&T case, see Steve Coll, *The Deal of the Century: The Breakup of AT&T* (1986).

[25] The case is *Aspen Skiing Co. v. Aspen Highlands Skiing Corp.* (1985).

[26] For background, see *The New York Times*, Oct. 22, 1995, sec. 3, p. 1.

[27] See *The New York Times*, April 25, 1996, p. D1. For biographical background, see *The Washington Post*, April 13, 1995, p. D12.

[28] See *The New York Times*, Sept. 13, 1996, p. D1.

[29] For a profile, see *The Wall Street Journal*, May 18, 1998, p. A1.

[30] *The Washington Post*, March 24, 1998, p. C5.

[31] For a profile of David Boies, see Amy Singer, "A Firm Of His Own," *The American Lawyer*, May 1998, p. 62.

[32] See *The New York Times*, June 9, 1998, p. A1; *The Wall Street Journal*, June 9, 1998, p. A3.

[33] Peter Passell, "Do Mergers Really Yield Big Benefits?", *The New York Times*, May 14, 1998, p. D1. See also Peter Passell, "When Mega-Mergers Are Mega-Busts," *The New York Times*, May 17, 1998, p. E18.

[34] *The Wall Street Journal*, May 7, 1998, A10.

[35] See *CQ Weekly*, May 16, 1998, p. 1301. Senate action is regarded as less likely.

[36] See *The Washington Post*, April 7, 1998, p. C2.

[37] *The Chicago Tribune*, May 13, 1998, p. A1.

[38] See *The Wall Street Journal*, March 4, 1997, p. A1.

[39] *The Wall Street Journal*, May 14, 1998, p. A10.

[40] Peritz, op. cit., p. 3.

Bibliography

Selected Sources Used

Books

Bork, Robert H., *The Antitrust Paradox: A Policy at War With Itself*, Basic Books, 1978.

Bork, a Yale law professor at the time, helped provoke a thorough re-examination of antitrust doctrine with his controversial thesis that antitrust laws have no justification except to promote "consumer welfare" — defined in terms of productive efficiency. The book includes detailed source notes.

Gellhorn, Ernest, and William E. Kovacic, *Antitrust Law and Economics in a Nutshell*, West Publishing, 1994.

This primer, written for a legal audience, covers the major topics in antitrust law, including horizontal and vertical restraints, mergers, price discrimination and so forth. It includes the text of the key parts of the Sherman and Clayton acts as well as a table of cases. Gellhorn, a former law school professor and dean, is an attorney in Washington; Kovacic is a professor at George Mason University School of Law.

High, Jack C., and Wayne E. Gable (eds.), *A Century of the Sherman Act: American Economic Opinion, 1890-1990*, George Mason University Press, 1992.

The book includes 17 articles — most of them critical of antitrust policy — written by leading economists dating from the early 20th century through the mid-1980s. High and Gable are professors at George Mason University.

Peritz, Rudolph J.R., *Competition Policy in America, 1888-1992: History, Rhetoric, Law*, Oxford University Press, 1996.

Peritz, a professor at New York Law School, synthesizes the history of antitrust law with other political, economic and intellectual trends from the adoption of the Sherman Act in 1890 through the Reagan and Bush presidencies. The book includes detailed source notes. For a number of articles discussing and critiquing the book, see "Symposium: Provocations and Reflections Upon Competition Policy in America," *The Antitrust Bullet*, Vol. 42, No. 2 (summer 1997), pp. 239-456.

Shenefield, John H., and Irwin M. Stelzer, *The Antitrust Laws: A Primer* [3d ed.], American Enterprise Institute Press, 1998 [forthcoming].

This 142-page primer, written for a business audience, provides a compact overview of antitrust laws, agencies and concepts. It includes a two-page suggested list of further readings. Shenefield, a former assistant attorney general for antitrust, is now a Washington lawyer; Stelzer, an economist, is director of regulatory policy studies at the American Enterprise Institute in Washington.

Sullivan, E. Thomas [ed.], *The Political Economy of the Sherman Act: The First One Hundred Years*, Oxford University Press, 1992.

This anthology includes 15 excerpted articles by leading scholars and policy-makers representing major developments in the political, economic and intellectual debates about antitrust policy. Sullivan is dean of the University of Minnesota law school. He is also co-author with Herbert Hovenkamp of the University of Iowa law school of an antitrust casebook, *Antitrust Law, Policy, and Procedure* (Michie Publishing, 3d ed., 1994).

Articles

Lowenstein, Roger, "Trust in Markets: Antitrust Enforcers Drop the Ideology, Focus on Economics," *The Wall Street Journal*, Feb. 27, 1997.

The 3,350-word article gives an excellent overview of the development of antitrust policy from passage of the Sherman Act in 1890 through President Clinton's first term. The article was part of a series entitled "Amalgamated America." A later article analyzed enforcement policies by antitrust agencies. See John R. Wilke and Bryan Gruley, "Merger Monitors: Acquisitions Can Mean Long-Lasting Scrutiny by Antitrust Agencies," *The Wall Street Journal*, March 4, 1997, p. A1.

FOR MORE INFORMATION

Information and documents about the antitrust suit against Microsoft Corp. and the company's response can be found at the following world wide web sites: **Justice Department**, www.usdoj.gov/atr; **states** [National Association of Attorneys General], www.naag.org; **Microsoft**, www.microsoft.com.

Cato Institute, 1000 Massachusetts Ave., N.W., Washington, D.C. 20001; (202) 842-0200; www.cato.org. The libertarian think tank has published a number of monographs critical of government regulation of the marketplace.

Center for Study of Responsive Law, P.O. Box 19367, Washington, D.C. 20036; (202) 387-8030; www.csrl.org. The center's Consumer Project on Technology studies competition issues in the computer industry.

Consumers Union of the United States, 1666 Connecticut Ave., N.W., Suite 310, Washington, D.C. 20009; (202) 462-6262; www.consumersunion.org. Consumers Union, publisher of *Consumer Reports*, lobbies on a range of consumer issues.

8 Utility Deregulation

ADRIEL BETTELHEIM

For years, residents and businesses in Harrisburg, Pa., didn't have to think about how they received their electricity. Pennsylvania Power & Light had a monopoly on power sales, and monthly bills from the big utility were an accepted fact of life.

Then, last January, state officials opened Pennsylvania's retail power market to competition. Since deregulation, Harrisburg-area consumers have been flooded with direct-mail brochures and radio and television advertising from power retailers urging them to compare prices. No less than 13 suppliers sought to power the Hershey Foods Corp.'s famed chocolate-manufacturing plants. The sprawling Milton S. Hershey Medical Center shopped around and saved $350,000 per year on electricity.

Already, residential consumers in the area are seeing average rate reductions of 9 percent, with industrial customers reaping even bigger savings, according to regulators. That's encouraging news in a state that historically had some of the highest electric rates in the nation.

"We're feeling pretty good about where we sit," says John Quain, chairman of the Pennsylvania Public Utility Commission. "I don't know what the learning curve is, and whether everyone will switch to the lowest-cost supplier. But they're beginning to understand how to shop for a brand-new commodity."

The experience in south-central Pennsylvania may soon be repeated around the country as state regulators and lawmakers embrace electric competition. A total of 24 states have implemented or approved plans to open their power markets to competition, and at least as many others are studying proposals. (*See map, p. 150.*)

Advocates say deregulation will

From *The CQ Researcher,*
January 14, 2000.

Digital Stock

bring lower electric bills, better service and such market innovations as allowing consumers to pick environmentally friendly sources of energy. It also does away with regulators' century-old practice of granting utilities monopolies on providing service in certain areas if they pledge to serve every customer.

But the long-term prospects for nationwide electricity deregulation remain murky. Federal lawmakers have yet to develop a national plan for opening the $220 billion power industry to competition. Congress remains sharply divided on key issues — such as whether to reimburse incumbent utilities for costs they incur in the free market and how much authority to grant the Federal Energy Regulatory Commission (FERC).

Without federal involvement, states can craft deregulation plans, but there is no single entity to oversee the interstate trading of electricity, reserve power for contingencies or monitor antitrust issues. Critics say the indecision is delaying the benefits consumers are expected to reap in the unbridled market, and leaves a patchwork quilt of local laws and regulations governing power sales.

Meanwhile, some states that implemented deregulation plans are being

criticized for allowing utilities to recover costs too quickly, negating most of the savings that deregulation promised. In California, consumer groups tried to scrap the state's deregulation plan, but their ballot initiative in the November 1998 elections was decisively beaten.

"It's an extraordinarily messy process," says Adam Thierer, an economic policy fellow at the Heritage Foundation. "States are making up rules as they go along, and many prospective competitors are sitting on the sidelines because of all the legal uncertainty. It's the opposite of when telecommunications, airlines, railroads and trucking were deregulated.[1] The states are leading the charge, and there are no national rules to connect it all."

"Progress is being made in some states, and some consumers are benefiting, but the market is completely irrational and localized," says Gerald R. Alderson, president of Wattage Monitor, a Reno, Nev., company that tracks deregulation efforts in various states. "The federal government has to do something — it's complete fiction that electricity is a commodity bound by state borders."

Congress made its latest attempt at sorting out the market on Oct. 27, when the House Commerce Energy and Power Subcommittee cleared a deregulation plan authored by the panel's chairman, Rep. Joe L. Barton, R-Texas. But the plan was opposed by most Democrats on the subcommittee, as well as the Clinton administration and an assortment of environmental, consumer and electric industry groups. Even Commerce Committee Chairman Thomas J. Bliley Jr., R-Va., expressed doubts about his fellow Republican's plan and is expected to introduce a rival version early this year.[2] A White House deregulation plan proposed to Congress last year also lacks sufficient support.

Such uncertainty and upheaval is

Competition in Power Industry Gaining Support

Twenty-four states have opened or plan to open their power markets to competition, and many others are studying proposals. Advocates say deregulation will bring lower electric bills and better service. But federal lawmakers have yet to develop a national plan for opening the $220 billion power industry to competition.

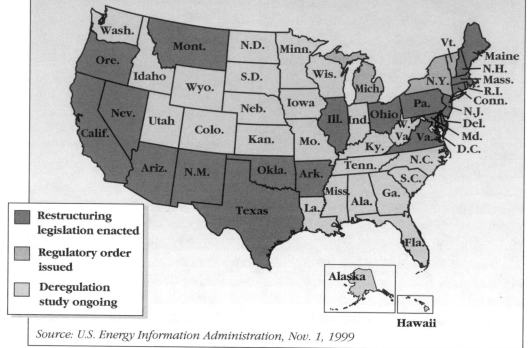

Restructuring
legislation enacted

Regulatory order
issued

Deregulation
study ongoing

Source: U.S. Energy Information Administration, Nov. 1, 1999

ties won some concessions, such as when FERC allowed the companies to recover "stranded costs" incurred on unprofitable power plants and power supply contracts if their customers switched to new suppliers.

Though those moves collectively restructured the wholesale electric market, they didn't directly address retail power sales to consumers, which have largely been left to the states. New Hampshire approved a retail competition pilot program in 1995, and Rhode Island, Massachusetts, Maine, Connecticut, New York, Pennsylvania, Illinois, Montana and California each followed with their own deregulation plans. To date, Pennsylvania's has drawn the biggest response, with more than 470,000 of the state's 5.3 million electric customers switching suppliers. [5] Most of the states with plans had historically high electric costs, in part because utilities there built expensive nuclear plants.

Some states with lower-than-average power costs have resisted opening their markets, fearing consumers' electric bills will rise. In October, a Colorado board that advises the state's General Assembly recommended against opening the $2.3 billion power market there to outside competition, meaning consumers are unlikely to have the ability to choose their power supplier for several years. One recent study showed residential consumers in the state paid 7.5 cents per kilowatt-hour in 1998, while the national average was 8.3 cents. In September, a Nebraska task force similarly recommended against deregulation, at least until a viable wholesale market is established and prices stabilize. Nebraska is the only state served entirely

nothing new for the electric power industry, an amalgam of some 3,100 investor-owned utilities, municipal power companies and rural cooperatives that are governed by a complex set of legislative and regulatory mandates. Most of the utilities don't actually generate power but buy wholesale electricity from other companies and distribute it to consumers. The largest utilities own and operate an extensive network of high-voltage transmission lines that are linked to permit electricity trading between generating companies. [3]

The push to bring competition to the system began during the energy crisis of the 1970s, when high oil prices drove up electric companies' costs of operating fossil fuel-powered plants and led to numerous rate increases. In an effort to diversify energy sources, Congress

in 1978 passed a series of measures forcing big utilities to buy power produced from renewable energy sources, such as hydroelectric, solar and wind power. The mandates, combined with the economic pressures of constructing new power plants, effectively created a new electric power sector consisting of small, independent generators. [4]

Deregulation efforts intensified during the free-market years of the Reagan administration in the 1980s, though utility companies at first successfully fought off efforts to bring competition to bulk power sales. Congress eventually passed the Energy Policy Act of 1992, which required utilities to open their transmission lines to all sellers of electricity and rolled back New Deal-era regulations to help new generating companies to sell power to utilities. Incumbent utili-

by publicly owned power, and residential rates there are 24 percent below the regional average. [6]

Few expect a consensus to develop soon on either the state or federal levels. The looming 2000 elections and potential political fallout from a major industry restructuring make congressional action unlikely. More states, including Virginia and Maryland, will introduce deregulation plans next year. But others are waiting to see what, if any, federal laws are laid down in the next several years. Nervously watching all of the activity are the utilities themselves, which in some deregulation states are being forced to sell power plants and take other cost-cutting steps to be competitive in open markets. Experts believe even partial deregulation will prompt a shakeout, in which the highest-cost companies could be forced out of business.

"The only reprieve provided by the prevailing 'go-slow' restructuring environment is the opportunity for vulnerable utilities to make up for any time that may have been lost through a failure to address competitiveness issues," write Standard & Poor's utility analysts David Bodek and Elizabeth Isaacs. "If utilities bury their heads in the sand, it is unlikely that they will be able to preserve financial strength." [7]

As the push for electricity deregulation continues, here are some questions being asked:

Will consumers benefit in a freer electricity market?

When California authorities approved a plan to deregulate the state's $20 billion electric market in 1996, it was cheered as long-overdue relief for consumers, who were paying some of the highest rates in the nation. The first-in-the-nation plan gave customers an immediate 10 percent rate rollback and promised to bring competition to a market then dominated by three big electric utilities.

But just over two years later, consumers' groups were so upset with the plan that they drafted a ballot initiative for the November 1998 elections to overturn deregulation. Though households got their rate reduction, residential ratepayers discovered new charges on their bills, including "transition charges" to help utilities recover costs associated with unprofitable nuclear plants and contracts. Consumer groups say the net effect was residential ratepayers saved just 1 to 3 percent on their bills. [8]

The experience in California illustrates one of the pitfalls of deregulation: Consumers frequently don't immediately realize savings because state regulators allow incumbent power suppliers to charge their customers for costs associated with operating in a competitive market. These stranded costs, in utility parlance, are often linked to money-losing generating plants, power supply contracts and debts that the companies took on to serve their customers, but that can't be recovered if the customers choose other electricity suppliers. Estimates of total stranded costs vary widely, from $10 billion to as much as $500 billion. The faster regulators allow utilities to recover stranded costs, the bigger the transition charges passed on to customers.

Utilities and their supporters say they are entitled to recover the costs because they built power plants and transmission lines — sometimes under orders from regulators — on the assumption they would serve all of the customers in their service areas on demand. "These costs were accumulated under rules of the game that limited profits and imposed various service obligations in return for a protected market," says Philip R. O'Connor, former chairman of the Illinois Commerce Commission and now a principal in the Chicago office of Coopers & Lybrand. "In the course of deregulating other industries,

policy-makers have achieved reasonably orderly transitions by considering the significant financial interests that investors, customers and others built up over the years."

But some consumers and advocacy groups contend small ratepayers are being forced to subsidize utilities' unprofitable investments while the utilities are simultaneously striking cut rate deals with big power users. In California, factories and other industrial power users could cut their costs by as much as 33 percent over four years, according to energy marketing experts, because utilities discounted rates to lock the big customers into long-term contracts.

"It is quite clear that residential ratepayers will only benefit from restructuring if vigorous policies that protect their economic interests are implemented," states a recent report by the Consumers Union and Consumer Federation of America. [9] The organizations estimate consumer bills in deregulation states could rise 10 to 20 percent because of such cost-shifting.

Stranded costs aren't the only factor affecting electric bills. Legislators and regulators in states that deregulate their power markets often separate the rate to generate electricity at the power plant from the rate to deliver it to consumers. The generation rate, called the "standard offer," is set by regulators in the hope it will be low enough to guarantee rate cuts but high enough to attract new power suppliers. However, in Massachusetts and Rhode Island, experts say policy-makers set the rate too low, leaving prospective competitors with few economic incentives to enter the market. In Rhode Island, only 1,992 of the state's 456,000 electric customers had left their utility for a competitor by mid-1999. [10]

Robert Burns, senior research specialist at the National Regulatory Research Institute (NRRI) in Columbus, Ohio, says most states haven't

Demystifying Deregulation

Following are some frequently asked questions about electricity deregulation:

Why the big fuss about electricity deregulation? — Because electricity is big business. Electricity sales in the United States generate an estimated $220 billion a year in revenue. As various states open this vast industry to competition, they are breaking up a system in which power companies were treated as regulated monopolies for most of this century. Similar deregulation of airlines, telecommunications and other industries is credited with bringing lower prices, improved service and market innovations. Advocates hope it will do the same in the power business.

Does deregulation mean not having to deal with your local utility ever again? — Hardly. Even if a residential customer switches power suppliers, the local utility will continue to transmit electricity over its wires to the residence. If there is an outage due to a storm, the ratepayer still must call the local utility. But the local utility essentially becomes a power shipper; the electricity that is being transmitted is a commodity that the consumer ordered from another vendor.

How can consumers compare rates? — Electricity usage frequently is measured in kilowatt-hours. Monthly bills list the current charge. In states with deregulation, utility commissioners or state consumer advocates have set up Web sites and phone services allowing consumers to check which vendors serve their areas and what rate each offers. Consumers in affected areas also likely will be besieged with advertising from utilities. Customers who consider changing suppliers need to ask whether there are transition fees or other charges associated with the switch.

Will every service area in a state be deregulated at the same time? — Probably not. Outlying areas that aren't served by big electric companies typically are on different schedules and will get electric choice later. Municipally owned utilities decide on their own whether their customers will have a choice of vendors. Some states like New Hampshire inaugurated pilot programs in particular service areas.

Will consumers have the option of obtaining power from environmentally friendly energy sources? — Many residents in deregulated states can buy "green power." However, "green" can be expensive. In Philadelphia, customers recently were paying 6.2 cents per kilowatt-hour (kwh) for 100 percent renewable energy, compared with an average of 5.7 cents per kwh paid by regular residential customers.

---

left enough "headroom" to guarantee new competitors will make a profit, thus limiting true consumer choice. Pennsylvania is the exception because it set a standard offer high enough to ensure that competing companies would enter the market and drive prices down. But, Burns notes, the success of electricity deregulation can't be measured simply by how many customers switch, or by how many companies rush to serve a particular service area.

"The first states that embarked on deregulation were concerned about getting retail prices down, especially for large commercial customers. If you measure the situation by that criteria, it has been a success," Burns says. He says residential customers in certain states may have to band together to obtain enough market power to get price concessions.

"If you lump households together and get several hundred or thousand customers, you may have a big enough load to make a transaction," Burns says.

Should FERC have the authority to regulate the newly unfettered electric market?

Individually, they're known as the Texas Interconnection, New England Power Pool and the Western Power Grid. Collectively, they're regional portions of the complex network of generators, power lines and substations that bring electricity to North America — a system with more than 700,000 miles of towers and wires spanning the United States and Canada. [11]

Deregulation is bringing major changes to this segment of the electric industry. Under the old system, one utility could own generators, transmission lines and distribution networks and essentially operate as a "vertically integrated" monopoly in a particular region. Now, specialized companies own pieces of the power

grid and are breaking down the old market barriers. Transmission companies that move the power bid for electricity from generating companies in carefully timed auctions. And federal regulators must keep track of the complex web of interstate energy sales, monitoring usage and making sure there is enough electricity left over for contingencies, such as a widespread power outage.

The specter of further electricity deregulation has sparked a heated debate over what role FERC will have in the new market. Specifically, lawmakers are divided over whether FERC will have enough authority to police market-power abuses, and whether the agency should have more of a role designating new transmission lines and regional power alliances. This last role is particularly important, as more states move to deregulation and regional segments of the power grid are thrown open to more competitors.

"FERC is trying to bring utilities together on a regional basis and set up some kind of oversight in the new market," says Burns. "There's a real need for a mechanism that allows the market to exist. Otherwise you'll have occasions where there isn't adequate capacity, and that can lead to major regional power outages."

Such shortages contributed to the blackouts that briefly shut down parts of Chicago last summer. Lack of capacity, and inadequate contingency plans to rush excess power to where it is needed, also contributed to two major failures of the Western Power Grid in 1996, and to the infamous 1965 New York City blackout that left 30 million people in the Northeast and Canada without electricity.

Some of the current concern is prompted by utilities' moves to merge transmission holdings into independent system operators (ISOs) that will run regional pieces of the nationwide power grid. FERC historically has judged the merits and problems with such mergers and determined whether they benefit consumers. The reviews have turned up pricing discrepancies; to move power 500 miles from Boston to Washington, transmission utility Southern Companies pays more than three times what it costs to move the same amount of power across 500 miles of its own lines elsewhere in the country. [12]

However, Barton's legislation passed by the House Commerce subcommittee in October would subject FERC's merger review to time limits. The agency also could not order divestiture of a regional system's assets to remedy discriminatory pricing. [13] Barton's legislation addressed criticism in some quarters that FERC's merger reviews duplicate the antitrust function of other government agencies, such as the Department of Justice and Federal Trade Commission. However, Democrats on the

subcommittee contend the Barton bill doesn't give FERC enough muscle to curb market abuses.

FERC Commissioner William Massey, without directly criticizing the Barton bill, warned a recent electric industry conference that the road to deregulation is not smooth and that FERC must provide "tough but fair" analysis of each merger's effects on competition. Massey also noted that, unlike other antitrust agencies, FERC allows public participation. "I remain convinced that all market stakeholders working in good faith with regulators can make all of the pieces fit together," Massey told the Electricity Consumers Resource Council. [14]

However, some argue that expanding FERC's role in the deregulated market amounts to nationalizing the electricity transmission sector. Critics say it essentially would give the federal government power to configure and make rules for combinations of individual utilities' transmission lines known as regional transmission organizations (RTOs) — a power the critics believe ultimately would lead to price regulation.

"It is all but certain that RTOs would evolve into regulatory or quasi-regulatory bodies whose decision making will be based on political rather than market forces," writes Thomas M. Lenard, vice president for research at the Progress & Freedom Foundation, a free-market think tank. "We should think twice before adopting such a framework because there is no reason to believe we know how to operate a centralized regulatory system for transmission any better than the current regulatory system has been operated." [15]

FERC Chairman James J. Hoecker and Commissioner Massey recently suggested that Northeastern utilities might want to form a single RTO to increase efficiencies in the power market and avoid Balkanizing the power grid. But such a move could

create confusion over whether FERC, states or the utilities actually have authority over electricity generation. For instance, would FERC simply have jurisdiction over power lines, or could it mandate that consumers in an area can choose their power supplier? And would such mandates pre-empt individual states' deregulation plans?

"We need to have all transmission under one set of rules," says former FERC Chairman Elizabeth Moler, now general counsel for the consumer group Americans for Affordable Electricity. "Nothing is more critical to the nation's well-being than a reliable power supply. This is a classic interstate commerce issue. Individual states cannot guarantee the reliability of the interstate grid — FERC must have the authority to do so." ■

BACKGROUND

PUHCA and PURPA

Deregulating the power market will likely involve scaling back or repealing a series of federal mandates that govern the flow of electricity from generating plants to the light switches in people's homes. They include a New Deal-era measure enacted to break the grip of powerful interstate holding companies that once controlled more than 75 percent of the nation's electric generating capacity, and a major law enacted during the administration of President Jimmy Carter to encourage development of alternative energy sources.

The Public Utility Holding Company Act of 1935 (PUHCA) forced the breakup of the holding companies and gave the Securities and Exchange Commission authority to require utilities to restrict electric power genera-

"Green Power" Gaining Support

The prospect of being able to choose one's power supplier is creating a burst of environmental awareness in some states that have adopted electricity deregulation plans. In fact, consumers are even getting appeals from divine sources.

The Pennsylvania Council of Churches recently issued a statement on global warming, urging persons of faith to buy electricity from renewable sources. Continuing to buy from polluting sources would contribute to environmental degradation — an act of violence to God's creation, according to the group, which includes representatives of Protestant faiths, the Greek Orthodox Church and the Philadelphia Board of Rabbis. [1]

Deregulation not only offers customers a choice of electricity suppliers but also some semblance of control over the power sources. Concern about the effects of coal-powered and nuclear power plants on the environment are leading power marketers to offer "green power" options.

Buying green power basically involves paying more to support the production of more renewable energy. The electricity that arrives in the customer's home is the same mix of power generated from various sources that other ratepayers receive. However, if enough customers sign up for the environmental option, more power from renewable sources will enter a region's distribution grid and contribute a greater percentage to the power mix.

One of the leading renewable energy suppliers is Green Mountain Energy Resources, which sells two renewable energy plans on its Web site, GreenMountain.com. One plan called "Wind for the Future" promises 100 percent renewable energy, 25 percent of which will come from new wind turbines. Green Mountain says that if half of all California households choose one of its plans, reduced fossil fuel emissions will keep 16.5 billion tons of carbon dioxide out of the air each year.

The sales pitch appears to be getting attention. In California, municipalities including Santa Monica, San Jose and San Diego all opted for green power. And some local utilities are beginning to offer green power options. The Los Angeles Department of Water and Power, a city-owned utility that derives 70 percent of its power from coal and nuclear sources, recently offered a clean-energy option promising that, if enough customers sign up, it will support building new wind and solar generating stations. [2]

One plant that recently went into service is Solar 2000, a 132-kilowatt solar-powered plant in Mendocino County, Calif. It is selling all of its generated power to Green Mountain under a multiyear purchase agreement. "This market will continue to grow as electricity suppliers educate customers about their opportunities ... in deregulated marketplaces," says James Torpey, president of GPU Solar, a developer of independent generating plants that operates the plant.

But many environmentalists warn that green power efforts won't have much of an effect if they don't receive government support. And they face a fight over such funds with the much more powerful electric utility industry, which bristles at criticisms of its plants and says power companies have undertaken expensive, voluntary initiatives to cut harmful emissions. The industry wants tax credits and other incentives to continue the work and fewer federal environmental mandates.

"Much has already been accomplished on a voluntary basis to meet global climate concerns and to increase efficiency and productivity," says Thomas R. Kuhn, president of the Edison Electric Institute, a trade group representing large investor-owned utilities. "These achievements need to be recognized and rewarded if they are to serve as a model for future advances."

[1] See "Penna. Churches Get Into Global Warming Debate," *The Electricity Daily*, Nov. 24, 1999, Vol. 13, No. 100. See Mary H. Cooper, "Global Warming Update," *The CQ Researcher*, Nov. 1, 1996, pp. 961-984.

[2] See William Booth, " 'Green' Power, an Electric Idea?" *The Washington Post*, Oct. 17, 1999, p. A1.

tion and transmission to a defined geographic area. The law also limited transactions between electric utilities and their parent companies, practically eliminating the participation of non-utilities in wholesale power sales.

The Carter-era measure is the Public Utility Regulatory Policies Act of 1978 (PURPA), which required utilities to purchase power from small power projects that used renewable sources of energy. The law propped up the price paid to these "qualifying facilities" by requiring utilities to pay what it would cost them to generate the same amount of electricity at their own plants. [16]

Deregulation advocates believe these laws, and a series of FERC orders dealing with the interstate flow of electricity, actually are slowing down the industry's transition from a regulated monopoly to a competitive service. PUHCA is blamed for being antiquated, and for preventing utilities from diversifying in order to improve profits. Critics say it also has already achieved its goal of making holding companies manageable both in size and accountability. However, consumer groups and many smaller publicly owned power companies say the law still may be necessary, because it protects against anti-competitive behavior at a time when utilities are merging to increase their market share.

PURPA, meanwhile, has been targeted for repeal because it is blamed for being anti-competitive and driving up consumer power bills. Critics say its power-purchasing requirements run counter to the goal of having a free electricity market, also noting that contracts to buy power from qualifying facilities are not cost-effective and result in higher consumer prices. Defenders of the law say there is no guarantee that a free market will promote development of alternative energy, adding that PURPA makes it easier for small energy generators to compete with big electric utilities.

The Clinton administration's electricity deregulation plan and various congressional proposals endorse doing away with the laws but differ on how to assure more open markets. One approach could involve imposing a federal "open access" requirement, similar to what was implemented in telecommunications deregulation, that would require utilities to open their power lines to rivals to give competitors direct access to consumers. The Heritage Foundation's Thierer says such a policy would assure that consumers have a choice in electricity providers. But, he notes, it would require continuous policing by regulators to assure that rivals are granted access to networks on non-discriminatory terms. He predicts lawsuits and court battles would ensue. [17] "Open access is kind of a transitional mechanism to get out of a regulatory logjam," Thierer says. "It's a deregulation 'halfway house' that has great promise, but also great problems."

An arguably more controversial approach would be mandatory divestiture, in which the federal government would order utilities to split off their generating facilities from transmission and distribution lines. An incumbent utility operating in both segments of the power business would be required to sell one part, thus opening the market to more competition. The approach has been tried on the state level; Rhode Island mandated that its utilities sell their power plants,

1900s-1960s

A series of federal laws lays out rules for the interstate transmission of electricity. Power companies gain monopolies in service areas in exchange for rate regulation.

1935
Congress passes the Federal Power Act, which regulates wholesale electric power rates, and the Public Utilities Holding Company Act (PUHCA), which forces the breakup of large industrial trusts that control most of the nation's generating capacity.

1935-1945
Nearly 300 public power systems and 800 rural cooperatives are formed, bringing power to areas that had no electric service. Dams and federal power administrations supply the electricity.

1954
The Atomic Energy Act allows private power companies to use nuclear energy.

1965
The worst power failure in American history blacks out much of the Northeast.

———— • ————

1966-1980s
An oil embargo drives up energy prices, prompting the federal government to push conservation initiatives and the development of renewable-energy resources.

1973
The Organization of Petroleum Exporting Countries launches a worldwide embargo, driving up electric utilities' costs.

1978
The Public Utilities Regulatory Policies Act (PURPA) requires utilities to use renewable energy.

1979
A near meltdown at the Three Mile Island nuclear plant in Pennsylvania shakes public confidence in nuclear energy, gradually halting a national power plant expansion program.

———— • ————

1990s
The push to bring competition to the electricity industry intensifies.

1992
The National Energy Policy Act opens the interstate transmission system to competition by allowing power producers to compete to sell electricity to utilities.

1996
FERC issues Order 888, requiring utilities to open their transmission lines to competing electric generators. New Hampshire launches a pilot program to allow competition. California, Rhode Island, Pennsylvania, Arizona and Massachusetts soon follow suit.

1999
House Commerce Subcommittee on Energy and Power passes electricity-restructuring plan.

and outside companies have rushed to buy the facilities. However, the success of such a plan depends on whether regulators would set rates for generating and transmitting electricity that are high enough to make profitable margins for new entrants.

Any broad deregulation plan also will have to deal with the federal government's own electric utilities. Huge entities like the Tennessee Valley Authority (TVA) sell subsidized power, and lawmakers are still divided over how to incorporate them into a restructured electricity market without crushing private utilities that haven't benefited from federal subsidies. Rep. Barton's bill in the House would limit the reach of the TVA and its ability to compete outside of its service area. [18]

"We here in Congress need to finish our job," Commerce Committee Chairman Bliley says. "There are federal issues that must be addressed if we are to bring about a fully open and competitive electricity power that benefits all Americans. In order to do our part, we must pass a comprehensive electricity power bill that is good for all consumers, improves reliability and ensures open and robust competition." ∎

CURRENT SITUATION

Big Savings?

Though the average consumer may gain the ability to choose electricity suppliers under deregulation, it's unlikely that individuals acting singly will reap big savings. Residential households and small businesses use scant amounts of electricity compared with big industrial users and wield little clout with suppliers — unless they band together with other buyers to form a block of purchasers.

A byproduct of the deregulatory push is the rise of "aggregators," or power brokers, who represent groups of customers and negotiate with energy suppliers to get the lowest price for electricity. The aggregators can help consumers navigate the increasingly complex market for buying power and, in a larger sense, speed up deregulation by involving more customers in a particular region.

"If an aggregator can lump you with several thousand other customers, you create a big enough load to be able to make a profitable transaction," says NRRI analyst Burns. "It doesn't really pay for a utility or the consumer to switch just one person's load because of economies of scale and the fact the power company usually will levy high transaction costs to pay for the change in service."

In Massachusetts, state and local government agencies and nonprofit foundations formed PowerOptions, a buying consortium that now comprises about 5 percent of the Massachusetts power market. The contract it negotiated with power suppliers last year is expected to save members some $33 million below what they would have paid individually after deregulation.

Such efforts are believed to be contributing to a nationwide decline in electricity rates. The Energy Department reports the average price of electricity fell 1.6 percent in 1998 to 6.7 cents per kilowatt-hour. Average monthly residential bills fell 2 percent, despite a 4.8 percent increase in monthly electricity consumption. Other factors contributing to the decline include so-called demand-side management programs, which encourage consumers to modify their patterns of electricity consumption. [19]

Rising Internet Use

Another trend in deregulated markets is the increased use of the Internet to make energy sales. On-line electric sales were expected to exceed $1 billion in 1999, and could reach $100 billion by 2004, according to Forrester Research. [20]

A new service on the Web, Houstonstreet.com of Portsmouth, N.H., takes advantage of the fact that power companies in deregulated markets are forming partnerships with distributors to create a single entity to serve ratepayers. The service allows power users and utilities to buy and sell electricity anonymously at openly listed prices.

A similar service aimed primarily at residential ratepayers is utility.com of Albany, Calif. The company acts both as an aggregator and virtual power company, allowing customers to pay their bills automatically, monitor their power usage and even adjust their home thermostats via on-line software. The service operates in California and Pennsylvania and is targeting states like Maine that soon will have deregulated markets.

Utility.com Chief Executive Officer Chris King likens the on-line services to those that vend books, toys and software on the Internet, except that the product is a vital commodity. "Take books, CDs, toys and pets. Add those together, multiply them by three and you get the size of the market. It's that big," King says. [21] ∎

OUTLOOK

Action in Congress?

Congress will get another chance to make sense of the myriad laws governing the electricity industry when

At Issue:

Should federal regulators be given expanded power to police the unfettered electricity market?

ALAN H. RICHARDSON
Executive Director, American Public Power Association

FROM TESTIMONY BEFORE THE HOUSE COMMERCE ENERGY AND POWER SUBCOMMITTEE, OCT. 6, 1999.

*t*he market power problems that exist, as well as those that we can now predict with a great degree of certainty, can only be addressed by Congress. These are interstate commerce problems that simply cannot be addressed by the individual states.

Federal antitrust laws work well to remedy problems in mature markets. But they are not well suited to guide the transition to competition for industries, such as the electric utility industry, that start from highly concentrated monopolies. Antitrust laws alone cannot convert such industries to ones capable of being controlled by competitive forces. . . .

The identification of such problems in any modern industry is hard, but in the electric utility industry . . . it is extremely difficult. Electricity is a real-time product. . . . It cannot be stored. This makes transactions in the electricity market very vulnerable to subtle discriminations such as capacity reservations on existing transmission facilities and manipulation of such seemingly innocuous events as unscheduled maintenance of strategically located generation and transmission facilities. For these reasons, the antitrust agencies have generally favored structural remedies. . . .

Congress held out the promise of competitive wholesale electric markets when it enacted the Energy Policy Act of 1992. This promise was reaffirmed when the act was implemented aggressively by the Federal Energy Regulatory Commission. But FERC has now acknowledged that its approach, reflected in Order 888, is deficient in many respects. Its current proceeding on regional transmission organizations is an attempt to address some of these deficiencies. Other deficiencies are apparent as well, including the absence of solid, clear legal authority under which FERC can effectively remove obstacles in the interstate commerce of electricity. . . .

Congress should also act to ensure the reliability of the electric utility system. Voluntary reliability standards are no longer adequate. . . .

And finally, Congress must act to address U.S. Tax Code provisions that are inconsistent with the new utility environment being brought about by state restructuring legislation. Public power's "private use" problem is a clear example of this. The operational limits imposed on publicly owned utilities with facilities financed by tax-exempt bonds by statutory private-use requirements are simply incompatible with the demands of the new market. . . .

THOMAS M. LENARD
Vice President for Research, Progress & Freedom Foundation

FROM *INVESTOR'S BUSINESS DAILY*, OCT. 26, 1999. USED WITH PERMISSION.

*s*urprising as it may be, there was a time when deregulation actually meant reducing the role of the regulator. . . . Sadly, this approach seems to have been lost, if not forgotten. After passage of the 1996 Telecommunications Act, the Federal Communications Commission assumed more authority, not less. Now Congress appears poised to make the same mistake with respect to electricity.

The House Commerce Committee is about to mark up an electricity "deregulation" bill that would vastly increase the authority of the Federal Energy Regulatory Commission and could, in the process, virtually nationalize the transmission sector. The vehicle for this policy is HR 2944, introduced by Joe Barton, R-Texas, chairman of the House Energy and Power Subcommittee.

The Barton bill reflects the interests of the large power marketers, who, quite naturally, would like to be able to transport their product over long distances inexpensively. To this end, the bill would encourage owners of transporters of electricity to transfer control of their facilities to "disinterested" third parties called independent system operators [ISOs] or regional transmission organizations [RTOs], which will operate them in the "public interest." . . .

. . . Except when entirely voluntary, the RTO concept is fundamentally flawed and counterproductive to the development of a competitive electricity sector. As their name suggests, RTOs are regional combinations of individual utilities' transmission systems. Their geographic configuration, governance structure and operating procedures would all require FERC approval, and they would operate the transmission grid under FERC's continuing regulatory scrutiny. All this would mean a large increase in the size and purview of FERC. . . .

. . . In fact, the most revealing single provision of this legislation is one that would give FERC direct authority to order utilities to build new transmission facilities. To give the regulator such unprecedented authority — even the old ICC never had the authority to order the railroads to lay new tracks — is an implicit admission of how far this legislation has departed from any concept of a market-based approach. . . .

Federal legislation that removes federal barriers to competition would be desirable. But the states will do better on their own than with a federal bill that adds more regulation than it removes.

lawmakers return from their winter recess this month. But many observers say prospects for drafting a nationwide deregulation plan soon are unlikely because of the major policy differences — and lawmakers' reluctance to pass sweeping legislation affecting a vital industry in an election year.

Democrats, some utilities and environmental groups continue to press for federal "date-certain" mandates, which would require all states to open their power markets to competition and mandate that the utilities buy a certain percentage of electricity from renewable sources. Such legislation would also give the federal government oversight over the interstate electric grid. But most Republicans believe such plans don't square with their anti-regulatory leanings and oppose sweeping mandates.

House Commerce Committee Chairman Bliley, who questioned aspects of Rep. Barton's plan, is expected to use the power of his chairmanship to upstage his fellow Republican and unveil his own deregulation plan. Bliley has indicated he is concerned about consumer protections in the deregulated market and may work with influential Democrats like Rep. Edward J. Markey, D-Mass., to draft tougher language giving the federal government a more prominent role policing market abuses.

But Democrats, who are hoping to regain control of the House of Representatives in the 2000 elections, aren't entirely united on electricity deregulation themselves. Rep. John D. Dingell, D-Mich., ranking Democrat on the Commerce Committee, has questioned the need for any federal legislation. [22]

On the Senate side, Sen. Frank H. Murkowski, R-Alaska, chairman of the Senate Energy and Natural Resources Committee, is working on a bipartisan deregulation plan that's narrower in scope than the Barton measure that passed the House subcommittee in October.

"There's such a state of flux, maybe the best step is [for Congress] to wait for most states to [draft deregulation plans], then try to arbitrate the situation," says the Heritage Foundation's Thierer.

Lawmakers aren't the only ones divided on a broad deregulation plan. Large investor-owned utilities, which historically have opposed a prominent federal role in the deregulated power market, are sparring with municipal utilities and rural co-ops, which generally favor more government protections. The sides are split on other issues, such as the use of tax-exempt financing by publicly owned utilities for future expansions.

Wattage Monitor's Alderson says that even after such sticking points are settled, it will take as long as a decade to determine whether deregulation is a success. Until then, change will come incrementally, with states pursuing their own initiatives.

"No market in any industry is deregulated in one year," Alderson says. "With phone deregulation, it took 10 years before everyone realized they had a choice in long-distance suppliers. And because the federal lawmakers can't agree, the [electricity] market won't even be able to benefit from national rules. Deregulation on a national scale is going to evolve very slowly." ∎

Notes

[1] For background, see David Masci, "The Future of Telecommunications," *The CQ Researcher*, April 23, 1999, pp. 329-352, and Kenneth Jost, "Antitrust Policy," *The CQ Researcher*, June 12, 1998, pp. 505-528;

[2] See Charles Pope, "House Subcommittee Moves Electricity Deregulation Bill With Big Issues Unresolved," *CQ Weekly*, Oct. 30, 1999, p. 2599.

[3] See "The Restructuring of the Electric Power Industry: A Capsule of Issues and Events," Energy Information Administration, 1998.

[4] For background, Kenneth Jost, "Restructuring the Electric Industry," *The CQ Researcher*, Jan. 17, 1997, pp. 25-48.

[5] See "One Year After Electric Deregulation, Few People Have Switched Suppliers," The Associated Press, Nov. 15, 1999.

[6] See "Customer Choice for Electricity Unlikely in Colorado in Near Future," The Associated Press, Oct. 18, 1999.

[7] See "Electric Market Restructuring: Expectations and Reality," *The Bond Buyer*, Oct. 25, 1999, p. 6.

[8] See Agis Salpukas, "California Vote Could Rewrite Electric Bills All Over U.S.," *The New York Times*, Oct. 25, 1998, p. A1.

[9] See Mark Cooper, "The Residential Ratepayer Economics of Electric Utility Restructuring," Consumers Union and Consumer Federation of America, July 1998.

[10] See Bob Wyss, "Electric Switch — R.I. Was First, But Pennsylvania Did It Best," *The Providence Journal-Bulletin*, Sept. 12, 1999, p. 1F.

[11] See John Casazza, "The Development of Electric Power Transmission," Institute of Electrical and Electronics Engineers, 1993.

[12] See "Hoecker and Massey Encourage the Northeast to Form Single RTO," *Foster Electric Report*, No. 176, p. 4 (Oct. 20, 1999).

[13] See Tom Tiernan, "With Legislative Time Running Out, FERC Authority Emerges as Key Issue," *Inside FERC*, Oct. 11, 1999, p. 1.

[14] See "Massey Questions FERC's Resolve Over Grid Management Influence," *The Energy Report*, Nov. 1, 1999.

[15] Op-ed piece, *Investor's Business Daily*, Oct. 26, 1999, p. A26.

[16] Jost, *op. cit.*

[17] See Adam Thierer, "Energizing America: A Blueprint for Deregulating the Electricity Market," *The Heritage Foundation Backgrounder No. 1100*, Jan. 23, 1997.

[18] Pope, *op. cit.*

[19] See Energy Information Administration, "Electric Power Annual 1998, Volume II," December 1999.

[20] See Peter Howe, "Electric Avenues: Net-Based Liaisons Emerge in Multipronged Landscape for Buying, Selling Energy," *The Boston Globe*, Nov. 14, 1999, p. E1.

[21] Quoted in "Utilities Take to Internet to Hawk Electricity," Reuters, Dec. 3, 1999.

[22] See Spencer Hsu, "Short-Circuiting the Electric Bill," *The Washington Post*, Oct. 17, 1999, p. H8.

Bibliography

Selected Sources Used

Books

Brennan, Timothy J. (ed.), *A Shock to the System: Restructuring America's Electricity Industry*, Resources for the Future, 1996.

A good overview of major trends in electricity restructuring, including a history of the industry and pertinent laws and regulations.

Smeloff, Ed, Peter Asmus and Amory Lovins, *Reinventing Electric Utilities: Competition, Citizen Action and Clean Power*, Island Press, 1996.

An easy-to-understand overview of electricity deregulation, including legal and technical aspects. Special emphasis on the future of energy, clean power and transportation.

Articles

"You've Got the Power," *The Washington Post*, Oct. 17, 1999, pp. H1-17.

A package of articles on electricity deregulation as Maryland, Virginia and the District of Columbia take up restructuring plans. Focuses on legislation, consumer issues and environmental impact.

Pope, Charles, "White House's Revamped Plan to Deregulate Electricity Gains Better Reception in Congress," *CQ Weekly*, April 17, 1999, p. 900.

The Clinton administration finds its plan to restructure the power industry is getting a warmer reception, but that the complexity of dismantling electricity monopolies makes the road ahead difficult.

Smith, Rebecca, "California's Electricity Deregulation Plan to Cost a Bundle," *San Jose Mercury News*, May 2, 1998, p. A1.

California's big three electric utilities expect to spend $1.1 billion carrying out the state's electric deregulation plan, a price tag at least double what anyone expected.

Tiernan, Tom, "With Legislative Time Running Out, FERC Authority Emerges as Key Issue," *Inside FERC*, Oct. 11, 1999, p. 1

As Congress nears adjournment for 1999, the future role of the Federal Energy Regulatory Commission is emerging as a contentious issue in electricity restructuring plans.

FOR MORE INFORMATION

Alliance to Save Energy, 1200 18th St., N.W., Suite 900, Washington, D.C. 20036; (202) 857-0666; www.ase.org. This nonprofit monitors developments in Congress and conducts educational programs.

American Public Power Association, 2301 M St., N.W., Washington, D.C. 20037; (202) 467-2900; www.appanet.org. This trade group representing publicly owned, locally controlled electric companies believes more federal involvement is necessary in a restructured electricity market.

Edison Electric Institute, 701 Pennsylvania Ave., N.W., Washington, D.C. 20004; (202) 508-5000; www.eei.org. This trade group representing large, investor-owned power companies historically has opposed extensive federal intervention in the domestic power market.

Energy Information Administration, 1000 Independence Ave., S.W., EI-30, Washington, D.C. 20585; (202) 586-8800; www.eia.doe.gov. This division of the Department of Energy forecasts domestic electricity usage and supply and demand for various energy sources.

Federal Energy Regulatory Commission, 888 First St., N.E., Washington, D.C. 20426; (202) 208-0383; www.ferc.gov. This branch of the Department of Energy oversees the interstate sale and transmission of electric power and regulates the operation of transmission lines.

Wyss, Bob, "Electric Switch: R.I. Was First, But Pennsylvania Did It Best," *The Providence Journal-Bulletin*, Sept. 12, 1999, p. 1F

A comparison of power-market restructuring plans in Rhode Island and Pennsylvania that attempts to explain why Pennsylvania's has led to more residential customers switching electric suppliers.

Reports and Studies

"Electric Power Annual 1998, Volume II," Energy Information Administration, December 1999.

A digest of electricity rates and usage in the United States in 1998.

"Fair Competition in Retail Electricity Markets," National Regulatory Research Institute, June 1998.

A report that examines the concept of "customer choice" and how retail electric customers can achieve the greatest benefits from deregulation.

Thierer, Adam, "Energizing America: A Blueprint for Deregulating the Electricity Market," *The Heritage Foundation Backgrounder No. 1100*, Jan. 23, 1997.

A conservative analysis of ways to break up the $220 billion electricity market, and potential benefits of deregulation.

9 Closing In on Tobacco

KENNETH JOST

F ew warnings about smoking are tougher than the one that recently appeared on the World Wide Web — and few have ever come from a less likely source.

"There is an overwhelming medical and scientific consensus that cigarette smoking causes lung cancer, heart disease, emphysema and other serious diseases in smokers," it cautions.

That's not all. Cigarette smoking "is addictive, as that term is used today," the message continues. "It can be very difficult to quit smoking, but this should not deter smokers who want to quit from trying to do so."

The latest anti-smoking message from the Surgeon General's office? Another blast from the anti-smoking groups that have battled the tobacco industry for more than 30 years?

Not even close. The blunt warnings are courtesy of the "people of Philip Morris" — the world's largest tobacco company — who produce one-sixth of the cigarettes smoked around the globe.

Since Oct. 12, the company's Web site (www.philipmorris.com) has included concessions about the health risks of smoking that the company's executives have disputed since the first scientific studies linked cigarettes to lung cancer in the early 1950s.

For good measure, the Web site provides quotes on the addictive nature of cigarettes from the Food and Drug Administration (FDA) and other official sources. It also includes a link to an American Cancer Society table showing that smoking causes 185,000 cancer deaths per year in the United States.

Philip Morris executives say the Web site represents an effort to be more "open" and "accessible" than the company has been in the past. "We knew that we had to — and we wanted to, frankly — talk about the issues con-

From *The CQ Researcher,*
November 12, 1999.

CQ Photo/Douglas Graham

fronting our company, and that includes tobacco," says Peggy Roberts, director of corporate communications.[1]

Some anti-smoking advocates welcomed Philip Morris' new candor. "It is a profound change," said David A. Kessler, the former head of the FDA and the architect of the agency's controversial effort to regulate tobacco products. "It really sets a new stage for regulation and legislation," added Kessler, now dean of the Yale University School of Medicine in New Haven, Conn.[2]

Other anti-smoking advocates had less positive reactions to the new Web site material. "I don't think very much of it," says John F. Banzhaf III, executive director of the Washington-based group Action on Smoking and Health and a 30-year veteran of anti-smoking advocacy. "It seems to me a belated and somewhat desperate attempt both to avoid legal liability in the future and perhaps to try to untarnish its virtually destroyed image."

The expansion of the Philip Morris Web site — and somewhat comparable moves by other U.S. tobacco companies — comes as the industry

is under siege as never before.[3] A year ago, the major U.S. tobacco companies completed agreements with state governments to pay $246 billion over a 25-year period to settle the states' costs of treating people with smoking-related illnesses. As part of the agreements, the companies agreed to significant restrictions on marketing and lobbying and to the creation of a national foundation to promote anti-smoking education programs. (*See table, p. 172.*)

Tobacco companies hoped the settlements would put the major anti-smoking legal battles behind them. But they included no restriction on private damage suits by smokers, ex-smokers or their families. Within several months, Philip Morris was hit with eight-figure jury awards in smoking-related suits. A California woman with inoperable lung cancer won a $51.5 million award in February; the amount was later cut in half. And the family of an Oregon man who smoked Marlboros for four decades before he died won an $81 million verdict in March.

Today, the big U.S. tobacco companies — Philip Morris, R. J. Reynolds, Brown & Williamson, Lorillard and Liggett Group — are facing a possible multibillion-dollar damage award in a class action suit filed on behalf of an estimated 500,000 sick Florida smokers. A state court jury in Florida in July found the tobacco companies had conspired to hide the danger and addictive nature of cigarettes. The ruling set the stage for the damages phase of the trial, which got under way on Nov. 1. A state appeals court upped the stakes for the companies by ruling on Oct. 20 that the panel may award punitive damages in a single lump sum instead of one worker at a time.[4]

Meanwhile, the industry is preparing for a Supreme Court showdown in its effort to block FDA regulation

Smoking by Youths Increased

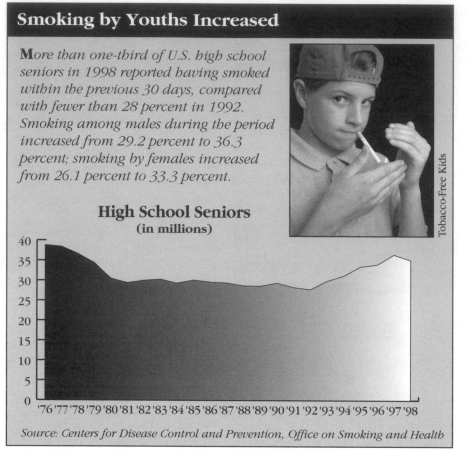

More than one-third of U.S. high school seniors in 1998 reported having smoked within the previous 30 days, compared with fewer than 28 percent in 1992. Smoking among males during the period increased from 29.2 percent to 36.3 percent; smoking by females increased from 26.1 percent to 33.3 percent.

Tobacco-Free Kids

High School Seniors
(in millions)

Source: Centers for Disease Control and Prevention, Office on Smoking and Health

of tobacco products. The FDA regulation, adopted in 1996, is aimed at reducing youth smoking through more stringent enforcement of minimum-age requirements for buying cigarettes and through restrictions on advertising and marketing practices. But the industry won a federal appeals court ruling last year that the agency has no statutory authority to regulate tobacco. The Supreme Court is set to hear arguments on Dec. 1 in the government's effort to overturn the decision and reinstate the challenged regulation. (see p. 169).

The most recent jolt for the tobacco industry came from a Justice Department suit seeking to recover smoking-related health-care costs for Medicare patients or other people in federal health programs. The suit, filed in federal court in Washington, D.C., on Sept. 22, includes fraud counts under the federal anti-racketeering law that theoretically could allow a court to order tobacco companies to turn over billions of dollars in so-called "ill-gotten gains" from the sale of cigarettes.

The tobacco companies bitterly denounced the suit, and some legal observers questioned the basis for the action. Still, many observers were speculating that the industry might feel obliged to settle the suit to avoid the distraction of a protracted legal battle with a powerful adversary and the risk of a gigantic judgment at the end.

The tobacco companies are also facing financial pressure, as the percentage of smokers in the United States continues to fall. About one-fourth of adults 18 years of age or older were smokers in 1997, according to the Centers for Disease Control and Prevention (CDC) — compared with 42.4 percent in 1965. Youth smoking, however, has been rising recently. In 1998 slightly more than one-third of high school seniors reported having smoked within the previous 30 days.

The overall decline in smoking reflects the accomplishments of the anti-smoking movement, which has grown over the past 30 years from a pesky thorn in the industry's side into a powerful lobbying force at the local and national levels. The tobacco industry has tried to counter the push for curbs on smoking in public places with campaigns emphasizing "smokers' rights" — themes also struck by two groups partly funded by the industry, the National Smokers Alliance and the American Smokers Alliance.

Some observers also say that the anti-smoking campaign has gone too far in impinging on the rights of people who choose to smoke. "What started out as primarily an educational movement that was aimed at persuading people not to smoke because it's unhealthy has become increasingly coercive over the years," says Jacob Sullum, a senior editor with the libertarian magazine *Reason* and author of a critical book about the anti-smoking movement. "You see smokers being pushed out into the cold, both literally and figuratively." [5]

"Many movements recognize the limitations of simply relying on public education," Banzhaf responds. "We don't rely on public education to prevent drunken driving. We lock people up. We don't rely on public education to get people to use seat belts and shoulder harnesses. We fine them. And we've historically used taxation to modify social behavior, both encouraging things that Congress regards as desirable and discouraging things that Congress felt were undesirable."

"All of the things that I've cited," Banzhaf concludes, "are far more coercive than the anti-smoking movement."

As the tobacco wars continue, here are some of the major questions being debated:

Should the Food and Drug Administration regulate tobacco products?

When smoking was being introduced into Europe in the 16th century, the French ambassador to Portugal, Jean Nicot, touted tobacco's use as a poultice to treat a variety of bodily ills.[6] Today, the chemically active ingredient in tobacco — nicotine — is more accurately recognized as an addictive substance that functions both as a sedative and a stimulant and has been shown to cause cancer in laboratory animals and is linked to cancer, heart disease and other illnesses in humans.

Despite its demonstrated effects on the body, however, tobacco is largely not covered by federal laws aimed at protecting consumer health and safety. Anti-smoking advocates view the FDA's plan to regulate tobacco as a long overdue correction to a legal loophole. Industry and pro-smoking groups counter that Congress never intended the agency to have jurisdiction over tobacco and that the FDA's plan represents an opening step toward banning tobacco altogether.

"Every product we consume or come into contact with — besides cigarettes — is regulated by the FDA," Banzhaf says. Similarly, he notes, other types of products are monitored by the Consumer Product Safety Commission.

Tobacco companies sharply dispute the picture of an unregulated industry. "Our products are among the most heavily regulated in the nation in terms of how they are manufactured, marketed, advertised and used," Brown & Williamson declares on its Web site (www. brownandwilliamson.com).

The company notes that the Department of Agriculture sets produc-

Adults Are Smoking Less

The percentage of adults 18 or older who smoke dropped almost 50 percent from 1965 to 1997, according to the most recent data from the Centers for Disease Control and Prevention. Smoking among male adults declined from 52 percent to 28 percent; adult female smoking declined from 34 percent to 23 percent.

Adults Age 18 and Over
(in millions)

Source: Centers for Disease Control and Prevention, Office on Smoking and Health

tion quotas and price levels for tobacco leaf; the Bureau of Alcohol, Tobacco and Firearms regulates cigarette manufacturers; and the Internal Revenue Service taxes the sale of cigarettes. In addition, federal law requires health warnings on cigarette packaging and advertisements, prohibits cigarette ads on radio and television and bans smoking on airplanes, in federally financed schools and in or around federal buildings. And states have myriad laws dealing with cigarettes, the company notes, including excise taxes, restrictions on smoking in public places and minimum-age requirements for purchasing cigarettes.

Anti-smoking advocates respond by emphasizing that none of the regulations limit the ingredients used in making cigarettes. "If I were making cigarettes, I could put in thalido-

mide, I could put in cyanide, I could put in anything I want," Banzhaf says.

Federal law, however, does require tobacco companies to disclose tar and nicotine content in cigarettes on packaging and to file annual reports with the Department of Health and Human Services on the ingredients used in making them.

To claim jurisdiction over tobacco products, the FDA had to fit cigarettes within the definitions used in its statutory charter: the Food, Drug and Cosmetic Act of 1938. The law gives the FDA power to regulate "drug delivery devices" and "drugs" — which are defined as substances or items "intended to affect the structure of any function of the body." The agency relied in part on newly uncovered evidence of the tobacco companies' long awareness of nicotine's effects to classify cigarettes as a "drug delivery device" under the law.

Some experts call the FDA's position legally sound. "Tobacco and tobacco products fit comfortably within the language of the statute," says Peter Rubin, a professor at Georgetown University Law Center. Lawyers for the tobacco companies disagree. "Common sense would tell you that a cigarette is neither a drug nor a medical device," said Bert Rein, a Washington attorney representing Brown & Williamson in the Supreme Court case." [7]

Tobacco companies also insist that the FDA regulation flies in the face of Congress' repeated refusal to give the agency authority over tobacco. "The issue here is who has the power to establish the social policies of the country," said Charles Blixt, executive vice president and general counsel of R.J. Reynolds. "Is it the elected officials in Congress or the unelected bureaucrats in the Food and Drug Administration?" [8]

But anti-smoking advocates contend that the FDA simply applied the statutory definitions to new information obtained from the tobacco industry's own files. "Congress deliberately included a very broad definition of drug," Banzhaf says. In any event, he adds, Congress had ample warning of the FDA's proposal and could have blocked the regulation if it had wanted to, he notes.

Finally, tobacco companies hint that the FDA has a hidden long-term goal — imposing a total ban on cigarettes and other tobacco products. "There's been an unwillingness on the part of the executive branch of the government to acknowledge that the tobacco industry has a right to exist," says Scott Williams, the industry's chief spokesman in Washington. Alternatively, tobacco companies worry that the FDA might require them to lower the tar and nicotine content in cigarettes to the point that consumers would no longer buy them.

The FDA, however, rejected a ban on tobacco products when it adopted the regulation. And Banzhaf says "no reputable anti-smoking organization" is suggesting a ban. As for lowering tar and nicotine levels, the FDA once considered such a step but backed off because of fears that people would smoke more and end up inhaling greater quantities of other toxic substances contained in cigarettes.

Should the tobacco industry pay the federal government for smoking-related health-care costs?

Tobacco company executives worried 20 years ago about being forced to reimburse government health programs for their costs in treating smoking-related diseases. "More industry antagonists are using an economic argument against cigarettes," warns a Philip Morris memo written in 1978 and uncovered by plaintiffs' lawyers many years later. "We must be prepared to counter this line of argument." [9]

The major U.S. tobacco companies capitulated to the argument a year ago when they agreed to pay state governments more than $200 billion over a 25-year period to cover the states' costs in treating people with smoking-related illnesses under Medicaid.

Now, the tobacco companies are facing a similar suit from the Justice Department. The suit seeks reimbursement for the estimated $20 billion per year that the government says it pays for health costs in the Medicare or other federal health programs.

"Each year, American taxpayers spend billions of dollars due to the actions of the cigarette companies," Attorney General Janet Reno said in announcing the lawsuit on Sept. 22. "Today's suit seeks to recover those expenses."

Tobacco companies were quick to denounce the suit as legally unsound and politically motivated. The law-

suit "is a cynical attempt to use the courts for political purpose," Brown & Williamson said in a prepared statement. "We are confident the courts will find this lawsuit to be meritless."

"We will not succumb to politically correct extortion," declared Greg Little, associate general counsel for Philip Morris. "We're right on the law. We're right on the facts. We will prevail in this lawsuit." [10]

Tobacco companies also adopted a combative stance toward the Medicaid reimbursement suits filed by state governments beginning in 1994. The industry sharply challenged the states' legal theories and vowed to defend the suits at trial. But none of the cases ever went to a jury, and the settlement in November cut off any final resolution of the issues.

The Justice Department suit faces significant legal questions. The suit relies on two federal statutes — the Medical Care Recovery Act and the Medicare Secondary Payer Act — that the government has used previously to recover medical costs in individual cases. The suit also claims that the tobacco companies' "false and misleading" statements on health issues amounted to a fraud on the public, punishable under the triple-damage provisions of the federal anti-racketeering law: the Racketeer Influenced and Corrupt Organizations Act, known as RICO.

The tobacco companies claim that the two cost-recovery statutes are inapplicable and do not override an earlier Supreme Court decision, *United States v. Standard Oil Company* (1948), which blocked the government from seeking reimbursement for medical costs from a third party. As for the RICO counts, the tobacco companies say the law targets organized crime, not lawful companies.

The tobacco companies and other critics also say the suit ignores the government's knowledge of the health risks from smoking, implying that it should have acted if smoking was so harmful. "No person or organization in the world has been more aware of the health risks associated with smoking than the federal government," Brown & Williamson's Web site argues.

The government, however, says the industry actively concealed the dangers from smoking. "The cigarette companies knew exactly what they were doing at all times — that their false and misleading statements would keep people smoking," David Ogden, acting assistant attorney general for the Civil Division, told reporters.

As with the FDA-regulation issue, the industry also claims that the suit is an end-run around Congress. "If people who smoke don't pay their own way, that's an issue for Congress to address," Little says. "It's not appropriate for the courts."

But anti-smoking groups say the courts are a proper forum for holding tobacco companies responsible. "There are a tremendous number of costs related to smoking that the public ends up paying for," says Mary Rouvelas, legislative counsel for the American Cancer Society. "This is one of the few cases where [wrongdoers] have engaged in ridiculous conduct without being held accountable for the damages attributable to their product."

Will additional tobacco regulations reduce smoking by young people?

Smoking by young people fell fairly consistently from the mid-1970s into the early '90s, but has been rising since 1992, according to the CDC. The FDA aimed its regulation of tobacco at strengthening enforcement of youth smoking restrictions and curbing marketing practices that draw youngsters to smoking. For their part, tobacco companies maintain that they do not target young people in their advertising and are actively working to discourage youth smoking.

The FDA sought to reduce youngsters' access to tobacco products by requiring age verification by photo ID of anyone under 27 purchasing cigarettes or smokeless tobacco. It also restricted a number of advertising and marketing practices, including limits on outdoor billboards near schools or playgrounds and restrictions on the use of brand names on promotional items or sponsored sporting or entertainment events.

Anti-smoking groups voice some ambivalence about the FDA regulation. "The rule is not the be-all and end-all of tobacco control, but it's an extremely important element in establishing a comprehensive tobacco policy in this country," says John Bloom, a health policy consultant for the cancer society.

Bloom says existing laws prohibiting the sale of cigarettes to minors have been poorly enforced. "This rule puts teeth into those laws," he says. The advertising restrictions, he says, would curb the kind of marketing strategies that "essentially prey upon the vulnerabilities of youth." "The rule is not perfect in this area," he says, "but it would go a long way in reducing the most offensive kinds of marketing."

Banzhaf says the FDA regulation would have "a significant but not overwhelming impact" on cigarette consumption by kids. He calls the restrictions "very mild" and says that more stringent steps are needed. "We're not going to have a big impact until we virtually ban cigarette

advertising and dramatically increase the price of cigarettes," he says.

The reasons for the increase in youth smoking over the past several years are not clear. William Novelli, president of the Washington-based National Center for Tobacco-Free Kids, cites a number of potential factors, including the relatively low cost of cigarettes in the United States compared to other industrialized coun-

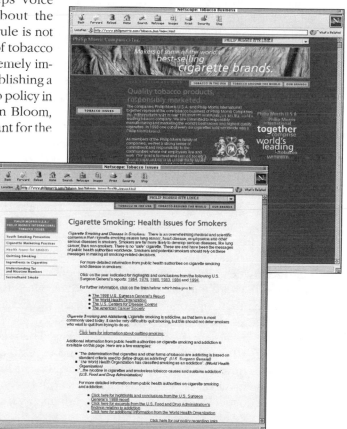

Extensive warnings about the health risks from smoking now appear on the Web site of Philip Morris, the world's largest tobacco company.

tries and what he calls the industry's "pervasive" advertising. He also notes the increase in the visible use of cigarettes by entertainers. "Smoking is really very pervasive in movies and music videos," he says.

Industry spokesmen profess having no explanation for the increase in youth smoking. "Clearly, it's far too high," says Tom Ryan, a spokesman for Philip Morris. "We don't know why kids are smoking. It's a very complex problem, and a complex problem requires a complex solution."

The settlement with the states includes a number of steps aimed at reducing youth smoking, including a complete ban on billboards. As part of the agreement, R.J. Reynolds agreed to drop its controversial "Joe Camel" cartoon figure, which critics said was evidently aimed at young people despite the company's insistent denials.

Novelli was disappointed that Philip Morris did not similarly agree to drop the famous Marlboro Man from its advertising. He and other anti-smoking advocates say the popular image is a major reason why Marlboro enjoys a disproportionate 60 percent market share among youth smokers — nearly three times higher than its 23 percent share among adults.

"We recognize that many of our critics believe that smoking rates among youth are a result of our marketing activities," Ryan responds, "but we are not aware that there is a body of research that supports this claim."

Ryan notes that Philip Morris earlier this year launched a $100 million campaign — independent of the master settlement with the states — aimed at producing what he calls "a measurable reduction in youth smoking." He adds, "We are ready to work with any individual or group that is sincerely committed to the reduction of youth smoking."

Anti-smoking groups are unconvinced. "These companies spend $5 billion a year on marketing," Novelli says, citing a figure that includes advertising as well as other promotional and distribution costs. "They create this tobacco environment, and then they spend $100 million telling kiddies not to smoke, and say they're doing their part." ■

BACKGROUND

Tobacco Under Fire

Tobacco came under fire from governmental authorities not long after it was introduced to Europe and then to the rest of the globe following Christopher Columbus' voyages at the end of the 15th century. James I of England authored an anonymous pamphlet in 1604 denouncing smoking as "a custome lothsome to the eye, hatefull to the Nose, harmefull to the brain, [and] daungerous to the Lungs." Later, he imposed a 4,000 percent duty on tobacco imported on Spanish ships. In Russia, tobacco users were exiled to Siberia; in China, traffickers were subject to execution. [11]

The anti-tobacco movement in America also dates to the 1600s. The Massachusetts Bay Colony enacted a law in 1634 prohibiting two or more persons from using tobacco together. Benjamin Rush, a noted early American physician, warned in an anti-tobacco tract in 1798 that a link existed between smoking or chewing and excessive drinking. With little in the way of hard medical data, however, tobacco's critics couched their arguments mostly in moralistic terms through the 1800s and early 1900s, often in sync with anti-liquor forces. The fieriest of the critics was Lucy Gaston, a schoolteacher from Illinois, who depicted cigarettes as the cause of indolence inside school and crime and immorality outside.

Gaston's National Anti-Cigarette League successfully agitated for laws banning cigarettes in a number of states, beginning with Washington in 1893. Seventeen years later, *The New York Times* noted the formation of the Non-Smokers Protective League by applauding efforts to reduce what the newspaper called "the general and indiscriminate use of tobacco in public places."

But the tobacco industry fought back hard, setting a pattern for the future. When Congress passed the Pure Food and Drug Act in 1906, tobacco was exempted. And the anti-cigarette laws were either repealed or unenforced until the last of them faded away in the 1930s.

Despite the anti-cigarette efforts, medical opinion through the 1800s did not oppose the use of tobacco, at least in moderation. By the 1930s, however, medical evidence against tobacco began to accumulate. In 1938, a Johns Hopkins University biologist found that smoking was associated with "a definite impairment in longevity . . . proportional to the habitual usage of tobacco by smoking." Seven years later, the American Cancer Society reported "a distinct parallelism between the incidence of cancer of the lung and the sale of cigarettes."

Then in the early 1950s, more detailed studies linking smoking to lung cancer were published — by U.S. researchers in the *Journal of the American Medical Association* in 1950 and by British physicians in the *British Medical Journal* in 1952. [12]

Another decade passed before Surgeon General Luther Terry issued his famous 1964 report — 387 pages long — concluding that cigarette smoking was "causally related" to lung cancer and tentatively endorsing the suspected link between smoking and heart disease.

"Cigarette smoking is a health hazard of sufficient importance in the United States to warrant appropriate remedial action," Terry's report said. The tobacco industry dismissed the report. "We don't accept the idea that there are harmful agents in tobacco," said Dr. Kenneth Lynch, chairman of the Tobacco Industry Research

Chronology

1950s Studies link cigarette smoking to lung cancer; first smoking suits against tobacco companies.

1950
U.S. researchers link cigarettes to lung cancer in *Journal of the American Medical Association*; British researchers follow with more detailed study in 1952.

1954
St. Louis factory worker becomes first smoker to sue tobacco companies for causing lung cancer; suit is dropped 13 years later.

1960s First federal initiatives against smoking.

1964
Surgeon General's report says cigarette smoking is "definite health hazard."

1965
Congress requires health warnings on cigarette packages and advertising, beginning Jan. 1, 1966.

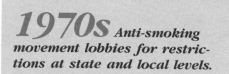

1970s Anti-smoking movement lobbies for restrictions at state and local levels.

1970
Congress bans cigarette advertising on radio and television.

1973
Arizona becomes first state to restrict smoking in public places.

1980s Tobacco companies face increased litigation from smokers, but avoid paying damages.

1987
Jury deadlocks in suit by family of Mississippi smoker Nathan Horton over his death from cancer; in retrial, jury holds American Tobacco Co. liable, but awards no damages.

1988
Jury awards $400,000 to husband of New Jersey smoker Rose Cipollone for her death from cancer; appeals court overturns award in 1990.

1990s Tobacco companies face increased pressure from litigation, federal regulation and disclosures from internal files.

1993
Environmental Protection Agency (EPA) labels "environmental tobacco smoke" (secondhand smoke) as a toxin and links it to cancer, heart disease; industry disputes report; federal court in 1998 orders EPA to reconsider.

1994
Mississippi becomes first state to sue tobacco companies for health-care costs related to smoking.

1995
Food and Drug Administration (FDA) proposes regulation to enforce age restrictions on buying cigarettes and limit advertising and marketing practices aimed at young people; regulation is adopted in August 1996, but challenged in court by industry, retailers.

1996
Liggett Group, smallest of major tobacco companies, settles claims with five states.

June 1997
Tobacco industry agrees to settle states' health-care reimbursement suits by paying $368 billion over 25 years; deal collapses by fall in face of opposition from anti-smoking groups. Four states — Mississippi, Florida, Texas and Minnesota — reach individual settlements in 1997 and early 1998 totaling $40 billion.

June 1998
Senate effectively kills settlement bill that would have cost tobacco companies more than $500 billion over 25 years.

August 1998
Federal appeals court in Richmond, Va., rules FDA has no authority over tobacco.

November 1998
Forty-six states embrace new 25-year, $206 billion settlement with tobacco companies; deal becomes final in November 1999, with payments to states due to begin before end of year.

September 1999
Justice Department sues tobacco companies for reimbursement of smoking-related costs in Medicare and other federal health programs; industry vows to fight suits; judge sets initial scheduling conference for Nov. 19.

Dec. 1, 1999
Supreme Court to hear arguments in FDA tobacco regulation case.

Committee's scientific advisory board.[13]

The Surgeon General's report quickly provided the impetus for the government's first regulatory initiative against smoking. The Cigarette Labeling and Advertising Act, passed by Congress in 1965, required all cigarette packs and advertisements to warn: "Caution: Cigarette smoking may be hazardous to your health."

Five years later, Congress mandated a stiffer message: "Warning: The Surgeon General has determined that smoking is dangerous to your health." (A series of four rotating warnings were required under legislation passed in 1984.) In addition, Congress banned cigarette advertising on radio or television, beginning in 1971.

Despite such setbacks, the tobacco industry was at the height of its power in Washington in the early 1970s, as Richard Kluger notes in his recent history of the tobacco wars, *Ashes to Ashes.* Tobacco lobbyists helped oust the stridently anti-smoking Surgeon General, Jesse Steinfeld, in 1972, and two years later helped engineer the downgrading of the Clearinghouse on Smoking and Health in the Department of Health, Education, and Welfare to a subsection of the CDC in Atlanta.

And when a federal judge ruled in 1975 that the Consumer Product Safety Commission had jurisdiction over tobacco, industry lobbyists went to Congress and got an amendment passed reversing the ruling and preserving tobacco's exemption from general consumer-protection laws.[14]

Lawsuits and Documents

Within a few years of the first studies linking cigarette smoking to lung cancer, tobacco companies began facing lawsuits from smokers, ex-smokers and their families — first a trickle and then a steady stream. Through the 1980s, the industry fended off the suits with artful legal defenses and aggressive litigation strategies. But the litigation helped bring to light damning evidence of the tobacco industry's knowledge of — and indifference toward — the health risks from smoking, directly from the files of the tobacco companies themselves.

The first lawsuit apparently came in 1954 when a 39-year-old St. Louis factory worker, Ira C. Lowe Jr., sued four tobacco companies.[15] He claimed cigarettes caused his lung cancer despite the companies' claim that they contained no harmful substances. The case was dropped 13 years later. The first case to reach a jury — in Louisiana — ended with a verdict for the tobacco company in 1958.

Two suits in the 1960s made more progress. A federal jury in Pittsburgh ruled in a suit brought by Ira Pritchard that cigarettes caused his lung cancer but refused to hold tobacco companies liable. Later, in a suit brought by the family of a Florida man, Edwin M. Green Sr., the state's Supreme Court ruled in 1963 that tobacco companies could be liable if cigarettes were shown to be the cause of his death. But a Florida jury rejected Green's claim the next year, finding that cigarettes were "reasonably safe and wholesome for human consumption."

The families of two lung-cancer victims won symbolic jury victories in the 1980s, but both ended with no money paid out by tobacco companies. In Mississippi, Nathan Horton, a 50-year-old carpenter, sued the American Tobacco Co. after he contracted lung cancer.[16] Horton's family continued the suit after his death in 1987. Pretrial rulings blocked some of the claims and forced his attorneys to argue only that the Pall Mall cigarettes he had smoked contained harmful additives. The first trial ended with a mistrial. In a retrial, a jury ruled that the tobacco company was responsible for Horton's death, but awarded nothing in damages.

A jury in New Jersey gave the Liggett & Myers Co. a bigger scare in 1988 in a suit brought by the family of Rose Cipollone, who had died of lung cancer in 1984 after chain-smoking mostly L&Ms for 30 years.[17] The jury found that the company had been negligent in failing to warn smokers of health risks prior to the 1965 labeling requirement but also found Cipollone mostly at fault for her death. On that basis, the panel awarded no damages to her estate but did order the company to pay $400,000 to her husband. That award, however, was overturned by a federal appeals court two years later.

The tobacco companies defended against the suits by arguing that the plaintiffs had, in legal parlance, "assumed the risk" of smoking even though they continued to cast doubt on the health hazards both in court and in public. Their defenses were undermined, however, by internal documents that surfaced because of the litigation. Cipollone's lawyer, Marc Edell, introduced evidence in the trial that tobacco companies had treated the health issue as a public relations problem and done little by way of scientific research. But Kluger says the evidence got little attention except in coverage by *The Washington Post*'s consumer affairs reporter, Morton Mintz.[18]

More extensive coverage resulted in 1994 thanks to a trove of 8,000 or more documents taken from the Brown & Williamson Co. by whistleblower Merrell Williams, a one-time smoker who became convinced of the company's duplicity while working as a paralegal at its Louisville, Ky., headquarters.[19] The boxloads of documents that Williams made off with eventually found their way to one of the lawyers in the

Horton case; a congressional sub-committee; several news organizations, including *The New York Times*; and an anti-smoking professor in California. The three-part series in the *Times* by Philip J. Hilts, which ran June 16-18, 1994, depicted the documents as showing that tobacco executives had publicly denied any health hazards from smoking even while privately debating the risks for 40 years.

Stanton A. Glantz, an economist and professor of medicine at the University of California in San Francisco, was among those who received the documents anonymously in 1994. He gave the documents more lasting exposure by posting them on the Internet the next year. The documents, Glantz noted in a 1996 book, "reveal that the tobacco industry's public position on smoking and health has diverged dramatically not only from the generally accepted position of the scientific community but also from the results of its own internal research."[20]

FDA Steps In

The tobacco companies' documents gave the FDA critical ammunition in its effort to assert jurisdiction over tobacco products. Kessler cited evidence that cigarette manufacturers changed nicotine levels in an attempt to addict smokers when he publicly suggested in February 1994 that the agency might regulate nicotine as a drug. In two later appearances be-

fore the House Energy and Commerce Health Subcommittee, Kessler asked for congressional "guidance" on the issue, warning that the FDA might have to ban cigarettes altogether because nicotine could not be found to be a "safe" drug as required under food and drug law.

Congress never seriously considered any legislation on the issue while under Democratic control, and Republicans showed no interest in the subject after they gained control of Congress in the November 1994 elections. Meanwhile, Kessler had received a recommendation from an FDA advisory panel in

Former FDA Chief David A. Kessler

CQ Photo/Douglas Graham

August that nicotine was an addictive drug and that it was the main reason why people smoked cigarettes.

Armed with the FDA recommendations, Kessler unveiled his proposal to regulate tobacco at a White House ceremony in August 1995, with President Clinton at his side. The rule made selling cigarettes or smokeless tobacco to anyone under age 18 a federal offense and imposed sweeping new restrictions on the tobacco industry's advertising and marketing practices. The proposal rejected a ban on cigarettes on the ground that it would lead to a black market.

The FDA formally adopted the rule a year later, in August 1996, after a voluminous rulemaking proceeding that drew more than 95,000 individual comments.[21] In its final form, the rule required retailers to verify by photo ID the age of anyone under 27 who was purchasing cigarettes or smokeless tobacco. It also banned vending machines or self-service displays except in facilities such as adult-only nightclubs that were completely inaccessible to minors. Originally, the FDA proposed banning all vending machines, but Clinton softened the restriction.

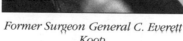

Former Surgeon General C. Everett Koop

CQ Photo/Douglas Graham

The regulation also prohibited all billboards within 1,000 feet of schools or playgrounds and limited other advertising — in stores or on buses, for example — to black-and-white, text-only message. The same "tombstone-ad" restrictions were imposed on ads in print publications with significant youth readership. And the regulation banned brand-name sponsorship of sporting or entertainment events and the sale or giveaway of products such as caps or gym bags emblazoned with tobacco brand names or logos.

The tobacco industry filed suit in federal court in North Carolina — in the heart of tobacco country — to try to block the regulation even before its adoption. The tobacco companies, along with a trade association of retailers, contended that the FDA lacked legal authority over tobacco and that the advertising restrictions in any event violated First Amendment protections for commercial speech.

Judge William L. Osteen Sr. put

the suit on hold until after the FDA completed action. Then, in April 1997, he issued a mixed ruling, holding that the statute gave the agency the authority to regulate access to tobacco but not to regulate marketing or promotion practices.

Both sides appealed, and the case came before a three-judge panel of the predominantly conservative 4th U.S. Circuit Court of Appeals in Richmond, Va., in June 1998. Outgoing Solicitor General Walter Dellinger personally argued for the government — an unusual appearance by the government's top appellate advocate in an intermediate-level court.

The court's 2-1 decision two months later gave the tobacco industry a clear-cut victory. "Congress did not intend to delegate jurisdiction over tobacco products," Judge H. Emory Widener Jr. wrote in the majority opinion. Widener criticized the FDA for engaging in a "mechanistic" reading of the statute and listed what he called a half-dozen "internal inconsistencies" in the agency's position — notably the FDA's failure to seek to ban tobacco although the agency is required to ban any product found to cause "serious adverse health consequences or death."

The Justice Department appealed to the Supreme Court. "Unless reversed by this Court," Solicitor General Seth P. Waxman wrote, "the panel's ruling will deprive the public of an unparalleled opportunity to prevent millions of children from beginning a highly addictive habit that often leads to premature death."

In response, the tobacco companies insisted the appeals court had correctly concluded that Congress gave the agency "no role" on tobacco issues. "FDA simply seeks to supplant enacted policy by disregarding stat-

utes with which it disagrees and short-circuiting an on-going political process," attorney Richard Cooper wrote.

The high court agreed on April 26, 1999, to hear the case in its next term. After both sides filed detailed briefs in the summer, the case was set for argument before the justices on Dec. 1.

Mississippi Attorney General Michael Moore initiated the first state suit against the tobacco companies in 1994.

Enter the States

Even as the tobacco industry was trying to block regulation by the FDA, it faced a new threat on a different front: lawsuits by state governments seeking to force tobacco companies to pay for the costs they incurred in treating indigent smokers and ex-smokers under the Medicaid program. Four years after the first of the suits was filed, the major U.S. tobacco companies sought to settle the litigation with historic agreements to pay states some $246 billion over a 25-year period and to accept an array of restrictions on advertising and

marketing practices.

Mississippi was the first of the states to take on the tobacco companies, filing suit in May 1994.[22] The state's attorney general, Michael Moore, said he got the idea from a law school classmate, Michael Lewis, whose secretary's mother, a smoker, had just died of heart disease. Moore put Lewis in touch with other attorneys, including Don Barrett, who had represented Nathan Horton in the unsuccessful suit against Liggett & Myers. The private lawyers took on the case for the state under a fee agreement calling for a percentage of any recovery, subject to court approval.

Moore said the suit was based on "a simple notion. You caused the health crisis: you pay for it."[23] The industry defense strategy that emerged was aimed at making the suit too burdensome to win. As author Michael Orey characterized the approach, the tobacco companies argued that the state would have to prove that each individual Medicaid recipient had an illness caused by smoking; the companies could then respond with their usual defenses of assumption of risk and comparative fault.[24]

Other states followed. Minnesota brought a broader suit in August 1994 — initiating litigation that would ultimately compile more than 30 million documents from tobacco companies in pretrial discovery. Florida filed suit in February 1995. By then, the Mississippi lawyers had survived an initial effort by the tobacco companies to have their suit thrown out of court.

In Florida, tobacco companies brought a constitutional challenge to a 1994 law that was aimed at undergirding the state's claim. The state Supreme Court, in June 1996, ruled the statute constitutional for the most part, though it narrowed the scope of the law somewhat. In

Secondhand Smoke a Hazy Issue

Joseph Avallone, Joseph Yaniak and Robin Taylor have each worked for 15 years or more in casinos in Atlantic City, N.J. Avallone has never smoked, and Taylor and Yaniak quit years ago. But they breathe in a lot of tobacco smoke. And they believe it puts them at increased risk of lung cancer, heart disease or other illnesses.

A number of governmental studies, including a major report by the Environmental Protection Agency (EPA) in 1993, support the view that secondhand smoke is hazardous to health. Most Americans apparently share that opinion. In a Gallup Poll completed in late September, more than 80 percent of the 1,039 people surveyed said they believe that secondhand smoke is either very harmful (43 percent) or somewhat harmful (39 percent) for adults.

The tobacco industry disagrees. It has a handful of scientific studies to support its stance as well as a federal court decision throwing out the EPA report because of procedural and substantive defects. And despite being on the defensive, the industry has been able to fend off some regulatory initiatives and to slow down lawsuits — such as one brought by Avallone, Yaniak and Taylor — that seek to force tobacco companies to pay damages or provide medical monitoring for workers exposed to secondhand smoke.

Anti-smoking groups can count many successes in their fight against what the government calls "environmental tobacco smoke" (ETS).[1] Smoking on all domestic airline flights has been banned since 1987. An order issued by President Clinton in 1997 prohibits smoking in federal office buildings. Virtually all the states and the District of Columbia limit smoking at restaurants and other public places.

On the other hand, only one state — California — meets the goal set by federal health officials 20 years ago of eliminating exposure to ETS by banning indoor smoking or limiting it to separately ventilated areas. And the U.S. Occupational Safety and Health Administration (OSHA) drew so much criticism when it proposed regulations in 1994 to bar smoking in most businesses or limit it to designated areas that the agency had to scrap the proposal.

In court battles, plaintiffs have only one victory — a partial one at that — in suits against the tobacco industry over secondhand smoke. Four tobacco companies — Philip Morris, R.J. Reynolds, Brown & Williamson and Lorillard — agreed in October 1997 to pay $349 million to resolve part of a class action brought in Florida by flight attendants who claimed their health had been damaged by exposure to ETS. The settlement included $300 million to fund a research center on smoking-related disease and $49 million to the lawyers who brought the suit. Individual flight attendants can still bring separate damage claims.

Juries have returned verdicts for tobacco companies in two individual suits brought by the families of lung cancer victims who blamed the deaths on secondhand smoke. Juries

in both cases — one in Indiana in March 1998, the other in Mississippi last summer — concluded that the plaintiffs had failed to prove that secondhand smoke caused the diseases.

The casino workers' suit, filed in a state court in New Brunswick, N.J., in April 1998, did not claim any present injuries. Instead, they said they feared their health was being compromised by exposure to secondhand smoke.[2] They originally sought damages, but then narrowed their claim to a demand for medical monitoring to be paid for by the tobacco companies. Judge Marina Corodemus in April refused to certify the suit as a class action — a ruling that could force separate, time-consuming trials on claims by each individual casino worker.

Meanwhile, the scientific debate continues. The EPA is appealing the July 1998 decision by federal Judge William Osteen in Winston-Salem, N.C., to "vacate" its 1993 report on secondhand smoke.[3] Osteen found that the EPA failed to comply with a congressional mandate to include industry representatives on an advisory panel that helped prepare the report, which was issued in the final days of President George Bush's administration. But Osteen also said the agency deviated from standard statistical practice so as to exaggerate the health risks of ETS.

Most recently, tobacco industry defenders have pointed to a 1998 study by an affiliate of the World Health Organization as discounting the dangers of secondhand smoke. In a study of 650 lung cancer patients in Europe, researchers for the International Agency for Research on Cancer found only "weak evidence" of a relationship between lung cancer and exposure to ETS.[4]

Another 1998 report by the New York-based American Council on Science and Health, a nonprofit consumer-education consortium, concluded somewhat similarly that secondhand smoke is "a weak risk factor" for lung cancer or heart disease among adults. But the report also said that exposure to ETS increases the risks for respiratory ailments among adults and for respiratory infections, ear infections, asthma and other respiratory symptoms among children.

The scientific evidence, the report concluded, "supports the adaptation of measures designed to reduce or prevent exposure to ETS," such as increasing ventilation and limiting levels of exposure through indoor smoking restrictions.[5]

---

[1] For background, see Richard Kluger, *Ashes to Ashes: America's Hundred-Year Cigarette War, the Public Health, and the Unabashed Triumph of Philip Morris* (1996); Richard L. Worsnop, "Indoor Air Pollution," *The CQ Researcher*, Oct. 27,1995, p. 959.

[2] For background, see *The New York Times*, May 25, 1998, p. B1.

[3] The case is *Flue-Cured Tobacco Cooperative Stabilization Corporation v. Environmental Protection Agency*.

[4] *Journal of the National Cancer Institute*, Vol. 90 (1998), pp. 1440-1450.

[5] American Council on Science and Health, "Environmental Tobacco Smoke: Health Risk or Health Hype?" 1998.

The Tobacco Settlement

The major U.S. tobacco companies agreed last November to pay $206 billion to 46 states over 25 years to settle claims for the states' costs of treating people with smoking-related illnesses. Previously, the tobacco companies agreed to pay $40 billion to four other states (Mississippi, Minnesota, Florida, Texas). The 46-state agreement includes an array of restrictions on advertising and marketing practices:

Research and Consumer Education

- Requires the industry to pay $25 million each year for 10 years to fund a charitable foundation to support studies in reducing teen smoking.
- Creates an industry-funded $1.45 billion advertising and education fund to counter youth tobacco use and educate consumers about smoking.

Targeting Youth

- Bans use of cartoons in the advertising and packaging of tobacco products.
- Prohibits targeting youth in advertising or promotions.

Access to Court Files

- Requires tobacco companies to open and maintain for at least 10 years, a Web site that includes all documents produced in smoking and health-related lawsuits.

Advertising

- Bans all outdoor advertising, including billboards, signs and placards in arenas, stadiums, shopping malls and video game arcades.
- Bans transit advertising of tobacco products.

Tobacco Merchandise and Sponsorships

- Bans distribution and sale of caps, T-shirts and other merchandise with brand-name logos.
- Bans payments to promote tobacco products in movies, television shows, video games and similar productions.
- Prohibits sponsorship of team sports/events with a significant youth audience.
- Bans tobacco brand names for stadiums and arenas.

Lobbying and Suppressing Research

- Prohibits manufacturers from conspiring to limit information or suppress research about the health hazards from the use of tobacco.
- Prohibits the industry from making any material misrepresentations regarding the health consequences of smoking.
- Prohibits tobacco companies from opposing proposed state or local laws intended to limit youth consumption of tobacco products.

Source: National Association of Attorneys General

CQ Photo/Scott J. Ferrell

Mississippi, Moore's suit also survived an effort by the state's Republican governor, Kirk Fordice, to have the suit dismissed. In West Virginia, however, the industry won a court ruling in 1995 that Orey says "gutted" the state's case.

The first break in the litigation came in December 1995, when Liggett & Myers, the smallest of the major U.S. tobacco companies, approached Barrett to talk about settling the case. Three months later, on March 13, 1996, Liggett became the first tobacco company ever to settle smoking-related lawsuits. The accord called for Liggett to pay five states — Florida, Louisiana, Massachusetts, Mississippi, and West Virginia — $1 million apiece plus between 2 percent and 7 percent of its pretax income for the next 24 years, the exact amount depending on the number of additional states that joined the agreement.

Fifteen months later — with most of the states now having filed similar suits — came a more dramatic breakthrough. A team of negotiators for the states reached an agreement with the remaining four tobacco companies in the suits — Philip Morris, R.J. Reynolds, Brown & Williamson, and Lorillard — to settle the litigation, at an eventual cost of $368 billion over 25 years. The accord, subject to congressional approval, called for advertising restrictions and mandatory labels acknowledging that cigarettes are both lethal and addictive.

Although the tobacco companies called the agreement "a bitter pill," they stood to gain significant protection against further litigation. Indeed, health groups and some prominent anti-smoking advocates, including Kessler and former U.S. Surgeon General C. Everett Koop, denounced the settlement as too weak. The critics complained that the agreement restricted the FDA's authority over tobacco, barred private litigants from seeking punitive damages from tobacco companies and did not provide sufficient penalties if they failed to reduce youth smoking.

Within months, the settlement collapsed. By then, Mississippi and Florida had negotiated separate settlements calling for payments by the tobacco companies of $3.4 billion and $11.3 billion, respectively. Texas and Minnesota followed in early 1998, netting settlements of $14.5 billion and $6.1 billion, respectively. (Subsequent changes upped the total settlements to $40 billion.)

Meanwhile, advocates of a national settlement crafted a tougher, $518 billion accord for Congress to act on. But the measure died in the Senate on June 17, 1998, when supporters — mostly Democrats — fell short of the 60 votes needed to overcome procedural hurdles to final action.

Despite lobbying against the bill in Congress, tobacco companies still wanted to settle the Medicaid litigation. An agreement finally came in November 1998. The accord called for the four tobacco companies to pay $206 billion to the 46 states that had not already settled — a lower figure than called for in the 1997 settlement or the congressional legislation.

The accord was weaker in other respects as well: It did not call, as the other proposals had, for financial penalties against the tobacco companies if youth smoking failed to decline by specified percentages over time. On the other hand, the agreement restricted tobacco advertising and promotions and included no protection against private damage suits.

Some anti-smoking advocates were still wary or critical. "We opposed the settlement," recalls Banzhaf of Action on Smoking and Health. "We thought it was far too generous to the industry." For their part, the companies issued a joint statement calling the settlement "a way to end this unique litigation and a common sense approach to address tobacco issues." ∎

CURRENT SITUATION

Clinton vs. Tobacco

A handful of lawyers in the Justice Department's Civil Division spent much of last year studying the possibility of the federal government's suing tobacco companies to recover the costs of treating smoking-related illnesses under Medicare and other federal health programs. The government attorneys were dubious, even after a team of plaintiffs' lawyers gave detailed presentations on the legal theories and strategies for such a suit. [25]

Industry lawyers fed those doubts with behind-the-scenes efforts to discredit the statutory basis for a federal suit. But in December Attorney General Reno quietly gave the go-ahead for a lawsuit. Lawyers for both the plaintiffs and the tobacco companies were kept in the dark about Reno's decision. They learned of the planned suit when the rest of the country heard of it in President Clinton's State of the Union address to Congress on Jan. 19.

"You know," Clinton said, "the states have been right about this: Taxpayers shouldn't pay for the costs of lung cancer, emphysema and other smoking-related illnesses; the tobacco companies should. So tonight I announce that the Justice Department is preparing a litigation plan to take the tobacco companies to court, and with the funds we recover, to strengthen Medicare."

Clinton had already personally identified himself with the tobacco issue in a way that no previous president had done. He had appeared with FDA Commissioner Kessler at White House ceremonies when the agency first proposed regulating tobacco in 1995 and when the tobacco regulations were adopted a year later. Cigarette smoking, Clinton said on Aug. 23, 1996, is "the most significant public health hazard facing our people." [26]

"His role has been enormous," says Novelli of the National Center for Tobacco-Free Kids. "He was the first president to take on the tobacco industry. Without him, there would have been very much less momentum."

Industry representatives view Clinton's moves less favorably. "The president announced in the State of the Union address that the litigation would be filed," says Philip Morris counsel Little. "That's unprecedented. Here you have an attempt to use the Justice Department to raise money."

"If people who smoke don't pay their own way, that's an issue for Congress to address," Little continues. "It's not an issue that's appropriate for the courts."

Novelli shrugs off the accusation of political motive. "It's good for a chuckle," he says. "There's a lot of political motive on the part of the tobacco industry. They still think they have a chokehold on the political process, and they scream whenever their hold is broken."

The tobacco companies have yet to file a formal response to the suit. The case was assigned to Judge Gladys Kessler, a 1994 Clinton appointee with a reputation for pushing lawyers to settle cases out of court. Kessler has set an initial scheduling conference for Nov. 19.

Meanwhile, lawyers are preparing for arguments before the Supreme Court in the FDA regulation case on Dec. 1. The two legal moves — the FDA case and the Medicare reimbursement suit — represent the federal government's most aggressive actions ever against the tobacco industry. Attorneys for the cigarette manufacturers voice confidence that they will prevail in both cases, but one longtime observer says the industry privately views each of them as a significant threat.

"I don't think the industry would have spent as much time and energy trying to discredit the suit even before it was filed if they had not been worried," says Mary Aronson, an expert on tobacco health policy.

As for the FDA, Aronson says the tobacco companies are worried less about the current regulation than about the potential for future restrictions. "As long as the FDA has authority over tobacco, the fear is that they'll remove nicotine from cigarettes," she explains. "And if we either remove nicotine or lessen the amount, then [the companies] will have a product that no one wants to use."

Spending the Money

When the tobacco industry agreed to pay 46 state governments $206 billion to settle smoking-related suits last year, anti-smoking groups had visions of major expansions of public-education programs. But a year later many of those groups are disappointed that state officials are not using the money primarily for smoking-cessation programs, but for a wide range of programs and government functions having nothing to do with smoking or public health.

Gov. Frank Keating, R-Okla., wants to use more than one-third of the state's share of the tobacco settlement to pay for education improvements. Michigan and Nevada are planning to use part of the proceeds for college scholarships. In Virginia, Democratic lawmakers want 40 percent of the state's share to go to building roads or other transportation improvements.

The states are "treating the $206 billion as a windfall," says cancer society consultant Bloom. "The money has a lot of potential, but it's not being realized as it now stands. A distinct minority of states are [setting up anti-smoking programs], but the rest are using the money for highways, prisons, tax cuts or whatever."

CDC officials echo the criticism. Speaking at the National Conference on Tobacco and Health in Kissimmee, Fla., in August, the officials said that only six out of 46 states in the November 1998 settlement have made major commitments to devote funds from the settlement to cutting down tobacco use. "This raises fundamental issues about where your moral values are," said Michael Eriksen, head of the CDC's Office on Smoking and Health. [27]

Maryland, one of the six states singled out by CDC officials, has established a fund to receive all payments from the tobacco settlement. [28] Under legislation proposed by the state's Democratic governor, Parris N. Glendening, and signed on April 27, the funds can be used for a wide range of smoking prevention and health-related programs, as well as for alternative crop development for tobacco farmers.

In New Jersey, Republican Gov. Christine Todd Whitman proposed and the Legislature agreed to devote about one-fifth of the money to anti-smoking initiatives and the remainder to a variety of health purposes.

Other states cited favorably by CDC officials included Hawaii, Minnesota, Vermont and Washington. Since the August conference, Louisiana has acted to create a permanent trust fund to receive proceeds from the settlement, with 75 percent of the money designated for health-related programs and education, including college scholarships.

Most governors have resisted calls to earmark funds strictly for anti-smoking activities and strongly opposed any sharing of the funds with the federal government. [29] "The states are allowed to decide, each state, what are the greatest needs in their states, and how to spend their tobacco settlement dollars," says Jean Henneberry, deputy director for health policy for the National Governors' Association.

States have actually not yet received any of the funds from the settlement, although the tobacco companies put $2.4 billion into es-

At Issue:

Should tobacco companies reimburse the federal government for health-care costs related to smoking?

RICHARD A. DAYNARD
Professor of law, Northeastern University School of Law

WRITTEN FOR *THE CQ RESEARCHER*, OCTOBER 1999.

*t*he Justice Department's landmark lawsuit against tobacco companies properly seeks to reimburse taxpayers for federal health-care expenditures caused by the companies' lethal products and deceptive conduct. The claim is similar to those brought by the states for their tobacco-caused Medicaid expenses. . . . The federal claim, for money paid to care for Medicare recipients, as well as for veterans, armed services members, federal civilian employees and their families, exceeds $20 billion per year. The federal claim is actually stronger than most of the settled states' claims, since federal statutes specifically authorize the federal government to recover its health-care payments from liable third parties.

The companies' liability has been amply demonstrated already. Following an eight-month trial in the first phase of the *Engle* class-action lawsuit in Florida, the jury concluded that the same tobacco companies committed fraud, fraudulent concealment, conspiracy to commit fraud and fraudulent concealment, and intentional infliction of emotional distress on their customers. The industry documents used in *Engle* and elsewhere, condemning the companies through the words of their own scientists, executives and lawyers, would likely lead the jury in the government's case to a similar conclusion.

These documents also demonstrate that the industry's disinformation campaign fooled the U.S. government as well as its citizens. For example, in 1963 Brown & Williamson's general counsel, reviewing secret research prepared for its parent company, concluded that "we are, then, in the business of selling nicotine, an addictive drug." The company made a deliberate decision not to share this with the Surgeon General's committee on smoking and health, with the result that its landmark 1964 report concurred with the industry's public position that smoking was a "habit" but not an "addiction." This mistake was not corrected until the 1988 report, 25 years after the industry knew better, with the result that both government and private anti-smoking efforts were substantially misdirected in the interim.

The industry's pattern of fraudulent behavior is not merely tortious: It also violates the Racketeer Influenced and Corrupt Organizations (RICO) Act. Hence, in addition to seeking recompense of taxpayer expenditures for tobacco-caused disease, the Justice Department is also exercising its civil law-enforcement powers under RICO to obtain disgorgement of the companies' ill-gotten gains and injunctive relief against continued industry misbehavior.

BROWN & WILLIAMSON TOBACCO CORP.

FROM "MEDICAL COST REIMBURSEMENT: THE MEDICARE LAWSUIT FILED BY THE GOVERNMENT IS MERITLESS," WWW.BROWNANDWILLIAMSON.COM

*i*n his 1999 State of the Union address, President Clinton threatened to "take the tobacco companies to court" to recover "hundreds of billions of dollars" in Medicare expenditures. The Department of Justice has now carried out the president's threat by filing a complaint against the leading U.S. cigarette manufacturers on Sept. 22, 1999. This lawsuit is strictly political, not legal. . . . [T]his suit by the federal government is unjustified and must fail for several reasons:

• Such a lawsuit is without legal authority, and in fact is foreclosed by already-existing law.

• Such a lawsuit is factually deficient because the federal government cannot credibly claim that it was misled about the health risks associated with smoking.

• Such a lawsuit must fail because there is not scientific basis for the government to claim that any wrongful conduct of the tobacco industry has increased health-care costs. In fact, the federal government actually has made money from the sale of cigarettes.

• Such a lawsuit should not be brought because it is bad public policy. . . .

The federal government's knowledge of the health risks associated with smoking is a critical touchstone in evaluating the federal government's suit for two reasons. First, the federal government would have to prove that the tobacco industry's conduct was responsible for increasing Medicare costs. As long as individual smokers and/or the federal government were aware of the health risks associated with smoking, however, responsibility would lie with the smokers and/or the government, not the tobacco companies. Second, the federal government would have to prove that the relevant statutes of limitations (legal bars against claims that are not pursued promptly) were suspended because the government was unaware of the health risks associated with smoking until shortly before it filed suit.

The federal government could not possibly make those showings. Indeed, it is fair to say that no person or organization in the world has been more aware of the health risks associated with smoking than the federal government. . . .

For years, United States courts and juries have routinely rejected suits against tobacco companies on the ground that individual smokers knew of the health risks associated with smoking. It would be incredible for the federal government to assert that it was less knowledgeable than those unsuccessful individuals.

crow in December. An action by the Virginia Supreme Court earlier this month dismissing a legal challenge to Virginia's approval of the settlement apparently means a sufficient number of states have approved the settlement, which will allow disbursement of the proceeds to start. North Dakota Attorney General Heidi Heitkamp says that the states may begin receiving money before the year is out. Tobacco distributors have filed legal challenges to the settlement in California and Pennsylvania, but Heitkamp voices confidence that they will be rejected.

Tobacco companies are saying little about the settlement, though both Philip Morris and R.J. Reynolds have posted some information about the agreement on their Web sites. The head of one of the smokers' groups, however, says the cost of the lawsuits, including the pending Justice Department suit, will be borne not by the industry but by smokers themselves. "These may be lawsuits against the tobacco industry, but the consumer is left to pay," says Thomas Humber, president of the National Smokers Alliance, which claims 3 million members.

Heitkamp says most of the non-economic provisions of the settlement — such as the ban on outdoor advertising — have already been implemented. The restrictions on tobacco-company sponsorship of events are being phased in over a three-year period.

"We like to think that some of these marketing restrictions have had some effect on consumption," Heitkamp says. In addition, the initial organizational steps have been completed for the foundation to fund programs on youth smoking and addiction, to be called the American Legacy Foundation.

Both Henneberry and Heitkamp acknowledge the controversies over the states' plan for spending the tobacco settlement funds, but they call for a wait-and-see attitude.

"From the public health standpoint there have been a number of disappointments in the number of states that have not dedicated all of the money to anti-smoking programs," Heitkamp says. "To be fair, you need to look at what all the states are doing. I think you have to say that the jury is out." ∎

OUTLOOK

"Still Under Attack"

Smoking has never been regarded as an unadulterated pleasure or a completely acceptable social practice. Long before the modern anti-smoking movement, youngsters had to sneak behind barns or hide in school bathrooms to smoke outside the view of their parents or teachers. Up until the post-World War II era, women who smoked were viewed as slightly dissolute.

As for health issues, some early tobacco company advertisements implicitly acknowledged the harsh side effects of smoking by touting their particular brand of cigarette as "milder" or "less irritating." And smokers themselves sometimes referred to cigarettes as "cancer sticks" even while they were lighting up.

Today, the health risks of cigarettes are well established and almost universally acknowledged — even on the Philip Morris Web site. President Clinton himself has declared smoking to be the leading preventable cause of death in the United States. In addition, apart from the recent proliferation of cigar bars, smoking has become more than a little déclassé. People who object to smoking no longer apologize for asking smokers to refrain. Instead, more and more public places and buildings are smoke-free zones, and smokers have to stand outside doorways — even in the cold or rain — to indulge their habits.

Still, the estimated 48 million U.S. adults who smoke create a good-sized market for cigarettes even without the huge international market for the leading American brands. The tobacco industry's clout in Washington has diminished, and the biggest U.S. tobacco companies are now emphasizing their other business lines: Kraft Foods and Miller Brewing for Philip Morris, Nabisco for R.J. Reynolds. But the tobacco concerns remain a major economic sector, with total employment of 41,000 people in 1997 and total revenue in 1997 of $34.5 billion.

Litigation and regulation remain significant threats for the industry. "The industry is still under attack," says tobacco health policy expert Aronson. "Even after all the big lawsuits have been resolved, the industry will still have to worry about policy issues in Congress and individual lawsuits. The individual suits are not going to go away."

Anti-smoking groups hope to weaken the tobacco industry further by reducing youth smoking and thus the companies' future market. Nearly 90 percent of adult smokers began smoking before age 18, according to the Surgeon General's 1994 report on smoking. "Most kids don't intend to remain smokers," says activist Banzhaf. "They don't realize the tremendous power of nicotine addiction."

Public health groups and anti-smoking organizations hope that the public education campaign being launched by the American Legacy Foundation will help turn around the recent increase in youth smoking.

Does Smoking Actually Save the Government Money?

D oes smoking really add billions of dollars to the country's total bill for health-care costs? Or does it actually save the government money?

The question lurks under the Justice Department's lawsuit seeking to force the tobacco industry to pay for treating smoking-related illnesses under Medicare and other federal health programs. Some critics of the suit contend that the government saves money in medical costs and retirement benefits because of smokers' shortened life spans.

"This is because the costs paid by government for many tobacco-related diseases are offset by savings to government retirement and health programs that otherwise would provide longer coverage and different end-of-life care," writes Todd Gaziano, a senior fellow in legal studies at the conservative Heritage Foundation." [1]

The National Center for Tobacco-Free Kids strongly criticizes what it terms the "death-benefit argument" as "immoral, mean-spirited and unjustifiable." The argument "embraces the unnecessary, premature deaths from tobacco use and fails to give any value to the lives that new investments in tobacco prevention would save," the center says in a three-page policy statement. [2]

Tobacco companies have yet to respond in court to the government's suit, which was filed in federal court in Washington on Sept. 22. So it is not known whether and to what extent they will raise the argument in their legal defense. But one of the companies — R.J. Reynolds Tobacco — appears to refer to the issue on its Web site.

In a section describing its position on the Justice Department suit, the company says that the Congressional Research Service (CRS) issued a report in June 1999 concluding that smokers "impose no net costs on the federal government." In that report and others, Jane G. Gravelle, a CRS senior specialist in economic policy, says that the government saves on the cost of old-age medical care, Social Security and nursing-home care because of the early death of smokers.

"Smoking has apparently brought financial gain to both the federal and state governments," Gravelle concludes in her most recent report, "especially when tobacco taxes are taken into account." [3]

The Justice Department claims in its suit that smoking-related illnesses cost the federal government about $20 billion per year in treating elderly patients under Medicare, veterans and other people covered by federal health programs.

Independent studies have come up with comparable figures. Researchers at the University of California estimated recently that smoking-related diseases cost the Medicare program about $14.2 billion in 1993. [4]

A team of Dutch researchers wrote the article most frequently cited for the view that smoking saves money in total health-care costs. They conclude that if all Dutch smokers were to quit, health-care costs would decline at first, but rise after a 15-year period. Eventually, they project, health-care costs would be 7 percent higher among men and 4 percent higher among women in a population where no one smoked. [5]

In its critique, the National Center for Tobacco-Free Kids says the "death-benefit" argument "places no economic value on life" and ignores as well the workplace productivity losses resulting from tobacco-caused illnesses.

"Investing in tobacco control," the center concludes, "reduces death and suffering, reduces the associated costs and enables our society to bear both the costs and the many benefits associated with more people living longer, healthier and more productive lives."

Tellingly, the Dutch researchers reached a similar conclusion. "Whether or not smokers impose a net financial burden ought to be of very limited importance," they wrote. "Smoking is a major health hazard, so the objective of a policy on smoking should be simple and clear: Smoking should be discouraged."

---

[1] Todd F. Gaziano, "Federal Litigation Against the Tobacco Industry: Elevating Politics Over Law," Heritage Foundation Backgrounder, July 30, 1999, p. 2 (www.heritage.org).

[2] National Center for Tobacco-Free Kids, "The Immorality (and Inaccuracy) of the Death Benefit Argument," Oct. 15, 1999 (www.tobaccofreekids.org).

[3] See Jane G. Gravelle, "The Proposed Tobacco Settlement: Who Pays for the Health Costs of Smoking?" Congressional Research Service, Oct. 12, 1999; memorandum to Rep. Ron Lewis, R-Ky., June 16, 1999.

[4] Zhang et al., "Cost of Smoking to the Medicare Program," *Health Care Financing Review*, Vol. 20, No. 4 (summer 1999), p. 179.

[5] Barendregt et al., "The Health Care Costs of Smoking," *New England Journal of Medicine*, Vol. 337, No. 15 (Oct. 9, 1997), p. 1052.

The tobacco companies themselves say they want to prevent youth smoking, favor stronger enforcement of minimum-age laws and will comply with the provisions of the settlement that restrict many of the types of advertising most likely to be seen by young people.

Adult smoking, meanwhile, has been declining, but the rate of decrease is tapering off. The tobacco companies continue to emphasize that they are manufacturing a "legal product" and are marketing it in a "responsible" way.

In the long term, Philip Morris spokeswoman Roberts says, she hopes for reduced tensions between the tobacco industry and its critics. "We hope that we're opening a dialogue and that we'll find some common ground with our critics and the public, and find areas where we can find solutions on youth smoking and other issues," she says. "We hope that in 10 years we will have an ongoing dialogue and that we'll have made some progress in some of these areas."

For his part, anti-smoking activist Novelli thinks the current developments could be the start of "a sea change" in the tobacco wars. "Ten years from now," he says, "we'll see some really strong reductions in the prevalence of smoking, and that will begin to pay off in terms of lives saved." ∎

Notes

[1] For other coverage, see the *Los Angeles Times*, Oct. 13, 1999, p. C1.

[2] Quoted in *The New York Times*, Oct. 13, 1999, p. A1.

[3] For earlier coverage, see Richard L. Worsnop, "Teens and Tobacco," *The CQ Researcher*, Dec. 1, 1995, pp. 1065-1088; "Regulating Tobacco," *The CQ Researcher*, Sept. 30, 1994, pp. 841-864.

[4] See *The New York Times*, Oct. 21, 1999, p. A21 (appeals court ruling); July 8, 1999, p. A1 (jury verdict).

[5] See Jacob Sullum, *For Your Own Good: The Anti-Smoking Crusade and the Tyranny of Public Health* (1998).

[6] See Richard Kluger, *Ashes to Ashes: America's Hundred-Year Cigarette War, the Public Health, and the Unabashed Triumph of Philip Morris* (1996), p. 9; Joseph C. Robert, *The Story of Tobacco in America* (1952), p. 4.

[7] Rein was quoted in "Supreme Court 2000: Privacy and Power," Oct. 3, 1999, www.msnbc.com.

[8] Quoted in *Richmond (Va.) Times Dispatch*, Oct. 3, 1999.

[9] Quoted in Michael Orey, *Assuming the Risk: The Mavericks, the Lawyers, and the Whistleblowers Who Beat Big Tobacco* (1999), p. 225. Orey does not identify the author of the memo or provide a specific citation.

[10] Quoted in *The New York Times*, Sept. 23, 1999, p. A1.

FOR MORE INFORMATION

Action on Smoking and Health, 2013 H St., N.W., Washington, D.C. 20006; (202) 659-4310; http://ash.org. The organization's executive director, John F. Banzhaf III, helped create the modern anti-smoking movement in the 1960s.

American Cancer Society, 1599 Clifton Rd., N.E., Atlanta, Ga. 30329; 1-800-ACS-2345; (404) 320-3333; www.cancer.org. The organization sponsors "The Great American Smokeout" and features tobacco-control information on its Web site.

National Center for Tobacco-Free Kids, 1707 L St., N.W., Suite 800, Washington, D.C. 20036; 1-800-284-KIDS; 202-296-5469; www.tobaccofreekids.org. The center describes itself as the largest non-government initiative to protect children from tobacco and secondhand smoke.

National Smokers Alliance, 901 N. Washington St., Suite 400, Alexandria, Va. 22314; 1-800-224-3322; (703) 739-1324; www.speakup.org. The smokers' rights organization claims 3 million members.

Office on Smoking and Health, Centers for Disease Control and Prevention, 1600 Clifton Rd., Atlanta, Ga. 30333; (770) 488-5705; www.cdc.gov/tobacco. The office is the federal government's clearing-house for information on tobacco and health.

Philip Morris Companies Inc., 120 Park Ave., New York, N.Y. 10017; (212) 880-5000; www.philipmorris.com. The world's largest tobacco company recently added new material on tobacco issues to its Web site along with links to sites maintained by other organizations, including anti-smoking groups.

[11] See Robert, *op. cit.,* p. 6; Kluger, *op. cit.,* p. 10.

[12] See Robert, *op. cit.,* pp. 255, 271; Kluger, *op. cit.,* pp. 134-136.

[13] Quoted in *ibid.,* pp. 258 (report), 260 (Lynch).

[14] *Ibid.,* pp. 364-377.

[15] See "Key Developments in the Tobacco Debate," *Facts on File*, June 19, 1997, p. 451, and additional references cited there. Other background drawn from Kluger, *op. cit.* See index entries for "liability suits."

[16] Some background drawn from the extensive account of the lawsuit and trial in Michael Orey, *Assuming the Risk: The Mavericks, the Lawyers, and the Whistleblowers Who Beat Big Tobacco* (1999), pp. 3-143.

[17] Some background drawn from the detailed account in Kluger, *op. cit.,* pp. 639-677.

[18] Kluger cites coverage in the Post on Jan. 25, 1987, and Jan. 5, 6, 29, and 30, 1988.

[19] See Orey, *op. cit.,* pp. 147-216.

[20] Stanton A. Glantz et al., *The Cigarette Papers* (1996), p. 2. Claimed contradictions are summarized in a table at pp. 15-17. The documents can be found at http://www.library.ucsf.edu/tobacco.

[21] The regulations can be found in the *Federal Register*, Vol. 61, No. 168 (Aug. 28, 1996), or on the FDA's Web site: www.fda.gov/opcacom/campaigns/tobacco/tobregs.htm.

[22] Background drawn from Orey, *op. cit.,* pp. 227-357. For a more critical account, see Jacob Sullum, *For Your Own Good: The Anti-Smoking Crusade and the Tyranny of Public Health* (1998), pp. 207-215.

[23] Quoted in *The New York Times*, May 24, 1994, p. A1.

[24] Orey, *op. cit.,* pp. 278-280.

[25] See *The Wall Street Journal*, Sept. 24, 1999, p. B1, and *Legal Times*, Sept. 27, 1999, p. 1.

[26] Quoted in *The New York Times*, Aug. 24, 1996, p. 1.

[27] Quoted in *The New York Times*, Aug. 25, 1999, p. A12.

[28] Information from National Governors' Association, www.nga.org (tobacco settlement, state activities).

[29] See *The New York Times*, Feb. 23, 1999, p. A19.

Bibliography

Selected Sources Used

Books

Glantz, Stanton A., John Slade, Lisa A. Bero, Peter Hanauer and Deborah E. Barnes, *The Cigarette Papers*, **University of California Press, 1996.**

The book provides substantial excerpts, with narration and analysis, from internal documents of the Brown & Williamson Tobacco Co. relating to smoking and health issues. Glantz, the lead author, is a professor of medicine at the University of California in San Francisco. The book includes chapter reference notes and a categorized list of documents used in preparing the book. The electronic version of the book and 8,000 pages of source documents are on the Web: www.library.ucsf.edu/tobacco.

Hilts, Philip J., *Smokescreen: The Truth Behind the Tobacco Industry Cover-up*, **Addison-Wesley, 1996.**

Hilts, a former health and science reporter for *The New York Times*, writes a strong critique of the tobacco industry's actions and statements on health issues based on internal documents unearthed during smoking litigation and other reporting. The book includes chapter notes and a two-page bibliography.

Kluger, Richard, *Ashes to Ashes: America's Hundred-Year Cigarette War, the Public Health, and the Unabashed Triumph of Philip Morris*, **Knopf, 1996.**

Kluger, a well-regarded author of two other works of social history, traces the history of the tobacco industry from the days of Christopher Columbus through the modern legal and regulatory wars in the United States. The 807-page book includes detailed chapter notes and a five-page bibliography.

Mollenkamp, Carrick, Adam Levy, Joseph Menn and Jeffrey Rothfeder, *The People vs. Big Tobacco: How the States Took on the Cigarette Giants*, **Bloomberg Press, 1998.**

The authors, reporters with the Bloomberg financial news service, detail the states' suits against U.S. tobacco companies through the abortive settlement in summer 1997. The book includes an eight-page chronology, source notes and the text of the proposed 1997 settlement.

Orey, Michael, *Assuming the Risk: The Mavericks, the Lawyers, and the Whistleblowers Who Beat Big Tobacco*, **Little, Brown, 1999.**

Orey, an editor at *The Wall Street Journal*, provides accounts based on his coverage while at *American Lawyer* magazine of two major smoking-related suits, both in Mississippi: the unsuccessful private suit by the family of Nathan Horton and the successful litigation brought by Mississippi Attorney General Michael Moore.

Pringle, Peter, *Cornered: Big Tobacco at the Bar of Justice*, **Henry Holt, 1998.**

Pringle, a British journalist, recounts the story of the "third wave" of tobacco litigation in the 1990s through the industry's abortive settlement with the states in 1997, with emphasis on the lawyers involved. The book includes source notes and a three-page bibliography.

Robert, Joseph, *The Story of Tobacco in America*, **Knopf, 1952.**

This early history provides a good account, from a favorable perspective, of the development and growth of the U.S. tobacco industry, with a few hints of the beginnings of the modern debate over smoking and health. The book includes 14 pages of bibliographical notes.

Ryback, Deborah Caulfield, and David Phelps, *Smoked: the Inside Story of the Minnesota Tobacco Trial*, **MSP Books, 1998.**

The Minneapolis reporters covered Minnesota's suit against the tobacco industry and recount the litigation from its beginnings through the aborted trial and settlement.

Sullum, Jacob, *For Your Own Good: The Anti-Smoking Crusade and the Tyranny of Public Health*, **Free Press, 1998.**

Sullum, an editor at *Reason* magazine, traces the history of tobacco from the 15th century to today and then attacks the anti-smoking movement on both factual and ideological grounds. The book includes detailed source notes and a seven-page bibliography.

White, Larry C., *Merchants of Death: The American Tobacco Industry*, **Beech Tree/Morrow, 1988.**

Journalist White provides a sharply critical account of the tobacco industry through the midway point of the so-called second wave of smoking-related suits and the beginning of diversification by the major U.S. tobacco companies.

Reports and Studies

Centers for Disease Control and Prevention, "Cigarette Smoking Among Adults — United States, 1997," *Morbidity and Mortality Weekly Report*, **Nov. 5, 1997, pp. 993-996 (www.cdc.gov).**

The government's latest survey found that 24.7 percent of all adults were cigarette smokers as of 1997, while the figure was higher — 28.7 percent — among young adults ages 18-24. An accompanying article, "Ten Great Public Health Achievements — United States, 1990-1999 Tobacco Use," notes the reduction in smoking prevalence and enactment of smoking restrictions and indoor air laws at the national, state, and local levels.

10 High-Impact Litigation

KENNETH JOST

Chicago has one of the nation's strictest gun-control ordinances. Even so, local police recover some 17,000 illegal firearms every year. Many are sold by dealers in the nearby suburbs — just outside Chicago's jurisdiction.

When Mayor Richard M. Daley called for a new crackdown on the flow of illegal guns, city lawyers dug into the law books and came up with a novel strategy: Sue the suburban gun dealers for creating a public nuisance.

"It's a very ancient concept — conduct that threatens public health and safety," explains Lawrence Rosenthal, the city's deputy corporation counsel. "A factory upstream that releases pollutants legally can be held liable downstream where that pollution is illegal." Similarly, outside gun dealers could be prosecuted for helping to put firearms on Chicago streets.

To launch the crackdown, police planned a sting operation in 1998. Undercover police officers posing as drug dealers, gang members or survivalists found many suburban dealers willing to sell them guns, even though the officers identified themselves as Chicago residents.

"The dealers were only too glad to sell them," Rosenthal recalls, though it is widely known that the Windy City virtually outlaws private possession of handguns.

The sting came to light when the city filed a path-breaking $433 million civil damage lawsuit seeking to recover some of the costs of gun-related crime from gun dealers and from gun manufacturers themselves. The evidence, Rosenthal says today, "makes clear that the industry's claim that it can't be held responsible [for

Newsmakers/Todd Buchanan

illegal gun trafficking] is a fraud. They will sell the weapons no matter how clear the notice is that they are going to be used illegally."

Since Chicago's suit was filed in November 1998, more than two dozen other city and county governments have also gone to court against the gun industry. (*See map, p. 182.*) The suits follow the model of the state governments' recent successful legal attack against the tobacco industry — and prompt similar criticisms that the litigation amounts to extortion against a lawful industry and an end-run around normal legislative and regulatory processes. [1]

The debate over the government-sponsored suits comes as judges, lawyers and legal experts also ponder how the courts can best deal with another type of high-impact, complex litigation — so-called class actions. Proponents say these kinds of mass suits give consumers and others an essential weapon against wrongdoing by private businesses. But business interests say class actions more often amount to legal blackmail

by forcing businesses into big settlements in order to avoid high litigation costs and unfavorable publicity.

Some of the gun suits follow Chicago's example in accusing manufacturers and dealers of creating a public nuisance. Others claim that gunmakers are violating product-liability laws by failing to incorporate safety features in guns and refusing to crack down on illegal sales by dealers.

Lawyers for gunmakers dismiss the allegations. "There is absolutely no basis for a cause of action against legally made, legally sold products as a public nuisance against the manufacturer," says Anne Kimball, a Chicago attorney representing two of the gunmakers — Smith & Wesson Corp. and Sturm, Ruger & Co. — in the Chicago suit and several others.

As for the product liability claims, Kimball says courts in Illinois and other states repeatedly have rejected such claims in private damage suits filed over the years. "Product-liability law is aimed at defective products," Kimball says. "You're not talking about defective products here."

More broadly, Kimball contends the suits are "an abuse of the judicial system" because they raise issues that belong in legislative bodies, not in the courts. In addition, the legal actions are counterproductive, she insists. "They serve a very negative purpose in focusing on litigation rather than focusing on law enforcement and how to prevent violence," Kimball says. "They do not forward the ball of either preventing violence or increasing consumer education and safety."

So far, gunmakers are besting the local governments in court. Judges last fall ruled against officials in Cincinnati, Miami-Dade County, Fla., and Bridgeport, Conn. In a fourth case, a

From *The CQ Researcher,* February 11, 2000.

The Lawsuits Heard 'Round the Country

Thirty local jurisdictions around the country have sued gun manufacturers since 1998 seeking damages for gun-related violence or changes in gun design or marketing practices. Judges have granted gunmakers' motions to dismiss three of the suits, in Bridgeport, Conn., Cincinnati and Miami-Dade County. A judge in Atlanta allowed the city's suit to proceed; the industry filed a separate suit in a higher court to block the suit.

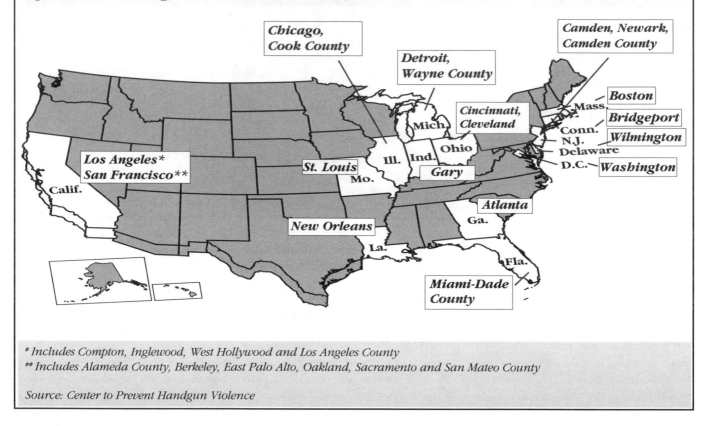

* Includes Compton, Inglewood, West Hollywood and Los Angeles County
** Includes Alameda County, Berkeley, East Palo Alto, Oakland, Sacramento and San Mateo County

Source: Center to Prevent Handgun Violence

---

judge allowed part of a suit filed by the city of Atlanta to proceed but threw out claims regarding product liability. Defendants have filed motions to dismiss Chicago's suit as well; a Cook County Circuit judge was scheduled to begin arguments on the motions on Feb. 10.

The legal offensives against the gun and tobacco industries break new ground by bringing the power of government to bear not on a single company — as in a typical antitrust or consumer-protection suit — but against an entire industry. The suits have cheered liberal health and safety advocates while disconcerting business interests and conservative legal organizations.

"It serves the public interest to use the litigation process for state or local governments to seek recoupment of costs due to the liability of others," says David Vladeck, director of the liberal Public Citizen Litigation Group. "There is an important legitimating effect to these cases when the plaintiff is not simply one individual seeking damages, but a local government seeking to vindicate broader interests."

But a spokesman for the U.S. Chamber of Commerce calls the new type of suits "enormously ominous."

"The cities are trying to get what amounts to extrajudicial remedies by posing such a threat to the gun industry that they will agree to restrictions on marketing or particular safety features that would generally not be the aim of litigation," says James Wootton, head of the Chamber's Institute for Legal Reform.

In both cases, Wootton adds, governments have a conflict of interest in seeking revenue from private industry rather than through taxation. "There are enormous incentives for them to come up with theories that essentially strip the defendants of their rights or are so Draconian that the industry has no choice but to settle," he says.

An attorney who represents several cities in suits against the gun industry, however, insists that the legal actions ask the court to impose a traditional damage remedy based on well-established legal principles.

"Courts interpreting the common law dating back to the British system deal with whether people or entities are acting negligently, whether their negligence has injured others and, if so, what are the damages," says Jonathan Lowy, senior attorney with the legal action project of the Center to Prevent Handgun Violence. "This is exactly what courts do."

Unlike the government suits, class actions are private suits brought by a number of individual plaintiffs on behalf of a much larger "class" of people with ostensibly similar legal claims. Class actions are governed in federal courts by a complex civil-procedure rule — known as Rule 23 — that was written in the 1960s to help consumers consolidate piddling legal claims about shady business practices into an economically viable lawsuit.

Since then, environmental and product-liability attorneys also have used the device to try to hold companies liable for injuries that they attribute to the companies' operations or products. One recent example is the wave of suits filed on behalf of women claiming medical injuries from silicon breast implants.

Consumers Filed the Most Class-Action Suits

Consumer disputes accounted for a quarter of the 1,000 private class-action suits that resulted in published judicial decisions in 1995 and 1996, according to the Rand Corporation. Tort cases — which have accounted for most of the controversial cases in recent years, such as breast-implant suits — were only 9 percent of the total.

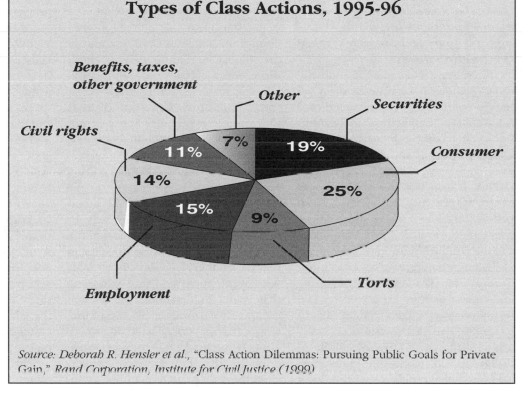

Types of Class Actions, 1995-96

- Benefits, taxes, other government — 11%
- Civil rights — 14%
- Other — 7%
- Securities — 19%
- Consumer — 25%
- Torts — 9%
- Employment — 15%

Source: Deborah R. Hensler et al., "Class Action Dilemmas: Pursuing Public Goals for Private Gain," Rand Corporation, Institute for Civil Justice (1999)

Industry lawyers defending the suits often have contended that the plaintiffs' lawyers had little evidence of real injuries or scant proof of the companies' responsibility. As in the breast implant suits, however, companies often agree to pay multimillion-dollar settlements to resolve the suits rather than fight the cases through costly trials and appeals.

Both types of "high-impact" litigation generate debate not only about the particular outcomes but also regarding the role that courts should play in dealing with broad public-policy issues.

"Laws are supposed to be enacted by legislatures," says Robert Levy, senior fellow in constitutional studies at the libertarian Cato Institute in Washington. The gun and tobacco suits, he says, are instead "government-sponsored litigation as a substitute for legislation that failed."

"The common law has always put the courts in a policy-making role," responds Vladeck, who is also a visiting professor at Georgetown University Law Center in Washington. "That's the way our product-liability and tort law have always been shaped."

The local governments' suits against the gun industry ensure that the debate over the courts' role will continue. And whether or not the suits are successful, their example may spawn further rounds of government-sponsored litigation against other industries. As the number of class actions being filed continue to grow, here are some of the questions being debated:

Does the new wave of government-sponsored litigation against private industries serve the public interest?

When state governments and the tobacco industry completed the $246 billion settlement of the Medicaid reimbursement litigation in November 1998, both sides issued statements depicting the move as positive. States saw the agreement as a landmark for holding the industry accountable for tobacco-related health problems while the companies called the deal a common-sense way to put the litigation behind them.

The agreement also had its critics, though. In particular, conservative and business-oriented advocates denounced the tobacco deal as an improper use of the courts to bully a lawful industry into a multibillion-dollar payoff to public treasuries. Today, these critics view the local governments' suits against gunmakers as more of the same.

"The idea is not to go to trial," Levy says. "It's to extort money or some other public-policy goals by settling. It's simply blackmail — blackmail masquerading as law."

Public-interest advocates scoff at the criticism. "I always laugh when someone accuses the government of strong-arming a big industry like the tobacco industry or the gun industry," Vladeck says. "There's a tremendous resource imbalance that cuts in the other direction. I don't think the tobacco industry was strong-armed by the government. What scared the tobacco industry

was losing big and losing all at once."

Critics also view the court suits as a means of circumventing legislative bodies unwilling to enact regulatory policies supported by executive officials. "The idea is that through litigation, you are going to get a result that you are unable to get through the legislative process," Wootton says.

Rosenthal acknowledges that Chicago officials turned to the courts out of frustration at the defeat of gun-control measures in Congress and in the Illinois legislature. "Gun control represents a classic failure of the legislative process," Rosenthal says. "Most legislators represent districts that do not experience the concentrated firearms violence that is found in the central cities. That's why the nation's mayors have been so consistently frustrated."

But Rosenthal also says the litigation is justified as the only way to hold gunmakers responsible for the damage their products inflict. "A big market out there consists of criminals who want guns, and any company that wants to maximize profits will compete for those sales," Rosenthal says. "If they don't have to worry about being held liable for what those criminals do, they are going to do everything they can to get guns in the hands of criminals."

Kimball, the gun companies' lawyer, heatedly denies the accusation "The last thing that firearms manufacturers want is for their products to be used by criminals," she says. "Number one, it is against the law. And, number two, it is bad business."

Critics also denounce the role that private attorneys have played in both the tobacco and gun litigation. State governments — beginning with Mississippi, the first of the states to sue tobacco manufacturers — hired private attorneys to wage the litigation and agreed to fee arrangements based on the eventual recovery. (*See story, p. 192.*) Today, private lawyers also

are being used in some of the gun litigation and, typically under contingency-fee agreements. In Chicago, though, Rosenthal says private lawyers aiding the city's suit are donating their time.

Levy argues that the suits essentially are being "concocted" by private lawyers and strongly criticizes allowing lawyers to collect a contingency fee rather than being paid according to a standard, hourly fee.

Lowy disagrees. "Before the success of the tobacco suits, it would have been difficult for many states to justify paying large hourly rates for those risky cases," he says.

Finally, critics also fear the tobacco and gun litigation will establish precedents for governments to try to collect damages from other industries. "These suits are like suing the auto industry because cars are used by criminals, drug abusers and children," Kimball told a forum cosponsored by the Chamber of Commerce last June. "It would be like suing automobile makers because cars move too fast or because toddlers, in the absence of safety devices, can crawl from the back seat. It doesn't make sense." [2]

But Lowy insists that the gun suits merely are seeking to enforce laws on the books against selling guns to criminals. "We're asking the courts to recognize a policy that is already well established," Lowy says. "That has absolutely nothing to do with hamburgers, matches, or knives or any other product that the industry claims it's being compared with."

One academic expert, however, acknowledges that the suits open up the possibility of additional claims. "It's not immediately clear where the line is," says Stephen Yeazell, a University of California at Los Angeles law professor and author of a history of the development of class-action suits. "As with any new kind of claim, there are interesting stopping-point problems."

Do private class-action suits serve the public interest?

Tobacco companies for years had an unbroken record of paying out no damage awards in smoking-related health suits. In recent years, though, the industry has had some significant setbacks in large, class-action suits filed on behalf of people claiming smoking-related injuries.

State courts in Florida have allowed two major class actions to proceed. In one, tobacco companies agreed in October 1997 to a $349 million settlement in a suit filed on behalf of flight attendants exposed to second-hand tobacco smoke. In a second case — filed on behalf of all smokers and ex-smokers in the state — a jury in July 1999 found tobacco companies liable for smoking-related health problems and is now hearing evidence in a punitive damage claim that could reach hundreds of millions of dollars.

Supporters see such consolidated legal actions as an essential tool for consumers to take on big businesses. But critics insist the suits often force businesses to settle even dubious actions in order to avoid huge litigation costs, unfavorable publicity and potentially whopping damage awards.

Legal experts find some truth in both views. "A lot of defendants say they are victims of blackmail, and a lot of plaintiffs say this is the only thing that protects the little guy from corporate America," says Richard Marcus, a civil-procedure expert at the University of California's Hastings College of Law in San Francisco. "Both of those assertions have some validity in some instances, but as generalizations they're just too broad."

Civil-procedure rules in federal and state courts set out a complex of con-ditions for a suit to be "certified" as a class action. Besides basic prerequisites — many potential class members with similar claims, legally and factually — courts generally must find that a class action is either necessary or preferable to reach a just solution.

Critics say judges, especially in state courts, interpret those criteria too liberally, forcing defendants to try to respond to impossible-to-pin-down allegations and evidence. "We've given the legal system a lot

Chicago Mayor Richard M. Daley asked city lawyers to find a new tactic to stem the flow of guns on streets. They suggested suing gun dealers for public nuisance.

Newsmakers/Tim Boyle

of leeway with the hope that some sort of rough justice is done," says Walter Olson, a senior fellow with the conservative Manhattan Institute on Policy Research. "The more cases that come, the rougher the justice looks to be."

From an opposite perspective, critics also complain that plaintiffs often end up with little in the way of compensation while their attorneys make off with big fees. "There are some outrageous examples where attorneys are walking off with huge attorney fees with very little benefit to the consumer," says Linda Mullenix, a leading civil-procedure expert at the University of Texas Law School. The settlement in the flight attendants' secondhand smoke suit, for example, called for tobacco companies to pay $300 million to set up a research foundation and pay lawyers $49 million while giving individual plaintiffs no compensation at all.

Liberal public-interest advocates share some of those concerns. "We have a lot of problems with the way class actions are being handled," says Vladeck of Public Citizen. "Lawyers bring these class actions, and they settle them for what I call the 'homogenized rate' — people with the most serious injuries tend to collect less than they ought to, and the people with the least serious injuries collect more than they ought to."

For the courts, the class-action rules can add to the litigation burden by attracting suits that would never be brought as individual claims. At times, though, class actions help the courts by consolidating claims that otherwise would have to be handled individually at much greater time and expense.

Businesses also have mixed views about class actions. Historically, business groups and their supporters criticized the procedure. In recent years, though, some companies have started to view the class action as a useful tool to negotiate so-called global settlements with plaintiffs' attorneys in an effort to put legal disputes behind them, even at the expense of hundreds of millions of dollars.

Despite the controversies, there is

Study of Class-Action Suits...

According to a 1995 suit filed by angry customers, Great Western Financial Corp. misled them into thinking their investments in one of the California bank's mutual funds were federally insured.

The bank denied the accusation, but two years later agreed to pay $17 million to settle the suit. Some 7,500 class members received an average of $1,478 each to compensate them for investment losses blamed on the bank's allegedly misleading solicitations. The attorneys who brought the case received $5.2 million in court-approved fees. [1]

The Great Western case, with its graphic illustration of the claimed benefits and costs of class-action suits, was one of 10 cases studied by researchers at the Rand Corporation's Institute of Civil Justice. Their preliminary conclusions lend support to both the advocates and critics of class actions.

The researchers end, however, by cautioning against legislative rule changes. Instead, they advocate placing primary responsibility on judges to better manage class actions, deter wrongdoing and ensure fair compensation in worthy cases and prevent abuses by class-action attorneys or lawyers for defendants.

On the positive side, the researchers rejected the criticism that class actions typically produce little compensation for plaintiffs and that lawyers "routinely" collect the major share of settlements as fees. All of the cases studied produced hefty sums in total compensation for plaintiffs. When Louisiana-Pacific settled a suit over defective siding for $470 million, class members got an average of $4,367 in compensation. Two big insurance companies, Allstate and Farmers, paid $25 million to settle an overcharging dispute. The average compensation per class member in that case was small, though: only $5.75.

Class-action attorneys received "substantial fees" in all of the suits, the researchers said, but the amount and their share of the awards "varied dramatically." Fees ranged from 5 percent to 50 percent of the total. But in eight of the cases studied, the fees amounted to one-third or less of the total award. Overall, the researchers conclude, fees were "a modest share of the negotiated settlements."

Substantively, the suits involved allegations that the researchers concluded could be viewed as "blameworthy" or as "trivial or even trumped-up." The researchers also said they could not fully evaluate the validity of the accusations. The report notes that in many instances government investigations were inconclusive and that at the time of settlements there was "considerable uncertainty regarding the defendants' culpability and plaintiff class members' damages."

Still, the researchers said that in six of the cases the litigation was "associated with changes in the defendants' business practices." In four of those cases, they added, the evidence "strongly suggests" that the changes resulted "directly or indirectly" from the lawsuits.

Unequivocally, the researchers described class actions as "costly." They estimated the costs for class-action lawyers — including fees, expenses and the costs of notice and no consensus today on rewriting the federal rule. Congress, however, has passed legislation to restrict class-action suits in the securities field and is now considering a bill to allow defendants to move class actions from state to federal courts.

"There simply isn't an ideal solution," says Jay Tidmarsh, a professor at Notre Dame Law School in South Bend, Ind., who has studied tort class actions for the Federal Judicial Center. "It's a very hard problem that's very likely to occupy us for the next 10 to 15 years." [3]

Does high-impact litigation improperly inject the courts into policy-making roles?

Robert B. Reich served for four years as a liberal stalwart in President Clinton's Cabinet as secretary of Labor. But today, as an academic and sometimes columnist, Reich criticizes the administration for using the courts to go after the tobacco and gun industries.

"Fed up with trying to move legislation, the White House is launching lawsuits to succeed where legislation failed," Reich, now professor of social and economic policy at Brandeis University, wrote in a recent column. "The strategy may work, but at the cost of making our frail democracy even weaker." [4]

Reich's criticism came a month after Housing and Urban Development Secretary Andrew M. Cuomo said on Dec. 8 that the administration was prepared to sue gunmakers on behalf of the nation's public housing authorities if the companies did not agree to demands to make guns safer. Earlier, the Justice Department on Sept. 22 had sued the major U.S. tobacco companies seeking unspecified amounts — probably in the billions of dollars — as reimbursement for smoking-related health costs in the Medicare program.

The same criticism about alleged misuse of the courts comes, vocally and more predictably, from conservative advocates and interest groups. "Laws are supposed to be enacted by legislatures," says Levy of the Cato Institute. Referring to the local governments' suit against the gunmakers, Levy says, "Here we have government-sponsored litigation as a substitute for legislation that failed."

...Advises Against Changing Rules

administration — amounted to more than $500 million in three cases and at least $10 million each in five others. Defense lawyers declined to provide figures on their costs, but the researchers said those also were likely to be "large." Assessing whether the benefits outweigh the costs, however, "turns out to be enormously difficult," the report concludes. The various issues, the researchers say, are "matters of judgment."

The report finds little merit in most of the major proposals for changing class-action rules. One proposal — dubbed the "just ain't worth it" rule — calls for federal judges to weigh the likely costs and benefits of a suit before certifying it as a class action. After noting the "ambiguity" of the evidence in the cases they studied, the Rand researchers said any attempt to adjudicate the underlying dispute at such an early stage would yield "unpredictable outcomes."

The researchers also rejected the idea of requiring class members to "opt in" to a suit as opposed to the current procedure, where someone has to take an affirmative step to "opt out" of a suit once it is certified as a class action. The proposal would lead to smaller classes and smaller aggregate settlements, the researchers say, which in turn would "discourage attorneys from bringing the suit." In addition, they say it is a "worrisome possibility" that minority and low-income individuals would be "disproportionately affected" by an opt-in requirement.

The report is somewhat equivocal about a third proposal to broaden federal court jurisdiction over class actions.

The House of Representatives passed a bill last year aimed at shifting more class actions from state to federal courts. Supporters contend that federal judges scrutinize class-action allegations more carefully and argue that suits with nationwide implications belong in federal court anyway. The Rand researchers say there is "no empirical basis" for giving federal judges higher marks for handling class actions than state judges. But they acknowledge that it might help eliminate "duplicative" litigation by allowing some state court class actions to be removed to federal courts and consolidated with suits on the same issue.

In the end, though, the researchers say judges can improve class actions under existing rules. "Judges hold the key to improving the balance of good and ill consequences of damage class actions," the researchers conclude. They say judges should "scrutinize proposed settlements more closely," both when the agreements are reached and as they are carried out.

In addition, the report says judges "should reward attorneys only for actual accomplishments." "The single most important action that judges can take to support the public goals of class-action litigation," the researchers say, "is to reward class-action attorneys only for lawsuits that actually accomplish something of value to class members and society."

---

[1] Background drawn from Deborah R. Hensler et al., "Class Action Dilemmas: Pursuing Public Goals for Private Gain" (executive summary), Rand Institute for Civil Justice, Nov. 1, 1999, p. 2. See *The Wall Street Journal*, Feb. 4, 1997; April 26, 1995, p. C20.

"All these lawsuits involve a repudiation of the democratic process," says John Langbein, a conservative professor at Yale Law School. "They all arise in circumstances in which the legislature did not produce the result that these people want."

Supporters of the tobacco and gun lawsuits insist that — except for the innovation of the government's role in the litigation — they follow well-established legal theories of liability that have historically derived from court decisions more than from legislatures. "People and companies have to do what they reasonably can to prevent foreseeable injuries to others," says gun-control advocate Lowy. "Companies can't put their heads in the sand if there are reason-

able ways to prevent injuries."

"The common law has always put the courts in a policy-making role," says Vladeck, pointing to a string of 20th-century decisions by state courts now widely accepted as the basis for suits involving unsafe products. "That's the way our product-liability and tort law have always been shaped," Vladeck continues. "It would be antithetical to our law and our common-law tradition to have it shaped in any other way."

Whether the courts are fashioning new rules of liability or not, judges clearly have been forced in some of the mass tort suits to devise new types of compensation schemes involving millions — even billions — of dollars for plaintiffs numbering in the thou-

sands or tens of thousands. The most massive of such litigation — claims brought by workers for alleged medical injuries due to asbestos exposure — has spawned more than 150,000 cases in federal courts, with 80,000 filed in the past decade alone.

Asbestos companies have worked with plaintiffs' attorneys to try to resolve the litigation by fashioning settlements with complex formulas for compensating plaintiffs already injured and paying damages to potential future claimants. Twice in the past few years, though, the U.S. Supreme Court has overturned settlements approved by lower federal courts. In one case, the high court in 1997 ruled that a $1.3 billion settlement by a consortium of 20 asbestos companies was unfair to future claimants. Then last year, the court threw out a $1.5 billion settlement by a former asbestos manufacturer, saying the company had unfairly sought to limit its overall liability. [5]

Mullenix says that the mass tort-compensation tactics reflect policy-making not so much by courts as by lawyers and others even farther removed from the political process. "It's private legislation by a lot of unelected people who are affecting aggregate rights and settlements with very little involvement by the judiciary," Mullenix says. [6] In both of the Supreme Court cases, however, some of the justices have noted critically that Congress has failed to act on proposals to legislate a compensation scheme to handle asbestos claims.

The various forms of consolidated legal actions "probably put the courts in a policy-making posture," concludes UCLA law Professor Yeazell, "but we've rather intentionally designed a system in which the courts are regularly put into that position.

"We are a relatively unregulated economy in contrast to other industrialized countries," Yeazell adds. "What that means is that default regulation occurs essentially through private litigation. We've set the courts up to do exactly that. The courts become the default regulators, and they have been for 200 years." ∎

BACKGROUND

"Group Litigation"

Precursors of the modern class action can be found in what Professor Yeazell calls "medieval group litigation" dating back as far as the 13th century. [7] Judges in England routinely allowed groups of people to bring suits in common, Yeazell explains. Parishioners might sue their rector over what tithes they owed, for example, or villagers might sue the lord of the manor over various kinds of disputes. In contrast to the plaintiffs in a modern class action, however, these were "pre-existing social groups," Yeazell notes. "They had some type of cohesion outside the litigation itself."

A second type of group action arose in the 18th century in response to the newly created business form of joint stock companies — precursors of the modern corporation. Many joint stock companies began with wild speculation and ended in financial disaster for hapless investors. A notorious example was the so-called South Sea Bubble, an ill-capitalized foreign-trade venture. It collapsed, triggering endless litigation. In one suit, a Chancery Court judge in 1722 allowed two officers of a company that invested money in the venture to bring suit against the company's former treasurers on behalf of all the proprietors. As Yeazell notes, the action resembles what is now called a shareholder's derivative suit, designed to recoup a company's losses from officers or managers for financial wrongdoing.

With the advent of modern corporation law in the 19th century — which allows incorporated businesses to be sued directly rather than through their officers — judges in England began to see less need for such group legal actions. Meanwhile, judges in the United States were allowing group legal actions in a few instances, but only sporadically, according to Yeazell.

In one pre-Civil War case, the Supreme Court allowed a suit between Northern and Southern conferences of Methodist ministers over how to divide pension funds when the church group split over the issue of slavery. Later in the 19th century, courts allowed businesses fighting the labor movement to join trade union members as defendants in joint legal actions for trespass, interference with business or the like. As with corporations, however, the recognition of trade unions as unincorporated associations in the 20th century reduced the need for such joint suits.

Class actions received their first, formal recognition in 1938 with the adoption of the Federal Rules of Civil Procedure. The rule divided class actions into three types: true, hybrid and spurious. The "spurious" class action was the closest to the kind of self-constituted litigation that attracts the most attention and controversy today. But it had limited importance under the 1938 rule because a class could include only people who voluntarily joined the suit — in modern parlance, an "opt-in" requirement rather than an "opt-out" proviso.

Three years later, however, an influential law-review article envisioned a wider role for class actions. Law Professor Harry Kalven Jr. and attorney Maurice Rosenfield depicted class actions as an essential supplement to government regulation of financial markets. Such suits, brought on behalf of large numbers of small shareholders, would help ferret out instances of impropriety and force wrongdoers to give up their financial gains. Kalven and Rosenfield limited their discussion to securities cases, but Yeazell notes the idea had "no inherent limitation." [8]

The strength of the Kalven-Rosenfield proposal depended, however, on eliminating the need to get the consent from every individual member of a class to be joined to the suit. But the language of the federal rules blocked that route, as did a Supreme Court decision in 1940 that seemed to bar a court from creating a mandatory class. Some judges over

Chronology

Before 1900

Courts in England and the United States recognize some types of "group litigation," but the use of such consolidated suits is infrequent.

1900s-1950s

Use of group litigation expands somewhat in the United States.

1938

Federal Rules of Civil Procedure adopted. Rule 23 allows plaintiffs to collect damages as well as obtain injunctions in class actions, but the criteria are difficult to meet.

1941

Influential law review article calls for expanded use of class actions as aid to enforcement of securities regulation.

1960s-1970s

Federal rules are amended to ease use of class actions. Class suits become more common and accepted as courts slowly shift from skepticism to acceptance.

1966

Overhaul of Rule 23 makes it easier to bring class actions by including class members in suits unless they take affirmative step to "opt out" of the litigation; rule lets judge approve class action if "superior" to individual adjudication of claims.

1974

U.S. Supreme Court decision requires class-action attorneys to notify individually all potential class members, an expensive and burdensome requirement (*Eisen v. Carlisle & Jacquelin*).

1980s

Use of class actions declines in face of judicial hostility and anti-lawsuit backlash.

1988

Total number of class actions in federal courts has declined by 80 percent since 1975.

1990s

Class actions increase, widely used in securities and mass tort cases. State governments win huge settlement from tobacco industry. Local governments sue gunmakers.

1994

Mississippi becomes first state to sue tobacco companies for health-care costs.

1995

Private Securities Reform Act sets new requirements for class-action securities suits in federal court. Congress follows in 1996 with second law to block lawyers from taking class actions to state courts instead.

1996

Federal courts' Advisory Committee on Civil Rules proposes significant revisions to class-action rules but changes are shelved in face of widespread opposition. Congress passes Prison Litigation Reform Act, easing the way for an end to court control over prisons.

1997

Supreme Court ruling in asbestos-exposure litigation makes it harder for businesses to negotiate "global settlement" of claims in class actions (*Amchem Products, Inc. v. Windsor*).

1998

New Orleans and Chicago become first of 30 jurisdictions to sue gun manufacturers. The suits seek damages and changes in design and marketing. States reach settlement with tobacco industry calling for nearly $250 billion over 25 years.

1999

Clinton administration in December threatens to file nationwide suit against gun industry on behalf of public housing authorities, but defers action to try to negotiate regulatory changes with industry. Judges dismiss cities' gun suits in three cases and bar part of complaint in fourth case; cities appeal. Private attorneys file antitrust class actions against Microsoft after judge's preliminary ruling that company was guilty of monopolistic practices.

2000s

Washington, D.C., becomes 30th local jurisdiction to sue gunmakers on Jan. 20. Attorneys discuss consolidating private suits against Microsoft.

the next 25 years circumvented the consent requirement, Yeazell writes, but for the most part the class action's development was frozen until a new rule was written.

Liberalizing the Rules

The new class-action directive — Rule 23 — was written against the backdrop of three diffuse social movements: the civil rights revolution, fully formed by the 1960s, and the incipient consumer and environmental movements. The framers of the new rule sought not only to correct what was seen as the obscurity of the existing rule but also to channel institutional reform litigation and small consumer claims into consolidated court suits. For better or worse, they succeeded. Rule 23 resulted in what Yeazell describes as "a flowering — or, depending on one's view, a plague — of class actions." [9]

The rule's four prerequisites for a class action look to the size and common interests of the potential class and the named plaintiffs' ability to typify and represent the entire class. Judges have the authority to certify a class action in three situations — "engagingly" known, Yeazell quips, as 23(b)(1), 23(b)(2) and 23(b)(3) suits. In the first category are suits where all of the parties are necessary to ensure a complete and consistent adjudication — for example, all the creditors of a wrongdoing business. The second category entails legal action brought to reform institutions, such as suits regarding school desegregation, prison conditions, state mental-health care and the like. These class actions are the most numerous and, procedurally, the least controversial.

The third category is the most controversial because it gives lawyers the widest berth to create a class for litigat-

ing purposes while giving judges the greatest leeway to determine whether a class action is the "superior" method for "fair and efficient adjudication." A 23(b)(3) class action can be created out of small-figure claims arising from allegedly fraudulent consumer practices or out of bigger antitrust claims stemming from allegations of anti-competitive business practices. The consolidation of claims — especially smaller claims — may be essential to give lawyers the financial incentive and ability to wage what can be a long and expensive court fight.

The growth of class actions in the first decade or so after the adoption of the rule created a backlash among business interests. Class actions were "often denounced as making it too easy for plaintiffs to force defendants to the wall," says the University of California's Marcus.

Yeazell agrees. "There was an initial, very strong defendants' reaction to this," he says. "They weren't happy about it." Harvard University law Professor Arthur Miller, in a law-review article published in 1979, complained that cases too often were certified on the basis of "conclusory assertions," settlements approved without "in-depth" examination and attorneys' fees petitions granted without being carefully scrutinized. [10]

The Supreme Court and lower federal courts also appeared to evince some hostility toward the invigorated class-action rule. Some trial judges appeared reluctant to certify class actions or to award attorneys' fees. The Supreme Court issued a number of restrictive rulings. In the most important, the court in 1974 held that individual notice must be given to all class members in a 23(b)(3) suit. In the specific case, that meant sending individual notices to some 2 million investors, whose claims averaged $70; the shareholder bringing the suit considered the requirement prohibitively expensive. In other rulings, the high

court limited the ability to bring class actions brought under state law into federal court by enforcing requirement that each plaintiff's claim must satisfy the minimum jurisdictional amount of $10,000. [11]

By the mid-1970s, though, judges had begun adapting to the new rule, and some of the abuses began to die out, according to Professor Miller. The rules remained largely unchanged despite a number of proposals for revisions in Congress and in the federal courts' rule-making bodies. As the decade ended, Miller wrote, the period was "characterized by increasing sophistication, restraint and stabilization in class-action practice."

Class-Action Cycles

Class-action suits declined through the 1980s to the point where leading experts were pronouncing them all but dead. In the past decade, however, class actions have increased in number and in importance — particularly in mass torts and securities litigation. Congress responded by passing legislation to curb private, securities class actions. The federal courts' rule-making body also considered rules changes, but the deep divisions that emerged resulted in the shelving of all but one minor change.

The decline in class actions can be seen in statistics from federal courts, which had been viewed as more hospitable than state courts to such suits. The number of class actions filed in federal courts declined from 3,061 in 1975 to 1,568 in 1980 and only 610 in 1987. [12]

"Class actions had their day in the sun and kind of petered out," Paul Carrington, a leading civil-procedure expert and then-dean of Duke University Law School, told *The New York Times* in early 1988. The decline was linked to the appointment of more conservative judges by President Ronald Reagan, a stricter approach to approving class actions and awarding attorneys' fees and a general backlash against what was termed the "litigation explosion." [13]

Beginning in the 1990s, however, some lawyers began using class actions to sue defendants in some types of mass tort cases — most dramatically, in the asbestos exposure litigation. The authors of Rule 23 actually had advised against using the class-action device in such suits except in limited circumstances. Many judges refused to certify such class actions, but — as a recent Rand Corporation study points out — many judges and lawyers became convinced over time that class actions "offered vehicles for efficiently resolving the large numbers of such suits." [14]

A second category of class actions also began to increase by the end of the '90s: securities litigation. The suits typically were brought by investors — represented by lawyers from a small but active specialty bar — against corporations, investment firms or accounting firms.

The plaintiffs' lawyers and other consumer advocates said the suits helped protect investors from shady schemes as well as from misleadingly optimistic information put out by stock issuers and their advisers. Critics said the suits often were filed by "professional plaintiffs" with only a nominal stake in the company and really were controlled by lawyers who had more interest in collecting fees than in protecting small investors.

Congress responded to intense lobbying by business groups, Wall Street firms and accountants by passing two laws aimed at curbing securities class actions. The first of the measures — the Private Securities Reform Act of 1995 — set out a host of new substantive and procedural provisions governing securities class actions. Among the more significant changes was one aimed at allowing large, institutional investors to take control of federal court class actions away from individual investors and plaintiffs' attorneys.

The law also gave investment firms and accountants a so-called safe harbor aimed at protecting them from potential liability for investor losses blamed on overly optimistic forecasts of a company's earnings.

The law had the unintended result of encouraging lawyers to file securities cases in state rather than in federal courts. To stop that trend, Congress passed a law a year later that essentially required all class actions involving nationally traded securities to be brought in federal rather than in state courts.

Meanwhile, both Congress and the federal courts had deadlocked over broader changes for mass tort cases or other class actions. The Advisory Committee on Civil Rules issued a collection of proposals in 1996 — many of them viewed as favorable to defendants. The rules provoked what the Rand report terms "a full-scale political battle."

The committee responded by tabling all the proposed changes except an evenhanded revision that allowed either plaintiff or defendant to take an immediate appeal of a judge's decision to certify or deny class-action status.

Chief Justice William H. Rehnquist then appointed a new working group in 1998 specifically to consider the mass tort issue. The group's report, issued in February 1999, acknowledged dissatisfaction with the current situation but avoided any specific recommendations. Instead, it called on Rehnquist to appoint a committee to study the issue. So far, Rehnquist has not done so. ∎

CURRENT SITUATION

Showdown on Guns

Fifteen months after the first of the local government suits against the gun industry, the mayor of the District of Columbia announced that the nation's capital city would join the legal assault as the 30th jurisdiction to seek to recover damages from firearms manufacturers for gun-related violence.

"We're supposed to have the toughest gun prohibitions in the nation, and yet our streets are flooded with guns," Mayor Anthony A. Williams said at a Jan. 20 news conference. The lawsuit specified no damage figure, but a city lawyer said the amount would be "astronomical." Williams said the suit would "provide the industry with a powerful incentive to reform its distribution practices." [15]

Advocates for the gunmakers predicted that the District's suit, along with the others, would fail. "The industry feels very strongly that it not only adheres to federal, state and local regulations but goes beyond them in attempts to assist law enforcement," Robert Delfay, president of the National Shooting Sports Foundation, a gun-manufacturers' trade association, told *The Washington Post*. "A judge who does his job will throw this case out."

So far, judges, in fact, are siding with the gun industry more often than with the city governments. Judges in Cincinnati, Miami and Bridgeport, Conn., granted motions by the gun manufacturers to dismiss complaints filed by those three cities. In addition, a judge in Atlanta dismissed part of

Are Billions for Tobacco Attorneys . . .

The story of the tobacco industry's $246 billion settlement with state governments is a parade of horrors for critics of government-sponsored litigation. In their eyes, state governments ganged up on the tobacco industry, extorted an unimaginable sum under a phony theory of legal liability, forced the industry to agree to regulatory changes repeatedly rejected by elected lawmakers and made smokers pay for the whole thing through significantly higher prices for cigarettes.

But nothing sticks in the critics' craw as much as the billions of dollars that plaintiffs' attorneys will rake in for their role in the litigation. The total amount — already in excess of $10 billion — "is a staggering sum without compare in human history," says Yale University law Professor John Langbein. "Never in history have lawyers been paid so much to do so little."

Defenders of the tobacco litigation, however, insist that plaintiffs' lawyers earned those fees by taking a gigantic legal risk, gambling millions of dollars of their own money and ultimately winning a major victory for public health.

"Some lawyers made a fortune," says John Coale, a prominent Washington trial lawyer. "They earned it. Like CEOs who make hundreds of millions of dollars when they produce a beneficial product, lawyers who fought tobacco earned their fees by serving the public good." [1]

Tobacco companies agreed to pay attorneys' fees on top of the $246 billion to be paid to states over the next 25 years, ostensibly as reimbursement for past health-related costs due to smoking. The fees are to be determined state by state either through agreement with the industry or by three-member arbitration panels established under the settlement. The fees are to be paid over time, subject to a $500 million per year cap under the terms of the settlement.

In the first of the fee arbitrations, private attorneys involved in three of the first state suits to be filed — in Mississippi, Florida and Texas — were awarded fees totaling $8.2 billion. The fees averaged about 25 percent of the estimated amounts the states will receive. Since then, fee awards have been a substantially smaller percentage of the state recoveries. Attorneys in the Illinois suit, for example, were awarded only 1.3 percent of that state's share of the settlement.

In announcing the first decisions, the panel's chairman, John Calhoun Wells, acknowledged the fees were "substantial." But Wells, a non-lawyer and former chairman of the Federal Mediation and Conciliation Service, said that without the private attorneys' work "there would be no multibillion-dollar settlements for the states to reimburse tobacco-related health expenses and provide funds for educational efforts to reduce youth smoking."

Tobacco Attorneys' Fees

Eighteen states reached fee agreements with the lawyers who represented them. But state officials and lawyers deadlocked over payments in nine states (below), sending the disputes to arbitration.

Arbitration Panel Decisions

State	Amount Awarded to Attorneys (in $ millions)	Percent of State Settlement Received by Attorneys	Amount Awarded to State (in $ millions)	Vote
Mississippi	$1,430	35%	$4,100	2-1
Texas	3,300	19%	17,400	2-1
Florida	3,430	26%	13,200	2-1
Massachusetts	775	9.3%	8,300	2-1
Hawaii	90	6.5%	1,380	3-0
Illinois	121	1.3%	9,100	3-0
Iowa	85	4.5%	1,900	3-0
Kansas	54	3.2%	1,700	3-0
Louisiana	575	12.8%	4,500	2-1
TOTAL	**$ 9,860**			

Note: Industry-appointed arbitrator Charles Renfrew dissented in the Mississippi, Texas, Florida and Louisiana awards, saying each was too large. State-appointed arbitrator Harry Huge dissented in the Massachusetts case, saying the award was too small.

. . . "Clearly Excessive" or "Entirely Justified"?

The written decisions in the Florida and Texas cases — 12 pages each — stressed the "unprecedented" nature of the tobacco suits and what was described in the Florida case as "the enormity of the time, labor and effort required." Lawyers in both cases had written contracts with the states calling for 25 percent contingency fees if the suits were successful.

The Mississippi lawyers had no specific contingency-fee agreement. The arbitration panel announced the award in that case — $1.4 billion, or more than one-third of the state's share of the settlement — in a one-paragraph order without elaboration.

The industry-appointed arbitrator, Charles Renfrew, dissented in each of the rulings. Renfrew, a former federal judge and deputy U.S. attorney general, called the fee awards "clearly excessive and to me incomprehensible." He said he would have set fees in the three cases at $2.2 billion total.

Lawyers in the fourth of the early state suits — Minnesota's — negotiated a fee agreement totaling $558 million for their work in representing the state and the Blue Cross/Blue Shield settlement. That represents 9.1 percent of the state's $6.1 billion settlement. As of late July, another 17 states reportedly had reached fee agreements totaling $450 million. [2]

The lawyers who will receive the biggest fees have defended the awards without apology. Richard Scruggs, the lead private lawyer in the Mississippi suit, called the $300 million in fees his firm will get "entirely justified." "We took an enormous risk and got an unbelievable result for the citizens of Mississippi," Scruggs told The Associated Press in late July. [3]

Joe Rice, managing partner of the South Carolina-based plaintiffs' firm Ness Motley Loadholt Richardson & Poole, similarly cites the gamble in taking on the litigation. "This law firm risked its financial livelihood to pursue the tobacco companies at a time when the industry hadn't lost or settled a single case," Rice told The Dallas Morning News in late October. Partner Ron Motley was one of the principal lawyers in the national settlement. The firm will receive $330 million for its work in the Texas case and, according to the newspaper, as much as $3 billion in total for representing 30 other states. [4]

State attorneys general generally defend the fee awards. "I am convinced the cigarette companies would still be undefeated in court" without Motley's and Rice's work, Florida Attorney General Bob Butterworth told the Dallas newspaper.

Critics, however, continue to attack the fees as unjustified. They point to the fact that many of the lawyers have close political connections. Scruggs, for example, is the brother-in-law of Mississippi Sen. Trent Lott, the Republican majority leader. They also strongly denounce the use of contingency-fee contracts — even though the percentage recovery agreements are not being precisely carried out in the arbitrations or settlements. And they contend the legal work in most of the later state suits was minimal and risk-free.

In the Illinois case, at least, the arbitrators appeared to agree. The panel unanimously reduced a $900 million request to $121 million after noting that there was "relatively little activity" in the state's suit.

Michael Horowitz, director of the Hudson Institute's Project for Civil Justice Reform in Washington, calls the fees "manifestly unethical." He is urging a change in the federal tax code to include "unreasonable" attorney fees under a 200 percent penalty provision currently applied to excessive payments to some corporate officers. [5]

Despite the controversy, however, the arbitration panel is continuing to acknowledge the instrumental role played by private attorneys in bringing about the tobacco settlement. In its most recent decisions, the panel on Jan. 31 awarded $575 million to lawyers in 13 firms — including Ness Motley — for work in the Louisiana suit. In addition to the risks and complexity of the litigation, the majority credited the lawyers' "early involvement, planning and recruitment of other states" with helping to assemble the attorneys general into "a unified force."

The panel estimated the lawyers devoted 75,000 to 80,000 hours to the Louisiana case over a six-year period. Based on that estimate, the fee represents about $700 per hour. Renfrew, in dissent, called the award "grossly excessive."

---

[1] Coale made his remarks on June 22, 1999, at a forum "The New Business of Government-Sponsored Litigation," cosponsored by the Federalist Society, Manhattan Institute and U.S. Chamber of Commerce.

[2] *The Wall Street Journal,* July 30, 1999.

[3] The Associated Press, July 31, 1999.

[4] *The Dallas Morning News,* Oct. 31, 1999.

[5] "The Tobacco Fee Scandal: A Precedent-Based Reform Proposal," Hudson Institute, undated briefing book.

that city's suit while reserving judgment on the rest of the complaint.

In the first of the rulings — in the Cincinnati case — Hamilton County Court of Common Pleas Judge Robert Ruehlman on Oct. 7, 1999, rejected all of the arguments that city governments have used as the premise for the suits. Ruehlman said the city's suit was too general and that product-liability laws did not allow recovery for damages resulting from a third party's illegal use of an otherwise lawful product. The judge also rejected the public-nuisance counts of the suit, saying the gun manufacturers had "no ability to control . . . criminal or reckless misuse of firearms by third parties." Finally, Ruehlman also said the city had no authority to "recover for expenditures for ordinary public services [that] it has the duty to provide."

Judges in the Miami-Dade County and Bridgeport cases similarly sided with all of the main arguments the gun industry put forth. In her Dec. 13 ruling, Dade County Circuit Judge Amy Dean said the effort to impose new regulatory requirements on gun manufacturers also was improper because of a state law pre-empting local governments' authority over firearms. Two days earlier, Superior Court Judge Robert F. McWeeny had dismissed the Bridgeport case. He said the city had no legal standing to bring the suit under state law and added a tart critique of the cities' financial motive for filing the suits. "When conceiving the complaint in this case," McWeeny wrote, "plaintiffs must have envisioned such settlements as the dawning of a new age of litigation

during which the gun industry, liquor industry and purveyors of 'junk' food would follow the tobacco industry in reimbursing government expenditures and submitting to judicial regulation."

The cities' only victory so far was a partial and limited one. Fulton County State Court Judge Gino Brogdon issued a two-page

Dade County Mayor Alex Penelas displays the "Saturday Night Special" that an 11-year-old Florida boy accidentally killed himself with. Penelas was announcing the county's suit against gunmakers.

Center to Prevent Handgun Violence

order on Oct. 27 dismissing the strict liability counts in the Atlanta suit but reserving judgment on negligence claims. He also rejected for now the gun industry's arguments that a newly enacted state law barred cities from bringing such suits. The gun industry filed a separate suit before a different judge invoking that statute to block the suit; arguments were held on Jan. 28. The Louisiana Legislature passed a similar law to try to block a suit by the city of New Orleans; a judge has the issue under advisement.

Meanwhile, Cook County Circuit Court Judge Stephen Schiller was scheduled to begin hearing arguments

on Feb. 10 on the gun industry's effort to dismiss the Chicago case. Both sides filed voluminous legal memoranda to make their respective cases. In its brief, the city reiterated that the gun manufacturers and dealers should be required to pay damages for circumventing gun-control laws. "Defendants know that there is great demand for illegal firearms in Chicago," the city's attorneys wrote, "and the defendants knowingly exploit that illegal demand."

Gun manufacturers in response denied that the city had linked them to any illegal gun trafficking and insisted the suit did not belong in the courts. The city's allegations, Kimball wrote in a joint brief for the defendants, "implicate public-policy choices involving competing views of society and questions regarding the 'causes' of urban violence, which are appropriately resolved by legislatures, as the elected representatives of the people."

Taking Cases to Court

Environmental activists have squared off against agricultural and biotechnology firms for years over the safety of genetically modified foods. With little success to show for their efforts in legislative or regulatory forums, the activists took a new tack in December. They helped launch a class-action suit, brought in the name of six farmers, that questions the safety of genetically modified crops developed by the St. Louis-based agribusiness firm Monsanto. [16]

The suit, filed Dec. 15 in federal court in Washington, claims that

At Issue:

Should gunmakers pay damages to local governments for gun-related violence and injuries?

JONATHAN LOWY
Senior attorney, Center to Prevent Handgun Violence

WRITTEN FOR *THE CQ RESEARCHER*

Should taxpayers alone bear the immense costs incurred by governments because of gun violence, or should their load be shared by those responsible for the underground gun market, who now profit from it and are able to prevent much of the resulting damage? Thirty local governments that have filed suit against the gun industry have decided that it is time gunmakers help, rather than hinder, the effort to end gun violence and contribute to the damage caused by their irresponsible conduct.

Gunmakers are not liable for gun violence simply because they make and sell guns but because they fail to do so responsibly. As they sell weapons designed to kill people — which juveniles, criminals and citizens of several cities are banned from possessing — gunmakers must take care to prevent deaths and not to circumvent gun laws. The industry violates both duties.

The industry's lax distribution of guns facilitates the thriving, unregulated market that arms those barred from legally possessing handguns. Gunmakers supply guns sold at gun shows in mass sales of 10, 20 or 100 guns at a time, in "straw purchases" and by corrupt dealers — despite knowing many of these guns are headed for the streets. Instead of implementing safety devices that could save hundreds of lives every year, gunmakers design for concealability and lethality and boast of "fingerprint resistant" finishes. Because guns are uniquely exempt from the Consumer Product Safety Act, holding gunmakers accountable in court is the only way to encourage them to design guns responsibly.

The industry chooses not to supervise dealers or make its products safer but to lobby Congress to allow its irresponsible conduct. Then it pockets the profits, while taxpayers pick up the tab. The result? More than 30,000 lives lost from guns each year. Local governments must spend vast sums to repair bullet holes instead of repairing playgrounds, to buy metal detectors for schools instead of textbooks.

The mounting toll in dollars and lives lost to guns has not motivated the industry to act responsibly. The threat of legal liability has. Since the first city filed suit, various gunmakers have announced they would ban sales at gun shows, make personalized handguns and cut off sales to disreputable dealers. The industry previously had deemed such crime-reducing measures impossible. If litigation by cities and counties is successful, gunmakers will be forced to do far more to stop gun violence, and the burden on taxpayers will be eased.

DAVID KOPEL
Research director, Independence Institute, Denver, Colo.

WRITTEN FOR *THE CQ RESEARCHER*

abusive lawsuits against firearms companies are an assault on America's republican form of government. Firearms laws should be made by our lawmaking bodies: by state legislatures and Congress. As pointed out by former Labor Secretary Robert B. Reich — who supports strict gun control — the lawsuits are thinly disguised efforts to end-run legislative decisions about what kind of gun laws are best.

All of the lawsuits are orchestrated by Sarah Brady's litigation organization, the Center to Prevent Handgun Violence, and all of them are premised on her belief that — as she said in 1993 — "To me, the only reason for guns in civilian hands is for sporting purposes." For example, many of the lawsuits complain that handgun manufacturers have improved their products too much. In the last decade, handgun companies, responding to consumer demand, produced models that are smaller, have larger ammunition capacity and greater accuracy and firepower.

It is lawful to use guns for protection. Smaller guns with greater firepower obviously are valuable for law-abiding persons carrying a handgun for protection or in a car. In the home, a smaller gun might be easier for the particular person to hold, easier to store in a particular place or easier to keep concealed from children.

Other assertions about how guns should be designed — with magazine disconnects or with so-called safety devices that prevent the gun from working reliably in an emergency — likewise are based on a theory that guns should not be used for protection.

Charges that gunmakers deliberately sell guns to criminals or children ignore the fact that guns are the most-regulated consumer product in America. Every retail purchase must receive permission from the FBI, based on the FBI's determination that the buyer is not a criminal and is old enough to buy the gun legally.

The lawsuits also show contempt for the First Amendment by targeting trade associations that engage exclusively in activities such as public education and lobbying.

If handguns are to be banned, the decision should be made by the legislature, not by trial lawyers, anti-gun lobbies and a few mayors who abuse the legal system to drive companies into bankruptcy through high litigation costs. Although the lawsuits are so legally frivolous that it is unlikely any plaintiff will be awarded a single dollar, the cost of defending suits is astronomical. Already, several firearms manufacturers have been bankrupted by litigation costs.

Monsanto gave farmers false assurances about the safety and marketability of a new breed of bioengineered seeds and that the company illegally is trying to control the market for genetically modified agriculture. Lawyers for Monsanto denounced the suit, arguing that the company's products are safe and denying any anti-competitive practices.

The suit is just one of many recent cases that provide fresh confirmation of the 150-year-old observation by French writer Alexis de Tocqueville that political disputes in the United States frequently end up in court. The suit was the brainchild of Jeremy Rifkin, president of the Foundation on Economic Trends and a longtime opponent of gene-altered food. "This is the beginning of a new chapter in the debate over genetically modified foods," Rifkin said at a Washington news conference after the suit was filed.

The health-care industry also finds itself embroiled in a new wave of class-action litigation to add to its difficult lobbying battles in Congress and in state legislatures around the country. Lawsuits filed last fall in federal courts in Mississippi, Pennsylvania and Florida and in state court in California charged the biggest health maintenance organizations (HMOs) with a variety of undisclosed policies or practices that unjustifiably short-changed customers on medical care. [17]

The suits have been brought by a consortium of a dozen law firms around the country put together by Richard Scruggs, a Mississippi attorney who was a key lawyer in the tobacco litigation. After filing the first of the suits against Aetna on behalf of a class of 18.3 million subscribers, Scruggs said the action aims to "change forever the way this HMO operates."

Microsoft Corp. also faces a barrage of class-action lawsuits at the same time it is defending itself against a combined antitrust suit filed in

federal court in Washington by the Justice Department and 19 states. Some 70 lawsuits had been filed as of December — coming hard on the heels of a preliminary ruling by federal Judge Thomas Penfield Jackson that the firm had been guilty of monopolistic practices. Lawyers in the cases are talking about how to consolidate them, but there is jockeying among the attorneys for control.

The suits against Microsoft represent a return of the common practice of years past of private actions following Justice Department antitrust enforcement efforts. The work dried up in the 1980s, according to Professor Marcus, with decreased antitrust activity by the Reagan Justice Department. Other types of class actions also apparently are increasing, according to the recent Rand report. Despite a lack of quantitative data, Rand researchers said there has been "a surge" in class actions in the past several years, particularly in state courts.

The apparent increase invigorated reform efforts in Congress during the past year. Sens. Charles E. Grassley, R-Iowa, and Herb Kohl, D-Wis., introduced a multipart bill in February 1999 aimed at curbing attorneys' fees and stiffening penalties for "frivolous" suits. The bill is pending. Meanwhile, the House passed in October a narrower bill that would make it easier to transfer a class action from state to federal court. For its part, the Justice Department opposed the bill. "Nothing magically changes by moving [class-action cases] to federal court," the department said in testimony in July. [18]

The Rand researchers also cast doubt on many of the proposed reforms to class-action rules. And despite the controversies over the procedure, the researchers concluded: "History suggests that damage class actions for some purposes will remain a feature of the American civil-litigation landscape." ∎

OUTLOOK

Other Targets?

More than 300,000 Americans die every year from poor diet and physical inactivity, according to health experts — roughly 10 times the number killed with guns. Critics blame the food industry for luring youngsters into high-fat, high-sugar, low-nutrition diets that they carry with them into adulthood.

Business groups conjure up the possibility of government-sponsored suits against fast-food "spokesman" Ronald McDonald to show what they consider the absurd logic of the legal theories used in the tobacco and gun litigation. Food manufacturers, however, are not a likely target: The industry has a large number of companies, none of them easy to depict as corporate "villains" comparable to tobacco companies and gun manufacturers.

Still, Professor Kelly Brownell of the Yale University School of Public Health sees a parallel with the tobacco and gun disputes. "Food companies can anticipate that the social climate, sooner or later, will turn against them," Brownell remarked at a forum on government-sponsored litigation cosponsored by the Chamber of Commerce last summer. To guard against a public backlash and pre-empt possible litigation, Brownell says food companies should start now "to help consumers make intelligent choices" about nutrition and diet.

That kind of frustration with industry practices underlay the states' successful suits against the tobacco industry and the cities' pending litigation against gun manufacturers. Business interests say the frustration is unjustifiable. Tobacco companies claim they have been working toward the regulators' major stated goal of reduced smoking among teenagers. And gun manufacturers similarly maintain they are working to make guns safer and cooperating with federal law enforcement officials in regulating firearms dealers.

In any event, business interests and other critics strongly insist the government-sponsored suits are simply improper vehicles for dealing with these kinds of issues. "We can't have coordinated litigation for extortionate purposes," says the Cato Institute's Levy. "And we can't be ignoring what is a centerpiece of the American Constitution: the separation of powers. We've co-opted the legislative process and given it to the courts."

Defenders of high-impact litigation, however, insist that lawsuits are often the only effective way to address social problems. "The day politicians step forward and do the right thing is the day lawyers will be put out of the social-reform business," John Coale, a prominent plaintiffs lawyer, remarked at the Chamber forum. "Politicians have failed us and continue to do so."

Predictions about the gun suits — among opposing lawyers and from outside observers — vary sharply. "We're going to win some of these cases against the industry," says Lowy of the Center to Prevent Handgun Violence. Kimball, the gun companies' attorney, disagrees. "There's no basis for these suits," she says.

For his part, Public Citizen's Vladeck sees some possibility that cities may win some of the suits. "These are very difficult cases, and I understand why people are skeptical," Vladeck says. "On the other hand, from what I've seen of the [evidence], I would say that there's a chance that they'll win."

But David Kopel, a longtime gun-control opponent and research director of the Denver-based Independence Institute, disagrees. "Most of the suits will never get to trial, and of those that do, none will result in a victory for the plaintiffs," he says. Still, Kopel says the costs of litigation will "drive more and more gun companies into bankruptcy and force the remaining companies to raise prices, thus making self-defense less affordable to poor people."

Whatever the outcome of the gun litigation, supporters discount the business lobby's warning about a rash of similar industrywide suits. "State and local governments by and large don't like to put themselves in an adversarial posture toward business,"

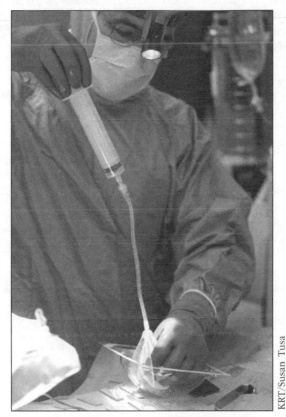

The nationwide scare — and class-action suits — over silicone breast implants prompted many women to try saline implants instead. Dr. Paul Eisenberg of Detroit drains one of the devices before insertion.

KRT/Susan Tusa

Vladeck says. "These suits are time-consuming, expensive and risky. They require significant resources, which, if you don't prevail, are lost. There are a lot of reasons why local governments are quite wary of bringing this high-stakes litigation."

Coale agrees. "There may be people out on the fringes who are going to go after Ronald McDonald, but you are not going to get a group of 60 to 70 well-heeled law firms to help," he remarked last summer. "I think that the day of the tort bar massing together and going after an industry is coming to an end. It is just not worth the effort."

Nonetheless, the state of Rhode Island in October launched what business-minded critics fear could be the start of a broad legal offensive against the paint industry for medical injuries attributable to the toxic effects of lead paint.

The suit, filed by Rhode Island Attorney General Sheldon Whitehouse, contends the industry continued marketing lead paints despite knowing the health risks since the 1930s. The complaint seeks damages for tax money spent treating people made ill by lead and for a program to remove lead from homes and buildings in the state.

The state retained a Rhode Island law firm — along with one of the main tobacco-case firms, South Carolina's Ness Motley Loadholt Richardson & Pool — to assist in the case on a contingency-fee basis. Officials of the companies called the lawsuit unjustified and said that lead paint has not been used in residential interiors since the 1950s and residential exteriors since the '70s.

Plaintiffs' lawyers also show no hesitation in taking big issues into courts through private lawsuits, like the coordinated attacks on HMOs or the class action against Monsanto over genetically engineered food. In the latest legal offensive, a consortium of more than 20 law firms filed an antitrust class-action suit in federal court in Washington, D.C., on Feb. 8 charging tobacco companies with illegally fixing prices charged to wholesalers. Spokesmen for tobacco firms said the suits were unjustified and denied any antitrust violations.

The lead lawyer in the litigation is Michael Hausfeld, whose firm, Cohen, Milstein, Hausfeld & Toll, is also vying for control of the private antitrust actions against Microsoft. Hausfeld is also the lead attorney in the suit against Monsanto. His aggressive approach exemplifies a new approach among class-action lawyers that rankles corporate lawyers. "It's something new in the next stage," attorney Victor Schwartz remarked in a recent profile of Hausfeld in *The Wall Street Journal*. Sophisticated plaintiffs' lawyers, Schwartz continued, "are playing off politics, anticipating the industries that will be vilified, then attacking en masse." [19]

UCLA's Yeazell agrees that businesses should expect no letup in the legal attacks from class-action lawyers. "You're going to see a continuing entrepreneurial plaintiffs' bar: well capitalized, well organized and very sophisticated," Yeazell says. "They're going to keep pushing at the envelope." ∎

Notes

[1] For background, see Kenneth Jost, "Closing In on Tobacco," *The CQ Researcher*, Nov. 12, 1999, pp. 977-1000.

[2] Federalist Society, Manhattan Institute, U.S. Chamber of Commerce, "The New Business of Government-Sponsored Litigation: State Attorneys General and Big City Lawsuits," June 22, 1999. Transcript provided by Manhattan Institute.

[3] Jay Tidmarsh, *"Mass Tort Settlement Class Actions: Five Case Studies,"* Federal Judicial Center (1998).

[4] Robert B. Reich, "Don't Democrats Believe in Democracy?," *The Wall Street Journal*, Jan. 12, 2000, p. A22. The article originally appeared in *The American Prospect* in the issue dated Jan. 17, 2000.

[5] The cases are *Ortiz v. Fibreboard Corp.* (1999) and *Amchem Products, Inc. v. Windsor* (1997). See Kenneth Jost, *The Supreme Court Yearbook, 1998-1999*, pp. 94-95; *The Supreme Court Yearbook, 1996-1997*, pp. 62-66.

[6] See Linda S. Mullenix, "Resolving Aggregate Mass Tort Litigation: the New Private Law Dispute Resolution Paradigm," *Valparaiso University Law Review*, Vol. 33, No. 2 (spring 1999), pp. 413-447.

[7] See Stephen C. Yeazell, *From Medieval Group Litigation to the Modern Class Action* (1987).

[8] *Ibid.*, p. 232. See Harry Kalven Jr. and Maurice Rosenfield, "The Contemporary Function of the Class Suit," *University of Chicago Law Review*, Vol. 8 (1941), p. 684.

[9] Yeazell, *op.cit.*, p. 237. For discussion of the writing and early interpretation of Rule 23, see *ibid.*, pp. 238-266.

[10] Arthur Miller, "Of Frankenstein Monsters and Shining Knights: Myth, Reality, and the 'Class Action Problem,'" *Harvard Law Review*, Vol. 92 (1979), p. 664, cited in Richard L. Marcus and Edward F. Sherman, *Complex Litigation: Cases and Materials on Advanced Civil Procedure* (3d ed.), (1998), p. 212.

[11] The notice case is *Eisen v. Carlisle & Jacquelin* (1974). The other cases are *Zahn v. International Paper Co.* (1973) and *Snyder v. Harris* (1969).

[12] See Douglas Martin, "The Rise and Fall of the Class-Action Lawsuit," *The New York Times*, Jan. 8, 1988. Other background drawn from this article and from Marcus and Sherman, *op. cit.*, pp. 212-213.

[13] For background, see Kenneth Jost, "Too Many Lawsuits?" *The CQ Researcher*, May 22, 1992, pp. 433-456.

[14] Deborah R. Hensler et al., "Class Action Dilemmas: Pursuing Public Goals for Private Gain" (executive summary), Rand Institute for Civil Justice, Nov. 1, 1999, p. 2.

[15] See *The Washington Post*, Jan. 21, 2000, p. A1; *The Washington Times*, Jan. 21, 2000, p. A1.

[16] Background drawn from *The New York Times*, Dec. 16, 1999, p. C1; *The Washington Post*, Dec. 16, 1999, p. E1. For background on the issue, see Kathy Koch, "Food Safety Battle: Organic vs. Biotech," *The CQ Researcher*, Sept. 4, 1998, pp. 761-784.

[17] See *U.S. Law Week*, Vol. 68, No. 14 (Oct. 19, 1999), pp. 2214-2215; Vol. 68, No. 18 (Nov. 16, 1999), pp. 2285-2286.

[18] See *U.S. Law Week*, Vol. 67, No. 30 (Feb. 16, 1999), p. 2471; Vol. 68, No. 5 (Aug. 10, 1999), p. 2068.

[19] Paul M. Barrett, "Why Americans Look to the Courts to Cure the Nation's Social Ills," *The Wall Street Journal*, Jan. 4, 2000, p. A1.

Bibliography
Selected Sources Used

Books

Marcus, Richard L., and Edward F. Sherman, *Complex Litigation: Cases and Materials on Advanced Civil Procedure* (3d ed.), West Publishing, 1998.

The chapter on class actions in this law-school casebook includes a brief overview of recent history and a number of leading court decisions on class-action requirements and procedures. Marcus is a professor at Hastings College of Law, University of California at San Francisco; Sherman is dean of Tulane University Law School.

Yeazell, Stephen C., *From Medieval Group Litigation to the Modern Class Action*, Yale University Press, 1987.

Yeazell, a professor at the University of California at Los Angeles Law School, traces the history of the class action from its precursors in medieval England to the sporadic use of comparable forms in the United States in the 19th century to its exponential in the late 20th century. The book includes detailed notes and a five-page table of cases.

Articles

Jost, Kenneth, "Closing In on Tobacco," *The CQ Researcher*, Nov. 12, 1999, pp. 977-1000.

The report traces the state governments' litigation against the tobacco industry from the initial suit in 1994 through the final settlement in 1998 and its subsequent implementation. The report includes a bibliography listing some of the major books on the state suits.

Kopel, David, "Abusive Lawsuits Against the Second Amendment," Independence Institute, updated. Jan. 24, 2000 (http://i2i.org).

This issue backgrounder, written by the research director of the Denver-based anti-gun control advocacy group, criticizes government-sponsored litigation against gunmakers and discusses bills pending in the Colorado legislature to prohibit such suits.

Mullenix, Linda S., "Resolving Aggregate Mass Tort Litigation: the New Private Law Dispute Resolution Paradigm," *Valparaiso University Law Review*, Vol. 33, No. 2 (spring 1999), pp. 413-447.

Mullenix, a professor at the University of Texas Law School, argues that mass tort suits have given rise to a new form of dispute resolution that carries the imprimatur of judicial oversight and approval but actually is in the hands of lawyers and other private parties.

Siebel, Brian, "City Lawsuits Against the Gun Industry: A Roadmap for Reforming Gun Industry Misconduct," *St. Louis University Public Law Review*, Vol. 18 (2000: forthcoming) (http://www.handguncontrol. org/legalaction/review.pdf).

This law review article, written by a senior attorney with the Center for the Prevention of Handgun Violence, details the local government lawsuits against U.S. and foreign gunmakers and the legal theories used in attempting to force them to pay damages for gun-related injuries.

Reports and Studies

Advisory Committee on Civil Rules and the Working Group on Mass Torts, "Report on Mass Tort Litigation," Federal Judicial Center, Feb. 15, 1999.

The 72-page report finds that mass tort suits present problems for both plaintiffs and defendants and pose a strain on the legal system. It concludes those problems will only intensify unless reforms are implemented and in general recommends a combination of legislation, rules and case management. But the committee stops short of urging specific solutions. A volume of appendices includes detailed reports on testimony by a range of experts and advocates at four public meetings conducted by the working group during 1998.

Hensler, Deborah R. et al., "Class Action Dilemmas: Pursuing Public Goals for Private Gain" (executive summary), Rand Institute for Civil Justice, Nov. 1, 1999, p. 2.

The report describes the controversies over the use of class actions in the United States since the writing of the current federal rule in 1966 significantly liberalizing the standards for filing and litigating them. Hensler, the lead author, is a well-respected expert on civil litigation. The 37-page executive summary can be found on the Web at www.rand.org. The full report, which includes detailed discussion of 10 representative class actions, is scheduled for publication in March.

Tidmarsh, Jay, "Mass Tort Settlement Class Actions: Five Case Studies," Federal Judicial Center, 1998.

The 100-page report examines settlements in five highly publicized mass tort cases, including suits over asbestos exposure and breast implants, and assesses federal courts' role in managing the litigation. Tidmarsh, a law professor at Notre Dame University, prepared the report for the Federal Judicial Center, the federal courts' research arm.

11 Patients' Rights

KENNETH JOST

Minnesota computer executive Patrick Shea thought he should see a cardiologist. He had been experiencing shortness of breath and dizzy spells. And heart disease ran in his family.

But Shea's physician assured him a specialist wasn't necessary and refused to give him the written referral required by his health plan. Instead, he told Shea that his problems were stress-related and that he was too young to have heart problems.

Later, while on an overseas business trip, Shea suffered chest pains so severe that he was hospitalized and had to return home. But his doctor still dismissed his concerns.

Shea never saw a specialist. He died in March 1993, less than a year later, leaving his wife Dianne with two young children and troubling questions. He was 40. An autopsy disclosed that Shea had suffered from arteriosclerosis — blocked arteries — which might have been corrected with cardiac bypass surgery.

"We repeatedly asked for referral to a cardiologist," Dianne later told a Minnesota legislative committee. "Not only were our pleas ignored, we were assured time and time again that our fears were unfounded."

In the months that followed, Dianne sought to discover how a man who had always followed his doctor's advice could die of an undiagnosed disease. What she found shook her confidence not only in their own doctors but also in the health care that more than 150 million Americans receive today from so-called managed-care systems: health maintenance organizations (HMOs) and similar network health-care plans. [1]

Supporters say managed care helps provide affordable, high-quality health care at a time when patients,

Originally published February 6, 1998. Updated by Adriel Bettelheim, December 1, 2000.

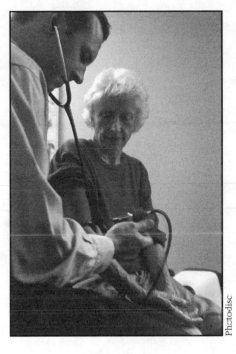

Photodisc

health-care providers, insurers and employers are all straining to keep down costs. But Dianne became convinced from the inquiry she and her lawyers made that cost controls helped kill her husband.

She claims in a wrongful death lawsuit that Shea's doctor had an undisclosed financial conflict of interest in refusing to refer him to a cardiologist because he received extra compensation from their HMO, Medica, for not sending patients to specialists.

The defendants in the federal court suit — Shea's doctors, their HMO clinic and Medica — deny that the doctors' compensation in any way depended on rejecting Shea's request to see a specialist. "Sheer speculation," Medica's lawyers say. The defendants also deny they were negligent in failing to diagnose Shea's heart disease. A trial in the case is expected later this year. [2]

Dianne Shea, meanwhile, has begun advocating reform of managed care. She urged the Minnesota Legislature to require health insurers to

disclose their "payment methodology" — information she says that might have prompted Shea to ignore his doctor's advice and see a cardiologist. "People have to understand that health care is a business," she says. "Just as we would never buy an investment blindly, we just cannot trust our doctors blindly."

The state Legislature last year passed a weakened version of Shea's proposal, requiring disclosure of the financial arrangements only on the patient's request. Minnesota thus became one of more than 30 states to pass legislation in the past three years aimed at strengthening the rights of patients enrolled in managed care — by far the dominant form of health care in the United States. *(See chart, p. 202.)*

Congress is also considering legislation that would impose far-reaching regulations on managed-care systems and possibly make it easier to sue health insurers for malpractice. Consumer and patient advocacy groups as well as the American Medical Association (AMA) are generally backing the proposals as part of an envisioned "Patients' Bill of Rights." However, the proposals are strongly opposed by health-care insurers and employers, who so far have thwarted any large-scale reform effort.

The efforts reflect a widespread belief that patients are being harmed in the shift away from traditional "fee-for-service" health insurance, which gave consumers greater freedom in choosing their own doctors and doctors greater freedom in prescribing treatment that insurers would pay for.

"Patients feel less personally taken care of, that they have interactions with too many health-care providers, that there's too much red tape in getting access to the specialists," says Myrl Weinberg, president of the National Health Council, a coalition

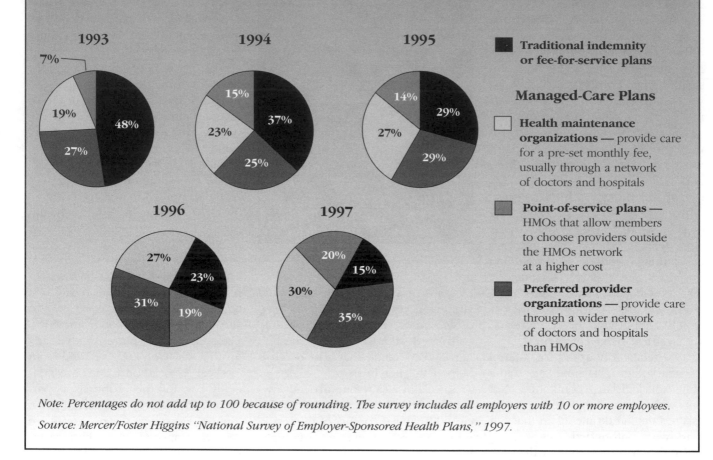

Managed-Care Plans Continue to Grow

The number of workers in managed-care health plans outnumbered those in traditional plans by nearly 6-to-1 in 1997, reflecting the continuing shift away from traditional plans in recent years.

1993
7%
19%
48%
27%

1994
15%
37%
23%
25%

1995
14%
29%
27%
29%

1996
27%
23%
31%
19%

1997
20%
15%
30%
35%

■ **Traditional indemnity or fee-for-service plans**

Managed-Care Plans

□ **Health maintenance organizations** — provide care for a pre-set monthly fee, usually through a network of doctors and hospitals

▨ **Point-of-service plans** — HMOs that allow members to choose providers outside the HMOs network at a higher cost

■ **Preferred provider organizations** — provide care through a wider network of doctors and hospitals than HMOs

Note: Percentages do not add up to 100 because of rounding. The survey includes all employers with 10 or more employees.

Source: Mercer/Foster Higgins "National Survey of Employer-Sponsored Health Plans," 1997.

of more than 40 patient advocacy groups, such as the American Cancer Society and American Heart Association, as well as major drug manufacturers and health insurers.

But health insurance industry officials insist that patients actually receive better care under managed-care plans.

"There's a tremendous possibility [with HMOs] to receive better, more integrated care," says Karen Ignagni, president of the American Association of Health Plans (AAHP). She says greater coordination among health-care providers also enhances accountability. "We've put in place the beginnings of quality measurement so that we can ensure significant improvements," she says.

Critics of managed care generally stop short of blaming it for an overall decline in the quality of health care. "For the most part, the studies have shown that the care is relatively the same," says Thomas Reardon, an Oregon physician and chairman of the AMA's Board of Trustees.

But the critics cite cases like Shea's to argue that managed-care plans have an incentive to skimp on care at the patient's expense. "There are pluses and minuses," says Adrienne Mitchem, legislative counsel for Consumers Union. "Some of the minuses are the overriding cost pressures. With traditional fee-for-service, you had the financial incentives to overtreat. With managed care, you have the financial incentives to undertreat."

Managed-care advocates indeed take credit for helping contain health-care cost increases, which rose at double-digit rates in the late 1980s and early 1990s — and now feel unjustly blamed for the difficulties that patients and providers face in adjusting to the changes.

"The public said to do something about health-care inflation, and we've been largely successful in doing that," says former Rep. Bill Gradison, R-Ohio, president of the Health Insurance Association of America (HIAA), which includes companies offering both managed care and fee-for-service insurance.

"Now, patients are saying, 'Hold on, we don't like the way you're doing it,'" Gradison continues. "The pace of change is bewilderingly fast and off-putting to a lot of people, and I mean not just the patients but the providers as well."

Gradison warns that new regulations "run the risk of increasing the cost of health plans and discouraging innovation." But critics say some changes are needed. "Managed care can do a lot of things well, but it needs to be regulated differently than we're now regulating it," says Lawrence Gostin, a health-law expert at Georgetown University Law Center.

The proposal with the most bipartisan support in Congress is a managed-care bill sponsored in the House by Reps. Charlie Norwood, R-Ga., and John Dingell, D-Mich. Norwood, a dentist, says he wants to "reverse what's going on in this country in health care." But while the measure won the support of 68 Republicans in 1999, Republican leaders have refused to endorse it.

"We've gone from patients having the right to choose their own doctors to patients being denied care and being denied the right to choose their own doctors to save money," Norwood says. "I don't oppose managed care, but I think there needs to be rules and regulations."

President Clinton also strongly endorsed managed-care reform. "Medical decisions ought to be made by medical doctors, not insurance company accountants," Clinton said in his 1998 State of the Union address. The line drew bipartisan applause from lawmakers that continued as Clinton spelled out his proposal:

"I urge this Congress to reach across the aisle and write into law a consumer bill of rights that says this: 'You have the right to know all your medical options, not just the cheapest. You have the right to choose the doctor you want for the care you need. You have the right to emergency room care, wherever and whenever you need it. You have the right to keep your medical records confidential.' Now, traditional care or managed care, every American deserves quality care."

Clinton's plea covered the main parts of a "Patients' Bill of Rights" issued by a 34-member commission he created in 1997. But he made no specific reference to one of its most contentious recommendations: a proposal to give patients greater ability to contest decisions by health plans to deny coverage for medical treatment.

Earlier, the administration also proposed separate legislation aimed at protecting patients' medical information. The privacy issue has become increasingly worrisome as computers have become more capable of accessing the most personal information. But the administration's proposals were widely criticized as too weak — in particular for giving law enforcement agencies broad discretion to obtain medical records without a patient's consent (see p. 206).

When Congress and state legislatures continue to ponder managed-care reform, these are some of the questions likely to be considered:

Should managed-care health plans be required to make it easier for patients to see specialists outside the plan's network of physicians?

The most visible difference between managed-care health plans and traditional fee-for-service insurance involves choosing a doctor and deciding when to seek treatment. Traditional insurance plans leave those choices to the patient; managed-care plans limit the patient's options.

Typically, a patient who enrolls in an HMO, like Patrick Shea, selects a "primary-care provider" from its network of doctors. That doctor then functions as a "gatekeeper" — overseeing the patient's health care and deciding when the patient needs to be referred to a specialist. [3]

The earliest group-health plans, in the 1920s and '30s, centralized medical decisions both to improve health care and lower costs. But since the federal government began promoting HMOs in the '70s, and later as for-profit managed-care plans came to dominate the industry, the emphasis increasingly has been on cost.

Critics, including patients, doctors and some outside observers, say the result has been to deny patients needed care in some cases. "Obviously, you can cut costs by cutting services," says George Annas, a professor of health law at Boston University, "but that wasn't the idea."

Managed-care health plans do take credit for helping hold down costs, but they insist that the quality of care has not suffered. "I don't know of many physicians who are devoted more to controlling costs than to care delivering," says AAHP President Ignagni.

Access to specialists is the most frequent source of friction between patients and health plans. Health plans control costs by limiting the number of specialists in the plan and the number of referrals to specialists outside the plan; they may pay their primary physicians in ways that create incentives to minimize the number of referrals. For patients, those incentives may create minor burdens — for example, a woman's need to get a referral for routine obstetric care — or more serious disputes.

Critics say the industry has been

States Where Patients Get Special Treatment

Specialist care — *At least thirty states make it easier for people in managed-care health plans to see certain specialists; all but Kentucky allow women either to designate an obstetrician-gynecologist as their primary-care provider or see an ob-gyn without a referral:*

Alabama, Arkansas*, California, Colorado, Connecticut, Delaware, Florida**, Georgia***, Idaho, Illinois, Indiana, Kentucky****, Louisiana, Maine*****, Maryland, Minnesota, Missouri, Mississippi, Montana, Nevada, New Jersey, New Mexico, New York, North Carolina, Oregon, Rhode Island, Texas, Utah, Virginia and Washington

External review — *Eleven states allow health-care patients to appeal coverage decisions to outside bodies:*

Arizona, California, Connecticut, Florida, Minnesota, Missouri, New Jersey, Rhode Island, Texas, New Mexico and Vermont

Post-mastectomy care — *Thirteen states require coverage of post-mastectomy inpatient care:*

Arkansas, Connecticut, Florida, Illinois, Maine, Montana, New Jersey, New Mexico, New York, North Carolina, Oklahoma, Rhode Island and Texas

Gag-rule ban — *Thirty-six states bar insurers from limiting doctors' communications with patients about treatment options:*

Arkansas, California, Colorado, Connecticut, Delaware, Florida, Georgia, Idaho, Illinois, Indiana, Kansas, Maine, Maryland, Massachusetts, Minnesota, Missouri, Montana, Nebraska, Nevada, New Hampshire, New Jersey, New Mexico, New York, North Carolina, Ohio, Oklahoma, Oregon, Rhode Island, South Carolina, Tennessee, Texas, Utah, Vermont, Virginia, Washington and Wyoming

* also covers optometrist or ophthalmologist; ** also covers chiropractor, podiatrist, dermatologist; *** also covers dermatologist; **** only covers chiropractor; ***** also covers nurse-practitioner, nurse-midwife

Sources: American Association of Health Plans, National Conference of State Legislatures.

making it more difficult for health-plan subscribers to see specialists. "Managed-care plans are increasingly using payment systems that discourage providers from referring patients to specialized care," John Seffrin, president of the American Cancer Society and chairman of the National Health Council, told the president's patients' rights commission last year.

"For the patient, it is difficult to know what they need to do" to see a specialist, agrees Weinberg, the council's president.

Industry officials, however, say that managed care — with its "gatekeeper"

physician and network of specialists — actually simplifies decisions for patients. "Unlike the old days, where you went to the phone book, now you have the ability to seek care through a network of professionals working together," Ignagni says.

Moreover, she points out that many plans in recent years have given consumers more options — for example, "point-of-service" (POS) plans that allow enrollees to see physicians outside the plan's network if they pay part of the cost through a higher deductible or a percentage of the fee. "We recognize that [a closed-plan HMO] doesn't meet the needs of all consumers," she says, "and that's why these other products have been developed."

Still, state and federal legislators are seeking ways to assure patients easier access to specialists. Some 30 states require health plans to give women the option of selecting an obstetrician as their primary-care provider. *(See table, at left.)* A number of states are considering bills to establish a procedure for a "standing referral" to a specialist for patients with chronic or life-threatening diseases or conditions. In Congress, Norwood and a number of other lawmakers have endorsed similar provisions.

Annas says health plans should be required to pay specialists whenever a subscriber must go outside the network. "I don't think that would happen very often," he says. "But it's not really a health plan if it doesn't offer the full range of medical services."

Norwood's bill, as well as some bills in the states, also includes a provision requiring health plans to offer a "point-of-service" option. Some critics say that would harm patients by undercutting the ability of HMOs to control costs and reduce premiums.

"The way HMOs keep costs down is by hiring physicians who practice conservatively" and don't order a lot of tests, says John Goodman, president of the National Center for Policy

Analysis, a free-market think tank in Dallas. "You can lower your premiums by joining an HMO that employs doctors who practice conservative medicine. If you take away the HMO's ability to do that, you take away one of the options that people have."

For their part, industry officials argue against any regulatory requirements, saying that market forces will drive health plans to give patients more choices for getting to a doctor of their choice. "Many plans are moving in that direction," Gradison says. "The question is whether the law should require that in every case, and my answer would be no."

But Paul Starr, a professor of sociology at Princeton University and author of a well-regarded history of the medical profession, says the industry cannot be counted on to give patients adequate choices for health care.

"We need legislation because whatever they're doing today doesn't guarantee what they'll do tomorrow," says Starr, who was an adviser for President Clinton's unsuccessful national health-care initiative in 1993 and '94. "They can just as easily withdraw access as provide it."

Should health plans be subject to medical malpractice liability?

When Ron Henderson died in a Kaiser Permanente hospital in Dallas in 1995, his family sued the HMO and several of its doctors for not diagnosing his heart disease.

Kaiser denied any wrongdoing and depicted Henderson as an overweight smoker who had ignored doctors' instructions. But the family's lawyers turned up embarrassing evidence of Kaiser's efforts to control costs by limiting hospital admissions in cardiac cases. In December 1997, Kaiser settled the case for $5.3 million. [4]

Kaiser was subject to a malpractice suit because, unlike most HMOs, it directly employs the physicians and nurses in its clinics. Courts have held that HMOs that contract with individual doctors or medical groups are shielded from malpractice suits on the theory that the doctor rather than the health plan is actually providing the care. But a new Texas law seeks to erase that distinction. [5]

"I can see no reason why a private, very profitable enterprise ought not be held accountable for mistakes that are made when everybody else is," says Texas state Sen. David Sibley, a conservative Republican and oral surgeon.

The new Texas law, which took effect on Sept. 1, was strongly pushed by the state medical association but vigorously opposed by health insurers. Geoff Wurtzel, executive director of the Texas HMO Association, called the law "bad policy" and blamed its enactment on what he termed "medical politics."

"In 1995, the Legislature overwhelmingly agreed that the threat of being sued didn't produce a better standard of care," Wurtzel said, referring to a restrictive malpractice law passed that year. "But all of a sudden, if it was HMOs, liability was OK."

Texas was the only state to directly subject health plans to malpractice liability. But Missouri opened the door to malpractice suits against HMOs by repealing a law that gave health plans a defense against malpractice. And Rhode Island and Washington, among others, have created commissions to study the issue.

The Texas law was challenged in federal court by the Aetna insurance company on the grounds that it is pre-empted by the federal law that governs employee benefits, including health insurance.

That law — known as ERISA, short for the Employee Retirement Income Security Act — is also now at the center of the legislative debate in Congress. Reform bills such as the one proposed by Norwood and Dingell would provide that ERISA does not pre-empt state laws dealing with malpractice liability,

as some federal courts have held. Those courts have held that health-plan subscribers who feel they were wrongly denied medical care can sue the plans only for reimbursement of the value of the care they did not receive. [6]

Norwood says there is no justification for shielding health plans from malpractice suits. "If you're a health-plan accountant or administrator and you want to make decisions about medical necessity," Norwood explains, "then you have to be responsible about those decisions in a court of law."

The AMA, a strong supporter of limiting medical malpractice suits in the past, supports the change. "When I make a decision, I as a physician accept accountability and liability," says Reardon. "When the plan makes a decision to provide or not to provide treatment, they should have the same responsibility and liability, especially when they're overriding a recommendation from the treating physician."

But the health insurance industry is adamantly opposed. "That's a perfect example of raising the costs of insurance with little, if any, discernible effect on the quality of the care," says the HIAA's Gradison. "It's a boon for the trial lawyers; I don't think it's a boon for the patients at all."

"All of the data suggest that consumers are not the beneficiaries of the current system," says AAHP President Ignagni. "We don't do families very much good if we provide them in the end with a situation that is designed to maybe provide compensation, maybe not, vs. trying to set up a situation that is built on quality improvement in which injuries don't occur in the first place."

One patients' group voices a similar interest in improving medical care without resorting to litigation. "We feel [litigation] is not necessarily the most productive way to resolve problems," says Weinberg of the National Health Council. Instead, Weinberg

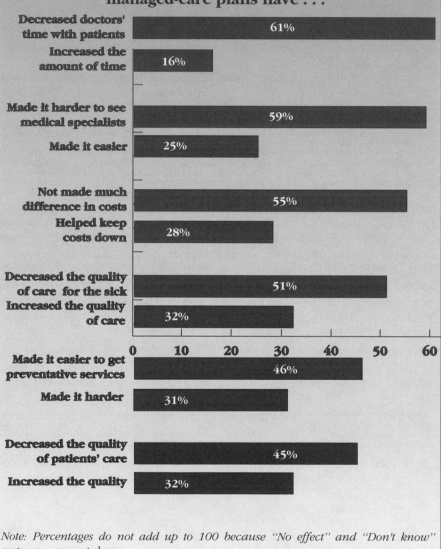

The Downside to Managed Care

A majority of Americans believe health maintenance organizations (HMOs) and other managed-care plans have had some adverse effects on health care, according to a 1997 survey. Overall, though, two-thirds of the respondents in managed care gave their plans an A or B, compared with three-fourths of the people with traditional health insurance coverage.

Percent of Americans who say HMOs and other managed-care plans have . . .

Decreased doctors' time with patients	61%
Increased the amount of time	16%
Made it harder to see medical specialists	59%
Made it easier	25%
Not made much difference in costs	55%
Helped keep costs down	28%
Decreased the quality of care for the sick	51%
Increased the quality of care	32%
Made it easier to get preventative services	46%
Made it harder	31%
Decreased the quality of patients' care	45%
Increased the quality	32%

Note: Percentages do not add up to 100 because "No effect" and "Don't know" responses are not shown.

Source: "Kaiser/Harvard National Survey of Americans' Views on Managed Care," November 1997.

says her group favors strong complaint-resolution procedures, such as the use of ombudsmen.

Other consumer groups go further and call for some independent external review of treatment decisions. "When a patient is denied coverage, it's ludicrous to think that they can appeal to the same system that denied them," says Mitchem of Consumers Union. But her group also favors malpractice liability for health insurers. "We want to ensure that there's some type of remedy that consumers can have access to," she says.

Health insurers are balking at any requirement for outside review procedures. "Some plans are doing this," Gradison says. "The question is whether it should be required by law."

Experts differ sharply on the potential effects of subjecting HMOs to malpractice liability. "If you apply tort liability to HMOs, you'll force them to do things that are not cost-effective," Goodman says. "You'll force them to waste money."

But Barry Furrow, a professor of health law at Widener University School of Law in Wilmington, Del., says that the threat of liability would result in better medical care by forcing managed-care administrators to focus more on quality than on costs. "You want to shift the competition more away from price and toward quality," Furrow says.

Are stronger safeguards needed to protect the privacy of patients' medical records and information?

The ongoing transformation from a paper-based health-care system to one that relies on electronic records has spawned an intense debate over who has access to individuals' medical histories and whether the information could be used to deny employment or health insurance. Recent cases of identity theft, hacker attacks on commercial Internet sites and more innocent technological snafus have reinforced a perception that personal information is not secure.

The Department of Health and Human Services (HHS) was expected at the end of 2000 to release guidelines that will allow government agencies, law enforcement and government researchers expanded access to medical databases. The guidelines stem from the Health Insurance Portability and Accountability Act of 1996, which, among other things, mandated Congress to develop national medical privacy standards by August 1999. When lawmakers missed the deadline, the task fell to HHS, which says its standards also will address consumer rights to see medical records and outline penalties for violating patient privacy. Privacy groups, such as the Andover, Mass.-based Coalition for Patients' Rights say the draft rules will not give patients any meaningful control over their medical histories and may allow doctors, insurers and other parties to share information without prior consent.

An early Clinton administration patient-privacy proposal, developed in 1997, spends nearly 40 pages detailing and justifying exceptions to the general rule prohibiting disclosure of patient records without the patient's consent. The list includes exceptions to disclose information necessary for the patient's health care, for payment and for internal oversight of the patient's treatment. The recommendation also calls for permitting disclosure of individually identifiable information to public health authorities for "disease or injury reporting, public health surveillance or public health investigation or intervention."

Most controversially, the administration also said that law enforcement or intelligence agencies should be able to obtain such information, without a court order, if needed for "a legitimate law enforcement inquiry" or — in the case of intelligence agencies — if needed for "a lawful purpose."

HHS Secretary Donna E. Shalala disputed advance reports that the proposal broadened law enforcement access to patient information. [7] She said the provision simply restated existing law. But Sen. Tim Hutchinson, an Arkansas Republican, said the proposal gave patients less privacy than existing federal law for bank records, cable television and video store rentals. Sen. Patrick J. Leahy of Vermont, the committee's ranking Democrat, was also critical. "There is divided opinion in the administration," Leahy said, "and right now the anti-privacy forces are winning on the key issue of law enforcement access to medical records." [8]

"HHS completely dropped the ball" on the issue, says Georgetown's Gostin. "They made an unforgivable mistake."

Gostin also faulted the privacy recommendations from the president's commission, issued two months after Shalala's testimony on Capitol Hill. The report called for permitting disclosure of patient information for purposes of "provision of health care, payment of services, peer review, health promotion, disease management and quality assurance." It addressed law enforcement only obliquely, saying law enforcement agencies "should examine their existing policies to ensure that they access individually identifiable information only when absolutely necessary."

"Everybody's in favor of privacy," Gostin says. "But the devil's in the details, and these don't provide any details. It basically does nothing."

For their part, however, health industry and business groups saw the administration's proposals as unduly restrictive. "The industry is very concerned about interrupting the flow of health information," said Heidi Wagner Hayduk, a consultant on privacy issues for the Healthcare Leadership Council, a coalition of major insurers, hospitals and drug companies. Medical innovation would be "stifled," she warned, if health-care providers and researchers were required to obtain patient authorization "every time information changes hands." [9]

Health-care industry groups also said federal legislation should pre-empt any state laws setting stricter protections for patient privacy. The administration's proposal would leave state laws unaffected, as would a stricter bill introduced by Leahy. But Sen. Robert F. Bennett, a Utah Republican, has introduced a bill that would set a single federal standard on the issue.

The administration also has endorsed a separate privacy proposal affecting the health insurance industry: a bill to bar health insurance companies and managed-care plans from discriminating against people on the basis of their genetic make-up. [10] The proposal has been pushed by a number of bioethics and privacy-advocacy groups, which point to studies documenting instances of genetic discrimination by, among others, employers and insurers.

The genetic privacy bill has languished in Congress for several years. Vice President Al Gore announced the administration's support for also banning genetic discrimination in the workplace. [11]

The administration's medical-records privacy proposal drew additional criticism at a second Senate Labor Committee hearing on the issue. Two medical groups, the AMA and the American Psychiatric Association, both called for stronger protection than the administration supported, while witnesses representing drug manufacturers and the American Hospital Association said the proposal went too far.

Such praise as the administration received for its proposal has been typically begrudging, at best. Boston University's Annas says the administration deserved credit for proposing a federal law guaranteeing patients the right to see their own records. And Robert Gellman, a privacy consultant who led Shalala's outside advisers on the recommendations, stressed that the package would be "stronger than any comparable state law." [12] But both men also faulted the law enforcement provisions, among other exceptions. "The administration," Annas concludes, "has a long way to go." ■

BACKGROUND

Health Insurance

Health care became widely available to most Americans, and a financially secure profession for most doctors, only in the recent past. [13] Well into the 20th century, routine health care was a luxury available only to well-to-do Americans. And many doctors had only modest incomes, since they did not see enough patients often enough to have a lucrative practice.

Two 20th-century developments changed the face of health care in the United States: widespread private health insurance and government-funded medical programs. Together, the two developments produced the mythic image that forms the backdrop of today's debate over medical care. In that idealized vision, most Americans enjoyed the services of a family doctor, a Marcus Welby figure who

gave skilled and compassionate care from birth to death with little concern about fees. And the government stepped in to provide care for those few who could not afford medical services. But the two developments also contained the germs of the cost problems that beset the health-care system today.

Private insurance entered the health field tentatively, limited at first to covering accidental injury and death. By the late 19th and early 20th centuries, however, many employers were providing limited medical care for their workers — motivated as much to reduce absenteeism caused by illnesses as to promote their employees' welfare.

The labor scarcities of World War II prompted some employers to begin offering health insurance as a benefit for workers. Labor unions, strengthened by New Deal legislation in the 1930s, included demands for health benefits in contract negotiations. And the postwar economic boom allowed major U.S. corporations to grant the demands.

Through the 1950s, more and more big corporations were including health benefits in union contracts; other employers followed suit. By the end of the decade, around two-thirds of the population at least had hospitalization insurance. [14]

The bill for these benefits was largely invisible. The expense was not a big cost item for employers, at least initially. For employees, the benefits were not taxed: In fact, the amounts did not even appear on pay stubs. As a result, many critics and observers contend, no one — neither business, labor, insurers nor health-care providers — had much incentive to watch the bottom line.

A second problem — access to care — was also somewhat obscured. With so many Americans sharing in the widened availability of health

care, it was easy to overlook those who were not: the elderly, the poor and the uninsured.

Government's Role

The government's initial moves to help provide health care were also tentative and limited. Some local governments began including medical benefits for the poor in general welfare programs in the early 20th century, and a New Deal program helped bring health care to some rural areas during the Depression. Throughout the century, progressives and labor interests called for compulsory national health insurance, but the efforts were blocked by business interests and, most important, the medical profession.

The two big federal health programs, Medicare and Medicaid, were enacted over the continuing opposition of the medical profession in the brief moment of liberal triumph in the 1960s. Congress had passed a limited bill to provide health insurance for the elderly poor in 1960, but the program proved to be unpopular. President Lyndon B. Johnson put the issue of health care for the elderly at the top of his Great Society agenda and pushed legislation through the overwhelmingly Democratic Congress in 1965.

As enacted, Medicare included the original idea of a contributory insurance program to cover hospitalization for the elderly (Part A) plus a similar plan for doctors' services (Part B). In addition, the law established the framework for Medicaid, the federal-state health-care program for the poor and the disabled.

Some doctors talked of boycotting Medicare, but they quickly realized that the program was — as Starr writes — "a bonanza," guaranteeing payment for medical services that

Chronology

Before 1950

Earliest forms of managed care are organized; employers begin to offer hospitalization insurance to workers.

——— • ———

1960s
Federal government establishes free health insurance for the elderly (Medicare) and a joint state-federal program to provide health care for low-income persons (Medicaid).

——— • ———

1970s
The Nixon administration backs the creation of health maintenance organizations (HMOs) to control health-care costs.

1973
The Health Maintenance Organization Act provides funds and regulatory support for HMOs, but also includes some coverage mandates that slow their growth.

1976
Congress eases some regulations on HMOs; two years later, Congress votes increased funding.

——— • ———

1980s
HMOs grow rapidly, gaining support from employers and consumers worried about spiraling increases in health-care costs.

1985
Supreme Court rules that Employee Retirement Income Security Act (ERISA) supersedes state laws regulating private employers' health plans (*Massachusetts Mutual Life Insurance Co. v. Russell*); some lower federal courts interpret decision as barring malpractice suits against managed-care plans.

——— • ———

1990s
Backlash against managed care grows.

1993
President Clinton proposes National Health Security Act, aimed at providing health insurance for all Americans; plan is assailed by business interests, medical lobby and Republicans.

1994
Clinton health-care plan dies in Congress.

1995
Many states pass laws requiring managed-care plans to allow women to designate ob-gyns as their primary-care provider.

Aug. 21, 1996
Clinton signs law making it easier for people to keep their health insurance when they lose or change jobs, start their own business or get sick; bill includes provision to facilitate sharing of patient information among health-care providers, but also requires government to develop privacy-protection guidelines by 1999.

September 1996
Congress responds to criticism of "drive-through deliveries" by requiring health insurance plans to cover at least 48 hours of hospital care for new mothers.

May 1997
Texas enacts legislation subjecting health maintenance organizations to medical malpractice liability; Aetna insurance company challenges law in federal court as pre-empted by ERISA.

July 1997
House and Senate conferees agree on provision in budget bill to bar Medicare-eligible HMOs from imposing "gag rules" on doctors by preventing them from discussing treatments or specialists that the plan would not pay for.

Sept. 11, 1997
Health and Human Services Secretary Donna E. Shalala presents medical-information privacy legislation to Congress; proposal is faulted by lawmakers, advocates and experts.

October 1997
Two House subcommittees hold hearings on Patient Access to Responsible Care Act sponsored by Rep. Charlie Norwood, R-Ga.

Nov. 19, 1997
Proposed "Patients' Bill of Rights" is issued by President Clinton's Advisory Commission on Consumer Protection and Quality in the Health Care Industry.

January 1998
Managed-care plans continued to grow in 1997 despite complaints about their services; coalition of health insurance and business lobbies announces plans for advertising campaign against managed-care reform legislation; Clinton urges Congress to pass consumer bill of rights.

June 2000
Supreme Court rules patients cannot sue managed-care plans for malpractice under ERISA.

Are Elderly Americans "Trapped" by Medicare?

Lawmakers and rival interest groups are clashing over the ability of senior citizens to see the physician of their choice outside the federal Medicare system. [1]

Conservatives want to get rid of a policy that largely prevents doctors and patients from arranging for Medicare-covered services outside the system's reimbursement scheme. They view the issue as a simple question of patients' rights.

"When you're sick, the federal government should not stand in the way of your getting the medical treatment you want," says Sen. Jon Kyl, an Arizona Republican who took up the issue after a constituent's complaint last year and forced a limited amendment to the law through Congress.

But the Clinton administration, Democratic lawmakers and the nation's largest senior citizens' group all argue that totally lifting the restriction would create the risk of gouging senior citizens and threaten the viability of the federal government's 33-year-old health insurance program for the elderly.

Seniors "would lose much of the financial protection that they are currently provided under Medicare" if the policy were eliminated, according to Rep. Pete Stark, a California Democrat and veteran legislator on health-care issues.

The dispute stems from a policy adopted by the Health Care Financing Administration (HCFA), the Health and Human Services agency that administers the Medicare program. For many years, the HCFA has prohibited doctors participating in the Medicare program from letting patients pay them out of their own pockets for services covered by Medicare.

Defenders of the policy say Medicare is acting just like any other insurer by requiring participating doctors to limit their fees to its schedule for reimbursements. Medicare reimbursements are sometimes markedly lower than prevailing fees for some services.

"Private payment would undermine the whole rationale for the Medicare fee schedule," says John Rother, legislative director of the American Association of Retired Persons (AARP). The 30-million-member organization strongly opposes lifting the ban.

Critics say the ban is bad for senior citizens and also bad for the Medicare program. They say it prevents senior citizens who can afford it from picking a particular doctor, for example, or from getting treatment without going through government red tape.

As for Medicare itself, these critics say that letting well-off seniors pay for some services themselves would strengthen the financially beleaguered insurance program. Supporters counter that lifting the ban would result in a two-tiered system — with one group of doctors for well-to-do seniors and another for Medicare patients.

Kyl won Senate passage on a party-line vote of an amendment to narrow the policy last summer as part of the Medicare reform provisions of the balanced-budget bill. [2] But the Clinton administration reportedly threatened to veto the entire bill over the issue. The result was a limited compromise that allows physicians to accept private payments for Medicare-covered services if they "opt out" of the Medicare program for two years. Critics say that few doctors could afford to drop out of the Medicare program.

A conservative senior citizens' organization is challenging that law in federal court in Washington. [3] United Seniors Association, a 60,000-member group founded in 1992, claims the law violates senior citizens' constitutional rights.

United Seniors President Sandra Butler says the new law makes health care less accessible for senior citizens. "Because seniors will be barred from contracting privately, many health- and life-saving services will be difficult for them to obtain, if they could obtain them at all," Butler says.

But Rother says few seniors agree. "I don't think I have a single letter in my file asking for the privilege of paying more for the services that Medicare already covers," he says. "This is not a patient-driven concern."

Medical groups are also divided on the issue. The American Medical Association (AMA) strongly supports Kyl's effort this year to repeal the restriction on private payments. "Medicare patients deserve the same rights as other patients to purchase health care directly from their physicians — without interference from the federal government," the AMA says.

But the American College of Physicians, which represents about 100,000 internists, opposes Kyl's bill. It says the measure "could threaten the viability of Medicare as an insurance program that offers accessible, affordable high-quality care."

---

[1] For background, see *USA Today*, Nov. 26, 1997, p. A6 and "Retiree Health Benefits," *The CQ Researcher*, Dec. 6, 1991, pp. 930-953.

[2] See *Congressional Quarterly Weekly Report*, June 28, 1997, p. 1529.

[3] The case is *United Seniors Association v. Shalala*, pending before U.S. District Judge Thomas F. Hogan.

---

many doctors had previously provided for free or for reduced fees. [15] Medicare and Medicaid closed the biggest gaps in health-care access, but liberals still said health care was too costly and favored broader national health insurance to ensure access for all.

Under President Richard M. Nixon, however, the federal government took a different tack to deal with the intertwined issue of access and costs. It backed a free-enterprise solution to the problems: a scheme being pushed by a physician-turned-health-care reformer in Minnesota that came to be called a "health maintenance organization" or HMO.

Rise of Managed Care

Managed care had its origins in ideas pushed by socially conscious health-care reformers in the early 20th century. [16] In one form — known as cooperative or prepaid group health plans — consumers paid a modest annual fee to one or more doctors to cover their families' preventive and sick care. The medical profession opposed the idea, however, and succeeded in getting laws passed in many states to bar consumer-controlled cooperatives.

Then during World War II, California industrialist Henry J. Kaiser set up two prepaid group health plans for his company's employees, known as Permanente Foundations. Unlike the health-care cooperatives, Kaiser's plans flourished — and served as the forerunner for what is today the country's largest HMO, Kaiser Permanente.

The Nixon administration saw in HMOs an appealing alternative to the liberal-backed national health insurance plans. Administration officials were sold on the idea by Paul M. Ellwood, today regarded as the father of managed care. Ellwood, a Minneapolis physician, argued that the traditional fee-for-services system penalized health-care providers who returned patients to health. He met with the administration's key health policy-makers on Feb. 5, 1970, to make his case for organizations to provide members comprehensive care for prepaid amounts. At that meeting Ellwood coined the phrase "health maintenance organizations." [17]

Financial and regulatory help were needed to put the idea into effect. The administration initially found money to help launch HMOs beginning in 1970, without specific congressional authorization, even as it was asking Congress to pass a law to promote the plans. The law enacted three years later — the Health Maintenance Organization Act of 1973 — provided more money, $375 million over five years, for grants and loans to help start up HMOs. [18] More important, the law required all businesses with more than 25 employees to offer at least one HMO as an alternative to conventional insurance if one was available.

At the same time, though, the act established requirements that proved to be regulatory obstacles to the growth of HMOs. It required HMOs to offer not only basic hospitalization, physicians' services, emergency care and laboratory and diagnostic services but also mental health care, home health services and referral services for alcohol and drug abuse.

These requirements, combined with the government's delay in promulgating regulations to implement the law, stunted the growth of HMOs, according to Starr's account. At the same time, the medical profession viewed the idea with skepticism or hostility. But Congress eased some of the burdens in 1976, and then provided another shot of money in 1978: $164 million over three years. [19] By then, HMOs were starting to take off in the market. At the end of the decade, HMOs had enrolled 7.9 million members — double the figure in 1970. Still, the number represented only 4 percent of the population and — as of the early 1980s — was expected to grow only to 10 percent of the population by 1990. [20]

In fact, enrollment in HMOs more than tripled over the next decade, reaching about 25 million in 1990. Despite a decade of rapidly rising health-care costs, HMOs had to keep fees down and provide good service in order to attract customers. Most faced business losses, and some went bankrupt. But they were generally regarded as successful in containing cost increases, enough so that traditional fee-for-service health plans began copying some of their practices, such as utilization review, where insurers scrutinized doctors' fees and practices.

Meanwhile, the once comfortable relationship between patients and doctors had become badly frayed. The growth of specialized medicine had weakened the bond with the old-style family doctors — who now likely as not called themselves "internists." The rise in doctors' income created a distance between an increasingly well-to-do profession and its patient-customers. And the increase in malpractice litigation led many physicians to adopt "defensive-medicine" practices to guard against the threat.

Managed-Care Backlash

The 1990s saw managed care reach a dominant position in the health insurance market. By 1993, most workers covered by employer-provided health insurance were enrolled in some form of managed care — either an HMO, a preferred provider organization (PPO) or a "point-of-service" (POS) plan. As of 1995, industry figures estimated a total of 150 million people nationwide were in a managed-care plan. Managed care was also credited with helping to bring down the rate of increase in health-care costs. But the decade also witnessed a growing backlash against managed care as many doctors chafed under cost-cutting pressures from HMO administrators, and many patients complained of delays in receiving — or outright denials of — needed medical care.

The consumer backlash against HMOs manifested itself most dramatically in court. A small number of HMO enrollees won whopping verdicts or settlements in suits claiming that their health plans had wrongfully denied or delayed necessary medical care. In California, the family of Helene Fox, who died of breast cancer after her HMO, Health Net, refused to pay for a bone marrow transplant, collected a $5 million settlement after a jury awarded her $89 million. In Georgia, Lamona and James Adams won a $45 million jury award in a suit that blamed Kaiser Permanente for the botched handling of a bacterial infection that forced doctors to amputate their infant son's arms and legs; the company later settled for an undisclosed sum. [21]

A mid-decade survey produced statistical evidence of the consumer dissatisfaction with HMOs, at least in comparison with traditional fee-for-service health plans. The survey, conducted for the Robert Wood Johnson Foundation by researchers at Harvard University and Louis Harris and Associates, found that significantly more HMO subscribers than fee-for-service plan subscribers complained about their medical care.

The complaints came only from small minorities: For example, 12 percent of HMO subscribers said their doctors provided incorrect or inappropriate medical care, compared with 5 percent of fee-for-service plan subscribers. Still, the higher levels of dissatisfaction with HMOs prompted a cautionary note from the survey's director. "Consumers need to be aware that all health plans don't treat you the same way when you are sick," said Robert Blendon, chairman of the department of health policy management at Harvard's School of Public Health. [22]

Health-care providers were also voicing dissatisfaction with managed care. In one incident, Massachusetts internist David Himmelstein attacked the HMO that he worked for, U.S. Healthcare, in an appearance on Phil Donahue's nationally syndicated television program in November 1995.

Himmelstein charged that the company rewarded doctors for denying care and forbade them from discussing treatment options with patients. The company — later acquired by Aetna — responded by terminating its contract with Himmelstein just three days after the TV show. But it reinstated him in February 1996 after a storm of criticism and also modified its contracts to permit doctors to discuss payment methods with patients.

Himmelstein's comments reflected the concerns that many doctors and hospital administrators had about managed care. "This is all about cost, not improving patient care," a doctor told *Wall Street Journal* reporter George Anders in a 1994 interview. "You survive in managed care by denying or limiting care," William Speck, chief executive of Presbyterian Hospital in New York, told Anders in June 1995. "That's how you make money." [23]

As the complaints escalated, state and federal lawmakers took up the issues. By mid-decade, hundreds of bills were being introduced in state legislatures around the country. The earliest legislation dealt with specific problems — like allowing women to select an ob-gyn physician as their primary-care provider, or prohibiting health-care plans from imposing "gag clauses" on physicians. Congress in 1996 passed a provision requiring health insurance plans to cover at least 48 hours of hospital care for new mothers — prohibiting so-called "drive-through maternity stays." [24]

Lawmakers also have responded to the growth of Medicare managed care. By the end of 1999, an estimated 6.3 million Medicare beneficiaries, or about 16 percent, were enrolled in some variety of managed-care plan, instead of in a traditional fee-for-service program. The Medicare managed-care option was viewed as attractive by some, because the plans could cover services that the traditional Medicare program

would not, most notably prescription drugs. A program called Medicare+Choice, approved by Congress in 1997 as part of the Balanced Budget Act, allows beneficiaries to choose a managed-care plan that provides all health services for a monthly fee that is set by the Medicare program and sometimes supplemented by a small premium from the beneficiary.

While Medicare+Choice was promoted as a potential boom in health care, the program went into turmoil in the fall of 1998, when health plans — faced with lower-than-expected reimbursements from Medicare — withdrew from the program. Forty-three major health plans quit the program in 1999, in a move that affected some 415,000 seniors, and left 45,000 of them with no managed-care option at all. Another 41 plans left in 2000, affecting about 327,000 beneficiaries. Analysts believe such pullouts will continue in regions where the plans determine they cannot make a sufficient profit. But lawmakers are divided on whether reimbursement rates should be adjusted to reflect higher medical costs, and, if so, by how much. ■

CURRENT SITUATION

Reform Efforts

A June 2000 U.S. Supreme Court decision on patients' rights to sue their health plans clarified one important aspect of the debate over managed-care overhaul, but did little to resolve political differences.

Justices in *Pegram v. Herdrich* ruled that a patient cannot sue a health plan under the Employee Retirement Income Security Act of 1974 (ERISA) because the plan offered bonuses to physicians to hold down costs. Justices said a decision in a patient's favor would have undermined the fundamental structure of the managed-care system, adding that it is up to Congress, not the courts, to set guidelines for insurers and patients. "The federal judiciary would be acting contrary to the congressional policy of allowing (health maintenance) organizations if it were to entertain (a) claim portending wholesale attacks on existing HMOs solely because of their structure," wrote Justice David H. Souter.

The suit stemmed from a claim by a Bloomington, Ill. woman, Cynthia Herdrich, that her physician, Lori Pegram, compromised her treatment in 1991 after she complained of abdominal pain. Instead of immediately sending Herdrich for a diagnostic ultrasound at a nearby clinic, Pegram scheduled the test for eight days later at a less expensive clinic 50 miles away. During the delay, Herdrich's appendix burst. During oral arguments in February 2000, Herdrich's attorney tried to convince justices that they should expand the right of patients to sue under ERISA by allowing Herdrich to claim Pegram failed to meet her duties as a trustee who controlled her health plan's administration of benefits.

The case was closely watched because ERISA — a law primarily designed to protect workers' pension rights — has long been criticized as a liability shield for health insurers. Most courts have held that an individual injured by an ERISA denial of care can only sue in federal court, and then only to recover the cost of the denied benefit and assorted court costs. The high court, in denying the right to sue, explored several other legal possibilities. In a lengthy footnote to the ruling, justices indicated

Managed-Care Reforms Get Qualified Support

Most Americans support several of the frequently mentioned proposals to make managed care more user-friendly. But their support drops when they are asked to consider potential consequences of the changes such as higher premiums.

Percentage of Americans who want health plans to ...

	Favor	Oppose
Provide more information about how health plans operate	**92%**	**6%**
If higher premiums result	58%	34%
If the government gets too involved	55%	38%
If employers drop coverage	54%	43%
Allow appeal to an independent reviewer	**88%**	**9%**
If higher premiums result	63%	32%
If the government gets too involved	51%	41%
If employers drop coverage	49%	45%
Allow a woman to see a gynecologist without a referral	**82%**	**16%**
If higher premiums result	63%	34%
If the government gets too involved	51%	43%
If employers drop coverage	48%	47%
Allow people to see a specialist without a referral	**81%**	**18%**
If higher premiums result	58%	39%
If the government gets too involved	47%	48%
If employers drop coverage	46%	51%
Pay for an emergency room visit without prior approval	**79%**	**18%**
If higher premiums result	62%	33%
If the government gets too involved	52%	41%
If employers drop coverage	48%	47%
Allow people to sue health plan directly	**64%**	**31%**
If higher premiums result	58%	34%
If the government gets too involved	55%	38%
If employers drop coverage	54%	43%

Note: Percentages do not add up to 100 because all respondents did not answer.

Source: Kaiser/Harvard "National Survey of Americans' Views on Managed Care," January 1998.

that health plans may have a responsibility to disclose details about coverage decisions to their patients — a move that could lead to class-action lawsuits claiming the plans breached their ERISA responsibilities by failing to tell patients about their financial structure.

The decision did little to settle a long-running impasse between congressional Democrats and Republicans over managed-care overhaul. Discussions to merge House and Senate bills fell apart in mid-2000 precisely over the issue of a patient's right to sue and how employers might be liable for an insurer's decision about medical care. However, in an indication of the increased political potency of the issue, Senate Republicans in June 2000 went on record in favor of expanding patients' rights to sue, in limited circumstances, during a vote on an amendment to the fiscal 2001 Labor, Health and Human Services and Education appropriations bill. The move, which came in response to a rival Democratic amendment designed to embarrass the GOP on the issue by making them appear to be protecting insurers, endorsed a limited right to sue managed-care plans for damages — an issue Senate Republicans staunchly opposed when the Senate considered and passed a managed-care bill in 1999.

The concession would allow lawsuits against managed-care companies in two instances: unreasonable delays in essential medical care and the failure to cover treatment that an independent physician deemed necessary and said the plan should cover. Patients could not win punitive damages, but could recover unlimited economic damages and as much as $350,000 for pain and suffering. But GOP and Democratic lawmakers continued to disagree over who should be covered by the new rules. The new proposal would limit most

protections to the approximately 56 million Americans in self-insured health plans that are not covered by state patient protection laws. Democrats and some House Republicans who support the Norwood-Dingell managed-care overhaul bill want broader protections and want the lawsuits to be handled in state courts, not federal courts. They also oppose the $350,000 cap on non-economic damages.

The Senate vote was not enough to revive stalled House-Senate talks on a managed-care overhaul bill. The House-passed provision combined the Norwood-Dingell measure with separate legislation featuring so-called "access" provisions that many Republicans believe will give more people affordable coverage. The provisions include an expansion of a pilot program for medical savings accounts (tax-exempt accounts used for medical expenses) and the creation of insurance-purchasing groups, which supporters believe will allow people to get health coverage for more affordable rates. Many Democrats were skeptical of the provisions, saying they doubted the proposals would reduce the ranks of the uninsured. The House provision also would allow patients to sue in state courts for damages. Health plans would be protected from punitive damages if they passed an external review. The House measure notably would cover all 191 million privately insured Americans.

Disagreements between Democrats and Republicans — and between House and Senate Republicans — doomed prospects for a compromise. Lawmakers said there was the possibility of reviving the measures in the 107th Congress, particularly with Democrats picking up seats and pressing for more health-related legislation.

Norwood says he introduced the original managed-care bill despite his

aversion to federal regulation. "It turns my stomach to turn this over to the Labor Department," he said, referring to the agency that would have principal responsibility for implementing the bill's provisions. "But it makes me even more nervous not to do anything."

Among its major provisions, Norwood's bill would require health plans to give consumers an option to buy "point-of-service" coverage — allowing them to select their own doctor for an additional cost. It would also require adequate access to specialists and emergency care, require internal grievance procedures and subject managed-care companies to medical malpractice liability for negligent treatment decisions.

Despite professed support from a majority of the House, Republican leadership remains unenthusiastic. House Majority Leader Dick Armey of Texas as far back as 1998 wrote a strongly worded letter to GOP members urging opposition to the forthcoming recommendations from President Clinton's health-care commission. Even though Armey did not refer to Norwood's bill, he called for restricting rather than expanding medical malpractice liability and recommended medical savings accounts rather than regulatory changes to give consumers more health-care choices. [25]

For its part, the health insurance industry is gearing up for an all-out lobbying campaign to defeat Norwood's bill or anything much like it. "It's our No. 1 issue," says HIAA's Gradison. "It's very bad public policy."

In a two-page lobbying flier, the AAHP warns that Norwood's bill would represent "the single, largest expansion of tort liability in memory," establish "federal price controls" and make it harder for families to get "affordable" health coverage. But Ignagni also hints at the possibility of supporting some legislative changes. "We intend to be very involved and will provide whatever information that we can," she says.

At Issue:

Has the rise of managed care hurt patients' rights?

ADRIENNE MITCHEM
Legislative counsel, Consumers Union

*a*mericans are experiencing a true crisis in confidence in today's managed-care industry. Consumers' faith is shaken because of signs that managed care may be sacrificing quality health care to boost profits.

As managed care replaced the old fee-for-service system, the financial incentives driving the health-care industry have turned upside down. This revolution, replacing incentives to overtreat patients with incentives to undertreat, has provoked a strong backlash. Nearly three in five Americans in a recent poll believe managed-care plans make it harder for people who are sick to see a specialist.

But this revolution also creates an opportunity to reintroduce a simple and old-fashioned idea: consumer protection laws. Responding to grass-roots uprisings, states have passed laws giving consumers tools to help them be smart shoppers, ensure accountability when costly mistakes are made, provide more access to specialist and emergency care and guarantee a fair system to review patient disputes.

A presidential advisory commission has developed a "Consumer Bill of Rights," spurring a flurry of bill introductions on Capitol Hill and the promise of a healthy debate about nationwide reform. On one side is a multimillion-dollar scare campaign, funded by industry, designed to preserve the status quo. On the other, a coalition of consumer groups and individual Americans who have been burned by the current system and want change.

A scorecard of principles for reform from Consumers Union will help measure who wins:

• The linchpin for consumers is an appeals system that gives patients access to an independent entity to settle disputes over medically necessary care when benefits are denied, terminated or delayed. The current system, where the managed-care company serves as both judge and jury for every appeal, is stacked against patients.

• Another vital component is full disclosure. Plans should be required to provide consumers with information to help them understand all of their alternatives for treatment, not just the cheapest.

• Consumers also want assurance that they will not be holding the bag for medical mistakes. Families shouldn't shoulder the financial burdens of medical negligence because industry is unaccountable for its actions.

* Finally, a consumer bill of rights should set minimum standards for all managed-care plans. Voluntary provisions won't suffice. When you get sick, doctors, not accountants, should call the shots.

Congress can restore consumer confidence in the managed-care system by passing enforceable and loophole-free legislation that includes a fair review process, full disclosure and accountability. Anything less falls short of true reform.

KAREN IGNAGNI
President, American Association of Health Plans

*h*ealth plans have advanced the cause of patients' rights with important patient protections that weren't available under the old system. Health-care practices and procedures have been made far more accountable — ensuring that the great majority of patients get the right care, at the right time and in the right setting — and appeals systems are in place to make sure that any patient who disagrees with a coverage or treatment decision has effective recourse.

Discussions of patients' rights should start with the fact that, from a patient's perspective, all other rights are meaningless without access to care. Under the old system, health care was being priced beyond reach. So one of the most important victories that health plans have won for patients' rights is to make health coverage more affordable for millions of working Americans.

Once assured of coverage, you should have the right to be protected against inappropriate care. Health plans promote quality care by emphasizing prevention and early diagnosis and monitoring practice patterns in order to do away with the wide variations in quality that did so much to make the old system not just costly but often downright dangerous. This commitment to accountability represents a major advance in patient protection.

But what if a conflict arises about what's covered or whether a particular treatment is in order? Despite critics' claims, disputes are rare and are usually resolved satisfactorily. Still, there's room for improvement — and health plans are participating in a nationwide initiative to continually improve care by identifying consumer concerns and developing patient-centered solutions. This, too, represents an unprecedented commitment to patients' rights.

Consumers should be wary of much that is being touted today as "consumer protection." For example, efforts to make health plans liable for individual practitioners' actions would simply clog the courts (at taxpayer expense) and enrich trial lawyers (not patients). At the same time, such efforts would adversely affect care by forcing health plans to act defensively, causing higher costs without producing better outcomes. Does that protect patients' rights? No — it just turns back the clock.

And we can't afford that. The health-care revolution that's in progress today was a necessary answer to the costly flaws of the old system. If the revolution has imperfections, the answer is to correct them — not to roll back progress or micromanage plans. Health plans are fully committed to making sure consumers are informed and their concerns met. That way, we can protect patients' rights without smothering innovative health care under layers of inflexible regulations and unproductive litigation.

Estimated Costs of Reform Vary Widely

Two studies — one funded by an industry group, the other by a patient-consumer coalition — reached dramatically different conclusions about the likely cost impact of the original and most widely supported managed-care reform proposal in Congress. But the industry's substantially higher estimate depends on interpretations of the bill, the Patient Access to Responsible Care Act (PARCA), that its sponsor says are wrong.

A report prepared for the insurance-business Health Benefits Coalition by the Washington consulting firm of Milliman & Robertson projected the bill would raise health insurance premiums by 23 percent. [1]

A study prepared for the Patient Access to Responsible Care Alliance — also known as PARCA — by Muse & Associates predicted a rate increase of between 0.7 to 2.6 percent. [2]

The reports made strikingly similar predictions about the effects of some provisions. Both reports, for example, predict little if any effect from provisions requiring emergency care coverage, easing referrals to specialists or giving consumers a choice between types of managed-care plans.

The industry-funded study, however, predicted substantially higher costs for three provisions in the bill:

• No payments to providers as an inducement to reduce or limit medically necessary services. Milliman & Robertson assumed the provision would prevent health plans from negotiating discount rates with providers and projected a 9.5 percent cost increase as a result. Muse & Associates noted that newly drafted report language specifically denied any intention to bar discounts; on that basis, it predicted no cost impact. Difference: 9.5 percent.

• Equal reimbursement for out-of-network providers. Milliman & Robertson say the provision could have no impact if interpreted to apply only to doctors' fees, but could raise premiums by 11 percent if it prevented point-of-service (POS) plans from requiring enrollees to pay a higher deductible for using an out-of-network provider. The firm then averaged the two figures to produce a "best estimate midpoint" of 5.5 percent. Muse & Associates says

the bill would not bar higher deductibles for using a doctor outside the network. Difference: 5.5 percent.

• No discrimination against health professionals. Milliman & Robertson says the provision could require health plans to cover services of professionals not now covered, such as chiropractors or acupuncturists. Muse & Associates said new report language stipulates the bill will not have that effect. Difference: 5.5 percent.

In addition, the industry-funded study predicted that because of its projected increases, some customers would drop their coverage — raising rates still further for consumers still in plans. The consumer-funded study predicts a much smaller effect. Difference: 4.5 percent. [3]

The Muse study predicted only a slight increase from a provision subjecting group health plans to medical malpractice liability; the Milliman-Robertson study did not analyze the provision.

Milliman & Robertson qualified its study by stating that several of its projections "depend heavily on interpretation of PARCA." For its part, Muse & Associates noted that its study took account of legislative changes made after the Milliman & Robertson study was completed.

Rep. Charlie Norwood, R-Ga., the main sponsor of PARCA, says the industry-funded study is based on a misreading of his bill. "The assumptions made are neither reasonable nor honest," he says.

But the Health Benefits Coalition, the business group that released the study, is standing by its predictions. "We have other studies that show that mandates at the state level have raised rates," a spokeswoman says, "and we expect federal regulation to be even more costly."

---

[1] Milliman & Robertson Inc., "Actuarial Analysis of the Patient Access to Responsible Care Act (PARCA)," released Jan. 21, 1998.

[2] Muse & Associates, "The Health Premium Impact of H.R. 1415/S.644, the Patient Access to Responsible Care Act (PARCA)," Jan. 29, 1998.

[3] Milliman & Robertson says its individual cost estimates total more than its "composite" prediction of 23 percent because some PARCA provisions overlap.

OUTLOOK

Weighing the Costs

The intense partisanship and narrow margins facing the 107th Congress make it difficult to predict whether any managed-care reform proposals will be enacted into law. Health-insurance groups such as AAHP and HIAA along with big-business lobbies such as the U.S. Chamber of Commerce and National Federation of Independent Businesses continue to argue that sweeping reforms would be bad medicine for patients. Specifically, they say legislation giving patients the expanded right to sue managed-care plans for health decisions will drive up premiums and force some small businesses to drop health insurance coverage for their employees.

Norwood and other reform advocates say such arguments are to be expected. "This is pretty normal,"

Norwood says. "The insurance companies stay in the background and try to push the Chamber of Commerce into the front. Yes, that will be formidable opposition. The problem is that they don't have the people on their side, and we do."

Indeed, studies show the public increasingly supports many provisions included in managed-care bills in Congress and in state legislatures. One 1998 survey by the Kaiser Family Foundation and Harvard University found substantial majorities in favor of such proposals as allowing people to appeal to an independent reviewer, to see a specialist or to sue health plans directly. (See poll, p. 109.)

The survey also indicated, however, that public support for those ideas drops significantly if people are asked about the consequences forecast by opponents, such as higher premiums, and reduced health-insurance coverage. "Support may fall if the public comes to see (the proposals) as part of a larger government health-reform plan that could result in employers dropping coverage of higher health insurance premiums," says Drew Altman, president of the Kaiser Family Foundation. Many of the major companies in the industry have been very profitable during the past decade, but in 1997 some of the biggest — including Kaiser, Aetna and Oxford Health Plans Inc. — reported losses. [26] The pressure on the industry has eased somewhat because of the slowing pace of health-care inflation. Managed-care companies also are finding other places to cut costs — for instance, dropping out of the Medicare program in areas where reimbursements lag far behind actual costs of treatment.

Even so, some insurers are beginning to raise premiums in anticipation of accelerating increases in health-care costs over the new few years. [27] Many of the price hikes are

(See poll, p. 109.)

linked to the flood of expensive new drugs hitting the market. The cost debate will turn in part on which side managed to convince the public and lawmakers that it has "credible experts" on its side, experts say. The debate already has produced dueling studies on the issue. (See story, p. 112.) One study prepared for the insurance industry and a coalition of business groups projected a 23 percent increase in health insurance premiums if Norwood's proposal were enacted. A rival study for the Patient Access to Responsible Care Alliance forecast a "slight increase" in managed-care premiums of from 0.7 to 2.6 percent. [28]

In Minnesota, however, Dianne Shea believes that the debate over patients' rights should not turn on costs. "This is the richest country in the world, and we're arguing about how to provide health care for everyone," she says. "Isn't it the right of

every American to have health care?"

"We've come up with a solution to every problem in this country," Shea concludes. "I know we can come up with a way to provide good health care to people." ∎

Notes

[1] The American Association of Health Plans reported that nearly 150 million Americans belonged to managed-care plans at the end of 1995, the most recent year surveyed: 58.2 million in HMOs and 91 million in preferred provider organizations (PPOs). See "1995 AAHP HMO and PPO Trends Report." An annual survey of employer-provided health-benefit plans released last month shows that the percentage of employees enrolled in managed-care plans rose in 1996 and 1997. See Mercer/Foster Higgins "National Survey of Employer-Sponsored Health Plans." In his State of the Union address on Jan. 27, President Clinton said that 160 million Americans are in managed-care plans today.

FOR MORE INFORMATION

American Association of Health Plans, 1129 20th St., N.W., Suite 600, Washington, D.C. 20036; (202) 778-3200; www.aahp.org. The trade association represents health maintenance organizations (HMOs) and similar network health-care plans.

American Medical Association, 1101 Vermont Ave., N.W., 12th Floor, Washington, D.C. 20005; (202) 789-7400; www.ama-assn.org. The AMA, with 300,000 members, is the nation's largest physicians' group; it supports some managed-care reform proposals.

Consumers Union of the United States, 1666 Connecticut Ave., N.W., Suite 310, Washington, D.C. 20009; (202) 462-6262; www.consumersunion.org. Consumers Union, publisher of Consumer's Report, lobbies on health issues in Washington and in state capitals.

Health Benefits Coalition, 600 Maryland Ave., S.W., Washington, D.C. 20004; (202) 554-9000. The ad hoc coalition, comprising 31 business trade associations, opposes managed-care reform bills in Congress.

Health Insurance Association of America, 555 13th St., N.W., Suite 600E, Washington, D.C. 20004; (202) 824-1600; www.hiaa.org. This trade association represents 250 of the country's major for profit health insurance carriers.

Patient Access to Responsible Care Alliance, 1111 14th St., N.W., Suite 1100, Washington, D.C. 20005; (202) 898-2400. The ad hoc coalition of 70 patient, provider and consumer-advocacy groups supports the major managed-care reform bill in Congress — the Patient Access to Responsible Care Act (PARCA).

[2] The 8th U.S. Circuit Court of Appeals ruled on Feb. 26, 1997, in *Shea v. Esensten* that the suit could proceed. The court ruled that Shea could sue her HMO under the federal benefits protection law known as ERISA for failing to disclose its system for reimbursing doctors.

[3] For background, see "Managed Care," *The CQ Researcher*, April 12, 1996, pp. 313-336.

[4] See *The Dallas Morning News*, Dec. 23, 1997, p. 1C and *The Washington Post*, Dec. 20, 1997, p. D1.

[5] For background on the debate over medical malpractice litigation, see "Too Many Lawsuits," *The CQ Researcher*, May 22, 1992, pp. 433-456.

[6] For background, see Barry R. Furrow, "Managed Care Organizations and Patient Injury: Rethinking Liability," *Georgia Law Review*, Vol. 31, winter 1997, pp. 419-509, and Clark C. Havighurst, "Making Health Plans Accountable for the Quality of Care," *ibid.*, pp. 587-647.

[7] See *The New York Times*, Sept. 10, 1997, p. A1.

[8] See *The New York Times*, Sept. 12, 1997, p. A24.

[9] PBS, "The NewsHour With Jim Lehrer," Sept. 16, 1997.

[10] For background, see "Medical Screening Raises Privacy Concerns," *The CQ Researcher*, Nov. 19, 1993, p. 1023. For opposing views on the issue, see *USA Today*, April 19, 1996, p. 13A.

[11] See *USA Today*, Jan. 20, 1998, p. 1A.

[12] Quoted in *The Washington Post*, Sept. 12, 1997, p. A1.

[13] Some background is drawn from Paul Starr, *The Social Transformation of American Medicine: The Rise of a Sovereign Profession and the Making of a Vast Industry* (1982).

[14] See *ibid.*, p. 334.

[15] *Ibid.*, pp. 369-370.

[16] Some of this material can also be found in "Managed Care," *The CQ Researcher*, April 12, 1996, pp. 324-327.

[17] Starr, *op. cit.*, p. 395.

[18] See 1973 *Congressional Quarterly Almanac*, pp. 499-507.

[19] See 1976 *Congressional Quarterly Almanac*, pp. 544-548, and 1978 *Congressional Quarterly Almanac*, pp. 576-580.

[20] Starr, *op. cit.*, p. 415.

[21] Details of the Fox and Adams case, along with citations to contemporaneous news accounts, can be found in George Anders, *Health Against Wealth: HMOs and the Breakdown of Medical Trust* (1996). Health Net had argued in the Fox case that the bone marrow transplant was not covered because it was an experimental procedure; Kaiser contended that it provided proper care in the Adams case.

[22] See "Sick People in Managed Care Have Difficulty Getting Services and Treatment," Robert Wood Johnson Foundation, June 28, 1995.

[23] Anders, *op. cit.*, pp. 42, 47.

[24] See 1996 *Congressional Quarterly Almanac*, pp. 10-85. The provision was included in the fiscal 1997 appropriations bill for the Veterans Administration, Department of Housing and Urban Development and other agencies. For a critical view of the impact of the law, see *Newsweek*, Aug. 4, 1997, p. 65.

[25] For background, see *Congressional Quarterly Weekly Report*, Nov. 22, 1997, pp. 2909-2911.

[26] See *The Wall Street Journal*, Dec. 22, 1997, p. A1 (Kaiser) and *The Washington Post*, Jan. 4, 1998 (Aetna, Oxford).

[27] See *The New York Times*, Jan. 11, 1998, p. A1.

[28] Milliman & Robertson, Inc., "Actuarial Analysis of the Patient Access to Responsible Care Act (PARCA)," released Jan. 21, 1998; Muse & Associates, "The Health Premium Impact of H.R. 1415/S.644, the Patient Access to Responsible Care Act (PARCA)," Jan. 29, 1998.

Bibliography

Selected Sources Used

Books

Anders, George, *Health Against Wealth: HMOs and the Breakdown of Medical Trust*, Houghton Mifflin, 1996.

Anders, a reporter for *The Wall Street Journal*, provides a strongly written, critical account of the impact of health maintenance organizations on patients' rights. The book includes detailed source notes.

Annas, George J., *The Rights of Patients: The Basic ACLU Guide to Patient Rights* [2d ed.], Humana Press, 1989.

This American Civil Liberties Union handbook, updated in 1989, gives an overview of patients' rights in such areas as informed consent, medical records, privacy and confidentiality and medical malpractice. The book includes source notes and an eight-page list of organizations and other references. Annas is a professor of health law at Boston University's schools of medicine and public health.

Goodman, John C., and Gerald L. Musgrave, *Patient Power: Solving America's Health Care Crisis*, Cato Institute, 1992.

Goodman and Musgrave argue strongly that the country's health-care "crisis" calls for free-market solutions — reducing government regulation, diminishing the role of insurance and giving individual consumers and patients greater responsibility for paying for their health care. Goodman is president of the National Center for Policy Analysis, a free-market think tank in Dallas; Musgrave is president of Economics America Inc., a consulting firm in Ann Arbor, Mich.

Patel, Kent, and Mark E. Rushefsky, *Health Care Policies and Policy in America*, M.E. Sharpe, 1995.

The book gives an overview of contemporary health-care issues. It also includes a brief chronology (1798-1995) and a 23-page bibliography. Patel and Rushefsky are professors of political science at Southwest Missouri State University.

Starr, Paul, *The Social Transformation of American Medicine: The Rise of a Sovereign Profession and the Making of a Vast Industry*, Basic Books, 1982.

This widely praised study traces the history of the U.S. medical profession and health-care system from the 1700s through the birth and emerging growth of managed care in the 1970s and early '80s. Starr, a professor of sociology at Princeton University, has been an adviser to President Clinton on health-care policy. The book includes detailed source notes.

White, Joseph, *Competing Solutions: American Health Care Proposals and International Experience*, Brookings Institution, 1995.

White compares the U.S. health-care system with those in other countries, including Australia, Canada, France, Germany, Great Britain and Japan. He is a research associate in governmental studies at the Brookings Institution.

Articles:

Langdon, Steve, "Critics Want More 'Management' of Managed Care Industry," *Congressional Quarterly Weekly Report*, March 15, 1997, pp. 633-640.

The article provides an overview of legislative developments on managed care at the start of the 105th Congress, along with summaries of major bills, legislative activity in selected states and a glossary.

Reports and Studies

Advisory Commission on Consumer Protection and Quality in the Health Care Industry, *Consumer Bill of Rights and Responsibilities: Report to the President of the United States*, November 1997.

The 72-page report by the 34-member commission appointed by President Clinton contains recommendations dealing with such issues as choice of providers and health plans, complaints and appeals and confidentiality of health information. A list of references and selected reading are included.

Computer Science and Telecommunications Board, National Research Council, *For the Record: Protecting Electronic Health Information*, National Academy Press, 1997.

This book-length report details a scientific panel's findings and recommendations on protections for electronic health information. The book includes an 11-page bibliography as well as detailed source notes.

Kaiser Family Foundation/Harvard University, *National Survey of Americans' Views on Managed Care*, Nov. 5, 1997; *National Survey of Americans' Views on Consumer Protections in Managed Care*, Jan. 21, 1998.

The first survey found that majorities of the public are concerned about key aspects of managed health care. The second found majority support for many of the major reform proposals currently being debated, but support dropped when people were asked about potential consequences of changes, such as higher insurance premiums.

12 Embryo Research

ADRIEL BETTELHEIM

Last fall, teams of scientists working separately at the University of Wisconsin and Johns Hopkins University made a groundbreaking discovery — and kicked up a tempest.

The researchers isolated from human embryos and fetuses a primitive variety of cells that are capable of developing into virtually every kind of tissue in the body. The so-called stem cells could provide valuable tools for curing ailments such as Parkinson's disease and diabetes, if scientists can learn how to train them to grow into a desired healthy body part.

"These findings . . . bring medical research to the edge of a new frontier that is extraordinarily promising," National Institutes of Health (NIH) Director Harold Varmus said, echoing the optimism that swept the scientific community. "It is not too unrealistic to say that this research has the potential to revolutionize the practice of medicine and improve the quality and length of life."

But while the findings generated headlines and drew comparisons to landmark moments in 20th-century science, they also reignited a simmering legal and ethical debate over embryo research. Scientists, theologians, politicians and government officials have sparred in recent months over whether a 1995 federal ban on funding research on embryos should apply to stem cells. Congress and the NIH are attempting to devise new guidelines in light of the developments. But officials first must arrive at a consensus on such thorny philosophical questions as when life begins, and whether an embryo has the same moral status as a person.

"It's a watershed issue that cuts

deeply into the future of the biomedical community," says Ronald M. Green, chairman of the Ethics Institute at Dartmouth College. "Science is forcing us to rethink our ethical, moral and religious considerations, but all the recent developments make it difficult to draw lines in the sand."

Human stem cells are hardly the first scientific discovery in recent years to challenge people's beliefs in this way. The advent of recombinant DNA technology in the 1970s led to developments allowing scientists to clone sheep and other mammals, raising the very real but unsettling prospect that human beings also could be replicated. [1]

Around the same time, scientists developed a deeper understanding of how DNA carries chemical messages, allowing them to identify specific human genes linked to diseases, and, possibly, certain types of behavior. That has raised questions about how much of our existence is predetermined, and whether science should be allowed to intervene via techniques such as gene therapy. [2]

The stem cell discovery could potentially have even more profound meaning, because it offers a glimpse at human life in its simplest form. The microscopic clumps of cells are found in the interior of days-old embryos before they develop rudimentary nervous systems and are capable of achieving something resembling awareness.

When isolated in culture dishes, the cells — through a still-unknown mechanism — can grow into specific body parts, such as brain cells or heart muscle. They also can replicate indefinitely in the laboratory, providing a potentially endless source of replacement tissue. Scientists have watched with amazement as some of the cells spontaneously evolve into tiny bundles of beating heart muscle, clumps of nerves or even hair and teeth. [3]

However, scientists don't yet know how to make a stem cell "committed" to becoming a particular body part. And they still aren't sure whether the spare body parts they create won't be rejected by the patient's immune system — a problem that frequently arises in organ transplants.

Some of the stem cells were extracted from spare embryos created in fertility clinics that were deemed unsuitable for implantation in the womb. Others came from the gonads of aborted fetuses. Because of uncertainties over whether the existing funding ban applies to stem cells, the University of Wisconsin and Johns Hopkins scientists relied on private funding for their work, including financing from Geron Corp., a Menlo Park, Calif., biotechnology firm with a strong interest in anti-aging products.

Most scientists believe the stem cells are biologically closer to other types of cells — say, blood cells — than to a complete embryo. They argue the government should fund research into how the cells can be coaxed into becoming a specific type of tissue, pointing to the wide-ranging health benefits that could follow. With this knowledge, researchers say they could perform tasks like creating new bone and cartilage cells for patients suffering from osteoporosis

From *The CQ Researcher*, December 17, 1999.

or arthritis, or nerve cells for stroke victims or people with spinal cord injuries.

"The world would be better off if public funding were available, because it would allow the best biomedical scientists in academia to enter the field," says James A. Thomson, the University of Wisconsin biologist who first isolated the human stem cells and used them to grow heart tissues. "Although a great deal of basic research needs to be done before these cells can lead to human therapies, I believe in the long run they will revolutionize many aspects of transplantation medicine."

However, anti-abortion groups and many Catholic theologians oppose using taxpayer money to fund the work, arguing the scientists are destroying life to advance their research. The critics, who believe that life begins at conception, contend the stem cells, however primitive, are distinct entities that have the same moral status as humans. They criticize the researchers for playing up the biological qualities of the stem cells while paying less attention to the methods that extract them from embryos. And they worry that advances in cloning will soon lead scientists to create embryos specifically so they can extract their stem cells.

"These embryos are far beyond conception; fertilization has taken place and we have a genetically unique individual," says C. Ben Mitchell, senior fellow at the Center for Bioethics and Human Dignity, a nonprofit group in Bannockburn, Ill., that is leading the fight against federal funding. "Giving an embryo a different moral status based on the time of gestation is simply an act of arbitrariness. There's no scientific evidence to point to a specific time when the moral status moves higher."

Public figures and advocacy groups are already joining the debate. Groups advocating for victims

of various diseases have mounted a major lobbying push in favor of federal funding, even going as far as recruiting the help of conservative Sen. Strom Thurmond, R-S.C., an abortion foe whose daughter suffers from juvenile diabetes, and 33 U.S. Nobel Prize winners.

Opponents, including the National Conference of Catholic Bishops, have issued strongly worded position papers supporting the ban, saying any researcher who understands the origin of the stem cells is "morally complicit" in their destruction. Those coming out against federal funding include no less than 70 members of Congress and former Surgeon General C. Everett Koop.

Lawmakers considering what to do must first consider the 1995 ban, authored by Rep. Jay Dickey, R-Ark. that prohibits spending federal money on any biomedical research involving human embryos outside the womb.[4] The ban, which didn't contemplate the extraction of stem cells, has been attached for the past four years as a rider to the annual bills that fund NIH.

Congress could elect to expand the ban so it explicitly mentions stem cell research. Lawmakers also could take the more dramatic step of extending the ban to privately funded research — a move that experts say would almost certainly would trigger legal challenges because it could infringe on individuals' reproductive rights. Congress also could elect to simply let the ban stand and defer to NIH on the issue of stem cell research — a move that appears increasingly likely given the sharp philosophical divide over the issue.

NIH in December released draft guidelines recommending the funding of stem cell research based on a legal opinion by Harriet Rabb, general counsel of the U.S. Department of Health and Human Services (HHS).[5] The opinion states that stem

cells "do not have the capacity to develop into a human being, even if transferred to the uterus." As a result, Rabb wrote, destruction of the cells during the course of research wouldn't constitute the destruction of an embryo. President Clinton's National Bioethics Advisory Commission and the American Association for the Advancement of Science (AAAS) have similarly endorsed federally funded stem cell research.

To get around the issue of the current funding ban, NIH said it would not use federal funds to create embryos for research but would support studies that use embryos developed by private sources. Moving with caution, the agency is seeking public comment on the draft guidelines and has assembled an oversight panel to review grant proposals.

"The ethical and social issues associated with stem cell research are complex and controversial and require thoughtful discourse in public fora to reach resolution," Varmus says.

But critics say the NIH's preliminary decision reflects a concerted effort to defy the funding ban and present a new definition of an embryo. "The researcher's temptation is to think that if something technically can be done it ethically should be done," Richard Doerflinger, associate director for policy development for the National Conference of Catholic Bishops, told a Senate Appropriations subcommittee hearing on stem cell research last December. "A civilized society will appreciate the possibilities opened up by research, but will insist that scientific progress must not come at the expense of human dignity."[6]

Geron is watching the debate closely. It wants to learn how to convert a patient's ordinary cells into stem cells that then can be used for transplantation and self-repair. The company announced in May that it

At the Beginnings of Life

The isolation of human embryonic stem cells, shown below, represents a landmark in biomedical research and offers the highest-resolution view yet into early human development. Controversy arises because stem cells are isolated from aborted fetuses or early-stage embryos.

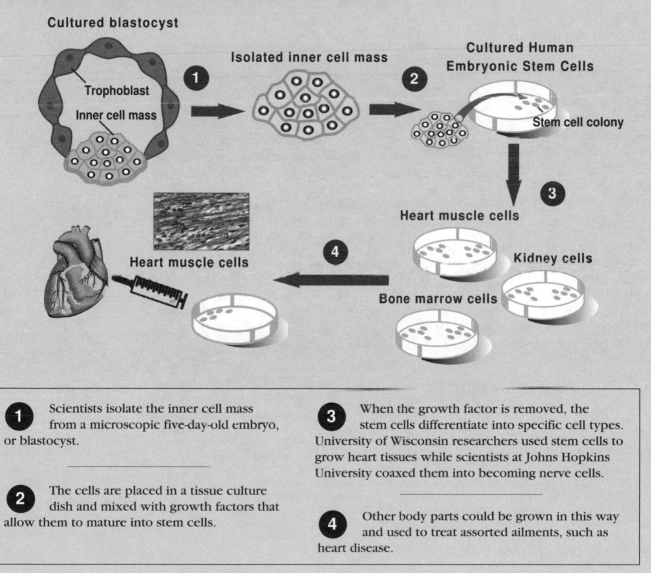

Culturing Human Embryonic Stem Cells

Cultured blastocyst

Trophoblast

Inner cell mass

1

Isolated inner cell mass

2

Cultured Human Embryonic Stem Cells

Stem cell colony

3

Heart muscle cells

4

Heart muscle cells

Kidney cells

Bone marrow cells

1 Scientists isolate the inner cell mass from a microscopic five-day-old embryo, or blastocyst.

2 The cells are placed in a tissue culture dish and mixed with growth factors that allow them to mature into stem cells.

3 When the growth factor is removed, the stem cells differentiate into specific cell types. University of Wisconsin researchers used stem cells to grow heart tissues while scientists at Johns Hopkins University coaxed them into becoming nerve cells.

4 Other body parts could be grown in this way and used to treat assorted ailments, such as heart disease.

Source: University of Wisconsin–Madison

formed a $20 million research alliance with the Roslin Institute of Scotland, which first focused worldwide attention on cloning in 1997 by creating Dolly, a cloned sheep. But Geron has denied it is interested in creating cloned human embryos.

Geron's involvement has made some observers uneasy because it operates entirely outside the scope of the funding ban and, by extension, without any federal oversight. Dartmouth ethics expert Green, among others, believes federal funding of stem cell research would ensure that other companies entered the field, and that NIH or some other federal authority would oversee the scope of the work.

"You would have a serious ethical issue if some company, not necessarily Geron, were deliberately creating embryos only to dismember them, and reaping huge financial benefits," Green says.

Geron says it convened its own ethics panel for advice on how to proceed, adding it understands the moral questions and general unease swirling around stem cell research.

"We are sensitive to the ethical issues surrounding our respective technologies," Geron President and Chief Executive Officer Thomas Okarma said in announcing the alliance with the Roslin Institute. "Both our organizations have been and remain committed to pursuing these technologies in an open and responsible manner."

As scientists, ethics experts, religious leaders and government officials continue to debate stem cell research and what it means for broader experiments involving human embryos, here are some questions they are asking:

Is the use of stem cells from embryos morally or ethically wrong?

The isolation of human stem cells created tensions between two of the modern world's most important ethical commitments: curing disease and protecting human life. For many, resolving the issue hinges on draw-

ing a series of careful distinctions about the source and nature of the stem cells.

The Johns Hopkins researchers' technique of extracting stem cells from aborted fetuses has stirred up slightly less controversy because the research didn't affect the ultimate fate of the embryos. Notwithstanding the separate and incendiary national

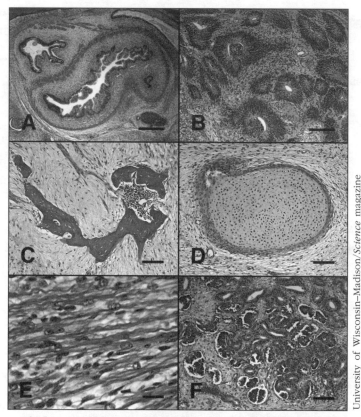

The human embryonic stem cells isolated at the University of Wisconsin–Madison randomly differentiated into a variety of cell types: (A) gut, (B) neural, (C) bone marrow, (D) cartilage, (E) muscle and (F) kidney.

University of Wisconsin–Madison/Science magazine

debate over abortion, using stem cells from already-dead fetuses has been likened to the well-established medical practice of obtaining donor tissue from cadavers. Many experts additionally believe this research would currently qualify for federal funding because of the wording of the congressional ban on embryo research. [7]

The University of Wisconsin team's

use of spare embryos from fertility clinics is much more controversial. About 16,000 embryos are created in clinics each year, the majority of which are deemed unsuitable for transplantation in the mothers' wombs. They typically are stored in liquid nitrogen and eventually discarded. However, using them to obtain stem cells involves the direct destruction of the embryos — an act that is expressly singled out in the congressional funding ban.

President Clinton's 17-member National Bioethics Advisory Commission believes the federal government should fund researchers using these two extraction techniques because a ban would conflict with the ethical goals of medicine — namely healing, prevention of disease and research. But the panel draws a distinction between the use of existing embryonic tissue and the hypothetical creation of a "research embryo" strictly so it can be used as a source of stem cells. The ethics panel says "there is no compelling reason" to generate an embryo for purposes other than creating a child, and recommends against using taxpayer funding for research using embryos produced for research purposes. [8]

Harold Shapiro, president of Princeton University and chairman of the ethics panel, says coming to some moral agreement on issues of birth and death is difficult because science is constantly evolving and testing individuals' beliefs. The result, he says, is anxiety about the future direction of technology and, in some cases, a temptation to "stop" science.

"We need new sources of reflection to enrich the ongoing ethical debates," Shapiro said. The "nervousness, ethical malaise, anxiety or even foreboding reflect, I believe, a shared understanding that humankind's destiny will not be decided in full in the laboratory or at the genetic level, where we have a lot more confidence in our ability to find solutions." [9]

Some theologians parse the ethical question differently, drawing distinctions not between the source of the embryos but between whether they exist inside or outside of the womb. Four leading theologians took this tack in October, when they wrote to Congress contending that human stem cell research can be conducted ethically and in harmony with religious principles.

"According to our religious beliefs, all human life must be protected," the theologians wrote. "However, they also indicate that there is a significant difference between an embryo suspended in liquid nitrogen that will never be implanted inside a womb, and an unborn child who is already in the womb." The group added that religious teachings stressing compassion for the sick further justify federal funding of the research.*

Theologians also are re-evaluating the question of precisely when life begins, postulating that such a thing as a "pre-embryo" may exist. Following this line of thinking, it may be permissible to extract stem cells before the embryo reaches some critical developmental milestone in which it becomes a distinct entity — for instance, the point at which it is capable of dividing in two to form twins.

* The letter was signed by Margaret Farley, a Roman Catholic nun and professor of Christian ethics at Yale University Divinity School; Nancy Duff, a Presbyterian theologian and associate professor at the Princeton Theological Seminary; Rabbi Elliott Dorff, professor of philosophy at the University of Judaism in Los Angeles; and Abdulaziz Sachedina, an Islamic scholar at the University of Virginia.

However, opponents of stem cell research contend such distinctions are designed to achieve political compromises and don't address the broader ethical issues surrounding experiments on human subjects. The critics say society must rigorously apply those principles or face the prospect of treating people as things.

"Members of the human species who cannot give informed consent should not be the subjects of an experiment unless they personally may benefit from it, or the experiment carries no significant risk to harming them," says the National Conference of Catholic Bishops' Doerflinger. He notes that U.S. law already allows for such considerations, permitting states to pass statutes prohibiting harmful experiments on human embryos, despite prohibitions on restricting access to abortions.

The Center for Bioethics and Human Dignity rejects using compassion for the sick as justification for conducting stem cell research, saying the Bible teaches that people are not free to pursue good ends through immoral or unethical means.

"We must not sacrifice one class of human beings to benefit another," says the center's Mitchell, citing as an example the use of data from Nazi medical experiments on concentration camp inmates to gain insights into human physiology.

Both groups believe the correct ethical approach would be to find alternate sources for stem cells. Indeed, lab techniques have been identified that could stimulate growth and specialization of stem cells extracted from adult tissues, bone marrow or umbilical-cord blood. However, scientists say those stem cells aren't biologically equivalent to the ones found in embryos and are less capable of evolving into the desired tissue.

Experts believe the debate over ethics will continue but that new

scientific discoveries will gradually make the potential applications of stem cell research overshadow the moral reservations. Arthur Caplan, director of the Center for Bioethics at the University of Pennsylvania, predicts patient-advocacy and disease-related interest groups will besiege undecided lawmakers with evidence that stem cell research can create such medical miracles as virus-free blood or help repair spinal-cord damage until the politicians give in. "That lobby, I think, will overwhelm moral reservations," Caplan said. [10]

Should stem cell research be eligible for federal funding?

To patient-advocacy groups, Michelle Puczynski is a living argument for federal funding of stem cell research. The 15-year-old from Toledo, Ohio, was 13 months old when she was diagnosed with juvenile diabetes. Since then, she has taken 16,500 injections of insulin simply to survive. The advocates, who invited Puczynski to a Washington news conference in May, say the government should bankroll research into how stem cells can be grown into insulin-producing pancreatic cells. Such cells could then be injected into Michelle's body to begin reversing the debilitating condition.

"Events in the lab are overcoming the fear of the unknown," says Daniel Perry, executive director of the Alliance for Aging Research and head of Patients' Cure, a Washington-based coalition of 35 patient organizations advocating federal funding. "This debate needs to include the voices of people who face tragic and catastrophic illnesses — conditions that potentially could be relieved."

But Congress has been leery about giving its blessing to new varieties of developmental biology. The 105th Congress took up a measure to ban a process known as somatic cell nuclear transfer that could be used to

Stem Cells' Unlimited Potential

Researchers believe that human embryonic stem cells can be grown into a variety of body parts, enabling them to fight many common afflictions.

Cells Derivable From Stem Cells	Target Diseases
Insulin-producing cells	Diabetes
Nerve cells	Stroke, Parkinson's disease, Alzheimer's disease, Spinal cord injury
Heart muscle cells	Heart attacks, Congestive heart failure
Liver cells	Hepatitis, Cirrhosis
Blood cells	Cancer, Immunodeficiencies
Bone cells	Osteoporosis
Cartilage cells	Osteoarthritis
Eye cells	Macular degeneration
Skin cells	Burns, Wound healing
Skeletal muscle cells	Muscular dystrophy

Source: Geron Corp.

create a human embryo. The process involves replacing the nucleus of an egg cell with another cell that wouldn't multiply if left in its original state. The remaining part of the egg cell can "program" the new nucleus to multiply. Scientists believe the process could help them clone cells that could treat cancer, heart disease and other conditions, but lawmakers expressed serious concerns about creating carbon copies of living or dead people. The Senate finally voted against taking up the bill because it was too broadly written. [11]

Defenders of stem cell research this year tried to insert a measure in a Senate spending bill that would have permitted government-supported research on spare stem cells donated by couples who went through in-vitro fertilization. But the provision was stripped out by Sen. Arlen Specter, R-Pa., chairman of the Senate Appropriations subcommittee that controls NIH's budget, who said the issue should be decided outside the budget process. Specter and Senate Majority Leader Trent Lott, R-Miss., indicated they will introduce legislation in February to define the conditions for federally supported stem cell research. [12]

The 1995 congressional funding bars the use of federal money for research in which embryos are "destroyed, discarded or knowingly subjected to risk, injury or death" but doesn't specifically mention stem cells. One key question surrounding the ban and its effect on the current research is whether stem cells can develop into embryos on their own and, thus, should fall under the funding ban. The answer appears to be "maybe."

Scientists at the University of Toronto in 1993 grew entire mice out of stem cells. But the scientists first wrapped the stem cells in an envelope of genetically modified cells that couldn't grow into part of the fetus but helped the stem cells attach to the wall of the female mouse's uterus. Without this kind of artificial protection, many scientists believe the stem cells alone aren't capable of evolving into a person. [13]

"Embryonic stem cells on their own can't make certain embryonic tissues, they can't form an embryo and we aren't cloning here," says John Gearhardt, director of the division of developmental genetics at the Johns Hopkins School of Medicine. He is the scientist who coaxed stem cells isolated from the gonads of aborted fetuses into becoming nerve cells.

But Gearhardt points out there are

different kinds of stem cells. He believes the ones he and the University of Wisconsin's Thomson isolated are "pluripotent" stem cells, meaning they are capable of becoming a wide array of human tissues but cannot become cells of the placenta or other tissues needed for implantation in the womb.

However, the scientists can't be sure. That is because very early in development, an embryo is also believed to possess "totipotent" stem cells that can form every kind of cell in the body. The researchers can't test whether the cells they isolated are totipotent because it would involve injecting the stem cells into another embryo to create a test environment to determine whether the cells retain all of their developmental powers. That would conflict with virtually all accepted ethical guidelines.

Rep. Dickey, the author of the congressional funding ban, says that such uncertainties are precisely why the ban should be applied to stem cells. He says scientists should study stem cells in animals and in less controversial adult cells without getting involved in politically volatile embryo research. He adds NIH's preliminary indications that it will fund stem cell research are a deliberate attempt to flout the law.

"Any NIH action to initiate funding of such research would violate both the letter and spirit of the federal law banning federal support for research in which human embryos are harmed or destroyed," Dickey wrote Secretary of Health and Human Services Donna E. Shalala in May.

Dickey has numerous allies. Sen. Sam Brownback, R-Kan., calls the research "immoral, illegal and unnecessary," adding, "there are better, more promising avenues to follow in order to continue our fight against some of the diseases with which we are battling." Brownback issued a highly critical position paper on stem cell research this summer that was endorsed by Catholic and Protestant anti-abortion leaders.

Despite the passionate feelings, political realities are thwarting the critics from enacting legislation. Dickey in September indicated he would draft an amendment to NIH's

The use of human embryonic stem cells in medical research is rekindling the debate over whether fetuses should be considered human beings. Above, abortion foes from Operation Rescue protest at an abortion clinic in Niagara Falls, N.Y., last April.

fiscal 2000 spending bill that would have extended the ban to stem cells. But he was talked out of the move by House Majority Whip Tom DeLay, R-Texas, who was seeking to eliminate controversial amendments in an effort to speed up the budget process. The fight will likely continue during the next Congress.

"Congress is crossing a moral Rubicon, and the people fighting the abortion wars see [stem cell research] as a kind of proxy for the fight over when does life begin," says the Alliance for Aging Research's Perry. "We're taking a middle-of-the-road

approach and hoping NIH will release its guidelines soon so we can develop a funding policy through an honest, thorough and open process."

Are the potential benefits of stem cell research being oversold?

A hiker suffers a serious heart attack in a remote part of a national park. By the time he reaches a hospital, only one-third of his heart is still working. Eager to return to active life, he provides doctors with a sample of his skin cells, which are then injected into specially prepared, donated human eggs. The eggs are grown in a lab for a week, developing into early-stage embryos that yield stem cells that are a perfect genetic match for the patient. Doctors grow the stem cells into heart-muscle cells, inject them into the patient and watch as the new cells begin to replace old damaged ones. Before long, the patient is restored to health.

This hypothetical scenario — outlined recently in *Scientific American* magazine by Roger Pedersen, a stem cell researcher at the University of California at San Francisco — illustrates the tremendous potential for therapeutic cures arising from stem cell research. If it were possible to control how stem cells differentiate into body parts, Pederson writes, the resulting cells could potentially help repair damage from Parkinson's disease, diabetes and other debilitating conditions that result from the death or damage of one or several cell types. [14]

But observers caution there are huge scientific hurdles ahead, and that significant health benefits from the current research may not be seen for decades, if ever. In particular, some worry that researchers — under pressure to produce and deliver results for politicians, potential investors and the public — may be hyping the field's potential before they even know whether stem cell-based transplantation works in humans.

"I hate to be the skunk at the garden party, but the probability of success simply isn't guaranteed," says Charles Jennings, editor of *Nature Neuroscience*, a scientific journal. "The brain, for example, has a hundred-billion neurons in an incredibly complicated array, firing 10 to 100 actions every second. You just can't expect to go patch up the holes in it with cellular putty-filler."

Jennings and others question whether stem cell researchers are moving too quickly toward human clinical trials without fully understanding the underlying science and possible risks. Without knowing precisely what kind of brain cells govern certain neurological functions, for example, the skeptics say it will be difficult to pinpoint a cure for Parkinson's disease — a progressive disorder characterized by the loss of dopamine-producing neurons in the brain. It also will be hard to recruit patients for trials on potential therapies. To test the efficacy, scientists will need one group that receives transplanted cells and another control group that receives a placebo. But skeptics question how many people will be willing to volunteer to have holes drilled into their heads or needles injected into their brains, on the chance they may receive an unproven treatment.

"Neural transplantation is quite risky," Jennings says. "And once the new cells are implanted, it's difficult to monitor physiological changes because you can't just decide to biopsy that part of the brain. It raises major concerns."

Some patient advocates have elected to remain silent on stem cell research until the outcome of experiments and the political debate become clearer. The American Cancer Society last summer pulled out of the Patients' Cure coalition, reportedly over internal policy disagreements. The organization also had received a letter from Cardinal William Keeler of Baltimore asking the cancer society to reconsider its membership. Officials denied that pressure from the Roman Catholic Church influenced their decision, saying they were conducting their own analysis of the issue and at some point in the future would issue a policy statement. [15]

Even some lawmakers generally sympathetic to scientific causes are openly expressing reservations about endorsing a major government role in stem cell work. Specter describes the issue as "fuzzy" — intriguing because of the medical potential but also fraught with troubling legal and moral implications. "I don't think you can rush to judgment on it," he says. "This is obviously on the cutting edge."

Most scientists acknowledge there are concerns but defend pushing forward, saying stem cell research is doing more than just promising future cures. It also is offering insights into events that can't be studied directly in the human embryo. The University of Wisconsin team, for example, has observed how stem cells differentiate into the three primary "germ lines" in the body, and subsequently into arrays of tissue cells, including cartilage, bone, muscle and neural and gut cells. Understanding these steps will yield new insights into birth defects, infertility and miscarriage, according to Thomson. And testing how specific, differentiated cells respond to certain drugs will allow researchers to sort out which medications are helpful or harmful. [16]

"We're not just a bunch of cowboys looking to stick strange cells into the heads of people," says Ronald McKay, a leading stem cell researcher and chief of the laboratory of molecular biology at the National Institute of Neurological Disorders and Stroke in Bethesda, Md. "This work has appeal to many different segments of the scientific community because stem cells give us a tool to look at very complex cellular functions."

Many researchers in the field are now focusing on chemicals that can act as growth factors and stimulate stem cells to produce specific kinds of cells. Researchers at Washington University School of Medicine in St. Louis, for example, found that the vitamin A derivative retinoic acid seems to stimulate a set of genes in stem cells to make them produce neurons while inhibiting genes that trigger other types of cell formation. [17]

Gearhardt of Johns Hopkins and other prominent researchers take pains to note that stem cell work is not a new, hype-driven branch of science but builds on more than a half-century of pioneering work in developmental biology. Viewed in this context, he says it is reasonable to expect careful, steady progress, but no breathtaking applications overnight.

"Our work is simply an extension of work that's gone on for decades," Gearhardt says. "We're taking discoveries that go back to the 1930s and '40s and just applying them to humans." ■

BACKGROUND

Early Breakthroughs

Scientific breakthroughs like the discovery of penicillin and the

Chronology

1960s *Biologists studying mice begin to postulate how "master cells" existing in embryos can create different kinds of tissue. However, they can't isolate the cells. Meanwhile, other types of fetal research yield a vaccine against measles and improved treatment of blood diseases.*

———— • ————

1970s *Embryo research accelerates and becomes a public issue.*

1973
The U.S. Supreme Court recognizes the constitutional right to abortion in *Roe v. Wade*.

1975
The U.S. Department of Health and Human Services (HHS) bars research on live fetuses but allows studies on dead fetuses or their tissues if permitted by state law.

———— • ————

1980s *Scientists continue their studies and begin transplanting fetal tissue. Anti-abortion groups oppose the use of biological materials from aborted fetuses.*

1981
Researchers in England and the United States derive stem cells from mouse embryos at an early stage. This allows them to begin developing cultures in laboratories to prompt the stem cells to form certain tissues.

1988
Scientists at the University of Colorado perform the first fetal tissue transplant on a patient with Parkinson's disease. HHS imposes a moratorium on federal funding of fetal tissue transplant research.

———— • ————

1990s *New discoveries offer a detailed view of early human development — and fan controversies.*

1993
Scientists at the University of Toronto announce they grew an entire mouse from individual stem cells extracted from mouse embryos. The experiment proves stem cells can grow into an entire healthy organism. President Clinton, in one of his first acts as president, removes prohibitions on fetal tissue research.

1994
A panel of experts convened by the National Institutes of Health (NIH) concludes that public funds should be spent on embryo research, as long as the embryos in question were not created strictly for research purposes. President Clinton soon after announces that his administration will forbid taxpayer funding for research with human embryos, regardless of their source.

1995
Congress incorporates language in the spending bill that funds NIH forbidding taxpayer funding for research with human embryos, regardless of their source.

The ban is included in subsequent annual spending bills. University of Wisconsin researchers isolate the stem cells of a monkey and discover unique properties inherent to primates.

November 1998
Scientists at the University of Wisconsin and Johns Hopkins University announce that they isolated human embryonic stem cells for the first time.

Jan. 19, 1999
NIH Director Harold Varmus announces the federal government can pay for some stem cell research, as long as publicly funded researchers don't grow the cells themselves.

May 4, 1999
Geron Corp., in Menlo Park, Calif., forms an alliance with the Roslin Institute of Scotland to blend stem cell research with the cloning technology that produced Dolly the sheep in 1997.

June 28, 1999
The National Bioethics Advisory Commission recommends that federally funded scientists be allowed to extract stem cells from human embryos, as well as conduct research on embryos derived by others.

Aug. 18, 1999
The American Association for the Advancement of Science endorses private and public research on stem cells, citing the potential medical benefits to individuals.

polio vaccine have long given Americans hope that other still common afflictions such as cancer, heart disease and mental illness could be stopped, too. In fact, progress has come painfully slow. Consider that when President Richard M. Nixon signed the National Cancer Act in 1971, marking the official declaration of war on the disease, many scientists believed they were within a decade of curing or controlling the disease. Nearly 30 years later, scientists are still learning the basic underpinnings of the disease and how to prevent specific cancers. [18]

It is precisely because of this incremental nature of scientific research that the isolation of human embryonic stem cells is both a watershed event and only the latest development in nearly a half-century of research into human tissue growth and transplantation. It may take many more decades — if ever — before the knowledge is harnessed into practical therapies that allow the body to replicate parts of itself.

The idea of a "master cell" that could prompt many kinds of tissue growth began to gain currency in the 1960s, when scientists noticed that cancerous cells in mice could form several different types of tissue. The discovery had limited research applications, however, and scientists for nearly two decades were unable to create non-cancerous, self-renewing stem cells from mouse embryos.

In 1981, researchers at the University of Cambridge in England and the University of California at San Francisco were able to derive stem cells from mouse embryos at an early, 100-cell stage. This allowed scientists to begin tinkering with cultures that could allow the cells to multiply. They also were able to combine mouse stem cells with separate embryos, giving rise to a genetically hybrid mouse. But the researchers soon learned there were major differences in developmental biology between mice and humans, leading to research on higher mammals.

In 1995, the University of Wisconsin's Thomson isolated the stem cells of a monkey. The work was notable because Thomson soon noticed unusual characteristics as he closely examined the behavior of stem cells. For instance, he found that primate stem cells quickly differentiated into various tissues unless they were grown in tissue culture dishes along with a special type of mouse cell called a "feeder cell" that prevents them from specializing. Scientists don't yet understand how the feeder cells work — a hurdle that will have to be overcome if they are ever to generate enough tissue for commercial purposes. [19]

Thomson subsequently applied his primate stem cell extraction technology to spare embryos from fertility clinics, which enabled him to perform the first successful extraction of human stem cells in February 1998. Around the same time, Johns Hopkins' Gearhardt also isolated and cultured human stem cells. Gearhardt's work arose out of two decades of research on how genetic errors give rise to Down's syndrome, a condition that occurs when one of an embryo's chromosomes copies itself once too often.

"It feels great [to be first], but it's just the beginning," Thomson says. "Up until this point, we've had no way to study questions about human development during the early weeks so we can see all of the critical decisions being made in the body plan. This gives us a nice source of material to study."

The University of Wisconsin and Johns Hopkins each patented the respective extraction techniques the scientists used and then licensed them to Geron. The biotech company believes it could be on the cusp of a financial bonanza if the stem cells can be harnessed to provide anti-aging products. But company President Okarma acknowledges this will involve much more research, including developing a much better understanding of human development. [20]

Unanswered Questions

One big question is why are stem cells so active in embryos but hardly in evidence after birth? Each of the body's cells carry the organism's unique genetic code imprinted in DNA and, theoretically, could use it to create replacement tissue during adulthood. But other than regenerating skin cells and occasionally mending some bone fractures, the human body outside of the womb typically does not take advantage of this option. In contrast, salamanders and certain other animals can regrow tails and limbs. [21]

Another focus is the cellular mechanism that shuts off stem cell division, which centers on the portion of a chromosome called a telomere. Cells are born with a length of telomere that gets shorter each time a cell divides. Conventional human cells divide about 50 times, then die of old age — a driving factor in the broader phenomenon of human aging. However, Geron scientists have perfected a way of building telomeres back up with an enzyme called telomerase. Scientists using the enzyme have been able to make stem cells divide 200 times or more, creating healthy cells that could increase the life span. But it's still unclear whether they can make enough cells to save a patient suffering from the late stages of conditions such as Alzheimer's disease or cirrhosis of the liver.

Longer term, stem cell research could be used to replace a human

Religious Views Vary on Stem Cell Research

Stem cell research, and the broader issue of using fetal tissue for biomedical purposes, has prompted a broad spectrum of religious views. The following sampling is culled from a one-day workshop organized by the National Bioethics Advisory Commission last May at Georgetown University. [1]

■ **Catholicism** — Roman Catholics view human life as a continuous progression from single-cell embryos to death, according to Edmund D. Pellegrino, director of the Center for Clinical Bioethics at Georgetown University Medical Center. Catholics therefore object to extracting stem cells from aborted fetuses or spare embryos from fertility clinics, believing that those who do are destroying the equivalent of a human being. They also are highly skeptical about designating just those embryos that are past a certain stage of development as human beings, viewing the practice as arbitrary.

A differing view is offered by Margaret Farley, a Catholic nun and professor of Christian ethics at Yale University Divinity School. Farley believes a case can be made for stem cell research and raises the possibility that embryos in their earliest stages of development may not constitute an individual human entity. She believes the break point may be when the embryo develops the first signs of a nervous system and can begin to respond to its surroundings, usually around 14 days after conception.

■ **Judaism** — Jewish law doesn't bestow legal status on embryos outside the womb. Moreover, it doesn't recognize fetuses as a human beings until they emerge from the uterus, regarding them during the first 40 days of gestation "as if they were simply water," according to Rabbi Elliot Dorff, professor of philosophy at the University of Judaism in Los Angeles. Therefore, current stem cell research is permissible, and even in keeping with the Jewish tradition of accepting both natural and artificial means to overcome illness. Judaism still prohibits abortions except when absolutely necessary, but it wouldn't frown on using stem cells extracted from a fetus to save other people's lives if the abortion were performed for sufficient reason.

■ **Islam** — Islamic law doesn't provide a universally accepted definition of "embryo" or define specifically when the fetus becomes a moral-legal being, according to Abdulaziz Sachedina, professor of Islam in the department of religious studies at the University of Virginia. A majority of Shiite and Sunni scholars divide pregnancies into two stages by the end of the fourth month, when they believe ensoulment takes place. Therefore, Sachedina says, research using stem cells from early-stage embryos is an act of faith in God, so long as the purpose is to improve human health.

■ **Eastern Orthodox** — This faith has a long tradition of encouraging medical healing but believes it should be done according to God's will, not our own, according to Demetrios Demopulos, pastor at Holy Trinity Greek Orthodox Church in Fitchburg, Mass. Therefore, embryos shouldn't be sacrificed in experiments, no matter how worthy the goal is. Demopulos says the prohibition on research using human embryos should be upheld in the public sector and even extended to the private sector.

■ **Protestantism** — Protestant faiths are split on stem cell research. Gilbert C. Meilaender Jr., a Christian ethicist at Valparaiso University in Indiana, says using stem cells from aborted fetuses or spare embryos is an example of the strong using the weak. Society is trying to benefit some members at the expense of others who have already been condemned to die, in this view.

However, Ronald Cole-Turner, a professor of theology at the Pittsburgh Theological Seminary and chair of the United Church of Christ committee on genetics, believes stem cell research should continue because it promises great benefit. His major concern is that the medical benefits will be distributed only by means of the market and won't be available to underprivileged members of society.

[1] See "A Look At . . . Science and Religion," *The Washington Post*, June 13, 1999, p. B3.

body's faulty genes with healthy DNA. Biologists currently perform gene therapy by loading the healthy DNA onto viruses that provide a means of transport. However, the body's immune system often rejects these treatments. This has frustrated medical efforts to weed out recessive genes that cause conditions like sickle-cell anemia. However, stem cell-based gene treatments have the potential to be far more efficient because they could carry the patient's own DNA with only the undesired, recessive gene altered. With stem cells' capacity to multiply, some genetic diseases that are now incurable could be defeated. However, such techniques would likely prompt a new debate over medical ethics because they would essentially alter human heredity. [22]

Oversight System

The prospect of stem cell researchers tinkering with human genetics has prompted differing views of how far the government should go in regulating the field. If federal funding for stem cell research is approved, the AAAS believes existing government agencies can oversee potential applications of the technology. The Food and Drug Administration would have the authority to regulate the development and use of human stem cells used as biological products to diagnose, treat or cure a disease. Similarly, the National Bioethics Advisory Commission and the separate Recombinant DNA Advisory Committee could work with physicians, patient disease groups, religious leaders, Congress and funding agencies like NIH to assure that appropriate safeguards are in place, the AAAS says.

The bioethics commission believes there should be a system of national oversight supplemented by local independent review boards to ensure that research can proceed under specific conditions. The ethics panel believes supervision of scientists who derive stem cell lines should begin at the local level so the university or other sponsoring institution and other interested parties take responsibility for ensuring the researchers' ethical conduct. The local boards also could review consent documents and oversee the sharing of research materials with foreign institutions.

On a national level, the ethics panel is urging HHS to establish a national oversight panel of scientists and representatives from other fields to ensure that research is conducted in an ethically acceptable manner. "In an ethically sensitive area of emerging biomedical research, it is important that all members of the research community, whether in the public or private sectors, conduct the research in a manner that is open to appropriate public scrutiny," the ethics panel says in its report endorsing federal funding of stem cell research.

Echoing some of the panel's conclusions, Dartmouth ethics expert Green says, "We need to have federal funding of this research, but the best researchers have to remain under open scrutiny as they continue to develop the field. Scientists have to be aware of the need to draw ethical lines, and that people [opposed to their work] aren't just a bunch of medieval anti-Copernicans." ∎

CURRENT SITUATION

Startling Discovery

Until recently, most scientists dismissed the notion that transplanting brain cells could cure serious head injuries or neurological disorders such as Alzheimer's and Parkinson's diseases. Now they are reconsidering the possibilities in light of some startling new evidence.

Researchers in Sweden and the United States over the past year have uncovered pathways in which the brain produces a small but consistent number of new nerve cells, contradicting the long-held belief that the adult brains of humans and other primates can only lose cells, not gain them. [23] At the center of the activity are neural stem cells that can grow into a wide variety of brain cells.

The news was startling because scientists previously thought that the complexity of the human brain prevented the constant production of new cells; essentially, the addition of extra cells would only disrupt the organ's orderly flow of electrical signals. But researchers working with adult macaque monkeys found that stem cells appear to stimulate creation of new nerve cells in the fluid-filled ventricles deep in the brain. The new cells then migrate over a week or more to the cortexes, where they subsequently send out connections to other nerve cells. The researchers now are trying to interrupt production of the new cells to see if the animals' behavior changes.

"Doctors might ... be able to stimulate stem cells to migrate into areas where they usually do not go and to mature into the specific kinds of nerve cells required by a given patient," neuroscientists Gerd Kempermann and Fred H. Gage of the Salk Institute for Biological Studies in La Jolla, Calif., wrote recently in *Scientific American*. "Although the new cells would not regrow whole brain parts or restore lost memory, they could, for example, manufacture valuable amounts of dopamine [the neurotransmitter whose depletion is responsible for the symptoms of Parkinson's disease] or other substances."

The findings have inspired a new burst of research into the brain's functions, long one of the biggest mysteries in biology. But while the discoveries ignited popular interest and inspired news headlines such as "Can I Grow a New Brain?" researchers caution that the brains of Alzheimer's victims and stroke patients don't appear to try to repair themselves, indicating the regenerative efforts may not be enough to overcome the most serious brain injuries. And they dismiss the futuristic scenario of whole-brain transplants as virtually impossible due to the sheer number of cells and the complex ways they are arrayed. [24]

If the latest research continues to appear promising, scientists expect to give animals various tests and learning tasks to see whether they can influence the stem cells to channel brain cells to various parts of the organ. One study performed on rats showed that if the rodents were trained in tasks involving a brain part called the hippocampus, which influences learning, memory and emotion, more new cells migrated to the part.

Key Questions About Stem Cells and Embryos

Following are some of the questions being raised by ethicists and other concerned Americans about current embryo research:

Why is so much attention being focused on stem cells? Scientists for decades knew that the cells existed, but only recently have been able to isolate them in laboratories. Watching how the cells differentiate into body parts gives researchers the best glimpse yet into the mysteries of early human development. Furthermore, learning how to "train" the cells to evolve into desired tissue could bring a host of promising new medical treatments. But some religious leaders and anti-abortion groups oppose the practice of extracting the cells from embryos and aborted fetuses, which they believe have the same moral status as a human being. Moreover, they worry that scientific advances may prompt researchers to clone embryos strictly so they can be tapped for their stem cells.

Can't scientists obtain stem cells from another source? Yes. Stem cells can also be extracted from adult tissue or from biological materials like umbilical cord blood. However, biologists say these stem cells are different from the ones that are extracted in the embryonic stage and display less of a tendency to differentiate. Thus, their usefulness in research is limited. Opponents of embryonic research say federal money should be directed toward finding new uses for this variety of stem cells.

Isn't there already a ban on using embryos in federally funded research? Yes. President Clinton and Congress have both forbidden taxpayer funding for research with human embryos, regardless of their source. However, lawmakers have also enthusiastically supported research on fetal tissue, as long as investigators don't have a connection with the abortion that provides the tissue source. This has created a curious dichotomy and made it more difficult for lawmakers to sort out whether stem cells actually fall under a funding ban, and whether Congress even has the legal authority to weigh in on the research.

Will stem cell research eventually allow people to clone themselves? It's not inconceivable. However, most experts believe stem cell technology will be primarily used to generate an endless supply of spare parts, such as heart muscle tissue, bone or cartilage. It also could be used in tandem with gene therapy to eliminate undesirable genetic traits in a person that give rise to diseases. That poses a new set of ethical questions, such as are we creating a new bioengineered subspecies of man.

Why are Geron Corp. and other biotechnology companies so interested in the field? Some of the companies want to turn people's ordinary cells into stem cells, then treat them so they can replicate indefinitely. This could provide a source of replacement tissue for deteriorating and diseased tissue and help reverse the aging phenomenon. Other companies want to study how stem cells differentiate to prevent miscarriages and birth defects or help infertile people conceive children.

While stem cells are showing new promise for brain research, they simultaneously are being shown to have less-than-anticipated utility in other areas of medicine. New research is showing that a cancer treatment consisting of high doses of chemotherapy accompanied by stem cell transplants may be no better than ordinary chemotherapy for women with advanced stages of breast cancer. [25]

The regimen was thought to be effective for patients whose breast cancer had spread to other parts of the body. Aggressive chemotherapy would kill the tumor, along with the undesired side effect of killing healthy bone marrow. Afterward, rapidly dividing stem cells previously filtered from the patient's blood would be transplanted back into the body to take up the bone marrow's function and grow new blood cells. Breast cancer is the primary reason such "autotransplants" are now performed. However, a recent study of 1,188 women with metastatic breast cancer treated in North America, Brazil and Russia found the treatment could not reverse the disease in the most serious cases.

"Everyone expected this to be the miracle," says Mary Horowitz, scientific director of the Autologous Blood and Marrow Transplant Registry of North America at the Medical College of Wisconsin and one of the study's authors. [26] She said the results would help breast cancer patients make more informed decisions, perhaps discouraging those with slim odds of survival from trying it as a last resort. ■

OUTLOOK

Future of Cloning

As science continues to challenge people's definitions about what it means to be human, it is likely that more controversial public policy decisions will be made surrounding issues of birth and death. Embryo research provides an important crucible, in the opinion of many experts, because it challenges society to find ethically acceptable applications of its rapidly expanding knowledge about the human condition.

The scientific discoveries surrounding stem cells actually are less of a concern to many people than the potential applications of the work — and what limits should be placed on the technology. Such worries were raised last fall when a Worcester, Mass., company, Advanced Cell Technology, created stem cells by cloning the nucleus of a human cell into a cow egg. The cow eggs are much easier to obtain than human eggs and could provide a more practical way of transplanting a person's own stem cells to replace damaged tissue.

However, critics worried that the company had created a strange cow-human hybrid and called for new controls on cloning technology. Company officials responded that the cells in question could not possibly grow into a viable creature and that they were strictly interested in biomedical applications. [27]

Cloning is the likely "next step" in the stem cell saga.

Science journalist Gregg Easterbrook, a senior editor at *The New Republic*, writes that, while stem cell research is in itself scientifically promising, it really serves as a means of accumulating the technical know-how to eventually clone human beings. This may not be something to necessarily fear, in Easterbrook's view, because cloned individuals could not be created as anything but

babies and would still be subject to the character-shaping effects of their generation's particular upbringing. Dictators would not be able to make carbon copies of themselves, as has been suggested in popular fiction and Hollywood movies. Instead, there would be beneficial effects, such as providing the means for infertile people to conceive and raise children.

"We should not be squeamish about cloning just because it mixes reproduction, technology and the new," Easterbrook writes. "Owing to the stem cell breakthrough, there now stands the prospect that our children

Harold Varmus, director of the National Institutes of Health, discusses the possible uses of stem cells during hearings before the Senate Appropriations Subcommittee on Labor, Health and Human Services and Education on Dec. 2, 1999.

will not only live healthier lives but that their children will be the final generation of Homo sapiens, supplanted by Homo geneticus or whatever comes next. . . . If all goes well, the advent of control over our own cells might offer our grandchildren many things we would wish for them." [28]

Bioethicist Dorothy C. Wertz of the Shriver Center in Waltham, Mass., predicts human cloning will become a treatment primarily used in fertility clinics, similar to egg donation or in-vitro fertilization. She notes both of those techniques were initially criti-

cized as ethically unacceptable but gradually became commonplace.

"The most likely use of cloning would be by people who cannot have children in the usual way and who want to have a child who is like themselves, rather than inviting an unknown stranger's genes into the family," Wertz wrote in the *Gene Letter*, a scientific journal. "Eventually, cloning on a limited basis will become an accepted reproductive technology." [29]

But such acceptance won't begin without more clear-cut rules governing reproductive medical research. President Clinton in 1994 prohibited federal funding from being used to clone human beings, saying, "each human life is unique, born of a miracle that reaches beyond laboratory science." [30] Federally funded scientists could extract DNA from fetal tissue until late last year, when NIH temporarily banned work that used fetuses to create stem cells. Meanwhile, it isn't clear whether Congress or any federal agency can regulate embryo research done in private — or the donation of embryos from thousands of fertility clinics.

Dartmouth ethics expert Green says a widespread ban on cloning and similar technologies won't work because no one will get all countries to agree on what is ethical science. People who want to seek out cloning procedures will travel to countries where the technology is tolerated, while research in countries with cloning bans will be stifled. He believes it's better to permit such research but subject it to strict ethical guidelines.

"There's a deep ethical need to draw lines, defend human life but not just be ignorant and resistant to

At Issue:

Should the federal government fund research involving stem cells derived from embryos remaining after infertility treatments?

NATIONAL BIOETHICS ADVISORY COMMISSION

FROM "ETHICAL ISSUES IN HUMAN STEM CELL RESEARCH," EXECUTIVE SUMMARY, SEPTEMBER 1999.

*r*esearch involving the derivation and use of human ES [embryonic stem] cells . . . remaining after infertility treatments should be eligible for federal funding. An exception should be made to the present statutory ban on federal funding of embryo research to permit federal agencies to fund research involving the derivation of human ES cells from this source under appropriate regulations that include public oversight and review. . . .

The current ban on embryo research is in form of a rider to the appropriations bill for the Department of Health and Human Services (DHHS), of which the National Institutes of Health (NIH) is a part. The rider prohibits use of the appropriated funds to support any research "in which a human embryo [is] destroyed, discarded or knowingly subjected to risk of injury greater than that allowed for research on fetuses in utero." . . . .

The ban, which concerns only federally sponsored research, reflects a moral point of view either that embryos deserve the full protection of society because of their moral status as persons or that there is sufficient public controversy to preclude the use of federal funds for this type of research. . . . In our view, the ban conflicts with several of the ethical goals of medicine and related health disciplines, especially healing, prevention and research. These goals are rightly characterized by the principles of beneficence and non-maleficence, which jointly encourage pursuing social benefits and avoiding or ameliorating potential harm.

Although some may view the derivation and use of ES cells as ethically distinct activities, we do not believe that these differences are significant from the point of view of eligibility for federal funding. That is, we believe that it is ethically acceptable for the federal government to finance research that both derives cell lines from embryos remaining after infertility treatments and that uses those cell lines.

Although one might argue that some important research could proceed in the absence of federal funding for research that derives stem cells from embryos remaining after infertility treatments (i.e., federally funded scientists merely using cells derived with private funds), we believe that it is important that federal funding be made available for protocols that also derive such cells.

Relying on cell lines that might be derived exclusively by a subset of privately funded researchers who are interested in this area could severely limit scientific and clinical progress.

RICHARD M. DOERFLINGER

Associate director for policy development, Secretariat for Pro-Life Activities, National Conference of Catholic Bishops

FROM TESTIMONY BEFORE THE SENATE APPROPRIATIONS SUBCOMMITTEE ON LABOR, HEALTH AND HUMAN SERVICES AND EDUCATION, DEC. 2, 1998.

*i*n discussions of human experimentation, the researcher's temptation is to think that if something technically can be done it ethically should be done — particularly if it may lead to medical benefits or advances in scientific knowledge. A civilized society will appreciate the possibilities opened up by research but will insist that scientific progress must not come at the expense of human dignity. When this important balance is not maintained, abuses such as the Tuskegee syphilis study or the Cold War radiation experiments become a reality.

In deciding whether to subsidize various forms of human experimentation, legislators are not merely making an economic decision to allocate limited funds. On behalf of all citizens who pay taxes, they are making a moral decision. They are declaring that certain kinds of research are sufficiently valuable and ethically upright to be conducted in the name of all Americans — and that other kinds are not.

By such funding decisions, government can make an important moral statement, set an example for private research and help direct research toward avenues which fully respect human life and dignity as they seek to help humanity. . . .

A remaining question involves the other avenues for advancing stem cell research, or for advancing the medical goals to which this research is directed, without exploiting developing human beings. Last year, for example, we proposed to Congress that there may be nine promising alternatives to the use of cloning to provide stem cells — and eight of these seem to involve no use of embryonic stem cells at all.

In the same few weeks that these embryo experiments garnered such national attention, significant advances were reported in two of these areas: the use of growth factors to help hearts grow new replacement blood vessels and the use of stem cells from placental blood to treat leukemia and other illnesses.

It would be sad, indeed, if Congress' attention were to focus chiefly on those avenues of research which garner front-page news precisely because they are ethically problematic. Instead, Congress has an opportunity to use its funding power to channel medical research in ways which fully respect human life while advancing human progress.

change," Green says. "If we can't develop a basic understanding of things like stem cells, it will be an impediment to our progress as a society." ∎

Notes

[1] See David Masci, "The Cloning Controversy," *The CQ Researcher*, May 9, 1997, pp. 409-432.

[2] See Adriel Bettelheim, "Biology and Behavior," *The CQ Researcher*, April 3, 1998, pp. 289-312.

[3] For background, see Roger A. Pedersen, "Embryonic Stem Cells for Medicine," *Scientific American*, April 1999, pp. 68-73.

[4] See *CQ Almanac 1995*, pp. 11-55-11-60.

[5] See Charles Marwick, "Funding Stem Cell Research," *Journal of the American Medical Association*, Vol. 281, No. 8, p. 224 (Feb. 24, 1998).

[6] Testimony before the Senate Appropriations Subcommittee on Labor, Health and Human Services and Education, Dec. 2, 1998.

[7] For background, see Sarah Glazer, "*Roe v. Wade* at 25," *The CQ Researcher*, Nov. 28, 1997, pp. 1033-1056.

[8] See National Bioethics Advisory Commission, "Ethical Issues in Human Stem Cell Research," September 1999.

[9] From the Andre Hellegers Lecture, Kennedy Institute of Ethics, Georgetown University, December 1998.

[10] Quoted in Paul Smaglik, "Stem Cell Scientists Caution Clinical Applications Remain Years Away," *The Scientist*, Vol. 12, No. 23, Nov. 23, 1998, p. 1.

[11] See *CQ Almanac 1998*, p. 19-3.

[12] See Paulette Walker Campbell, "Fight Over Stem Cell Research Is Unlikely to Tie Up Spending Bill," *The Chronicle of Higher Education*, Oct. 15, 1999, p. A36.

[13] See Gina Kolata, "When a Cell Does an Embryo's Work, a Debate Is Born," *The New York Times*, Feb. 9, 1999.

[14] Pedersen, *op. cit.*

[15] See "Two Republicans Endorse Stem Cell Research Funding," Reuters, July 30, 1999.

[16] See Nicholas Wade, "Scientists Cultivate Cells at Root of Human Life," *The New York Times*, Nov. 6, 1998, p. A1.

[17] Pedersen, *op. cit.*

[18] See Adriel Bettelheim, "Cancer Treatments," *The CQ Researcher*, Sept. 11, 1998, pp. 785-808

[19] See Rick Weiss, "Stem Cell Discovery Grows Into A Debate," *The Washington Post*, Oct. 9, 1999, p. A1.

[20] See testimony before the Senate Appropriations Subcommittee on Labor, Health and Human Services and Education, Dec. 2, 1998.

[21] See Gregg Easterbrook, "Medical Evolution," *The New Republic*, March 1, 1999, pp. 20-25.

[22] Easterbrook, *op. cit.*

[23] See Gerd Kempermann and Fred H. Gage, "New Nerve Cells for the Adult Brain," *Scientific American*, May 1999, pp. 48-53.

[24] See David Brown, "Brain Regenerates Cells, Study Says," *The Washington Post*, Oct. 15, 1999, p. A2.

[25] See Philip A. Rowlings et al., "Factors Correlated With Progression-Free Survival After High-Dose Chemotherapy and Hematopoietic Stem Cell Transplantation for Metastatic Breast Cancer," *Journal of the American Medical Association*, Vol. 282, No. 14, (Oct. 13, 1999), pp. 1335-1343.

[26] Quoted in Marilynn Marchione, "Study Shows When Treatments for Breast Cancer Are Most Effective," *Milwaukee Journal Sentinel*, Oct. 13, 1999, p. 1.

[27] See Faye Flam, "Despite Objections, Hopes Rise for Material That Could Repair Human Ailments," *The Philadelphia Inquirer*, June 27, 1999.

[28] Esterbrook, *op. cit.*

[29] See "Conclusion: The Future of Cloning," *Gene Letter*, Vol. 3, Issue 1, August 1998

[30] See "Human Cloning Discouraged," The Associated Press, March 4, 1997.

FOR MORE INFORMATION

Center for Bioethics and Human Dignity, 2065 Half Day Road, Bannockburn, Ill. 60015; (847); 317-8180, www.bioethix.org. This non-profit group is spearheading opposition to federally funded stem cell research on material derived from embryos, arguing the work entails destroying human beings.

Geron Corp., 230 Constitution Dr., Menlo Park, Calif. 94025; (650) 473-7700; www.geron.com. This biotechnology company funded the recent research into stem cells and licensed patents from the academic institutions where the work took place. It hopes to combine stem cell technology with cloning to create new anti-aging products.

National Institutes of Health, 1 Center Dr., Building 1, Suite 126, Bethesda, Md. 20892; (301) 496-2433; www.nih.gov. This branch of the Department of Health and Human Services supports and conducts biomedical research into causes and prevention of disease and would oversee federally supported research on stem cells and embryos. It now is devising guidelines on stem cell research.

Bibliography

Selected Sources Used

Books

Cook-Deegan, Robert, *The Gene Wars: Science, Politics and the Human Genome*, W.W. Norton, 1996.
The former director of the Biomedical Ethics Advisory Committee gives a firsthand account of efforts to launch the Human Genome Project and the politics surrounding the biomedical research community.

Lyon, Jeff, and Peter Gorner, *Altered Fates: Gene Therapy and the Retooling of Human Life*, W.W. Norton, 1996.
Two reporters explore the possibility of curing thousands of genetic conditions by transplanting properly coded genes for defective ones. They also explore the genetic roots of aging, psychology and intellect and discuss the biomedical possibilities from cloning human embryos.

McGee, Glenn, (ed.)., *The Human Cloning Debate*, Berkeley Hills Books, 1998.
Numerous perspectives on the promise and challenges from cloning in the wake of the 1997 creation of Dolly, the sheep. Special emphasis on the philosophical implications of human cloning.

Quesenberry, Peter J. (ed.), *Stem Cell Biology and Gene Therapy*, Wiley-Liss, 1998.
A somewhat technical look at stem cell research and gene therapy. Topics covered include preparations of stem cells, possible therapies and new clinical applications.

Articles

"Comment: Stem Cell Research," Mary Woodard Lasker Charitable Trust, 1998.
A comprehensive review of key scientific, policy and ethical issues surrounding stem cell research and how it may relate to the 1995 congressional ban on embryo research. Included are perspectives from politicians, religious leaders, government officials and prominent scientists.

Hoffman, Paul, "Can I Grow A New Brain?" *Time*, Nov. 8, 1999, p. 94.
This portion of *Time*'s Visions 21 series focuses on the use of neural stem cells to repair damage and even re-create parts of the brain.

Marwick, Charles, "Funding Stem Cell Research," *Journal of the American Medical Association*, Vol. 281, No. 8, p. 224 (Feb. 24, 1999).
Account of how the National Institutes of Health decided it can fund research on stem cells from human embryonic tissue, despite the statutory ban on research involving human embryos.

Pedersen, Roger A., "Embryonic Stem Cells for Medicine," *Scientific American*, April 1999, pp. 68-73.
A stem cells researcher at the University of California at San Francisco details the far-reaching potential of stem cell-derived therapies if scientists are able to coax the cells into making perfectly matched tissues for transplantation.

Smaglik, Paul, "Stem Cell Scientists Caution Clinical Applications Remain Years Away," *The Scientist*, Nov. 23, 1998, p. 1.
Biologists still have years of work before patients will receive either stem cell-derived tissue transplants or stem cell-based gene therapy, scientists agree.

Wade, Nicholas, "Scientists Cultivate Cells at Root of Human Life," *The New York Times*, Nov. 6, 1998, p. A1.
The first report of the isolation of human embryonic stem cells and an early analysis of the thicket of ethical and legal questions that the discovery prompted.

Weiss, Rick, "Stem Cell Discovery Grows Into A Debate," *The Washington Post*, Oct. 9, 1999, p. A1.
The new field of stem cell research faces major tests in the laboratory and in Congress as the fiscal 2000 federal budget cycle draws to a close.

Reports

American Association for the Advancement of Science, "Stem Cell Research & Applications," Aug. 18, 1999.
After hearing from scientists, religious leaders and government officials, the association endorses federally funded stem cell research, saying it holds enormous potential for contributing to mankind's understanding of basic human biology.

National Bioethics Advisory Commission, "Ethical Issues in Human Stem Cell Research," September 1999.
A White House ethics panel examines pressing issues surrounding stem cell research and concludes the federal government should have a funding and oversight role.

13 Medical Mistakes

SARAH GLAZER

Karl Shipman's fall from a ladder in 1997 should have ended in straightforward treatment for his broken wrist.

But after the 64-year-old internist's accident, almost everything that could have gone wrong did, according to his daughter Debra Malone, a nurse. First, Shipman's doctors misdiagnosed as back strain an infection in his wrist that had spread to his spine.

When his condition worsened, Shipman went to the intensive-care unit of Presbyterian-St. Luke's Medical Center, the Denver hospital where he had practiced for 35 years. There, according to Malone, a nurse who lacked intensive-care training and an intern just out of medical school failed to recognize his worsening condition. By the next morning, when a physician trained in critical care came on duty, Shipman was suffering from shock, respiratory failure and cardiovascular collapse. He died 18 days later.[1]

Shipman's case illustrates how flaws in the American system of medical care — the most technologically advanced medical system in the world — often combine with human mistakes to cause death and injury. In fact, more people die each year from medical mistakes in American hospitals than are killed in car crashes or by breast cancer or AIDS. (See table, p. 246.)

Experts have known that medical errors are widespread for more than a decade. But the problem has received a new dose of attention from the public and Congress following a recent report from the prestigious Institute of Medicine (IOM) confirming the extent of the phenomenon

From *The CQ Researcher*, February 25, 2000.

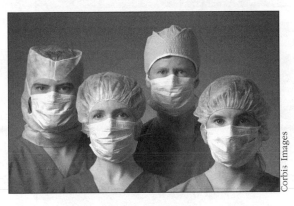

Corbis Images

and urging reforms.[2] And on Feb. 22, President Clinton added his voice to the call for mandatory reporting of errors. (See "At Issue," p. 253.)

Shipman's case also illustrates how a hospital's refusal to admit mistakes often puts it in an adversarial position with patients and their families and blocks improvements. A blue-ribbon panel appointed by the IOM argues that the failure to acknowledge and analyze mistakes deprives hospitals of important information that could help prevent similar mistakes in the future.

The antagonism that such an attitude creates among patients' families was painfully clear last December, when Malone told a congressional committee investigating medical mistakes about her father's death.

"The pain of our loss is compounded by the knowledge that his death was probably preventable," she said. "What became even more upsetting was the stonewalling, defensive posture the hospital took when I attempted to address these issues with them. The risk-management office assured me that they had reviewed the case and found nothing wrong with the care my father received."[3]

Yet federal and state health officials probing Shipman's death found deficiencies in eight areas, especially the hospital's failure to assure that all its nurses were competent. Even then, the hospital issued an official statement con-

tending, "the care and treatment provided was appropriate."[4]

The stand taken by Presbyterian-St. Luke's is all too common, some in the profession say. "The culture of this is that hit-and-run is OK if you don't get caught. If the patients don't sue you, you've gotten off," says Steve S. Kraman, chief of staff at the Veterans Affairs Medical Center in Lexington, Ky. The facility is one of the few hospitals in the nation that informs patients and their families if they are victims of medical error and offers to compensate them. (See story, p. 248.)

Kraman says hospitals fear that admitting mistakes will spark a double-whammy: Patients will file malpractice suits, and malpractice insurers will drop the hospital from coverage. In addition to suits, medical experts say individual doctors and nurses who are honest with patients face the prospect of being ostracized by their colleagues or fired.

The solution is to create an atmosphere in hospitals that fosters less blame, not more, according to the IOM report. "We have punitive environments in our hospitals," says IOM committee member Lucian Leape, an adjunct professor at the Harvard School of Public Health. "If something goes wrong in a hospital, the assumption is frequently that somebody screwed up, and they should be made to pay. Punishing the person turns out not to be very effective at preventing someone else from doing the same thing later. It's a system that's been used for the last hundred years, and it's gotten us where we are today — which is an incredibly unsafe system."

The IOM points to the aviation industry as its model for safety reform, noting that pilots can report errors anonymously to the National Aeronautics and Space Administra-

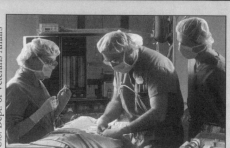

U.S. Dept. of Veterans Affairs

When Doctors Are Disciplined

Doctors in the United States committed more than 14,000 offenses for which disciplinary action was taken by a state medical board in 1995 or 1996. More than one-third of the offenses were for substandard care or resulted in a criminal conviction.

OFFENSE	NUMBER	PERCENT
Criminal conviction	2,545	18.1%
Substandard care, incompetence or negligence	2,531	18.0
Misprescribing or overprescribing drugs	1,632	11.6
Substance abuse	1,566	11.1
Professional misconduct	1,576	11.2
Noncompliance with a board order	953	6.8
Noncompliance with a professional rule	1,233	8.8
Practicing without a license	477	3.4
Practicing without a controlled-substance license	55	0.4
Providing false information to medical board	384	2.7
Sexual abuse of or sexual misconduct with a patient	425	3.0
Physical or mental impairment	365	2.6

Note: Percentages do not add to 100 because only major categories of offenses are listed.

Source: Public Citizen Health Research Group, "16,638 Questionable Doctors," 1998

produced infections from improperly sterilized equipment. "There's not a hospital that publicly releases the names of doctors whose privileges they've suspended or revoked, which is usually done for ineptitude or negligence."

The dilemma faced by policymakers is how to balance the public's right to know with the creation of a blame-free, mistake-admitting culture. Consumers and large employers want to know hospitals' error rates so they can put market pressure on hospitals and doctors to improve patient safety. But the American Medical Association (AMA) and the American Hospital Association (AHA) counter that disclosure would only foster fear of lawsuits among doctors and nurses, making them even more secretive. And that would undermine the long-term public goal of finding out what causes errors and how to prevent them, the health industry lobbies contend.

As state and federal lawmakers, the Clinton administration and medical professionals contemplate legislation dealing with medical mistakes, here are some of the questions they are asking:

tion (NASA). "The way aviation got so safe was to recognize that you didn't keep planes from crashing by punishing pilots but by redesigning the planes and the procedures and experience," says Leape, co-author of a landmark 1991 study of the high medical-error rate in New York state. "We have to take that approach in health care."

For example, simply having a doctor specially trained in critical care on duty at Presbyterian-St. Luke's' intensive care unit might have saved Shipman's life. Research suggests this step alone could reduce patient deaths by 10 percent, according to Leapfrog, a group of leading U.S. employers who are launching an

effort to steer their workers to hospitals with safer practices.

But a blame-free atmosphere alone won't satisfy consumer advocates. Many consider it an outrage that prospective patients can't find out which hospitals or doctors have the best — and worst — performance records.

"The No. 1 reason these mistakes occur is because hospitals are not accountable," says Charles B. Inlander, president of the People's Medical Society, a consumers' group in Allentown, Pa. "There's no public disclosure of these mistakes. Not a single hospital in the country publicly reports its drug errors to any authority," nor its rate of hospital-

Should hospitals be required to report their medical errors?

In diluted form, potassium chloride is commonly used as an additive to intravenous solutions to replace potassium in critically ill patients. The solution is never supposed to be injected full strength. Yet each year, fatal accidents occur when hospital staffers mistakenly inject full-strength potassium chloride into severely ill patients. [5]

After Massachusetts hospitals reported several such incidents to the Massachusetts Board of Registration in Medicine, the board recommended that hospitals only stock their patient-care units with diluted potassium chloride prepared by the hospital pharmacy.

IOM panel member Leape points to Massachusetts as a model of how a state can learn from its mistakes. Hospitals there have been required to report unexpected deaths and major complications of treatment to the board since 1987, along with preventive steps they are taking.

By examining approximately 500 reports a year, the state board has identified problems ranging from chemotherapy overdoses to infections caused by certain types of endoscopic equipment used to visualize the interior of organs. It has followed up with safety alerts and guidelines to hospitals. [6]

"Most people feel this has been effective in getting hospitals to take responsibility and to make changes," Leape says. Expanding the system nationwide, he believes, "would make it possible to collect data and aggregate it and learn from it. It would make it easier for parties that have facilities in more than one state [to correct mistakes] and it would make it easier to get together and inform consumers."

Taking a cue from the aviation industry, where pilots' identities are destroyed within 72 hours after they report an error to NASA, the IOM report recommended that hospitals encourage a similar approach. [7] Near-misses — errors not resulting in serious harm — should be reported on a voluntary basis, the IOM recommends, with the information confidential and

protected by law from public scrutiny. To encourage information-sharing nationwide, the panel recommended that Congress create a Center for Patient

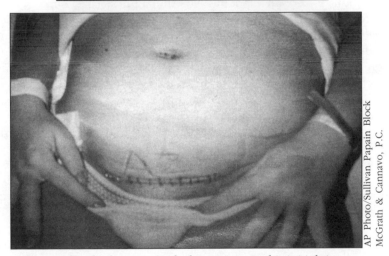

Allan Zarkin (top), a New York obstetrician, cut his initials into a patient's abdomen with a scalpel after performing a Caesarean section on her last year. It was months before his license was suspended. He faces assault charges and a $5 million lawsuit.

Safety within the federal government to track such patient safety reports, research the cause of mistakes and dis-

seminate information on ways to prevent errors.

But, some panel members observe, deaths or serious injuries from medical errors are more akin to the devastation from a plane crash, where passengers die, and the public expects to learn findings of the investigation. For mistakes that hurt people, the panel made its most controversial recommendation — creation of a nationwide mandatory reporting system to collect such information.

About one-third of the states now require hospitals to report treatment-related deaths and injuries to state health departments [8] State agencies would continue to be the primary collectors of that information under the recommendation. However, the panel wants to extend the system to all states and to make reporting standards uniform so the information could be shared among hospitals and state agencies.

The recommendation has strong support from consumer groups, which have been pushing for stronger reporting systems at the state level. But the AMA opposes mandatory reporting, arguing that it could open hospitals and doctors to malpractice litigation.

"If the fear of litigation continues to pervade efforts to improve patient safety and quality, our transformation into a culture of safety on behalf of our patients may never be fully realized," Nancy W. Dickey, immediate past

Three Mistakes — Three Victims

Willie King's wrong leg was amputated in 1995. Surgeon Rolando Sanchez said he realized he was removing the wrong leg after he had started cutting through the muscle of the 51-year-old diabetic, a retired equipment operator, at University Community Hospital in Tampa. Two months later, the hospital was stripped of its accreditation needed to receive Medicare and Medicaid funds. After the incident attracted national headlines, the state of Florida beefed up enforcement of its program requiring hospitals to report mistakes. Sanchez's license was suspended for six months The state Board of Medicine noted King's other leg probably would have been amputated anyway. King sued, and the hospital settled the lawsuit for $900,000. Five months later, Sanchez was accused of amputating a woman's toe without her consent, and his license was again suspended for six months. In July 1998 the state rescinded Sanchez's license for putting a catheter into a major vein of the wrong patient. He was permitted to resume his medical practice in April 1999.

❑ **Ben Kolb**, 7, died on Dec. 13, 1995, after going into the hospital for an operation to remove a benign tumor from inside his ear. A lab investigating the case later discovered that the anesthetic syringe had been filled mistakenly with topical adrenaline, a medication that is never supposed to be injected. The death spurred changes at Martine Memorial Medical Center in Stuart, Fla., which took the unusual step of informing Ben's family that his death was due to a mistake. A special filtering device is now used to transfer medications directly to a syringe and must occur under the observation of two nurses.

❑ **Betsy Lehman**, 39, a health columnist for *The Boston Globe*, died on Dec. 3, 1994, of a chemotherapy overdose at Dana-Farber Cancer Institute, where she was being treated for breast cancer. Lehman's physician mistakenly misread the dose, leading to fatal heart damage. The mistake was not discovered until February 1995, when hospital clerks were doing a routine review of records. The case made front-page headlines in the *Globe* on March 23, 1995.

president of the AMA, told the Senate Committee on Health Education, Labor and Pensions on Jan. 25.

The AHA, often an ally of the AMA, has not joined it in opposing mandatory disclosure, although it shares the AMA's concerns about liability. "The reporting systems that are in place now are inadequate," says AHA Senior Vice President Richard Wade. There is too great a fear of retribution among doctors and other hospital staff to report honestly to state agencies or hospital administrators under current systems, he says.

"You need to create a set of protections so you make it safe for people to report," Wade says. "The traditional systems for error reporting have been search and destroy. As the IOM said, this should not be about blame-fixing and finding the guilty party and firing them."

The failure of existing systems to protect patients' safety has led to the unfair singling out of nurses as scapegoats, when the real problem was a systemic failure within the hospital, according to the American Nurses Association, which supports mandatory reporting. The group points to the case of three registered nurses in Colorado who were charged with criminally negligent homicide after a medication error resulted in the death of an infant in 1996. After a physician had ordered a single, intramuscular dose of penicillin, a hospital pharmacist mistakenly sent up a much larger dose. The neonatal nurse changed the medication to intravenous to avoid sticking the child repeatedly with such a large dose. Two of the three nurses pleaded guilty and received two years' probation and 24 hours of public service. The third nurse was acquitted.

Contending that state mandatory-reporting systems have not demonstrated that they can reduce medical errors, the AMA argues against instituting mandatory reporting on a national level. IOM panel members concede they have no hard proof of the effectiveness of reporting because there have been no studies at the state level. In the two states with the most extensive reporting systems — Florida and New York — consumer advocates and state officials say inaccurate and sometimes dishonest reporting have been problems.

In Florida, which has the country's oldest and most comprehensive reporting system, hospitals reported some 5,091 patient injuries in 1998. But Ray McEachern, president of the Association for Responsible Medicine in Tampa, Fla., says Florida hospitals are "scofflaws" when it comes to the reporting system because virtually nobody reports their mistakes or errors accurately. And he says the state government is "aiding and abetting the cover-up by hiding the identity of the wrongdoers."

McEachern founded the patients-rights group in 1993 after a doctor's mistake left his wife, Pat, partially paralyzed. For the first 10 years the law was in effect, the state made no attempt to enforce it, McEachern contends. The number of errors reported doubled statewide in 1996, the year after the state began conducting on-site audits at hospitals.

Anna Polk, who directs the risk-management program that enforces the law for the Florida Agency for

Health Care Administration, concurs that Florida hospitals don't report their errors accurately, but she adds, "It's not simply Florida, it's anywhere."

Hospital administrators learn of only 5 to 10 percent of the errors occurring at their own institutions, according to studies cited by Polk. She attributes Florida's under-reporting in part to a culture of silence and a fear among hospital staff that retribution from colleagues could destroy their careers.

"There can be very serious reprisals for nurses or other professionals for reporting. You just don't tell on each other. That's part of the traditional taboo that's been in place forever," Polk says. "Some doctors have told me they've suffered a loss of referrals" after discussing another doctor's mistakes in hospital meetings.

Consumers like McEachern say the solution is to strengthen Florida's reporting system, not do away with it. The state needs a tough system of verification backed up by stiff fines and criminal penalties for doctors or hospitals that fail to report errors honestly, he argues.

In New York state, where treatment-related injuries are reported more extensively than anywhere in the country — at a rate of 15,000 to 20,000 a year — the system has been plagued by underreporting, critics say, and is now in its third redesign.

"Having a collection system doesn't reduce errors; you have to act on it," says Blair Horner, legislative director of the New York Public Interest Research Group (NYPIRG), a consumers' organization.

"In New York, there's no evidence that there's been an aggressive effort to reduce errors in health-care settings."

Betsy Lehman, a Boston Globe *health columnist, died in 1994 at the Dana-Farber Cancer Institute (top) when her doctor mistakenly quadrupled her chemotherapy dosage. A clerk discovered the error three months later.*

New York's reporting system was already in place in 1991 when Harvard researchers reported that close to 7,000 patients had died in one year from negligence in New York hospitals — more than died in murders or car crashes combined in New York City, according to Horner. [9] Yet even those startling statistics "never triggered any kind of patient-safety program," Horner observes "No one has argued the number has changed."

The bizarre case of physician Allan Zarkin has highlighted further flaws in the New York system. Last year, after performing a Cesarean, Zarkin carved his initials into the patient's abdomen. Zarkin continued to practice in New York City for four months after the incident before his license was suspended. According to state officials, the hospital did not file the mandatory report on the incident to the state bureau of hospitals. Zarkin has not denied the charge, but his lawyers say he suffers from Pick's disease, an Alzheimer's-like degeneration of the brain's frontal lobe. [10]

"Zarkin's like the poster child of what can go wrong. The hospital didn't even report the incident to the state Health Department in a way that would have allowed the health commissioner to yank his license through an emergency proceeding," Horner says. "It was a classic failure of the system to protect the public. Zarkin is the most outrageous example of what happens in hospitals every day."

Horner sees the IOM report as an opportunity to push the New York state legislature to strengthen and expand its reporting program, improve the disciplinary system and create whistleblower protection for hospital workers who see mistakes or miscreant behavior. "I doubt [Zarkin] was in there by himself," Horner says. "Why didn't someone stop him? It's not that other physicians don't see what's going on. They chose not to report it."

But IOM panel member Donald M. Berwick says the public perception that most errors are caused by people like Zarkin is inaccurate. A major finding of the IOM report is that most safety problems pervade even the best organizations. "So we're not going to solve the problem by firing some docs or closing some hospitals," says Berwick, president of the Institute for Healthcare Improvement, a private organization in Boston that trains hospital staff in safer practices.

However, Berwick warns, an environment of mandated reporting and reprisal would be "pretty toxic to real improvement. Mandatory reporting will improve trust and a sense in the public that we're not hiding things," and that's the main reason the panel recommended it, he says. "But the main route to safety is through voluntary reporting and deep study about why the hazards exist."

Should reports of medical errors be made public?

Crane operator Mark Baas of Allentown, Pa., was scheduled to undergo open-heart surgery when he stumbled across a booklet that may have saved his life. It listed the bypass success rates of surgeons and hospitals throughout Pennsylvania, and to Baas' surprise ranked both his hospital and his surgeon with a minus sign. The symbol meant that more patients died there than would be expected given their risk of death before surgery. Baas also noticed that a nearby hospital rated a diamond for its surgical program, indicating its

mortality rate was within the expected range. The booklet also gave a "plus" rating to one of the hospital's doctors, signifying that he performed better than expected. Baas had his operation at the second, diamond-rated facility without incident. [11]

The booklet Baas consulted was published by the Pennsylvania Health Care Cost Containment Council, an independent state agency created in 1986 to help labor unions and businesses throughout the state find cost-effective health care. The council has reported on mortality rates, average length of hospital stays and the cost of up to 60 common medical procedures.

Some consumer advocates and major employers want similar information about the medical-error rates at hospitals that they are about to patronize. "By law, we get more information about funeral homes, bank loans and refrigerators than we do about a hospital or a doctor," says Inlander of the People's Medical Society. He argues that Pennsylvania's system for reporting mortality rates and complications from surgery — known as performance outcomes — should be the model for reporting medical errors. He points to studies showing market pressures have forced hospitals to improve and become safer.

Under the Pennsylvania system, hospitals with poor ratings have tended to lose market share at first. But in subsequent years they improved the most if they were under competitive pressures from nearby hospitals with better ratings, researchers at the University of Pittsburgh and Carnegie Mellon University concluded. Between 1992 and 1997, when ratings for coronary bypass surgery were reported annually, the state's overall death rate from the procedure dropped 26 percent, according to Joe Martin, communications director of the cost-containment council.

The IOM's proposal that hospitals be required to report their mistakes to government agencies has led many observers to assume that such reports would be available to the public in much the same form that Baas found. However, the IOM report is vague on the question of whether mandatory reports of serious harm would be available to the general public in a form that clearly identified individual doctors or hospitals.

Currently, even states that require reporting of mistakes do not disclose hospitals' or doctors' error rates. In Florida, state law forbids the agency that collects data to reveal the number of mistakes reported by an individual hospital. In New York, the state is not legally barred from releasing the number of adverse events reported by an individual hospital, but it has never done so. In most states, consumer information has been limited to the total number of adverse events reported statewide, and is sometimes broken out by type of accident.

Consumer advocates argue that members of the public should know a hospital's error rate so that they can make wise choices before receiving patient care. The IOM report has given new impetus to consumer groups in New York to lobby for making more information about hospitals and doctors accessible to consumers.

"I think the only way to get institutions to act is to make the information publicly available," says NYPIRG's Horner. His group is lobbying to beef up New York's reporting system with aggressive auditing and penalties for not reporting. As for hospital report cards on error rates, "Once we know the data is valid," he says, "then it should be reported."

Authors of the IOM report stress that the most important contribution of a national reporting system in their view would be the ability to standardize the collection of errors across

Preventing Mistakes the Modern Way

New York's Montefiore Medical Center has turned to high technology to reduce mistakes from a major source of problems. The big facility in the Bronx requires all prescriptions to be entered on a computer.

If a patient is allergic to the prescribed medication, the word "Allergy" pops up on the screen in red letters — and the computer describes how the patient may react to the incorrect drug. And if a drug is prescribed that could interact with one the patient is already taking, the computer flashes "Interaction" and warns that blood tests should be monitored to avoid a dangerous complication.

Instead of pulling out a paper chart to check a patient's prescribed medication, nurses at the hospital check a hand-held computer clamped onto their rolling equipment table. Doctors at Montefiore can write prescriptions on their home computers, at their office or on a wireless hand-held computer in the patient's room. Not only that, if one of their patients walks into any of Montefiore's 35 outpatient centers, the medical staff can pull up his most recent prescriptions and entire medical history.

Montefiore is among only 1 percent of U.S. hospitals that require all drug and patient orders to be entered directly into a computer.

Yet about 20 percent of hospitals have the technological capacity to do so, according to Arnold Milstein of the Leapfrog Group. The group of leading employers, including General Motors, is using its market power to encourage more hospitals to adopt the system. A study at Brigham and Women's Hospital in Boston found that direct computer entry by doctors reduced the rate of serious medication errors by more than half. [1]

If such a system had been in place at Boston's Dana-Farber Cancer Institute in December 1994, it could have prevented the mistaken chemotherapy dose that killed 39-year-old *Boston Globe* reporter Betsy Lehman, some experts believe. Dana-Farber's computer system was set to go into operation a few months after Lehman died. [2]

Perhaps the most obvious problem the system corrects is doctors' notoriously illegible handwriting. "A lot of mistakes go with paper order entry," says Robert Lynn, a kidney specialist at Montefiore. "I've had orders not followed because people can't read my handwriting."

The system also avoids the kinds of mistakes that used to arise if there was a discrepancy between the prescription sent to the pharmacy and the paper order the nurse was consulting. "Now everyone's looking at the same screen," nurse Christine Imperio says, because the doctor's order arrives simultaneously at the computers in the pharmacy and nurse's station. The warning signals in the program make it "harder to order the wrong dose," she adds.

Not surprisingly, the system has glitches. Lynn complains that it takes longer to enter batches of orders than to scribble them on a piece of paper. The red-letter "Interaction" warning comes up so frequently in the program, he says, that hospital staffs tend to ignore it.

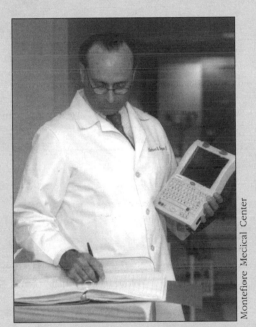

Dr. Matthew A. Berger of Montefiore Medical Center, New York City, uses a hand-held computer to write prescriptions.

Montefiore Medical Center

Matthew A. Berger, medical director of Montefiore's clinical information system, says the system permits a large hospital like Montefiore to track how long it takes a patient to receive a test or an antibiotic from the time it is ordered and to improve its overall procedures. Moreover, hospital staff cannot erase orders to cover up mistakes, a well-recognized problem for state regulators overseeing hospitals. [3]

"You wouldn't run a big bank or a business without an inventory-control system. That's why a big hospital is willing to put up $10-$20 million for this," Berger says. Training staff on the system is costly, he says, requiring two weeks of initial training followed by two weeks of follow-up help.

Cost is the main reason the system has not been more widely adopted, according to Richard Wade, a spokesman for the American Hospital Association. "More than 40 percent of hospitals are in some kind of financial difficulty," he says. "One-third to one-half of our hospitals couldn't think of anything that expensive today." For rural hospitals, he adds, "It may not be the most effective use of the money in a 20-bed hospital."

---

[1] David W. Bates et al., "Effect of Computerized Physician Order Entry and a Team Intervention on Prevention of Serious Medication Errors," *Journal of the American Medical Association*, Oct. 21, 1998, pp. 1311-1316.

[2] Michael L. Millenson, *Demanding Medical Excellence* (1997), p. 91.

[3] Robert Gray Palmer, "Altered and 'lost' medical records," *Trial*, May 1999, pp. 31-36.

The High Toll of Medical Mistakes

Between 44,000 and 98,000 people die each year because of mistakes in medical treatment in hospitals, according to two recent studies. Medical errors ranked eighth among the top causes of death in the United States in 1997, even when the lower estimate is used.

Heart disease	727,000
Cancer	540,000
Stroke	160,000
Lung disease	109,000
Accidents	96,000
Pneumonia and flu	86,000
Diabetes	63,000
Medical errors	44,000
Breast cancer	42,000
Suicide	31,000
Kidney disease	25,000
Homicide	20,000
AIDS	17,000

Sources: Centers for Disease Control and Prevention; Institute of Medicine

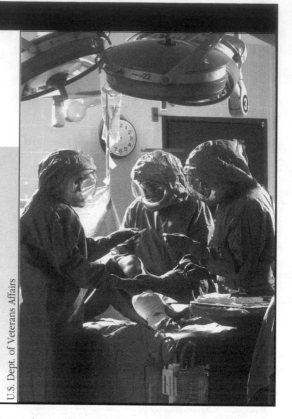

U.S. Dept. of Veterans Affairs

state lines. That way the medical profession could learn what kinds of practices across the nation are causing errors and could help hospitals learn how to prevent them by sharing that information.

Most state laws consider the information in internal hospital reviews of physicians' competency as privileged and unavailable to patients or the public. But a recent investigation by the *Philadelphia Inquirer* of records at the Medical College of Pennsylvania Hospital opened during a bankruptcy proceeding revealed hundreds of cases of patients killed or injured by medical errors. Neither the patients nor their families, however, had been informed. In one case, doctors operated on the wrong side of a patient's chest; he died three months later. The family learned of the mistake from the Inquirer. [12]

The IOM panel wrestled with the conflict between providing a non-punitive atmosphere, where doctors feel free to report mistakes, and the public's right to know, several panel members say. "We have to balance the very real need for accountability with the reality that reporting is often punishment — and often unjustified," says Leape, who opposes identifying doctors involved in mistakes. "Our feeling is we should hold the institutions responsible," he says, "and that's where the reporting level ought to be."

Lowell S. Levin, a professor emeritus of public health at Yale University, believes hospital errors should be visible. "After all, these are mainly public institutions," he says. "If not publicly owned, they're publicly supported. And as taxpayers and citizens we're entitled to full disclosure of all that goes on within the walls of these institutions."

Powerful groups with very different interests in the availability of such information are primed to clash over how much should be made public. In response to the IOM report, a group of leading employers, including General Motors Corp., has launched an effort to steer its employees to hospitals with the lowest rates of error-caused death or serious injury. The Leapfrog Group is a steering committee of The Business Roundtable in Washington, D.C., which represents 100 of America's leading corporations, employing approximately 10 million Americans.

The error rates reported by the IOM "imply that every hour one of our member-company enrollees suffers an avoidable death and five suffer an avoidable disability due to hospital errors," said Leapfrog member Arnold Milstein, medical director of the Pacific Business Group on Health. [13]

Milstein says he would like to see hospital-by-hospital reporting of deaths and serious injuries publicized. Leapfrog is developing purchasing standards to guide companies in choosing health-care providers with the best quality and safety records.

According to Milstein, the group wants to send hospitals and health plans a blunt message: "Depending on your performance, we'll encourage our people to use you, discourage our people from using you, we'll exclude you or we'll vary how much we pay you."

The AMA and AHA insist such information should remain confidential because it could open the medical profession to lawsuits and also could give the public a misleading picture of which hospitals are most dangerous. Both organizations caution that hospitals that report the highest death and injury rates may be those with sicker populations or ones that perform more difficult surgeries.

"Whatever we do has to have a degree of honesty with the public where it's useful information and it's not something that frightens the public and unfairly paints a picture of what may be happening," says the AHA's Wade.

A mandatory reporting system is unlikely to provide a reliable report card along the lines the business groups are hoping for, some experts believe. "To try to say, based on the number of error reports you get through mandatory reporting, that you will show that one hospital is better than another is wishful thinking and will do a great disservice," Leape cautions. "It will penalize those hospitals that are honest and report their errors and let the ones that cheat get away with it."

Whether or not statistics are published for each hospital, doctors and hospitals fear malpractice lawyers would engage in a feeding frenzy to try to subpoena any information collected by state health departments as part of pretrial discovery. Any approach to improving patient safety, the AMA has testified, should include "federally guaranteed legislative protection from discovery for all aspects of information gathered to improve patient safety." [14]

But does the risk of a lawsuit justify withholding the information, particularly from a patient who has been seriously injured? "Should the injured party have a right to know? Our answer is yes," says the IOM panel's Berwick. " The committee's view is that there is a moral obligation to reveal that. Right now, hospitals would object to even that. Although they might say it's ethical to tell them, they'd say it's unrealistic to tell them because of the malpractice climate."

Some legal experts agree that public release of hospital errors could influence litigation. "If five people come to your law office Thursday and ask if you'll take their cases, and one of them says he was injured in a hospital with pretty bad numbers to begin with, that might seem like a better target of opportunity," says Thomas W. Mayo, an associate professor of law at Southern Methodist University who specializes in health care.

But Mayo doubts that publicizing such information would initiate a flood of lawsuits. He points to the federal government's former practice of reporting mortality levels at hospitals providing Medicare. For several years, those reports were published annually in local newspapers. They came in for harsh criticism from hospitals for failing to adjust the statistics according to the relative sickness of each hospital's population. Even so, "The sky didn't fall in with those numbers being reported every year," Mayo says, in terms of malpractice claims against hospitals with comparatively worse data.

Only a tiny percentage of injured patients ever file malpractice suits, and of those a very small percentage wins, experts agree. [15] Under lobbying pressure from the medical profession, several states have passed tort-reform laws placing caps on damages a patient can win in a medical malpractice suit or placing other hurdles to filing. Those laws have dampened lawyers' interest in bringing such cases to court. "Across the board, malpractice suits are down, especially in states with historically high rates of malpractice filings — Florida, New York, Texas, California — because of tort-reform measures," Mayo observes.

In Pennsylvania, individual physician ratings have not led to a single lawsuit, according to Martin of the cost-containment council. New York publicizes mortality rates for coronary-artery bypass surgeries for each surgeon and each hospital. The publicity has not spurred malpractice suits in New York, according to the designer of the system, Edward Hannan, chairman of the Department of Health Policy Management at the State University of New York at Albany.

Some experts remain skeptical that confidentiality protection will make much difference in encouraging honest reporting of errors. In Florida, for example, although state law makes hospital reports of errors confidential, hospitals still underreport, Polk notes.

Is the current system of disciplining doctors working?

To consumer advocate Horner, prospective patients in New York have to act like James Bond to find out if any complaints have been filed against the doctor they're considering using. Like virtually all the states, New York won't release information on pending complaints — only those that have resulted in final action. [16] Even then, many consumers don't know where to find the information, Horner says. In some states, the state board can take years to reach a decision on a complaint while the doctor is still practicing — two-and-a-half years on average in Virginia, for example. [17]

But conscientious consumers in New York would have to work even

When Honesty Is the Cheapest Policy

Kentucky farmer Claudie Holbrook, 67, died of a blood clot in his lung in 1997 because he had been getting the wrong formulation of blood-thinning medicine for several months.

But the Veterans Affairs Medical Center in Lexington, Ky., didn't try to cover up the Army veteran's death. Hospital officials informed the family that the hospital's medication error was responsible. The hospital's attorney also explained that the family could file a lawsuit against the hospital, offered to help fill out the paperwork and proposed a monetary settlement as an alternative. [1] Even more surprising, Holbrook's family decided not to sue.

Contradicting the conventional wisdom among hospitals that admitting errors is an invitation to lawsuits, the big hospital has discovered it can limit the costs associated with malpractice suits by reporting mistakes to patients or their families as soon as possible and offering reasonable compensation. In a study comparing the Kentucky hospital with 35 similar veterans' hospitals from 1990 to 1996, the Kentucky hospital paid less than all but seven other facilities. In five of the hospital's 88 malpractice claims for hospital errors involving death or injury during that period, the patients probably would not have learned of the mistake if the hospital had not told them, according to the study's lead author, Steve S. Kraman, the facility's chief of staff. [2]

Holbrook's family received an indication that Holbrook had been getting the wrong medication about a week before he went into the hospital with the fatal blood clot.

After an error killed Claudie Holbrook in 1997, the Veterans Affairs Medical Center in Lexington, Ky., admitted responsibility and offered to compensate his family.

Holbrook family

A supervisor for the home-nursing agency that was monitoring Holbrook's blood told the family he had the wrong medication. The hospital's pharmacy mistakenly had supplied Holbrook with a blood thinner that was one-tenth the strength needed to combat his blood-clotting disorder, according to Kraman. The mistake apparently came about because the pharmacy was not accustomed to sending the high-concentration version home with a patient, Kraman says.

Holbrook's daughter Sandy Reynolds, the main family member responsible for injecting her father with the blood-thinner twice a day over a 13-month period, remembers being wracked with guilt, anger and questions about his medication as she drove her father to the hospital one final time that morning in February 1997. In two previous visits to the hospital, she says, the medical staff found her father's blood at dangerous levels of viscosity but still didn't catch the medication mistake. If the hospital had not later admitted its mistake, the Kentucky business-woman says, "I would have been madder than hell and I would have sued them."

Instead, the hospital's attorney and a hospital nurse visited the family several weeks after Holbrook's death and, in Reynolds' words, admitted "they were responsible for my dad's death." It was an emotional scene, and Reynolds broke down crying. "The people that came out and dealt with us were very friendly and caring, and patted and hugged and cried a little bit. It appeared as if they were truly sorry," Reynolds recalls.

One of the reasons the family decided not to sue was that the compensation the hospital offered was similar to

harder to uncover a doctor's malpractice history. That's because they would have to travel to every court-house in the state where a suit has been filed. The state collects that information but doesn't make it available.

Horner's group has been lobbying the state's legislature to pass a bill

known as "Lisa's Law," in memory of Lisa Smart, a 30-year-old woman who died in 1997 during routine gyneco-logical surgery at Beth Israel Medical Center in Manhattan. An assisting surgeon was on probation with the state at the time. The bill would expand the information currently available on the state Health

Department's Web site by including a doctor's malpractice history, educa-tional background and any dismissal from a hospital staff.

Lisa's Law is modeled after a Massachusetts law that makes a doctor's malpractice history pub-licly available on a comparative basis with other doctors in the same

the amount their attorney told them to expect from a lawsuit, Reynolds says. The settlement of $50,000 was modest, Reynolds concedes. But she said that next to an apology, the most important thing to her was the hospital's commitment to make sure that kind of mistake never happened again. "If we can get one pharmacist to check the zeros, one doctor to think twice, then Dad didn't die without a purpose," she says.

In response to Holbrook's death, the hospital has made several changes. It has placed the high-concentration blood-thinner in a different section of the pharmacy from the low-dose version to avoid mix-ups, according to Kraman. It has placed more pharmacists on duty during the pharmacy's busiest time of day. Now no patient leaves the hospital without an individual consultation with the pharmacist in a private booth on how to use prescribed medicine. And University of Kentucky faculty are teaching the case to medical students as an example of how medical errors can happen.

What most injured patients and their families want are an apology and a promise that the problem will be fixed to prevent future errors, Kraman has found. "Sometime if they get the first two, they don't want monetary compensation. They've resisted occasionally, and we've had to talk people into accepting it," Kraman says. The hospital has only been forced to pay malpractice judgments twice in the 13 years since initiating its tell-and-pay approach.

The hospital initiated its rather radical policy in 1987 after losing two malpractice judgments totaling more than $1.5 million. A policy advising veterans' hospitals to inform patients of their rights to file claims for hospital-caused injuries has been buried in the policy manual of the Department of Veterans Affairs (VA) since 1995. But hospital attorney Ginny Hamm says Lexington is the first in the system to carry out the policy aggressively. Partly in response to the publication of Kraman's article last December, the VA is considering a new policy of actively informing patients of error-caused injuries, according to VA spokesman Terry Jemison. "In recent months we've become much more committed to a corporate atmosphere of reporting errors" at all VA hospitals, Jemison says.

The Kentucky hospital's experience seems to confirm

several studies finding that almost all medical malpractice cases involve a breakdown in the physician-patient relationship. Almost half of newborn-related injury lawsuits in Florida were motivated by a suspicion of a cover-up or a desire for revenge, one study found. [3]

In an accompanying editorial, Albert W. Wu of Johns Hopkins University School of Medicine, in Baltimore, Md., called the Lexington center's approach "the rare solution that is both ethically correct and cost-effective." But Wu also raised some questions about how well the VA's experience would transfer to non-federal hospitals. The VA's patients consist mainly of "older men of limited means, a group that may have finite expectations and a low level of litigiousness," Wu noted. In the Veterans Affairs system, patients can also qualify for compensation without a finding of negligence if their injuries are "service connected." [4]

Hospitals that are privately insured would probably have to persuade their insurance companies that a policy of open disclosure would cost them less in liability and litigation costs than the usual policy of keeping mum, Kraman concedes. But he's convinced that "one lawsuit with a cover-up" could cost 10 times more than the value of the case. "If you make errors and hide in the bushes hoping no one will sue you, it will be impossible for [an injured patient's] lawyers to ignore that," Kraman says. "If you identify the errors and fairly compensate the patients, then there's nothing for the lawyers to do."

---

[1] Under the Federal Tort Claims Act, a veteran can sue a VA hospital for compensatory damages. The United States government is not liable for punitive damages. However, federal judges have wide discretion on awarding damages and some judgments have been in the millions of dollars. In order for the Lexington VA hospital to offer a payment to an injured patient, the patient must first file a claim under the Tort Claims Act and the hospital must offer to settle it before it reaches court.

[2] Steve S. Kraman and Ginny Hamm, "Risk Management: Extreme Honesty May Be the Best Policy," *Annals of Internal Medicine*, Dec. 21, 1999, pp. 963-967.

[3] Cited in Albert W. Wu, "Handling Hospital Errors: Is Disclosure the Best Defense?" *Annals of Internal Medicine*, Dec. 21, 1999, pp. 970-972.

[4] *Ibid.*, p. 971.

specialty. [18] The Medical Society of New York strongly opposes posting doctors' malpractice histories, contending that the data can be misleading because some specialties have higher rates of malpractice suits, as do doctors who take on high-risk cases. The society also argues that there could be internal

politics behind a doctor's dismissal from a hospital. [19]

The issue has taken on greater urgency in New York because of the Zarkin case. At the time that he cut his initials in a patient's abdomen, the Department of Health had already received at least two patient complaints about the doctor, one well

over a year old. But neither the abused patient nor a clinic director who hired Zarkin after the incident could have known that, because health officials were not permitted to say he was being investigated until his license was officially suspended. [20]

Consumer advocates have long argued that the self-policing approach of state medical boards is inadequate for disciplining negligent doctors, in large part because doctors form the majority of every medical board in the country. "It's the foxes guarding the chicken coops because the boards are predominantly physicians," Inlander says. "They are not protecting the public; they are protecting the industry."

The number of doctors disciplined is very low compared with those thought to be negligent or substandard. In 1985, *The New England Journal of Medicine* concluded that 5 percent of the nation's doctors "ought not to be practicing." But that year less than one-half of 1 percent were disciplined.[21] According to the Public Citizen Health Research Group, only 2,731 doctors nationwide were subject to serious discipline in 1996. By contrast, the consumers' group estimates that some 80,000 patients are killed and 234,000 injured as a result of negligence in hospitals.[22] The group's director, Dr. Sidney Wolfe, calls that a "worrisome discrepancy."

Furthermore, consumers argue, disciplinary action is too soft. Only 32 percent of the physicians disciplined for substandard care, incompetence or negligence in 1996 had to stop practicing, even temporarily, according to the Health Research Group.[23]

Wide discrepancies among states' rates of discipline seem to reflect how tough a state's board is on doctors, rather than the quality of its professionals. "People who live in a state with poor doctor discipline such as Massachusetts are at risk of being injured or killed by doctors who would have been thrown out of the practice of medicine in states that are more aggressive like Vermont," Wolfe asserts.

Dr. James Winn, executive vice president of the Federation of State Medical Boards, disputes these criti-

cisms. He says it is not clear what portion of negligence incidents each year is caused by doctors, as opposed to nurses and other hospital professionals. Winn also disagrees that the boards are soft on doctors. "Medical boards come into play when there is a pattern of care that is obviously substandard," Winn says. "I've seen no medical boards giving out a weak slap on the wrist for those kind of doctors."

But Winn believes the boards are hobbled by insufficient reporting of bad doctors. Citing the 1991 Harvard study in New York, Winn notes that only a tiny percent of the state's 7,000 deaths and 877 disability cases caused by negligence resulted in lawsuits. "If it didn't result in a lawsuit, I can guarantee it didn't get reported to the medical board," Winn says. "You can't turn around and say the medical board is doing a weak job because they're not disciplining people they don't even know about."

Currently, the federation believes hospitals are not reporting all cases of negligence to state medical boards, according to Winn, although he says he's not sure how widespread underreporting is. Under a 1986 law establishing a National Practitioner Data Bank, hospitals must report to the data bank and to their state medical boards whenever they deny hospital privileges to a doctor for more than 30 days. Hospitals are required to consult the data bank before hiring a doctor to find out whether the doctor has ever lost hospital privileges, had his license suspended in another state or been the subject of malpractice suits. But hospitals are often reluctant to suspend privileges for fear the doctor will sue them, Winn says.

"We are aware of situations where lawyers for the [disciplined] physician and lawyers for the hospital board create a settlement of a problem [of substandard care] where the

doctor just moves to another locality or state so that they avoid any reporting requirement," Winn says. "So the incident doesn't get reported; the guy just gets out of town."

One of the data bank's main purposes was to keep doctors whose licenses had been lifted by one state from jumping to another state to practice, unbeknown to a state board or hospital. However, under pressure from doctors, Congress closed the only national repository on doctors' disciplinary records to the public. This remains a sore point with consumers.

"Here you are gathering all the information about the lousy things doctors do, and it's closed to the public because the AMA moaned, groaned and donated," Inlander says. "It turns out to be one of the most anti-consumer pieces of legislation ever passed." ∎

BACKGROUND

Common Malady

The plague of medical mistakes in modern American medicine is actually old news. In *Demanding Medical Excellence*, author and health consultant Michael L. Millenson quotes a doctor as early as 1955 describing accidents produced by well-intentioned therapy as "one of the commonest conditions" in a hospital. But Millenson argues that doctors tended to view such accidents as the inevitable cost of practicing increasingly complex modern medicine.[24]

In the 1970s, a sudden surge in malpractice premiums raised the question of whether the cause was improved lawyering or declining doctoring. A large-scale study backed

Chronology

1950s *Some doctors acknowledge that well-intentioned physicians are injuring patients in hospitals, but the medical profession takes no active steps to combat mistakes.*

1955
Journal of the American Medical Association publishes article by David Barr calling accidents from medical treatment one of the "commonest" conditions in hospitals.

———— • ————

1970s *Malpractice insurance premiums skyrocket, raising questions about how much litigation stems from faulty medical care.*

1978
Study of California hospitals backed by California Medical Association finds medical treatment is killing more Americans per year than in the entire Vietnam War.

———— • ————

1990s *Widely publicized cases of patients killed or hurt by hospital mistakes and new studies finding widespread errors raise public awareness of medical mistakes.*

1991
Harvard study of New York hospitals is published in *New England Journal of Medicine* finding substantial number of patients die from medical errors

— 98,000 each year nationwide in today's terms.

1992
Harvard study is corroborated by study of Colorado and Utah hospital patients who die from errors — or 44,000 Americans each year.

1993
Ray McEachern founds a patients'-rights group, the Association for Responsible Medicine in Tampa, Fla., after a doctor's mistake leaves his wife, Pat, partially paralyzed.

February 1995
Willie King, a retired equipment operator, has the wrong leg amputated at a Tampa hospital.

March 1995
Boston Globe reports that health columnist Betsy Lehman died from a chemotherapy overdose because of a hospital staff error.

December 1995
Seven-year-old Ben Kolb enters Stuart, Fla., hospital for minor ear operation and dies after being injected with the wrong medication.

1996
The number of medical errors reported at Florida hospitals doubles a year after the state began conducting on-site audits at hospitals.

September 1999
Philadelphia Inquirer series reports hundreds injured and 66 killed by errors at a Philadelphia hospital after records are opened in bankruptcy proceedings.

Nov. 29, 1999
Institute of Medicine issues

report urging the nation to cut the death and injury rate from medical errors.

———— • ————

2000 *Members of Congress and administration officials study ways to implement Institute of Medicine proposals to reduce errors.*

Jan. 25, 2000
Senate Appropriations Subcommittee on Labor holds hearings on medical errors.

Jan. 26, 2000
Senate Committee on Health, Education, Labor and Pensions holds first of a series of hearings on medical mistakes.

Feb. 8, 2000
Sens. Arlen Specter, R-Pa., and Tom Harkin, D-Iowa, introduce legislation encouraging states to report hospital errors. The bill would give grants to states to collect information on medical errors and to pass it on to the federal Agency for Healthcare Research and Quality. Responding to concerns of the American Medical Association and the American Hospital Association, all information collected by the federal government would be barred from use in pretrial discovery or Freedom of Information Act inquiries.

Feb. 22, 2000
President Clinton calls for mandatory reporting of medical errors.

by the California Medical Association sampled over 20,000 medical charts from 23 California hospitals in 1974. It concluded that one patient in 20 was harmed by treatment. On a nationwide basis, the California study suggested hospital care produced 121,000 deaths every year. [25]

If that statistic was right, it meant that medical treatment was killing twice as many Americans in a single year as died in the Vietnam War.

The 1991 Harvard study, which reviewed 30,000 of New York's 1984 hospital discharges, reported figures similar to the California findings. Extrapolated on a nationwide basis to current-day figures — the more than 33 million admissions to U.S. hospitals in 1997 — the Harvard study suggests that as many as 98,000 patients die each year from medical errors. [26] This figure has been widely quoted as the upper end of the range reported by the IOM study.

Disability or prolonged hospitalization caused by medical management occurred in 3.7 percent of the hospitalizations, the New York study found. The proportion of such "adverse events" attributable to errors and therefore preventable was 58 percent. Twenty-eight percent of the "adverse events" were linked to negligence. Of those, almost 14 percent resulted in death, and almost 3 percent caused permanent, disabling injuries. Drug complications were the most common adverse event, followed by wound infections and technical complications. [27]

The Harvard findings have since been corroborated by a study of hospital discharges in Colorado and Utah in 1992. Extrapolation to current nationwide hospital admissions led the IOM to its lower-range estimate that at least 44,000 Americans die in hospitals each year as a result of preventable medical errors. [28] Although the Harvard findings have been widely quoted since the

IOM report came out last year, at the time of their publication in 1991, the headlines announcing the study "changed nothing at all," Millenson writes. The following year, a study of Harvard's own hospitals found injuries from preventable drug errors were "common." [29]

Perhaps more effective in shaking up public complacency about hospital treatment was a *Boston Globe* report in March 1995 that a young health columnist for the newspaper, Betsy Lehman, had died of a chemotherapy overdose. Lehman's death at Boston's Dana-Farber Cancer Institute had been due to a rather simple mistake: Her physician believed that the figure showing the total dose of the chemotherapy drug over a four-day period was the amount to be given each day for four days. [30]

Even more horrifying, the error was only discovered three months later by Dana-Farber clerks — not clinicians — during a routine review of the records. [31]

A series in the *Philadelphia Inquirer* in September of last year also shook up health-industry observers. The newspaper's search of medical records at the Medical College of Pennsylvania hospital found that hundreds of patients had been seriously injured and at least 66 had died after medical mistakes from 1988 to 1989. The paper discovered that its numbers mirrored estimates by Harvard's Leape that 1 million patients nationwide are injured each year by errors. [32]

The series also highlighted the fact that patients are rarely informed of mistakes. In a 1991 study, researchers at the University of California found only 24 percent of medical residents told patients or their families of mistakes. [33]

It's not clear whether medical errors are on the rise, but some observers fear the problem may be growing as more drugs are pre-

scribed, technology becomes more complex and untrained staff are put in jobs beyond their competency. From 1983 to 1993, medication errors produced a twofold increase in inpatient deaths and an eightfold increase in outpatient deaths, according to the IOM. [34]

Starting in the 1990s, hospitals searching for ways to cut overhead actually had cleaning and maintenance staff handle some tasks once performed by nurses, giving them minimal training to operate or interpret results from complex machinery, says Mary Foley, president of the American Nurses Association.

"You do wonder whether we are back to the way it is in the Middle East, where you need a family 'sitter' to sit there and make sure everything is handled correctly," Foley says. "Someone terribly ill is the last person who can look up and say, 'Is that the right antibiotic?' " ∎

CURRENT SITUATION

Harsh Criticism

The existing system of hospital regulation has come in for harsh criticism from consumers' groups. Most of the mud slinging has been aimed at the main body charged with inspecting and accrediting hospitals, the Joint Commission for Accreditation of Healthcare Organizations.

"The joint commission is essentially a wholly owned subsidiary of the hospitals," says Public Citizen's Wolfe, noting that hospitals pay the commission to inspect them. "It does a lousy job. It should be abolished."

At Issue:

Should hospitals be required to report deaths and serious injuries resulting from their medical mistakes?

BILL CLINTON
President of the United States

FROM STATEMENT DELIVERED AT THE WHITE HOUSE, FEB. 22, 2000

*l*ast December, I directed our . . . health-care quality task force to analyze the [Institute of Medicine] study [and] to report back with recommendations about how we can follow the suggestions they made to protect patients and promote safety. This morning I received the task force report, and I am proud to accept all its recommendations.

Our goal is to . . . reduce preventable medical errors by 50 percent within five years. Today I announce our national action plan to reach that goal. . . .

First . . . I propose the creation of a new center for quality improvement and patient safety. My budget includes $20 million to support the center, which will invest in research, develop national goals, issue an annual report on the state of patient safety and translate findings into better practices and policies.

Second, we will ensure that each and every one of the 6,000 hospitals participating in Medicare has patient-safety programs in place to prevent medical errors, including medication mistakes. . . .

Third, as we seek to make sure that the right systems are in place, we need to make sure they are working. Today I am releasing our plan for a nationwide state-based system of reporting medical errors, to be phased-in over time. This will include mandatory reporting of preventable medical errors that cause death or serious injury and voluntary reporting of other medical mistakes. . . .

We also wanted to replace what some call a culture of silence with a culture of safety — an environment that encourages others to talk about errors, what caused them and how to stop them in the first place. So we'll support legislation that protects provider and patient confidentiality, but that does not undermine individual rights to remedies when they have, in fact, been harmed. . . .

Finally, I'm . . . calling on the Food and Drug Administration to develop new standards to help prevent medical errors caused by drugs that sound similar or packaging that looks similar. In addition, we'll develop new label standards that highlight common drug interactions and dosage errors.

Taken together, these actions represent the most significant effort our nation has ever made to reduce medical errors. It's a balance, a common-sense approach based on prevention, not punishment, on problem solving, not blame-placing.

NANCY W. DICKEY, M.D.
Immediate past president, American Medical Association

STATEMENT, FEB. 22, 2000

*t*he AMA supports President Clinton's goal of reducing health-system errors and improving patient safety, and we agree with many of his proposals.

However, we are concerned that the proposal for mandatory reporting will not improve patient safety and may, in fact, have the perverse result of driving errors underground. Effective aviation safety programs have taught us that a culture of safety is created by avoiding a culture of blame. The same principle holds true for the health system.

The AMA and the medical-specialty societies have been pioneers in the effort to reduce health-system errors. Based on our work, we agree with many of the president's proposals for steps that the private sector and government can take to improve patient safety.

We support the president's call for increased funds to research errors and disseminate the findings to improve health care. We also concur with the proposal to modify pharmaceutical packaging and marketing practices to reduce medication errors. Prompt action is needed on many consensus areas for improving patient safety.

However, the AMA is opposed to the expansion of mandatory reporting of medical errors. There is no evidence to show that mandatory reporting improves patient safety. Before we expand data collection activities, we need to analyze existing state systems to determine the most effective use of finite resources.

The AMA appreciates President Clinton's statement of support for protecting the confidentiality of peer-review activities.

But we are concerned that the protections do not go far enough to promote the type of information sharing that would help create a culture of safety where all members of the health system can learn from and prevent errors.

About 70 percent of the organization's funding comes from the fees it collects for inspections, but that's not much different from an accounting firm whose clients pay it by the audit, responds commission President Dennis S. O'Leary.

In Wolfe's view, the IOM's call for a nationwide, mandatory-reporting system for medical errors is a "an indirect slap at the joint commission because if they were doing their job, they would get these data and make them public."

Over the past three years, less than 1 percent of the 5,000 hospitals the organization inspects have failed to receive accreditation. The commission's efforts to get hospitals to report serious injuries or deaths from errors are equally unimpressive. Over a five-year period, the organization received fewer than 500 reports from the 5,000 hospitals it inspects, fewer than would be expected from one large hospital, critics say.

"These are pathetically small numbers," O'Leary agrees. "We are a classic example of why voluntary reporting doesn't work." Hospitals "are afraid to report in the absence of confidentiality protections, because they think it will create a feast for trial lawyers."

The AHA's Wade confirms that hospitals became increasingly mistrustful of the joint commission once states used the organization as a proxy for state licensure, and the federal government tied conditions for participating in Medicare to accreditation. "The hospitals say they're paying the joint commission to be a consultant," Wade says. "They ask 'Are you a performance-improvement consultant or the cop from Washington, D.C.?'"

Both organizations say the solution to honest reporting is providing federal guarantees of confidentiality so hospital staff won't be afraid to report errors. O'Leary adds that he thinks it is just a matter of

time before mandatory reporting goes into effect.

Like an Army base that gets a new coat of paint just before inspection, hospitals spend months getting ready for the joint commission's regular, announced inspections every three years. That may be one reason the commission rarely flunks a hospital for accreditation, critics charge. Even for "surprise" inspections, hospitals are routinely given at least 24 hours' notice. In the wake of the IOM report and an extremely critical report from the inspector general of the Department of Health and Human Services (HHS) last year, the commission has announced that it will start making surprise inspections without prior notice this year.

Doctors' Offices

While most estimates of medical errors focus on hospitals, injurious mistakes could be occurring at an even higher rate in doctors' offices, some consumer advocates believe. "The worst place to have anything done is the doctor's office," Inlander says. "No one is monitoring them."

In recent years, patients have been undergoing a growing range of elective surgeries, from laser eye surgery to knee operations, in doctors' offices and other types of outpatient clinics. Such facilities are rarely subject to state requirements for reporting error-related injuries. Most don't have to undergo any kind of licensing inspection. As a result, there's little hard data about what happens.

Nevertheless, some recent reports are disturbing. The death rate for liposuction, the popular cosmetic surgery performed mainly in doctors' offices and clinics, is 20 to 60 times higher than the death rate for all operations performed in hospitals, according to a recent study. In liposuction, fat is sucked out of the thighs, bellies and other parts of the

body, usually by plastic surgeons. More than 170,000 people undergo the procedure each year. The study, published in *Plastic and Reconstructive Surgery*, found that for every 5,000 liposuction procedures from 1994 to 1998, one patient died. [35]

Harvard's Leape calls that death rate "pretty scary." The IOM panel has recommended that mandatory reporting of medical errors should be required initially of hospitals but eventually should be expanded to walk-in settings as well. Leape says the few studies of major procedures performed outside hospitals suggest "their risk of errors and injuries is about the same as in the hospital," and possibly even worse. ■

OUTLOOK

Doctors vs. Consumers?

As Congress begins drafting legislation aimed at tackling medical errors, the interests of hospitals and doctors already are colliding with those of consumers and employers. On Feb. 8, the first major bill — the Medical Error Reduction Act of 2000 — was introduced by Sens. Arlen Specter, R-Pa., and Tom Harkin, D-Iowa. It would keep all medical information collected by the federal government confidential. The bill would give grants to states to collect information on medical errors and to pass it on to the federal Agency for Healthcare Research and Quality. Responding to concerns of the AMA and AHA, all information collected by the federal government would be barred from use in pretrial discovery or from inquiries under the Freedom of Information Act.

Clinton's Medical-Error Initiative

On Feb. 22, President Clinton announced he was endorsing virtually every recommendation of the Institute of Medicine, including its goal of reducing preventable medical errors by 50 percent within five years. The president's initiative included:

❑ Support for a nationwide system of mandatory reporting for hospitals, phased in over three years. The president is urging state health agencies to require that hospitals report any errors causing death or serious injury, with hospitals publicly identified.

❑ Encouraging the development of voluntary reporting of errors that do not harm patients.

❑ Support for legislation that protects hospital analyses of medical errors and the identity of doctors from legal discovery for malpractice suits. But the president said patients or their family members should have access to information about an error that caused them serious injury or death.

❑ Regulations requiring the more than 6,000 hospitals participating in Medicare to carry out programs to reduce errors, such as computerized drug prescribing by doctors.

❑ New standards to be developed by the Food and Drug Administration to help prevent medical errors caused by drug names.

❑ Creation of a new Center for Quality Improvement and Patient Safety.

❑ The use of computerized order entry for drugs at all Veterans Affairs hospitals this year.

❑ A mandatory error-reporting system in the 500 military hospitals and clinics system serving over 8 million patients.

Such "closed-to-the-public" provisions make Inlander suspicious of efforts to create a national collection system. "The only other time the feds did anything like this was when they created the National Practitioner Data Bank — and it's closed to the public," he observes. Consumers should have access to individual hospitals' error rates, Inlander says, because "That's the only thing that's going to help me [as a consumer]. I'm the one that has to go in there."

To answer some of the questions raised about the relative merits of public disclosure and mandatory vs. voluntary reporting, Specter and Harkin have proposed demonstration projects at 15 hospitals throughout the nation. One-third of the facilities would have to inform HHS of any medical errors; one-third would also inform the patient and/or his family; and the rest would only inform HHS of errors on a voluntary basis.

On Feb. 22, President Clinton called for a nationwide system of reporting medical errors, similar to the system used by airlines to report aviation safety hazards. Rather than trying to impose a federal requirement now, he is pressuring the states to adopt mandatory reporting require-ments within three years. Clinton endorsed virtually all of the recommendations made in November by the Institute of Medicine. [36]

Previous statements by administration officials had worried some lawmakers about the administration's commitment to mandatory reporting. [37] Several administration officials recently said they were not convinced of the effectiveness of mandatory reporting or were concerned that disclosing hospitals' and doctors' names could inhibit reporting. [38] However, the president sided with consumers in proposing that hospitals be publicly identified when reporting mistakes that cause harm.

Sens. Joseph I. Lieberman, D-Conn., and Charles E. Grassley, R-Iowa, are drafting legislation that may require hospitals to report all medical mistakes as a condition of receiving Medicaid and Medicare funds. And Sen. Edward M. Kennedy, D-Mass, is developing legislation to encourage reporting of medical mistakes along the lines of the IOM report. [39]

No matter what the government does, big-business leaders say they are committed to putting economic pressure on hospitals to become safer. The Leapfrog business group will urge employers to reward hospitals that take at least three steps shown to save lives:

• requiring doctors to enter prescriptions on a computer;

• issuing report cards showing mortality and complication rates for surgical procedures, as Pennsylvania does; and

• keeping specially trained personnel on duty in intensive-care units.

The attention to medical errors also has given publicity to new technologies that could help prevent mistakes, such as putting bar-coded wrist bands on patients to identify them and packaging medication with bar-coded labels. [40]

For its part, the IOM has proposed a raft of practical solutions, from periodically re-examining doctors and nurses to stocking only diluted solutions of dangerous drugs on patient wards. Taken together, the IOM says the steps it is proposing could help the nation reduce medical errors by at least 50 percent over the next five years. As evidence, it points to the aggressive, successful efforts to build a safe aviation system.

Meanwhile, the IOM appears to have achieved its immediate goal: "to break [the] cycle of inaction." [41]

Notes

[1] Testimony of Debra Malone, Hearing on Medical Mistakes, Dec. 13, 1999, U.S. Senate Appropriations Subcommittee on Labor, Health and Human Services, Education and Related Agencies, transcript by Federal Document Clearing House, pp. 21-23.

[2] Linda T. Kohn et al., eds., "To Err is Human: Building a Safer Health System, Committee on Quality of Health Care in America," Institute of Medicine, National Academy Press (1999).

[3] Malone, *op. cit.*, p. 21.

[4] Ann Schrader, "Officials Find Hospital Errors Led to '97 Death; Presbyterian-St. Luke's Cited in 8 Areas," *Denver Post*, April 14, 1999, p. B-01.

[5] Kohn, et al., *op. cit.*, p. 167.

[6] The program is described in Lucian L. Leape et al., "Promoting Patient Safety by Preventing Medical Error," *Journal of the American Medical Association*, Oct. 28, 1998, pp. 1444-1447.

[7] Kohn et al., *op. cit.*, p. 109.

[8] Sixteen states and the District of Columbia have a law requiring hospitals to report unexpected patient deaths or serious injuries from medical treatment, according to a March 1999 phone survey conducted by the Joint Commission on Accreditation of Healthcare Organizations: Alabama, Alaska, District of Columbia, Florida, Idaho, Iowa, Louisiana, Massachusetts, Minnesota, Nevada, New Jersey, New York, Pennsylvania, Tennessee, Texas, Washington and Wisconsin. According to the Institute of Medicine, additional states with mandatory reporting systems include California, Colorado, Kansas, Mississippi, Rhode Island and South Dakota.

[9] Troyen A. Brennan et al. "Incidence of Adverse Events and Negligence in Hospitalized Patients," *New England Journal of Medicine*, Feb. 7, 1991, p. 373. The study estimated 6,895 deaths from negligent care in New York in 1984.

[10] Jennifer Steinhauer and Edward Wong, "How Doctor Got Work after Carving into Patient," *The New York Times*, Jan. 27, 2000, pp. B1, B5.

[11] This incident is described in Michael L. Millenson, *Demanding Medical Excellence* (1997), pp. 208-209.

[12] Andrea Gerlin, "Mum is often the word when caregivers stumble," *Philadelphia Inquirer*, Sept 14, 1999.

[13] Statement by Arnold Milstein, MD, Medical Director, Pacific Business Group on Health on Behalf of The Business Roundtable before the Senate Committee on Health, Education, Labor and Pensions, Jan. 25, 2000.

[14] "Statement of the American Medical Association to the Senate Committee on Health, Education, Labor and Pensions, by Nancy W. Dickey, M.D., immediate past president. Re: Preventing Health System Errors," Jan. 25, 2000, p. 3.

[15] For example, a study of a Chicago hospital found that almost 18 percent of patients had a serious adverse event related to inappropriate care but only 1 percent of them filed a claim for compensation. Cited in Albert W. Wu, "Handling Hospital Errors: Is Disclosure the Best Defense?" *Annals of Internal Medicine*, Dec. 21, 1999, pp. 970-971.

[16] According to the Federation of State Medical Boards, Kentucky is the only state where complaints against a doctor are a matter of public record prior to investigation and action by the state medical board.

[17] Kohn et al., *op. cit.*, p. 123.

[18] Other states that provide data on malpractice claims include California, Florida, Idaho and Tennessee, according to Public Citizen's Health Research Group. California, Florida, Idaho and Massachusetts report disciplinary actions taken by hospitals against physicians on the state medical boards' Web sites.

[19] Jennifer Steinhauer, "Albany Bill Would Help Patients Learn Doctors' Discipline Records," *The New York Times*, Dec. 27, 1999, p. 1.

[20] Steinhauer and Wong, *op. cit.*

[21] Millenson, *op. cit.*, p. 70.

[22] Public Citizen's Health Research Group, "15,638 Questionable Doctors — 1998 Edition."

[23] *Ibid.*

[24] Millenson, *op. cit.*, p. 56.

[25] *Ibid.*, p. 58-59.

[26] Kohn et al., *op. cit.*, p. 1.

[27] *Ibid.*, p. 25.

[28] *Ibid.*, p. 26.

[29] Millenson, *op. cit.*, p. 63.

[30] *Ibid.*, p. 52, 54.

[31] *Ibid.*, p. 52

[32] Andrea Gerlin, "Health Care's Deadly Secret: Accidents Routinely Happen," *Philadelphia Inquirer*, Sept. 12, 1999.

[33] Cited in Gerlin, "Mum is the Word," *op cit.*

[34] Kohn et al., p. 28.

[35] Cited in Robert Davis, "Liposuction death rate 'unacceptable,' " *USA Today*, Jan. 18, 2000, p. 1A.

[36] "Moving Fast on Patient Safety," (editorial), *The New York Times*, Dec. 8, 1999, p. 22.

[37] U.S. Senate press release, "Senators Push Federal Agencies to Move More Aggressively on Medical Errors in Major Programs: Lieberman, Grassley, Kerrey, Nickles send letters demanding reports from HHS, DOD, OPM and VA on action plans," Feb. 8, 2000.

[38] Robert Pear, "U.S. Health Officials Reject Plan to Report Medical Mistakes," *The New York Times*, Jan. 24, 2000, p. 14.

[39] See Mary Agnes Carey and Rebecca Adams, "Deadly Medical Mistakes: Congress Urged to Go Slow in Weighing Legislative Fix," *CQ Weekly*, Jan. 29, 2000, p. 188.

[40] See Milt Freudenheim, "Corrective Medicine: New Technology Helps Health Care Avoid Mistakes," *The New York Times*, Feb. 3, 2000, pp. C1, C26.

[41] Kohn et al., *op. cit.*, p. 3.

FOR MORE INFORMATION

Agency for Healthcare Research and Quality, 2101 Jefferson St., Suite 501, Rockville, Md. 20852; (301) 594-1364; www.ahcpr.gov. This recently renamed arm of the Department of Health and Human Services supports research to improve quality and decrease errors in health care.

Institute of Medicine, 2101 Constitution Ave. N.W., Washington, D.C. 20418; (202) 334-2000; www.nationalacademies.org. This arm of the National Academy of Sciences published "To Err is Human," an influential report on medical errors.

National Patient Safety Foundation at the AMA, 515 North State St., 8th Floor, Chicago, Ill. 60610; (312) 464-4848; www.npsf.org. This American Medical Association group studies why errors occur in health care.

People's Medical Society, 462 Walnut St., Allentown, Pa. 18102; (610) 770-1670; www.peoplesmed.org. This national consumer organization aims to make the health-care system more responsive to consumers.

Bibliography
Selected Sources Used

Books

Inlander, Charles B., and Ed Weiner, *Take this Book to the Hospital With You*, St. Martin's Paperbacks, 1997.
Published by the People's Medical Society, this book offers tips on protecting oneself in the hospital and has a section on hospital-caused injuries.

Millenson, Michael L., *Demanding Medical Excellence: Doctors and Accountability in the Information Age*, University of Chicago Press, 1997.
This well-written book by a former *Chicago Tribune* journalist contains chapters on the growing understanding of medical errors and on efforts by Salt Lake City's LDS hospital to prevent mistakes.

Articles

Brennan, Troyen A. et al., "Incidence of Adverse Events and Negligence in Hospitalized Patients: Results of the Harvard Medical Practice Study I," *The New England Journal of Medicine*, Feb. 7, 1991, pp. 370-376.
This landmark study of New York hospital patients established the basis for today's estimate that 98,000 patients nationwide die annually from medical errors.

Freudenheim, Milt, "Corrective Medicine: New Technology Helps Health Care Avoid Mistakes," *The New York Times*, Feb. 3, 2000, p. C1.
This article discusses high-tech measures being taken by hospitals to combat mistakes.

Gerlin, Andrea, "Health Care's Deadly Secret: Accidents Routinely Happen," *The Philadelphia Inquirer*, Sept. 12, 1999; Part I of a four-part series. The entire series can be accessed at http://health.philly.com/specials/mistakes/hosp12.asp.
The *Inquirer*'s series on "Medical Mistakes" was touched off when bankruptcy proceedings opened the records of the Medical College of Pennsylvania, revealing that errors had injured hundreds of patients.

Kilborn, Peter T., "Ambitious Effort to Cut Mistakes in U.S. Hospitals," *The New York Times*, Dec. 26, 1999, p. 1A.
Reactions to an Institute of Medicine report on medical errors — from business groups, the hospital accrediting agency and members of Congress — constitute "the most ambitious effort ever to confront mistakes in the nation's hospitals," the author concludes.

Kraman, Steve S., and Ginny Hamm, "Risk Management: Extreme Honesty May be the Best Policy," *Annals of Internal Medicine*, Dec. 21, 1999, pp. 963-967.
In Lexington, Ky., the Veterans Affairs hospital's unusual policy of informing patients when they are the victims of medical mistakes appears to control malpractice costs.

Pear, Robert, "U.S. Health Officials Reject Plan to Report Medical Mistakes," *The New York Times*, Jan. 24, 2000, p. 14.
Some federal health officials express doubts about the value of a mandatory reporting system for medical errors as the administration conducts a review of the Institute of Medicine's proposals.

Shapiro, Joseph P., "Doctoring a Sickly System," *U.S. News & World Report*, Dec. 13, 1999, p. 60.
The Veterans Affairs hospital system is becoming a model for quality improvement, the article says, such as scanning bar-coded wristbands on patients to check against medication mistakes.

Reports and Studies

Demian, Larry et al., Survey of Doctor Disciplinary Information on State Medical Board Web Sites, Public Citizen Health Research Group, Feb. 2, 2000, www.citizen.org/hrg/publications/1506.htm.
This report by a consumer group found that 10 states provide no information on their Web sites.

Kohn, Linda T. et al., eds., To Err Is Human: Building a Safer System, Institute of Medicine, National Academy Press, 1999.
This report by an IOM blue-ribbon panel gained widespread media attention for pointing out that more people die in hospitals than car crashes. It proposes mandatory reporting of hospital medical errors.

Office of the Medical Inspector, Veterans Health Administration, Department of Veterans Affairs, Special Report: VA Patient Safety Event Registry: First Nineteen Months of Reported Cases Summary and Analysis; June 1997 through December 1998, July 15, 1998.
The VA's first systematic attempt to require reports of medical mistakes from VA hospitals documented almost 3,000 incidents of medical errors and adverse events from medical treatment.

Public Citizen Health Research Group, 16,638 Questionable Doctors, March 1998, www.citizen.org/hrg/qdsite/PUBLICATIONS.
This report rates states according to the toughness of disciplinary measure they take against doctors whose competence is under question.

14 Internet Privacy

DAVID MASCI

Every day, millions of on-line consumers turn to the Internet to find everything from tips on travel to advice on healthy eating.

Many click on the popular GeoCities site. Not surprisingly, GeoCities wants something in return: marketable personal information. To encourage visitors to fill out questionnaires and reveal their names, incomes and other personal data, GeoCities offers them free E-mail accounts and their own Web home page.

In the past, GeoCities promised that the personal information being collected would not be shared "with anyone without your permission." But on Aug. 13, 1998, the Federal Trade Commission (FTC) accused GeoCities of breaking its promise.

"GeoCities has misled its customers, both children and adults, by not telling the truth about how it was using their personal information," said Jodie Bernstein, director of the FTC's Bureau of Consumer Protection, in a statement released that day.

According to the commission, GeoCities shared information about more than 2 million of its Web users with outside parties without receiving or even asking for permission. The data was used to create advertisements and solicitations personalized to appeal to the original GeoCities visitors.

"GeoCities was collecting all this sensitive information and the people [who had completed questionnaires] didn't realize what was going on," says Deirdre Mulligan, staff counsel at the Center for Democracy and Technology. "They didn't know what they were giving away."

Of course, much of the Internet, almost by definition, is not private.

From *The CQ Researcher,*
November 6, 1998.

AP Photo/Murrae Haynes

Indeed, the new medium connects people around the world in a way that few could have dreamed about. Created by the Pentagon in the 1970s as an alternate means of communication during wartime, the net now offers tens of millions of ordinary people access to an amount of information that would dwarf what is stored in the Library of Congress.

The Internet has been hailed as the most important communications development since Guttenburg invented movable type more than 500 years ago. As with the advent of printing, the creation of the Internet has led to an information explosion that is rapidly transforming almost every sphere of life, from education to communications to retail commerce.

The number of people on-line is growing exponentially. Just four years ago, there were only about 3 million Internet users around the world, mostly in the United States. At the beginning of this year, the number had ballooned to nearly 60 million in the U.S. alone and more than 100 million worldwide. [1]

Along with an increase in the number of people on-line has come a corresponding growth in commercial use. Established retailers and a host of newcomers have created Web sites to hawk everything from rare books to sex toys. By the end of last year, 10 million people worldwide had purchased a product or service on-line. [2]

But the Internet, like most new tech-

nologies, presents challenges as well as tremendous opportunities for society. Every day, millions of Americans disclose personal information about themselves when they buy goods or services from an on-line business or simply visit Web sites. In many cases, companies that operate these sites offer few or no assurances as to how this information will be used. Many, in fact, trade or sell consumers' names and addresses and other data to retailers and marketers. Other companies have sprung up solely for the purpose of collecting and selling personal information.

The growth of such on-line enterprises has prompted many policymakers and others to question whether they have the right to acquire and, more importantly, pass on personal data to third parties. And if so, should the Web sites be required to tell consumers what they intend to do with the birth dates, E-mail addresses and telephone numbers they are collecting?

According to an FTC study released on June 4, only 14 percent of commercial Web sites publicly disclosed their privacy policies. At the same time, 92 percent, collected personal information from users who visited them. [3] Another survey, conducted by *Business Week* in March, found that non-users of the Internet cite privacy concerns as their main reason for not going on-line. [4]

For its part, GeoCities acknowledged no wrongdoing and paid no fine. Yet, as part of a settlement with the FTC, it did agree to establish and enforce a new privacy policy. Now, when on-line consumers complete the GeoCities' questionnaire, they are told that the information will be released to outside parties.

Indeed, the FTC could not force GeoCities to stop passing on personal information. It is only empowered to act against what it sees as "deceptive

Most Web Sites Collect Personal Information

The vast majority of Web sites collect personal information from on-line consumers, and most collect several types of information, such as name, address, Social Security number and birth date.

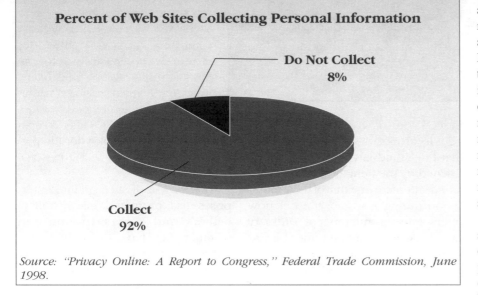

Percent of Web Sites Collecting Personal Information

Do Not Collect
8%

Collect
92%

Source: "Privacy Online: A Report to Congress," Federal Trade Commission, June 1998.

practices," such as claiming you're not passing on private information when you actually are. "We are not trying to tell them what their privacy policies ought to be," said Toby Levin, staff counsel at the FTC. [5]

That's part of the problem, say many privacy advocates. They point out that because there is no law protecting privacy on-line, Web sites are not obligated to do so. In fact, say some, the GeoCities case may end up doing more harm than good. "It has had a perversely undesirable effect in that it has convinced companies on-line not to post privacy policies so as to avoid any [FTC] scrutiny," says Jason Catlett, president of Junkbusters Corp., a New Jersey on-line-privacy protection firm. In other words, if there is no posted policy, there can be no deceptive practices.

Privacy advocates like Catlett say that the current system, where Web sites establish and enforce their own privacy policies if at all, is terribly flawed. They are urging the Clinton administration and Congress to step in with legislation aimed at protecting consumer privacy on-line. "We need to lay down some rules, simple do's and don'ts, for on-line privacy," says Jerry Berman, executive director at the Center for Democracy and Technology, a civil liberties group that focuses on technology issues. Among other things, such rules would give consumers the right to see the information collected about them and the ability to stop its dissemination to third parties.

In addition, Berman and others favor the creation of a privacy agency within the federal government to enforce the new rules and advise businesses on how to establish effective privacy policies. The FTC, they say, does not have the staff to police the Internet for evidence of deceptive practices (its current mandate), let alone enforce new privacy laws. [6]

Privacy advocates admit that there are Web sites, usually created by large businesses, that do have adequate privacy policies. But the majority of on-line sites offer consumers little or no protection when it comes to maintaining the confidentiality of personal information.

The computer and retail industries argue, however, that government regulation is unnecessary and unrealistic. To begin with, they say, the Internet is still taking shape, making talk of rigid rules on privacy unrealistic. "At this stage, trying to nail down some policy with legislation might not work and could end up retarding the growth of on-line commerce," says Russ Bodoff, the general manager for the Better Business Bureau On-line, an industry group that aims to make self-regulation work.

Bodoff says that his organization and others like it have helped hundreds of Web sites create and enforce privacy standards. Already, supporters of self-regulation say, most of the biggest and most well-known sites have privacy policies. "With a little bit of guidance, self-regulation can be as effective as legislation," Bodoff claims.

Finally, self-regulation boosters argue, the on-line industry has an interest in guaranteeing privacy since consumers who feel abused by Web sites won't visit them again. Says Chet Dalzell, a spokesman for the Direct Marketing Association: "Marketers and retailers on-line know that they have to extend a certain amount of privacy and make sure transactions are secure in order to ensure that customers will visit or shop at their Web site."

As Dalzell suggests, privacy doesn't just entail creating a policy or rules to protect the confidentiality of information. Transactions and other communications must be secure from those who do not want to follow any rules that might be set.

Computers, as well as phones and other communications tools, secure the transfer of data by using encryption technology. Encryption software protects information by scrambling it into an unreadable code at its source and unscrambling it when it is received.

Encryption is already widely used on-line in the United States to protect everything from sensitive E-mail to credit card numbers. But the intelligence and law-enforcement communities are wary of the potential for the misuse of this technology.

Currently, the United States bans the export of powerful encryption technology. The intelligence community argues that such controls are needed to keep powerful technology out of the hands of America's enemies, who would use it to thwart U.S. intelligence-gathering efforts.

"If this were easily obtainable, our ability to keep apprised of what terrorists and other enemies were doing would be severely hampered," says Dan Smith, chief of research for the Center for Defense Information, a pro-defense think tank. The ban should be kept in place even if it only delays states like Iraq and Libya from acquiring sophisticated encryption technology. "At least we have more time . . . to stay one step ahead of them," he says.

At the same time, the law-enforcement community is pressing Congress to require software makers to install a "key" or "back door" in their encryption programs, making it possible for state and federal officers to decode encrypted data. "When we obtain a court-ordered warrant, we should be able to access the encrypted information, just like we can wiretap phones and search homes today," says Charles Barry Smith, a special agent and encryption expert at the FBI. Most programs today contain no such key, often making data retrieval difficult if not impossible.

Smith and others say that criminals and terrorists are increasingly using computers to store information and to communicate with each other. And, they claim, strong encryption programs are already hampering law

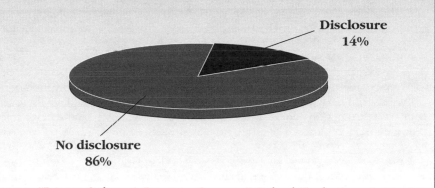

Few Sites Disclose Information Policy

Less than 15 percent of the Web sites that collect personal information tell consumers who is collecting the information and how it will be used.

Percent of Web Sites With an Information Disclosure

Disclosure 14%

No disclosure 86%

Source: "Privacy Online: A Report to Congress," Federal Trade Commission, June 1998

enforcement's efforts to conduct surveillance and gather evidence in many cases.

But privacy advocates and the computer industry oppose both existing and proposed limits on encryption technology. To begin with, they argue, export controls are merely hurting American companies, which are losing this segment of the overseas software market to European and Asian corporations. "By hamstringing U.S. companies, we've simply created an opportunity for foreign firms to take over a market that should be ours," says Solveig Singleton, director of information studies at the CATO Institute. Some of this advanced, foreign encryption is available to America's enemies, defeating the purpose of the export limits in the first place.

In addition, privacy advocates argue, the proposed "key" to allow law enforcement to unlock encrypted information defeats the whole purpose of protecting your data. "It doesn't make any sense: Why would you want encryption that could be opened by a third party?" asks Marc

Rotenberg, director of the Electronic Privacy Information Center, which promotes on line privacy and other civil liberties.

Questions concerning encryption or the regulation of Web sites will take on increasing importance as more and more people spend more and more time on-line. Other privacy concerns also have come to the fore. For instance, many experts, including some in the business community, supported the recent successful effort in Congress to enact legal protections for children's privacy on-line. Many of the same people also favor some sort of special protection for medical records and other very sensitive information.

As these and other issues are debated, here are some of the questions Internet experts are asking:

Should the federal government set privacy standards for the Internet?

On Friday, July 31, Vice President Al Gore delivered what was dubbed as a "major" speech on Internet pri-

Data-Collection Business Is Booming

In today's hyperconnected world, it's not difficult to find personal information about someone. Most search engines have "people finders" or "personal locators" that supply telephone numbers, street addresses, and even directions to people's houses. For a little money, say $25, one can obtain someone's Social Security number, previous addresses and possibly their driving record.

And that's just the tip of the iceberg. "Most people don't realize how much information about them is out there," says Deirdra Mulligan, staff counsel at the Center for Democracy and Technology.

"We should be worried about this," agrees Mary Griffin, counsel for the Consumers Union of the United States. "People just don't know how little privacy protection they have when it comes to this stuff."

Particularly worrisome, say privacy advocates like Griffin, are the hundreds of companies in the United States today that devote themselves to collecting an unfathomable amount of information about almost everyone in the country. Some can provide detailed financial histories, including information about bank accounts, credit card balances and loans. Others offer employment records or track buying habits.

"They have gone on an information-collecting binge," says Charles Morgan Jr., chief executive for Arkansas-based Acxiom Co., one of the largest information-collection firms in the country. "There's just this insatiable appetite for more information to make better decisions." [1]

The information these firms collect is used for a variety of purposes, from running credit checks to creating marketing campaigns. And the data comes from a huge number of sources. When someone fills out a credit-card application, registers with a club, completes a survey or enters a contest, there is a good chance that the information they have given will end up with one or more of these firms. Much of the information also comes from government agencies. "With so much public information on-line, it's easy to find out a lot about someone," says Pamela Rucker, a spokeswoman for the National Retail Federation.

There has long been a wealth of information available about Americans. After all, the United States has always been a consumer-driven and legalistic society. But until recently, there was no affordable way to collect, store and retrieve this data. Computers — and later the Internet — changed that. "The information was always there, but it took technology to enable them to use it properly," Rucker says.

And the opportunities offered by technology have led to an explosion of new data-collection firms. In the last five years alone — the period paralleling Internet growth — the number of firms has increased by a factor of 10. Today, there are more than 1,000 companies collecting and selling information. [2]

Many observers complain that the rush to collect personal information that has followed the computer and Internet revolutions has not been accompanied by proper efforts to protect privacy. "Technology is clearly ahead of policy here," Griffin says. Jason Catlett, president of Junkbusters Corp., a privacy-protection firm, agrees. "What we have is really a form of surveillance."

Griffin and others think that anyone who collects information from a consumer should be required to give the consumer the option of prohibiting disclosure to outside parties. For example, she says, "When you filled out a credit-card application, there would be a box you could check giving you the right to stop the transfer of that information to others."

But those who collect and use the information counter that the services they provide are integral to the flow of modern commerce in the Information Age. For example, they say, when people apply for credit cards or auto insurance, credit checks can be run almost instantaneously. Consumers may value their privacy, but they value convenience even more. "Consumers don't want it tomorrow, they want it now or yesterday," Rucker says.

---

[1] Quoted in Robert O'Harrow, "Data Firms Getting Too Personal?" *The Washington Post*, March 8, 1998.

[2] *Ibid.*

---

vacy at the White House. Gore, who has long had an interest in the Net and is the administration's point man on technology issues, addressed computer industry executives, privacy advocates and others. "Privacy is a basic American value — in the Information Age and in every age," Gore said. "And it must be protected." [7]

The vice president went on to say that the nation needed a "Privacy Bill of Rights," so as to guarantee that Web sites do not acquire and use information in ways that are unfair to consumers. "You should have the right to choose whether your personal information is disclosed," Gore said. "You should have the right to know how, when and how much of that information is being used; and you should have the right to see it yourself."

But while Gore called for new legislation to protect children's privacy on-line, he stopped short of asking Congress to codify his Bill of Rights. Instead, he urged the on-line industry to step up its efforts at self-regulation, a policy long supported by the Clinton administration. [8]

For many privacy advocates in attendance that day, like the Electronic Privacy Information Center's Rotenberg, Gore's speech "came up short." According to Rotenberg and others, the vice president should have used the address to call for comprehensive privacy legislation. "The time has come to establish certain privacy protections in law, period," Rotenberg says.

Rotenberg and others argue that legal protections are needed because the on-line industry has shown — after being given years to establish and enforce effective privacy standards — that it is incapable of policing itself. "The industry is clearly not doing enough on its own," says Berman of the Center for Democracy and Technology.

While Berman admits that there are "some companies, usually big, established ones, that play by the rules, many don't recognize privacy concerns at all." A lot of these bad actors are "small start-ups that aren't aware that they have a responsibility to consumers." Like Rotenberg, Berman argues that "we will probably need some legislation to establish some minimum privacy benchmarks."

Those benchmarks, Berman says, include the protections mentioned by Gore: the right to choose whether your personal information can be disseminated and, if permission is given, to know how the data will be used. In addition, Berman says, "there has to be accountability, some sort of punishment for [the site] or remedy for the individuals" who have had their privacy violated.

Finally, opponents of self-regulation say, there should be an agency or office to oversee and, if necessary, enforce privacy protections. "You need an office with some staff and resources and authority to make some decisions," Rotenberg says, adding that the president could appoint a "privacy czar" patterned after the drug czar, a position created in 1987 to coordinate the war against illegal narcotics.

Currently, the FTC has a role in overseeing privacy issues on-line. But while the agency has studied the issue and made recommendations, it has no authority to regulate the fair use of information on the Internet. Indeed, all it can do is prosecute deceptive or fraudulent practices. In the case of privacy, that means that if a Web site posts a policy but does not follow its own rules, the agency can prosecute it for deceiving the site's users.

But, says Beth Givens, director of the Privacy Rights Clearinghouse, a privacy advocacy group in San Diego, even in the deceptive-practices arena, the agency does not have the resources to prosecute any but the most egregious cases. "If the FTC gets enough complaints about someone, they may eventually decide to do something," she says. "But if Jane or John Q. Grievance wants redress, the FTC is not strong enough to help."

The FTC's weakness points to the need for a new privacy agency, she and others say. It would not only enforce new privacy laws but also represent the United States in the international arena. "This is something that could actually be good for business," says Robert Gellman, a privacy consultant in Washington, D.C., who opposes comprehensive privacy legislation but favors a privacy agency. For instance, he says, such an office could negotiate with the European Union as it begins implementing the on-line privacy directive that it put into effect in October. (*See story, p. 266.*) "Right now, we really have no one to speak for us on this issue except the FTC, and they're only interested in privacy when they get a headline out of it," Gellman says, adding that most other developed countries already have a privacy agency or office.

But many supporters of self-regula-

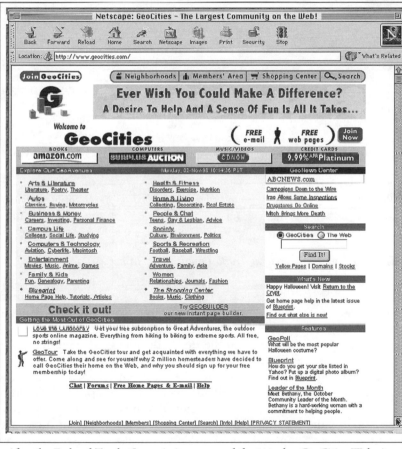

After the Federal Trade Commission accused the popular GeoCities Web site of misleading on-line visitors, it agreed to disclose that it releases personal information about visitors to outside parties.

Types of Personal Information Collected

More than half of the nation's Web sites collect four types of personal information from on-line customers.

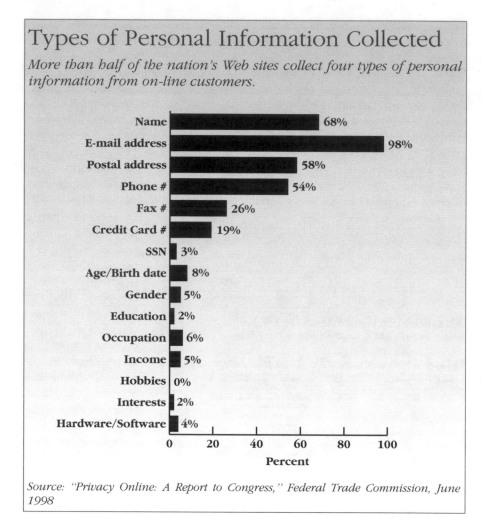

Type	Percent
Name	68%
E-mail address	98%
Postal address	58%
Phone #	54%
Fax #	26%
Credit Card #	19%
SSN	3%
Age/Birth date	8%
Gender	5%
Education	2%
Occupation	6%
Income	5%
Hobbies	0%
Interests	2%
Hardware/Software	4%

Percent

Source: "Privacy Online: A Report to Congress," Federal Trade Commission, June 1998

tion claim that privacy agencies and laws would be nothing less than Orwellian. "The government shouldn't try to be big brother," said Ira Magaziner, one of President Clinton's leading advisers on the Internet. Regulations, Magaziner said recently, are "a knee-jerk reaction of the industrial age, when government was expected to protect you. In the digital age, there are new paradigms; one of them is to empower people by giving them the tools to protect themselves." [9]

Others who oppose government action point out that most Web sites are now trying to post and enforce privacy policies. "The majority of Web sites where there is shopping and things like that have privacy policies posted," says Dalzell of the Direct Marketing Association (DMA). Indeed, several organizations, including the DMA and the Better Business Bureau (BBB), have created privacy guidelines for members. Some groups, like the BBB, even have a "seal of approval" for sites that meet their standards.

Supporters of self-regulation also point out that Web sites will protect consumer privacy if for no other reason than it's good business. "Consumers will only go where they feel comfortable, and businesses on-line and elsewhere know that," says Mark Uncapher, vice president of the Information Technology Association of America, an industry group. "That fact, more than anything else, will drive self-regulation."

Other opponents of government action argue that privacy restrictions might put many sites out of business, since the personal information they receive is sometimes a substantial source of revenue, especially for less well-established businesses. According to CATO's Singleton, people who favor protecting privacy sometimes forget that it also "entails limiting the kind of information businesses can exchange with each other," she says. "Now that may not sink a big company, but many businesses on the Web are small and not profitable," she adds.

For example, Singleton says, many magazines are trying to stay afloat by selling targeted advertising, which appeals to the specific interests of each user. "Regular banner ads aren't lucrative," she says. But in order to sell targeted adds, the site must know something about the users, such as their interests, age and education.

Finally, and perhaps most important, self-regulation boosters argue, it is premature to talk about privacy regulation because the Internet is still in its infancy. "E-commerce was born just a few years ago, so this is a new area where marketers are still learning and struggling to determine the right formula," Dalzell says.

Gellman, while less optimistic about the promise of self-regulation, agrees that a comprehensive law on privacy would be hard, if not impossible, to write for the Internet at this or any time. "It's so hard to distinguish between industries, types of records and other things that writing rules would be very difficult," he says. "I mean, should the rules for access to medical records be the same as those for pizza delivery records?"

Uncapher agrees, adding that even if effective rules for today could be drafted, it would be counterproductive at this stage in the Internet's development to try to pin down a lasting policy. "The medium is growing so quickly," he says, "that it's impossible to come up with hard-and-fast rules on something like privacy."

But privacy advocates counter that the Internet is not beyond the grasp of effective regulation. "That argument is a cop-out because no change that would come, no growth in the Net, would obviate the need for basic protections, like requiring [Web sites] to disclose how they're using the information they gather," Givens says.

Rotenberg agrees that the argument against regulation is specious. "They don't think it's possible to enact legal safeguards for privacy because the technical changes are coming too fast," he says. "But they do believe in legal safeguards for copyrights and patents, which also concern fast-changing technology."

In addition, Givens, Rotenberg and others argue, consumers alone will not drive privacy policy. For one thing, they say, many people don't think or care about privacy issues. Others are simply not aware that their personal information is being taken and used by the Web sites they visit. "We could do all the best consumer education in the world," Givens says, "but there will always be people who will be vulnerable to abuse and deception."

Should encryption technology be free from export and other restrictions?

A recent television advertisement depicts a man working at a computer while his wife reads the newspaper. "Hon, do we have encryption software on our computer?" she asks. "Yeah," he says. "That makes it safe to do our bills on here. Encryption locks our private information." His wife then points out that "Washington" wants to acquire the "key" to encryption programs, making everyone's sensitive information open to possible government scrutiny. "Should we trust Washington bureaucrats with the key to our private lives?" she asks. [10]

The commercial is reminiscent of the famous "Harry and Louise" spot, in which another anxious husband and wife worried about President Clinton's plans to overhaul the nation's health care system. That advertisement is credited with helping kill the health-reform initiative.

The fact that "Harry and Louise" are now talking about encryption at

---

Today, with millions of shoppers using credit cards on-line and millions more sending important information via E-mail, encryption has become a major tool of commerce.

---

all is testament to how far the Information Age has penetrated daily life. Until the 1990s, encryption technology was largely the provenance of the national-security community, a technology used to protect sensitive data from the Soviet Union and other unfriendly powers. Today, with millions of shoppers using credit cards on-line and millions more sending important information via E-mail, encryption has become a major tool of commerce.

Encryption software protects data by scrambling it into an unreadable code. Only someone with companion software can decode the message and read the data. As the husband in the television commercial says, this allows consumers to send their credit card number or a sensitive document on the Internet, secure in the knowledge that it will be seen only by those authorized to see it.

And security is important. When someone sends an E-mail message or purchases something with a credit card on-line, the information is often routed through a number of computers — sometimes more than a dozen. At any one of these junctures, the data can be intercepted and downloaded by a third party without anyone else's knowledge.

Currently, there are no limits on the use of encryption technology in the United States. Any person or company can buy the most powerful program available. Indeed, many companies that have a presence on the Web are employing powerful encryption programs to ensure that transactions are secure.

But export controls limit the sale of much of the more powerful encryption programs overseas, even to America's closest allies in Europe and Asia. These controls, which have been in place for decades, are meant to keep the technology out of the hands of America's enemies by keeping it close to home. Less powerful encryption programs can be exported. Indeed, the Clinton administration recently eased up on some of these export restrictions. Still, the most powerful, and hence popular, U.S. encryption products are generally not available overseas.

In addition to export controls, the law-enforcement community, led by the FBI, has been pushing for new laws that would

Europe Protects On-line Privacy

While policy-makers in the United States debate the need for formal on-line privacy protection, their counterparts in the European Union (EU) have already embraced it.

The Directive on Personal Data Protection has been hailed as a model for the United States. It incorporates the basic principles espoused by American privacy advocates, giving individuals significant control over the use of sensitive personal information about them, such as health and financial records.

The directive gives EU citizens the right to see any information a Web site has collected about them. It also requires data collectors to inform citizens how the information will be used and empowers individuals to prohibit sites from passing on data to third parties.

But American businesses, and others, argue that the EU directive could severely hamper both traditional and Internet commerce in Europe and the United States. In particular, American companies complain about a provision in the law prohibiting the export of sensitive information to countries, like the U.S., that do not have similar privacy protections.

If that provision were enforced and the United States did not enact its own privacy-protection law, the flow of credit card numbers, addresses and similar information from Europe could grind to a halt, and with it much transatlantic commerce. "The potential for disruption here is enormous," says Chet Dalzell, a spokesman for the Direct Marketing Association.

Hoping to avoid a trade war, U.S. Commerce Department officials have proposed what is known as a "safe harbor" approach, allowing continued export of information to those U.S. companies with in-house privacy policies that meet EU standards. "We say, 'Let's create a situation where, if companies agree to follow certain data practices, they can be held harmless under the new directive,' " says David Aaron, under secretary of Commerce.

But, so far, U.S.-E.U. negotiations have produced no agreement. European officials call the safe harbor approach impractical. "The prevailing message from Brussels right now is that the EU is unwilling to do a deal with each American company," says Jason Catlett, president of Junkbusters, an on-line privacy-protection firm based in Green Brook, N.J. Catlett and others say that the Europeans hope that the United States will enact its own Internet privacy law.

Officials in both camps say that for the time being, no action is likely to be taken against American companies and others on-line. For one thing, the new directive, which went into effect on Oct. 25, still must be approved by the legislatures in each of the 15 member states of the European Union. So far, only two countries, Greece and Portugal, have formally ratified the directive, although, according to the European Union, 10 others are in the process of doing so presently.

Still, many predict, there could be trouble as early as next year if no agreement is reached. "I don't think the EU would cut off American Web sites, because we so dominate the Web right now," Catlett says. "But I do think they would pursue big, individual companies like Citibank or IBM and force them to shut down a large part of their Web traffic to and from Europe."

allow government officials to unscramble encrypted data, so long as they obtained a search warrant. Many existing programs allow only those who have purchased the encryption software to unscramble the data. Not even the manufacturer of the program has the means to decode what its customers have encrypted. The law-enforcement community wants encryption makers to be required to include a "key" or "back door" that would allow the company to unscramble data encrypted by its product in cases where the authorities obtained a valid search warrant.

Many high-technology companies and privacy advocates argue that restrictions on encryption of any kind — both existing and desired — are unnecessary and harmful. To begin with, they say, the current export restrictions are shortchang-

ing consumers who buy encryption programs either alone or bundled into a software package. This is done to ensure that the software can be exported to other markets.

"If they installed stronger encryption features in the software, they would have to repackage these things for export," Rotenberg says. In other words, companies are intentionally "dumbing down" encryption protection to ensure that it is not affected by the export controls.

As a result, Rotenberg and others say, many on-line consumers and businesses are now much more vulnerable to an invasion of privacy, even though the technology to better protect them is readily available. Indeed, they point out that the Justice Department estimates that computer secu-

rity breaches cost American companies and consumers $7 billion in 1997.

Intentionally putting weak encryption into larger software packages is also hurting the software makers, who are losing markets to companies in other technologically sophisticated countries in Europe and Asia. These foreign software makers are already filling the niche in the encryption market left open by the absence of competition from the United States. "Other countries are happy to use U.S. export controls as an excuse to outsell U.S. companies in this field," says CATO's Singleton.

In addition, opponents argue, export controls are not preventing the technology from falling into the wrong hands. "Today there are companies in other countries with strong encryption technology, much of it developed by software engineers who were educated in the United States," Singleton says. "So it's foolish to think that preventing strong encryption from leaving the United States is going to stop people from getting their hands on this technology."

But others disagree, arguing that America's strong encryption technology is still the world's best and thus should not be fully exportable. "It's clear that this technology could do great harm if it fell into the wrong hands, and so must be controlled," says Eugene "Red" McDaniel, president of the American Defense Institute.

McDaniel worries that the U.S. intelligence community would be unable to keep track of the nation's enemies if encryption technology were exported. "It could be devastating," he says.

The Center for Defense Information's Smith agrees. "This stuff could severely hamper our efforts to collect foreign intelligence by making it hard to nearly impossible to listen in on what our enemies are doing," he says.

Smith acknowledges that other companies in other nations undoubtedly are working on strong encryption and that American export controls may only delay the technology from falling into the wrong hands. Still, he argues, delay is reason enough to maintain the tight controls.

"We are clearly the most advanced in this area, and so even if we only delay the wrong people from getting hold of strong encryption," he says, "something good will have come from the [export] restrictions. If, say, Iraq doesn't get good encryption for a few more years because of these controls, at least the NSA [National Security Agency] has more time to come up with ways to crack these stronger [encryption] codes."

Others point out that American industries that need strong encryption, like banking, are able to buy the best

in the world. And, says the FBI's Smith, echoing the industry argument, since most ordinary people don't buy software solely for encryption, export controls will be less likely to hurt software companies. "You buy Lotus Notes for what it does, not because it has strong encryption," he says, referring to a popular IBM software program. "The U.S. dominates about 70 percent of the world software market, not because it makes good encryption but because of the quality of the software and what it does."

And if some consumers get weaker encryption protection as a result of the export laws? "That's a small price to pay for our keeping this stuff away from potential enemies," says Smith of the Center for Defense Information.

Similarly, the FBI's Smith and others in the law-enforcement community argue that their proposal to require all encryption technology to have a "back door" is a small price for businesses and consumers to pay for protection against society's dangerous criminals. FBI Director Louis Freeh told the House Select Committee on Intelligence in September 1997 that without "a viable key management infrastructure that supports immediate decryption capabilities for lawful purposes, our ability to investigate and sometimes prevent the most serious crimes and terrorism will be severely impaired." [11]

Freeh and others point out that gaining access to computer records has helped solve or prevent countless crimes. For example, he says, World Trade Center bomber Ramsey Youseff used a computer to store his plans to destroy 11 U.S. airliners. If the information had been protected by a strong encryption program, it might not have been recoverable.

Now, they say, commercially available encryption technology is beginning to thwart investigations. "We're starting to see its use in the area of terrorism, where both domestic and international terrorists are using commercially available encryption soft-

ware to encrypt stored files and E-mails, and we're being frustrated at being able to gain plain-text access," Smith says. "In some of these cases, we don't know what they're talking about," he adds.

Law enforcement officials say that being prevented from accessing encrypted information upsets the balance between the need for privacy and the legitimate needs of the police. "We have the right to engage in a reasonable search after showing probable cause and pursuant to a warrant," Smith says. "This takes that away from us."

But privacy advocates argue that providing a "key" to encryption programs defeats the whole purpose of securing information in the first place. "The idea that you regulate encryption because it might cause the FBI problems is nonsense," Rotenberg says. "It's like saying that we should regulate typewriters because they may be used in a criminal act."

CATO's Singleton agrees, adding that requiring software makers to include a "key" to access encrypted messages in "real time," or as they're being sent, could be terribly burdensome for the software maker. "To allow the intercept of real-time communications is a technical feat that would require a lot of money and work," she says. ∎

BACKGROUND

Early Privacy Efforts

The value of privacy, or the right to be left alone, has long been recognized in the United States as a fundamental right. The U.S. Constitution's Bill of Rights recognizes privacy a number of times when it prohibits what it terms "unreasonable" search and seizure and allows defendants to refuse to incriminate themselves. Today, there is large body of statute and common law aimed at safeguarding individuals from unreasonable state interference.

But, according to privacy advocates, statute and common law have not kept apace with technological change. "There basically is no right to privacy on the Internet," Givens says. Still, there are principles that have come down during the last 25 years governing the fair use of a person's personal information or data.

The first glimmer of recognition that some sort of fair-use standards were needed came in 1973, when the Department of Health, Education and Welfare (HEW) created a task force to study the effect that computerization of medical records would have on privacy. The task force produced a "Code of Fair Information Practices," which set down several basic principles aimed at safeguarding personal privacy, including:

• Ensuring that the existence of personal databases is publicly known;

• Providing ways for people to learn what kind of information about them is in a database and how it is being used;

• Ensuring that individuals can check the accuracy of information about themselves and prevent the administrators of the database from using that information for purposes other than those for which it was collected;

• Providing guarantees that the information will not be misused. [12]

The HEW principles have formed the basis for later efforts to protect information privacy. For instance, Congress largely codified them when it passed the Privacy Act of 1974. Although the act's title implies broad, sweeping privacy coverage, it actually only applies to federal agencies when they collect data from individuals.

In 1980, the HEW principles were again largely incorporated in another set of privacy standards, this time drafted by the Organization of Economic Cooperation and Development (OECD). The Paris-based organization, which is a forum for some of the world's richest countries (including the United States), adopted "Guidelines on the Protection of Privacy and Transborder Flows of Personal Data." The guidelines did not have the force of law and instead were developed to aid nations in harmonizing their privacy policies. [13] They have been influential, most notably within the European Union, which issued its Directive on Protection of Personal Data in June 1995.

The "Cookie" Monster

According to privacy advocates like Rotenberg, the phenomenal rise of Internet use has not been accompanied by a corresponding increase in the level of privacy awareness. "It hasn't kept pace with the technology," he says. Mulligan of the Center for Democracy and Technology agrees, adding: "A lot of people, when they're typing this stuff into their computers, think it's private, like they're using a typewriter or something."

But what exactly happens when someone logs on and begins "surfing the Net?" Just as there is a lack of consumer awareness of the extent to which personal data may be used by third parties, there is often a corresponding fear that by simply visiting a Web site one forfeits one's E-mail address and other confidential information.

In fact, when users visit a Web site, their browser usually releases very little detailed, personal information about them. From the visitors' Web browser, the site can determine what kind of computer and Web browser is being used. The visitors' browser also reveals the last site they visited and, if they're at work, the name of their company. [14]

In addition, someone's browser releases its host E-mail address, such as aol.com or nyu.edu. With this information, the Web site could send an E-mail to everyone at the host address, a technique known as "spraying."

Not revealed is what would be considered more personal information: someone's name, phone number and home address. In almost all cases, E-mail addresses also remain confidential, unless the visitor is using a very old Web browser, some of which do reveal the user's E-mail in full.*

But Web sites do have ways of extracting a little more information about on-line users without asking anyone to disclose anything. For instance, the site can deposit a small amount of code in the user's hard drive, known as a "cookie." While a cookie cannot pry a person's name or E-mail address from them, it can track everything they do each time they're on the site.

The cookie allows the site to determine if the user is a return visitor and, if so, what they have done each time they have visited. So, for instance, Yahoo or another commonly used search engine might know that, say, user No. 8954 reads the Bible, has an interest in sailing and checks the stock price of IBM each day. This, in turn, allows the site to select specific advertisements to suit the particular user's interests. [15]

"People pick up all kinds of cookies all the time and immediately begin collecting all kinds of information about you," says Catlett, comparing them with parasites.

---

*There are a number of special programs capable of retrieving some E-mail addresses, but they are not commonly used.

Chronology

1960s-1980s

Early computer networks created by the military and universities eventually evolve into the Internet. The federal government and others begin considering privacy rights in the Information Age.

1969
Pentagon's Defense Advanced Research Projects Agency (DARPA) establishes ARPANET, a precursor to the Internet.

1973
A privacy task force created by the Department of Health, Education and Welfare (HEW) develops basic principles to safeguard personal health information stored on computers.

1974
Congress passes the Privacy Act, which applied the HEW task force's principles to government records.

1980
The Organization of Economic Cooperation and Development establishes privacy standards based largely on the HEW principles.

1984
Pentagon gives up control of the Internet.

1990-2000

The increased use of personal computers and modems leads to the dramatic growth of Internet use. Privacy advocates begin calling for legal protections for Internet users.

1991
The Center for Media Education is founded.

1992
The Privacy Rights Clearinghouse is founded.

1994
There are 3 million Internet users worldwide.

1995
The European Union (EU) adopts the Directive on Personal Data Protection.

1996
Congress passes the Health Insurance Portability Act, which requires new federal standards to protect health records to be in place by August 1999.

1997
According to the FTC, Internet businesses spent almost $1 billion for on-line advertising.

March 1997
FBI Director Louis J. Freeh urges a Senate committee to set limits on encryption software.

December 1997
An estimated 10 million people have purchased something over the Internet.

January 1998
The number of Internet users is estimated at 60 million in the United States alone.

June 1998
The FCC releases a report to Congress on Internet privacy.

August 1998
The FCC settles with the Web site GeoCities for alleged privacy violations.

Oct. 21, 1998
Congress passes legislation aimed at protecting children's privacy on-line.

Oct. 25, 1998
The EU's Directive on Personal Data Protection takes effect.

1999
Deadline for Congress to enact new standards to protect health records.

2000
FTC estimates that Internet advertising spending will total $4.35 billion.

Many Children's Sites Don't Provide Disclosure

Nearly 90 percent of the Web sites targeted at children collect personal information from children, but nearly half don't provide information-disclosure statements.

Percent of Web Sites Collecting Personal Information From Children

Do Not Collect
11%

Collect
89%

Percent of Children's Web Sites With an Information-Practice Disclosure

Disclosure
54%

No Disclosure
46%

Source: "Privacy Online: A Report to Congress," Federal Trade Commission, June 1998

But there are ways to fight back. A program offered free by the Junkbusters Corp. prevents cookies, blocks out banner ads and protects attempts to pry an E-mail address from the user.

Some Internet experts say that the obsession with on-line confidentiality is misplaced. "What are we protecting consumers from, free coupons?" asks CATO's Singleton. "Targeted advertisements are actually an advantage to consumers because they speak to their interests."

But Catlett says the idea that consumers are being so closely tracked on-line is scary. "They're building these enormous profiles of where people are browsing and what they're looking at, that can be used to hurt them," he says. For example, Catlett predicts, on-line browsing records will be subpoenaed. "You know, it's like leaving behind radioactive material that can be traced," Catlett says. "The only reason it exists is because it's a windfall for the marketers." ■

CURRENT SITUATION

Medical Records

A family member is suddenly hospitalized while on vacation, thousands of miles from home. Instead of calling hometown doctors and hospitals in a search for relevant health records, the treating physician simply pulls up the patient's medical history on the Internet.

If the scenario sounds a little far-fetched, it shouldn't. Health-care providers, insurance companies and others are already putting personal medical information on-line. Indeed, there are companies that provide secure sites on the Web where individuals can store medical information for themselves and their fami-

lies. "Because my kids have allergic reactions to medication, I have always been concerned over what would happen if they needed care when I wasn't available," says Leslie Lee, a housewife from Menlo Park, Calif., who recently put her family's health records on-line. [16]

For many consumers like Lee, on-line access to health records is a valuable and worthwhile service. But privacy advocates worry that using the Internet to store and access sensitive medical information could lead to profound breaches of privacy. "Many health-care providers and others already sell or give medical records away," Rotenberg says, pointing out, for example, that a lot of pharmacies sell prescription lists to pharmaceutical companies. "The Internet, of course, raises a host of new privacy concerns," he adds.

These concerns range far and wide. For instance, epidemiologists have recently expressed interest in tapping medical record databases for research purposes. Should they gain access, and, if so, how would the information be controlled? And what rules would govern access for law-enforcement officials?

Computer-industry representatives say that while there are legitimate concerns, the situation should not turn into a privacy nightmare. "There is already a consensus today that parties that have no role in the person's health-care process — basically if they're not in the payment stream — shouldn't have access to the records," says Uncapher of the Information Technology Association.

Today, the presence of medical records on-line is still small, but growing fast. For instance, while only 16 percent of the nation's hospitals use the Internet to store and access patients' records, the number is almost double what it was two years ago. [17]

Currently, there are no nationwide laws to protect the confidentiality of medical records, although some states, like California, offer limited privacy protections. That is likely to change in the near future. In 1996, Congress passed the Health Insurance Portability and Accountability Act, which mandated new federal standards to protect the confidentiality of medical records by August of 1999. If Congress doesn't act by that date (and so far it hasn't), the law authorizes the Department of Health and Human Services (HHS) to do the job for them via regulations.

In August, HHS announced standards that it would like to see either passed by Congress or promulgated as regulations. Among the proposals put forth by the agency were requirements that companies lock access to

records, train employees in privacy standards and develop a security plan to ensure medical-record safety.

"Electronic medical records can give us greater efficiency and lower cost, but those benefits must not come at the cost of loss of privacy," said HHS Secretary Donna Shalala.

Protecting Children

Children who visit the Liberty Financial Company's Web site for

The Federal Trade Commission says 89 percent of all children's Internet sites collect personal information on children, but only 23 percent advise children to get a parent's permission before releasing information. Above, sixth-graders log-on in DeepHaven, Minn.

young people can learn a number of things about managing money, from how to open a savings account to the rudiments of investing. The site also offers kids a chance to win prizes, but only after they complete a survey that asks their E-mail address, age, sex and whether they own any stocks, bonds or other forms of wealth.

Peter P. Morgan, senior vice president for Liberty, says that the survey allows his company to better tailor the site to children's needs and that the information is not sold or even

saved. "From our perspective, this site was meant to be an educational site for the benefit of kids and parents who want to teach [them] about economics,' " he says. [18]

But others see tremendous potential for sites like Liberty's to violate a child's privacy. "Children are so easily manipulated and their good will can be abused," says Katharina Kopp, a senior policy analyst at the Center for Media Education, a children's advocacy group. "When it comes to protecting their privacy, they cannot make rational decisions and are incapable of protecting their rights," she adds.

Kopp and other children's advocates say that there are a huge number of sites directed at kids. Some, like the Liberty site, are owned by companies that don't generally sell products or services to children. So why worry about them? According to Kopp, "marketers have long realized that kids can influence purchases, not only of children's items but adult purchases too." For instance she says, oil giant Chevron has created a Web site for children because the company knows that kids can convince their parents to buy their gasoline. In addition, she says, sites like Chevron's can acclimate children to a company brand so that when they become adults they will choose Chevron over other products."

Currently, about 10 million children under age 18 use the Internet regularly, more than five times more than in 1995. A recent survey by the Westin group found that 97 percent of parents oppose the selling or use

Protecting Yourself On-Line

Many Web sites post privacy policies aimed at allaying any concerns that on-line visitors might have. But others don't have such policies or, if they do, don't post them. Still, privacy advocates say, there are some things that Internet users can do to protect their privacy, such as:

• Check to see if the Web site you are visiting has a posted privacy policy. If it doesn't, there is no way of knowing how the information you give will be used. If a site does post a policy, check to see the limits it places on their ability to transfer your information to others.

• Download one of the many privacy-protection programs available on the Internet. They can block attempts to "steal" your E-mail address or shield your hard drive from "cookies," the code that many Web sites use to track someone's past and present activity on the site. Some, like the Junkbusters program cost nothing.

• Clean out your Web browser's memory cache after each session. The cache keeps a record of the Web sites you've visited, making it easy for others to trace your steps. Your browser's Preference folder should offer the option to empty the cache.

• Encrypt your on-line messages. Intercepting and reading E-mail is not that difficult. A good encryption program can make snooping much harder.

---

of information gathered from children. In the same survey, 80 percent of parents objected to Web sites requesting a child's name and address, even if that information is only going to be used internally. [19]

In a report released in June, the FTC determined that 89 percent of all children's sites it surveyed collected information on children. Of these, only 23 percent advised children to get their parents' permission and fewer than 10 percent attempted to require such permission. [20]

In the same report, FTC Chairman Robert Pitofsky called on Congress to act to protect children's privacy. "The Commission recommends legislation that would place parents in control of the on-line collection and use of personal identifying information from their children," he wrote. He went on to recommend that Web sites receive parental consent before getting information from children 12 and under. For older children, the commission recommended that the site notify parents before taking any information.

Pitofsky's call did not go unheeded on Capitol Hill. In October Congress added language that closely paralleled the FTC proposal to its fiscal 1999 omnibus spending bill. That measure was signed into law on Oct. 21.

OUTLOOK

Will Government Act?

Most privacy advocates predict that legal protection will eventually be extended to personal information on-line. "It is generally the case that when a new technology comes along, it takes time to sort the rules out," Rotenberg says. "But we usually end up with some sort of privacy protection, and I think that will be the case here."

Congress already has acted to protect children's privacy. Some action on medical record privacy is expected in the near future.

But Rotenberg and others also believe that more comprehensive privacy protections may be enacted soon. Their optimism stems in part from a belief that the Clinton administration is slowly shifting its position on Internet privacy from one of self-regulation to at least limited government oversight. "I think Gore may be in the process of changing his mind," Rotenberg says. "His hope is still that self-regulation will work, but that we should prepare for something else if it doesn't."

Givens of the Privacy Rights Clearinghouse agrees that government is likely to soon lose patience with industry attempts at self-regulation. "The government is starting to say, 'We've given you a chance and it hasn't worked out all that well,'" she says. Indeed, in testimony in July, FTC Chairman Pitofsky told a House Commerce subcommittee that Congress should give the on-line industry until the end of 1998 to have an effective privacy policy in place. "If it does not work out, we believe Congress should seriously consider legislation," he said.

Others think that the European Union's new directive on on-line privacy may prod the business community into focusing more closely on privacy protection. "U.S. [on-line] firms may face some fines as the [EU] member states begin implementing the directive, and that might get them on board in favor of some sort of privacy regulation," Rotenberg says.

But others say that talk of imminent regulation is premature. "I think for now, legislative energy will be focused on protecting children and medical records," says Uncapher of the Information Technology Association. "I think the government is going to give self-regulation more of a chance, give it more time."

CATO's Singleton agrees, adding

At Issue:

Should the federal government set privacy standards for the Internet?

DEIRDRE MULLIGAN

Staff counsel, Center for Democracy and Technology

FROM TESTIMONY BEFORE THE SENATE COMMERCE, SCIENCE AND TRANSPORTATION SUBCOMMITTEE ON COMMUNICATIONS, SEPT. 23, 1998.

*t*he Center for Democracy and Technology (CDT) believes that it is time for Congress and relevant stakeholders to develop a bipartisan, national privacy policy for the Internet. While efforts at self-regulation continue, and are a necessary component of the electronic marketplace, legislation will speed the adoption of Fair Information Practices across the market, provide a level playing field, and ensure that bad actors are deterred.

Toward this end, CDT has called for legislation enabling the Federal Trade Commission to develop rules to protect the privacy of both adults and children. . . .

The Federal Trade Commission Report "Privacy Online: A Report to Congress" found that, despite increased pressure from the White House to develop meaningful self-regulation and growing public anxiety about privacy on the Internet, companies continue to collect personal information on the World Wide Web without providing even a minimum of consumer protection. . . .

While self-regulation is a necessary part of any effective privacy regime on the global Internet, structural flaws in a purely self-regulatory system and specific difficulties that arise from the nature of the Internet suggest that self-regulation alone will result in incomplete protection. The four primary shortcomings of industry self-regulation in the privacy area have been: 1)the failure to incorporate core elements of fair information practice into substantive guidelines; 2) the lack of oversight and enforcement; 3) the absence of legal redress to harmed individuals; and, 4) the inability to set enforceable limits on government access to personal information.

Self-regulatory efforts to provide privacy protections on the Internet, to date, continue to exhibit these structural flaws. . . .

If Congress acts soon, it can protect privacy, build upon and improve the ongoing activities in the private sector, establish a level playing field and create a structure for oversight and enforcement of privacy practices on the Internet. Failure to act will result in continuing consumer distrust of the Internet, inadequate attention to individual privacy in the marketplace, and a legal framework that in some instances actually punishes those moving in the right direction while creating no incentive for self-regulatory activities. . . . However, we must also recognize that legislation will not on its own provide complete privacy protection. Privacy protection must build upon the strengths of existing efforts—self-regulatory and technical—but fold them into a comprehensive system of enforceable privacy protections.

STEVEN J. COL

Senior vice president and general counsel, Council of Better Business Bureaus Inc. and BBBOnline Inc.

FROM TESTIMONY BEFORE THE HOUSE COMMERCE SUBCOMMITTEE ON TELECOMMUNICATIONS, TRADE AND CONSUMER PROTECTION, JUNE 21, 1998.

*t*he question posed so frequently in recent weeks by many in the executive and legislative branches, probably including some committee members, and by others closely following the on-line privacy-protection issue, is "has self-regulation of online privacy worked?" . . .

The better question for the subcommittee and the Congress as a whole to ask itself is not whether self-regulation of on-line privacy "has" worked, but rather whether self-regulation of on-line privacy "can" work, and is it "likely" to work sooner and better than other alternatives?

Let me explain. The Internet is moving at warp speed. What we know now about the technology, the type and number of content and marketing and advertising providers, the marketing techniques used, consumer access to and use of the medium and the extent to which privacy is jeopardized and is protected, is very, very different than the state of our knowledge just a year ago. . . .

Add to this equation the fact that the so-called Internet industry is many industries, and is not the cohesive force some would suggest. It is ISPs and browsers, and software companies, and on-line "cookie" companies and stockbrokers, and auto dealers, and computer sellers, and so on. Users are equally diverse, including sophisticated computer users, mainstream novices, business personnel, grandmothers and children.

Expectations that this environment would produce in this, the consumer Internet's infancy, a cohesive, organized, fully developed, comprehensive, ubiquitous and completely effective and funded program to protect and enforce on-line privacy may be naive. The point is, we are all learning, and we are developing techniques and responses to emerging issues as our learning progresses.

And, make no mistake about it, an exclusive legislative alternative to a self-regulatory approach is no better, and maybe is much worse. It won't be speedy and it won't have the nimbleness required to respond to the changing technology and cast of players. I dare say that had the Congress passed an omnibus privacy-protection law last year, covering all aspects of the Internet marketplace as it existed at that time, we would be testifying today before an oversight committee to discuss whether the government has adequately enforced the law, or whether the law required substantial change to accomplish its purposes.

that government attempts to enact comprehensive privacy regulation on the Internet would be fiercely resisted. "For years and years, businesses have enjoyed tremendous freedom in this area," she says, "and they're not going to let it go easily." ■

Notes

[1] Figures cited in Federal Trade Commission Associate Director David Medine's testimony before the House Judiciary Subcommittee on Courts and Intellectual Property, March 26, 1998.

[2] *Ibid.*

[3] Federal Trade Commission, "Privacy On-Line: A Report to Congress," June 1998, p. 23.

[4] Medine, *op. cit.*

[5] Quoted in Joel Brinkley, "Web Site Agrees to Safeguards in First On-Line Privacy Deal," *The New York Times,* Aug. 14, 1998.

[6] For background, see "Regulating the Internet," *The CQ Researcher,* June 30, 1995, pp. 561-584.

[7] Quoted in Ed Murrieta, "Gore: Protect Privacy," *Wired News,* July 31, 1998.

[8] Quoted in *Ibid.*

[9] Quoted in Deborah Scoblionkov and James Glave, "Magaziner: Back Off, Big Brother," *Wired News*, July 22, 1998.

[10] Quoted in Rajiv Chandrasekaran, "Harry and Louise Have a New Worry: Encryption," *The Washington Post*, July 28, 1998.

[11] Testimony before the Senate Judiciary Subcommittee on Technology Terrorism, and Government Information, Sept. 3, 1997.

[12] Beth Givens, "A Review of the Fair Information Principles: The Foundation of Privacy Policy," Privacy Rights Clearinghouse, October 1997.

[13] *Ibid.*

[14] Elizabeth Weise, "Revealing Secrets About Privacy on the Web," *USA Today*, June 24, 1998.

[15] *Ibid.*

[16] Quoted in "Doctors and Patients Now Access Medical Records On-Line," *Business Wire*, Aug. 24, 1998.

[17] Milt Freudenheim, "Medicine at the Click of a Mouse; On-Line Health Files are Convenient. Are They Private?" *The New York Times*, Aug. 12, 1998.

[18] Quoted in Pamela Mendels, "Internet Sites for Children Raise Concerns on Privacy," *The New York Times*, July 4, 1998.

[19] Cited in testimony by David Medine, associate director, FTC, before the House Judiciary Subcommittee on Courts and Intellectual Property, March 26, 1998.

[20] FTC Report, *op. cit.*

FOR MORE INFORMATION

Business Software Alliance, 1150 18th St. N.W. Suite 700, Washington, D.C. 20036; (202) 872-5500; www.bsa.org. This organization of software companies promotes the growth of the software industry worldwide.

Center for Democracy and Technology, 1634 Eye St., N.W. Suite 1100, Washington, D.C. 20006; (202) 637-9800; www.cdt.org. The center lobbies for civil liberties, including the right of privacy, in the computer and communications media.

Center for Media Education, 1511 K St., N.W. Suite 518, Washington, D.C. 20005; (202) 628-2620; www.cme.org/cme. The center promotes the responsible use of new technologies for children.

Electronic Privacy Information Center, 1718 Connecticut Ave. N.W., Suite 200, Washington, D.C. 20009; (202) 544-9240; www.epic.org. The center conducts research on the impact of the computer revolution on civil liberties, such as privacy.

Bibliography

Selected Sources Used

Books

Brin, David, "The Transparent Society: Will Technology Force Us to Choose Between Privacy and Freedom?" Addison Wesley (1998).

Brin, known more as a science fiction writer than a social commentator, argues that it is not possible to protect privacy in our technologically advanced society. But instead of limiting the ability of technology to guard privacy, the author proposes what he calls "reciprocal transparency," or complete openness. If companies or the government can collect information about citizens, Brin argues, they should fully know what that information is and where it's going.

Articles

Clark, Charles S., "Regulating the Internet," The CQ Researcher, June 30, 1995.

Clark's piece, while a bit dated, is an excellent introduction to the debate over Internet policy, including privacy protection.

Clausing, Jeri, "Critics Contend U.S. Policy on the Internet Has Two Big Flaws," The New York Times, June 15, 1998.

Clausing outlines the problems privacy advocates and others have with the Clinton administration's decision not to push for formal privacy protections on-line. This passivity, they say, will ultimately slow the commercial growth of on-line commerce.

Freudenheim, Milt, "Medicine at the Click of a Mouse; On-Line Health Files Are Convenient. Are They Private?" The New York Times, Aug. 12, 1998.

The article discusses the privacy implications of putting people's health records on-line.

Glover, K. Daniel, "Do You Have the Right to Be Left Alone?" IntellectualCapital.com, Aug. 27, 1998.

This on-line article gives a good overview of some parts of the basic debate over privacy protection in the Information Age.

Gruenwald, Juliana, "Who's Minding Whose Business on the Internet?" CQ Weekly, July 25, 1998.

Gruenwald chronicles recent efforts in Congress to regulate privacy on-line. She writes that lawmakers are facing increasing pressure to do something to guard consumer privacy, especially with regard to children.

Hansell, Saul, "Big Web Sites to Track Steps of Users," The New York Times, Aug. 16, 1998.

Hansell describes how big Web sites like Lycos-Tripod are collecting and storing information about Internet users' likes and dislikes in order to produce targeted advertisements.

O'Harrow Jr., Robert, "Data Firms Getting Too Personal?" The Washington Post, March 8, 1998.

O'Harrow gives a detailed and well-researched account of the data-warehousing industry. The article makes clear how easy it is for data-collection firms to collect even very personal information about almost anyone.

Mendels, Pamela, "Internet Sites for Children Raise Concerns on Privacy," The New York Times, July 4, 1998.

The article chronicles the growing concern over the potential for Web sites to violate the privacy of minors. Particularly worrisome for privacy advocates are those sites directed specifically at young people.

Quittner, Joshua, "No Privacy on the Web," Time, June 2, 1997.

Quittner gives a good summary of the debate over whether to regulate privacy on-line.

Wise, Elizabeth, "Revealing Secrets About Privacy on the Web," USA Today, June 24, 1998.

Wise provides an easy-to-read account of what can and cannot be learned about someone when they visit a Web site.

Reports and Studies

Federal Trade Commission, "Privacy On-Line: A Report to Congress," June 1998.

An exhaustive examination of on-line privacy issues by the closest thing the United States has to a privacy agency. In particular, the report details concerns regarding the privacy of children on the Internet.

Smith, Robert Ellis, "War Stories: Accounts of Persons Victimized by Invasions of Privacy," Privacy Journal, 1997.

Smith, publisher of the journal, has collected hundreds of tales of privacy invasions, both on- and off-line.

15 Digital Commerce

ADRIEL BETTELHEIM

Illinois manufacturer Arnie Koldenhoven went looking for a few tons of steel coils recently — but not in the usual places. Instead of poring over price lists from local mills or comparison shopping by phone, the president of Arrowhead Steel simply clicked on a new Internet auction site fast becoming the talk of the steel industry.

Almost instantly, Koldenhoven was presented with a choice of three suppliers. He keyed in his bid and within minutes was linked with Weirton Steel, a West Virginia company that unloads its surplus stock online.

"It's kind of the next step in our business," says Koldenhoven, who makes parts for cars, office furniture and high-tech equipment. "Fifteen years ago, the fax machine relieved us from having to rely entirely on the mail or phone calls. This will make us even more efficient — and help us handle more material in less time."

Business-to-business transactions like Koldenhoven's are fueling a dramatic surge in U.S. Internet commerce, transforming the World Wide Web from a domain of chat rooms, weather reports and pornography into a powerful selling tool. Indeed, Forrester Research in Cambridge, Mass., estimates that Internet business trade will explode from $43 billion in 1998 to $1.3 trillion by 2003 — 9 percent of all business sales in the United States.

Companies increasingly are using the Internet for everything from scheduling truck and rail shipments to ordering parts and designing telecommunications equipment. The online transactions save time and cut costs by reducing the need for expensive sales staffs, in-house computer networks and voluminous paper records. [1]

From *The CQ Researcher*, February 5, 1999.

AP Photo/Bob Galbraith

Industry experts foresee many more Internet business applications within the next five years. Farms will be able to take round-the-clock orders for crops from food processors and grocery chains. Utilities will use the Web to buy most of their electricity and gas and to schedule shipments. Construction firms and government agencies will bid out contracts online. Drug and medical supply companies will use the Internet to replenish hospital chains.

The availability of more goods is being accompanied by a profusion of new services, thanks to the vast array of customized software available on the Internet. The technology allows a Wall Street company to connect with a client in Japan using a real-time translation service. An energy trader in Houston can route a telephone call to the Middle East through an online transcription service and get a text version of his conversation delivered via e-mail. And Web-based auctions like the one Koldenhoven used are bringing together small- and medium-sized businesses from every corner of the world.

"It's not sexy, but it's where the action is," says Forrester business analyst Steve Bell. "We're at a point where the number of businesses online has reached critical mass, meaning the market is going to grow dramatically."

But many problems loom. Sticky questions about how to tax goods and services in the borderless realm of cyberspace could imperil future state and municipal tax collections.

The government has yet to define what is appropriate online speech — a particularly touchy issue in a medium where pornography is widely available and annual sales of X-rated material exceed $900 million, according to best estimates. [2] Moreover, politicians and government regulators appear to be uncertain how to protect users against online fraud and unscrupulous business practices.

The rise of business-to-business transactions has generally been overshadowed by the incessantly hyped boom in consumer-driven Internet purchases. Online sales to individuals have turned electronic retailers like bookseller Amazon.com and eBay, the popular consumer auction service, into household names — and stock market darlings. Internet retailers accounted for at least $3 billion in sales during the recent holiday shopping season.

Surprisingly, however, consumer transactions account for less than one-quarter of Internet commerce (and only a tiny fraction of all retail sales). The lion's share of online commerce is business-to-business transactions. According to Zona Research, in Redwood City, Calif., they account for 77 percent of online sales and will be the driving force behind significantly greater use of the Internet in the next decade.

"We're seeing the emergence of online market-makers, who can act as intermediaries between buyers and sellers, offer a contract, coordinate bids, do language services and arrange shipping, all in one place," says Zona chief economist Jack Staff. "It makes doing business more efficient, with less potential for mistakes."

The dynamic environment is prompting intense jockeying by computer companies that provide links to the Internet and offer software and consulting for digital commerce. In one notable move, America Online Inc. (AOL) struck an agreement to

Surge Expected in U.S. Online Commerce

The total value of Internet commerce in the United States is expected to grow from less than $50 billion in 1998 to more than $1.3 trillion by 2003. Computers and electronics will continue to lead the field, but quantum increases are expected in transactions involving motor vehicles, petrochemicals and other industries.

Value of U.S. Internet Commerce (In $ Billions)

Industry Sectors	1998	1999	2000	2001	2002	2003
COMPUTING & ELECTRONICS	$19.7	$50.4	$121.4	$229.1	$319.1	$395.3
MOTOR VEHICLES	3.7	9.3	22.7	53.2	114.3	212.9
PETROCHEMICALS	4.7	10.3	22.6	48.0	96.8	178.3
UTILITIES	7.1	15.4	32.2	62.9	110.6	169.5
PAPER & OFFICE PRODUCTS	1.3	2.9	6.4	14.3	31.1	65.2
SHIPPING & WAREHOUSING	1.2	2.9	6.8	15.4	32.7	61.6
FOOD & AGRICULTURE	0.3	3.0	6.3	13.1	26.7	53.6
CONSUMER GOODS	1.4	2.9	6.1	12.7	26.0	51.9
PHARMACEUTICAL & MEDICAL	0.6	1.4	3.5	8.5	20.0	44.1
AEROSPACE & DEFENSE	2.5	6.6	14.8	25.6	34.0	38.2
CONSTRUCTION	0.4	1.6	3.4	7.0	14.2	28.6
HEAVY INDUSTRIES	0.1	1.3	2.5	4.7	8.7	15.8
INDUSTRIAL EQUIPMENT	14.1	1.3	2.4	4.5	8.5	15.8
TOTAL (IN $ BILLIONS)	$43.1	$109.3	$251.1	$499.0	$842.7	$1,330.8

Source: Forester Research Inc.

acquire Netscape Communications Corp. in a complicated $4.2 billion deal that also involves Sun Microsystems. AOL — an online service primarily known for its chat rooms, e-mail and news and weather reports — hopes to gain the 70 million people who surf the Internet using Netscape's browser software, then help small and large businesses to create virtual shops to sell to them.

"It will allow more [business] partners to get to market faster," AOL President and Chief Operating Officer Robert Pittman told reporters after the deal was announced. "Simply put, what we are doing is we are going to companies that are expert at building brick-and-mortar stores and giving them the tools they need to build virtual stores."

Assuming the deal is completed, the enlarged AOL will join elite company. It will directly compete with computer industry colossus Microsoft Corp., whose Windows software has become the industry standard for personal computers. Both will try to grab market share from IBM Corp., regarded as the current digital commerce market leader because of its sophisticated software products and consulting services. [3]

Another significant deal is AT&T's proposed $31.8 billion acquisition of cable television giant Tele-Communications Inc. (TCI). The combination, if approved by federal authorities, would create a new outlet for obtaining high-speed Internet access through TCI's cable systems. That would make it easier for computer users to make transactions and transfer large amounts of digital data. [4]

The various deals envision a day within the next decade when high-capacity digital networks provide a seamless link in cyberspace. Consumers and business people will be able to click on the Internet from their televisions, watch TV shows on their desktop computers and make phone calls from either device. The services will be brought to offices and homes by satellite, wireless, microwave, cable TV and telephone technologies, all linked in one giant network.

But such innovations are posing difficult questions for regulators and lawmakers. Should companies have to pay sales taxes on the goods and services they purchase online, as they would in face-to-face transactions? If not, will a de facto tax-free zone in cyberspace siphon business away from traditional merchants and erode local governments' tax bases? Can the federal government regulate advertising claims and the type of speech used in Internet marketing? Could sensitive information exchanged in electronic transactions —say, a company's sales estimates or an individual's medical records — fall into the hands of unscrupulous operators?

Digital commerce currently is free from most government interference, and the Clinton administration hopes it stays that way. The White House last November released a lengthy policy report that called for no new regulations on electronic transactions. Instead, it urged Internet companies to regulate themselves. President Clinton also called on government agencies to develop incentives for private companies to create high-speed networks that carry voice, video and data transmissions faster.

Congress has taken a similar tack, passing legislation last year by Sen. Ron Wyden, D-Ore., and Rep. Chris-

"To subject the Internet to a crazy-quilt of inconsistent local and state taxes would have a chilling effect on the growth of that marketplace."

— *Sen. Ron Wyden, D-Ore.*

topher Cox., R-Calif., that places a three-year moratorium on states and localities imposing new taxes on Internet transactions and establishes a panel to study ways to create a uniform tax. "To subject the Internet to a crazy-quilt of inconsistent local and state taxes would have a chilling effect on the growth of that marketplace," Wyden says.

Many policy analysts believe the minimalist approach makes sense. They note past efforts to regulate prices and entry in industries such as transportation wound up stifling competition and not serving the public interest. Indeed, the analysts say the whole point of digital commerce is to decentralize business entrepreneurship, empowering citizens while reducing the power of governments.

"Policy-makers should let markets, rather than governments, address any problems associated with digital technology," Brookings Institution economics scholar Robert Litan and Cato Institute Chairman William Niskanen argue in their 1998 book *Going Digital.* "The digital revolution is overwhelmingly a private-sector phenomenon and should remain so."

But critics say there are many legitimate areas for regulation, such as privacy and security, and argue more should be done to protect consumers in the lawless frontier of cyberspace. Some Web sites, such as the popular GeoCities site, have drawn fire from the Federal Trade Commission (FTC) for compiling personal information about users and distributing it to third parties. Hackers also have infiltrated commercial Web sites, forcing companies to create firewalls, identity cards and user passwords to secure their networks. [5]

"On certain issues, the administration is just not doing enough," says Marc Rotenberg, director of the Washington-based Electronic Privacy Information Center, a nonprofit group that addresses Internet issues. "It can be fairly asked whether the administration's policy was based on self-regulation or on promoting business interests."

More difficult questions face Clinton administration antitrust officials, who must develop rules for the rapidly changing market. The Department of Justice says it's willing to move against high-tech market abuses that limit innovation, reduce quality or raise prices, and currently is pressing a closely watched federal antitrust suit against Microsoft. The suit charges the Redmond, Wash., corporation with violating a 1995 federal court decree by allegedly requiring computer manufacturers to license Microsoft's new Internet browsing software as an integral part of the company's Windows operating system.

However, administration officials acknowledge that making broad rules for the digital market isn't always clear-cut. Indeed, in still maturing industries, where the next great product seems to appear each week, it's difficult to agree on what constitutes market domination or unfair trade practices. Justice Department officials concede that they may have to take a less paternalistic view and tolerate some joint ventures and near-monopoly conditions until enough competitors emerge. The officials haven't signaled, for instance, whether they will challenge the AOL-Netscape merger — a combination some critics believe limits consumer choice and concentrates power in the market for Internet browsers and gateways.

Assistant Attorney General Joel Klein, the Justice Department's antitrust chief, told a recent Brookings Institution telecommunications conference that antitrust enforcement in high-tech industries should be "modest in scope and surgical in application," adding that each case is different and has to be appraised on its merits. "I'm not here to tackle big corporations or get in the way of economic efficiencies," Klein said.

As government officials ponder

The FCC "hasn't made the Internet the object of its smothering affection yet, but it's just a matter of time. It is in the nature of regulators to find new things to regulate."

— *Rep. Michael G. Oxley, R-Ohio*

responses to the rapid changes coming to the digital marketplace, these are some of the questions that are being asked:

Should the government take a hands-off approach to regulating digital commerce?

"We will do nothing that undermines the capacity of emerging technologies to lift the lives of ordinary Americans," President Clinton, flanked by digital-commerce executives, declared on Nov. 30 at a White House event showcasing his administration's Internet policy.

Clinton essentially favors a hands-off policy when it comes to the Internet, viewing it as a global medium that creates high-paying jobs and now accounts for up to one-third of the nation's annual economic growth, according to Department of Commerce estimates. The White House — and many in Congress —believe regulations would only stifle creativity and create obstacles to further growth. Instead, they are calling on Internet companies to police themselves and adopt voluntary good-business standards that ensure fair pricing and access.

But self-regulation may not be easy. The Internet's very omnipresence and the host of cyberspace issues up for discussion make it difficult for politicians to avoid adopting some guidelines for the marketplace.

The fear of cyberspace predators capturing and selling personal information has fueled calls for privacy laws and stronger encryption software to scramble users' data. The profusion of Internet pornography twice prompted Congress to pass laws intended to protect minors from viewing cyberporn and questionable speech, though the first effort was struck down as unconstitutional. And even the White House has backed laws making it a crime to develop technologies that could help people circumvent copyright laws or steal intellectual property.

Ira Magaziner — architect of President Clinton's failed health-care plan and, until recently, the administration's Internet czar — insists government, in general, must show restraint and have faith that market forces will correct abuses. In a recent interview in *The New Republic*, Magaziner termed the Internet "as close to a pure marketplace as we've seen," where consumers have access to an almost limitless number of sellers. Competition is assured because a worldwide set of vendors exists, and the barriers to setting up a Web site are comparatively low. In short, buyers and sellers, acting in their own self-interest, will ensure the market prospers and grows, he says. [6]

Others are more skeptical. Privacy advocates say technological advances have made it increasingly easy for online marketers to collect information about individuals and businesses and store it in databases. One way is through the use of "cookies," bits of computer code that can be deposited on a user's computer hard drive to track everything the person does on a Web site. While a cookie can't uncover a user's name or e-mail address, it has an effect similar to following someone down the aisles of a store: It profiles buying habits and stores the information in a database. Later, the information can be used to sell the person something.

Other technologies collect information as people charge groceries, make toll-free phone calls and fill out warranty cards. And as software gets more sophisticated — and databases are linked — the opportunities for surveillance grow. Rotenberg of the Electronic Privacy Information Center says online consumers and businesses will be increasingly vulnerable to security breaches because transactions are typically routed through a number of computers. At any one connection, data can be intercepted and downloaded by a third party.

"Privacy legislation usually comes in response to new technologies, and I'd like to see that apply across the

Not Taxing Internet Sales Could Cost Billions

If the federal government doesn't require Internet commerce to be taxed, consumers may take their business to cyberspace, hurting local merchants and eroding communities' tax bases. The potential loss in tax revenue by 2003 could be 20 percent of current local sales taxes, according to some estimates.

Potential Sales-Tax Losses From Electronic Commerce

States	Total U.S. Sales Tax Revenue 1996 ($Billions)	Potential Tax Loss From 20% Decline ($Billions)
Less-Populated States (< 2 million)	$7.2	$1.4
Populated States (2-4 million)	14.1	2.8
More-Populated States (4-7 million)	29.5	5.9
Most-Populated States (> 7 million)	72.2	14.4

Sources: National League of Cities, National Conference of State Legislatures, National Governors' Association

Internet," Rotenberg says. "There are measures to protect cable subscribers, prevent junk faxes and curb telemarketers. I'd like to see an end to the double standard for the Internet."

The current lack of U.S. Internet privacy laws could trigger a trade dispute with European countries, which have adopted strong consumer privacy laws that address the Internet's potential to be a medium for fraud and other problems. A European Union accord that went into effect last year requires any countries or companies that trade personal data with Europe to recognize the tougher standards. That could affect U.S. banks, travel companies and Internet merchants, which now can move large amounts of consumer data around the world without being sub-

ject to similar laws.

"[Europe] has given an ultimatum to Washington: Adopt strong privacy laws, or stand the risk of losing countless billions of dollars of business," Simon Davies, director general of Privacy International, a London-based advocacy group, wrote recently in *The Daily Telegraph*. [7]

The Department of Commerce has tried to broker a compromise, encouraging U.S. companies to adopt voluntary privacy codes in return for European grants of immunity from their privacy laws. But European governments have resisted, and the dispute may head to the courts if both sides can't reach mutually acceptable protections.

A related privacy debate surrounds U.S. export controls on encryption software. There are no limits on the

High-Income Families Spend Most Online

Households that earned over $50,000 in 1998 accounted for nearly three-quarters of total online retail spending, compared with only about half of all U.S. retail spending. Affluent households will continue to dominate online spending in the next decade, though less so.

Percentage of Household Online Spending

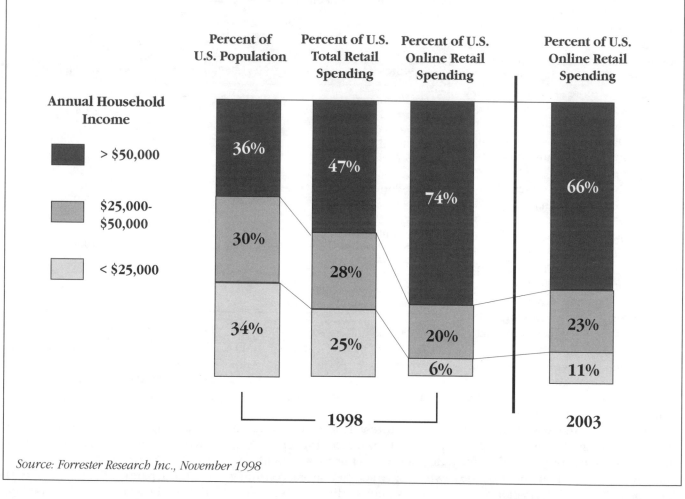

Source: Forrester Research Inc., November 1998

use of encryption technology in the United States, and many digital marketers use the most powerful software available to scramble sensitive data into unreadable code. However, the Clinton administration limits the foreign sale of the most powerful encryption programs, fearing they will fall into the hands of America's enemies. Some in Congress are urging the administration to loosen the

restrictions and help boost global electronic commerce. The administration has granted a few exceptions — such as for electronic-banking software — but so far is resisting lifting the ban.

Another subject of growing debate is the potential of the Federal Communications Commission (FCC) to regulate the Internet. Many lawmakers are calling for a broad overhaul of

the agency's oversight powers, precisely so it won't be able to impose rules hindering electronic commerce.

The FCC "hasn't made the Internet the object of its smothering affection yet, but it's just a matter of time," Rep. Michael G. Oxley, R-Ohio, a member of the House Commerce Telecommunications Subcommittee, said earlier this year. "It is in the nature of regulators to find new things to regulate."

Many in Congress blame FCC regulations for preventing the increased competition in the phone market that was promised in the Telecommunications Act of 1996. Specifically, lawmakers say the FCC makes it more difficult for phone companies to introduce new high-bandwidth digital services. Regulators on the federal and state levels say the problem rests with local phone companies that have been slow to open their monopoly markets.

Though the FCC has shown some interest in regulating the Internet, it could more immediately find itself setting rules for accessing the global network. A pending case would allow GTE Corp., Bell Atlantic Corp. and other local phone companies to build high-speed data networks with some restrictions. America Online also has asked the agency to require AT&T to give rival Internet providers access to the high-speed networks it plans to build as part of its acquisition of TCI.

One area of Internet commerce where lawmakers favor more regulation is the sending of "spam," or unsolicited e-mail. Online marketers frequently send unauthorized bulk e-mails, angering users and prompting comparisons to aggressive telemarketing phone schemes. Congress is contemplating rules that would better identify commercial e-mail and allow computer users to opt out of receiving the messages. The Ralph Nader-affiliated Consumer Project on Technology has suggested that unsolicited e-mail be tagged to discourage scam artists or pornographers from disguising the messages they send. However, Magaziner and some Clinton administration officials think such proposals could discriminate against computer users who want to receive without any strings attached.

"There are a lot of ways the government can get involved in regulation, but one has to keep in mind the larger issue of where the industry and technology is," says economist Staff. "This is a nascent technology, and we have a long tradition of encouraging industries through little or no regulation. The Clinton administration should be taking a laissez-faire approach; they don't have much of a choice."

Should taxes be levied on Internet transactions?

A computer user in New York City logs on to the World Wide Web using an Alexandria, Va.-based Internet service provider and finds the home page for Amazon.com in Seattle. The user decides to send a book as a gift to a relative in Georgia, paying for the purchase with an online banking service in Charlotte, N.C. Which state gets to tax the transaction?

Currently, none. The ability of digital commerce to hopscotch borders has created a set of difficult policy questions for governments. Simply put, the nation's 30,000 taxing authorities — cities, counties, special taxing districts — want to collect a cut of surging Internet sales but lack a simplified system to levy taxes. Internet merchants fear taxes will scare away potential customers and argue digital commerce will be stymied by myriad local tax laws.

Congress, apparently unwilling to referee the dispute, last October passed the Internet Tax Freedom Act, which imposes a three-year moratorium on new Internet taxes. The measure also created a 19-member advisory commission of business-persons and state leaders to try to devise a uniform taxing policy by 2001. The law, signed by a supportive President Clinton as part of the omnibus appropriations package passed in the final days of the 105th Congress, grandfathered already-passed taxes on Internet transactions in 11 states and Washington, D.C. [8]

Taxation is perhaps the most con-troversial issue surrounding digital commerce and one filled with legal implications. Online sellers technically are subject to the same taxes as other businesses. But because the Internet has no single location, it's difficult to establish the precise place where a transaction takes place. Also, the items being sold aren't necessarily physical goods, but screenfuls of information that might more appropriately be categorized as a "service." Some states make this distinction, choosing not to tax downloaded software and Internet access the way they tax other telecommunications services. Other states do. The muddled picture extends to foreign trade, where goods are often subject to tariffs but services aren't. All of this is forcing would-be regulators to reappraise their basic definition of commerce. [9]

"The problem with existing state and local tax structures is that they are horse-and-buggy laws that were developed to address a manufacturing-based economy," says R. Scot Grierson, senior manager for state and local taxes at KPMG Peat Marwick in Costa Mesa, Calif. "They are not readily applied to sophisticated electronic technologies."

There are some legal precedents for taxing long-distance sales. A long-running dispute between states and mail-order companies led to a U.S. Supreme Court decision (in *Quill Corp. v. North Dakota*) that usually prevents states from collecting sales tax on interstate transactions. A state's sales tax can generally be collected only when the buyer and seller have a physical presence in the state — for instance, if the retailer has a headquarters, outlet or warehouse in the state. The question is whether a similar standard should apply to Internet commerce.

James McQuivey, senior analyst at Forrester Research, believes Congress acted correctly because it would be

The Art of the Personalized Pitch

Customers of the Internet music retailer CDNow get more than a screenful of new album releases when they click on its Web site. The popular service also offers them a personalized "Wish List" of recommended purchases based on their stated preferences, past buys and ratings on artists and CDs. The company says the feature essentially creates an individualized music store for each of its 600,000 customers.

Other cyberspace ventures, including bookseller Amazon.com and the Web portal Excite Inc., also use one-on-one pitches to boost sales. At a time when regulators and lawmakers view the Internet as a mass medium, digital marketers increasingly are personalizing it by targeting ads and features at individual users. In the process, they are challenging the decades-old notion that mass marketing is the most effective way to reach consumers.

"I don't think it will mean the death of advertising because ads are too entrenched in our culture," says senior analyst James McQuivey of Forrester Research in Cambridge, Mass. "But you could see selling becoming more specialized. Automakers are excited about using the Internet to show customers individual models and let them try out different options. They'll be able to suggest that drivers in regions with icy or wet weather consider anti-lock brakes."

When Jupiter Communications surveyed 25 top online merchants last year, the New York market researcher found 40 percent already were offering personalized features, and 93 percent intended to have some form of personalization on their Web sites by the end of 1999. Experts say that while aggressive pricing is perhaps the single, biggest factor involved in getting people to make their first online purchases, customized services keep them coming back and allow retailers to develop loyal followings. [1]

McQuivey credits Amazon.com with perfecting the personalized pitch by establishing a popular feature that recommends book titles as potential purchases based on users' interests. The feature is built around a technology called "collaborative filtering," which uses mathematical formulas to predict what customers will buy based on previous purchases, stated preferences and the preferences of other people who bought the same title.

Dell Computer Corp., one of the most successful high-tech online retailers, has used personalization to create more than 1,500 customized home pages for its most loyal customers so that they have fast access to special sales and billing information.

American Airlines' Frequent-Flyer program creates personal profiles of members to accelerate online booking. The profiles contain members' home airports, frequently flown routes and seating and meal preferences. And Kmart recently introduced www.thatperfectgift.com to encourage holiday shoppers to build a Christmas gift list and help them select appropriate items.

The personalization extends beyond individual sites to the Internet portals that serve as gateways to the online shopping bazaar. The portals use software to match a user's stated interest with selected advertising. For example, someone who uses a portal to access a site about Colorado vacations may be presented with a banner ad for skis. Excite, Yahoo! and other portals also offer personalized services, such as weather reports and horoscopes.

Despite the appeal, not everyone is enamored with personalization. Some users worry about their purchasing profiles getting swapped among online retailers. The concerns have prompted Netscape's and Microsoft's popular browsers to offer features that turn off "cookies," the data files that track Web surfers' online movements. Other software allows users to list sites from which they will accept cookies. And a San Diego service called The Anonymizer allows people to surf the Web and send e-mail anonymously.

"Ultimately, this will make transactions more efficient, but I still think people will go out shopping for the experience," says Forrester's McQuivey. "There's nothing like testing out how a leather chair feels, or trying on clothes, in person."

---

[1] For background, see Robert Hof, Heather Green and Linda Himelstein, "Now It's Your Web," *Business Week*, Oct. 5, 1998, pp. 164-176.

---

unfair and burdensome to require out-of-state firms to comply with thousands of local tax rates that could lead to multiple taxation. "You hope this is something that could be phased in slowly because the industry is still evolving," McQuivey says.

But critics say putting off the tax issue has serious implications. States believe keeping the Internet tax-free, even for a few more years, could spell economic ruin. Sales taxes account for as much as 40 percent of all state revenues. The National Governors' Association estimates that if sales over the Internet reach $300 billion by 2002, as has been projected, states and local governments will lose up to $20 billion in potential revenues. That would amount to more than 15 percent of current total sales taxes.

"States first need to adopt uniform tax definitions and a single tax rate per state," says Raymond Scheppach, the association's executive director. "Once that is settled, they can come to Congress to get the right to compel out-of-state sellers to collect the tax."

The association agreed, nonetheless, to the three-year moratorium so state governments could try to establish a single tax or a simplified system to apply to Internet sales. A pilot program is under way in Washington, Idaho and Utah, with more studies planned with the National Tax Association.

One possible solution would involve states applying a single tax, say 5 percent, to online sales. The states would then redistribute proceeds to local governments in proportion to their share of statewide sales-tax collections from local businesses. The local governments would no longer be able to design their own sales taxes. And online merchants wouldn't have to deal with myriad local tax rates and definitions of what is taxable.

Austan Goolsbee, a professor of economics at the University of Chicago Graduate School of Business, says there already is strong evidence that customers are flocking to the Internet for the tax advantages. A recent study Goolsbee completed on the purchasing habits of online consumers found that the number of online shoppers and the dollar amounts they spend would decline 25 percent and 30 percent, respectively, if they were charged sales tax.

"People who live in locations with high sales taxes are significantly more likely to buy things over the Internet," Goolsbee says. [10]

Critics also note that the Internet's current tax-free status widens the so-called "digital divide" between information haves and have-nots. The critics cite market surveys showing that approximately 80 percent of U.S. households with incomes over $100,000 have personal computers, while PCs are only

found in 25 percent of households with incomes below $30,000. Thus, a person with a credit card, a computer and an Internet-access account can avoid taxation on goods and services that would be taxed for someone who bought them from a neighborhood store.

"Sales-tax liability [will] be more and more concentrated among the lowest-income segments of the population," Michael Mazerov and Iris Lav

Cisco Systems President John Chambers addresses a conference on Internet commerce last Nov. 30 in Washington. President Clinton and eBay CEO Meg Whitman are at left

of the Washington-based Center on Budget and Policy Priorities wrote in a lengthy critique of the tax moratorium last year. The two analysts believe states will likely raise sales taxes to make up for revenues lost to the Internet, and that the moratorium gives online merchants less incentive to embrace a uniform policy on Internet taxation.

The 19-member commission that will have a major say in any new taxes on the Internet was designed to have equal numbers of industry and government representatives. But local government agencies are complaining that the group is unfairly tilted in favor of big business, with

representatives from corporations like Time Warner, MCI Worldcom and Netscape. Peat Marwick's Grierson says skepticism is mounting over whether the commission will recommend widespread changes or keep the status quo.

The commission "is still missing some business representation from Main Street," Grierson says. "Hopefully, they'll make some recommendations to solve this, but there's a chance they'll leave things as is."

Should the government try to regulate Internet content?

Thousands of Internet surfers logged onto the Internet in September when the House made public intimate details of President Clinton's sexual affair with Monica Lewinsky, as contained in a report by independent counsel Kenneth Starr.

At the same time, a House Commerce subcommittee was approving legislation that could make it a federal offense for a commercial Web site to publish sexually graphic content if it were deemed harmful to minors under age 17. [11] The apparent contradiction illustrated the dilemma over whether to regulate Internet content, a debate that could affect the future of commercial speech on the World Wide Web.

The legislation was eventually passed by Congress as the Child Online Protection Act and signed into law as part of the $500 billion omnibus appropriations bill last October. It would set penalties of up to six months in prison and a fine of $50,000 for businesses that make any indecent online communications for commercial purposes. On Feb. 1, a federal judge in Philadelphia, heeding arguments by civil liberties groups that the law could result in the censoring of free speech, issued a preliminary injunction blocking the statute from taking effect. Judge Lowell Reed, who had issued a temporary restraining order in November so the arguments could be heard, said the fears were "reasonable, given the breadth of the statute." The U.S. Department of Justice, which defended the law, said it was reviewing the decision. The groups claim the statute violates First Amendment guarantees of free speech and is a form of censorship.

The suit is more than just a free-speech battle. The outcome will help define the parameters of commercial speech on the Internet and could have a significant effect on digital marketers of all stripes, from medical Web sites and art dealers to online booksellers and, of course, the robust Internet pornography business. [12]

The law marks the second time Congress has tried to limit access to adult online material. The first attempt, included in the 1996 Telecommunications Act, was invalidated by the U.S. Supreme Court a year later because justices ruled portions of the law were too broad and could restrict speech in cyberspace. The Department of Justice, which is defending the new law, says it is much more narrowly written and only applies to commercial Web sites. The 1996 measure applied to all online material, including e-mail.

"It is not appropriate that there is still no legal protection for children from indecent material," says Ohio Rep. Oxley, the lead sponsor of the measure in the House. Oxley and other supporters say making the Internet more family-friendly will only enhance the medium's economic, educational and societal potential. And they note the statute is espe-

cially timely because recent congressional legislation mandates that school classrooms and libraries be wired to the Internet.

It's easy for anyone to come across pornography on the Internet. Literally tens of thousands of adult Web sites are in operation, selling live video sex, raunchy videotapes and sexual paraphernalia. Many use alluring but non-sexual search terms —such as "red light" and "Monica Lewinsky" — to snag casual Internet surfers using browsers. Forrester Research says online pornography accounted for an estimated $925 million in sales last year, and that revenues are growing 30-40 percent per year.

Opponents of the new law contend it's potentially harmful to more than just the pornography business. "The [new] law will seriously stifle the creativity and new business models that are starting to thrive on the Web," Christopher Hansen, an attorney for the American Civil Liberties Union (ACLU) and one of the lead lawyers challenging the law, said before preliminary hearings in the case began last month.

Specifically, opponents object to a provision in the law that requires an electronic-verification system to be put in front of any questionable material. Such a gateway — for instance, a credit-card verification device intended to establish that the person accessing the site is an adult — would be expensive to implement and could be unreliable, Hansen argues. The nuisance of being checked could also drive away potential customers, he adds.

The law makes exceptions for works that have political, scientific or artistic merit. But some online businesses say it will be difficult to decide what is appropriate for children and worry that it will be applied too broadly.

The Internet industry has tried to address the pornography problem it-

self by offering technology that can block objectionable material on home computers. Microsoft offers filtering software on its Web browser that allows parents to block adult Web sites. AOL has set up a children's viewing zone. The companies, eager not to appear to be defending pornography, say they would prefer to leave regulation of cyberspace in the hands of consumers, though they might favor a narrowly written law specifically targeting hard-core online pornographers.

Other industries have broader concerns. Christopher Finan, president of the American Booksellers Foundation for Free Expression, one of the groups challenging the new law, wrote recently in *Newsday* that the law could restrict transmission of obstetrical and gynecological information on medical Web sites, or limit whether an art dealer can place paintings of nudes on the Internet. Booksellers, led by Powell's Books of Portland, Ore., worry it will restrict sales of some material dealing with alternative sexual lifestyles or pornography.

"Opposing this law doesn't mean that plaintiffs do not care about the problem of unintended exposure of minors to inappropriate material," Finan says. "But if bookstores and other businesses cannot post material about sexual topics that is of interest to adults, then Oxley's law will make the Internet fit only for children." [13] ∎

BACKGROUND

Bell's Vision

When Alexander Graham Bell demonstrated the first telephone at Philadelphia's Centennial Exhibi-

Chronology

1930s-1950s

Early computers process and record data electrically and make computational decisions based on wiring and information encoded in their circuitry.

1939
John Vincent Atanasoff builds an electronic digital computer in Ames, Iowa, using concepts that later become central to the development of modern computers.

1946
Engineers at the University of Pennsylvania begin operating the first digital computer: ENIAC (electronic numerical integrator and computer).

1948
Scientists at Bell Labs introduce the transistor.

1958
Texas Instruments scientists invent the integrated circuit, a group of transistors implanted on a single chip of silicon.

———— • ————

1960s-1980s

The advent of the microprocessor ushers in the era of the personal computer. The nascent Internet takes shape, though it is largely restricted to government and academic use.

1969
The U.S. Department of Defense Advanced Research Projects Agency completes ARPAnet, a computer network designed to withstand nuclear attacks that allows messages and data to be sent coast-to-coast.

1971
Intel introduces the 4004, the first microprocessor. The device puts computer memory and processing ability on a single silicon chip, shrinking personal computers to desktop size.

1975
An early personal computer, MITS' Altair, is sold as a mail-order kit for $397.

1983
Radio Shack introduces the first laptop computer.

1986
The National Science Foundation develops NSFNET, a successor to ARPAnet that links supercomputers around the country and that allows scientists to exchange data and send electronic messages.

1989
Scientists at the European Center for Nuclear Research (CERN) in Switzerland develop a method of requesting Web files and documents, called hypertext transmission protocol (HTTP). This marks the beginning of the World Wide Web.

———— • ————

1990s *Internet use explodes with the advent of browsers and the privatization of government networks. A new form of business, digital commerce, allows businesses and consumers to buy and sell online.*

1993
Mosaic, an early Web browser that works with the most widely used computers, is developed by the National Center for Super-computing Applications. The National Science Foundation begins privatizing its network.

1994
More than 10,000 Web sites are in operation; about 3.2 million host computers are connected to the Internet. Developers of Mosaic move to Silicon Valley and establish Netscape, maker of the Navigator Web browser. Microsoft agrees with the U.S. Department of Justice to abandon several business practices that help it dominate the market for PC operating systems.

1995
The first commercial Web sites begin to appear. About 45 million people worldwide now have access to the Internet. Microsoft declares it will focus product development on the Internet market, soon unveiling its Explorer browser that competes with Navigator.

1997
America Online acquires rival Internet service CompuServe in a three-way deal. The company soon announces it has 10 million members worldwide. The Justice Department launches a suit against Microsoft for violating its decree and engaging in anti-competitive behavior to grab a dominant share of the Web browser market.

1998
Mergers and consolidations hit the industry as forecasts of digital commerce increase. AOL, with 14 million subscribers, says it will buy ailing Netscape. Microsoft focuses on more electronic-commerce offerings. The value of online transactions rises to more than $30 billion.

tion in 1876, many sensed the device would bring dramatic changes to everyday life. But Bell and others viewed it, first and foremost, as a tool of commerce. The idea of personal coast-to-coast communication apparently was never considered. After all, the then-dominant telegraph wasn't used in homes.

The digital commerce boom of the 1990s is helping fulfill Bell's vision. The ability to send large volumes of information over wires — specifically, fiber-optic cable — is shifting business away from traditional merchants and service providers. Now, business contracts, sales orders and inventory requirements can be translated into digital code that can be blasted around the world at the speed of light.

The modern era of electronic commerce began in the 1960s, when several industry groups began to develop electronic data interchange (EDI) systems. These networks used a common computer language to transmit large volumes of business data over phone lines. Spinoff applications soon followed. Banks realized the advantages of linking remote sites to centralized data centers and began introducing credit-card processing systems in the early 1970s. These systems married the latest integrated banking services with new technology, speeding up transaction times and making shopping more convenient.

Another wave of development came in the mid-1980s with the introduction of automated teller machines (ATMs) at banks around the country. Consumers at first balked at using the contraptions, preferring the comfort of making deposits and withdrawals in person. But the ATMs foreshadowed Internet commerce by demonstrating how secure networks could allow people to access individual bank accounts via host computers.

Internet Pioneers

The advent of the World Wide Web in 1989 and the commercialization of the Internet in 1991 brought digital commerce into full bloom. Companies set up early Web sites to advertise products, recruit workers or build brand loyalty among customers. Not surprisingly, the sites were especially popular among people with technology backgrounds, who could hunt for jobs in the booming computer industry or access technical data for their home computers. The strength of advertising on the Web grew as casual computer users began gradually surfing the Internet with improved browser software — which uses search terms to steer people to particular sites — and more formal entry points like the Netscape or Yahoo! portals.

The earliest sites were drab by today's standards. Many contained just words, without graphics, pictures or links to other sites. A number catered to specific audiences, such as the Wire Networks' Women's Wire, a women-only site launched in 1994 with $1.2 million in seed capital that now competes with more than a dozen similar Web publications.

Gradually, Web software and marketing became more sophisticated. Cisco Systems Corp., a San Jose, Calif., maker of telecommunications network equipment, set up one of the first sophisticated electronic commerce sites in summer 1996. The site allowed engineers to use the site like an electronic drafting table to design products online using Cisco hardware. They then could place orders for the devices they had created, as well as check on invoices and account information. Online sales for the first year totaled just over $100 million; the company now handles in excess of $3 billion in

Internet orders annually.

Another high-tech company that gravitated to the Web early is Dell Computer Corp., which now reaps about $2.2 billion a year in online sales — nearly 15 percent of the company's total revenues. The Round Rock, Texas, company began posting sales literature and technical support information for its personal computers on its Web site in 1994. In mid-1996 it installed software that allowed customers to configure their own computers and order them online. The orders still had to be retyped into computers that ran the rest of Dell's business. But the success — early orders ran about $100,000 per week — convinced Dell, and eventually other computer makers, that the Internet was a successful tool for personalizing business.

Pornographers also were online pioneers. Starnet Communications of Vancouver, B.C., was among the first to use its Web site to show live erotic videos in 1995. Seattle-based Interactive Entertainment Group took the concept further, leasing adult entertainment to some 1,400 Web sites and building its business to approximately $50 million in revenues last year. Despite the continued growth prospects for pornography, Forrester Research says some operators are turning their attention to the next wave: Internet gambling. [14]

The Online Boom

More mainstream consumer sites started to flourish in the mid-1990s as computer tinkerers began to develop variations on online commerce. In 1995, Pierre Omidyar, a French-born Silicon Valley computer programmer, set up a home page called Web Auction to help his girlfriend sell Pez dispensers. The goal was to create an automated service

Shopping Was Never Like This

Click on an Internet Web site, and chances are you'll find an opportunity for interactive digital commerce. Increasingly sophisticated software — and forecasts of a trillion dollar online economy by the next decade — have made the World Wide Web a veritable shopping bazaar. The following examples reflect just a fraction of the products and services available online:

Real Estate — The real estate brokerage Coldwell Banker offers a service called Personal Retriever on its Web site (www.coldwellbanker.com) that creates a portfolio of house listings in specified locales. The user goes through a menu that asks about the time frame for the transaction, the user's price range, annual income, age and number of kids. Then the user enters particulars about the desired house, such as the number of bedrooms and baths. The Web site returns with house listings that meet the criteria, and offers updates by e-mail.

A search for seacoast property near Rockland, Maine, reveals one shortcoming: The properties are limited to Coldwell Banker listings, and currently there are no properties for sale. Moving up the coast, the Web site reveals two properties in Hancock County that fall into the price range. If a listing looks particularly inviting, the user can then click on a mortgage calculator to determine monthly payments.

Auctions — The popular eBay auction site (www.eBay.com) offers thousands of items, from baseball cards to weapons, in a traditional auction format. Users who register and receive a password can bid on items, ask the seller questions and contact other potential bidders. One recent auction in the coins and stamps category featured a 1930 U.S. Standing Liberty Quarter with a rare error —the die was rotated 10 percent in the wrong direction. The first bid was for the minimum required, $1. But over the next five days, 17 bidders upped the ante to $52. The consensus seemed to be that the coin would be a unique addition to any collection.

Some of eBay's auction items might raise eyebrows. The erotica section features listings for nearly 7,000 X-rated books, videos, magazines and adult toys — some accompanied by snapshots of the items. eBay recently announced it was adopting new measures to beef up security on the site, but they may not fully address the sale of such material on the site. [1]

Natural Gas — One of the promising commercial Web sites is Altra Energy Technologies' Altranet (www.altranet.com). This Houston-based Web site is a pioneer in digital energy trading, allowing commodities brokers and utilities to strike deals for natural gas shipments, schedule them on pipelines and check market prices. Forrester Research estimates $4.9 billion of natural gas was traded online last year. When registered users with IDs post a deal on the Web site, it is instantly displayed to other traders on the network.

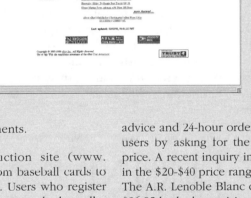

When a dealer sees a favorable deal, he clicks a "data cell" and hits the entry key, and the transaction is consummated. The Web site eliminates the need to rely on market makers or other middlemen, who arrange shipments but sometimes have unreliable or questionable pricing.

Wine — Some digital commerce sites offer know-how and helpful suggestions but aren't always practical. The Virtual Vineyard site (www.virtualvineyard.com) is a hit with wine fans, who enjoy the advice and 24-hour ordering features. A gift selector prompts users by asking for the type of gift, the occasion and the price. A recent inquiry into Valentine's Day wine suggestions in the $20-$40 price range turned up three recommendations. The A.R. Lenoble Blanc de Blancs Grand Cru Champagne for $26.95 looked promising, and the accompanying tasting chart detailed its intensity, body, acidity and complexity. However, a request to ship the product to a Maryland address was unsuccessful because the state prohibits shipment of wine direct to consumers. When an alternate address in Washington, D.C., was provided, the service added $8.95 for shipping and advised it will take 10 to 15 days for the wine to arrive.

---

[1] For background, see Lisa Napoli, "Net Auctioning Has Dark Side," *The New York Times*, Jan. 18, 1999.

---

that allowed an unlimited number of sellers to auction items 24 hours a day — and collect a small fee for each sale. The venture proved hugely successful with pack rats and collectors and became eBay, which now holds a dominant position in online auctions over competitors such as Yahoo! and Home Shopping Network's First Auction.

"We've really seen three waves of development in electronic commerce sites," says Zona Research economist Staff. "The first was in the early and mid-1990s, when companies wanted to save paperwork and money and put their catalogs online. The second wave, which is happening now, consists of companies that are using the sites to make sales above and beyond the traditional methods. The third wave, which we're starting to see with the auctions, is using the Web as a market maker and serving as an intermediary between buyers and sellers. This is creating transactions that wouldn't have otherwise taken place."

The Internet's myriad applications have made it by far the most rapidly adopted technology in this century. Radio had been in existence for 50 years before 50 million people tuned in. Television took 13 years to reach that point. Sixteen years after the first home computer kits came out in the mid-1970s, 50 million people owned PCs. But once it was opened to the general public, the Internet broke that barrier in four years. [15]

But large corporations still have technical concerns. Because the Internet is a public network that connects smaller networks and service providers, there is no single entity to ensure that a message leaving one point arrives at its destination. For this reason, some businesses have set up "extranets," or virtual private networks on the Internet, that limit access to a prequalified set of businesses. One example is Automotive Network Exchange (ANX), which links Chrysler Corp., Ford Motor Co. and General Motors Corp. with their regular parts suppliers and distribution channels.

Some retailers view the Web as a way of expanding sales to a younger, more affluent audience. Celebrity homemaker Martha Stewart, who launched a site in 1997, surveyed 4,700 customers who responded to an online questionnaire and found the average age

was 30 with an income of $65,000. By contrast, readers of her magazine, *Martha Stewart Living*, averaged 41 and $58,000 in income. [16]

But some studies suggest it will be difficult to expand online shopping's allure without offering price breaks. New York-based Jupiter Communications surveyed 50,000 households last year and found that 65 percent of the people with Internet access who browsed or surfed the Web didn't make purchases. Instead, they often checked prices on goods and services, then purchased them from traditional retailers and service providers. The vast majority said online prices — not privacy concerns — were the major barrier to buying something, hinting that off-line businesses were more flexible and willing to deal.

"Aggressive pricing on select items will get customers in the door, and is a crucial step to help win the next phase of the customer acquisition battle," says Jupiter analyst Evan Cohen. "Vendors shouldn't slash prices across the board, but strategic discounting will help." ∎

CURRENT SITUATION

Business Worries

As the Internet influences more aspects of daily life, the potential for problems and legislative remedies increases. Soon Internet-related provisions will be part of banking, agriculture and education bills. Senate Judiciary Committee Chairman Orrin

G. Hatch, R-Utah, has raised the prospect that criminal and civil rights codes may be amended during the current Congress to address electronic privacy concerns. And the Web already has been a focus of recent copyright and trade legislation.

But lawmakers may find it difficult to define priorities because consumer and business use of the Internet involves different sets of political considerations. Surveys show consumers generally want new laws to protect their online privacy and safeguard against fraud. But such an interventionist approach doesn't please online businesses, which tend to believe in letting the market solve its own problems.

"Businesses tend to work with established partners again and again — they know each other, they can install software to authenticate who everyone is," says Forrester analyst Bell. "It's actually in their interest to provide lots of sensitive information to a supplier or client. They have fewer concerns [about privacy] than an online consumer."

Even so, market-based solutions could prove elusive because not everyone views digital commerce as a cure-all. This is particularly true in financial services and banking, where the rise of discount online brokerages has given investors the option of bypassing brokers and other traditional middlemen.

The tensions were evident last October, when Merrill Lynch & Co. Vice Chairman John Steffens called online trading a "threat to Americans' financial lives" and compared it with gambling. Steffens was frustrated by the rise of brokerages like Charles Schwab and E*Trade, which offer do-it-yourself investing for nominal fees and have eaten into traditional brokerages' commissions. Soon after, Merrill Lynch made its extensive database of corporate investment research available free on

At Issue:

Should Congress permanently ban new state and local taxes on Internet commerce?

ADAM THIERER
WALKER FELLOW IN ECONOMIC POLICY, THE HERITAGE FOUNDATION

FROM "SPARE INTERNET FROM TAXATION?" THE WASHINGTON TIMES, JULY 11, 1997. REPRINTED WITH PERMISSION.

Show me an untaxed corner of the economy, and I'll show you a politician eager to plunder a "new source of revenue." So it is with the Internet, which has America's 30,000 state and local taxing jurisdictions drooling with anticipation at the thought of shaving a slice from this promising new industry.

Absent from their calculations is the fact that subjecting interactive technologies to 30,000 different sets of tax collectors would hobble one of the fastest-growing segments of the U.S. economy. . . .

[T]here is another barrier to local officials taxing the Internet: the U.S. Constitution. The Founding Fathers wisely included a section in the Constitution that prevents states and localities from taxing interstate commerce, which is exactly what electronically transmitted information is. When a good or service enters the stream of interstate commerce, the "Commerce Clause" gives Congress the power to prohibit state or local actions that interfere with the free flow of that commerce.

While the founders could not have envisioned the development of modern, technologically advanced sectors of the economy such as the Internet, the Constitutional framework they outlined for basic commercial activities still applies. State and local officials may not like it, but their taxing authority ends at the geographical boundaries of their jurisdictions.

Moreover, even if states and localities had the proper authority to tax the Internet, they would run into a host of practical problems. Electronically transferred information travels across the Internet far too quickly for regulators to monitor and, more importantly, does so in a way that respects no geographic boundaries. It is virtually impossible to know the points at which the billions of daily Internet transactions begin and end. Consequently, state and local attempts to tax such intangible electronic commerce would result in a confusing and overlapping set of tax laws. . . .

The proliferation of satellite-based technologies and the wireless transmission of information will only add to the confusion. As an increasing amount of Internet traffic is transmitted wirelessly across the United States and around the world, the jurisdictional claims of states and localities certainly will lose credibility. States and localities will have to be content with taxing firms that provide Internet services within their jurisdictions. Anything more than that becomes legally and logistically problematic.

RAYMOND C. SCHEPPACH
EXECUTIVE DIRECTOR, NATIONAL GOVERNORS' ASSOCIATION

FROM TESTIMONY BEFORE SENATE FINANCE COMMITTEE, JULY 16, 1998.

Today, only 11 states have taxes on Internet access. . . . Nevertheless, congressional committees continue to consider legislation to address the "problem" of state and local taxes potentially threatening the future growth and development of the Internet. . . .

The fear that 30,000 taxing jurisdictions could threaten the development of the Internet is an unfounded one. Most transactions take place between two parties — a buyer and a seller. Occasionally multiple parties are involved, but it is nearly always a small and manageable number. The only taxes that could be involved in such a transaction are the taxes of the states and cities in which those parties are located. In fact, in nearly every case, the purchaser's location alone determines the tax consequences of a transaction. The concern that multiple jurisdictions will somehow be taxing single transactions has yet to be demonstrated. Before federal legislation is adopted to prevent such a problem, there should be some evidence of a problem. . . .

We have noticed that none of these proposed bills to protect the Internet has included restrictions on federal taxing authority, for instance, the collection of the federal airline ticket tax for tickets sold over the Internet. Apparently what is good for the states and cities is not good for the federal government. We also notice that at the same time there is pressure to stop state and local taxation of Internet access, the federal subscriber line charge on individual telephone lines increases by the number of lines into a household. Thus, if a family decides to get a second line to permit them to make greater use of the Internet, the federal tax on that line is $5.40 per month, compared with $3.50 for the primary phone line. . . .

Today, more than 90 percent of most products are sold in stores, and if products are sold in a state that has a sales tax on that particular product, those sales are taxed. These taxes are what pay for the schools and hospitals, police services and roads that our citizens depend on. . . . However, if a product is sold into a state by a vendor with no physical presence in a state, the sales tax is not collected. The tax is due, but it can't be collected. This unfairness must be corrected, and our proposal for a streamlined, simplified sales tax with uniform definitions of goods and services across all participating states, simplified audit and collection procedures and one sales tax rate per state is designed to make the sales tax collective by remote vendors. . . .

Following the Leaders

The pending purchase of Netscape Communications Corp. by America Online Inc. — and concurrent strategic moves by Microsoft Corp. — will influence the direction of digital commerce for years to come. Here's why these three firms are so important to the online industry:

Netscape — Marc Andreessen and other engineers who developed the early Mosaic Web browser founded the company in California's Silicon Valley just five years ago. Netscape's Navigator browser, first shipped in late 1994, quickly became the preferred tool for computer users to surf the Internet. However, it has steadily lost market share to Microsoft's Explorer, a rival Web browser first introduced in 1996 that is included with Microsoft's Windows PC operating system. Netscape now distributes its browser for free (it is used by approximately 70 million people) and generates most of its revenues from selling digital-commerce and other software to corporations. The electronic-commerce software enables companies to create Web pages and process electronic transactions.

America Online — The Herndon, Va., company was founded as Quantum Computer Services in 1985 and has grown into the world's biggest Internet company, with 14 million subscribers. It acts as a combination service provider and portal, connecting people to the World Wide Web, providing e-mail and chat rooms and offering news, entertainment and commercial services. Now it wants to make the Internet more of a two-way medium, in which businesses interact directly with computer users. By absorbing Netscape and working with partner Sun Microsystems Inc., AOL wants to develop a full line of digital-commerce software and services and, ultimately, a new programming language to get around Microsoft's dominance of desktop computing. This could lead to the development of small devices that bring digital commerce and AOL services to people, without the need for a PC.

Microsoft — The 800-pound gorilla of the personal computer industry was founded in 1975 by Bill Gates and high school classmate Paul Allen. The Redmond, Wash., firm has become a market force through its Windows operating system, which runs in more than 90 percent of the personal computers sold today. Windows is the route most desktop computer users take to connect with the Internet. However, Microsoft has been slow to establish a presence in digital commerce. Gates is trying to build up market share with MSN, an online service that competes with AOL, and digital-commerce offerings that sell cars, travel and real estate. Microsoft also owns the Sidewalk network of local Web sites, which list entertainment and feature digital Yellow Pages. The company is the target of a U.S. Department of Justice antitrust suit. It charges that Microsoft violated terms of a 1995 court decree by using its market power in operating system software to boost its share of the browser market, at Netscape's expense. The company says it was only trying to improve its product offerings and give customers more for their money. The outcome will be significant; if Microsoft loses, some believe the government will force it to include rivals' browsers and other products on Windows — or even break up the company. If Microsoft loses, it is expected to appeal, meaning the case will likely drag on for years.

the Internet, hoping to steer more business to its brokers. [17]

Complaints about online trading have prompted the Securities and Exchange Commission (SEC) to pay more attention to the sector. The SEC has been flooded by hundreds of complaints from investors, who noted discrepancies between the stock prices quoted on their computer screens and what they ended up paying. SEC Chairman Arthur Levitt recently cautioned small investors who have flocked to the Internet to approach electronic investing with care. [18]

Fighting Fraud

Other financial-services professionals are worried about Internet rivals eroding their core business. Bankers note that E*Trade now offers online mortgages, insurance and credit cards. Charles Schwab is adding insurance and electronic bill payments to its Internet services. Industry-watchers wonder whether new electronic intermediaries handling vast amounts of customer information will be regulated the same way as banks and other financial institutions. They also question whether a surge in electronic cash transactions will make it difficult to monitor spending and lead to fraud and money-laundering.

Concerns about fraud also extend to the electronic auction services that are proving increasingly popular in the digital market. The services are built around the idea that businesses are as eager to bid on machine parts and computer equipment as consumers who seek Beanie Babies and sports memorabilia. [19]

However, the potential for abuse is great. Buyers can be victimized by sellers who don't deliver the advertised goods. Sellers also can fall victim to prank bids, or buyers who collaborate to lower prices. In one scenario, a buyer can make a very high bid on an auction item to scare off all other bidders, then withdraw it, allowing a collaborator to then come in with a much lower offer. Because many auctions are conducted anonymously, enforcement is difficult.

The FTC is looking at strengthening anti-fraud measures, particularly as they relate to international transactions. FTC Bureau of Consumer Protection Director Jodie Bernstein says the agency wants to "promote global understanding of the issues at stake and develop a thoughtful, proactive approach . . . for Internet retailing to reach its full potential."

However, electronic retailers appear content to try to safeguard themselves. eBay adopts a Better Business Bureau-style approach by asking buyers to evaluate sellers' promptness and honesty, then posting the evaluations on the site. "The point is to have reputation follow you electronically, whether it is good or bad," says eBay Chief Executive Officer Margaret Whitman.

Those measures may not be enough, however. The New York City Department of Consumer Affairs recently launched a fraud investigation into whether people who use eBay falsely labeled some sports memorabilia as "one-of-a-kind." The probe could decide whether an Internet auction service is accountable for unscrupulous clients. [20]

Other business-to-business sites utilize bank credit verification systems to check sellers' identities and credit. And Internet companies like Netscape are developing more transaction-security software, hoping to demonstrate to would-be regulators that the industry is serious about policing itself.

One area where Internet companies may not be able to escape looming regulation is in the market for

their very own stocks. Electronic retailers' shares have soared to unprecedented highs as investors realize the digital commerce market's potential. By mid-January, eBay's stock had risen 1,500 percent from its initial public offering price last September. Amazon.com's stock price doubled roughly twice a month before losing more than half its market value over eight trading days in January. The company had been valued at $29 billion — more than Sears, Roebuck & Co. — even though it hasn't turned a profit since its inception three-and-a-half years ago.

The National Association of Securities Dealers and the Securities and Exchange Commission (SEC) both have brought enforcement actions against speculators manipulating stock prices. And the Nasdaq stock exchange is working with the SEC to consider ways to limit volatility in the Internet sector, perhaps by changing the way initial public offerings (IPOs) are brought to market.

"There is a fair amount of downside risk for both market participants and investors with these kinds of swings," Nasdaq spokesman Scott Peterson said recently. [21] ∎

OUTLOOK

No Government Action?

While digital commerce grows at a breathtaking pace, the status quo of non-regulation persists on the Internet. That is likely to continue, in the opinion of many analysts, because government's cumbersome rule-making process and long-term planning can't possibly keep up with a surging market that defies most growth predictions.

Digital commerce's ability to confound even the high-tech experts was evident during the recent holiday season, when the Marketing Corporation of America estimated that U.S. consumers spent $8.2 billion online. That was nearly seven times the amount that it estimated was spent in 1997, and considerably more than pre-holiday industry estimates of from $2.3 billion to $3.5 billion. [22]

The marketing group says it arrived at the number by interviewing 2,000 online merchants and consumers. Craig Johnson, director of the group's electronic retail practice, says forecasts can underestimate totals because they rely on incomplete data from online merchants, or rely too much on consumer surveys that tend to overstate purchases.

It's difficult to even assess the size of the digital market that government is considering regulating. Estimates of total U.S. business and consumer purchases last year range from $31 billion to $51 billion, depending on the methodology used. Even calculating the number of people with online access varies widely: Media Metrix pegs the number of Americans connected to the Web at about 56.8 million, while the Marketing Corporation of America says it's more like 102 million.

The numbers are likely to surge further with the advent of programming technology that bypasses personal computers and links the Internet to small, handheld devices not unlike pagers. The intelligent devices will allow motorists to download driving directions from the Web while in their cars, check their stock portfolios on the subway or be reminded to pick up milk on the way home. And their cost will make the Internet — and digital commerce — available to an entirely different segment of the population that can't afford PCs.

All of the market uncertainty may

provide a good argument for government to avoid intervening until the market matures. *Going Digital* authors Litan and Niskanen point to the history of high-definition television — another technology with the potential to dominate the 21st century that surged on the scene in the 1980s, tempting regulators to set rules. The Bush administration had a choice of setting industry standards for HDTV transmitters and sets or allowing 20 or so domestic manufacturers to hash out rules for the market. The White House took a hands-off approach, prompting the companies to develop better technologies that eventually led to today's crisp, cinema-quality pictures.

"It is important not to assume that government action may be required to resolve every uncertainty or technological incompatibility associated with electronic commerce," the authors write. "Markets can do a far better job, more quickly, than can governments." ∎

FOR MORE INFORMATION

American Electronics Association, 601 Pennsylvania Ave. N.W., North Building, #600, Washington, D.C. 20004; (202) 682-9110, www.aeanet.org. This trade group for software, electronic, telecommunications and information technology companies concentrates on trade issues, including export controls of Internet-related products.

Electronic Privacy Information Center, 1718 Connecticut Ave. N.W., Suite 200, Washington, D.C. 20003; (202) 483-1140, www.epic.org. This civil liberties group focuses on computer privacy, encryption, information access and other cyberspace issues.

Internet Society, 11150 Sunset Hills Rd., Suite 100, Reston, Va. 20190; (703) 326-9880, www.isoc.org. A research and educational organization that promotes further development and availability of the Internet and its associated technologies.

Progress and Freedom Foundation, 1301 K St. N.W., Suite 550E, Washington, D.C. 20005; (202) 289-8928, www.pff.org. This conservative-leaning think tank studies how the digital revolution and Internet use affect public policy.

Notes

[1] See "Special Report: The Internet," *The Wall Street Journal*, Dec. 7, 1998, pp. R1-32.

[2] For background, see Charles S. Clark, "Regulating the Internet," *The CQ Researcher*, June 30, 1995, pp. 561-584.

[3] See Jared Sandberg, "Net Gain," and Steven Levy, "Xmas.com," *Newsweek*, Dec. 7, 1998, pp. 46-57.

[4] See Stephen Labaton, "AT&T Passes Hurdle in Plan to Buy TCI," *The New York Times*, Dec. 31, 1998, p. C1.

[5] For background, see David Masci, "Internet Privacy," *The CQ Researcher*, Nov. 6, 1998, pp. 953-976.

[6] Quoted in John Judis, "online Magaziner," *The New Republic*, Dec. 28, 1998, p. 27.

[7] Simon Davies, *The Daily Telegraph*, Jan. 21, 1999, p. 6.

[8] For background, see Eileen Shanahan, "www.taxfree.com," *Governing*, December 1998, pp. 34-38.

[9] For background, see "The Disappearing Taxpayer" and "Taxes Slip Through the Net," *The Economist*, May 31, 1997, pp. 15, 22.

[10] Austan Goolsbee, "In a World Without Borders: The Impact of Taxes on Internet Commerce," Working Paper, University of Chicago, 1998.

[11] See Alan Ota, "On-Line Smut Curb Criticized As Too Tough," *CQ Weekly*, Sept. 19, 1998, p. 2499.

[12] See Pamela Mendels, "online Smut Law Heads Into Court," *The New York Times*, Jan. 18, 1999, p. C3.

[13] See Christopher Finan, "New Internet Law Is Wrong for Adults," *Newsday*, Nov. 10, 1998, p. A45.

[14] See Sharon Waxman, "King of the World Wild Web," *The Washington Post*, Jan. 6, 1999, p. C1. For background, see Richard L. Worsnop, "Gambling Under Attack," *The CQ Researcher*, Sept. 6, 1996, pp. 769-792.

[15] See Mary Meeker and Sharon Pearson, "Morgan Stanley U.S. Investment Research: Internet Retail," Morgan Stanley & Co., May 28. 1997, p. 2-2-2-6.

[16] See Martha Stewart, "My Big Bet on the Net," *Newsweek*, Dec. 7, 1998, p. 53.

[17] For background, see Fred Vogelstein, "online Traders Beware!" *U.S. News & World Report*, Jan. 18, 1999, p. 41.

[18] See Stephen Labaton, "On-Line Trades Rise and So Do The Complaints," *The New York Times*, Jan. 28, 1999, p. A1.

[19] See Claudia Deutsch, "Business Explore online Auctions for Equipment, Parts," *The New York Times*, June 1, 1998.

[20] See Donna De La Cruz, "Web Site eBay Under Investigation," *The Associated Press*, Jan. 27, 1999.

[21] Quoted in Jennifer Files, "Internet Shares Climb to Higher Territory," *Dallas Morning News*, Jan. 12, 1999, p. 1D.

[22] See Maryann Jones Thompson, "New Total for online Holiday Shopping: $8 Billion," *The Industry Standard*, Jan. 15, 1999, www.thestandard.net.

Bibliography

Selected Sources Used

Books

Case, John, *Digital Future*, William Morrow, 1985.

A dated but revealing look at the evolution of the personal-computer market and how it began to affect delivery of goods and services, as it was happening.

Kalakota, Ravi, and Andrew Whinston, *Frontiers of Electronic Commerce*, Addison-Wesley, 1996.

A good overview of the emerging electronic-commerce market, with special attention to the way the Internet works, available technologies and regulations. Somewhat technical, but accessible to general readers.

Litan, Robert, and William Niskanen, *Going Digital!* Brookings Institution Press and Cato Institute, 1998.

Two respected policy analysts outline what they think U.S. lawmakers must do to assure that Information Age technology benefits the global economy. Both favor limited government intervention in digital-commerce markets.

Shurkin, Joel, *Engines of the Mind*, W.W. Norton, 1996.

A respected science writer outlines the evolution of the computer, focusing on the people who developed innovations like the transistor. He does not take up the Internet or digital commerce.

Articles

Hof, Robert, Heather Green and Linda Himelstein, "Now It's Your Web," *Business Week*, Oct. 5, 1998, pp. 164-176.

This overview explains how the Internet is moving toward one-to-one marketing, changing the way all companies will do business.

Judis, John, "Ira's Impractical Plan for the Internet," *The New Republic*, Dec. 28, 1998, pp. 27-32.

This profile of White House adviser Ira Magaziner includes the pros and cons of his plan calling for less government regulation of the Internet.

Sandberg, Jared, "Net Gain," *Newsweek*, Dec. 7, 1998, pp. 46-49.

America Online's deal to acquire Netscape is a high-stakes gamble on the Internet, digital commerce and how technology will affect Americans' lives, Sandberg says.

"Selling Points," *The Wall Street Journal Reports*, Dec. 7, 1998, pp. R1-R32.

A series of articles examining where Internet commerce is succeeding, barriers to further growth and what marketers are learning about online buying habits.

"The Disappearing Taxpayer," *The Economist*, May 31, 1997, p. 15.

The development of digital commerce raises the question of whether governments should continue to levy taxes in a world in which companies, assets and people are mobile.

Walker, Leslie, and Stephanie Stoughton, "Click! Click! Click!" *The Washington Post*, Nov. 22, 1998, p. H1.

A consumer's guide to online shopping and how Web-based buyers' services are still evolving.

Reports and Studies

***Is The New Global Economy Leaving State-Local Tax Structures Behind?* National League of Cities, National Conference of State Legislatures, National Governors' Association, 1998.**

The rise of digital commerce poses potential threats to the current state-local tax structure, argue three trade groups for local and state governments in this policy paper.

***Online Retail Strategies*, Forrester Research, 1998.**

This leading new-media market-research firm tracks digital commerce's growth spiral, analyzes retail categories and sizes up the potential market.

***The Emerging Digital Economy*, Technology Administration, U.S. Department of Commerce, 1998.**

This Clinton administration policy paper outlines reasons for minimal government intervention in Internet transactions and provides a history of electronic commerce.

16 Copyright and the Internet

KENNETH JOST

Nick Chupka has hundreds of music CDs in his collection, but he bought no more than two or three disks in the past year. Instead, the 21-year-old University of Maryland senior is doing what millions of other music fans are doing. He downloads songs from on-line digital music distribution networks — from Web sites with odd-sounding names like Napster, MyMP3.com and Gnutella.

Many music fans look on Napster — the most popular of the networks with a claimed 27 million users — as a magnificent boon. "It's a really good resource for pretty much finding any kind of music that you're looking for," says Chupka, who plans to teach American literature in high school. "It also provides a place where people can experiment and try things out. They don't have to buy a whole CD. They can try out a song and see if they like it."

The record industry, how

From *The CQ Researcher,* September 29, 2000.

Rock star Courtney Love supports free distribution of music via Napster and other on-line music-sharing sources. "Technology that exposes our music to a larger audience can only be a good thing," she says.

ever, is fighting the on-line services in court, accusing both Napster and MyMP3.com of violating copyright laws and threatening to erode the economic base for popular music. "It's blatant theft of other people's copyrighted works," says Cary Sherman, general counsel for the Recording Industry Association of America (RIAA), which represents the biggest U.S. labels.

But in Chupka's view, it's the recording industry that takes advantage — of performers as well as consumers like him. "I'm not a big fan of the recording industry at all," he says. "I would love for this whole digital music thing to do away with the recording industry as a whole."

Meanwhile, he's saving a whole lot of money on Phish, the Grateful Dead, the Disco Biscuits and his other favorite bands. "If I had to purchase all of those CDs, I can't even imagine all the thousands of dollars I would have had to spend," he says.

But more important to Chupka than the savings was "being able to get a lot of songs," including obscure, hard-to-find ones, he says.

In fact, Napster's so-called "music file-sharing community" collectively probably owns enough recordings to rival any institutional collection in the world. And accessing its growing, far-flung trove involves two simple steps: Log on to Napster.com, then type in the name of a favorite song or composition. In a cyber-instant, Napster's giant search engine finds the work on a member computer and provides the connection for downloading it to yours. (*See diagram, p. 298.*)

Which is exactly what the record industry sees as wrong. Napster "is an illustration of somebody who makes it easy and possible for you to walk out [of a record store] without paying for it," says Judith Saffer, an assistant general counsel of Broadcast Music Inc. (BMI), one of the two major music-licensing organizations.

But Napster's supporters insist the network is not violating the law. Instead, they say the service is legitimately exploiting the Internet's potential for so-called "peer-to-peer sharing."

"People can share music, share texts, share books, if they do it individually — in person, through the mail or the like," says David Boies, the nationally known litigator hired to represent Napster in the copyright-infringement case. "What the Internet does is to provide an efficient ability to do it on a broader scale. The question is whether the efficiency of the Internet means you should prevent people from doing on the Internet things that they can unquestionably do lawfully in other ways."

So far, the record industry is winning in court against both Napster and MyMP3.com. A federal judge in New York in April found MyMP3.com guilty of copyright infringement and last month ordered the service to pay the biggest record company, Univer-

How Napster Works

Napster.com enables computer users to download free music recordings via the Internet. Napster does not store MP3 files (standard, compressed music or video files that can be transmitted over the Internet), but searches for MP3 files on computers of Napster users; the Napster site includes a chat room and audio player.

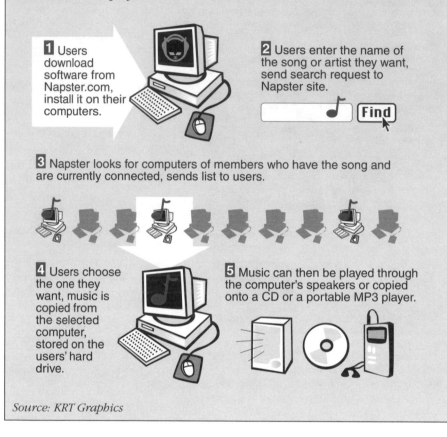

1 Users download software from Napster.com, install it on their computers.

2 Users enter the name of the song or artist they want, send search request to Napster site.

3 Napster looks for computers of members who have the song and are currently connected, sends list to users.

4 Users choose the one they want, music is copied from the selected computer, stored on the users' hard drive.

5 Music can then be played through the computer's speakers or copied onto a CD or a portable MP3 player.

Source: KRT Graphics

sal Music Group, $25,000 for each of the label's discs that the site had on its server. Meanwhile, a federal judge in San Francisco in late July found Napster guilty of contributory copyright infringement and ordered the file-sharing service shut down. But the federal appeals court in San Francisco blocked the shutdown order pending an appeal of the judge's preliminary injunction that will be heard on Oct. 2.

Similar copyright-related disputes are popping up all around the Internet. The movie industry is suing the publisher of a self-styled hacker magazine for posting on its Web site the computer code for hacking movie videodisks, or DVDs. The movie industry is also seeking to shut down a fledgling Web site that bills itself as "a virtual VCR" — with stored copies of television programs that users can download to their computers on demand. And news organizations, sports leagues, authors and a host of other copyright holders are either engaged in disputes over access to their material on the Internet or girding for conflict in the future. (*See story, p. 309.*)

The "copyright community" — the record and film industries, many intellectual-property lawyers and many academic experts — say the disputes are fueled by a Wild West-type mentality pervasive among many Internet advocates and users.

"There's a rather surprising camp of people out there who believe that violating copyright law is simply a new business strategy and that's OK because we shouldn't be bound by these antiquarian legal concepts," says Mark Radcliffe, a lawyer with one of Silicon Valley's leading intellectual-property firms.

But James Boyle, a copyright expert at Duke University Law School in Durham, N.C., says the record and film industries' complaints that the Internet is facilitating widespread "piracy" of their works are not well-founded. "What people are arguing about is what is mine and what is yours — exactly how much an intellectual-property owner should control," Boyle says. "When we talk about piracy, it sounds like we know what's mine and what's yours. That's not the situation we have here at all."

Experts on both sides, however, agree that the disputes are forcing some fundamental re-examinations of copyright-law principles that originated with the invention of the printing press and changed with each new technological innovation making copying easier and less expensive.

"It's pretty clear that this new medium is challenging old paradigms in a way that they can't withstand," says Meg Smith, a fellow at Harvard Law School's Berkman Center for Internet and Society. "It's becoming harder and harder to stretch existing law to accommodate what we can now do."

"The titanic struggle that's going on is one in which the copyright holders are desperately trying to hold on to the old regime, though I believe they understand the old regime is crumbling," says Michael Shamos, a computer and copyright law expert at Carnegie Mellon University in Pittsburgh. Copyright holders, Shamos says, "are trying to forestall the day when information, which wants to be free, will in fact be free."

As the copyright disputes are played out on the Internet, in the marketplace and in legislative and judicial arenas, here are some of the major questions being debated:

Are traditional copyright-law principles outmoded in the Internet age?

No one needed a copyright statute when monks copied books by hand and roving troubadours carried the popular music of the day in their heads. But then came the printing press. And a few centuries later the camera. And the phonograph. And then the photocopier.

Each technological breakthrough made it less and less expensive to copy creative works with greater and greater fidelity to the original. The achievements resulted in new and wider audiences for creative works but also posed some knotty problems about how to ensure fair compensation for authors, artists and composers.

The advent of digitized information seemingly offers the ultimate in inexpensive copying of information of all sorts. "The cost of copying a work on the Internet is one-quarter of a cent," Shamos says. "And it's diminishing. It's not going to go to zero, but it's going to get close."

Internet advocates say the changed economics can help or hurt copyright holders. "Cheaper copying means there are greater possibilities for so-called piracy," Duke's Boyle says. "Of course, it also lowers your cost of production, your cost of distribution, your cost of advertising. So

you really need better empirical evidence of what the overall effect is."

But copyright lawyers generally minimize the need for rethinking established legal principles. "As far as the copyright community is concerned, people's copyright rights are entitled to be protected no matter what the medium," says BMI's Saffer,

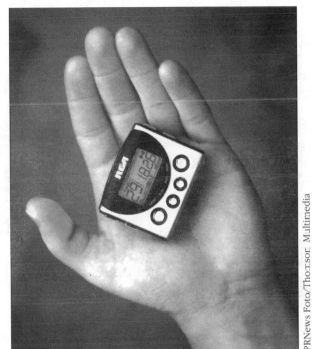

This tiny MP3 player produced by RCA was unveiled in June at the San Diego MP3 Summit in California. The miniature device can play audio MP3 files downloaded from a personal computer.

who also serves as chair of the American Intellectual Property Law Association's copyright committee. "Just because there's a new medium doesn't mean that you throw the rules away and start from scratch."

The most important legal principle under scrutiny is "fair use" — a doctrine first recognized in U.S. court decisions in the 19th century and written into federal law in a 1976 revision of the Copyright Act. "Fair use" represents a defense to a use or copying of a copyrighted work that otherwise would amount to a copyright

infringement. For example, the owner of a book can photocopy some pages of a copyrighted book for personal use — even if the book carries a stern warning against reproduction of any portion without the written consent of the author or publisher.

The 1976 law instructs courts to consider four factors in considering a fair use defense: first, "the purpose and character of the use" — for example, commercial on one hand or educational on the other; second, "the nature of the copyrighted work"; third, "the amount and substantiality of the portion used in relation to the copyrighted work as a whole"; and, fourth, "the effect of the use upon the potential market for or value of the copyrighted work."

The fourth factor — the effect on the market — is often decisive. In a pivotal 1973 decision, the U.S. Court of Claims upheld the National Library of Medicine's practice of routinely photocopying articles from scholarly journals for patrons on the ground that the publisher had failed to prove a reduction in subscription sales (*Williams & Wilkins v. The United States*). In another major decision, the U.S. Supreme Court in 1984 ruled that home videotaping of movies shown on television is a protected fair use in part because movie studios had failed to show that the practice reduced the audience for televised films (*Sony Corporation of America v. Universal City Studios, Inc.*).

Interest groups and experts alike approach the fair-use issue from different perspectives. "In my view, fair use is certainly subservient to the rights of the copyright owner," Shamos says. But Duke's Boyle argues that free-speech principles require a broader interpretation. "The Supreme Court has said several times that fair use is essential to the constitutionality of copyright," he says.

The fair-use issue figures in all of the current Internet-related copyright disputes, but there are also other legal issues that relate to laws enacted since the beginning of the digital age. Napster and MyMP3.com are citing a 1992 law — the Audio Home Recording Act — that sought to settle a dispute over copying of digital audiotapes by specifically authorizing non-commercial copying of a single digital audiotape. By contrast, the film industry is using a provision of a 1998 law — the Digital Millennium Copyright Act — to try to prohibit the posting of the DVD decryption code.

Whatever reading the courts give to those specific statutes, the broader — seemingly inescapable — challenge will remain to redefine fair use in a world where nearly perfect copying and instantaneously global distribution are possible at minimal cost.

"We've never looked at fair use where you have distribution costs that are essentially zero," concedes Smith of Harvard's Berkman Center. In contrast to other recognized fair-use examples, she says, "we're in a context where you can imagine the market being harmed."

For his part, Shamos acknowledges that copyright holders may have to do some rethinking to fashion a viable economic structure for the marketplace created by the new technology. "We need a mechanism for financial accountability for copying that manages to put an appropriate royalty in the copyright owner — where appropriate might be much lower on a per-copy basis if the number of people getting the work is much larger," Shamos says. "But if [royalties] get to zero, that will shut down the impetus for many [people] to be creative."

Are on-line music-distribution networks violating copyright laws?

The Napster phenomenon was drawing tens of thousands of Internet-savvy music fans last year before the non-wired world took much note.

Madonna presents the MTV Video Music Award for Best Rap Video to Dr. Dre, who along with Metallica and other artists opposes free music sharing. "To have yet one more way to strip an artist of making an honest living is just too much," he says.

When federal Judge Marilyn Hall Patel found Napster guilty of copyright infringement on July 26 and ordered the service shut down, however, the ruling was Page 1 news. And the ruling resulted in a sudden surge of traffic for Napster, boosting its Web site from the 31st to the 19th most visited on-line site for the week. [1]

Napster's 19-year-old founder, Shawn Fanning — whose "nappy" haircut gave the company its name — reacted to the ruling by digging in his heels. "We will keep fighting for Napster and for your right to share music over the Internet," Fanning said in a Webcast following the decision. For its part, the recording industry association said the ruling "sends a strong message to others that they cannot build a business based on others' copyrighted works without permission." [2]

Today, opposing attorneys echo the same sentiments. "What's at stake is the extent to which [music fans] are going to continue to have the convenient and efficient access to music that Napster offers," says Boies, who came to the Napster case fresh from his victory as special trial counsel for the government in its antitrust suit against Microsoft Corp.

But RIAA general counsel Sherman mocks Napster's argument that the company is advancing the cause of popular music. "The most amazing thing is they call themselves a music community," Sherman says. "They haven't spent a dime on creating music. They are simply taking advantage of the music that the record companies have invested in."

In her ruling, Judge Patel decisively rejected Napster's two central arguments. First, she said, Napster users were not engaging in a recognized "fair use" of their recordings. "It's not a typical personal use when music is distributed to many anonymous users," Patel said. Second, she found Napster liable for contributory infringement because copying copyrighted works outweighed any legal uses for the technology, such as promoting artists' works with their consent. "That was the whole reason for Napster's existence," the judge said.

Copyright experts are divided on whether Patel applied the right legal principles. Napster "has a small number of legitimate uses, but the overriding purpose is to enable people to obtain music without paying for it," says Shamos of Carnegie Mellon.

But Peter Jaszi, a professor at American University's Washington College of Law, says the Supreme Court's home videotaping decision protects a new technology from liability for contributory infringement if it has some substantial legitimate use.

"Judge Patel says most of the people using Napster are using it in a bad way, so the technology has to go down," says Jaszi, who signed an appellate brief in support of Napster. "She's got the basic criterion wrong."

The MP3.com case — the name stems from the now standard digital file-compression format devised by the Motion Picture Expert Group — also involves a mix of legitimate and allegedly illegitimate uses of the Internet for distributing music. Computer entrepreneur Michael Robertson started the company to give artists a chance to promote their music, but in January he launched an upgraded "Instant Licensing" service that allowed users on-line access to a library of some 45,000 popular music CDs.

Ostensibly, users first had to verify ownership of the CD — by registering at a store or uploading the CD themselves from their own computer. The record industry says the verification process is easy to evade — for example, by borrowing a CD from a friend. More broadly, though, the record companies claim the copying represented a clear violation of copyright-law principles.

U.S. District Court Judge Jed Rakoff in Manhattan agreed in a preliminary ruling on April 28. [3] Afterward, MP3.com settled with all but one of the record companies that had filed suit — for undisclosed sums reported to be about $20 million each. But Universal Music Group kept on with its suit, and the judge on Sept. 6 ordered MP3.com to pay $25,000 — a sum that could total $250 million — for each of the label's disks that it had uploaded.

Robertson continued to insist that the company was operating within copyright laws. "We built technology that lets people listen to their own CD collections," he told reporters. [4] But Jaszi calls MP3.com's defense "difficult." "MP3.com was actively involved in the unauthorized reproduction of music," he says, "and it was doing so without any clear privilege under the statute."

Even if record companies prevail against Napster and MP3.com, other file-sharing technologies and companies are on the horizon that observers say may prove more difficult to police. And many observers fault the record industry for being slow to recognize the potential of on-line distribution of music.

"Right now, they're just trying to fight the competition in court because they're not ready to fight with technology," says Smith, the Berkman Center fellow.

RIAA general counsel Sherman says the criticism is unwarranted. "Our companies want to be on the Internet in innovative ways, but sometimes you have to stand up for basic principles or get overridden," he says. "Hopefully, the principles that are established will result in the quicker establishment of a legitimate marketplace because the rules will be known that licenses have to be obtained."

Should courts block the dissemination of software to "decrypt" DVD movie disks?

The movie industry spent millions of dollars to develop an encryption software to prevent copying of DVD movie disks. But last fall, the industry's "Content Scrambling System" (CSS) software was hacked — by a 15-year-old Norwegian, Jon Johansen, working with two people he met under pseudonyms on the Internet. The movie industry is now in federal court trying to prevent the "DeCSS" decryption program from being broadly disseminated through the Internet.

The suit, filed in January by eight of the major U.S. motion picture studios, relies on a central provision of the Digital Millennium Copyright Act (DMCA) aimed at preventing the circumvention of technology to protect copyrighted material. [5] The anti-circumvention provision — codified as Section 1201 of the Copyright Act — provides that no one shall "offer to the public, provide or otherwise traffic in" a technology that is "primarily designed or produced" to circumvent a copyright-protection technology or that has only "limited commercially significant purpose" other than circumvention.

The statute broadly defines "circumvention" to include descrambling a scrambled work, decrypting an encrypted work or otherwise bypassing or removing a technological measure without the copyright owner's permission. The act allows certain exceptions — most significantly for so-called "reverse engineering." Under this exception, software developers are allowed, in effect, to decode an encryption software "for the sole purpose of" making the product compatible with a different computer operating system.

In fact, Johansen claimed that one of his purposes was to make it possible to view DVDs on VCRs using the new Linux operating system, not just on Windows-operated machines. The studios dismissed that explanation. They said that the DeCSS program was written for Windows-based software and that the industry was in the process of licensing manufacturers to produce Linux-based DVD players.

The studios did not take legal action against Johansen, however. They acted after the magazine *2600*, self-described as "The Hacker Quarterly," posted the DeCSS program on its Web site (www.2600.com). In their suit, the studios depicted the decryption software as the sort of piracy-enabling technology that Congress intended to shut off and the Web site posting as the kind of trafficking in circumvention technology that the law prohibited.

"We are determined to defend the technology that protects artists' and intellectual-property holders' rights," Jack Valenti, president of the Motion Picture Association of America (MPAA), said at the time. "If you can't protect that which you own, then you don't own anything."

The three defendants named in the suit — including the magazine's publisher, Eric Corley — countered by arguing that publishing the decryption software was legitimate because of the reverse-engineering exception.

"Congress certainly did not intend to destroy the traditional rights of the public by barring technologies that facilitate circumvention for lawful fair-use purposes," the defendants' lawyers wrote in one of their briefs.

In two rulings, U.S. District Judge Lewis Kaplan in Manhattan came down decisively on the studios' side — first in issuing a preliminary injunction on Jan. 20 and then in making the injunction permanent on Aug. 17.[6] Kaplan rejected the "fair use" defense, which he said Congress had not incorporated in the anti-circumvention provision, as well as broader free-speech arguments raised by the defense.

"There is no serious question that defendants' posting of DeCSS violates the DMCA," Kaplan wrote in his 89-page opinion in August.

Computer law expert Shamos, the studios' lead witness in the case, acknowledges that the statute may restrict the ability to write and distribute software, but he echoes Kaplan in saying that Congress envisioned that result.

"If the purpose of the software is merely to enable people to steal the copyrighted works of others," Shamos says, "Congress decided that it should be prohibited. It doesn't stop anybody who's legitimate, and it does stop people who are not legitimate."

But Jason Mahler, vice president and general counsel of the Computer and Communications Industry Association, disagrees. "Congress did not want to stand in the way of development of new technologies that might benefit consumers and everyone else but which may be used illegally," Mahler says. "You don't make cars illegal just because bank robbers can use them to get away with ill-gotten money."

Another critic, Smith of the Berkman Center for Internet and Society, says the ruling seems inconsistent with free-speech principles in other areas. "If you can publish bomb-making instructions, it's pretty shocking that you can't also publish instructions for decrypting something," Smith says.

She also criticizes the judge's decision to block the magazine not only from posting the computer code itself but also from providing links to other Web sites where the computer code can be found. "If we start chilling linking, then we really do lose a lot of the value of what the Internet is," she says.

For his part, Valenti strongly endorses the judge's ruling and dismisses all of the criticisms. "Right now, technology is being used illegitimately," Valenti says. "This magical technology allows you to bring this stuff down free of charge. We are working very hard to use technology legitimately and use it to defeat illegitimate technology." ■

BACKGROUND

"Exclusive" Rights

Copyright law in the United States has evolved over two centuries through a combination of legislative actions and judicial rulings laid over a marketplace for creative works periodically reshaped by technological advances. Lawmakers and judges, as well as the individuals and industries in the so-called creative community, have searched for an optimal balance between the two conflicting goals of rewarding creative endeavor while also protecting the public's interest in enjoying creative works.[7]

The Constitution viewed copyright in utilitarian terms — in contrast to the approach of some European countries that today still stress the "moral right" of authors. The framers authorized Congress to pass legislation to grant authors, "for limited times," "the exclusive right" to their "writings" in order to "promote the progress of science." (Art. I, Sec. 8, cl. 8.) In its first major copyright decision, the Supreme Court treated copyright as a statutory creation aimed primarily at serving the public interest and only secondarily at rewarding authors.[8]

Congress approved the first national copyright law in 1790, just a year after the ratification of the Constitution. The act allowed authors a 14-year copyright, renewable for a second 14-year term, subject to registering their work with a local district court and publishing a notice in local newspapers. Originally, only books could be copyrighted. But coverage was expanded through the 19th century, either by legislation or court rul-

Chronology

Before 1900
U.S. copyright law takes shape.

1790
Congress passes first copyright law, with 14-year term for literary works and option to renew for a second 14-year period; law is extended later to protect sheet music (1831), photographs (1865), works of art (1870) and musical performances (1897).

———— • ————

1900s-1960s
Copyright protection extended to new media; invention of photocopier challenges existing view on copyright infringement.

1909
Major revision of Copyright Act extends term to 28 years, with option to renew; provides protection for "piano rolls" as well as phonographs, subject to mandatory licensing provision. Law extended to cover motion pictures in 1912.

1918
Supreme Court rules International News Service guilty of "misappropriation" for republishing Associated Press news.

1960
Xerox Corp. introduces photocopier; copying of copyrighted materials becomes widespread.

———— • ————

1970s Photocopying
issue resolved; home video recording issue surfaces.

1973
Library photocopying of articles ruled legal by U.S. Court of Claims; ruling stands after Supreme Court deadlocks 4-4 in 1975.

1976
Major overhaul of Copyright Act extends term to life of author plus 50 years; codifies "fair use" defense, with four factors specified for consideration; permits library photocopying. Law had been extended earlier to cover sound recordings (1971).

———— • ————

1980s Movie studios
lose battle against home video recording.

1984
Home video recording of movies off broadcast television is ruled by Supreme Court to be legal "fair use."

———— • ————

1990 to Present Digital
revolution brings rash of disputes between copyright community and Internet advocates.

1992
Audio Home Recording Act permits individual, non-commercial copying of digital audiotapes; act requires royalties on sales of blank tapes and tape decks.

1993
CompuServe is sued by music publishers' group for establishing music bulletin board; settles suit in 1995 with agreement to pay licensing fees in the future.

1997
Movie studios introduce movies on DVD disks, with encryption software to prevent copying. Computer entrepreneur Michael Robertson launches MP3.com.

1998
Digital Millennium Copyright Act prohibits disseminating technology to circumvent software protection on CDs, DVDs and similar products.

May 1999
Shawn Fanning founds Napster.

October 1999
Norwegian teenager Jon Johansen "hacks" DVD encryption software.

Dec. 16, 1999
Record industry sues Napster for copyright infringement.

Jan. 14, 2000
Movie industry sues hacker magazine *2600* for disseminating DVD decryption software; judge issues preliminary injunction on Jan. 20 barring posting of computer code, permanent injunction on Aug. 17.

Jan. 21, 2000
Record companies sue MP3.com for copyright infringement; judge finds service guilty on April 2; imposes damages of $25,000 per disk on Sept. 6; further proceedings set for Nov. 13.

July 26, 2000
Judge finds Napster guilty of contributory copyright infringement and orders service shut down; appeals court blocks shutdown order two days later and schedules arguments for Oct. 2.

ing, to include prints, musical compositions, dramatic works, photographs, artistic works and sculpture.

A copyright dispute early in the 20th century serves as a harbinger of sorts of the end-of-century clashes over copyright on the Internet. The issue then was whether the statutory protection for "musical compositions" extended to piano rolls. The cylindrical devices with illegible scatterings of holes did not physically resemble copyrightable sheet music, but they served a similar purpose — and were viewed by composers and publishers as cutting into their markets. They asked the Supreme Court for copyright protection, but the justices in 1908 rejected their plea in a literalistic application of the Copyright Act.

Congress, which had already been working on overhauling the law, then stepped in. As part of the Copyright Act of 1909, lawmakers decided to provide copyright protection for piano rolls as well as the then-newfangled invention of phonograph records. But, as Stanford University law Professor Paul Goldstein explains, the law subjected this new right to a compulsory license.

"Once a copyright owner authorized a pianola or record company mechanically to copy his musical composition," Goldstein writes, "any other company was free to make its own recording of the composition by . . . paying the copyright owner two cents for each record it produced." [9]

The 1909 law expanded copyright to cover "all writings" — including speeches, for example — and extended the copyright term to 28 years, with the option of a 28-year renewal. The act disfavored authors and composers in another respect, however,

by preserving the formal requirements for securing a copyright that had been written into law in 1790 but eliminated in some European copyright acts.

Almost seven decades later, Con-

Michael Robertson, CEO and founder of MP3.com, testifies before a Senate Judiciary Committee on the future of digital music on July 11.

Reuters/Molly Riley

gress enacted another comprehensive revision of copyright law. The 1976 act expanded the scope of copyright to cover all written works, even if unpublished, and extended the duration of copyright to the life of the author plus 50 years. In addition, the formal notice and registration requirements were loosened, though not completely discarded. Most significantly perhaps, the law codified the judicially created doctrine of "fair use" as a defense to copyright-infringement claims.

The act listed four factors for courts

to consider in determining whether a claimed infringement was, in fact, a legal fair use but provided no guidance on how to weigh those factors. The issue had already emerged as pivotal in a copyright dispute over photocopying, and it was to become more important and more contentious in disputes still to come over videotaping and digital copying and distribution of copyrighted material.

Copying Rights

The invention of photocopiers and videocassette recorders (VCRs) allowed consumers to copy copyrighted material — at first books, articles and other printed matter, and then televised movies — with minimal effort and at minimal cost. Copyright holders turned to the courts for protection but were rebuffed in two legal showdowns that each reached the U.S. Supreme Court. [10]

The photocopying test case emerged in the 1960s in a dispute between a company that published medical journals and the government's National Library of Medicine, which had an assembly-line practice of photocopying articles from journals for patrons and other libraries. William Passano, president of Williams & Wilkins Co., the publishing firm, asked the library to pay two cents per page for copies; when the library turned him down, he filed a claim for compensation with the U.S. Court of Claims in 1968. The government contended that what it called the library's "longstanding practice of making copies for scholarly use" amounted to a protected "fair use."

A trial-level commissioner ruled in

Passano's favor in February 1972, saying that the library's photocopying reduced the market for subscriptions. In November 1973, however, the Court of Claims reversed the decision by a 4-3 vote. The majority found the evidence of reduced demand unpersuasive. Passano then took the case to the Supreme Court, which heard arguments in December 1974. Two months later, on Feb. 25, 1975, the court announced that the justices were deadlocked 4-4, with one justice recused; the tie vote left the Court of Claims' ruling in the government's favor on the books.

Congress then wrote the final word on the issue. The 1976 copyright revision specifically provided that libraries could reproduce a single copy of a work if the reproduction was not intended for commercial gain. In addition, it allowed libraries to make copies for interlibrary exchange — just as the National Library of Medicine had done — as long as the copying did not substitute for a subscription or purchase. And the law immunized libraries from liability for patrons' unsupervised use of copying machines as long as a copyright warning was posted nearby.

The VCR issue moved into the courts within a month after the copyright revision was signed into law in October 1976. Movie studios saw VCRs as a threat because they allowed consumers to record televised motion pictures and thereby reduced the studios' ability to charge broadcasters or cable channels for repeated showings. Two of the major movie studios — Universal City Studios and Walt Disney Productions — sued in federal court in Los Angeles in November 1976 to try to control the practice.

The studios targeted the Sony Corp., manufacturer of the then-dominant Betamax VCR, and argued that the company was guilty of "contributory infringement" by enabling consumers to copy copyrighted material. Sony adopted a fair-use defense. Judge Warren Ferguson rejected the studios' suit, saying that they had failed to show any adverse present or future effects from home video recording. In October 1981, however, the federal appeals court in San Francisco disagreed. It ruled that home video recording did not constitute fair use and that Sony could be held responsible for the copyright infringement.

The Supreme Court settled the issue with a 5-4 ruling in 1984. The majority said that home viewers' use of VCRs for "time shifting" — viewing a movie at a later time — amounted to fair use because it was a "non-commercial, nonprofit activity" that had "no demonstrable effect upon the potential market for, or the value of, the copyrighted work."

The VCR debate continues to this day. The movie studios insist that they lose millions of dollars from unauthorized copying of films. MPAA President Valenti also stresses that the studios were not trying to block the use of VCRs but only wanted to impose a royalty on all blank videotapes in order to compensate copyright holders. But law Professor Boyle notes that the VCR boom has proved to be a financial bonanza for movie studios. "They wanted a protectionist rule," Boyle says. "If they'd gotten it, videotapes would have been more expensive, and it would have taken a long time for the market to develop."

"Digital Millennium"

The digital revolution transformed the creation, storage and distribution of information, including all of the creatures of copyright — from books and periodicals to photographs, audio recordings and video. As Stanford's Goldstein observes, the very attributes that made the digital format so appealing — fidelity, compression and malleability — also posed daunting challenges to traditional ideas of copyright law based on works in fixed media that could not be reproduced without a loss of quality. [11]

Courts and lawmakers first grappled with a surprisingly difficult issue: what legal protection to give to computer programs themselves. [12] Initially, many software developers thought computer programs were patentable inventions, but a Supreme Court decision in 1972 cast doubt on that approach. Instead, Congress in 1980 followed a study commission's recommendation to provide for copyright protection for computer programs.

But, as American University's Jaszi observes, software "wasn't like the traditional subject matter of copyright. It's more mechanical, more practical." As a result, courts have somewhat limited the protection for computer programs under copyright — creating hurdles for plaintiffs in all but the most flagrant cases of copying. Meanwhile, though, patent protection was resurfacing as an option, thanks to a Supreme Court decision in 1981 that looked more favorably on that approach. Still, patent protection has its own problems: a difficult standard to meet for patentability and a shorter term (17 years) than the copyright period.

The introduction of digital audiotape technology (DAT) in the 1980s created another difficult issue for copyright holders — in this case, the music industry. [13] Composers, artists and record companies feared that the use of digital tape decks would enable consumers to produce masterquality copies of music tapes and thereby cause reduced sales and royalties. A protracted legal and lobbying battle between the music industry on the one hand and electronics manufacturers on the other ended in 1992 with the passage of the Audio Home Recording Act.

The law allowed "consumers" to

make single copies of sound recordings for "non-commercial use" without running afoul of copyright law. In return, manufacturers of digital tapes and tape decks must pay a royalty to the U.S. Copyright Office for distribution to copyright holders. In addition, the law prohibits the manufacture of digital tape decks that can copy copies — thus, reducing the potential for mass-quantity reproductions of original tapes.

The rise of the Internet posed another problem for copyright law: what liability, if any, Internet access providers might face for copyright infringement for the posting of protected materials by network users. Copyright holders feared the easy availability of copyrighted works on the Internet, but access providers contended they could not police users to prevent copyright infringements.

In an influential case (*Religious Tech. Center v. Netcom On-Line Comm. Corp.*), a federal court in San Francisco ruled in 1995 that Netcom, a major Internet access provider, was not directly liable for the posting of copyrighted materials on the network but might be "vicariously liable" if it knew of an infringement and failed to take steps to remove the protected material. Congress adopted a somewhat similar approach in a provision of the 1998 copyright revision by giving digital networks immunity from copyright liability if they remove protected material after receiving notice from the copyright holder.

The 1998 law — the Digital Millennium Copyright Act — was the culmination of a legislative initiative by the Clinton administration that began with the issuance of a so-called white paper in 1995 advocating a number of new protections to "update" copyright law for the digital age. The anti-circumvention provision emerged immediately as a focal point of dispute. The administration strongly sided with the movie and recording industries in calling for a ban on equipment, devices or software that could defeat copyright-protective encryption. A coalition of equipment manufacturers, libraries and consumer and user groups unsuccessfully opposed the proposal. The final version, which cleared Congress on Oct. 12, 1998, left Hollywood pleased.

"Passage of the legislation brings us a step closer to being able to utilize the Internet as a means of providing information and entertainment to consumers," MPAA spokesman Richard Taylor said. [14]

"Celestial Jukebox"

Internet advocates began dreaming of on-line entertainment — music, movies or books — as early as the start of the 1990s. They conjured up the image of a "celestial jukebox" — a phrase of uncertain origin that Stanford's Goldstein used in the subtitle of his 1994 book on the future of copyright. In his rendering, Goldstein imagined computer-linked networks that could deliver a film, recording or book instantaneously to a user's computer and automatically charge the subscriber for the service. [15]

But the businesses that did emerge at the end of the decade — MyMP3.com, Napster and Scour.com — omitted any charge to users or any licensing fee to copyright holders. The recording and film industries responded with litigation aimed, they insisted, not at killing the services but simply at ensuring proper compensation to composers, performers and music publishers and to film studios for their copyrighted materials.

Actually, the on-line service provider CompuServe was the first major company to feel the legal wrath of the music industry. CompuServe established an on-line bulletin board for users to share music by uploading files to the service or downloading files from it. The National Music Publishers' Association and its licensing subsidiary, the Harry Fox Agency, filed a class action copyright-infringement suit against CompuServe in 1993. In November 1995, CompuServe settled the suit by paying an undisclosed amount and agreeing to a licensing arrangement in the future. Association President Edward Murphy voiced the hope that other on-line services would reach similar agreements — "obviating the need for further legal actions." [16]

Murphy's hope proved illusory. Through the decade, the recording industry waged what one court called "a well-nigh constant battle" against so-called pirate Web sites with cease-and-desist letters and litigation. The comment by the federal appeals court in San Francisco came in a June 1999 decision that rejected the recording industry's attempt to outlaw a portable music player capable of playing audio MP3 files downloaded from a personal computer. [17]

In the midst of the record industry's battles, however, some independent record labels and unsigned artists were making fully legitimate use of the Internet to distribute and promote their music. And record companies themselves were professing interest in developing their own digital distribution businesses.

Napster and MP3.com beat the record companies to the punch. Napster went on-line in May 1999 as the brainchild of Fanning, a one-time Northeastern University computer science student inspired by his roommate's complaints about the difficulty of finding MP3 files on the Internet. [18] Fanning used money from his uncle and a venture-capital firm to get his music search-engine running. Word spread quickly through colleges and universities, high schools and middle schools throughout the country. By the end of the year, the Napster

Does Napster Reduce Sales of Music CDs?

When Napster's founder Shawn Fanning appeared on MTV's annual "Music Video Awards" program earlier this month, he was wearing a T-shirt from the band "Metallica," Napster's most vocal critic among performers.

"Nice shirt," his co-presenter, MTV's Carson Daly, said. "Actually, a friend shared it with me," Fanning replied. "I'm thinking about getting my own, though." [1]

The tongue-in-cheek routine referenced one of the sharpest disputes between Napster and the record industry: the effect that the on-line music-sharing network is having — if any — on retail sales of music CDs.

The record industry strongly argues that the massive, free downloading of what it calls "pirated" music files "displaces" CD purchases that Napster users would otherwise make. Napster and supporters insist that file "sharing" whets the appetite of Napster's "music community" to buy more, not fewer, CDs.

Record companies and Napster have both introduced a flurry of studies in the ongoing federal copyright-infringement case in San Francisco to try to substantiate their claims. The evidence points both ways. In ruling for the record companies, Judge Marilyn Hall Patel said that both major studies offered by the opposing sides were flawed. But she said the record industry's study was more credible and cited it in finding that "Napster use is likely to reduce CD purchases by college students." [2]

In the record companies' main exhibit, the Field Research Corp. found 500 Napster users among a nationwide sample of 3,200 college students. The major finding cited by the record companies: When asked why they used Napster, more than one-third of those responding — 34.4 percent — gave answers that "either explicitly indicated or suggested that Napster displaces CD sales."

Some of those answers were quite explicit — for example, "to get free music" or "don't have to buy CDs." But another common answer — "can get any song I want" — appears less clear in indicating reduced purchases. And the presentation of the study did not emphasize that more

The popular rock band Sugar Ray appears at a California record store to plug its latest CD.

than half of the respondents — 54 percent — gave reasons unrelated to CD purchases. The most common response — given by 30 percent of the Napster users — related to quick, easy and convenient access to music.

In a second study presented by the recording industry, the music sales-tracking company SoundScan similarly found a likely reduction in CD sales to college students. The study compared nationwide figures over several years with sales for the same periods around colleges that had banned student use of Napster. Nationally, sales increased 18 percent from 1997 to 2000, while sales around Napster-banned campuses declined 12 percent.

Napster's principal expert was Peter Fader, a marketing expert at the University of Pennsylvania's Wharton School. Fader conducted a survey of 1,600 Napster users, assembled evidence from other surveys and critiqued the two studies presented by the record companies.

Fader's survey — which covered all Napster users, not just college students — found that 28 percent had increased their CD purchases since using Napster. Only 8 percent said they bought fewer CDs, while 64 percent said their purchases had not changed.

Fader said other studies "create a virtual chorus of data refuting [record companies'] claims of substantial negative impact on music purchasing." Some studies did tend to buttress the conclusion that on-line music sharing stimulated sales. But at least one of the studies — at the University of Southern California, one of the campuses that banned Napster — found that more Napster users reported reducing their CD purchases than those who reported increased buying.

Whatever Napster's impact, the most recent sales figures give a rosy picture for the record industry. CD sales for the first six months of 2000 were 6 percent higher than for the comparable period in 1999. RIAA President Hillary Rosen said the numbers showed that despite the Internet's potential, "loyalty to the physical product remains."

---

[1] Quoted in *The Washington Post*, Sept. 8, 2000, p. C2.

[2] Some of the studies can be found on the respective Web sites: the Recording Industry Association of America (www.riaa.com) and www.Napster.com. Judge Patel's opinion is also at www.riaa.com.

"community" included at least 200,000 users; today, Napster says the number is 27 million.

MP3.com traced its origins back further, to a conventional search-engine service started in 1996 by Michael Robertson, a software entrepreneur with a degree in cognitive science from the University of California at San Diego. [19] Robertson learned of the MP3 software in October 1997, acquired rights to the domain name, renamed the company, and began offering up-and-coming artists a chance to distribute their music through the Internet. By spring 1999, MP3.com was drawing about 250,000 visitors a day. Then in January 2000, Robertson moved to draw more visitors by creating a library of tens of thousands of CDs on the MyMP3.com server for users to download.

The record industry landed on both services with both feet, filing lawsuits against Napster in December and against MP3.com in January. Lower court judges sided with the record companies, depicting MP3.com and Napster as nothing less than intellectual-property pirates. Judge Rakoff, in his initial ruling in late April, said that MP3.com's defense against the RIAA's copyright-infringement suit "amounts to nothing more than a bald claim that defendant should be able to misappropriate plaintiffs' property simply because there is a consumer demand for it." Three months later, Judge Patel was similarly dismissive of Napster's defenses. "Pirating be damned is the sense one gets," the judge said.

Meanwhile, the motion picture association was pressing its case against the hacker magazine *2600* for disseminating the DVD decryption program. In his ruling backing the film industry, Judge Kaplan characterized the magazine as part of "a movement that believes that information should be available without charge to anyone clever enough to break into the computer systems or data storage

media in which it is located."

Industry officials praised all three rulings, while defendants in each of the cases vowed to appeal. But many observers warned that whatever the ultimate court rulings, the industry's legal efforts would not stop the work of anti-encryption hackers or the proliferation of on-line music-distribution networks.

"Napster or no Napster, these services will exist," Mark Mooradian, a senior analyst at Jupiter Communications, told the *Los Angeles Times* following Patel's ruling. "The one thing this does is buys the [record] industry a little bit of time." [20] ■

CURRENT SITUATION

Facing Off in Court

The legal fight that *Newsweek* magazine labeled "the first great battle of the Internet century" goes before the federal appeals court in San Francisco on Oct. 2. [21] Both the record industry and Napster say the stakes extend far beyond young music fans' desire to skimp on their CD budgets.

The record companies that brought the copyright-infringement suit say a ruling to allow Napster's global file-sharing network would fundamentally transform copyright law.

"That would mean that one individual buying a CD could become the world-wide publisher of that music on the Internet without any compensation to the original creator," says RIAA general counsel Sherman. "It would mean that we would no longer have the music market that we've known before. And it

would have the same kind of disabling effect on other copyright holders."

For his part, Napster's lawyer says a ruling to uphold the lower court injunction against the network would undermine the Internet's potential to facilitate "peer-to-peer" information exchanges of all sorts — for music, text searches or general research.

"What's at stake is whether a peer-to-peer access service subjects itself to liability if it does not monitor or control the information that's being shared," Boies says. "Of course, if someone tries to monitor what's being shared, you have defeated the benefits of peer-to-peer technology."

In their massive legal briefs — 75 pages for the record companies, 66 for Napster — the opposing attorneys disagree sharply on the implications of the closest precedent from the Supreme Court: its 1984 decision in the Sony case upholding home videotaping of television programs. [22] Napster's attorneys argue that the file-sharing technology is legal because it is capable of "substantial non-infringing use" — quoting from the high court's decision. They say that both sampling and "space shifting" — moving a recording from one medium to another — amount to fair use under the copyright law.

But the record companies' lawyers counter that Napster users go beyond the "time shifting" of videotaped TV programs that the Supreme Court said was legal. Instead, the record companies' attorneys said, Napster users are creating permanent collections of music, or "librarying." That practice, they say, reduces sales for CDs and thus fails the fourth factor in the fair-use defense: the effect on the market for copyrighted works.

In the other on-line music case, attorneys for Universal Music Group and MP3.com are preparing for the damages phase of the trial, set to begin before Judge Rakoff in New York on Nov. 13. Universal claims MP3.com

Web Site Barred From Posting Papers' Articles

Jim Robinson, a Fresno, Calif., software developer, founded the Free Republic Web site four years ago to expose what he calls government corruption and the liberal media's role in covering it up. Now he finds himself locked in a copyright fight with two of the country's biggest newspaper companies over the right to post the full text of news articles for readers of his Web site to critique.

The *Los Angeles Times* and *The Washington Post* claim that Robinson and his Web site (www.freerepublic.org) are violating their copyrights by posting the full texts of stories from the papers. A federal judge in Los Angeles issued a preliminary ruling in favor of the papers in November. Once a final order is issued — expected soon — Robinson vows to appeal.

Robinson, a harsh critic of President Clinton, says the newspapers' legal actions did not surprise him. "I didn't think the liberal papers would appreciate our involvement with what we were doing, trying to get the real news out to the world, going through their articles for their lies and their cover-up," Robinson says. "So I figured they'd do whatever they could to try to stop us."

But Rex Heinke, the Beverly Hills lawyer representing the two newspapers, says they are simply trying to protect their intellectual property. "There's nothing new about the idea that newspapers or any other author who creates intellectual content wants to protect it from wholesale, full-text copying," says Heinke, a longtime media and entertainment-industry lawyer.

News organizations have, in fact, been involved in copyright-related litigation throughout the 20th century. In one important case, The Associated Press won an injunction against the rival International News Service for copying AP dispatches from East Coast newspapers and telegraphing the contents to INS subscribers on the West Coast.

The Supreme Court in 1918 held that even though "facts" could not be copyrighted, the INS's practice amounted to "misappropriation" of the AP's intellectual property. (*International News Service v. Associated Press*).

Today, the Internet aggravates news organizations' copyright problems by enabling anyone to copy the news and distribute it not just across the country but around the globe.

"Eighty years ago, there weren't that many people who could make a business model out of using telegrams and telegraphs to get copy distributed," says George Galt, the AP's current director of business affairs. "Now that that infrastructure is in place, it's much easier to do."

Heinke agrees that the Internet raises the stakes in the Times' and Post's dispute with Robinson's Web site.

"What is disturbing here is the scale of the copying and the ability to widely disseminate it and the fact that the defendants are archiving these articles so that they're building a library of thousands of articles," he says.

Robinson bills his Web site as "a fast-moving forum" for "breaking news and up-to-the-minute updates." The Web site's home page continues, "Most importantly, visitors are encouraged to comment on the news of the day here, and especially to contribute whatever information they may have to help others better understand a particular story."

Robinson's lawyer says posting the full text of newspaper articles is essential to his purpose. "When an event occurs on day one and it's described in an article in *The Washington Post* on day two, we believe it's important to be able to critique the Post's coverage of that event," says Brian Buckley, a Los Angeles attorney. "And the only way to do that is to post the full text of the Post's coverage of that event."

The Times and the Post, along with the Post's on-line subsidiary, brought the copyright-infringement claim against Robinson in September 1998. Robinson defended his practice under the copyright doctrine known as "fair use," a judicially created defense that was codified into a four-factor test in the federal Copyright Act in 1976.

In November 1999, U.S. District Judge Margaret Morrow rejected Robinson's fair-use defense. She said the full-text postings failed three of the four fair-use factors, including the effect on the newspapers' markets. She noted that the newspapers' Web sites charged users $1.50 per story to access archived articles.

Morrow also rejected Robinson's claim that blocking his Web site from posting the full text of stories infringed users' First Amendment rights. "Their speech is in no way restricted by denying them the ability to infringe on [the newspapers'] exclusive rights in the copyrighted news articles," the judge wrote. [1]

Buckley says the ruling will have "a chilling effect" on free expression. "When Congress passed the fair-use statute, it did so to encourage free speech, particularly regarding important discussions of public interest," he says.

But Heinke insists that the newspapers are not trying to silence their critics or stifle debate. And he says the Internet itself offers a solution to the dispute.

"If people want to read an article, all Free Republic members have to do is to post the hypertext link to the article, and users can click on it and read it for themselves," Heinke says. "This in no way limits their ability to comment or criticize."

---

[1] Morrow's 28-page opinion in *Los Angeles Times v. Free Republic* is dated Nov. 8, 1999. For coverage, see the *Los Angeles Times*, Nov. 9, 1999.

uploaded between 5,000 and 10,000 of its disks. At $25,000 per CD, that could amount to a staggering award of $125 million to $250 million. MP3.com contends the number is lower — about 4,700 — and also plans to challenge the eligibility of virtually all of Universal's copyright registrations. [23]

Meanwhile, the movie industry has its hands full with Internet-related copyright disputes. Attorneys for hacker journalist Corley gave notice on Sept. 18 that they will appeal Judge Kaplan's decision to enjoin posting the DeCSS decryption software or providing links to Web sites where the computer code can be found. Martin Garbus, the New York City First Amendment litigator who represents Corley, says he will argue that posting the code is protected under the First Amendment and "fair use" and that the movie industry failed to show any harm from the posting — arguments the judge rejected at trial.

Even if the injunction is upheld, Garbus warns that the copyright holders may be unable to stop the spread of security-circumventing software. "The culture is out there, and it's going to be moving at a fast speed," Garbus says. But Leon Gold, the New York lawyer representing the film industry, thinks court enforcement of the law can bring hackers to heel. "I very much think it will be brought under control in that way," he says.

The film industry is also litigating two other important cases. Along with the record industry, it filed suit to stop another on-line file-sharing site, Scour.com, which offers both music and movie files — "Napster for movies," as the MPAA's Valenti calls it. The case was filed in federal court in New York, but attorneys for Scour are seeking to have it moved to Los Angeles.

In the other case, the major movie studios in June sued a Web-based TV-playback service called RecordTV.com. David Simon, a computer programmer in California, said he launched the site

after his daughter complained she was missing episodes of one of her favorite cartoon programs. [24] The case is pending; the film industry earlier used legal action to force a Canadian "Webcaster" to shut down.

Getting to Market

Record industry executives have seen the future, and it's on the Net. Now the major record companies are scrambling to catch up with the "kids" who saw the future first.

The big-five record companies have all announced initiatives for digital distribution of music. On Sept. 6, Warner Music Group became the last of the five to air its plans, the same day as the damages ruling in the MP3.com suit. Universal, EMI, Sony and Bertelsmann's BMG unit all came out with rudimentary announcements earlier in the summer.

The plans vary in their details, but for the moment have two general features: Fans will be able to download songs for a price — perhaps $2 apiece — or pay a monthly subscription fee for unlimited downloading. In the future, more elaborate offerings may become available, according to the RIAA's Sherman. As one example, a company might offer free sampling of current releases, but encrypt the tracks to prevent copying and to "time out" after a specified period — perhaps 24 hours.

"Ultimately, record companies have to win this battle in the marketplace," Sherman says. "We have to develop a marketplace that will attract consumers, works perfectly, is priced reasonably, doesn't have a threat to security or privacy — and people must know that the money that they spend is going ultimately to the artists who create the music they love."

Napster officials say they welcome the music industry's initiatives while

insisting that they wanted all along to strike a licensing agreement with the major labels. "It's a positive step for the industry to license its music," says attorney Boies. "We have tried to arrange such a license with the music industry. The record labels have thus far refused to do that." (Record industry officials say Napster was never serious about making a deal.)

Industry observers have doubts about the record companies' prospects. "There is no proof that the music industry will ever come up with a way to securely and conveniently deliver music on-line and entice people to pay for it," *Los Angeles Times* reporter Chuck Phillips wrote in mid-July, prior to the Napster ruling. Two days after the decision, *The Wall Street Journal* said the record companies' Internet efforts were "widely viewed as late and relatively timid." [25]

The record industry is seeking to solve the technological problem with its so-called "Secured Digital Music Initiative" — an effort to devise a universal encryption software for music recordings. "The idea is to create some base level of protection so that legitimate commerce on the Internet is not totally displaced by a totally piratical marketplace," Sherman says. But many computer experts doubt that any security software can be made totally hacker-proof.

As for economics, record companies face an uphill struggle to persuade music fans to pay for on-line music as long as they can get it for free from other sources. And even if Napster's file-sharing network is shut down, other on-line options will develop that will be difficult, if not impossible, to control. The Gnutella Web site allows users to network directly with other computers with no centralized library like MP3.com and no centralized directory like Napster. With more advances in compressing digital files, it may be possible in the longer-term future to exchange music files

At Issue:

Is Napster's music file-sharing service legal under copyright laws?

DAVID BOIES
ATTORNEY FOR NAPSTER INC.

WRITTEN FOR THE CQ RESEARCHER, SEPTEMBER 2000

*n*apster, the fastest-growing application in the history of the Internet and the largest community of music lovers in the world, respects copyright and the interests of recording artists. The record companies, however, have repeatedly refused Napster's offers of a reasonable license and opposed a compulsory license. At its heart, therefore, the Napster controversy is about whether the major record companies or Napster will control Napster's peer-to peer technology.

Far from harming the industry's copyrights, Napster has enhanced their value by increasing sales and exposing music fans to new music. Napster threatens only the record companies' dominance over traditional channels of distribution and promotion.

Napster is legal, first, because its users' conduct is legal. Napster users engage in the non-commercial, person-to-person sharing of music, a right protected under the Audio Home Recording Act of 1992. Second, because Napster is "capable of substantial non-infringing uses," it is not liable under the Supreme Court's home videotaping case for any potentially infringing use of the technology that it cannot control without destroying the technology's benefits.

Countless bands have already used Napster to become better known, and more than 25,000 artists currently authorize their music to be shared via Napster.

Napster is also widely used for other fair uses, including transforming music a user already owns into a more convenient format ("space-shifting") and previewing music to decide whether to buy it.

Compliance with the record industry's demands would eliminate these uses and destroy Napster by requiring it to eliminate its decentralized peer-to-peer architecture. Further, under the Digital Millennium Copyright Act, even if Napster has general knowledge that some of its users engage in copyright infringement, it is not liable for infringements as long as it follows certain prescribed procedures.

As a result of Napster's compliance with these procedures, it terminated hundreds of thousands of users who the band Metallica claimed were engaged in infringing conduct.

During the home videotaping dispute two decades ago, the head of the motion picture industry compared the Betamax to the Boston Strangler in its potential impact on filmmaking. Instead, home VCRs created the video rental market, which now accounts for half of that industry's profits.

Today, we cannot and should not allow similar unfounded predictions of doom to deny the public the benefit of new technologies — such as Napster.

HILARY ROSEN
PRESIDENT AND CEO, RECORDING INDUSTRY ASSOCIATION OF AMERICA

WRITTEN FOR THE CQ RESEARCHER, SEPTEMBER 2000

*t*he important issue is not whether a single company violates copyrights. Napster plainly does. The real question is how best to build the infrastructure for on-line music. The recording industry's answer is to embrace both new technology and the creative process.

Across the Internet, new sites and business models are proliferating that make music accessible on-line while respecting the copyright protection at the heart of the creative process. Artists, labels and entrepreneurs are offering music on-line on the basis of subscription models, Web-casting and pay-per-download arrangements. Others who own copyrighted material are choosing to make it available at no cost.

As exciting as these innovations are, the most thrilling ones are those we cannot even imagine yet. As they have for decades, new technologies and business models will continue to transform how music is distributed, and the recording industry — whose business is finding new ways to make music available to more people — will continue to embrace them. We welcome new approaches — including peer-to-peer models like Napster's — that respect copyright law.

Copyrights and royalties are not incompatible with an infrastructure for on-line music. To the contrary, they are a prerequisite for it. Protection for intellectual property is the foundation of innovation, a fact that Napster — which itself has posted copyright notices — apparently understands.

One need not debate the finer points of copyright law to know that trafficking in stolen copyrighted works is a foundation of Napster's business. Anyone who reads Judge Marilyn Hall Patel's thoughtful opinion will understand that.

The broader issue is neither a single company nor even just the pocketbooks of the artists off whose creativity it is living. It is that Napster's effort to legitimize the widespread theft of copyrighted material threatens the future of on-line music itself. If intellectual property is not protected on-line, there will be a substantial disincentive for making it available there. And if creativity itself is devalued by the contention that there is no harm in stealing its fruits, the inspiration to produce music in the first place will be diminished.

Does Napster violate copyrights? It obviously does. But that is not the issue. This case will someday be seen as little more than a speed bump on the road to a vibrant on-line music community paved with an embrace of technology and respect for creativity. That is a destination toward which the recording industry is leading the way.

Metallica v. Chuck D.

Rock groups and artists have divided over the Napster issue. The heavy-metal band Metallica is suing Napster and individual Napster users for copyright infringement. But some performers support Napster — including Chuck D., co-founder of the rap group Public Enemy, which used the Internet to establish itself.

> **"This is not about Metallica versus the Internet. We know that the Internet is the future in terms of spreading your music to your fans, and we're excited about that. But we want to control how that's done, just like we've always controlled what we make."**
>
> *— Lars Ulrich*
> *Metallica drummer*

Reuters/Molly Riley

AP Photos/Stacey Zaferes

> **"I just go by logic — that people will want to hear something before they buy it. If I got turned on by an artist after I heard something for free, I would go out and buy it. That's too logical for people in the music industry to understand."**
>
> *— Chuck D.*
> *Public Enemy co-founder*

simply as e-mail attachments — defying efforts by the recording industry or law enforcement to control.

Record companies have a stake in selling CDs the old way — in $15 jewel-box packaging — even while Internet sales take off. By one estimate, Internet sales of music are expected to climb from less than $1 billion this year to $3.4 billion by 2004. But the Internet will still constitute less than one-fifth of the projected $19 billion in sales by that time. "People like the recording industry have this difficult dance to do — maintaining the current business while accommodating the incredible demand for distribution from one digital source," attorney Radcliffe says.

The movie industry is farther away from Internet marketing, largely because downloading a film is far more difficult and time-consuming than downloading a song. But the MPAA's Valenti insists the studios view the Internet in the long run as a boon to the industry.

"We're trying to embrace it," Valenti says. "Our companies are working on business models. But you can't put it up there if you know that like Napster everybody can bring it down for free." ■

OUTLOOK

Whither Copyright Law?

Official Washington took a long, hard look at copyright law over the past five years — first to prepare for the World Intellectual Property Organization conference in 1996 and then to work on the 1998 law aimed at implementing the treaty adopted at the international meeting. Despite the prolonged review, the head of the U.S. Office of Copyright concedes today that Napster caught federal policy-makers by surprise.

"I don't think anybody had the foresight to foresee a Napster, or Gnutella, or FreeNet or the other types of things," Marybeth Peters, the U.S. Register of Copyrights, told the *Washington Internet Daily* earlier this month. "We weren't that visionary." [26]

No great vision is required today to see that the Internet is on the way to becoming an even more important source of distribution for all sorts of copyrighted material — not only music and news but also books and movies. But there are no easy predictions about what business models

the recording industry and others that depend on copyrights are likely to devise to try to keep the creative process — and their companies — financially viable and healthy.

One thing is clear, at least to the industries battling over copyrights: There will be dire consequences if they lose their current legal battles. "If [the courts] exile or shrink copyright," says MPAA President Valenti, "it will be Armageddon time because without copyright protection who is going to invest the huge amounts of money into creative work if they can be burglarized at any moment."

Internet advocates say the record and music industries' fears are exaggerated. "There's a lot of hoopla that the whole music industry is going down the tubes, that there won't be anything left of the movie industry," says copyright expert Boyle. "This is fantasy. I see no sign of a collapse. On the contrary, I see a lot of opportunities."

With their creative talent, record and film libraries and existing distribution networks, the established companies have significant advantages in exploiting those opportunities, but intellectual-property attorney Radcliffe says they may also have some disadvantages. "Many of those industries are dominated by large companies, whose main claim to fame is that they've built up the infrastructure — which costs so much to do," Radcliffe says. "Now, when you distribute digitally, all that advantage is going to become a disadvantage."

On the other hand, the two on-line music networks — MP3.com and Napster — have yet to prove that they have viable, long-term business models. MP3.com makes some money from selling CDs, but free downloading is its biggest draw. Napster has no revenue and only vaguely outlined plans about how to "monetize" the massive customer base represented by its millions of users. And both face serious questions about their futures

if they lose their current court fights.

Still, MP3.com and Napster may be blazing a path for themselves and others to make a business off the Net. For the record companies, the challenge will be to design on-line products that fans want and to find a price that they will pay — either per song or on a subscription basis.

Carnegie Mellon's Shamos, an e-commerce expert, also sees another possible financial model: a royalty paid into a government-administered fund by all Internet service providers (and passed on to consumers as part of their monthly fee) and then distributed to copyright holders whose works are accessed from the Web.

"Once you have a viable collective model for funneling money from a lot of people into a collective source, it enhances production of creative work," Shamos says.

American University law Professor Jaszi, however, warns against the emergence of a "pay-per-use" system. "The large content industries would like to take us toward a pay-per-use environment, in which all kinds of information is monitored, and we're billed on a per-drink basis," Jaszi says. "That has some obvious advantages for some consumers in some situations. But there are also some dangers."

Jaszi says current copyright law reflects a different approach, in which consumers "buy chunks of information and then make free use of it after that." That approach, he says, "encourages a sometimes inefficient but ultimately a productive use of information."

Jaszi says, the copyright battles will continue for a while.

"It's clearly the beginning of a story, not the end," Jaszi says. "No matter who comes out on top, there's going to be another round of legislative activity afterwards. And in those legislative rounds, the question of how we want our copyright system to look is going to be the central question." ■

Notes

[1] *CNET News*, Aug. 4, 2000. Patel's 46-page written opinion in *A&M Records, Inc. v. Napster, Inc.*, dated Aug. 10, can be found at the Recording Industry Association of America's Web site, www.riaa.com.

[2] See *The Wall Street Journal*, July 28, 2000, p. B1 (Fanning's statement); July 27, 2000, p. A8 (RIAA statement).

[3] Rakoff's 10-page written opinion in *UMG Recordings, Inc. v. MP3.COM, Inc.*, dated May 4, 2000, can be found at the Recording Industry Association of America's Web site, www.riaa.com.

[4] Quoted in *The New York Times*, Sept. 7, 2000.

[5] For background, see *The New York Times*, July 31, 2000; *The Village Voice*, week of Aug. 2-8, 2000. Materials on the case can be found on the Web sites of the Motion Picture Association of America (www.mpaa.org) and the Electronic Frontier Foundation (www.eff.org).

[6] Kaplan's two written opinions in *Universal City Studios, Inc. v. Reimerdes* can be found on the Motion Picture Association of America's Web site, www.mpaa.org.

[7] Background drawn from Paul Goldstein, *Copyright's Highway: From Gutenberg to the Celestial Jukebox* (1994), and Robert P. Merges, Peter S. Menell, Mark A. Lemley and Thomas M. Jorden, *Intellectual Property in the New Technological Age* (1997). See also Paul Goldstein, *Copyright, Patent, Trademark and Related State Doctrines* (4th ed., 1997).

[8] See Merges et al., *op. cit.*, p. 327. The decision is *Wheaton v. Peters* (1834); for a discussion, see Goldstein, *Copyright's Highway*, pp. 53-55.

[9] *Ibid.*, p. 67.

[10] Background drawn from *ibid.*, pp. 78-128 (photocopying), pp. 129-164 (VCRs).

[11] Background drawn from *ibid.*, pp. 197-236.

[12] For a brief overview, see *ibid.*, pp. 815-816.

[13] For background, see 1992 *CQ Almanac*, pp. 192-193.

[14] Quoted in 1998 *CQ Almanac*, p. 22-9.

[15] Goldstein, *Copyright's Highway, op. cit.*, pp. 28-29. Goldstein says he was unable to track down who coined the term "celestial jukebox."

[16] *Patent, Trademark and Copyright Journal* (BNA), Vol. 51, p. 48 (Nov. 9, 1995).

[17] The case is *Recording Industry Association of America v. Diamond Multimedia Systems, Inc.*, decided June 15, 1999, by the 9th U.S. Circuit Court of Appeals.

[18] Background drawn from *The New York Times*, March 7, 2000. Fanning was nicknamed "Napster" in high school because of his haircut.

[19] Background drawn from *The New York Times*, April 11, 1999. See also *Boston Globe*, Jan. 28, 2000.

[20] Quoted in the *Los Angeles Times*, July 27, 2000, p. A9.

[21] See Steven Levy, "The Noisy War Over Napster," *Newsweek*, June 5, 2000, p. 46.

[22] See *The Wall Street Journal*, Sept. 13, 2000, p. B1.

[23] See *The New York Times*, Sept. 7, 2000, p. C1.

[24] See *The Wall Street Journal*, June 30, 2000, p. A1.

[25] *Los Angeles Times*, July 17, 2000, p. A1; *The Wall Street Journal*, July 28, 2000, p. A1.

[26] The full text of the interview appeared in another Warren Publishing Co. publication, *Audio Week*, Sept. 11, 2000.

FOR MORE INFORMATION

American Intellectual Property Law Association, 2001 Jefferson Davis Highway, Suite 203, Arlington, Va. 22202; (703) 415-0780; www.aipla.org. The national bar association comprises about 10,000 lawyers who represent owners or users of intellectual property.

Berkman Center for Internet and Society at Harvard Law School, 511 Pound Hall, 1563 Massachusetts Ave., Cambridge, Mass. 02138; (617) 495-7547; http://cyberlaw.harvard.edu/. The center was founded in 1995 "to explore and understand cyberspace, its development, dynamics, norms, standards and need or lack thereof for laws and sanctions."

Computer and Communications Industry Association, 666 11th St., N.W., Suite 600, Washington, D.C. 20001; (202) 783-0070; www.ccianet.org. CCIA is a nonprofit trade association of computer and communications firms, including equipment manufacturers, software developers, telecommunications and on-line service providers and others.

Electronic Frontier Foundation, 1550 Bryant St., Suite 725, San Francisco, Calif. 94103; (415) 436-9333; www.eff.org. EFF is a nonprofit, non-partisan organization that seeks to protect civil liberties, including freedom of expression and privacy, in the arena of computers and the Internet.

Motion Picture Association of America, 1600 I St., N.W., Washington, D.C. 20006; (212) 293-1966; 15503 Ventura Blvd., Encino, Calif. 91436; (818) 995-6600; www.mpaa.org. The MPAA, founded in 1922, is the trade association of the U.S. motion picture industry, representing producers and distributors.

Recording Industry Assn. of America, 1330 Connecticut Ave., N.W., Suite 300; Washington, D.C. 20036; (202) 775-0101; www.riaa.org. The RIAA represents the major recording companies that produce 90 percent of the recorded music produced and sold in the United States.

Bibliography

Selected Sources Used

Books

Boyle, James, *Shamans, Software, and Spleens: Law and the Construction of the Information Society*, Harvard University Press, 1996.
Boyle, a law professor at Duke University, criticizes what he calls the "author-centered" theory of intellectual property and urges instead "a large-scale restriction on intellectual-property rights, an expansion of the public domain and a greater sensitivity to the needs of both sources and audiences." The book includes 58 pages of notes.

Goldstein, Paul, *Copyright's Highway: From Gutenberg to the Celestial Jukebox*, Hill and Wang, 1994.
Goldstein, a law professor at Stanford University, provides a readable account of the development of copyright law and recent copyright issues, including photocopying, home video recording, and digital copying and distribution on the Internet. The book includes 17 pages of chapter notes.

—, *Copyright, Patent, Trademark and Related State Doctrines: Cases and Materials on the Law of Intellectual Property (4th ed.)*, Foundation Press, 1997.
Goldstein's law school casebook covers the range of federal and state intellectual-property law, including copyright. One chapter covers intellectual property of computer programs.

Menges, Robert P., Peter S. Mcnell, Mark A. Lemley and Thomas M. Jorde, *Intellectual Property in the New Technological Age*, Aspen Law & Business, 1997.
This law school casebook includes a thorough overview of copyright law and a separate chapter on intellectual-property protection of computer software. The authors are all professors at the University of California's Boalt Hall School of Law at Berkeley.

Articles

Brown, Glenn, "Running for Cover," *The New Republic Online* (www.tnr.com), July 27, 2000.
Brown analyzes the music industry's effort to police digital on-line music networks in the light of composers' turn-of-the-century copyright-infringement claim against "piano rolls." Brown has worked on digital music issues for the Berkman Center on Internet and Society at Harvard Law School.

Clark, Charles S., "Clashing Over Copyright," *The CQ Researcher*, Nov. 8, 1996, pp. 985-1008.
The report gives an overview of Internet-related copyright disputes before the advent of on-line digital music distribution networks.

Harmon, Amy, "Free Speech Rights for Computer Code?" *The New York Times*, July 31, 2000, p. C1.
The article gives an overview of the movie industry's lawsuit seeking to block the dissemination of the computer code for "decrypting" movie videodisks or DVDs.

Levy, Steven, "The Noisy War Over Napster," *Newsweek*, June 5, 2000, pp. 46-53.
The cover story gives an overview of the technological, legal and economic aspects of the rise of on-line music networks. In an accompanying opinion piece, Lars Urich, drummer for Metallica, explains the band's reasons for opposing Napster; other rock performers, both pro- and anti-Napster, are quoted in the main article.

Swishcr, Kara, "Move Over, Beethoven: A music-industry lobbyist and a high-tech CEO square off about the changes to come," *The Wall Street Journal*, April 17, 2000.
The article consists of a joint interview with Hillary Rosen, president and CEO of the Recording Industry Association of America, and Rob Glaser, chairman and chief executive officer of RealNetworks, Inc., of Seattle, the leading maker of technology that allows consumers to listen to music over the Web.

Reports

Spaulding, Michelle, "The ABCs of MP3: A Crash Course in the Digital Music Phenomenon," *Berkman Center for Internet and Society at Harvard Law School* (http://cyberlaw.harvard.edu/).
The 10-page report gives an introduction to the development of digital music networks and the legal controversies over the phenomenon. The report is part of a larger "briefing book" assembled by the Berkman Center that includes a variety of other backgrounders and position papers on the subject.

How to Write a Research Paper

This guide to writing a research paper is arranged in five parts: the first section outlines six steps that will help you write a paper—from getting ready to choose a topic to writing and revising. The second part discusses library research, and the third and fourth give tips on using the Web to conduct research. Finally, you will find a list of links to useful online resources. The Internet is constantly changing. Be aware that some of the resources noted here may no longer be available; however, you should be able to find most of them and what is included here will give you a good idea of the information that is available.

Six Steps to Writing a Research Paper

Step 1   Getting Started

Goal: Preparing for the assignment and getting ready to choose a topic

UNDERSTAND THE ASSIGNMENT. Read over the instructions for the assign ment to make sure you fully understand what the instructor has in mind and on what basis you will be graded.

CONSIDER THE PROCESS YOU'LL USE. The paper is your final *product,* but a research paper involves an extensive *process* before you can generate the product. If you focus too quickly on the end product, you may miss some of the important research steps and find yourself writing a paper

Adapted, with permission, from *A+ Research and Writing for High School and College Students,* copyright 1997 by Kathryn L. Schwartz. Published by the Internet Public Library: http://www.ipl.org.

without enough understanding of the topic. Browse over the rest of the steps suggested here to get an idea of the process and think about how you'll approach each step. Start a journal or notebook and begin jotting notes about not only "what" you plan to do but also "how" you plan to do it.

SET YOUR DEADLINES FOR EACH STEP OF THE ASSIGNMENT. Ideally, you will have at least four weeks from the date it's assigned to complete a research paper of seven or eight pages (2,000 to 2,500 words). Shorter papers requiring fairly simple research (four or five pages—1,500 words) may not require four weeks' "lead time," while a fifteen-page or longer paper might be a semester-long project.

THINK ABOUT POSSIBLE TOPICS: The word "topic" is used variably by many teachers of writing and research to mean anything from the very general "subject matter" to the very specific "thesis statement." Here, the term *topic* is broadly defined, while *focus* means a narrower perspective on the topic, and *thesis* statement is the main point of your paper, which cannot be determined until after research and analysis is complete.

INFO SEARCH—BROWSE, READ, RELAX. Start by thumbing through the textbooks or course pack for the class in which your paper was assigned. Browse the table of contents, chapter headings and subheadings to get an overview of the subject matter. Visit your library and browse in the catalog and reference room to find out what sources are held by the library that may relate to your class. Browse some of the subject-indexed sources on the Internet with the same purpose.

RELATE YOUR PRIOR EXPERIENCE AND LEARNING. The process of successful research and writing involves build-

ing on what you know. You don't need to know a *lot* about a subject to use it as your topic, but choosing one you're totally unfamiliar with could be a mistake. It may take so much time and effort to become informed about the subject that you don't really have time to get into the depth required by your assignment.

JOT DOWN YOUR QUESTIONS AND IDEAS ABOUT POSSIBLE TOPICS. Use your notebook to starting recording questions that interest you or ideas for possible topics.

You'll end up with a list of ideas and musings, some of which are obviously ridiculous and not reasonable topics for your paper, but don't worry about that at this point. Think about things that interest you and that build upon some experience or knowledge you have or build upon things you're presently learning in class.

BRAINSTORM, ALONE AND WITH OTHERS. Toss ideas around in your mind. Bounce ideas off of your classmates, your teacher or your siblings and parents to get their reactions and ideas. Many times another person will have a fresh perspective you might not have thought of, or something they say will trigger an idea for you.

Step 2   Discovering and Choosing a Topic

Goal: Discovering and choosing a topic for your research

INFO SEARCH—READ FOR OVERVIEW OF VARIOUS TOPICS. Use the notes you've made and the thinking you've done so far to select some areas for general reading. Use the library's reference room—encyclopedias, dictionaries, almanacs—to get an overview of possible topics (even if your instructor has told you that you can't use an encyclopedia as a reference—that's not important at this stage).

Explore CD-ROM tools in your library, like newspaper and magazine indexes, searching with key words representing your topic ideas. Explore the Internet by using several of the resources organized by subject.

Remember to keep your concept of topic rather broad at this stage— you can look for a focus later, after you know something about the topic.

CONTINUE THINKING AND JOTTING DOWN QUESTIONS AND IDEAS IN YOUR NOTEBOOK. As you read, ideas and questions may strike you—write them down, or you'll lose track of them. Look for issues that interest you, that arouse your curiosity or your passion. Consider the audience for your research paper: what kinds of things have been discussed in class that seemed to interest the class and the instructor? What kinds of issues were touched upon but could use further study and elaboration?

INFO SURVEY—WHAT PRINT AND ELECTRONIC RESOURCES ARE AVAILABLE? When you've narrowed your choices down, make a quick survey of the research resources that will be available to you on each potential topic. How much information seems to be available in your library's catalog? If it's a current topic, is there information in newspaper and magazine indexes and are those newspapers and magazines held by your library? Is there much authoritative information on your topic on the Internet? Is the available information slanted to one side of an issue versus another? How much work will it take to get the information you need if you choose a particular topic?

TRY DIFFERENT TOPICS ON FOR "SIZE." The topic you choose should "fit" in several important respects: your interests and knowledge, the purpose of the assignment, the type of paper

(report, issue, argument), the length of the paper. Don't worry too much about having a broad topic at this point. Look for topic ideas at Researchpaper.com (http://www. researchpaper.com/) or in your library. Ask the reference librarian if the library has books of suggested topics like Kathryn Lamm's *10,000 Ideas for Term Papers, Projects, Reports & Speeches* (New York: Macmillan, 1995).

Step 3   Looking for and Forming a Focus

Goal: Exploring your topic; finding and forming a focus for your research

INFO SEARCH—EXPLORING YOUR TOPIC. Before you can decide on a focus, you need to explore your topic, to become informed about the topic, to build on your knowledge and experience. You'll be locating books, articles, videos, Internet and other resources about your topic and reading to learn! You're looking for an issue, an aspect, a perspective on which to focus your research paper.

This is the first step in which you'll probably be checking books out of the library. Encyclopedias won't be much help here. You're looking for treatments of your topic that are either more comprehensive or more specific than an encyclopedic treatment, with various authors' summaries, analyses and opinions. But, until you've chosen a focus, you're not really on a mission of gathering information. If you gather information on the topic as a whole, you'll waste a lot of time doing it and have way too much to sort through when you are ready to write your paper. Resist the temptation to "gather" until you've chosen a focus. Now you'll be using the library's online catalog, online indexes and the Web search engines along with the reference room and

the subject-based Web directories.

INFO SEARCH—PRELIMINARY NOTE TAKING. As you read, start taking notes of what you're learning about your topic—concepts, issues, problems, areas where experts agree or disagree. Keep track of the bibliographic references for the information you're using, and write down a note or two of what's contained in the book, article, Website, etc. There's nothing more frustrating than knowing you read something earlier about a particular point and not being able to locate it again when you decide it's something you need.

Find out what kind of citations are required by your instructor and make sure you're recording what you'll need to do your bibliography.

PURPOSEFUL THINKING ABOUT POSSIBLE FOCUSES. While you're learning about your topic, intentionally look for possible focuses in the material. You could spend enormous amounts of time reading, especially about an interesting topic, without being any closer to a focus unless you purposefully keep that goal in your mind while you read.

CHOOSING A FOCUS OR COMBINING THEMES TO FORM A FOCUS. Try your choices of focus on for "size" as you did your topic. Which ones fit the assignment, the size, scope and type of the paper? Think about which of your possible focuses has the best chance for making a successful paper. If you find several themes within your topic that separately are too small to support the entire paper, can they be combined to form a focus?

Step 4   Gathering Information

Goal: Gathering information that clarifies and supports your focus

INFO SEARCH—FINDING, COLLECTING AND RECORDING. This is the step most people think of when they think of "library research." It's a hunt for information in any available form (book, periodical, CD, video, Internet) which is pertinent to your chosen focus. Once you know the focus of your research, there are lots of tools and strategies to help you find and collect the information you need.

Your information search should be focused and specific, but pay careful attention to serendipity (finding, by chance, valuable things you weren't even looking for). Keep your mind open to continue learning about your focused topic.

Now is the time to carefully record your sources in the bibliographic format required by your instructor. Every piece of information you collect should have bibliographic information written down before you leave the library. You should also pay attention to the quality of the information you find, especially if you're using information you find on the Internet. Now is also the time to learn the details of using search engines. Many of the sources you will want to use are online, whether in the library or on the Internet.

THINK ABOUT CLARIFYING OR REFINING YOUR FOCUS. As you gather information about your focused topic, you may find new information that prompts you to refine, clarify, extend or narrow your focus. Stay flexible and adjust your information search to account for the changes, widening or narrowing your search, or heading down a slightly different path to follow a new lead.

START ORGANIZING YOUR NOTES. Start organizing your notes into logical groups. You may notice a gap in your research, or a more heavy weighting to one aspect of the subject than what you had intended. Starting to organize as you gather information can save an extra trip to the library. It's better to find the gap

now instead of the night before your paper is due.

THINK ABOUT WHAT YOUR THESIS STATEMENT WILL BE. The thesis statement is the main point of your paper. The type of thesis statement you'll be making depends a lot on what type of paper you're writing—a report, an issue analysis, an advocacy paper or another type. As you gather specific information and refine your focus, intentionally look for a main point to your findings. Sometimes, a thesis emerges very obviously from the material, and other times you may struggle to bring together the parts into a sensible whole. The tricky part is knowing when to stop gathering information—when do you have enough, and of the right kind? Seeking a main point as you research will help you know when you're done.

Step 5 Preparing to Write

Goal: Analyzing and organizing your information and forming a thesis statement

ANALYZE AND ORGANIZE YOUR INFORMATION. The word "analyze" means to break something down into its parts. A meaningful analysis identifies the parts and demonstrates how they relate to each other. You may have information from different sources that examines different aspects of your topic. By breaking down the information, you may be able to see relationships between the different sources and form them into a whole concept. When you're trying to make sense of the information coming out of your research process, you often have to look at it from different perspectives and sometimes have to step back and try to get a "big picture" view. Some ways to do this are to try out different organization patterns: compare and contrast, advantages and disadvantages, starting from a narrow premise and building on it,

cause and effect, logical sequence.

CONSTRUCT A THESIS STATEMENT AND TRY IT ON FOR "SIZE." Before beginning to write the paper, write the thesis statement. Boil down the main point of your paper to a single statement. Sharon Williams and Laura Reidy at the Hamilton College site (http://www.hamilton.edu/academic/Resource/WC/Intro_Thesis.html) give this explanation of the thesis statement:

A well-written thesis statement, usually expressed in one sentence, is the most important sentence in your entire paper. It should both summarize for your reader the position you will be arguing and set up the pattern of organization you will use in your discussion. A thesis sentence is not a statement of accepted fact, it is the position that needs the proof you will provide in your argument. Your thesis should reflect the full scope of your argument—no more and no less; beware of writing a thesis statement that is too broad to be defended within the scope of your paper.

Another way to summarize the nature and function of the thesis statement is that it is a single sentence, usually in the first paragraph of the paper, which:

- declares the position you are taking in your paper,
- sets up the way you will organize your discussion, and
- points to the conclusion you will draw.

WEED OUT IRRELEVANT INFORMATION. Now that you have all those wonderful notes and citations from your research, you're going to have to get rid of some of them! No matter how profound and interesting the information is, if it doesn't relate to and support the thesis you've chosen, don't try to cram it into the paper—just set it aside. You'll have an easier time writing if you do this weeding before you start.

INFO SEARCH—FILL IN THE GAPS. Once you've identified which of your research notes you'll use, you may see some gaps where you need an additional support for a point you want to make. Leave enough time in your writing plan for an extra trip to the library, just in case.

Step 6 Writing the Paper

Goal: Writing, revising and finalizing the paper

THINK ABOUT THE ASSIGNMENT, THE AUDIENCE AND THE PURPOSE. To prepare for writing, go over once more the requirements of the assignment to make sure you focus your writing efforts on what's expected by your instructor. Consider the purpose of the paper, either as set forth in the assignment, or as stated in your thesis statement—are you trying to persuade, to inform, to evaluate, to summarize?

- Who is your audience and how will that affect your paper?
- What prior knowledge can you assume the audience has about the topic?
- What style and tone of writing are required by the audience and the assignment—informal, scholarly, first-person reporting, dramatized?

PREPARE AN OUTLINE. Try to get a "model" outline for the type of paper you're writing, or look at examples of good papers to see how they were organized. The Roane State Community College Online Writing Lab (Jennifer Jordan-Henley) gives an example of an outline for a paper written to describe a problem. See http://www2.rscc.cc.tn.us/~jordan_jj/OWL/Research.html:

- Introduction
  Statement of the Problem
  Thesis Sentence
- Body: Paragraphs 1 and 2
  History of the Problem (Include,

perhaps, past attempts at solutions. Work in sources.)
- Body: Paragraphs 3 and 4
  Extent of the Problem (Who is affected? How bad is it? Work in sources.)
- Body: Paragraphs 5 and 6
  Repercussions of the Problem (Work in sources.)
- Body: Paragraphs 7 and 8
  Future solutions (not necessarily your own. More sources.)
- Conclusion
  Summarize your findings

WRITE THE ROUGH DRAFT—VISIT THE OWLS. Here's where the Online Writing Labs, or OWLs, excel—there are many dozens of great articles on every aspect of writing your paper. The Links to Online Resources pages (p. 325) have classified these by topic so that you can browse easily and pick out articles you want to read. The entire Links for Writing section will be helpful, and specifically the sections on:

- Title, introduction and conclusion
- Writing style and technique
- Grammar and punctuation

KNOW HOW TO USE YOUR SOURCE MATERIALS AND CITE THEM. See the section Citing Sources on the Links page (p. 325). There's also a nice section on using sources in the middle of the article entitled "Writing a General Research Paper" (http://www2.rscc.cc.tn.us/~jordan_jj/OWL/Research.html) from the Roane State Community College Online Writing Lab (Henley, 1996). The section, "What Happens When the Sources Seem to be Writing My Paper For Me?" describes how to break up long quotations and how to cite an author multiple times without letting the author take over your paper, and it links to both the MLA and the APA style requirements for partial quotations, full quotations, indented quotations, in-text quotations, and paraphrasing.

HAVE OTHERS READ AND CRITIQUE THE PAPER. Read your paper out loud, to yourself. See if the arguments are coherent, logical and conclusive when read aloud. Have several experienced people read and critique your paper. If your school has a writing lab, use the tutors or helpers there as critics.

REVISE AND PROOFREAD. See the "Revision Checklist" section of the article The Research Paper (http://www.chesapeake.edu/Writingcenter/respaper.html) from Chesapeake College. The checklist asks some general questions to help you step back and take a look at the overall content and structure of the paper, then drills down to paragraphs, sentences and words for a closer examination of the writing style. Almost all the OWLs have very large sections on grammar, sentence and paragraph structure, writing style, proofreading, revising and common errors.

Browse some of the larger OWLs like Purdue University and University of Victoria and see the linked articles on Revising and rewriting (p. 325).

Learning to Research in the Library

Get to know your library

Libraries build their collections based on what they think their patrons will need, so the collections of reference materials, fiction and non-fiction will differ between a public and an academic library. Be aware of what kind of collection you're working with, and make arrangements to visit a different library if necessary.

Learn to browse—understand the classification scheme in your library

A library's classification scheme is a system by which books are organized to be placed on the shelves.

Browsing the shelves is an important step when you're trying to get ideas for your research project, so it's worth the effort to become familiar with your library's system.

Most libraries in the U.S. use either the Dewey Decimal system or Library of Congress system, while Britain uses the UDC and other countries use various systems. All of the systems attempt to "co-locate" books with similar subject matter. In a smaller library, many times you can bypass the catalog as a starting point and go directly to the shelves for a first look at your topic, so long as you have a chart of the classification scheme as a guide.

Remember, though, that a book can have only one location in a library. Some books cover more than one subject and the cataloguer has to choose one place to locate the book. Also, non-book materials such as videos and films, will be located in a different section of the building and could be missed by simply shelf-browsing the book collection.

Learn how online library catalogs work

A library catalog is a listing of all the items held by a particular library. A cataloguer examines the item (book, video, map, audio tape, CD, etc.) and decides how it will be described in the library's catalog and under what subject it will be classified. When the item is entered into the library's online catalog database, information is entered into different fields, which are then searchable by users.

Library catalogs usually treat a book as a single "item" and catalog it that way, even if it might be a book of poetry or a book of essays by different authors. You can't find a reference to a particular poem in the library catalog, nor to a particular essay within a book of essays. The same is true of magazines, journals and newspapers. The library catalog will tell you if the library keeps a particular periodical in its collection, but will not list all the articles within the periodical, nor will it necessarily even list all the issues of the periodical which are kept. There are other publications in the reference room which will help you retrieve these individual items, but usually not the library catalog.

Most catalogs are searchable by author, title, subject and keyword. Some of the important things you need to know about the information in those fields are discussed below.

SEARCHING THE CATALOG BY SUBJECT AND KEYWORD. The subject field of a catalog record contains only the words or phrases used by the cataloguer when assigning a subject heading. If the library is using Library of Congress Subject Headings (LCSH), for example, the subject heading for a book about how playing football affects the players' bodies would probably be assigned the subject heading "Football—physiological aspects." Unless you type in that entire phrase as your search term, you won't find the book by searching the subject field.

Subject field searching can be very helpful, but you must find out how the subject you're looking for is worded by using the subject manuals or getting help from the reference librarian. Once you zero in on an appropriate subject heading, a search in the catalog will give you a list of all the items in the library's collection categorized under that heading, so you can browse the collection online. Note also that most items are classified under one or two *very specific* subject headings, rather than under many subjects. The keyword field of a library catalog generally searches several fields in the database record— the author, title and description fields. The description is any information about the catalogued item which may have been entered by the cataloguer. *This is not the full text of the book, nor is it an abstract (summary) of the book but rather a short paragraph containing information the cataloguer thought would be helpful to a user.* This is *not* like searching for keywords in an indexed database like Alta Vista on the Internet, where every word in a document has been recorded.

For this reason, keyword searching alone could miss an item pertinent to your research project if the keyword you use was not included in the short paragraph written by the cataloguer. It's best to use a combination of keyword searching and subject-field searching to make a comprehensive search of the library catalog.

SEARCHING OTHER LIBRARIES' CATALOGS. There are lots of library catalogs on the Internet—but so what? You can search the catalog of a library in Timbuktu, but that doesn't get you the book. Remember that library catalogs do not have full text of books and documents but are just a database with descriptions of the library's holdings. There are a few, and will be more, actual online libraries where you can go to read or search full text documents. Just don't confuse these special resources with a library catalog, which is very different.

Find out how to search for journals and newspapers at your library

Most libraries have either print, CD-ROM or online (either in the library or sometimes on the Web) indexes of magazine, journal and newspaper articles (referred to as periodicals) available for users. Some of these are abstracts of the articles, which are short summaries written to describe the article's contents in enough detail so that a reader can decide whether or not to seek out the full text. Some of these sources may be in the form of full text, where the entire articles have been entered into the database.

The databases will include particular periodicals published within a span of time (for example, a popular newspaper index goes back 36 months for certain major newspapers). Know what the database you're searching contains and whether it's represented as abstract or full text.

Note that these resources, whether print or digital, contain information about periodicals which may not be held by your library. If the database does not have full text articles, you may find an article right on point to your topic, but that particular newspaper or journal may not be in your library's collection. Check out your options with the reference desk if you need an article that's not in your library's collection.

Bibliography surfing

Web surfing is finding an interesting Web page and then using the hyperlinks on that page to jump to other pages. If you find the first page interesting, chances are you'll also be interested in the pages the author has chosen to link to. Librarians and researchers have been doing this for a long time, in the print medium. It's a valuable tool for identifying sources on your chosen topic.

What you do is use the bibliography provided at the end of an encyclopedia article, journal article or book that you've found particularly pertinent to your topic and follow the bibliographic references much as you would hyperlinks on the Web. Since you're locating items that influenced the author of the original article and to which he or she referred, they're likely to be "on point" to your topic. Then use the bibliography at the end of *those* cited articles to find even *more* items, and so on.

Consult the reference librarian for advice

Several times above, you've been advised to consult the reference librarian. Reference librarians can help save you a lot of time because they know their library's collection very well—both the reference collection and the nonfiction collection—and can often tell you "off the top of their heads" whether or not the library has a particular item you're looking for. They are also skilled searchers, both of the library's catalog and of online resources such as CD-ROM, online databases and the Internet. In addition, they're trained in teaching others to use these resources and are glad to do so.

Learn about search syntax and professional search techniques

To be successful at any kind of online searching, you need to know something about how computer searching works. At this time, much of the burden is on the user to intelligently construct a search strategy, taking into account the peculiarities of the particular database and search software.

Learning to Research on the Web

Cyberspace is not like your library

When your search term in one of the popular search engines brings back 130,000 hits, you still wonder if the *one* thing you're looking for will be among them. This can be an enormous problem when you're trying to do serious research on the Internet. Too much information is almost worse than too little, because it takes so much time to sort through

it to see if there's anything useful. The rest of this section will give you some pointers to help you become an effective Internet researcher.

Get to know the reference sources on the Internet

Finding reference material on the Web can be a lot more difficult than walking into the Reference Room in your local library.

The subject-classified Web directories described below will provide you with your main source of links to reference materials on the Web. In addition, many public and academic libraries, like the Internet Public Library (http://www.ipl.org), have put together lists of links to Web sites, categorized by subject. The difficulty is finding Web sites that contain the same kind of substantive content you'd find in a library. See the links to *Reference sources on the Web* (p. 325) for a list of some Web-based reference materials.

Understand how search engines work

Search engines are software tools that allow a user to ask for a list of Web pages containing certain words or phrases from an automated search index. The automated search index is a database containing some or all of the words appearing on the Web pages that have been indexed. The search engines send out a software program known as a spider, crawler or robot. The spider follows hyperlinks from page to page around the Web, gathering and bringing information back to the search engine to be indexed.

Most search engines index all the text found on a Web page, except for words too common to index, such as *a, and, in, to, the* and so on. When a user submits a query, the search engine looks for Web pages containing the words, combinations, or phrases asked for by the user. Engines may be programmed to look for an exact match or a close match (for example, the plural of the word submitted by the user). They may rank the hits as to how close the match is to the words submitted by the user.

One important thing to remember about search engines is this: once the engine and the spider have been programmed, the process is totally automated. No human being examines the information returned by the spider to see what subject it might be about or whether the words on the Web page adequately reflect the actual main point of the page.

Another important fact is that all the search engines are different. They each index differently and treat users' queries differently. The burden is on the searcher to learn how to use the features of each search engine.

Know the difference between a search engine and a directory

A search engine lets you seek out specific words and phrases in Web pages. A directory is more like a subject catalog in the library—a human being has determined the main point of a Web page and has categorized it based on a classification scheme of topics and subtopics used by that directory. Many of the search engines have also developed browsable subject catalogues, and most of the directories also have a search engine, so the distinction between them is blurring.

Jack Solock, special librarian at InterNIC Net Scout, classifies Web directories into categories based on the amount of human intervention (see "Searching the Internet Part II: Subject Catalogs, Annotated Directories, and Subject Guides" at http://rs.internic.net/nic-support/nicnews/

oct96/enduser.html). The categories he uses are subject catalogs, annotated directories and subject guides.

A subject catalog classifies Web pages into subject categories and uses excerpts from the Web page as a short description. An annotated directory divides sites by subject but also contains analysis of the site by an editor, librarian or subject specialist, who writes a description to assist the user. A subject guide attempts to provide a selection of sites relating to a particular subject that represent high quality resources, thus representing the highest level of human intervention of the three types because it involves building a collection of sites to represent a subject area.

Mr. Solock categorizes the following resources:

- Yahoo, BUBL and Galaxy as *subject catalogs*,
- Magellan, Lycos Top 5% and InterNIC Directory of Directories as *annotated directories* and
- Argus Clearinghouse and the WWW Virtual Library as *subject guides*.

Learn about search syntax and professional search techniques

To be successful at any kind of online searching, you need to know something about how computer searching works. At this time, much of the burden is on the user to intelligently construct a search strategy, taking into account the peculiarities of the particular database and search software.

Learn some essential browser skills

Know how to use your browser for finding your way around, finding your way back to places you've been before and for "note-taking" as you

gather information for your paper. A large part of effective research on the Web is figuring out how to stay on track and not waste time—the "browsing" and "surfing" metaphors are fine for leisure time spent on the Web, but not when you're under time pressure to finish your research paper.

URLs. UNDERSTAND THE CONSTRUCTION OF A URL. Sometimes a hyperlink will take you to a URL such as http://www.sampleurl.com/files/howto.html. You should know that the page "howto.html" is part of a site called "www.sampleurl.com." If this page turns out to be a "not found" error, or doesn't have a link to the site's home page, you can try typing in the location box "http://www.sampleurl.com/" or "http://www.sampleurl.com/files/" to see if you can find a menu or table of contents. Sometimes a file has been moved or its name has changed, but the site itself still has content useful to you—this is a way to find out.

If there's a tilde (~) in the URL, you're probably looking at someone's personal page on a larger site. For example "http://www.bigsite.com/~jonesj/home.html" refers to a page at www.bigsite.com where J. Jones has some server space in which to post Web pages.

NAVIGATION. Be sure you can use your browser's "Go" list, "History" list, "Back" button and "Location" box where the URL can be typed in. In Web research, you're constantly following links through to other pages then wanting to jump back a few steps to start off in a different direction. If you're using a computer at home rather than sharing one at school, check the settings in your "Cache" or "History list" to see how long the places you've visited will be retained in history. This will determine how long the links will show as having been visited before. Usually, you want to set this period of time to cover the full time frame of your research project so you'll be able to tell which Web sites you've been to before.

BOOKMARKS OR FAVORITES. Before you start a research session, make a new folder in your bookmarks or favorites area and set that folder as the one to receive new bookmark additions. You might name it with the current date, so you later can identify in which research session the bookmarks were made. Remember you can make a bookmark for a page you haven't yet visited by holding the mouse over the link and getting the popup menu (by either pressing the mouse button or right clicking, depending on what flavor computer you have) to "Add bookmark" or "Add to favorites." Before you sign off your research session, go back and weed out any bookmarks that turned out to be uninteresting so you don't have a bunch of irrelevant material to deal with later. Later you can move these bookmarks around into different folders as you organize information for writing your paper—find out how to do that in your browser.

PRINTING FROM THE BROWSER. Sometimes you'll want to print information from a Web site. The main thing to remember is to make sure the Page Setup is set to print out the page title, URL, and the date. You'll be unable to use the material if you can't remember later where it came from.

"SAVING AS" A FILE. Know how to temporarily save the contents of a Web page as a file on your hard drive or a floppy disk and later open it in your browser by using the "file open" feature. You can save the page you're currently viewing or one which is hyperlinked from that page, from the "File" menu or the popup menu accessed by the mouse held over the hyperlink.

COPYING AND PASTING TO A WORD PROCESSOR. You can take quotes from Web pages by opening up a word processing document and keeping it open while you use your browser. When you find text you want to save, drag the mouse over it and "copy" it, then open up your word processing document and "paste" it. Be sure to also copy and paste the URL and page title, and to record the date, so you know where the information came from.

BE PREPARED TO CITE YOUR WEB REFERENCES. Find out what form of bibliographic references your instructor requires. Both the MLA and APA bibliographic formats have developed rules for citing sources on CD-ROM and the Internet. Instructions for citing electronic sources are available at many libraries, including the Purdue University Online Writing Lab (http://owl.english.purdue.edu/Files/110.html).

Skills for Online Searching

There are many sources on the Web to help you learn search skills. Many of the concepts for using Web search engines also apply to searching online library catalogs and CD-ROMs. This section of the manual will get you started and point you to other online sources where you can learn more.

Learn how search syntax works

Search syntax is a set of rules describing how users can query the database being searched. Sophisticated syntax makes for a better search, one where the items retrieved are mostly relevant to the searcher's need and important items are not missed. It allows a user to look for combinations of terms, exclude other terms, look for various forms of a word, include synonyms, search for phrases rather than single words. The main tools of search syntax are these:

BOOLEAN LOGIC. Boolean logic allows the use of AND, OR and NOT to search for items containing both terms, either term, or a term only if not accompanied by another term. The links below and all the Web search engines "search help" have a lot of good examples of Boolean logic. Tip: NOT can be dangerous. Let's say you want to search for items about Mexico, but not New Mexico, so you use NOT to exclude the word *New* from your retrieved set. This would prevent you from retrieving an article about *New regulations in Mexico* because it contained the word *New,* though that wasn't what you intended.

WILDCARDS AND TRUNCATION. This involves substituting symbols for certain letters of a word so that the search engine will retrieve items with any letter in that spot in the word. The syntax may allow a symbol in the middle of a word (wildcard) or only at the end of the word (truncation). This feature makes it easier to search for related word groups, like *woman* and *women* by using a wildcard such as *wom*n*. Truncation can be useful to search for a group of words like *invest, investor, investors, investing, investment, investments* by submitting *invest* rather than typing in all those terms separated by OR's. The only problem is that *invest** will also retrieve *investigate, investigated, investigator, investigation, investigating.* The trick, then is to combine terms with an AND such as *invest* AND stock* or bond* or financ* or money* to try and narrow your retrieved set to the kind of documents you're looking for.

PHRASE SEARCHING. Many concepts are represented by a phrase rather than a single word. In order to successfully search for a term like *library school* it's important that the search engine allow syntax for phrase searching. Otherwise, instead of get-

LINKS TO ONLINE RESOURCES

http://www.ipl.org/teen/aplus/links.htm
Go online to link to over a hundred Web pages that will help you with your research and writing project.

Links for Research

Reference sources on the Web
http://www.ipl.org/teen/aplus/referenceweb.htm
A chart of some of the online reference books available free on the Web

Web directories and subject-classified resources
http://www.ipl.org/teen/aplus/linksdirect.htm
Yahoo, Argus, IPL et al.

Search engines and their "search help" pages
http://www.ipl.org/teen/aplus/linksengines.htm
Alta Vista, Excite, Lycos et al.

Other links for learning to research
http://www.ipl.org/teen/aplus/linksother.htm
Online articles, online library and research instruction

Links for Writing

OWLs on the Web
http://www.ipl.org/teen/aplus/linksowls.htm
Links to Online Writing Labs (OWLs) "handouts"

OWL Handouts by Topic:

Common types of papers
http://www.ipl.org/teen/aplus/linkscommon.htm
Research papers; persuasive essays; narrative essays; cause/effect essays; how to write summaries and more

Papers on special subjects
http://www.ipl.org/teen/aplus/linksspecial.htm
Film, drama and book reviews; writing about poetry; scientific and lab reports; abstracts and others

Planning and starting the writing assignment
http://www.ipl.org/teen/aplus/linksplanning.htm
The writing process; ideas; journal writing; overcoming obstacles

The topic
http://www.ipl.org/teen/aplus/linkstopic.htm
Several articles from the OWLs

Title, introduction and conclusion
http://www.ipl.org/teen/aplus/linkstitle.htm
Several articles from the OWLs

Thesis statement
http://www.ipl.org/teen/aplus/linksthesis.htm
Articles from many points of view

Organizing information
http:///www.ipl.org/teen/aplus/linksorganizing.htm
Taking notes; outlining; organizing by cubing, mapping and more

Writing style and technique
http://www.ipl.org/teen/aplus/linkswritingstyle.htm
Audience and tone; logic and developing arguments; sentences, words and phrases; paragraphs; coherence, clarity, conciseness; transitions; gender-fair writing; writing on the computer other style and technique issues

Citing sources
http://www.ipl.org/teen/aplus/linkciting.htm
Paraphrasing, summarizing and plagiarism; using quotations; styles of citation

Grammar and punctuation
http://www.ipl.org/teen/aplus/linksgrammar.htm
Links to grammar handbooks

Revising and rewriting
http://www.ipl.org/teen/aplus/linksrevising.htm
How to proofread, edit and revise; short proofreading and editing checklists; critiques and peer review

ting documents about library schools you could be getting documents about school libraries or documents where the word *library* and *school* both appear but have nothing to do with a library school.

PROXIMITY. This allows the user to find documents only if the search terms appear near each other, within so many words or paragraphs, or adjacent to each other. It's a pretty sophisticated tool and can be tricky to use skillfully. Many times you can accomplish about the same result using phrase searching.

CAPITALIZATION. When searching for proper names, search syntax that will distinguish capital from lower case letters will help narrow the search. In other cases, you would want to make sure the search engine isn't looking for a particular pattern of capitalization, and many search engines let you choose which of these options to use.

FIELD SEARCHING. All database records are divided up into fields. Almost all search engines in CD-ROM or online library products and the more sophisticated Web search engines allow users to search for terms appearing in a particular field. This can help immensely when you're looking for a very specific item. Say that you're looking for a psychology paper by a professor from the University of Michigan and all you remember about the paper is that it had something about Freud and Jung in its title. If you think it may be on the Web, you can do a search in Alta Vista, searching for *Freud* AND *Jung* and limit your search to the *umich.edu* domain, which gives you a pretty good chance of finding it, if it's there.

Make sure you know what content you're searching

The content of the database will affect your search strategy and the search syntax you use to retrieve documents. Some of the different databases you'll encounter in your library and online research are:

REPRESENTATION OR SUMMARY OF A DOCUMENT. If a document has been summarized, like a library catalog entry where certain features like title and author have been recorded along with a sentence or two of description, don't expect to retrieve the document by looking for keywords in the text. A search is only searching what's in the database—the representation, not the document itself.

INDEX AND ABSTRACT OF A DOCUMENT. When a document like a journal article has been indexed and an abstract written, a human indexer has helped organize the document for easy retrieval. He or she has chosen some words, phrases and concepts that represent the subject matter of the document and has attached those to the database record as "descriptors." The specific terms usually come from a book of terms used by that database producer, to promote consistency between indexers.

The indexer, or possibly the author of the article, has written an abstract or summary of the article's content that is included in the database. Again, it's important to realize that you're not searching the entire text of the document but someone's representation of the document. If you can zero in on some of the database's descriptors that accurately describe the topic you're looking for, you can easily retrieve all the articles with the same descriptors. If you do a keyword search in this type of database without checking the permissible descriptors, you're hoping that the indexer will have used your keyword in the summary or that the author will have used it in the title of the article.

FULL TEXT OF A DOCUMENT. Searching full text documents gives you a good chance of retrieving the document you want, provided you can think of some key words and phrases that would have been included in the text. The problem is retrieving too many documents when you're looking for something particular, because common words and concepts can appear in documents irrelevant to your topic. This is one of the problems with Internet search engines that index the full text of Web pages. The more skilled you can become in your use of search syntax, the greater will be your success in finding relevant information in a full text database.

Index